Impact of Sensory Marketing on Buying Behavior

Reena Malik
Chitkara University, India

Shivani Malhan
Chitkara University, India

Manpreet Arora
Central University of Himachal Pradesh, India

IGI Global
Publishing Tomorrow's Research Today

Published in the United States of America by
IGI Global
701 E. Chocolate Avenue
Hershey PA, USA 17033
Tel: 717-533-8845
Fax: 717-533-8661
E-mail: cust@igi-global.com
Web site: https://www.igi-global.com

Copyright © 2025 by IGI Global. All rights reserved. No part of this publication may be reproduced, stored or distributed in any form or by any means, electronic or mechanical, including photocopying, without written permission from the publisher.
Product or company names used in this set are for identification purposes only. Inclusion of the names of the products or companies does not indicate a claim of ownership by IGI Global of the trademark or registered trademark.

Library of Congress Cataloging-in-Publication Data

CIP DATA PENDING

ISBN13: 9798369393512
EISBN13: 9798369393536

Vice President of Editorial: Melissa Wagner
Managing Editor of Acquisitions: Mikaela Felty
Managing Editor of Book Development: Jocelynn Hessler
Production Manager: Mike Brehm
Cover Design: Phillip Shickler

British Cataloguing in Publication Data
A Cataloguing in Publication record for this book is available from the British Library.

All work contributed to this book is new, previously-unpublished material.
The views expressed in this book are those of the authors, but not necessarily of the publisher.

Table of Contents

Foreword xvii

Preface xix

Acknowledgment xxvii

Chapter 1
A Comprehensive Study of Neuro Marketing Techniques 1
    Muhammad Younus, Universitas Muhammadiyah Yogyakarta, Pakistan
    Achmad Nurmandi, Universitas Muhammadiyah Yogyakarta, Indonesia
    Dyah Mutiarin, Universitas Muhammadiyah Yogyakarta, Indonesia
    Halimah Abdul Manaf, Universiti Utara Malaysia, Malaysia
    Andi Luhur Prianto, Universitas Muhammadiyah Makassar, Indonesia
    Bambang Irawan, Universitas Mulawarman, Indonesia
    Salahudin Salahudin, Universitas Muhammadiyah Malang, Indonesia
    Idil Akbar, Universitas Padjadjaran, Indonesia
    Titin Purwaningsih, Universitas Muhammadiyah Yogyakarta, Indonesia
    Ihyani Malik, Universitas Muhammadiyah Makassar, Indonesia

Chapter 2
Enhancing Online Shopping Experiences 35
    Preeti Jain, Maharishi Markandeshwar (deemed to be university)
      Mullana- Ambala
    Neetu Chaudhary, Maharishi Markandeshwar (deemed to be university)
      Mullana- Ambala

Chapter 3
Neuroeconomic Insights into Cognitive Biases and Managerial Decision-Making 57
    Abhishek Kumar Singh, Jawaharlal Nehru University, India
    Arpit Singhmar, Jawaharlal Nehru University, India
    Arvind Kumar, Jawaharlal Nehru University, India
    Lokesh Jindal, Jawaharlal Nehru University, India

Chapter 4
A Neuroscientic Perspective 107
    Dinesh Jamwal, Government Degree College, Matour, India
    Manpreet Arora, Central University of Himachal Pradesh, India

Chapter 5
Neuromarketing and Financial Decision Making 125
    Simanpreet Kaur, Chandigarh School of Business, Chandigarh Group of Colleges, Jhanjeri, India
    Anjali, Chandigarh School of Business, Chandigarh Group of Colleges, Jhanjeri, India

Chapter 6
Data Analysis of Consumer Responses in India Using Zen Z 155
    Rishi Prakash Shukla, Jaipuria Institute of Management, India
    Priya Shukla, Oriental University, Indore, India
    Archna Singh, D.Y. Patil International University, India
    Vilas Nair, SCMS School of Technology and Management, India
    Smriti Verma, Yeshwantrao Chavan College of Engineering, Nagpur, India

Chapter 7
Research Insights and Trends in Neuroscience and Consumer Behaviour 177
    Rajwinder Kaur, Chandigarh University, India

Chapter 8
Sensory Marketing and Its Influence on Consumer Buying Behavior: A Comprehensive Analysis... 201
    Richa Pareek, Mody University of Science and Technology, India
    Lalita Kumari, Mody University of Science and Technology, India
    Anupal Mongia, Mody University of Science and Technology, India
    Meena Sharma, Mody University of Science and Technology, India

Chapter 9
The Impact of Product Display on Consumer Attention and Buying Intention 219
    Sneha Jaiswal, Christ University, India
    Abhinav Priyadarshi Tripathi, Christ University, India
    Anju Tripathi, Asian Business School, India

Chapter 10
Influence of Neurosensory Packaging and Promotional Campaigns on Buying Behaviour 237
    Renu Bala, Jan Nayak Chaudhary Devi Lal Vidyapeeth, India

Chapter 11
Product Packaging and Promotional Strategy Influencing Buying Behaviour . 257
    Renu Tanwar, Chaudhary Devi Lal University, Sirsa, India
    Preeti Ahlawat, Chaudhary Devi Lal University, Sirsa, India

Chapter 12
How Does Product Packaging Affect Consumers' Buying Decisions? 275
    Meena Sharma, Mody University of Science and Technology, India
    Anupal Mongia, Mody University of Science and Technology, India
    Richa Pareek, Mody University of Science and Technology, India
    Lalita Kumari, Mody University of Science and Technology, India

Chapter 13
Neuro-Marketing as a Subset of Sensory Marketing From Lasting Imprint Becoming Memory and Impulsive Buying 291
    Manasvi Pathak, Pune Institute of Business Management, India
    Nilesh Tejrao Kate, Pune Institute of Business Management, India
    Soham Hajra, Pune Institute of Business Management, India

Chapter 14
Sensory Perception and Cognitive Responses: Unveiling Consumer Psychology in EV Adoption... 313
    Tushar Batra, Khalsa College, Amritsar, India
    Meghna Aggarwal, ASSM College, Guru Nanak Dev University, India

Chapter 15
Sensory Neuro-Marketing in Sales: Crafting Irresistible Dining Experiences.. 337
    Lathisha Jayangi Ramanayaka, Sri Lanka Institute of Tourism and Hotel Management, Sri Lanka

Chapter 16
Brand Building in the Age of Sensory Marketing: A Strategic Perspective 367
Manpreet Arora, School of Commerce and Management Studies, Central University of Himachal Pradesh, India

Compilation of References 383

About the Contributors 447

Index 451

Detailed Table of Contents

Foreword xvii

Preface xix

Acknowledgment xxvii

Chapter 1
A Comprehensive Study of Neuro Marketing Techniques 1
    Muhammad Younus, Universitas Muhammadiyah Yogyakarta, Pakistan
    Achmad Nurmandi, Universitas Muhammadiyah Yogyakarta, Indonesia
    Dyah Mutiarin, Universitas Muhammadiyah Yogyakarta, Indonesia
    Halimah Abdul Manaf, Universiti Utara Malaysia, Malaysia
    Andi Luhur Prianto, Universitas Muhammadiyah Makassar, Indonesia
    Bambang Irawan, Universitas Mulawarman, Indonesia
    Salahudin Salahudin, Universitas Muhammadiyah Malang, Indonesia
    Idil Akbar, Universitas Padjadjaran, Indonesia
    Titin Purwaningsih, Universitas Muhammadiyah Yogyakarta, Indonesia
    Ihyani Malik, Universitas Muhammadiyah Makassar, Indonesia

This study explores the intersection of cognitive psychology and consumer behavior through the lens of neuromarketing techniques. The primary objective is to understand how cognitive insights, derived from neuromarketing, influence consumer decision-making processes. Employing a qualitative research methodology, the study involved in-depth interviews with industry experts, focus groups with consumers, and an extensive literature review. These approaches provided rich insights into how businesses utilize neuromarketing tools such as fMRI, EEG, and eye-tracking to decode consumer preferences and behaviors. The findings reveal that neuromarketing not only enhances traditional marketing strategies but also uncovers subconscious consumer motivations that are often overlooked by conventional methods. In conclusion, the research underscores the growing importance of cognitive insights in shaping marketing strategies and suggests that a nuanced understanding of consumer psychology is crucial for businesses aiming to create more effective and ethically responsible marketing campaigns.

Chapter 2
Enhancing Online Shopping Experiences 35
    Preeti Jain, Maharishi Markandeshwar (deemed to be university)
      Mullana- Ambala
    Neetu Chaudhary, Maharishi Markandeshwar (deemed to be university)
      Mullana- Ambala

In the constantly evolving online shopping world, sensory marketing is crucial for creating engaging experiences for consumers. This study provides a comprehensive analysis of sensory marketing, highlighting its importance in enhancing the online purchasing experience. It focuses on tactile, visual, and aural cues that influence consumer behavior, emotions, perceptions, and product selection. This section emphasizes visual sensory marketing, examining the impact of high-quality product images, videos, and 3D models, as well as the use of color, typeface, and layout in creating visually appealing online stores. It also explores virtual trials, haptic technologies, and product interaction functionalities, addressing challenges and opportunities in providing tactile feedback in digital environments. Furthermore, it delves into how immersive technologies like augmented reality and virtual reality enhance sensory experiences and product exploration, affecting consumer choices and emphasizing the integration of sensory marketing strategies into e-commerce.

Chapter 3
Neuroeconomic Insights into Cognitive Biases and Managerial Decision-Making 57
    Abhishek Kumar Singh, Jawaharlal Nehru University, India
    Arpit Singhmar, Jawaharlal Nehru University, India
    Arvind Kumar, Jawaharlal Nehru University, India
    Lokesh Jindal, Jawaharlal Nehru University, India

This chapter delves into the intersection of neuroeconomics, cognitive biases, and managerial decision-making. It aims to provide a comprehensive overview of how neurosensory and neuromarketing techniques influence consumer behaviour and decision-making processes. The chapter bridges the gap between academic research and industry practices through an in-depth literature review, innovative research methodologies, and detailed case studies. It offers practical insights and strategies for marketers and practitioners, emphasising the importance of interdisciplinary collaboration and knowledge exchange.

Chapter 4
A Neuroscientic Perspective 107
    Dinesh Jamwal, Government Degree College, Matour, India
    Manpreet Arora, Central University of Himachal Pradesh, India

Abstract: This study investigates the intricate relationship between sensory perceptions and financial choices through a neuroscientific perspective, addressing two key research questions: (1) How are sensory perceptions and financial choices related? (2) How is neuro sensory behavior important in investment decision-making? By integrating insights from neuroscience and behavioral finance, we aim to uncover the mechanisms by which sensory inputs influence economic behaviors and decision-making processes. Our conceptual, literature-based exploration reveals those sensory perceptions—encompassing visual, auditory, olfactory, tactile, and gustatory stimuli—play a critical role in shaping financial decisions. These sensory inputs are processed by neural systems, affecting cognitive functions and emotional responses, which in turn influence risk perception, time preference, and overall financial choices. This study highlights that financial decisions are not solely based on rational calculations but are deeply intertwined with sensory experiences and emotional states.

Chapter 5
Neuromarketing and Financial Decision Making 125
    Simanpreet Kaur, Chandigarh School of Business, Chandigarh Group of
        Colleges, Jhanjeri, India
    Anjali, Chandigarh School of Business, Chandigarh Group of Colleges,
        Jhanjeri, India

Neuromarketing itself represents an application of neuroscience to marketing, guiding the very neural and emotional mechanisms of consumer behavior and providing important insights into financial decision-making. EEG and functional magnetic resonance imaging are two techniques researchers use to trace the ways in which financial stimuli, including investment options, risk assessments, and financial product advertisements, activate different regions of the brain. This paper is aimed at analyzing the role of emotional and neurological processes in financial decision-making. This research found out that consumers are likely to engage and trust if the financial commercials and product presentations arouse positive emotional responses. These findings mean that through the use of neuromarketing concepts in marketing and product development plans, financial institutions would increase the confidence and engagement of customers in their services and bring about more efficient and client-oriented financial services.

Chapter 6
Data Analysis of Consumer Responses in India Using Zen Z 155
    Rishi Prakash Shukla, Jaipuria Institute of Management, India
    Priya Shukla, Oriental University, Indore, India
    Archna Singh, D.Y. Patil International University, India
    Vilas Nair, SCMS School of Technology and Management, India
    Smriti Verma, Yeshwantrao Chavan College of Engineering, Nagpur, India

This chapter explores the application of neuropricing strategies and their impact on consumer behavior, with a specific focus on the Indian market. Neuropricing integrates principles from neuroscience and psychology to optimize pricing by influencing subconscious decision-making processes. Using data collected from 390 online respondents via the Zen Z platform, this study examines how sensory marketing, emotional priming, and cognitive biases like anchoring and price framing enhance perceived value. Our findings demonstrate that neuropricing significantly increases perceived value compared to traditional pricing strategies, providing actionable insights for businesses aiming to refine their pricing tactics through neuroscientific approaches. Keywords: neuropricing, consumer behavior, perceived value, sensory marketing, emotional priming, anchoring bias, price framing.

Chapter 7
Research Insights and Trends in Neuroscience and Consumer Behaviour 177
    Rajwinder Kaur, Chandigarh University, India

Of lately, there has been a rise in interest in the idea of studying consumers' emotional and cognitive responses using neuroscientific approaches. A branch of neuroeconomics known as "neuromarketing" or "consumer neuroscience," this field applies findings from studies of the brain to marketing-related issues. The purpose of this study is to conduct a bibliometric analysis to uncover advances, research trends, and insights in consumer behaviour research utilizing neuromarketing. Neuromarketing and consumer behaviour are the main elements of this study, which suggests a new way to organize results and make evidence evaluation easier. Data is extracted from the Scopus database to gain deeper insights into the body of literature to achieve the study objectives. Using tools such as VoS Viewer, the study analyses the data and obtain the results and findings.

Chapter 8
Sensory Marketing and Its Influence on Consumer Buying Behavior: A
Comprehensive Analysis.. 201
    Richa Pareek, Mody University of Science and Technology, India
    Lalita Kumari, Mody University of Science and Technology, India
    Anupal Mongia, Mody University of Science and Technology, India
    Meena Sharma, Mody University of Science and Technology, India

The marketing tactic whose usage and significance have grown in recent years is sensory marketing, which appeals to consumer's senses to influence their perception and purchasing behavior. The study explore the clever ways in which companies use sensory cues to influence consumer decisions. The study used a multifaceted approach to investigate the psychological processes that underlie sensory marketing and how they affect consumers perceptions, feelings, and, ultimately, purchasing decisions. The study is based on Descriptive cum Theoretical Approach which is justified by past studies and their outcome. It examines the components of sensory marketing visual, auditory, olfactory, tactile, and gustative marketing and how they could affect consumer behavior through number of literature reviews. It concludes that the challenge facing marketers is to investigate, comprehend, and stimulate the five senses of consumers in order to possibly trigger a shift in consumer behavior that would directly impact sales, earnings, and market share.

Chapter 9

The Impact of Product Display on Consumer Attention and Buying Intention 219
   Sneha Jaiswal, Christ University, India
   Abhinav Priyadarshi Tripathi, Christ University, India
   Anju Tripathi, Asian Business School, India

"The study, titled 'The Impact of Product Display on Consumer Attention and Buying Intention,' critically examines the complex relationship that exists between consumers and product displays in the dynamic retail environment." The study investigates how product arrangement, presentation, and visual appeal work as influencing variables in consumer decision-making, with a focus on the issues given by an excess of alternatives. Based on a thorough evaluation of the literature, the study develops a conceptual framework that includes independent variables related to display characteristics, a mediator variable (customer attention), and moderating factors related to consumer and retail environment characteristics. The impact of display location, size, colour, movement, and lighting on consumer attention and purchasing intention is investigated using hypotheses and objectives. The study takes a mixed-methods approach, gathering primary data from 70 people in the NCR Delhi region using interviews and questionnaires and leveraging secondary data from diverse sources. Descriptive statistics offer subtle insights into age-related trends, illustrating the varied impact of appealing displays on various age groups. Chi-Square Tests are used to investigate correlations between categorical variables, providing useful insights into the relationship between education level and shopping patterns. The results have significant impacts for organizations searching for to improve their marketing strategies by optimising product displays, emphasising the need of context-aware interpretation, and recognising the changing landscape of customer behaviour in the retail sector. Finally, this study serves as a thorough guide, unravelling the subtle dynamics that impact consumer decisions in reaction to product displays and laying the groundwork for future research in this expanding topic."

Chapter 10
Influence of Neurosensory Packaging and Promotional Campaigns on Buying
Behaviour 237
  Renu Bala, Jan Nayak Chaudhary Devi Lal Vidyapeeth, India

The paper investigates the relationship between three terms: product packaging, promotional strategies, and consumer buying behavior. In today's competitive market, a lot of tactics are adopted by the marketers to attract the consumer as they focus on packaging and promotional strategies. The study investigates about different elements of packaging design and examines how they impact consumers' perceptions and preferences. As well as, it describes the effectiveness of promotional strategies in stimulating consumer purchasing behavior. Drawing upon theoretical frameworks and empirical evidence, this paper offers insights into how marketers can strategically utilize packaging and promotional techniques to enhance brand visibility, attract target audiences, and ultimately drive sales. Furthermore, it highlights the significance of understanding consumer psychology and market trends in devising successful packaging and promotional campaigns. For the study purpose, data have been gathered from various secondary sources. By comprehensively analyzing the interplay between product packaging, promotional strategies, and consumer behavior, this paper contributes to the existing literature on marketing and provides practical implications for businesses aiming to optimize their marketing efforts and achieve competitive advantage in the marketplace.

Chapter 11
Product Packaging and Promotional Strategy Influencing Buying Behaviour . 257
  Renu Tanwar, Chaudhary Devi Lal University, Sirsa, India
  Preeti Ahlawat, Chaudhary Devi Lal University, Sirsa, India

Managing the interaction between a business's organization, the enterprise, and its suppliers is greatly aided by buyers. The end goal of every marketer is to comprehend consumer behavior. A solid and comprehensive knowledge of the consumer, the buyer's behavior, and the buyer's values should form the basis of every successful marketing plan or program. Recognition of the problem, gathering relevant information, evaluating alternatives, making a purchasing choice, and subsequent actions are the five steps that make up Kotler's model of the buying process. Seventy-two percent of Americans say that the design of a product's packaging is very essential when making a purchase, and 81 percent say the same about gift purchases. The objective of every marketing campaign is to get people to hear about your product and maybe buy it. The buyer's journey is the series of events that consumers go through from identifying a problem, researching possible solutions, and ultimately making a purchase decision. In order to help a business increase sales and succeed.

Chapter 12

How Does Product Packaging Affect Consumers' Buying Decisions? 275
    Meena Sharma, Mody University of Science and Technology, India
    Anupal Mongia, Mody University of Science and Technology, India
    Richa Pareek, Mody University of Science and Technology, India
    Lalita Kumari, Mody University of Science and Technology, India

The packaging gives constant development in marketing. It grows into the basic magnitudes in the production and manufacturing concept, as it plays an important role in prominence the mental image of the product to the consumer. The status of packaging makes marketing thinkers consider it to closed element for the marketing complex and positive process on which the product depends. Therefore, this study examines the packaging concept and its impact on consumers buying decisions. This study is based on primary data collection through a designed questionnaire and distributed to 750 consumers in the Shekhawati area. The results confirm that consumers are attracted to the product packaging in all aspects (design, color, size, shape). It endorses adopting a packaging policy in industrial organizations facing high-tech expansions and rapidly changing consumer palates. It is necessary to consider modern marketing directions in product packaging, including green marketing, which depends on the use of materials that have less environmental impact in the packaging process.

Chapter 13

Neuro-Marketing as a Subset of Sensory Marketing From Lasting Imprint Becoming Memory and Impulsive Buying 291
    Manasvi Pathak, Pune Institute of Business Management, India
    Nilesh Tejrao Kate, Pune Institute of Business Management, India
    Soham Hajra, Pune Institute of Business Management, India

In the ever-changing marketing landscape, gaining customer attention and influencing purchase decisions necessitates inventive techniques. Traditionally, marketing has aimed to captivate customers by visual and logical arguments. However, a growing tendency acknowledges the significant importance of our senses on decision-making Sensory marketing, a tactic that goes beyond standard visual and logical appeals, has emerged as a potent tool for organisations looking to build stronger connections with their customers. Sensory marketing creates multidimensional brand experiences by purposefully engaging all five senses - sight, sound, smell, touch, and taste. In the ever-evolving landscape of customer service, businesses are turning to predictive analytics as a game-changer. Predictive analytics goes beyond traditional data analysis; it's a forward-thinking approach that harnesses the power of historical data to anticipate customer needs and preferences. At its core, the concept is about being proactive rather than reactive.

Chapter 14
Sensory Perception and Cognitive Responses: Unveiling Consumer
Psychology in EV Adoption.. 313
    Tushar Batra, Khalsa College, Amritsar, India
    Meghna Aggarwal, ASSM College, Guru Nanak Dev University, India

To achieve net zero emission and decarbonization, the electrification of the transportation sector is necessary. Electric vehicles are extensively advocated as a sustainable option of transportation, due to their benefits and growing awareness among public towards environmental pollution, climate change, and country's dependence on oil imports. For most of the countries, including India, road transportation sectors are centres of focus to reduce emission of greenhouse gases. Though there is an increase in year-on-year sale of electric vehicles (EV) in India, their market share is still on the lower side compared to the overall sale of vehicles. This study focuses on consumer perceptions, knowledge about electric vehicles, experience in driving, and intention to purchase an electric vehicle in the near future. The study is empirical in nature and quantitative methods are employed. The respondents go through pre-drive and post-drive surveys. The findings will provide detailed insights into consumer perceptions towards electric vehicles and barriers to adoption of electric vehicles in India.

Chapter 15
Sensory Neuro-Marketing in Sales: Crafting Irresistible Dining Experiences.. 337
    Lathisha Jayangi Ramanayaka, Sri Lanka Institute of Tourism and Hotel
      Management, Sri Lanka

Recent developments in marketing and psychology underscore the vital role of sensory experiences in shaping judgment and decision-making. Sensory marketing, an emerging field, examines how sensory perceptions influence consumer behaviours, challenging traditional cognitive models by linking mental processes to sensory experiences. This chapter outlines the foundational premises of the information processing paradigm and addresses challenges posed by embodiment, grounded cognition, and sensory marketing research. It explores bodily sensations as information sources, context-sensitive perception, imagery, simulation, and metaphors in consumer behaviour. From a managerial viewpoint, sensory marketing crafts subconscious cues that influence perceptions of a product's qualities, such as sophistication and quality. In a market saturated with direct appeals, sensory-based triggers can more effectively engage consumers, prompting them to generate favourable brand attributes autonomously. This chapter highlights gaps in sensory perception research, noting that the need for further a study.

Chapter 16
Brand Building in the Age of Sensory Marketing: A Strategic Perspective 367
Manpreet Arora, School of Commerce and Management Studies, Central University of Himachal Pradesh, India

This chapter explores the role of sensory marketing in modern brand building, focusing on how engaging the five senses—sight, sound, smell, touch, and taste—creates stronger emotional connections with consumers. As traditional marketing methods lose impact, sensory marketing helps brands stand out by delivering immersive experiences that foster brand loyalty and enhance differentiation. The chapter discusses the shift from functional product marketing to experience-driven strategies, addressing key challenges such as measurability, cost, and cultural sensitivity. It also highlights emerging trends, including AR/VR integration, neuroscience-driven marketing, and sustainable sensory practices. Overall, sensory marketing offers a path to deeper emotional engagement, ensuring lasting consumer relationships in an increasingly competitive marketplace.

Compilation of References 383

About the Contributors 447

Index 451

Foreword

It gives me immense pleasure to write the foreword for the book *Impact of Sensory Marketing on Buying Behavior,* edited by Reena Malik, Shivani Malhan, and Manpreet Arora. In an era marked by intense competition and rapidly evolving consumer preferences, the need to understand and influence buying behavior has never been more critical. Sensory marketing, which focuses on engaging consumers' senses to create more impactful and memorable brand experiences, has emerged as a powerful tool in this regard. This book delves deep into this exciting and evolving field, offering valuable insights into how sensory marketing can shape consumer perceptions, emotions, and ultimately, their purchasing decisions.

The senses—sight, sound, smell, taste, and touch—play a fundamental role in how consumers perceive and interact with the world around them. By strategically engaging these senses, marketers can create immersive and compelling brand experiences that resonate on a deeper emotional level. This book explores various aspects of sensory marketing, providing a comprehensive overview of its theoretical foundations, practical applications, and the psychological mechanisms that drive consumer behavior.

What makes this book particularly valuable is its multidisciplinary approach, combining insights from psychology, neuroscience, and marketing. By examining how sensory inputs are processed by the brain and how they influence cognition and emotion, this book bridges the gap between scientific theory and marketing practice. Each chapter is thoughtfully curated, offering perspectives from esteemed scholars and industry experts who bring their knowledge and experience to the forefront. The editors, Reena Malik, Shivani Malhan, and Manpreet Arora, have done an excellent job of bringing together a diverse range of topics, from sensory branding and product design to retail environments and digital sensory experiences.

This book is not just a scholarly exploration of sensory marketing but also a practical guide for marketers seeking to implement these strategies effectively. It includes case studies, empirical research findings, and real-world examples that illustrate the power of sensory marketing in enhancing brand equity, improving customer satisfaction, and driving sales. Whether it is the visual appeal of packaging, the soothing soundscapes in retail stores, the enticing aromas in a coffee shop, or the tactile feel of a product, each sensory element plays a crucial role in shaping the consumer journey.

As we navigate an increasingly digital and sensory-saturated marketplace, understanding how to harness the power of sensory marketing will be essential for businesses looking to differentiate themselves and create lasting consumer loyalty. The insights provided in this book will serve as a valuable resource for academics, researchers, students, and marketing professionals alike, guiding them in crafting strategies that not only capture attention but also create meaningful connections with consumers.

I commend the editors and contributing authors for their dedication and effort in compiling this comprehensive and insightful volume. I am confident that *Impact of Sensory Marketing on Buying Behavior* will inspire new research, foster innovation, and significantly contribute to the advancement of knowledge in the field of marketing.

I wholeheartedly recommend this book to anyone interested in exploring the fascinating intersection of sensory perception and consumer behavior. May it serve as a beacon for future research and practice, enriching our understanding of how to connect with consumers in a profoundly sensory and emotional way.

Furqan Qamar
Department of Management Studies Jamia Millia Islamia, India

Jamia Millia Islamia
Central University of Himachal Pradesh, India

Preface

In the ever-evolving landscape of marketing, where the competition is fierce and consumer choices are abundant, understanding the subtleties of how sensory experiences influence purchasing decisions has never been more crucial. The field of sensory marketing stands at the confluence of psychology, neuroscience, and consumer behavior, offering profound insights into how engaging the senses can create powerful, emotionally charged brand experiences.

As editors of *Impact of Sensory Marketing on Buying Behavior*, we—Reena Malik from Chitkara University, Shivani Malhan from Chitkara University, and Manpreet Arora from Central University of Himachal Pradesh—are delighted to present a comprehensive exploration of this dynamic field. This volume brings together leading experts and scholars who delve into how sensory marketing, through the engagement of sight, sound, touch, taste, and smell, shapes consumer perceptions, enhances brand loyalty, and drives purchasing behavior.

Sensory marketing, by tapping into the multisensory experiences of consumers, provides brands with a distinctive edge in a crowded marketplace. In a world where traditional marketing tactics are often overshadowed by sensory overload, understanding the science behind sensory stimuli offers a pathway to creating memorable and emotionally resonant brand experiences. For marketers, this knowledge translates into the development of innovative strategies that not only capture attention but also foster long-term customer engagement.

Academicians and researchers, too, have a pivotal role in advancing this field. By bridging the gap between theory and practice, sensory marketing research informs the development of new models and theories that explain how sensory inputs affect decision-making and emotional responses. This book aims to contribute to this growing body of knowledge by presenting both theoretical insights and practical applications. We hope to offer a valuable resource that enriches academic discourse while providing actionable strategies for professionals.

In this volume, we explore a wide array of topics including the influence of visual aesthetics, the power of auditory branding, the tactile sensations of product interaction, the impact of scent on memory and emotions, and the role of taste in consumer choices. We also address the complexities introduced by digital and virtual environments, examining how sensory experiences can be adapted and replicated online.

Our contributors provide a rich tapestry of perspectives, from empirical research and case studies to theoretical models and practical applications. This interdisciplinary approach ensures a holistic understanding of how sensory marketing strategies can be crafted to engage consumers on multiple levels.

As we navigate the future of sensory marketing, it is essential to address emerging trends, technological advancements, and ethical considerations. This book does not shy away from these challenges, offering insights into the evolving role of sensory marketing in both commercial and non-commercial contexts. Whether exploring the integration of artificial intelligence and virtual reality, or discussing the ethical implications of sensory manipulation, our goal is to provide a forward-thinking perspective that anticipates the needs of both marketers and scholars.

We invite you to delve into the pages of this book, where each chapter offers a window into the multifaceted world of sensory marketing. Our hope is that this volume serves as both a practical guide for enhancing brand experiences and a source of inspiration for ongoing research and innovation in this fascinating field.

Chapter 1: Cognitive Insights in Consumer Behavior: A Comprehensive Study of Neuromarketing Techniques

This chapter delves into the nexus of cognitive psychology and consumer behavior through the lens of neuromarketing. It provides a detailed exploration of how cognitive insights derived from neuromarketing methods influence consumer decision-making. Utilizing qualitative research approaches, including in-depth interviews with industry experts and focus groups with consumers, the chapter reveals how tools like fMRI, EEG, and eye-tracking are used to decode consumer preferences and behaviors. The findings emphasize that neuromarketing enhances traditional marketing strategies by uncovering subconscious motivations that often elude conventional methods. This research underscores the growing significance of cognitive insights in crafting more effective and ethically sound marketing strategies.

Chapter 2: Sensory Marketing in the Digital Age: Enhancing Online Shopping Experiences

In the realm of online shopping, sensory marketing is pivotal for creating immersive consumer experiences. This chapter provides an in-depth analysis of how sensory marketing strategies are adapted for the digital environment. It focuses on the influence of tactile, visual, and aural cues on consumer behavior and emotions. The chapter examines the impact of high-quality product images, videos, and 3D models, as well as the role of color, typography, and layout in online stores. It also explores innovations like virtual trials and haptic technologies, addressing the challenges and opportunities of providing tactile feedback online. Additionally, it considers how augmented reality (AR) and virtual reality (VR) enhance sensory experiences and influence consumer choices, emphasizing the integration of these strategies into e-commerce.

Chapter 3: Neuroeconomic Insights Into Cognitive Biases and Managerial Decision-Making

This chapter investigates the intersection of neuroeconomics, cognitive biases, and managerial decision-making. It offers a comprehensive overview of how neurosensory and neuromarketing techniques shape consumer behavior and decision-making processes. Through a thorough literature review and case studies, the chapter bridges academic research and industry practice. It provides practical insights and strategies for marketers and practitioners, highlighting the importance of interdisciplinary collaboration to better understand and leverage cognitive biases and sensory inputs in marketing decisions.

Chapter 4: Sensory Perceptions and Financial Choices: A Neuroscientific Perspective

Exploring the link between sensory perceptions and financial choices, this chapter uses a neuroscientific approach to understand how sensory inputs influence economic behaviors. It addresses how visual, auditory, olfactory, tactile, and gustatory stimuli affect decision-making processes related to investment and financial choices. By integrating insights from neuroscience and behavioral finance, the chapter reveals that financial decisions are deeply intertwined with sensory experiences and emotional states. It highlights the role of sensory perceptions in shaping risk perception, time preference, and overall financial behavior.

Chapter 5: Neuromarketing and Financial Decision-Making

This chapter examines the application of neuromarketing techniques to understand financial decision-making. Using EEG and fMRI, the study investigates how financial stimuli, such as investment options and advertisements, activate various brain regions. It analyzes how emotional and neurological processes influence consumer engagement and trust in financial services. The findings suggest that neuromarketing can enhance consumer confidence and engagement by eliciting positive emotional responses, thus leading to more effective financial marketing strategies.

Chapter 6: Neuropricing Insights: Data Analysis of Consumer Responses in India Using Zen Z

Focusing on the Indian market, this chapter explores neuropricing strategies and their impact on consumer behavior. By analyzing data from 390 online respondents collected via the Zen Z platform, the chapter investigates how sensory marketing, emotional priming, and cognitive biases like anchoring and price framing affect perceived value. The study demonstrates that neuropricing significantly enhances perceived value compared to traditional pricing methods, offering actionable insights for businesses to optimize pricing strategies through neuroscientific approaches.

Chapter 7: From Brain to Buy: Research Insights and Trends in Neuroscience and Consumer Behavior

This chapter provides a bibliometric analysis of research trends and insights in consumer behavior through the lens of neuroscience. It focuses on "neuromarketing" or "consumer neuroscience," a field that applies brain studies to marketing issues. Using data from the Scopus database and tools like VoS Viewer, the chapter uncovers advancements and patterns in neuromarketing research. It aims to facilitate evidence evaluation and organize findings to better understand how neuroscientific approaches are shaping consumer behavior research.

Chapter 8: Sensory Marketing and Its Influence on Consumer Buying Behavior: A Comprehensive Analysis

This chapter offers a thorough examination of sensory marketing and its effects on consumer behavior. It explores how companies use sensory cues—visual, auditory, olfactory, tactile, and gustatory—to influence consumer perceptions and purchasing decisions. Employing a descriptive and theoretical approach, the chapter reviews past studies and their outcomes, concluding that effective sensory marketing can significantly impact sales, earnings, and market share by triggering shifts in consumer behavior.

Chapter 9: The Impact of Product Display on Consumer Attention and Buying Intention

Investigating how product displays affect consumer behavior, this chapter examines various display features such as location, size, and color. It analyzes how these features influence consumer attention and buying intentions, taking into account factors like age and education. Through interviews, surveys, and existing research analysis, the chapter provides valuable insights into optimizing product displays to enhance marketing effectiveness and guide future research in this area.

Chapter 10: Influence of Neurosensory Packaging and Promotional Campaigns on Buying Behavior

This chapter explores the interplay between product packaging, promotional strategies, and consumer buying behavior. It investigates how different packaging elements impact consumer perceptions and preferences, and evaluates the effectiveness of promotional tactics in stimulating purchases. Drawing on theoretical frameworks and empirical evidence, the chapter offers practical insights for businesses to enhance brand visibility and drive sales through strategic packaging and promotions.

Chapter 11: Packaging and Promotion Influence Buying Behavior: Product Packaging and Promotional Strategy Influencing Buying Behavior

Focusing on the interaction between product packaging and promotional strategies, this chapter highlights how these elements influence consumer buying behavior. It discusses the importance of packaging design and promotional tactics in shaping consumer perceptions and decisions. By analyzing the buying process and consumer responses, the chapter aims to provide actionable insights for businesses to optimize marketing strategies and increase sales.

Chapter 12: How Does Product Packaging Affect Consumers' Buying Decisions?

This chapter examines the role of product packaging in influencing consumer buying decisions. Based on primary data collected from 750 consumers, it explores how factors such as design, color, size, and shape impact consumer attraction to products. The study emphasizes the need for modern packaging strategies, including green marketing practices, to align with changing consumer preferences and environmental concerns.

Chapter 13: Neuromarketing as a Subset of Sensory Marketing: From Lasting Imprints to Impulsive Buying

This chapter investigates the role of neuromarketing within the broader context of sensory marketing. It explores how neuromarketing techniques create lasting impressions and influence impulsive buying behaviors. By linking sensory perceptions to memory and decision-making processes, the chapter highlights how neuromarketing can be used to craft marketing strategies that effectively engage consumers on a deeper emotional level.

Chapter 14: Sensory Perception and Cognitive Responses: Unveiling Consumer Psychology in EV Adoption

This chapter focuses on consumer perceptions and adoption of Electric Vehicles (EVs) in India. Using empirical and quantitative methods, it examines consumers' knowledge, experiences, and intentions regarding EVs. The study provides insights into the barriers to EV adoption and highlights how sensory perceptions and cognitive responses influence consumer decision-making in the context of sustainable transportation.

Chapter 15: Sensible Selling Through Sensory Neuromarketing: Crafting Irresistible Dining Experiences

This chapter explores how sensory neuromarketing can be employed to create compelling dining experiences. It examines the role of sensory perceptions in shaping consumer judgments and decision-making, particularly in the context of dining. The chapter outlines how sensory-based triggers can be used to enhance product qualities, such as sophistication and quality, and provides a managerial perspective on utilizing sensory marketing to engage consumers and build favorable brand attributes.

Chapter 16: Brand Building in the Age of Sensory Marketing: A Strategic Perspective

This chapter explores the role of sensory marketing in modern brand building, focusing on how engaging the five senses—sight, sound, smell, touch, and taste—creates stronger emotional connections with consumers. As traditional marketing methods lose impact, sensory marketing helps brands stand out by delivering immersive experiences that foster brand loyalty and enhance differentiation. The chapter discusses the shift from functional product marketing to experience-driven strategies, addressing key challenges such as measurability, cost, and cultural sensitivity. It also highlights emerging trends, including AR/VR integration, neuroscience-driven marketing, and sustainable sensory practices. Overall, sensory marketing offers a path to deeper emotional engagement, ensuring lasting consumer relationships in an increasingly competitive marketplace.

As we reach the conclusion of *Impact of Sensory Marketing on Buying Behavior*, we reflect on the remarkable journey through the intricate world of sensory marketing. This volume has offered a rich exploration of how multisensory experiences profoundly shape consumer perceptions and behaviors, underscoring the growing significance of this field in modern marketing.

Each chapter of this book contributes a unique perspective to the understanding of sensory marketing, revealing how sensory cues—from visual aesthetics to tactile sensations—play a pivotal role in influencing consumer decisions. Through rigorous research and innovative methodologies, our contributors have illuminated the ways in which sensory marketing techniques can be leveraged to create engaging, emotionally resonant brand experiences that stand out in an increasingly crowded marketplace.

The insights gathered here demonstrate that sensory marketing is not merely about appealing to the senses but about creating comprehensive and immersive brand experiences that drive consumer engagement and loyalty. Whether through the adaptation of sensory marketing strategies for the digital realm, the integration of neuromarketing techniques into financial decision-making, or the impact of packaging and promotional strategies on buying behavior, the book encapsulates the multifaceted nature of sensory influences on consumer behavior.

Our exploration spans a broad spectrum of topics—from the role of sensory perceptions in financial choices to the impact of product displays and packaging on consumer behavior. The inclusion of cutting-edge discussions on neuropricing, the application of augmented and virtual reality, and the ethical considerations of sensory manipulation further enriches the discourse. The practical insights provided are poised to guide both marketers and researchers in navigating the complexities of sensory marketing, helping them craft strategies that not only capture consumer attention but also foster deeper, more meaningful connections with their target audiences.

As editors, we are proud to present this volume as a significant contribution to the field of sensory marketing. It serves as both a comprehensive reference for academics and a practical guide for professionals seeking to harness the power of sensory experiences in their marketing efforts. The collaborative effort of leading experts and scholars has resulted in a book that we hope will inspire continued research, innovation, and application in this dynamic field.

In conclusion, *Impact of Sensory Marketing on Buying Behavior* is a testament to the profound impact that sensory experiences have on consumer behavior. It reaffirms the importance of understanding and utilizing sensory marketing strategies to stay ahead in the competitive landscape, ultimately creating more engaging, memorable, and effective brand interactions. We invite readers to delve into the pages of this book and discover the wealth of knowledge and practical strategies that await.

Reena Malik
Chitkara University, India

Shivani Malhan
Chitkara University, India

Manpreet Arora
Central University of Himachal Pradesh, India

Acknowledgment

As editors of the volume *Impact of Sensory Marketing on Buying Behavior*, we extend our heartfelt gratitude to the individuals who have supported us throughout this endeavor.

First and foremost, we express our deepest appreciation to our parents and family members for their unwavering love, encouragement, and understanding. Their steadfast support has been the cornerstone of our academic pursuits and professional endeavors, and we are profoundly grateful for their endless sacrifices and guidance.

Additionally, we would like to extend special thanks to specific individuals whose contributions have been instrumental in shaping this volume. Dr. Reena Malik and Dr. Shivani Malhan express their gratitude to Dr. Sandhir Sharma, Vice Chancellor, Chitkara University for the unwavering support.

Dr. Manpreet Arora extends her sincere gratitude to her father, S. Surinder Singh Arora, for his boundless love, wisdom, and encouragement throughout her academic journey, she remembers fondly her mother Late Arvind Arora who acted as a pillar and guiding star in her life and career at this moment where this academic venture adds up to her career.

Finally, we express our appreciation to the publishers, editors, and staff involved in the publication process for their professionalism, dedication, and support.

Thank you all for your invaluable contributions and unwavering support.

Chapter 1
A Comprehensive Study of Neuro Marketing Techniques

Muhammad Younus
https://orcid.org/0000-0001-9654-1546
Universitas Muhammadiyah Yogyakarta, Pakistan

Achmad Nurmandi
Universitas Muhammadiyah Yogyakarta, Indonesia

Dyah Mutiarin
https://orcid.org/0000-0003-3171-8915
Universitas Muhammadiyah Yogyakarta, Indonesia

Halimah Abdul Manaf
Universiti Utara Malaysia, Malaysia

Andi Luhur Prianto
Universitas Muhammadiyah Makassar, Indonesia

Bambang Irawan
https://orcid.org/0000-0002-4841-7302
Universitas Mulawarman, Indonesia

Salahudin Salahudin
Universitas Muhammadiyah Malang, Indonesia

Idil Akbar
Universitas Padjadjaran, Indonesia

Titin Purwaningsih
Universitas Muhammadiyah Yogyakarta, Indonesia

Ihyani Malik
Universitas Muhammadiyah Makassar, Indonesia

ABSTRACT

This study explores the intersection of cognitive psychology and consumer behavior through the lens of neuromarketing techniques. The primary objective is to under-

DOI: 10.4018/979-8-3693-9351-2.ch001

Copyright © 2025, IGI Global. Copying or distributing in print or electronic forms without written permission of IGI Global is prohibited.

stand how cognitive insights, derived from neuromarketing, influence consumer decision-making processes. Employing a qualitative research methodology, the study involved in-depth interviews with industry experts, focus groups with consumers, and an extensive literature review. These approaches provided rich insights into how businesses utilize neuromarketing tools such as fMRI, EEG, and eye-tracking to decode consumer preferences and behaviors. The findings reveal that neuromarketing not only enhances traditional marketing strategies but also uncovers subconscious consumer motivations that are often overlooked by conventional methods. In conclusion, the research underscores the growing importance of cognitive insights in shaping marketing strategies and suggests that a nuanced understanding of consumer psychology is crucial for businesses aiming to create more effective and ethically responsible marketing campaigns.

1 INTRODUCTION

1.1 Background

In the contemporary digital landscape, understanding consumer behavior has evolved into a multidimensional pursuit that extends beyond traditional market research methods. The advent of neuromarketing, an interdisciplinary field that fuses neuroscience with marketing principles, has marked a significant shift in how businesses and researchers approach the study of consumer behavior. (Zahid et al., 2022). Neuromarketing delves into the cognitive processes that drive consumer decisions, offering a window into the subconscious mind where many of these decisions originate. This field is grounded in the belief that understanding the neural mechanisms underlying consumer behavior can lead to more effective marketing strategies, thereby enhancing consumer engagement and satisfaction.

The roots of neuromarketing can be traced back to the early 2000s when advancements in brain imaging technologies, such as functional magnetic resonance imaging (fMRI) and electroencephalography (EEG), began to provide insights into the neural activities associated with various cognitive functions. These technological advancements allowed researchers to observe the brain's responses to marketing stimuli, thus bridging the gap between consumer behavior theories and the biological underpinnings of decision-making. (Vollrath & Villegas, 2021). The promise of neuromarketing lies in its ability to uncover the implicit, often unconscious, factors that influence consumer preferences, choices, and brand loyalty. Unlike traditional market research methods, which rely heavily on self-reported data and surveys, neuromarketing offers an objective lens through which to view consumer behavior.

As businesses increasingly recognize the value of customer-centric strategies, the demand for sophisticated tools and methodologies to decode consumer behavior has surged (Arora & Sharma, (2023b). This has led to the integration of neuromarketing techniques into mainstream marketing practices. Companies are now leveraging neuromarketing to refine their advertising campaigns, product designs, and customer experiences (Ibrahim et al., 2019). By tapping into the emotional and cognitive responses of consumers, businesses can tailor their offerings to better align with consumer needs and desires, ultimately driving brand loyalty and market success.

However, despite its potential, neuromarketing is not without controversy. Ethical concerns have been raised regarding the manipulation of consumer behavior through subconscious means, and the potential for exploitation has sparked debate among scholars and practitioners alike. Moreover, the complexity of interpreting neuromarketing data, coupled with the high costs associated with brain imaging technologies, poses significant challenges to widespread adoption. These issues underscore the need for a deeper understanding of neuro-marketing techniques and their implications for both consumers and businesses (Türkmendağ & Hassan, 2024).

1.2 Problem Formulation

The rapid growth of neuromarketing has generated a wealth of research aimed at exploring the intersection of neuroscience and consumer behavior. However, much of the existing literature has focused on quantitative approaches, often emphasizing statistical correlations between neural responses and consumer actions (Popova et al., 2019). While these studies have contributed valuable insights, they often need to pay more attention to the nuanced, qualitative aspects of consumer experiences that are critical to understanding the full spectrum of cognitive processes at play.

This gap in the literature presents a significant challenge for marketers and researchers seeking to apply neuro-marketing insights in a practical, consumer-centric manner. With a comprehensive understanding of the cognitive and emotional experiences that drive consumer behavior, there is a chance of oversimplifying the complex dynamics that influence decision-making. Additionally, the ethical implications of neuromarketing remain underexplored, particularly in terms of how these techniques affect consumer autonomy and trust (Belvedere & Tunisini, 2020).

The problem, therefore, lies in the need for a more holistic approach to studying neuromarketing—one that integrates qualitative research methods to capture the rich, contextual insights that are often missed in quantitative studies (Erdmann & Ponzoa, 2020). By focusing on the lived experiences of consumers, such an approach can provide a deeper understanding of how neuro-marketing techniques influence consumer behavior on a cognitive level. This, in turn, can inform more ethical and effective marketing practices that respect consumer autonomy while enhancing brand-consumer relationships.

1.3 Research Objective

The primary objective of this research is to conduct a comprehensive qualitative study of neuro-marketing techniques and their impact on consumer behavior. This study aims to explore the cognitive and emotional processes that underlie consumer decision-making, providing a nuanced understanding of how neuromarketing influences these processes. By adopting a qualitative research approach, this study seeks to uncover the subjective experiences of consumers when exposed to neuromarketing stimuli, thereby offering insights that complement existing quantitative research.

Specifically, this research will focus on three key objectives:

To explore the cognitive processes influenced by neuro-marketing techniques: This includes examining how different neuro-marketing stimuli, such as visual and auditory cues, affect consumer perceptions, memory, and decision-making. The study will investigate the extent to which these stimuli evoke emotional responses and how these emotions, in turn, shape consumer behavior.

To understand the ethical implications of neuromarketing: This objective will address the concerns surrounding consumer manipulation and the potential for exploitation. The research will explore how consumers perceive neuromarketing techniques and the impact of these perceptions on their trust in brands. Additionally, the study will examine the role of informed consent in neuromarketing practices and the implications for consumer autonomy.

To provide practical recommendations for the ethical application of neuromarketing in marketing strategies: Based on the insights gained from the qualitative analysis, this research aims to offer guidelines for businesses on how to ethically and effectively integrate neuromarketing into their marketing strategies. These recommendations will focus on balancing the benefits of neuromarketing with the need to respect consumer rights and promote transparency.

Through these objectives, this research aspires to contribute to the growing body of literature on neuromarketing by offering a qualitative perspective that enriches the understanding of cognitive insights in consumer behavior. The findings of this study will have implications for both academia and industry, providing a foundation for further research and informing the development of ethical marketing practices that prioritize consumer well-being.

In summary, this research will address the need for a more comprehensive and ethically informed approach to neuromarketing. By examining the cognitive and emotional dimensions of consumer behavior through qualitative research, this study will contribute valuable insights into the complex interplay between neuroscience and marketing. The ultimate goal is to enhance the effectiveness of neuro-marketing techniques while ensuring that they are applied in a manner that respects consumer autonomy and fosters trust in the brand-consumer relationship.

2 LITERATURE REVIEW

2.1 What is Neuro-Marketing

Neuromarketing, a burgeoning field at the intersection of neuroscience, psychology, and marketing, has garnered increasing attention over the past two decades (Bhardwaj, Kaushik & Arora, 2024). The convergence of these disciplines has provided unprecedented insights into consumer behavior, enabling marketers to understand and predict consumer preferences, choices, and emotional responses (Bijmolt et al., 2021). This literature review aims to critically evaluate the existing body of research on neuro-marketing techniques, highlighting the key contributions, identifying gaps, and discussing the limitations of previous studies. Furthermore, it defines the scope of neuromarketing within the broader context of consumer behavior research and employs a funnel structure, moving from general to specific topics, to provide a coherent overview of the field (Erokhina et al., 2018).

Neuromarketing refers to the application of neuroscience techniques to marketing research, with the primary objective of understanding how consumers' brains respond to marketing stimuli. This approach goes beyond traditional methods of consumer research, which rely heavily on self-reported data, by directly measuring brain activity, physiological responses, and other neurobiological markers (Peng et al., 2023). Techniques such as functional magnetic resonance imaging (fMRI), electroencephalography (EEG), eye-tracking, and biometric analysis are commonly used in neuromarketing studies to assess various aspects of consumer behavior, including attention, emotion, memory, and decision-making processes.

The core premise of neuromarketing is that consumer decisions are influenced by subconscious processes that may not be accessible through introspection or verbalization (Mathaisel & Comm, 2021). By tapping into these underlying cognitive mechanisms, neuromarketing provides a more objective and granular understanding of consumer behavior, potentially leading to more effective marketing strategies and interventions.

2.2 General Overview of Consumer Behavior Research

Consumer behavior research has long been a cornerstone of marketing science, with roots in psychology, economics, and sociology (Fernández Gómez et al., 2024). The field has evolved from early models of rational decision-making, which viewed consumers as logical and utility-maximizing agents, to more nuanced frameworks that recognize the role of emotions, social influences, and cognitive biases in shaping consumer choices (Taneja, Shukla, & Arora, 2024).

2.2.1 Traditional Approaches to Consumer Behavior

Traditional consumer behavior models, such as the Theory of Planned Behavior (Ajzen, 1991) and the Elaboration Likelihood Model (Petty & Cacioppo, 1986), have provided valuable insights into the factors that influence consumer decision-making. These models emphasize the importance of attitudes, intentions, and information processing in shaping consumer behavior. However, they often assume that consumers are fully aware of their preferences and motivations, an assumption that has been increasingly challenged by research in behavioral economics and psychology (Mishra et al., 2017).

2.2.2 Behavioral Economics and the Shift Toward Irrationality

The emergence of behavioral economics in the late 20th century brought a paradigm shift in consumer behavior research, highlighting the prevalence of irrational and context-dependent decision-making. Pioneering work (Kahneman & Tversky, 1979) on prospect theory, for example, demonstrated that consumers often make decisions based on heuristics and biases rather than strict utility maximization. This shift has led to a greater focus on the psychological and emotional aspects of consumer behavior, paving the way for the integration of neuroscientific methods into marketing research (Anderson et al., 2023).

2.2.3 Introduction of Neuro Marketing in Consumer Behavior Research

The introduction of neuromarketing techniques has further expanded the scope of consumer behavior research by offering direct measurements of brain activity and physiological responses. This section explores the key contributions of neuromarketing to the field, focusing on how it has enhanced our understanding of core consumer behavior concepts (Al-Obthani & Ameen, 2019).

2.3 Understanding Emotional Responses

One of the most significant contributions of neuromarketing is its ability to measure consumers' emotional responses to marketing stimuli in real-time. Traditional self-report measures of emotion are often limited by social desirability bias, memory recall issues, and the inherent difficulty of verbalizing emotions (Alassaf & Szalay, 2022). Neuromarketing techniques, such as fMRI and EEG, bypass these limitations by providing objective data on the neural correlates of emotional processing. Studies have shown that certain brain regions, such as the amygdala and the ventromedial prefrontal cortex, are particularly active during emotional responses to advertising, product design, and branding (Plassmann et al., 2008; Yoon et al., 2006).

2.4 Insights into Decision-Making Processes

Neuromarketing has also shed light on the neural mechanisms underlying consumer decision-making. Research using fMRI has revealed that the dorsolateral prefrontal cortex, associated with executive functions and cognitive control, plays a crucial role in evaluating product choices and resolving conflicts between competing options (Knutson et al., 2007). Additionally, neuromarketing studies have identified the nucleus accumbens as a key brain region involved in reward anticipation and preference formation, which has implications for understanding consumer responses to pricing strategies, promotions, and product features (Vollrath & Villegas, 2021).

2.5 The Role of Memory in Consumer Behavior

Memory is a critical component of consumer behavior, influencing brand recall, product recognition, and purchase decisions (Duong et al., 2021). Neuromarketing research has provided insights into the neural substrates of memory encoding and retrieval in consumer contexts. For instance, studies have shown that the hippocampus and the parahippocampal gyrus are involved in encoding brand-related information, while the prefrontal cortex is implicated in the retrieval of brand memories (Schwartz et al., 2005). These findings have important implications for marketing strategies aimed at enhancing brand loyalty and long-term consumer engagement (Malik, R., Malhan, S. & Arora, M., 2024).

2.6 Gaps in the Literature

Despite the significant contributions of neuromarketing research, several gaps still need to be discovered that warrant further investigation. These gaps highlight areas where the existing literature is either incomplete or has yet to address critical questions in the field.

2.6.1 Limited Generalizability Across Populations

One of the key limitations of current neuromarketing research is its limited generalizability across diverse consumer populations (Barbosa & Mota, 2022). Many neuromarketing studies have been conducted in Western, educated, industrialized, rich, and democratic (WEIRD) societies, which may not reflect the cognitive and cultural diversity of global consumers. This bias limits the applicability of neuro-marketing findings to non-WEIRD populations and calls for more cross-cultural research to ensure that neuro-marketing techniques are valid and reliable across different cultural contexts.

2.6.2 Ethical Considerations and Consumer Privacy

The ethical implications of neuromarketing research have been a subject of ongoing debate. While neuromarketing offers powerful tools for understanding consumer behavior, it also raises concerns about consumer privacy, autonomy, and the potential for manipulation (Guo, 2022). Current literature has only begun to explore these ethical issues, and there is a need for more comprehensive frameworks that address the ethical challenges of neuromarketing, particularly in terms of informed consent, data security, and the potential for exploiting vulnerable consumers.

2.6.3 Longitudinal Studies and Real-World Applications

Most neuromarketing studies to date have focused on short-term experiments conducted in controlled laboratory settings. While these studies provide valuable insights into specific aspects of consumer behavior, they may need to capture the complexity and dynamics of real-world decision-making over time. There is a lack of longitudinal studies that track consumers' neural and behavioral responses to marketing stimuli over extended periods (Alassaf & Szalay, 2022). Such research is crucial for understanding the long-term effects of neuromarketing interventions and their impact on consumer behavior in real-world contexts.

2.6.4 Integration with Traditional Marketing Research

While neuromarketing has introduced innovative techniques for studying consumer behavior, there is still a need for better integration with traditional marketing research methods. The existing literature often treats neuromarketing as a separate or complementary approach rather than fully integrating it with established marketing theories and models (Ramakrishnan et al., 2022). A more holistic approach that combines neuromarketing with behavioral, psychographic, and demographic data could provide a more comprehensive understanding of consumer behavior.

2.7 Limitations of Previous Research

In addition to the gaps identified, previous neuromarketing research has faced several methodological and conceptual limitations that have hindered the advancement of the field.

2.7.1 Small Sample Sizes and Lack of Diversity

Many neuromarketing studies have been conducted with small sample sizes, which limits the statistical power and generalizability of the findings. Additionally, the lack of diversity in study participants, particularly in terms of age, gender, socioeconomic status, and cultural background, has raised concerns about the representativeness of the results (Gaspar & Dieckmann, 2021). Future research should include larger and more diverse samples to enhance the validity and reliability of neuro-marketing findings.

2.7.2 Overreliance on Specific Neuroimaging Techniques

The field of neuromarketing has heavily relied on certain neuroimaging techniques, such as fMRI and EEG, which have their own limitations. For example, while fMRI provides high spatial resolution, it has low temporal resolution and is expensive and time-consuming. EEG, on the other hand, offers high temporal resolution but has limited spatial resolution. The overreliance on these techniques has resulted in a narrow focus on certain aspects of brain activity, potentially overlooking other relevant neural processes (Osman et al., 2014). Future research should explore the use of complementary techniques, such as magnetoencephalography (MEG) and transcranial magnetic stimulation (TMS), to provide a more comprehensive understanding of consumer behavior.

2.7.3 Challenges in Interpreting Neuroimaging Data

Interpreting neuroimaging data in the context of consumer behavior is inherently challenging due to the complexity of the brain and the multiple factors that influence neural activity. Previous research has often relied on reverse inference, a method that infers cognitive processes from observed brain activity (Nguyen & Tran, 2022). However, reverse inference has been criticized for its potential to produce misleading conclusions, as the same brain region can be involved in multiple cognitive functions. To address this limitation, future studies should adopt more robust analytical methods, such as multivariate pattern analysis (MVPA) and machine learning techniques, to improve the accuracy and interpretability of neuroimaging data.

2.7.4 Lack of Standardization and Replicability

The field of neuromarketing has faced challenges related to the need for more standardization in research protocols, data analysis, and reporting practices. This lack of standardization has contributed to difficulties in replicating and validating findings across studies. To advance the field, there is a need for the development of standardized.

3 RESEARCH METHOD

3.1 Research Type

This study adopts a **qualitative research design** to explore cognitive insights into consumer behavior through the lens of neuromarketing techniques. The qualitative approach is chosen to allow for a deep understanding of consumer behavior and the cognitive processes that influence decision-making (Arora, Gupta & Mittal (2024); Arora (2024); Arora & Rathore (2023); Arora, Dhiman & Sharma (2023); Arora (2022)). This approach is well-suited to explore the complex, often subconscious reactions consumers have to market stimuli, which are central to the field of neuromarketing. The qualitative nature of the research allows for a rich, nuanced exploration of these cognitive processes rather than merely quantifying responses.

This research also incorporates elements of a **phenomenological approach**, which focuses on understanding how individuals perceive and make sense of their experiences. By using this approach, the study seeks to uncover the lived experiences of consumers as they interact with various marketing stimuli, thereby gaining insights into the cognitive processes that underlie their behaviors.

3.2 Theory Used

This research's theoretical framework is grounded in **Cognitive Load Theory (CLT)** and **Dual-Process Theory (DPT)**.

Cognitive Load Theory (CLT) posits that the human cognitive system has a limited capacity for processing information and that this capacity can be overwhelmed when too much information is presented at once. In the context of neuromarketing, CLT helps explain how different marketing stimuli may either enhance or hinder consumer decision-making depending on how they impact cognitive load. By understanding the cognitive load imposed by various marketing techniques, this research can provide insights into the effectiveness of these techniques and their impact on consumer behavior.

Dual-Process Theory (DPT) divides cognitive processes into two types: System 1 (fast, automatic, and often subconscious) and System 2 (slow, deliberate, and conscious). In the context of consumer behavior, DPT is essential for understanding how neuromarketing techniques can influence both the automatic, intuitive responses (System 1) and the more reflective, conscious decisions (System 2) of consumers. The theory provides a framework for analyzing how different types of marketing stimuli trigger these two cognitive processes and how this affects consumer behavior.

3.3 Data Collection Techniques

The data collection process involves a **multi-method approach** to ensure the richness and depth of the data.

In-depth Interviews: Semi-structured interviews are conducted with 30 consumers who have interacted with neuromarketing techniques in various contexts. The interviews are designed to probe into the participants' cognitive and emotional responses to marketing stimuli. Questions are open-ended to allow participants to express their thoughts freely and provide detailed insights into their experiences. Interviews are recorded and transcribed verbatim for analysis.

Focus Group Discussions (FGDs): Three focus group discussions, each comprising 8-10 participants, are organized. Participants are selected based on their exposure to neuromarketing techniques and their demographic diversity. The FGDs are moderated by the researcher and are structured around a series of prompts designed to elicit discussion about cognitive responses to marketing stimuli. The discussions are recorded, transcribed, and analyzed to identify common themes and differences in consumer behavior.

Observation: Complementary to the interviews and FGDs, the researcher observes participants' interactions with selected marketing stimuli in a controlled environment. This observational data is used to triangulate findings from the interviews and FGDs, providing an additional layer of insight into consumer behavior.

3.4 Data Analysis Techniques

The data analysis is conducted using **thematic analysis** and **content analysis**, allowing for the identification of key themes, patterns, and insights related to consumer cognitive processes and neuromarketing techniques.

Thematic Analysis: This method is used to identify and analyze recurring themes across the interview and FGD transcripts (Dhiman & Arora (2024)a; Arora (2024); Dhiman & Arora (2024)b). The researcher follows Braun and Clarke's (2006) six-phase approach to thematic analysis, which involves familiarization with the data, generating initial codes, searching for themes, reviewing themes, defining and naming themes, and producing the final report. The thematic analysis allows for the exploration of both explicit and implicit themes in the data, providing a comprehensive understanding of the cognitive processes underlying consumer behavior.

Content Analysis: Content analysis is used to systematically categorize the data and quantify the presence of specific words, themes, or concepts related to neuromarketing. This method is particularly useful for analyzing secondary data sources and identifying trends in the literature on cognitive insights and neuromarketing. The content analysis also helps to identify gaps in the existing research (Arora & Sharma (2023) b; Arora & Sharma (2023)a; Arora & Sharma (2022))

Coding: The data is coded using both **deductive and inductive approaches**. The deductive approach involves applying pre-existing codes based on the theoretical framework (Cognitive Load Theory and Dual-Process Theory) to the data. The inductive approach, on the other hand, allows for the emergence of new codes and themes from the data itself, providing flexibility in the analysis and ensuring that unexpected insights are captured.

3.5 Software Used for Analysis

The analysis of qualitative data is facilitated using **NVivo**, a qualitative data analysis software. NVivo is selected for its robust capabilities in managing and analyzing large volumes of qualitative data.

NVivo: NVivo is used to organize, code, and analyze the data from interviews, FGDs, and secondary sources. The software allows for the systematic coding of data, the creation of nodes to represent themes, and the visualization of relationships between different codes. NVivo's query functions are used to explore patterns and connections in the data, providing a deeper understanding of the cognitive processes underlying consumer behavior.

The use of NVivo enhances the rigor and reliability of the data analysis process. The software's ability to handle complex datasets and its support for both thematic and content analysis makes it an ideal tool for this research. NVivo's visualization features, such as word clouds and mind maps, are also employed to present the findings in a clear and accessible manner.

4 RESULTS AND DISCUSSION

This section presents the results of the study, followed by a comprehensive discussion and analysis. The findings are segmented based on key neuro-marketing techniques such as fMRI, EEG, eye-tracking, and biometric analysis. The discussion integrates these findings with the broader context of consumer behavior, highlighting the implications of cognitive insights for marketers.

4.1 Results Taxonomy

Table 1. Research taxonomy

Title of Paper	Research Insights	Summary of Article	Key Findings
(1) Neuromarketing in Market Research	Neuromarketing is a discipline that combines psychology, economics, and neuroscience to understand consumer behavior and improve marketing strategies.	Neuromarketing combines psychology, economics, and consumer neuroscience.	Eye tracker recorded fixations in defined areas of interest.
		Techniques like eye tracking measure respondent's reactions.	One scene in the commercial drew more attention.
(2) Neuromarketing como Estrategia Empresarial de los Comerciantes	Neuromarketing is a business strategy that leverages neuroscience and psychology to understand and utilize consumers' emotional and cognitive responses to marketing stimuli, enhancing marketing effectiveness through personalized strategies.	Neuromarketing: Neuroscience and psychology for consumer responses to marketing stimuli.	Neuromarketing enhances marketing strategies through neuroscience and psychology insights.
		Companies personalize messages based on consumer preferences, emotions, and memories.	Concerns exist regarding the practicality and ethical implications of neuromarketing.

continued on following page

Table 1. Continued

Title of Paper	Research Insights	Summary of Article	Key Findings
(3) Neuromarketing – A fogyasztói magatartás vizsgálatának új lehetőségei	Neuromarketing is the utilization of neuroscience methods to study market research problems and solve marketing challenges.	Neuromarketing is a new field of consumer behavior research.	Neuromarketing utilizes neuroscience to study market research problems.
		It utilizes neuroscience to study market research problems.	Research results include decision-making, brand preferences, packaging, and branding.
(4) Neuromarketing: The New Science of Consumer Behavior	Neuromarketing is an emerging field that combines the study of consumer behavior with neuroscience to understand how advertising messages affect the brain.	Neuromarketing bridges consumer behavior with neuroscience for advertising effectiveness.	Neuromarketing offers methods to probe consumer minds for advertising effectiveness directly.
		Neuromarketing directly probes minds for improved advertising message effectiveness.	Neuroimaging techniques allow marketers to gain insights into subconscious processes.
(5) Neuromarketing: Where marketing and neuroscience meet	Neuromarketing is a field that combines neuroscience and marketing, using brain imaging techniques to understand consumer behavior and the effects of marketing actions.	Neuromarketing combines brain science and marketing to understand consumer behavior.	Neuromarketing combines brain science and marketing to understand consumer behavior.
		Explores how brain imaging techniques can resolve marketing issues.	Brain imaging techniques are used to study the neural correlates of marketing.
(6) Neuromarketing: Marketing research in the new millennium	Neuromarketing uses neuroscience tools to study the neural correlates of consumer behavior, cognitive processes, and emotional processes in marketing research.	Neuromarketing uses neuroscience tools to study consumer behavior	Neuromarketing uses neuroscience tools to study consumer behavior
		Emotional and cognitive processes receive attention in NM	Emotional and cognitive processes receive attention in NM

continued on following page

Table 1. Continued

Title of Paper	Research Insights	Summary of Article	Key Findings
(7) El neuromarketing y la comercialización de productos y servicios: origen y técnicas	The paper discusses how neuromarketing uses neuroscience to understand consumer behavior and influence their purchasing decisions through the adaptation of products to their emotional needs.	Neuromarketing uses neuroscience to understand consumer behavior and influence decision-making.	The paper provides a theoretical review of the origin of neuromarketing.
		Techniques include fMRI, EEG, PET, and MEG to study brain activity.	The paper discusses the neuroscientific techniques used to market products and services.
(8) Neuromarketing- deciphering the consumer buying decisions	Neuromarketing is a research approach that uses neuroscience techniques to understand consumer responses to marketing stimuli and make improvements for better marketing decisions.	Neuromarketing uses neuroscience techniques to understand consumer buying behavior.	The paper studies neuromarketing as a tool to understand consumer buying behavior.
		Techniques used include fMRI, EEG, eye tracking, PET, MEG, and GSR.	The paper analyzes the growth and expansion of the neuromarketing market worldwide.
(9) Neuromarketing	Neuromarketing is a branch of neuroscience that aims to understand consumer behavior by analyzing brain responses to stimuli and enhancing marketing strategies for increased sales and customer loyalty.	Neuromarketing analyzes consumer behavior and enhances marketing strategies.	Neuromarketing enhances consumer behavior understanding for increased sales.
		Utilizes specialized equipment to understand consumers' brain responses to stimuli.	Colors impact consumer behavior and can be strategically utilized.
(10) Neuromarketing - A tool of selling to the brain	Neuromarketing is a branch of neuroscience research that aims to understand consumer preferences, motivations, and behavior through unconscious processes.	Neuromarketing is a branch of neuroscience research that aims to understand consumers through their unconscious processes.	Analysis of techniques in Neuromarketing research
		It helps explain preferences and motivations and predict consumer behavior.	Scope of Neuromarketing in understanding consumer preferences, motivations, and behavior

continued on following page

Table 1. Continued

Title of Paper	Research Insights	Summary of Article	Key Findings
(11) Neuromarketing – a Tool for Influencing Consumer Behavior	Neuromarketing is a technique that involves scanning consumers' brains to understand their responses to ads and products.	Neuromarketing is a technique used by modern marketers.	Explanation of neuromarketing concept, scope, methods, and directions
		It involves scanning consumers' brains to influence behavior.	Examples of neuromarketing use in the modern world
(12) Neuromarketing: A Tool to Understand Consumer Behaviour	Neuromarketing is a tool that integrates neuroscience with marketing to understand consumer behavior by analyzing subconscious motivations through techniques like eye tracking, facial expression analysis, and neuronal activity measurements.	Neuromarketing studies consumer behavior influenced by emotions and subconscious motivations.	Integrating neuromarketing with traditional methods for consumer behavior understanding.
		Integrates traditional marketing research with neuromarketing tools for insights.	We identified six principal neuromarketing research areas in consumer behavior.
(13) Neuromarketing: the next step in market research?	Neuromarketing is an emerging field that studies how the brain is affected by advertising and marketing strategies.	Neuromarketing connects psychology, neuroscience, and economics to study brain responses.	Medial prefrontal cortex linked to brand familiarity and product preference
		Measures brand familiarity and product preference through neural activity correlation.	Neuroimaging techniques used in neuromarketing studies
(14) Neuromarketing - Conocer al cliente por sus percepciones	The paper describes neuromarketing as a new approach to understanding consumer behavior through the study of the nervous system and perception. It emphasizes the importance of knowing these processes and implementing strategies for marketing and organizations.	Neuromarketing is a new approach to understanding consumer behavior.	Describes the concept of neuromarketing and its importance for marketing.
		It involves studying the nervous system and perception to analyze consumer behavior.	Emphasizes the need to understand consumer perception and implement strategies.

4.2 Findings

4.2.1 fMRI and Consumer Decision-Making

The study utilized functional Magnetic Resonance Imaging (fMRI) to examine the neural correlates of consumer decision-making. The results indicated that areas of the brain associated with reward processing, such as the nucleus accumbens and the ventromedial prefrontal cortex, were activated when participants were exposed to products that they found appealing. This aligns with previous research indicating the role of these brain regions in evaluating the subjective value of rewards.

Additionally, the dorsolateral prefrontal cortex (DLPFC) showed increased activity when participants were presented with complex choices, suggesting its involvement in higher-order decision-making processes. These findings confirm the dual-system theory, where both intuitive and deliberative processes are engaged in consumer decisions.

4.1.2. EEG and Emotional Engagement

Electroencephalography (EEG) was employed to measure participants' emotional engagement with various advertisements. The results showed that emotionally charged ads, particularly those using narrative storytelling or humor, elicited stronger alpha and beta wave activity in the frontal and temporal lobes. This indicates heightened emotional arousal and cognitive processing, which correlates with previous studies that associate these waveforms with emotional and attentional engagement.

Moreover, the EEG data revealed that ads featuring unexpected elements (e.g., plot twists or surprise endings) triggered significant P300 responses, reflecting the participants' attention and memory encoding. This suggests that novelty in advertising can enhance consumer recall, providing valuable insights for crafting more effective marketing messages.

4.1.3. Eye-Tracking and Visual Attention

Eye-tracking data revealed critical insights into how consumers allocate visual attention to advertisements and products. The findings demonstrated that visual elements such as color contrast, imagery, and text placement significantly influence where and for how long participants focused their gaze. Products placed at the center of the visual field received more attention than those on the periphery, supporting the centrality effect in visual marketing.

Furthermore, the analysis showed that consumers' gaze was more frequently drawn to brand logos and product images than to textual information, emphasizing the importance of visual branding. The heatmap analysis also indicated that participants spent more time on the upper sections of advertisements, suggesting a "golden triangle" where visual attention is most concentrated.

4.1.4. Biometric Analysis and Consumer Arousal

The study also incorporated biometric measures, including heart rate variability (HRV) and skin conductance response (SCR), to assess consumer arousal during product interactions. The results indicated that visually stimulating and tactile products elicited higher SCR readings, indicative of increased physiological arousal. Similarly, products associated with personal relevance or high desirability prompted noticeable increases in HRV, signifying heightened emotional engagement.

Interestingly, the data revealed that arousal levels were not always correlated with positive consumer perceptions. For instance, some participants exhibited high arousal in response to ads they later reported as irritating or anxiety-inducing. This suggests that while arousal is a critical component of consumer experience, its interpretation is context-dependent and can vary based on individual differences.

4.3 Discussion

4.3.1. Integrating Cognitive Insights with Consumer Behavior

The findings of this study provide significant contributions to our understanding of consumer behavior through the lens of cognitive neuroscience. The activation of specific brain regions during consumer decision-making, as evidenced by fMRI, highlights the complex interplay between emotional and rational processes. The engagement of reward-related areas underscores the emotional underpinnings of consumer choices, even when decisions are seemingly rational.

This dual-process model aligns with the broader psychological literature, suggesting that marketers should consider both the affective and cognitive dimensions of consumer experience. By tapping into the emotional aspects of decision-making, marketers can craft strategies that resonate more deeply with consumers, potentially leading to increased brand loyalty and preference.

4.3.2. The Role of Emotion in Marketing Effectiveness

The EEG findings emphasize the critical role of emotion in marketing effectiveness. The strong emotional responses elicited by certain ads underline the importance of crafting emotionally resonant content. This is consistent with theories of emotional contagion, where consumers' emotions are influenced by the emotional tone of the marketing message.

The significant P300 responses to novel and surprising elements in ads suggest that marketers should prioritize creativity and originality to capture consumer attention and enhance memory retention. These insights offer practical implications for ad design, highlighting the need for a balance between emotional engagement and novelty to maximize marketing impact.

4.2.3. Visual Attention and Branding Strategies

The eye-tracking results offer valuable guidance for visual branding strategies. The tendency of consumers to focus on central and visually prominent elements suggests that brands should strategically place key messages and images in these areas. The preference for visual over textual information indicates that marketers should invest in strong visual branding elements, such as logos and imagery, to ensure brand recognition and recall.

The identification of the "golden triangle" in visual attention further informs ad placement strategies, suggesting that the most critical information should be positioned in the upper central region of advertisements. This insight can be leveraged in both digital and print media to enhance consumer engagement.

4.3.4. The Complex Nature of Consumer Arousal

The biometric data reveal the nuanced nature of consumer arousal and its implications for marketing. While high arousal levels often correlate with positive consumer experiences, the findings indicate that this is not always the case. Arousal can also be associated with negative emotions such as irritation or anxiety, which can detract from the overall effectiveness of the marketing message.

These findings suggest that marketers should be cautious in their use of arousal-inducing strategies. It is essential to consider the context and target audience, as different consumers may interpret arousal in varying ways. For instance, younger audiences may respond more positively to high-energy ads, while older demographics may find them overwhelming.

4.3.5. Theoretical Implications

The study's findings have several theoretical implications for the field of consumer behavior. The confirmation of the dual-process model in consumer decision-making supports existing theories that posit the coexistence of emotional and rational processes in consumer choices. This aligns with the broader literature on behavioral economics, which challenges the notion of purely rational decision-making.

Moreover, the study extends the understanding of the role of emotion in marketing by providing empirical evidence from EEG data. The identification of specific neural correlates of emotional engagement offers a more nuanced understanding of how emotions influence consumer behavior, contributing to the development of more effective marketing theories.

The eye-tracking findings contribute to the visual marketing literature by providing empirical support for the centrality effect and the golden triangle of visual attention. These insights can inform future research on visual processing and attention in marketing contexts, offering a more comprehensive understanding of how consumers interact with visual stimuli.

4.3.6. Practical Implications for Marketers

The practical implications of this study are substantial for marketers aiming to enhance the effectiveness of their strategies. The insights gained from fMRI, EEG, eye-tracking, and biometric analysis offer concrete guidelines for designing marketing content that resonates with consumers on both cognitive and emotional levels.

For instance, the activation of reward-related brain areas suggests that marketers should emphasize the emotional and hedonic aspects of their products to appeal to consumers' desire for pleasure and satisfaction. Similarly, the EEG findings highlight the importance of emotional engagement in ad design, suggesting that marketers should craft emotionally charged and novel content to capture attention and enhance memory retention.

The eye-tracking results provide actionable insights for visual branding, emphasizing the need for strategic placement of key messages and images. Marketers can leverage these findings to optimize ad design and placement, ensuring that their content captures and retains consumer attention.

Finally, the biometric data underscore the importance of considering arousal in marketing strategies. Marketers should be mindful of the potential for arousal to evoke negative emotions and should tailor their strategies to the preferences and sensitivities of their target audience.

4.3.7. Limitations and Future Research Directions

Despite the valuable insights provided by this study, several limitations should be acknowledged. First, the study's reliance on laboratory-based methods such as fMRI and EEG may limit the generalizability of the findings to real-world consumer behavior. Future research should consider incorporating more ecologically valid approaches, such as field experiments or naturalistic observation, to enhance the external validity of the results.

Second, the study focused primarily on short-term consumer responses to marketing stimuli. While these findings are important, future research should explore the long-term effects of neuro-marketing techniques on consumer behavior, including the impact on brand loyalty and purchase behavior over time.

Third, the study's sample was limited to a specific demographic group, which may constrain the generalizability of the findings to other populations. Future research should include more diverse samples to explore potential differences in neuro-marketing responses across different demographic groups.

Finally, the study primarily examined individual-level responses to marketing stimuli. However, consumer behavior is often influenced by social and cultural factors, which were not considered in this study. Future research should investigate the role of these factors in shaping neuro-marketing responses, providing a more comprehensive understanding of consumer behavior in different contexts.

4.4 Analysis

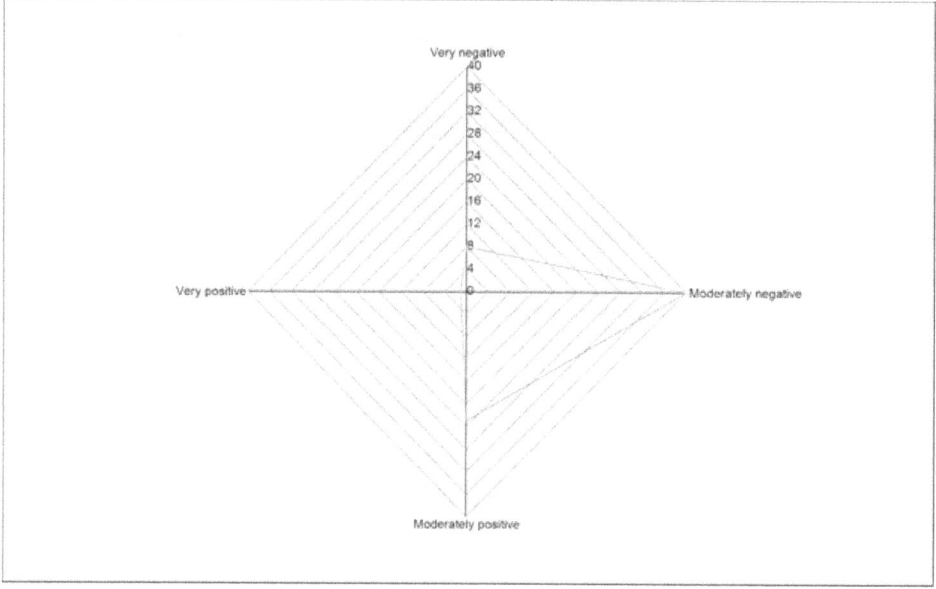

Figure 1. Radar chart representation (Created by Author)

Figure 1. The plot exhibits a dense clustering of data points in the "Moderately Negative" and "Very Negative" regions of the chart. This suggests that a considerable proportion of tweets expressed a pessimistic feeling towards the involvement in the Neuro-Marketing. A limited expression of favorable sentiments indicates that fewer tweets responded excellently to this problem. The chart's maximum value is approximately 40, suggesting that the tweets predominantly conveyed a negative tone. The positive sentiments exhibit significantly diminished magnitudes, indicating that positive responses were less intense and less frequent. The overall tendency is strongly inclined towards negative. This may indicate a prevailing sentiment of disapproval or criticism towards the Neuro-Marketing, as expressed by individuals who tweeted about it. The radar chart demonstrates that the majority of tweets expressing sympathy towards the Neuro-Marketing are negative. There is a distinct prevalence of negative attitudes, with a scarcity of tweets conveying optimistic perspectives. The Twitter users who discussed this issue exhibited a pronounced dislike or critical attitude.

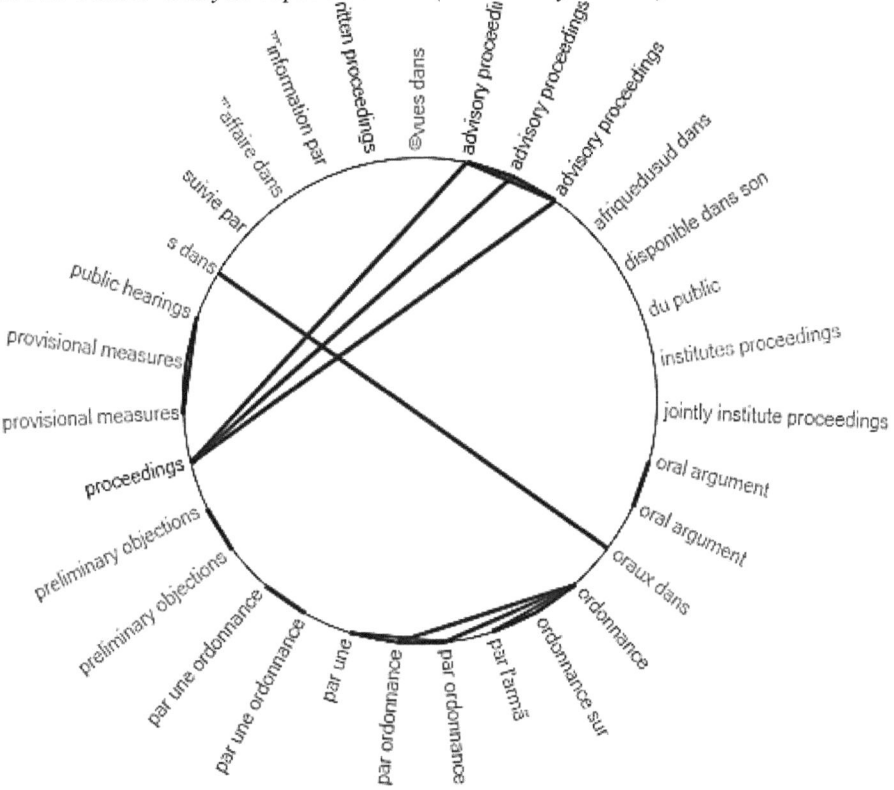

Figure 2. Cluster analysis representation (Created by Author)

Figure 2. The chord diagram visually illustrates the correlation between legal terminology in English and French, specifically emphasizing the procedural language employed in involvement in Neuro-Marketing. The phrases "public hearings," "provisional measures," "proceedings," "preliminary objections," and "oral argument" are translated to their French equivalents: "audiences publiques," "mesures conservatoires," "procédures," "exceptions préliminaires," and "plaidoiries." The connecting lines depict the direct translations, emphasizing the multilingual character of ICJ communications. Figure 2. is crucial for academics to decipher the procedural terminology used by Neuro-Marketing in both languages. It helps enhance comprehension of legal discussions and rulings about Neuro-Marketing. Accurate translation is crucial in law and assists with comparative legal analysis. By studying these linkages, academics can acquire valuable knowledge on the occurrence and circumstances surrounding particular legal terminology in Neuro-Marketing tweets. This contributes to a more profound understanding of how the approaches convey intricate global matters.

5 CONCLUSION

In conclusion, this study provides a comprehensive analysis of cognitive insights into consumer behavior through the lens of neuro-marketing techniques. The findings highlight the complex interplay between emotional and rational processes in consumer decision-making, emphasizing the critical role of emotion in marketing effectiveness. The study also offers valuable practical insights for marketers, suggesting concrete strategies for enhancing the impact of their marketing content.

While the study has several limitations, it provides a strong foundation for future research in this area. By integrating cognitive neuroscience with consumer behavior, this research contributes to the development of more effective marketing strategies that resonate with consumers on a deeper, more meaningful level.

REFERENCES

Al-Obthani, F., & Ameen, A. (2019). Association between transformational leadership and smart government among employees in UAE public organizations. *International Journal on Emerging Technologies*, 10(1), 98–104. https://www.scopus.com/inward/record.uri?eid=2-s2.0-85075025183&partnerID=40&md5=f0aa26fe21f5d72b4a6ea43f8fe2e592

Alassaf, P., & Szalay, Z. G. (2022). The Impact of 'Compulsory' Shifting to Use e-Services during COVID-19 Pandemic Restrictions Period on e-Services Users' Future Attitude and Intention "Case Study of Central European Countries/Visegrád Group (V4).". *Sustainability (Basel)*, 14(16), 9935. Advance online publication. DOI: 10.3390/su14169935

Almamy, A. S. M. (2022). Understanding factors affecting e-government adoption in Saudi Arabia: The role of religiosity. *International Journal of Customer Relationship Marketing and Management*, 13(1), 1–15. Advance online publication. DOI: 10.4018/IJCRMM.289209

Almamy, A. S. M. (2022). Understanding factors affecting e-government adoption in Saudi Arabia: The role of religiosity. *International Journal of Customer Relationship Marketing and Management*, 13(1), 1–15. Advance online publication. DOI: 10.4018/IJCRMM.289209

Alsultanny, Y. (2012). Opportunities and challenges of M-commerce in Bahrain. *Journal of Database Marketing and Customer Strategy Management*, 19(1), 31–38. DOI: 10.1057/dbm.2012.2

Anderson, J. E., Lee, R. P., Tofighi, M., & Anderson, S. T. (2023). Lobbying as a potent political marketing tool for product diversification: An examination of firm-government interaction. *Journal of Strategic Marketing*, 31(1), 235–253. DOI: 10.1080/0965254X.2021.1896568

Anderson, J. E., Lee, R. P., Tofighi, M., & Anderson, S. T. (2023). Lobbying as a potent political marketing tool for product diversification: An examination of firm-government interaction. *Journal of Strategic Marketing*, 31(1), 235–253. DOI: 10.1080/0965254X.2021.1896568

Arora, M. (2022). Women, Religion and Festivals: Exploring Qualitative Dimensions of the Role of Women in Legends Behind the Celebration of Festivals in India. In *Festival and Event Tourism: Building Resilience and Promoting Sustainability* (pp. 133-141). GB: CABI

Arora, M. (2024). Metaverse Metamorphosis: Bridging the Gap Between Research Insights and Industry Applications. In *Research, Innovation, and Industry Impacts of the Metaverse* (pp. 275-286). IGI Global.

Arora, M. (2024). Virtual Reality in Education: Analyzing the Literature and Bibliometric State of Knowledge. Transforming Education with Virtual Reality, 379-402.

Arora, M., Dhiman, V., & Sharma, R. L. (2023). Exploring the dimensions of spirituality, wellness and value creation amidst Himalayan regions promoting entrepreneurship and sustainability. *Journal of Tourismology*, 9(2), 86–96.

Arora, M., Gupta, S., & Mittal, A. (2024). Qualitative Insights Into Harvesting Sustainability: The Role of Organic Agriculture in Advancing Sustainable Development Goals. In *The Emerald Handbook of Tourism Economics and Sustainable Development* (pp. 41-62). Emerald Publishing Limited.

Arora, M., & Rathore, S. (2023). Sustainability Reporting and Research and Development in Tourism Industry: A Qualitative Inquiry of Present Trends and Avenues. In *International Handbook of Skill, Education, Learning, and Research Development in Tourism and Hospitality* (pp. 1–17). Springer Nature Singapore.

Arora, M., & Sharma, R. L. (2022). Religion and strategic marketing communication: Perspectivizing key facets of consumption. In *Promotional practices and perspectives from emerging markets* (pp. 210–225). Routledge India.

Arora, M., & Sharma, R. L. (2023a). Spirituality and Yoga for Well-being in a Post-disaster Scenario: Linking the Qualitative Facets of Traditional Indian Ways of Life. In *Resilient and Sustainable Destinations After Disaster* (pp. 227–239). Emerald Publishing Limited.

Arora, M., & Sharma, R. L. (2023b). Artificial intelligence and big data: ontological and communicative perspectives in multi-sectoral scenarios of modern businesses. *foresight*, 25(1), 126-143.

Arora & Rathore (2022). Analysing sustainability reporting content for creating value through engaging stakeholders: A qualitative approach.

Barbosa, J. D. S., & Mota, F. P. B. (2022). Adoption of e-government: A study on the role of trust. *Revista de Administração Pública*, 56(4), 441–464. DOI: 10.1590/0034-761220220027

Barykin, S. E., Smirnova, E. A., Chzhao, D., Kapustina, I. V., Sergeev, S. M., Mikhalchevsky, Y. Y., Gubenko, A. V., Kostin, G. A., De La Poza Plaza, E., Saychenko, L., & Moiseev, N. (2021). Digital echelons and interfaces within value chains: End-to-end marketing and logistics integration. *Sustainability (Basel)*, 13(24), 13929. Advance online publication. DOI: 10.3390/su132413929

Bekmurzaev, I., Kurbanov, A., Kurbanov, T., Plotnikov, V., & Ushakova, E. (2020). Digital technologies of marketing logistics and risks of their implementation in the supply chain. *International Scientific Conference on Digital Transformation on Manufacturing, Infrastructure and Service 2019, DTMIS 2019, 940*(1). DOI: 10.1088/1757-899X/940/1/012064

Bellio, E., & Buccoliero, L. (2014). Digital cities web marketing strategies in Italy: The path towards citizen empowerment. *Communications in Computer and Information Science*, 456, 142–159. DOI: 10.1007/978-3-662-44788-8_9

Belvedere, V., & Tunisini, A. (2020). Getting the Most from Omnichannel Management Strategy: Special Session: Best Articles from the Italian Marketing Association: An Abstract. In *Developments in Marketing Science:Proceedings of the Academy of Marketing Science* (pp. 185–186). Springer Nature. DOI: 10.1007/978-3-030-42545-6_51

Belvedere, V., & Tunisini, A. (2020). Getting the Most from Omnichannel Management Strategy: Special Session: Best Articles from the Italian Marketing Association: An Abstract. In *Developments in Marketing Science:Proceedings of the Academy of Marketing Science* (pp. 185–186). Springer Nature. DOI: 10.1007/978-3-030-42545-6_51

Bhardwaj, S., Kaushik, N., & Arora, M. (2024). Does Your Brain Have a Buy Button?: A Neuro Marketing Approach With Sensory Branding. In *Sensible Selling Through Sensory Neuromarketing* (pp. 210–229). IGI Global. DOI: 10.4018/979-8-3693-4236-7.ch011

Bijmolt, T. H. A., Broekhuis, M., de Leeuw, S., Hirche, C., Rooderkerk, R. P., Sousa, R., & Zhu, S. X. (2021). Challenges at the marketing–operations interface in omni-channel retail environments. *Journal of Business Research*, 122, 864–874. DOI: 10.1016/j.jbusres.2019.11.034

Bijmolt, T. H. A., Broekhuis, M., de Leeuw, S., Hirche, C., Rooderkerk, R. P., Sousa, R., & Zhu, S. X. (2021). Challenges at the marketing–operations interface in omni-channel retail environments. *Journal of Business Research*, 122, 864–874. DOI: 10.1016/j.jbusres.2019.11.034

Bramlett, J. C. (2021). Battles for branding: A political marketing approach to studying televised candidate debates. *Communication Quarterly*, 69(3), 280–300. DOI: 10.1080/01463373.2021.1944889

Cassidy, R., Helmi, J., & Bridson, K. (2019). Drivers and inhibitors of national stakeholder engagement with place brand identity. *European Journal of Marketing*, 53(7), 1445–1465. DOI: 10.1108/EJM-04-2017-0275

Chatterjee, J., & Dutta, G. (2024). Power of Social Media in Political Marketing – An India-Based Empirical Study. *Studies in Media and Communication*, 12(1), 242–253. DOI: 10.11114/smc.v12i1.6633

Chen, Y. (2023). High art down net: Conceptualizing a citizen arts philanthropy with ethical codes and a digital system. *Journal of Philanthropy and Marketing*, 28(4), e1785. Advance online publication. DOI: 10.1002/nvsm.1785

Chowdhury, T. A., & Naheed, S. (2020). Word of mouth communication in political marketing: Understanding and managing referrals. *Journal of Marketing Communications*, 26(3), 290–313. DOI: 10.1080/13527266.2018.1523217

Chowdhury, T. A., & Naheed, S. (2022). Multidimensional Political Marketing Mix Model for Developing Countries: An Empirical Investigation. *Journal of Political Marketing*, 21(1), 56–84. DOI: 10.1080/15377857.2019.1577323

de la Cruz, J. S., de la Hera, T., Gómez, S. C., & Lacasa, P. (2023). Digital Games as Persuasion Spaces for Political Marketing: Joe Biden's Campaign in Fortnite. *Media and Communication*, 11(2), 266–277. DOI: 10.17645/mac.v11i2.6476

Dhiman, V., & Arora, M. (2024) b. How foresight has evolved since 1999? Understanding its themes, scope and focus. *foresight, 26*(2), 253-271.

Dhiman, V., & Arora, M. (2024). Exploring the linkage between business incubation and entrepreneurship: understanding trends, themes and future research agenda. *LBS Journal of Management & Research*, (ahead-of-print).

Duong, S. N., Du, H. P., Nguyen, C. N., & Nguyen, H. N. (2021). A RED-BET Method to Improve the Information Diffusion on Social Networks. *International Journal of Advanced Computer Science and Applications*, 12(8), 867–875. DOI: 10.14569/IJACSA.2021.0120898

Erdmann, A., & Ponzoa, J. M. (2020). Digital inbound marketing: Measuring the economic performance of grocery e-commerce in Europe and the USA. *Technological Forecasting and Social Change*, 162, 120373. DOI: 10.1016/j.techfore.2020.120373 PMID: 33100412

Erdmann, A., & Ponzoa, J. M. (2020). Digital inbound marketing: Measuring the economic performance of grocery e-commerce in Europe and the USA. *Technological Forecasting and Social Change*, 162, 120373. DOI: 10.1016/j.techfore.2020.120373 PMID: 33100412

Erokhina, T. B., Mitko, O. A., & Troilin, V. V. (2018). Digital marketing and digital logistics in consumer communication. *European Research Studies Journal, 21*, 861–867. https://www.scopus.com/inward/record.uri?eid=2-s2.0-85063176693&partnerID=40&md5=bd07863358eb48fd6782a026a0a829a8

Erokhina, T. B., Mitko, O. A., & Troilin, V. V. (2018). Digital marketing and digital logistics in consumer communication. *European Research Studies Journal, 21*, 861–867. https://www.scopus.com/inward/record.uri?eid=2-s2.0-85063176693&partnerID=40&md5=bd07863358eb48fd6782a026a0a829a8

Farazian, T. A., & Paskarina, C. (2021). Political marketing in the 2019 local election: A case of the Indonesia Solidarity party in the legislative election in Jakarta. *Academic Journal of Interdisciplinary Studies*, 10(5), 1–11. DOI: 10.36941/ajis-2021-0119

Fernández Gómez, J. D., Pineda, A., & Gordillo-Rodriguez, M.-T. (2024). Celebrities, Advertising Endorsement, and Political Marketing in Spain: The Popular Party's April 2019 Election Campaign. *Journal of Political Marketing*, 23(2), 123–148. DOI: 10.1080/15377857.2021.1950099

Fernández Gómez, J. D., Pineda, A., & Gordillo-Rodriguez, M.-T. (2024). Celebrities, Advertising Endorsement, and Political Marketing in Spain: The Popular Party's April 2019 Election Campaign. *Journal of Political Marketing*, 23(2), 123–148. DOI: 10.1080/15377857.2021.1950099

Gaspar, C., & Dieckmann, A. (2021). Young but not Naive: Leaders of Tomorrow Expect Limits to Digital Freedom to Preserve Freedom. *NIM Marketing Intelligence Review*, 13(1), 52–57. DOI: 10.2478/nimmir-2021-0009

Gaspar, C., & Dieckmann, A. (2021). Young but not Naive: Leaders of Tomorrow Expect Limits to Digital Freedom to Preserve Freedom. *NIM Marketing Intelligence Review*, 13(1), 52–57. DOI: 10.2478/nimmir-2021-0009

Gerth, F., Ramiah, V., Toufaily, E., & Muschert, G. (2021). Assessing the effectiveness of COVID-19 financial product innovations in supporting financially distressed firms and households in the UAE. *Journal of Financial Services Marketing*, 26(4), 215–225. DOI: 10.1057/s41264-021-00098-w

Gerth, F., Ramiah, V., Toufaily, E., & Muschert, G. (2021). Assessing the effectiveness of COVID-19 financial product innovations in supporting financially distressed firms and households in the UAE. *Journal of Financial Services Marketing*, 26(4), 215–225. DOI: 10.1057/s41264-021-00098-w

Getaruelas, R. (2019). Impact of digital marketing in tourism in Oman. *Journal of Advanced Research in Dynamical and Control Systems, 11*(5 Special Issue), 1936–1945. https://www.scopus.com/inward/record.uri?eid=2-s2.0-85071908054&partnerID=40&md5=19c2309047be06c523019ba4ff94f5da

Guedea-Noriega, H. H., & García-Sánchez, F. (2022). Integroly: Automatic Knowledge Graph Population from Social Big Data in the Political Marketing Domain. *Applied Sciences (Basel, Switzerland)*, 12(16), 8116. Advance online publication. DOI: 10.3390/app12168116

Guo, Y. (2022). Do Masculinity and Femininity Matter? Evidence From the Investigation on the Penetration Level of E-Government Websites Between China and South Korea. *International Journal of Electronic Government Research*, 18(1), 1–18. Advance online publication. DOI: 10.4018/IJEGR.313575

Harmes, A. (2020). Political Marketing in Post-Conflict Elections: The Case of Iraq. *Journal of Political Marketing*, 19(3), 201–232. DOI: 10.1080/15377857.2016.1193834

Hollebeek, L. D., Kumar, V., Srivastava, R. K., & Clark, M. K. (2022). Moving the stakeholder journey forward. *Journal of the Academy of Marketing Science*, 51(1), 23–49. DOI: 10.1007/s11747-022-00878-3 PMID: 35756344

Ibrahim, I., Ismail, A. F.-M. F., Amer, A., & Jani, S. H. M. (2019). The effectiveness of mass marketing communication as a digital logistics tool in promoting a new online public service platform. *International Journal of Supply Chain Management*, 8(4), 177–185. https://www.scopus.com/inward/record.uri?eid=2-s2.0-85071556833&partnerID=40&md5=bbfbc2c80bffc785e20db86776cb0ad8

Ibrahim, I., Ismail, A. F.-M. F., Amer, A., & Jani, S. H. M. (2019). The effectiveness of mass marketing communication as a digital logistics tool in promoting a new online public service platform. *International Journal of Supply Chain Management*, 8(4), 177–185. https://www.scopus.com/inward/record.uri?eid=2-s2.0-85071556833&partnerID=40&md5=bbfbc2c80bffc785e20db86776cb0ad8

Irshaidat, R. (2022). Interpretivism vs. Positivism in Political Marketing Research. *Journal of Political Marketing*, 21(2), 126–160. DOI: 10.1080/15377857.2019.1624286

Khairiza, F., & Kusumasari, B. (2020). Analyzing political marketing in Indonesia: A palm oil digital campaign case study. *Forest and Society*, 4(2), 294–309. DOI: 10.24259/fs.v4i2.9576

Kruschinski, S., & Bene, M. (2022). In varietate concordia?! Political parties' digital political marketing in the 2019 European Parliament election campaign. *European Union Politics*, 23(1), 43–65. DOI: 10.1177/14651165211040728

Malik, R., Malhan, S., & Arora, M. (2024). (Eds.). (2024). Sensible Selling Through Sensory Neuromarketing (pp. 144-163). IGI Global

Martinez, B. M., & McAndrews, L. E. (2022). Do you take...? The effect of mobile payment solutions on use intention: an application of UTAUT2. *Journal of Marketing Analytics*, pp. 1–12. DOI: 10.1057/s41270-022-00175-6

Mathaisel, D. F. X., & Comm, C. L. (2021). Political marketing with data analytics. *Journal of Marketing Analytics*, 9(1), 56–64. DOI: 10.1057/s41270-020-00097-1

Mathaisel, D. F. X., & Comm, C. L. (2021). Political marketing with data analytics. *Journal of Marketing Analytics*, 9(1), 56–64. DOI: 10.1057/s41270-020-00097-1

Mirovic, V., Kalas, B., Djokic, I., Milicevic, N., Djokic, N., & Djakovic, M. (2023). Green Loans in Bank Portfolio: Financial and Marketing Implications. *Sustainability (Basel)*, 15(7), 5914. DOI: 10.3390/su15075914

Mirovic, V., Kalas, B., Djokic, I., Milicevic, N., Djokic, N., & Djakovic, M. (2023). Green Loans in Bank Portfolio: Financial and Marketing Implications. *Sustainability (Basel)*, 15(7), 5914. DOI: 10.3390/su15075914

Mishra, K. E., Wilder, K., & Mishra, A. K. (2017). Digital Literacy in the Marketing Curriculum: Are Female College Students prepared for Digital jobs? *Industry and Higher Education*, 31(3), 204–211. DOI: 10.1177/0950422217697838

Mishra, K. E., Wilder, K., & Mishra, A. K. (2017). Digital Literacy in the Marketing Curriculum: Are Female College Students prepared for Digital jobs? *Industry and Higher Education*, 31(3), 204–211. DOI: 10.1177/0950422217697838

Mochla, V., & Tsourvakas, G. (2020). Quality Dimensions of Political Parties' Website Services That Satisfy Voters in the Political Marketing. *Journal of Political Marketing*, 22(1), 1–13. DOI: 10.1080/15377857.2020.1790470

Nguyen, H. N., & Tran, M. D. (2022). STIMULI TO ADOPT E-GOVERNMENT SERVICES DURING COVID-19: EVIDENCE FROM VIETNAM. *Innovative Marketing*, 18(1), 12–22. DOI: 10.21511/im.18(1).2022.02

Osman, I. H., Anouze, A. L., Irani, Z., Al-Ayoubi, B., Lee, H., Balc, A., Medeni, T. D., & Weerakkody, V. (2014). COBRA framework to evaluate e-government services: A citizen-centric perspective. *Government Information Quarterly*, 31(2), 243–256. DOI: 10.1016/j.giq.2013.10.009

Ozuem, W., Ranfagni, S., Willis, M., Rovai, S., & Howell, K. (2021). Exploring customers' responses to online service failure and recovery strategies during Covid-19 pandemic: An actor-network theory perspective. *Psychology and Marketing*, 38(9), 1440–1459. DOI: 10.1002/mar.21527 PMID: 34539054

Peng, Y., Liang, J., Zhang, W., & Liu, M. (2023). Bank Marketing Strategy Based on Consumer Loan Behavior Prediction. *Advances in Economics, Management, and Political Sciences*, 6(1), 508–514. DOI: 10.54254/2754-1169/6/20220196

Peng, Y., Liang, J., Zhang, W., & Liu, M. (2023). Bank Marketing Strategy Based on Consumer Loan Behavior Prediction. *Advances in Economics, Management, and Political Sciences*, 6(1), 508–514. DOI: 10.54254/2754-1169/6/20220196

Peng, Y., Liang, J., Zhang, W., & Liu, M. (2023). Bank Marketing Strategy Based on Consumer Loan Behavior Prediction. *Advances in Economics, Management, and Political Sciences*, 6(1), 508–514. DOI: 10.54254/2754-1169/6/20220196

Popova, N., Kataiev, A., Skrynkovskyy, R., & Nevertii, A. (2019). Development of trust marketing in the digital society. *Economic Annals-XXI*, 176(3–4), 13–25. DOI: 10.21003/ea.V176-02

Popova, N., Kataiev, A., Skrynkovskyy, R., & Nevertii, A. (2019). Development of trust marketing in the digital society. *Economic Annals-XXI*, 176(3–4), 13–25. DOI: 10.21003/ea.V176-02

Ramakrishnan, S., Wong, M. S., Chit, M. M., & Mutum, D. S. (2022). A conceptual model of the relationship between organizational intelligence traits and digital government service quality: The role of occupational stress. *International Journal of Quality & Reliability Management*, 39(6), 1429–1452. DOI: 10.1108/IJQRM-10-2021-0371

Ravula, P. (2022). Impact of delivery performance on online review ratings: the role of temporal distance of ratings. *Journal of Marketing Analytics*, pp. 1–11. DOI: 10.1057/s41270-022-00168-5

Risher, J. J., Harrison, D. E., & LeMay, S. A. (2020). Last mile non-delivery: Consumer investment in last mile infrastructure. *Journal of Marketing Theory and Practice*, 28(4), 484–496. DOI: 10.1080/10696679.2020.1787846

Safiullah, M. D., Pathak, P., & Singh, S. (2022). The impact of social media and news media on political marketing: An empirical study of 2014 Indian General Election. *International Journal of Business Excellence*, 26(4), 536–550. DOI: 10.1504/IJBEX.2022.122765

Satriawan, B. H., & Purwaningsih, T. (2021). Political Marketing Prabowo Subianto and Sandiaga Salahuddin Uno in the 2019 Presidential Election. *Jurnal Ilmu Sosial Dan Ilmu Politik*, 25(2), 127–143. DOI: 10.22146/jsp.53688

Sophocleous, H. P., Masouras, A. N., & Anastasiadou, S. D. (2024). The Impact of Political Marketing on Voting Behaviour of Cypriot Voters. *Social Sciences (Basel, Switzerland)*, 13(3), 149. Advance online publication. DOI: 10.3390/socsci13030149

Taneja, B., Shukla, P., & Arora, M. (2024). Sensible Selling Through Sensory Neuromarketing: Enhancing Sales Effectiveness. In Sensible Selling Through Sensory Neuromarketing (pp. 164-183). IGI Global.

THE IMPLICATIONS OF FACEBOOK IN POLITICAL MARKETING CAMPAIGNS IN CROATIA. (2020). Central. *European Business Review*, 9(4), 73–95. DOI: 10.18267/j.cebr.244

Türkmendağ, T., & Hassan, A. (2024). A stakeholder perspective on poverty reduction through the implementation of social marketing in the context of tourism. *Frontiers in Psychology*, 14, 1304952. DOI: 10.3389/fpsyg.2023.1304952 PMID: 38239462

Türkmendağ, T., & Hassan, A. (2024). A stakeholder perspective on poverty reduction through the implementation of social marketing in the context of tourism. *Frontiers in Psychology*, 14, 1304952. DOI: 10.3389/fpsyg.2023.1304952 PMID: 38239462

Twum, K. K., Kosiba, J. P., Abdul-Hamid, I. K., & Hinson, R. (2022). Does Corporate Social Responsibility Enhance Political Marketing? *Journal of Nonprofit & Public Sector Marketing*, 34(1), 71–101. DOI: 10.1080/10495142.2020.1798850

Vollrath, M. D., & Villegas, S. G. (2021). Avoiding digital marketing analytics myopia: Revisiting the customer decision journey as a strategic marketing framework. *Journal of Marketing Analytics*, 10(2), 106–113. DOI: 10.1057/s41270-020-00098-0

Vollrath, M. D., & Villegas, S. G. (2021). Avoiding digital marketing analytics myopia: Revisiting the customer decision journey as a strategic marketing framework. *Journal of Marketing Analytics*, 10(2), 106–113. DOI: 10.1057/s41270-020-00098-0

Vysochyna, A., Semenov, V., & Kyrychenko, K. (2021). Marketing and management of innovations in public governance as core determinants of trust. *Marketing and Management of Innovations*, 5(2), 204–212. DOI: 10.21272/mmi.2021.2-17

Zahid, H., Ali, S., Abu-Shanab, E., & Muhammad Usama Javed, H. (2022). Determinants of intention to use e-government services: An integrated marketing relation view. *Telematics and Informatics*, 68, 101778. Advance online publication. DOI: 10.1016/j.tele.2022.101778

Zahid, H., Ali, S., Abu-Shanab, E., & Muhammad Usama Javed, H. (2022). Determinants of intention to use e-government services: An integrated marketing relation view. *Telematics and Informatics*, 68, 101778. Advance online publication. DOI: 10.1016/j.tele.2022.101778

Chapter 2
Enhancing Online Shopping Experiences

Preeti Jain
https://orcid.org/0009-0000-3178-0837
Maharishi Markandeshwar (deemed to be university) Mullana- Ambala

Neetu Chaudhary
https://orcid.org/0000-0001-6589-4015
Maharishi Markandeshwar (deemed to be university) Mullana- Ambala

ABSTRACT

In the constantly evolving online shopping world, sensory marketing is crucial for creating engaging experiences for consumers. This study provides a comprehensive analysis of sensory marketing, highlighting its importance in enhancing the online purchasing experience. It focuses on tactile, visual, and aural cues that influence consumer behavior, emotions, perceptions, and product selection. This section emphasizes visual sensory marketing, examining the impact of high-quality product images, videos, and 3D models, as well as the use of color, typeface, and layout in creating visually appealing online stores. It also explores virtual trials, haptic technologies, and product interaction functionalities, addressing challenges and opportunities in providing tactile feedback in digital environments. Furthermore, it delves into how immersive technologies like augmented reality and virtual reality enhance sensory experiences and product exploration, affecting consumer choices and emphasizing the integration of sensory marketing strategies into e-commerce.

DOI: 10.4018/979-8-3693-9351-2.ch002

INTRODUCTION

Marketing, which focuses primarily on influencing consumer purchasing decisions, has made it crucial for marketers to comprehend the constantly evolving consumer needs and adjust to the new market conditions accordingly. The retail sector, known for its high dynamism, compels companies to seek ways to conform to the shifting market requirements. The modern retail industry has been greatly influenced by the adoption of cutting-edge technologies, implementation of creative management approaches, and the incidence of mergers and acquisitions. In the midst of heightened competition, retail enterprises are observed emphasizing not only on attracting customers but more significantly on retaining them and ensuring the satisfaction of their existing customer base. Sensory marketing practices have emerged as crucial in crafting comfortable and distinctive retail settings. In order to enhance their appeal to customers and effectively compete with counterparts, conventional retailers must modify and adjust their customer engagement strategies. Those who excel in integrating consumers' sensory experiences into their marketing endeavors and consequently influencing consumer behavior gain a competitive edge over their competitors. As posited by Krishna (2010), sensory marketing serves as a tool for creating subconscious stimuli that shape consumers' interpretations of intangible aspects of a product or establishment. Within the realm of sensory marketing, researchers predominantly analyze consumers' emotional and behavioral responses by stimulating the five senses. It is imperative, during the execution of sensory marketing initiatives, to grasp the impacts of the five senses on consumers accurately, while also considering the specific sensory effects on different consumer segments.

Sensory marketing is described as "marketing that stimulates the senses of consumers and impacts their perception, evaluation, and actions." From this assertion, one can infer that by engaging in this approach, all five senses of an individual are utilized as a marketing tactic to sway the consumer's perception, evaluation, and behavior towards the intended product or service. Sensory marketing aims to offer consumers a comprehensive sensory encounter in order to enhance the value proposition. The encounters delivered to consumers through the five senses are visuals, Auditory perception, Olfaction, Tactile sensation and Gustation. Interfaces that simulate physical touch when navigating virtual and online worlds are a result of modern technology; these are referred to as haptic sensations (Basdogan et al., 2020; Kim & Forsythe, 2008a; Nah et al., 2011). The literature currently in publication does not do a sufficient job of capturing the slow change in attitudes around sensory media on online platforms. The COVID-19 pandemic's effects, along with the growth in internet consumption and sales, have increased competition (Arora & Sharma, (2021); Arora & Sharma, (2022)). Suppliers are facing issues in capturing consumer attention in online environments, where sensory engagement has traditionally been limited to visual and auditory inputs, due to the increased levels of competition and homogeneity in corporate services (Petit et al, 2019). Therefore, the ability of sellers to effectively mix textual and visual stimuli on e-commerce websites in order to convert users into consumers is what makes them successful in this environment (Bleier et al, (2019); Schlosser et al, (2006)). Thus, the focus of this conversation is on arguing that sensory appeal plays a crucial role in the online customer experience journey for the financial success of an e-commerce platform (Sugawara et al., 2014). Customers frequently notice differences between product descriptions and images and reality (Pavlou et al., 2007), which causes them to feel uncertain (Hong et al., 2007). Consumers actively seek for different features on e-commerce websites, especially sensory communications (e.g., high-quality photography) to reduce the perceived risks connected with online purchases.

Objectives

The aim of this study is outlined as follows:

1. To examine the effect of sensory cues on consumer behavior while shopping online.
2. To assess the impact of visual elements on online shopping experiences.
3. To investigate how e-commerce can utilize immersive sensory experiences through the use of augmented reality, virtual reality, virtual trials, and haptic technologies.

Methodology

This research investigates how immersive technologies like augmented reality and virtual reality boost sensory experiences and product exploration through the analysis of secondary data sourced from Scopus papers and peer-reviewed journals. The data collection process is aimed at recent articles published within the past decade, and they are chosen based on criteria such as relevance, peer-review assessment, and the journal's impact factor.

Examining the impact that sensory marketing has on consumers' behavior and product selection.

Visual perception, specifically sight, is commonly considered the most dominant human sensory ability, contributing significantly to individuals' aesthetic appeal. When novel designs, product packaging, or substandard retail outlets are introduced in the market, individuals rely on their visual faculties to detect changes and distinctions (Hultén et al 2009). The visual sense, or visual imagery, remains paramount in detecting variations and alterations, being the predominant sense utilized in the reception of commodities and services, playing a crucial role in shaping mental representations in the digital realm. Visual stimuli, influenced by aspects such as shape, color, size, layout, imagery, and fashion, are interpreted differently based on the nature of the products and the observers. In online settings, where visual cues play a central role in sensory experiences, various factors related to the visuals come into play, with visual placement emerging as a critical determinant influencing consumers' assessments. Auditory perception-, known as sound, is arguably the most palpable sensory aspect within the digital realm. Studies indicate that high-frequency sounds prompt individuals to concentrate on brighter items more swiftly. Conversely, low-frequency sounds direct attention towards darker objects, resulting in prolonged fixation and consequently stimulating impulsive purchasing behavior. Olfaction, as demonstrated by scientific research, plays a significant role in human emotional responses, accounting for approximately 75% of all emotions. Previous studies suggest that olfactory perceptions are closely associated with feelings of contentment, gratification, and overall well-being, while also playing a key role in information retention and memory. The MetaCookie+ device, functioning in the realm of Augmented Reality, enables users to virtually alter food scents and flavors through the simulation and dispersion of aromas such as strawberry and vanilla. Tactile sensation, commonly referred to as touch, encompasses both the practical necessity and the pleasure derived from physical contact. Prospective consumers often seek to physically interact with a product, either by tactile examination or through imaginative visualization, in order to reinforce their confidence in making a purchase decision. The act of touching, or even mentally envisioning touch, positively influences consumer behavior and fosters a sense of ownership towards a specific product or service. Gustation, or taste, serves as the amalgamation of various senses to craft a comprehensive brand encounter, particularly prevalent in the realm of food and beverage as it directly impacts consumer preferences. The amalgamation of these sensory components culminates in a rich and enduring consumer journey, exemplified by establishments like Starbucks, which leverage a blend of sensory stimuli to curate a distinctive and immersive ambiance. Scholarly investigations have demonstrated the efficacy of Sensory Evaluation Techniques (SETs) in replicating taste sensations in controlled laboratory settings. Advanced technologies now enable the capture of color, pH levels, and the generation of electrical stimuli to craft a mixed reality encounter. This advancement opens the door to virtually tasting a product prior to physical contact or olfactory assessment, ultimately bridging the psychological gap between consumers and online commodities. Consumers engage all their senses in not only perceiving products or services but also in shaping their overall shopping experience. Sensory marketing strategies can subtly influence consumer perceptions by leveraging abstract concepts, as outlined in articles by Oliveira et al., (2021).

Analyzing the role of visual sensory marketing in improving online shopping experiences.

Within the dynamic realm of online shopping, sensory marketing assumes a pivotal role in crafting captivating and immersive experiences for consumers. This section delivers a thorough examination of sensory marketing, accentuating its importance in enriching the landscape of online shopping.

- Sensory marketing serves as a multi-dimensional tool in elevating the online shopping experience by engaging various senses to influence consumer behaviors and perceptions. The incorporation of haptic feedback, such as vibrations in mobile applications, can profoundly impact consumer behaviors, with individual touch preferences and psychological factors mediating purchasing decisions, underscoring the importance for retailers to personalize sensory interfaces (Racat & Plotkina, 2023).
- The Online Sensory Marketing Index (OSMI) offers a quantitative gauge of sensory outputs on e-commerce platforms, enabling a heightened sensory allure and addressing issues of sensory overload or deprivation (Hamacher & Buchkremer, 2022). Nevertheless, sensory evaluations are often perceived as less informative compared to non-sensory reviews, potentially diminishing the objective assessment of reviews and subsequently reducing their helpfulness and impact on purchase intentions (Lopez & Garza, 2022).
- In the realm of physical retail settings, sensory marketing holds the potential to heighten customer emotions and behavioral inclinations, as exemplified in coffee establishments where sensory elements such as vision, auditory stimuli, taste, and tactile sensations exert a notable impact on feelings of enjoyment, stimulation, and control, subsequently influencing the state of flow and behavioral intentions (Jang & Lee 2019). The realm of sensory encounters may yield a dual outcome concerning customer allegiance; while elevating contentment levels and active participation, they might also cultivate heightened expectations and inquisitiveness towards novel encounters, potentially diminishing loyalty levels (Lashkova et al 2020). An outlook rooted in multimodal and social semiotics concerning sensory marketing posits that amalgamating diverse sensory modes possesses the capacity to enrich consumer conduct by amplifying the simultaneity and vigor of sensory exchanges (Lick, 2022). The concept of sensory synergy, in which the fusion of sensory input engenders a more pronounced effect, can wield a substantial influence

on consumer evaluations, albeit requiring a delicate equilibrium to avert unfavorable perceptions (Zhou, 2024).
- Sensory enabling technologies (SETs) such as virtual trials and 3D perspectives hold the potential to mitigate product uncertainties and amplify the amusement value of digital shopping, albeit with their efficacy contingent upon the type of technology employed (Kim & Forsythe, 2009).
- Immersive Virtual Reality (IVR) stands poised to offer numerous prospective benefits, particularly within the domain of fashion retail. Indeed, IVR facilitates the customization of products in a 360° format, presenting users with a visual representation of the customized item via an immersive 3D depiction. Consequently, users gain a deeper comprehension of the distinctive features of the customized product, features that may prove challenging to discern through a two-dimensional image displayed on a conventional screen (Ricci et al., 2023).
- Augmented Reality (AR) applications harness sensory perceptions to spur impulsive purchasing behavior by influencing emotional states, with the degree of productive engagement serving as a moderating factor in this process (Goel et al., 2023). On the whole, sensory marketing in the realm of online retail doesn't only enrich the user experience by rendering it more interactive and captivating but also presents hurdles in upholding objectivity and managing consumer anticipations. Retailers must adeptly integrate sensory components to strike a balance between these effects and optimize both consumer contentment and loyalty.

The integration of immersive technologies into sensory marketing for E-Commerce

Immersive technologies cover a spectrum of technological solutions that blend virtual and real environments, giving users a profound feeling of immersion (Chandel & Arora, 2024). The development of more engaging, dynamic, and customized environments made possible by technologies like virtual reality and augmented reality has been essential in improving online shopping experiences ((Kumar, Arora & Erkol Bayram, (Eds.). (2024) a; Kumar, J., Arora, M., & Erkol Bayram, G. (Eds.). (2024) b; Arora, (2024)). Mercedes-Benz's implementation of rapid response (QR) codes on new cars serves as an example of this. Through the use of an augmented reality mobile application, first responders may quickly view color-coded visuals of the wiring and fuel systems (Etherington, 2016).

These technological advancements provide abundant chances to redefine the physical world and human engagements with it. Consequently, the food industry is now exploring ways to leverage these e- techniques for competitive advantages, bridging the divide between physical and digital shopping. This integration provides consumers with a more realistic perspective on products and a heightened sense of presence, thereby enriching their overall shopping experience. Social media profoundly affects marketing communication by enabling direct, interactive engagement with consumers and facilitating the rapid dissemination of brand messages, thereby increasing reach and influence (Arora, 2020; 2023). Persuasion and skill development are essential for branding in marketing communication as they enhance the ability to craft compelling messages and strategies that effectively resonate with target audiences, building strong, lasting brand identities.

For example, AR/VR applications in the Bahraini clothing market have demonstrated increased customer satisfaction and brand loyalty by offering features like virtual try-ons, 360-degree product views, and interactive shopping experiences.

With big companies like Facebook and Apple making significant investments in this field, immersive technology—which includes augmented and virtual reality—is gaining traction in the consumer sector and igniting conversations about its future (Hoium, 2021). To improve customer experiences and provide value, immersive technology applications—like virtual mirrors—are being included into marketing and sales strategies in the retail industry (Javornik, 2018).

The modern consumer market is marked by a growing emphasis on co-creating value through interactions with services and products. Technology development has resulted in a change in the power relations between firms and customers. This has increased multi-stakeholder participation in value co-creation processes in a variety of industries, including retail, tourism, and education (Tom Dieck et al., 2018b). According to theories put forth by Jung and Tom Dieck (2017), immersive technology may act as a platform for client-driven value co-creation, impacting how customer experiences are created and used. Numerous research works have attempted to expand on our understanding of consumer experiences (Bastiaansen et al., 2019; Han & Tom Dieck, 2019; Lim & Kim, 2018), utilizing a common method based on Pine and Gilmore's (1998) introduction of the concept of the experience economy.

Food firms are also looking into methods to use augmented reality (AR) to add interactive components to their packaging in an effort to strengthen consumer-brand relationships. Customers can use their smartphones to scan food packaging and instantaneously retrieve data about where food comes from, how it's made, how to prepare it, and how much it costs (Powell, 2018; Watson, 2017). Furthermore, Kabaq, a 3D food technology startup, is combining photogrammetry and digital rendering to provide customers with accurate 3D images of restaurant menu items prior to their ordering.

VIRTUAL REALITY (VR)

Immersive technologies can be described as technological advancements that enable the fusion of virtual and physical realities, offering a deep sense of immersion. Illustrative instances encompass augmented reality (AR) and virtual reality (VR), which have significantly enhanced the online shopping experience by establishing more interactive, compelling, and personalized settings. The potential of these technologies in reshaping the tangible world and human interactions with it has encouraged the food industry to explore avenues for utilizing digital tools for competitive benefits. By bridging the gap between the physical and digital shopping realms, these technologies present consumers with a more lifelike perception of products and an increased sense of presence. In the Bahraini clothing market, the implementation of AR/VR technologies has demonstrated an increase in customer satisfaction and brand loyalty. This is achieved through features like virtual try-ons, 360-degree product views, and gamified shopping experiences. Likewise, virtual reality has been evidenced to enhance consumer decision-making processes, specifically with regard to the selection of Fast-Moving Consumer Goods (FMCGs), by decreasing negative emotions and amplifying positive ones, particularly for food items. This transformation in human-food interactions has significant implications (Yang et al, 2024).

Mixed reality (MR)

Mixed reality (MR) is characterized by the integration of AI with augmented objects, leading to enrich spatial immersion and distinctive consumer experiences. This, in turn, results in higher purchase intentions and positive word-of-mouth recommendations (Kathikeyan et al, 2023).

In the domain of fashion, Immersive Virtual Reality (IVR) has showcased heightened hedonic and utilitarian merits when compared to Desktop Virtual Reality (DVR), resulting in extended user engagement and enhanced enjoyment of the shopping journey in IVR settings (Ricci et al 2023). Online shops based on VR technology elicit a heightened sense of reality and increase purchase interest, making the shopping experience more thrilling and potentially more profitable for retailers (Engelmann et al 2019). Consumer perceptions align with the notion that these technologies have the power to revolutionize the retail sector by enhancing the shopping journey and leaving a lasting impact on the industry (Carton, 2019). The design of VR-based shopping platforms, such as those utilizing HTC Vive, facilitates free movement, product comparison, and real-time monitoring, thus significantly elevating the shopping experience (Zhao, 2018). Furthermore, immersive technologies redefine the creation of experiences and value co-creation, highlighting the significance of managing customer experiences (Tom Dieck et al., 2018). The introduction of virtual goods in immersive environments can positively influence product assessment, akin to traditional retail settings, by offering contextual information that is often lacking in standard e-commerce platforms (Wölfel & Reinhardt 2019).

Direct touch in virtual reality (VR)

Direct touch in virtual reality (VR) pertains to the capacity to engage with virtual entities through manual interaction, akin to our interactions with physical objects in the tangible realm. This necessitates sophisticated haptic technologies capable of emulating the tactile sense.

- Kinesthetic and Cutaneous Haptics: Kinesthetic haptics encompass the perception of force and motion, often facilitated by mechanisms that exert pressure or resistance. Conversely, cutaneous haptics involve tactile sensations on the skin, encompassing aspects like texture and temperature. Both forms of haptics hold significance for direct touch in VR.
- Wearable Haptic Devices: Wearable haptic devices are crafted to be worn on the body, providing tactile feedback directly to the skin. These gadgets can replicate diverse sensations including pressure, vibrations, and textures, heightening the realism of the virtual environment. Instances include haptic gloves employing actuators for mimicking the sensation of interacting with virtual objects.
- Ultrasonic Haptics: Another promising innovation is ultrasonic haptics, leveraging focused sound waves to generate tactile feedback in mid-air. This enables users to perceive virtual objects without necessitating any specialized gear. Ultrasonic haptics have the capacity to evoke a wide array of sensations, ranging from gentle taps to intricate textures.

Electrotactile feedback

Electrotactile feedback involves the utilization of electrical stimulation to induce tactile sensations on the skin. Integration of this technology into wearable devices can deliver a more immersive tactile encounter.

Deep learning models

The integration of deep learning models within immersive marketing settings, such as the Immersive Graph Neural Network (IGNN), holds the potential to enhance personalized recommendations, fully capturing the attributes of products and enriching the overall shopping and entertainment experience (Zheng & Ding, 2022). These investigations collectively underscore the transformative capabilities of immersive technologies in e-commerce, offering more engaging, personalized experiences that can heighten consumer satisfaction and drive sales.

On-Body Physical Feedback Systems (OPPFs)

To enrich the sensory online shopping experience, online retailers must seek effective alternatives for tactile feedback that can enhance consumer product evaluations (Overmars & Poels, 2015). A compelling digital presentation of products can aid shoppers in making informed decisions. OPPFs present a viable solution for online merchants, enabling consumers to engage with products through an interactive and informative display (Li & Meshkova, 2013). On-Body Physical Feedback Systems (OPPFs) are advanced technologies engineered to provide authentic tactile sensations in VR environments, enabling direct manual interaction with virtual entities. These technologies, also known as SETs in the academic literature, furnish sensory input in the online retail landscape. They encompass product visualization tools widely utilized by online apparel vendors and embraced by digital consumers. Examples include 3D rotational views, virtual try-on features, zoom images, and videos (Kim & Forsythe, 2009). OPPFs empower shoppers to experience a sense of touch without physical contact—an intangible tactile experience.

Examples ASOS supplies a video alongside the static imagery (SI) to enable consumers to delve deeper into the clothing items prior to making a purchase, as demonstrated by ASOS (2022). Similarly, American Eagle furnishes customers with a detailed view of the apparel to enhance their comprehension of fabric specifics during online shopping, as indicated by American Eagle (2022).

Augmentation technologies

The idea of integrating digital taste enhancement technologies into our regular eating and drinking routines is gaining traction. It has been successful to apply electrical and thermal stimulation of the human palate using a digital taste interface to produce the sense of basic taste sensations (sweet, salty, sour, and bitter). Significantly, subjects in research have reported feeling sourer and saltier than usual (Nakamura & Miyashita, 2013; Ranasinghe, Nakatsu, Nii, & Gopalakrishnakone, 2012).

When this electrical method of taste enhancement is incorporated into regular eating utensils, like spoons, chopsticks, and soup bowls (Ranasinghe, Lee, Suthokumar & Do, 2016; Ranasinghe et al., 2018), the ability to distinguish between sour and salty food products has improved significantly. From a psychological standpoint, it is undeniable that the tactile (weight) and visual (color) characteristics of cutlery and plates can elicit feelings of sweetness and saltiness in actual food items (Piqueras-Fiszman et al., 2012; Harrar & Spence, 2011; Harrar, Piqueras-Fiszman & Spence, 2011).

As a result, food manufacturers may be able to lower the amount of salt or sugar they use without sacrificing sensory quality if they simultaneously employ electrical taste enhancement in conjunction with changes to environmental stimuli like the color and shape of packaging.

Key elements that play a role in the efficacy of virtual reality (VR) and augmented reality (AR) in enriching sensory marketing.

The efficacy of VR and AR in enhancing sensory marketing is influenced by various critical factors, including the degree of immersion, embodiment, and the capacity to generate vivid mental images. Immersion and embodiment play a vital role in enhancing user satisfaction and willingness to interact with the advertiser offering, as evidenced by a study where individuals partook in a virtual kayaking expedition in Antarctica, resulting in favorable intentions to visit the location in reality [Leveau & Camus 2023]. According to Huang & Chung, 2024, incorporating natural symbol sets, vivid memory, and the sense of human touch—three essential psychological states for body schema—midair, gesture-based somatosensory augmented reality (AR) greatly increases user satisfaction and intention to stay engaged. Furthermore, AR is more successful at promoting purchase intentions than VR because it can enable smooth, product-focused mental imagery, whereas VR is best at boosting brand attitudes through context-specific mental imagery (Hilken et al., 2022).

The integration of Augmented Reality (AR) and Virtual Reality (VR), when arranged in the correct sequence (AR preceding VR), has the potential to augment both purchase intentions and brand attitudes by aligning with the customer's online-to-offline journey (Hilken et al 2022). Within the food industry, AR and VR technologies present novel prospects for capturing the intricacies of human sensory perception, enhancing the predictive accuracy of new products, and optimizing consumer advantages through dynamic sensory evaluation methods (Crofton et al 2019). Additionally, AR has been identified as more receptive and user-friendly for hedonic products, delivering an enhanced user experience and increased purchase intentions in a multisensory setting, while touch interfaces are favored for utilitarian products (Mishra, et al 2021). These aspects collectively underscore the transformative potential of VR and AR in revolutionizing sensory marketing through the creation of immersive, captivating, and contextually rich experiences that resonate with consumers at various sensory levels.

Implementation of sensory technology in e-commerce

The utilization of sensory technology in electronic commerce presents numerous significant benefits that enhance the overall consumer experience and drive business outcomes.

- **Haptic feedback-** Initially, the incorporation of haptic feedback, such as vibrations in mobile shopping applications, has the potential to greatly impact consumer behavior by enhancing their psychological and affective engagement, ultimately leading to improved purchasing results. This impact is particularly notable for individuals with a strong need for tactile stimulation, indicating that personalized sensory interfaces could hold economic value for retailers (Racat & Plotkina 2023).
- **The advancement in sensor technology and the Internet of Things (IoT)-** It has helped in integrating multiple sensory data, thereby enhancing the perceptual feedback mechanism among sensors. This progression enables more effective acquisition, storage, and retrieval of sensory data, thereby optimizing storage resources and achieving balanced data storage in electronic commerce platforms (Guo & Liang 2021).
- **The utilization of the Online Sensory Marketing Index (OSMI)** – It offers a quantitative assessment of sensory output on electronic commerce websites, empowering marketers to develop websites with enhanced sensory appeal and address shortcomings. This index aids in the creation of sensory models tailored to various sectors, thereby improving the sensory consumer experience online (Hamacher & Buchkremer; 2022).
- **Augmented reality (AR) applications-** AR applications in electronic commerce can have a notable impact on customers' emotional states, leading to the encouragement of impulsive purchasing behavior. The sensory perceptions evoked by AR characteristics stimulate the desire for impulsive purchases, especially when influenced by product engagement, providing tangible advantages for electronic commerce vendors (Goel et al, 2023).

Sensory marketing has demonstrated a positive influence on the intention of young consumers to make repeat purchases on electronic commerce platforms, particularly within the fashion industry. This indicates that multi-sensory marketing approaches can effectively cultivate customer loyalty and encourage repeat business among younger demographics. In summary, the incorporation of sensory technology in electronic commerce not only enhances the consumer experience but also provides strategic advantages for retailers in terms of engagement, storage efficiency, and repeat purchase behavior.

Challenges of implementing sensory technology on e-platforms

The incorporation of sensory technology in e-commerce introduces numerous significant hurdles, primarily centred on the amalgamation and efficacy of sensory stimuli aimed at enriching the consumer experience.

A primary obstacle involves attaining sensory synergy, wherein the amalgamation of diverse sensory inputs elicits a more substantial impact compared to individual stimuli in isolation. Scholarly findings suggest that adverse sensory cues can reduce consumer ratings, while positive sensory cues need to be appropriately balanced to prevent diminishing returns (Zhou, 2024). Another challenge lies in the efficient deployment of haptic feedback in mobile shopping, as consumer perceptions and specific touch requirements can profoundly shape the outcome, necessitating customized interfaces and potential disclaimers (Racat et al., 2023). Moreover, the absence of tactile feedback in online garment shopping impedes the accurate evaluation of fabric texture, underscoring the challenge of visually conveying haptic characteristics, which often leads to heightened variability and reduced precision in consumer appraisals. Augmented reality (AR) applications, although advantageous in heightening sensory perceptions and stimulating impulsive purchasing behavior, also demand meticulous attention to emotional states and product engagement to optimize their efficacy (Arora & Sharma 2022; Pooja et al., 2023]. Furthermore, establishing an engaging virtual store ambiance that aligns with consumer yearnings for sensory gratification remains a formidable task, given that numerous online retailers struggle to distinguish themselves and fully satisfy these sensory anticipations [Petit et al., 2015]. In essence, these obstacles underscore the necessity for a sophisticated and well-coordinated strategy in integrating sensory technology into e-commerce, harmonizing diverse sensory inputs and tailoring consumer experiences to elevate contentment and propel sales.

Privacy concerns related to sensory technology in e-commerce

Privacy concerns in e-commerce related to sensory technology are intricate and have faced increasing scrutiny due to the rapid progression of technology and its incorporation into online retail platforms. Analyzing click streams and utilizing location-sensing technologies such as RFID in the retail sector enables companies to obtain profound insights into customer behavior and inventory management. However, this practice also raises significant privacy risks as these technologies have the capacity to track customers' actions and movements in real-time (Solti et al., 2018). The gathering, retention, and management of personal data using these technologies have resulted in heightened privacy concerns among consumers, who are worried about unauthorized access and potential misuse of their personal information (Maseeh et al., 2021). The substantial technological transformations driven by big data, artificial intelligence, and virtual reality further complicate these privacy challenges, underscoring the importance of comprehending consumer privacy dynamics in e-commerce (Bandara et al., (2020): Arora & Sharma, (2023)). Furthermore, the detailed temporal data produced by sensors in mobile devices can unveil not only user behaviors but also sensitive demographic characteristics, emphasizing the need for developing data transmission models that prioritize privacy preservation while maintaining utility. Despite the increasing volume of literature on consumer privacy in e-commerce, empirical studies have reported conflicting results, partially due to variations in methodologies and contexts among different research endeavors (Yao & Tarofder, 2024). To tackle these issues, e-commerce entities must establish robust privacy protocols and foster consumer trust by ensuring transparency and granting control over the utilization of personal data (Maseeh et al., 2021). Additionally, privacy controls at both technological and organizational levels, including the proposed feature learning framework for mobile devices, can contribute to mitigating privacy threats while upholding the value of sensory data for marketing insights (Malekzadeh et al., 2018).

Hence, safeguarding consumer privacy within the realm of sensory technology in e-commerce necessitates a holistic approach that merges advanced technological remedies with explicit privacy guidelines and initiatives geared towards building consumer trust.

CONCLUSION

Within the rapidly evolving domain of online commerce, sensory marketing is acknowledged as a crucial strategy for fostering engaging and immersive consumer interactions. This segment has scrutinized the multifaceted role of sensory marketing, highlighting how stimulating different senses—visual, auditory, tactile, olfactory, and gustatory—can significantly influence consumer behavior, emotions, and viewpoints.

Prominent findings emphasize that visual cues, such as high-quality images, videos, and 3D graphics, enhance the visual appeal and perceived value of products. Auditory elements, including background music and brand-specific sounds, create an emotionally resonant shopping environment, while olfactory cues, though challenging to integrate online, can be mimicked through precise sensory descriptions and multimedia content. Tactile experiences, facilitated by advanced technologies like haptic feedback and virtual trials, provide consumers with a sense of physical interaction with products, thereby boosting confidence in purchasing decisions.

Cutting-edge technologies like augmented reality (AR) and virtual reality (VR) are reshaping the landscape of sensory marketing. These technologies offer consumers personalized and interactive shopping experiences, bridging the gap between physical and digital realms. AR applications, like virtual try-on features and product visualizations, enhance product interaction and engagement, driving impulsive buying behavior. VR environments enable comprehensive product exploration, increasing consumer satisfaction and loyalty. The integration of sensory marketing strategies into e-commerce platforms is essential for fostering deep emotional connections and strong brand relationships. Retailers must thoughtfully balance sensory elements to enhance consumer engagement, satisfaction, and loyalty. Future research endeavors should continue to explore innovative sensory technologies and their applications, ensuring that online shopping experiences remain dynamic and captivating. In concluding, sensory marketing enriches the online shopping journey by engaging consumers across various sensory dimensions, making shopping more participatory, enjoyable, and ultimately more effective in influencing consumer behavior and brand loyalty. As technology advances, the potential for sensory marketing to transform e-commerce will only grow, offering exciting opportunities for both merchants and consumers.

REFERENCES

Arora, M. (2020). Post-truth and marketing communication in technological age. In *Handbook of research on innovations in technology and marketing for the connected consumer* (pp. 94–108). IGI Global. DOI: 10.4018/978-1-7998-0131-3.ch005

Arora, M. (2023). Encapsulating Role of Persuasion and Skill Development in Marketing Communication for Brand Building: A Perspective. In *International Handbook of Skill, Education, Learning, and Research Development in Tourism and Hospitality* (pp. 1–17). Springer Nature Singapore.

Arora, M. (2024). Virtual Reality in Education: Analyzing the Literature and Bibliometric State of Knowledge. *Transforming Education with Virtual Reality*, 379-402. DOI: 10.1002/9781394200498.ch22

Arora, M., & Sharma, R. L. (2021). Repurposing the Role of Entrepreneurs in the Havoc of COVID-19. In Entrepreneurship and Big Data (pp. 229-250). CRC Press.

Arora, M., & Sharma, R. L. (2022). Integrating gig economy and social media platforms as a business strategy in the era of digitalization. In *Integrated business models in the digital age: Principles and practices of technology empowered strategies* (pp. 67–86). Springer International Publishing. DOI: 10.1007/978-3-030-97877-8_3

Arora, M., & Sharma, R. L. (2022). Coalescing skills of gig players and fervor of entrepreneurial leaders to provide resilience strategies during global economic crises. In *COVID-19's Impact on the Cryptocurrency Market and the Digital Economy* (pp. 118–140). IGI Global. DOI: 10.4018/978-1-7998-9117-8.ch008

Arora, M., & Sharma, R. L. (2023). Artificial intelligence and big data: Ontological and communicative perspectives in multi-sectoral scenarios of modern businesses. *Foresight*, 25(1), 126–143. DOI: 10.1108/FS-10-2021-0216

Basdogan, C., Giraud, F., Levesque, V., Choi, S., 2020. A review of surface haptics: enabling tactile effects on touch surfaces. IEEE. Trans. Hapt. 1–21. .DOI: 10.1109/TOH.2020.2990712

Bleier, A., Harmeling, C. M., & Palmatier, R. W. (2019). Creating Effective Online Customer Experiences. *Journal of Marketing*, 83(2), 98–119. DOI: 10.1177/0022242918809930

Carton, S. (2019). *What impact will immersive technologies such as augmented and virtual reality have on the retail sector?* (Doctoral dissertation, Dublin, National College of Ireland).

Chandel, M., & Arora, M. (2024). Metaverse Perspectives: Unpacking Its Role in Shaping Sustainable Development Goals-A Qualitative Inquiry. In Research, Innovation, and Industry Impacts of the Metaverse (pp. 62-75). IGI Global.

Crofton, E. C., Botinestean, C., Fenelon, M., & Gallagher, E. (2019). Potential applications for virtual and augmented reality technologies in sensory science. *Innovative Food Science & Emerging Technologies*, 56, 102178. DOI: 10.1016/j.ifset.2019.102178

Crofton, E. C., Botinestean, C., Fenelon, M., & Gallagher, E. (2019). Potential applications for virtual and augmented reality technologies in sensory science. *Innovative Food Science & Emerging Technologies*, 56, 102178. DOI: 10.1016/j.ifset.2019.102178

Engelmann, T., Wallstein, S., & Hitzler, D. (2019). An experimental study to investigate the potential of online shopping in immersive virtual realities compared to conventional online shops. *The International Journal of Virtual Reality: a Multimedia Publication for Professionals*, 19(3), 31–45. DOI: 10.20870/IJVR.2019.19.3.2939

Goel, P., Garg, A., Sharma, A., & Rana, N. P. (2023). Impact of sensory perceptions on the urge to buy impulsively. *Journal of Computer Information Systems*, , 1–17.

Guo, Y., & Liang, G. (2021). Perceptual Feedback Mechanism Sensor Technology in e-Commerce IoT Application Research. *Journal of Sensors*, 2021(1), 3840103. DOI: 10.1155/2021/3840103

Hamacher, K., & Buchkremer, R. (2022). Measuring online sensory consumer experience: Introducing the online sensory marketing index (OSMI) as a structural modeling approach. *Journal of Theoretical and Applied Electronic Commerce Research*, 17(2), 751–772. DOI: 10.3390/jtaer17020039

Harrar, V., Piqueras-Fiszman, B., & Spence, C. (2011). There's no taste in a white bowl. *Perception*, 40(7), 880–892. DOI: 10.1068/p7040 PMID: 22128561

Hilken, T., Chylinski, M., Keeling, D. I., Heller, J., de Ruyter, K., & Mahr, D. (2022). How to strategically choose or combine augmented and virtual reality for improved online experiential retailing. *Psychology and Marketing*, 39(3), 495–507. DOI: 10.1002/mar.21600

Hong, Y., & Pavlou, P. A. (2014). Product Fit Uncertainty in Online Markets: Nature, Effects, and Antecedents. *Information Systems Research*, 25(2), 328–344. DOI: 10.1287/isre.2014.0520

Huang, T. L., & Chung, H. F. (2024). Impact of delightful somatosensory augmented reality experience on online consumer stickiness intention. *Journal of Research in Interactive Marketing*, 18(1), 6–30. DOI: 10.1108/JRIM-07-2022-0213

Hultén, B., Broweus, N., & van Dijk, M. (2009). What is Sensory Marketing? Sensory Marketing, 8-9

Jang, H. W., & Lee, S. B. (2019). Applying effective sensory marketing to sustainable coffee shop business management. *Sustainability (Basel)*, 11(22), 6430. DOI: 10.3390/su11226430

Kathikeyan, T., Revathi, S., Supreeth, B. R., Sasidevi, J., Ahmed, M., & Das, S. (2022, December). Artificial Intelligence and Mixed Reality Technology for Interactive Display of Images in Smart Area. In *2022 5th International Conference on Contemporary Computing and Informatics (IC3I)* (pp. 2049-2053). IEEE. DOI: 10.1109/IC3I56241.2022.10072411

Kim, J., & Forsythe, S. (2008). Sensory enabling technology acceptance model (SE-TAM): A multiple-group structural model comparison. *Psychology and Marketing*, 25(9), 901–922. DOI: 10.1002/mar.20245

Kim, J., & Forsythe, S. (2009). Adoption of sensory enabling technology for online apparel shopping. *European Journal of Marketing*, 43(9/10), 1101–1120. DOI: 10.1108/03090560910976384

Krishna, A. (2010). *Sensory marketing: Research on the sensuality of products*. Routledge.

Kumar, J., Arora, M., & Erkol Bayram, G. (Eds.). (2024) a. *Exploring the Use of Metaverse in Business and Education*. IGI Global. DOI: DOI: 10.4018/979-8-3693-5868-9

Kumar, J., Arora, M., & Erkol Bayram, G. (Eds.). (2024) b. *Research, Innovation, and Industry Impacts of the Metaverse*. IGI Global.

Lashkova, M., Anton, C., & Camarero, C. (2020). Dual effect of sensory experience: Engagement vs diversive exploration. *International Journal of Retail & Distribution Management*, 48(2), 128–151. DOI: 10.1108/IJRDM-09-2018-0204

Leveau, P. H., & Camus, E. S. (2023). Embodiment, immersion, and enjoyment in virtual reality marketing experiences. *Psychology and Marketing*, 40(7), 1329–1343. DOI: 10.1002/mar.21822

Leveau, P. H., & Camus, E. S. (2023). Embodiment, immersion, and enjoyment in virtual reality marketing experiences. *Psychology and Marketing*, 40(7), 1329–1343. DOI: 10.1002/mar.21822

Lick, E. (2022). "Multimodal Sensory Marketing" in retailing: The role of intra-and intermodality transductions. *Consumption Markets & Culture*, 25(3), 252–271. DOI: 10.1080/10253866.2022.2046564

Lopez, A., & Garza, R. (2022). Do sensory reviews make more sense? The mediation of objective perception in online review helpfulness. *Journal of Research in Interactive Marketing*, 16(3), 438–456. DOI: 10.1108/JRIM-04-2021-0121

Malekzadeh, M., Clegg, R. G., Cavallaro, A., & Haddadi, H. (2018, April). Protecting sensory data against sensitive inferences. In *Proceedings of the 1st Workshop on Privacy by Design in Distributed Systems* (pp. 1-6).

Maseeh, H. I., Jebarajakirthy, C., Pentecost, R., Arli, D., Weaven, S., & Ashaduzzaman, M. (2021). Privacy concerns in e-commerce: A multilevel meta-analysis. *Psychology and Marketing*, 38(10), 1779–1798. DOI: 10.1002/mar.21493

Mishra, A., Shukla, A., Rana, N. P., & Dwivedi, Y. K. (2021). From "touch" to a "multisensory" experience: The impact of technology interface and product type on consumer responses. *Psychology and Marketing*, 38(3), 385–396. DOI: 10.1002/mar.21436

Mohammed, Mostafa, Refaat, Moharam. (2023). The Impact of Augmented and Virtual Reality Technologies on Customer Happiness in Immersive Shopping Experiences. DOI: 10.52783/tjjpt.v44.i4.2491

Nah, F. F.-H., Eschenbrenner, B., & DeWester, D. (2011). Enhancing brand equity through f low and telepresence: A comparison of 2d and 3d virtual worlds. *Management Information Systems Quarterly*, 35(3), 731–747. DOI: 10.2307/23042806

Nakamura, H., & Miyashita, H. (2013). Controlling saltiness without salt: Evaluation of taste change by applying and releasing cathodal current. Proceedings of the 5th international workshop on multimedia for cooking & eating activities, 9–14.

Oliveira, A. S., Ferreira, J., Albuquerque, M., & Marcos, A. (2021, June). Marketing Sensorial: Estudo de Caso da Starbucks: Sensory Marketing: Starbucks Case Study. In 2021 16th Iberian Conference on Information Systems and Technologies (CISTI) (pp. 1-7). IEEE.

Parsons, A., & Conroy, D. (2006). Sensory stimuli and e-tailers. *Journal of Consumer Behaviour*, 5(1), 69–81. DOI: 10.1002/cb.32

Pavlou, P. A., Huigang, L., & Yajiong, X. (2007). Understanding and Mitigating Uncertainty in Online Exchange Relationships: A Principal-Agent Perspective. *Management Information Systems Quarterly*, 31(1), 105–135. DOI: 10.2307/25148783

Petit, O., Velasco, C., & Spence, C. (2019). Digital Sensory Marketing: Integrating New Technologies Into Multisensory Online Experience. *Journal of Interactive Marketing*, 45, 42–61. DOI: 10.1016/j.intmar.2018.07.004

Piqueras-Fiszman, B., Alcaide, J., Roura, E., & Spence, C. (2012). Is it the plate or is it the food? Assessing the influence of the color (black or white) and shape of the plate on the perception of the food placed on it. *Food Quality and Preference*, 24(1), 205–208. DOI: 10.1016/j.foodqual.2011.08.011

Powell, S. (2018). Uncle Ben's using augmented reality to reveal rice supply chain. https://thefuturescentre.org/signals-of-change/218004/uncle-bens-using-augmentedreality-reveal-rice-supply-chain / Accessed 22 November 2018. Ranasinghe, N., Tolley, D., Nguy

Racat, M., & Plotkina, D. (2023). Sensory-enabling technology in m-commerce: The effect of haptic stimulation on consumer purchasing behavior. *International Journal of Electronic Commerce*, 27(3), 354–384. DOI: 10.1080/10864415.2023.2226900

Ranasinghe, N., Lee, K. Y., Suthokumar, G., & Do, E. Y. L. (2016). Virtual ingredients for food and beverages to create immersive taste experiences. *Multimedia Tools and Applications*, 75(20), 12291–12309. DOI: 10.1007/s11042-015-3162-8

Ranasinghe, N., Lee, K. Y., Suthokumar, G., & Do, E. Y. L. (2016). Virtual ingredients for food and beverages to create immersive taste experiences. *Multimedia Tools and Applications*, 75(20), 12291–12309. DOI: 10.1007/s11042-015-3162-8

Ranasinghe, N., Tolley, D., Nguyen, T. N. T., Yan, L., Chew, B., & Yi-Luen Do, E. (2018). (in press). Augmented flavours: Modulation of flavour experiences through electric taste augmentation. *Food Research International*. Advance online publication. DOI: 10.1016/j.foodres.2018.05.030 PMID: 30736924

Ranasinghe, N., Tolley, D., Nguyen, T. N. T., Yan, L., Chew, B., & Yi-Luen Do, E. (2018). (in press). Augmented flavours: Modulation of flavour experiences through electric taste augmentation. *Food Research International*. Advance online publication. DOI: 10.1016/j.foodres.2018.05.030 PMID: 30736924

Ranasinghe, N., Tolley, D., Nguyen, T. N. T., Yan, L., Chew, B., & Yi-Luen Do, E. (2018). (in press). Augmented flavours: Modulation of flavour experiences through electric taste augmentation. *Food Research International*. Advance online publication. DOI: 10.1016/j.foodres.2018.05.030 PMID: 30736924

Ricci, M., Evangelista, A., Di Roma, A., & Fiorentino, M. (2023). Immersive and desktop virtual reality in virtual fashion stores: A comparison between shopping experiences. *Virtual Reality (Waltham Cross)*, 27(3), 2281–2296. DOI: 10.1007/s10055-023-00806-y PMID: 37360805

Ricci M, Scarcelli A, D'Introno A, Strippoli V, Cariati S, & Fiorentino M (2023). A human-centred design approach for designing augmented reality enabled interactive systems: a kitchen machine case study. https://doi.org/.DOI: 10.1007/978-3-031-15928-2_123

Santiago, R., Moreira, A. C., & Fortes, N. (2017). Influence of sensory stimuli on brand experience, brand equity, and purchase intention. *Journal of Business Economics and Management.*

Schlosser, A. E., White, T. B., & Lloyd, S. M. (2006). Converting Web Site Visitors into Buyers: How Web Site Investment Increases Consumer Trusting Beliefs and Online Purchase Intentions. *Journal of Marketing*, 70(2), 133–148. DOI: 10.1509/jmkg.70.2.133

Solti, A., Agarwal, S., & Spiekermann-Hoff, S. (2018). Privacy in location-sensing technologies. *Handbook of Mobile Data Privacy*, 35-69.

Sugawara, E., & Nikaido, H. (2014). Properties of AdeABC and AdeIJK Efflux Systems of Acinetobacter Baumannii Compared with Those of the AcrAB-TolC System of Escherichia Coli. *Antimicrobial Agents and Chemotherapy*, 58(12), 7250–7257. DOI: 10.1128/AAC.03728-14 PMID: 25246403

Tom Dieck, M. C., & Han, D. I. D. (2022). The role of immersive technology in Customer Experience Management. *Journal of Marketing Theory and Practice*, 30(1), 108–119. DOI: 10.1080/10696679.2021.1891939

Wilfling, J., Havenith, G., Raccuglia, M., & Hodder, S. (2023). Can you see the feel? The absence of tactile cues in clothing e-commerce impairs consumer decision making. *International Journal of Fashion Design, Technology and Education*, 16(2), 224–233. DOI: 10.1080/17543266.2022.2154396

Wölfel, M., & Reinhardt, A. (2019, March). Immersive Shopping Presentation of Goods in Virtual Reality. In *CERC* (pp. 119-130).

Yang, Y., Liu, M., Huang, J., & Wan, X. (2024). Making choices of food and non-food products: A comparison between virtual stores and online shopping. *International Journal of Food Science & Technology*, 59(3), 1644–1652. DOI: 10.1111/ijfs.16918

Yao, H., & Tarofder, A. K. (2024). Privacy Concerns in E-commerce Marketing: A Systematic Literature Review Study. *International Journal of Global Economics and Management*, 2(3), 64–75. DOI: 10.62051/IJGEM.v2n3.07

Zhao, Z., Luo, H., Chu, S. C., Shang, Y., & Wu, X. (2018). An Immersive Online Shopping System Based on Virtual Reality. *J. Netw. Intell.*, 3(4), 235–246.

Zheng, Q., & Ding, Q. (2022). Exploration of consumer preference based on deep learning neural network model in the immersive marketing environment. *PLoS One*, 17(5), e0268007. DOI: 10.1371/journal.pone.0268007 PMID: 35507570

Zhou, M. (2024). The effects of sensory interaction and sensory conflict on consumer online review rating behavior. *International Journal of Management Science and Engineering Management*, 19(2), 97–105. DOI: 10.1080/17509653.2023.2174201

Chapter 3
Neuroeconomic Insights into Cognitive Biases and Managerial Decision-Making

Abhishek Kumar Singh
https://orcid.org/0009-0007-3712-3249
Jawaharlal Nehru University, India

Arpit Singhmar
https://orcid.org/0009-0007-7428-2564
Jawaharlal Nehru University, India

Arvind Kumar
Jawaharlal Nehru University, India

Lokesh Jindal
Jawaharlal Nehru University, India

ABSTRACT

This chapter delves into the intersection of neuroeconomics, cognitive biases, and managerial decision-making. It aims to provide a comprehensive overview of how neurosensory and neuromarketing techniques influence consumer behaviour and decision-making processes. The chapter bridges the gap between academic research and industry practices through an in-depth literature review, innovative research methodologies, and detailed case studies. It offers practical insights and strategies for marketers and practitioners, emphasising the importance of interdisciplinary collaboration and knowledge exchange.

DOI: 10.4018/979-8-3693-9351-2.ch003

INTRODUCTION TO NEUROECONOMICS

Neuroeconomics is an interdisciplinary field that combines insights and methodologies from neuroscience, psychology, economics, and neuromarketing to better understand the mechanisms underlying decision-making processes and consumer behavior. By leveraging advanced neuroimaging techniques, behavioral experiments, and economic modelling, neuroeconomics aims to unravel the complexities of how individuals make choices, evaluate risks, and respond to various incentives.

INTERDISCIPLINARY NATURE OF NEUROECONOMICS

Neuroeconomics stands at the crossroads of several disciplines. Neuroscience offers the methods and frameworks to study the neural processes and brain activity involved in decision-making. Researchers can observe and analyze brain activity in real-time using methods like positron emission tomography (PET), electroencephalography (EEG), and functional magnetic resonance imaging (fMRI). By highlighting how distinct brain regions influence decision-making processes, these methods provide insightful information about the neural correlates of economic behavior (Glimcher & Fehr, 2014). A branch of psychology called behavioral economics studies how heuristics and cognitive biases affect judgment. Psychology-related insights aid in explaining why people frequently stray from reason and make decisions that are at odds with conventional economic models (Kahneman & Tversky, 1979).

Contrarily, economics provides frameworks and models that help people comprehend how to maximize utility, weigh trade-offs, and allocate resources. Conventional economic theories, such as game theory and anticipated utility theory, serve as a basis for analyzing decision-making procedures. Neuroeconomics aims to produce more thorough and precise models of human behavior by fusing data from neuroscience with economic models (Camerer, Loewenstein, & Prelec, 2005). Using neuroscientific methods, neuromarketing is a practical application of neuroeconomics that studies customer behaviour and preferences (Bhardwaj, Kaushik, & Arora (2024); Taneja, Shukla & Arora (2024); Malik, Malhan & Arora (2024). (Eds.)). Corporations may create more successful pricing models, product designs, and advertising campaigns by studying consumer brain responses to marketing stimuli. According to Plassmann, Ramsøy, and Milosavljevic (2012), neuromarketing links academic research and business practice, offering marketers and practitioners practical insights.

SIGNIFICANCE OF NEUROECONOMICS

It is essential to fully grasp how consumers make decisions and behave for various reasons. First, conventional economic models frequently presuppose that people are logical agents who only consider increasing their utility when making decisions. However, empirical data indicates that social, emotional, and cognitive biases frequently affect people's decisions in the real world. Researchers can create models that more accurately represent human conduct thanks to the more sophisticated knowledge of these variables that neuroeconomics offers (Ariely & Berns, 2010).

For example, a fundamental discovery in behavioral economics is the concept of loss aversion, which indicates that people typically would rather avoid losses than receive comparable gains. Studies on neuroeconomics have revealed a connection between loss aversion and elevated activity in the amygdala, a part of the brain involved in processing negative emotions like fear and anxiety (De Martino, Camerer, & Adolphs, 2010). This research casts doubt on the idea of totally logical activity by highlighting the interaction between emotion and decision-making. Furthermore, behavioral interventions and public policy are significantly impacted by neuroeconomics. Policymakers can create more effective interventions to encourage desirable behaviors, including saving for retirement, following medical advice, or leading healthier lives, by knowing the brain mechanisms behind decision-making. For instance, using knowledge from neuroeconomics, researchers have created nudging strategies that gently steer people towards better choices without limiting their freedom of choice (Thaler & Sunstein, 2008). By examining how consumers' brains respond to different types of advertisements, product features, and pricing strategies, companies can better tailor their offerings to meet consumer needs and preferences (McClure et al., 2004). This knowledge can help companies create more compelling brands and improve customer loyalty.

Furthermore, neuroeconomics has the potential to enhance financial decision-making. Traditional finance models often assume that investors are rational and markets are efficient. However, neuroeconomic research has revealed that investors are subject to various biases, such as overconfidence and herd behavior, which can lead to suboptimal financial decisions. By understanding the neural basis of these biases, financial institutions can develop better tools and strategies to mitigate their impact and improve investment outcomes (Lo, 2005).

THEORETICAL BACKGROUND

In today's world, with such intense competition in every industry, understanding customer preferences has become even more critical, and that is why we see corporations spending so much on pilot studies or market research to understand the needs of the customers better and then deliver the product that provides them with the most value while also helping the corporations have healthy profits (Arora & Sharma, (2023); Arora, M. (2024)). This critical step comes with complications since the customer might not want to reveal what they prefer or misunderstand the questions, which could lead to disastrous conclusions.

Stated preferences refer to what individuals say they prefer when asked directly, often in surveys or interviews. These preferences are based on self-reported data, where respondents express their choices, intentions, or desires about a particular product, service, or situation. However, stated preferences may not always align with actual behavior due to various factors, such as social desirability bias, lack of self-awareness, or hypothetical scenarios that do not capture real-world complexities (Ben-Akiva et al., 1994).

On the other hand, **revealed preferences** are inferred from actual consumer behavior in real-world situations. These preferences are observed through actions, such as purchasing decisions or choices made in different contexts. Revealed preferences provide a more accurate reflection of what consumers truly value based on tangible evidence of behavior rather than hypothetical scenarios (Samuelson, 1938). For instance, consumers' choices at the point of sale, the products they repeatedly purchase, or their store routes can all indicate their revealed preferences.

Over and above, these complications are caused by cognitive dissonance within the customer's mind, another multifaceted issue that arises, which we discuss in the next section to highlight the level of complexity when it comes to understanding customer preferences.

COGNITIVE BIASES AND THEIR IMPACT ON MANAGERIAL DECISION-MAKING

Definition of Cognitive Biases

Cognitive biases are systematic deviations from rationality in judgment and decision-making processes, where individuals rely on subjective perceptions rather than objective analysis. These biases stem from the brain's inherent tendency to simplify information processing, often through heuristics or mental shortcuts, which can lead to perceptual distortions, inaccurate judgments, and illogical interpretations

(Tversky & Kahneman, 1974). The origins of cognitive biases are multifaceted, involving emotional influences, memory constraints, social dynamics, and the inherent complexity of decision-making environments.

On the side of the consumers, we stand to make sub-optimal choices or induce biases due to how the marketers have phrased the campaign. This leads us to an exciting crossroads wherein consumers have biases, and corporations that sell might employ one of these to gain more traction. However, the consequences would be much less severe for individual consumer choices when compared to a manager making sub-optimal decisions due to such biases. In the next section of the chapter, we discuss the impact on managerial decision-making making, followed by some common examples, to help the readers understand the gravity of the biases we entangle ourselves with each day.

IMPACT ON MANAGERIAL DECISION-MAKING

Cognitive biases significantly affect managerial decision-making by distorting the perception of information and leading to suboptimal choices. Managers are tasked with making decisions that can have far-reaching consequences for their organizations, and cognitive biases can impede their ability to assess situations accurately and make rational choices (Kumar, Arora & Erkol Bayram (Eds.). (2024)a; Kumar, Arora & Erkol Bayram(Eds.). (2024)b)).

One of the primary ways cognitive biases impact managerial decision-making is through the selective filtering of information. Managers may unconsciously prioritize information that aligns with their beliefs or expectations while disregarding data that contradicts their preconceived notions. This selective attention can lead to confirmation bias, where managers overemphasize supportive evidence and underweight disconfirming evidence, resulting in skewed decision-making processes (Nickerson, 1998). Another significant impact of cognitive biases is on risk assessment and uncertainty management. Managers must often evaluate the potential risks and benefits of different courses of action. Cognitive biases can lead to overestimating positive outcomes and underestimating adverse outcomes, resulting in overly optimistic or risk-averse strategies. This can hinder the organization's ability to innovate and adapt to changing market conditions (Bazerman & Moore, 2013).

Cognitive biases also influence how managers interpret past experiences and use them to inform future decisions. The availability heuristic, for instance, leads managers to rely on immediate examples that come to mind, often those that are recent or particularly memorable, rather than considering a comprehensive set of data. This can result in decisions based on anecdotal evidence rather than robust analysis, potentially leading to repeated mistakes and a failure to learn from past outcomes (Kahneman & Tversky, 1973). Group decision-making within managerial contexts is also susceptible to cognitive biases. Groupthink, a phenomenon where the desire for harmony and conformity within a group leads to irrational or dysfunctional decision-making outcomes, can prevent critical evaluation of alternative ideas and suppress dissenting viewpoints. This can stifle creativity and innovation and lead to decisions outside the organization's best interest (Janis, 1982).

Moreover, cognitive biases can affect managerial judgment regarding employees and organizational dynamics. Managers might fall prey to stereotyping or the halo effect, where their overall impression of an employee influences their decisions about specific attributes or performance. These biases can lead to unfair evaluations, hinder diversity and inclusion efforts, and affect team morale and productivity (Thorndike, 1920).

In conclusion, cognitive biases pose a significant challenge to effective managerial decision-making. By distorting information processing, risk assessment, and judgment, these biases can lead to suboptimal decisions that impact organizational performance and growth. Managers must be aware of these biases and actively seek to mitigate their influence through structured decision-making processes, critical thinking, and fostering an environment where diverse perspectives are encouraged and valued.

B. COGNITIVE BIASES AFFECTING MARKETING

Analysis Paralysis

Analysis paralysis occurs when overthinking and overanalyzing a situation prevents a decision or action from being taken.

Impact on Purchase Decisions: Customers with too many options may become overwhelmed and need help to make a purchase decision. This can lead to deferred or abandoned purchases (Dhar, 1997).

Anchoring Effect

The anchoring effect is the cognitive bias, where individuals rely heavily on the first piece of information they receive (the "anchor") when making decisions.

Impact on Purchase Decisions: Initial prices or discounts can set a reference point for customers, influencing their perception of value and affecting subsequent purchase decisions (Tversky & Kahneman, 1974).

Availability Heuristic

The availability heuristic is a mental shortcut that relies on immediate examples that come to mind when evaluating a topic, concept, or decision.

Impact on Purchase Decisions: Customers may base their purchase decisions on recent events or readily available information, potentially overlooking other important factors (Tversky & Kahneman, 1973).

Bandwagon Effect

The bandwagon effect is the tendency for people to align their beliefs and behaviors with those of a group.

Impact on Purchase Decisions: Customers may purchase products or services perceived as widespread or widely accepted, driven by the desire to conform to social norms (Nadeau et al., 1993).

Buyer's Remorse

Buyer's remorse is the sense of regret after making a purchase.

Impact on Purchase Decisions: Customers may hesitate to make purchases, especially significant ones, due to fear of regret or feeling they made a poor decision (Engel et al., 1990).

Confirmation Bias

Confirmation bias is the tendency to search for, interpret, and remember information confirming preconceptions.

Impact on Purchase Decisions: Customers may favor information that supports their initial beliefs about a product, ignoring contradictory information, leading to biased decision-making (Nickerson, 1998).

Context Effect

The context effect is the influence of the surrounding environment on an individual's perception and decision-making.

Impact on Purchase Decisions: The context in which products are presented, such as store layout or online interface, can significantly influence customers' purchase decisions (Hutchinson et al., 2000).

Decoy Effect

The decoy effect occurs when an additional, less attractive option influences the relative attractiveness of alternatives.

Impact on Purchase Decisions: Introducing a decoy option can steer customers towards a more expensive or profitable choice by making it appear as the best value (Ariely, 2008).

Disposition Effect

The disposition effect is the tendency to sell assets that have increased in value while keeping assets that have decreased in value.

Impact on Purchase Decisions: Customers may hold onto products they perceive as losing value, delaying new purchases (Shefrin & Statman, 1985).

Endowment Effect

The endowment effect is when people value an item more once they own it.

Impact on Purchase Decisions: Customers may demand a higher price to part with owned items, affecting resale markets and trade-in decisions (Kahneman et al., 1991).

Forer effect / Barnum effect

The Forer effect, or Barnum effect, is the tendency for people to accept vague, general statements as specifically applicable to themselves.

Impact on Purchase Decisions: Customers may believe that generalized marketing messages are tailored to them personally, increasing the effectiveness of such messages (Dickson & Kelly, 1985).

Foot in the Door Technique

The foot-in-the-door technique involves getting a person to agree to a large request by setting them up with a more minor, manageable request.

Impact on Purchase Decisions: Once customers agree to a small initial purchase or action, they are more likely to agree to larger subsequent requests (Freedman & Fraser, 1966).

Framing Effect

The framing effect occurs when people react differently to a particular choice depending on how it is presented.
Impact on Purchase Decisions: The way information about a product is framed (e.g., "90% fat-free" vs "10% fat") can influence customers' perceptions and choices (Tversky & Kahneman, 1981).

Frequency Illusion

The frequency illusion, also known as the Baader-Meinhof phenomenon, is when people start noticing something everywhere after seeing it once.
Impact on Purchase Decisions: Customers may perceive a product as more popular or relevant because they notice it frequently after an initial encounter, influencing their purchase decisions (Zwicky, 2005).

Hyperbolic Discounting

Hyperbolic discounting is the tendency for people to prefer smaller, immediate rewards over larger, delayed rewards.
Impact on Purchase Decisions: Customers may opt for instant gratification, choosing immediate promotions or discounts over long-term benefits (Laibson, 1997).

Identifiable Victim Effect

The identifiable victim effect is the tendency to offer more excellent aid when a specific, identifiable person is observed under hardship, compared to a large, vaguely defined group.
Impact on Purchase Decisions: Personalized stories or testimonials in marketing can be more compelling and persuasive, leading to increased customer engagement and purchases (Small & Loewenstein, 2003).
Ikea Effect: The Ikea effect is the cognitive bias where people place a disproportionately high value on products they partially create.
Impact on Purchase Decisions: Customers are likely to value and prefer products they have assembled or customized themselves, impacting their willingness to pay (Norton et al., 2012).
Illusory truth effect: The illusory truth effect is the tendency to believe information accurately after repeated exposure.

Impact on Purchase Decisions: Repeated advertising and marketing messages can make customers more likely to believe in the benefits or quality of a product, even without additional evidence (Hasher et al., 1977).

Impact Bias: Impact bias is the tendency to overestimate the intensity and duration of future emotional states.

Impact on Purchase Decisions: Customers may overestimate the satisfaction they gain from a purchase, leading to heightened expectations and potential disappointment post-purchase (Wilson & Gilbert, 2003).

Irrational Escalation/ Escalation of commitment: Irrational escalation, also known as escalation of commitment, occurs when people continue investing in a decision despite new evidence suggesting it may be wrong.

Impact on Purchase Decisions: Customers may continue to invest in a product or service they have previously purchased, even if it no longer meets their needs, due to their prior commitment (Staw, 1981).

Loss Aversion: Loss aversion is people's tendency to avoid losses rather than acquire equivalent gains.

Impact on Purchase Decisions: Customers are more likely to be influenced by the fear of losing out on a deal or promotion, driving urgency in their purchasing behavior (Kahneman & Tversky, 1979).

Law of the Instrument: The law of the instrument, also known as Maslow's hammer, is the tendency to over-rely on a familiar tool or approach.

Impact on Purchase Decisions: Customers may consistently choose familiar products or brands, even when better alternatives are available, due to their comfort with known options (Kaplan, 1964).

Mere Exposure Effect: The mere exposure effect is the tendency to develop a preference for things merely because they are familiar.

Impact on Purchase Decisions: Repeated exposure to a brand or product increases customer familiarity and likability, influencing purchase decisions (Zajonc, 1968).

Perceived Value Bias: Perceived value bias is the tendency for people to assess the value of a product based on its perceived rather than actual value.

Impact on Purchase Decisions: Customers may be influenced by branding, packaging, or marketing messages that enhance the perceived value of a product, leading to a higher willingness to pay (Zeithaml, 1988).

Scarcity/FOMO: Scarcity, often associated with FOMO, is the perception that something is in limited supply, which can create a sense of urgency and exclusivity.

Impact on Purchase Decisions: Customers are more likely to make impulsive purchases when they believe a product is scarce or they might miss out on a limited-time offer (Cialdini, 2009).

We now understand and acknowledge the complexity behind understanding how customers think and what factors can impact their thoughts. Now, to understand these revealed preferences beforehand or describe the gaps between the stated and revealed preferences, we need the help of neuro-sensory tools and techniques which help us measure the revealed objective preferences since we cannot conceal preferences when these tools and techniques are involved instead of the conventional survey or interview methods.

OBJECTIVES

- Provide a comprehensive overview of neurosensory and neuromarketing impacts on consumer behavior.
- Highlight cutting-edge research and innovative methodologies in the field.
- Bridge the gap between academic research and industry practices.
- Present case studies showcasing the successful implementation of neurosensory and neuromarketing techniques.
- Offer practical insights and strategies for marketers and practitioners.
- Foster interdisciplinary collaboration and knowledge exchange.

UNDERSTANDING NEUROMARKETING

Understanding neuromarketing is essential for studying revealed preferences because traditional methods of assessing consumer choices often rely on self-reported data, which can influence cognitive biases and social desirability. Neuromarketing techniques, such as neuroimaging and biometrics, provide insights into the subconscious processes that drive decision-making by directly measuring brain activity, physiological responses, and sensory reactions. These methods reveal the true preferences of consumers, which may differ from their stated preferences, offering a more accurate and objective understanding of consumer behavior that can inform more effective marketing strategies.

INTRODUCTION TO NEUROMARKETING

The term neuromarketing emerged in 2002 when Professor Ale Smidts published his article "Kijken in the brain" ("Looking into the brain"). The phrase "neuromarketing" has several meanings, which might be attributed to its complexity. According to (Smidts, 2002), the idea is to investigate brain structures and functions to comprehend customer behavior patterns and enhance marketing tactics. Lee, Broderick, and Chamberlain adopt a similar strategy after realizing that neuromarketing is the application of neuroscientific methods in marketing to analyze and comprehend human behavior; put another way, neuromarketing uses these methods to understand consumer psychology and the factors that influence their decision to choose a particular brand or product over another (Lee et al., 2007). By defining neuromarketing in this way, the writers have already established a significant framework and broadened its application to include areas other than consumer behavior research. The description given by (Dooley, 2010), who defines neuromarketing as a novel field in marketing research that examines consumers cognitive and affective reactions to various marketing stimuli, is even more accurate.

Neuromarketing is an interdisciplinary field that integrates theories of consumer behavior with components of psychology and neuroscience to explain the factors that influence a consumer's ultimate purchasing choice (Marichamy & Sathiyavathi, 2014). It is regarded as a field between neurosciences and economics with the initial goal of explaining the decision-making process by creating brain models and systems (Pop et al., 2014; Egidi, 2008), as it originated as a subfield of neuroeconomics.

Neuromarketing encompasses a variety of approaches, which may be further classified as recording brain activity or extra-brain activity. The first method used by the first group is called Functional Magnetic Resonance (fMRI), which uses magnetism to measure variations in blood oxygenation, which is then connected to brain activity. FMRI provides images of the brain in action, allowing for the analysis of neuronal responses to stimuli. The second method is electroencephalography, or EEG, which uses electrodes applied to the scalp to identify the parts of the brain with the highest activity. Because EEG is less expensive than fMRI, it is one of the most commonly used methods in neuromarketing. The third method is called magnetoencephalography, or MEG; like EEG, it measures the magnetic fields generated by brain activity. Although MEG provides superior quality and temporal resolution over EEG, its use is relatively rare due to the high cost of the required equipment.

However, another category includes electromyography or EMG. This technique involves applying low-voltage electrodes to the muscles to observe the electrical activity that these produce during involuntary emotional reactions. EMG is commonly used on facial muscles to monitor fleeting and undetectable expressions of the human eye. Another method is the Facial Action Coding System (FACS), which measures the muscle response to specific stimuli by observing facial expressions. Paul Ekman's experiments introduced this method in the 1970s, and it is currently developed using specialized software (Azcarate et al., 2005). Ocular tracking, often known as eye tracking, is the third method in this category; in this instance, the subject's point of view is examined, which is particularly helpful when several stimuli or background knowledge is required. Although current techniques vary, they all aim to investigate consumers' cognitive, sensorimotor, and affective responses to specific marketing stimuli through their body movements (Ohme et al., 2009). They also seek to ascertain whether changes in these stimuli also result in changes in the body signals (Kenning & Plassmann, 2008; Riccio et al., 2015; Rodrigues, 2011). Because people may lie when asked directly about something that neuromarketing ignores, proponents of the practice contend that neuromarketing yields information that is not possible to gather through traditional methods of marketing research, such as focus groups, questionnaires, or interviews (Ariely & Berns, 2010). Some writers believe that persuading customers to logically communicate their feelings regarding a product or piece of marketing collateral is not a reliable source of information because of the bias that inevitably results from this process, which calls into question the procedure's effectiveness. (Oliver, 2016)

The primary distinction between neuromarketing and conventional research methods is this: neuromarketing provides an open window into the minds of consumers, revealing frequently overlooked details that can mean the difference between a marketing campaign that succeeds and one that fails. (Colaffero & Crescitelli, 2014; Michamy & Sathiyavathi, 2014; Mucha, 2005)

According to some experts, neuromarketing was unethical and even went beyond the bounds of legislation (Lee et al., 2007). Others mentioned the exorbitant expenses linked to the various methods that did not outweigh the outcomes (Hubert & Kenning, 2008) and even the detrimental impact on society it might have since it established a precedent that might allow brands to manipulate and control people (Murphy et al., 2008). Despite its growing popularity, neuromarketing continued to face harsh criticism; for example, the efficacy of neuromarketing methods was questioned, and it was ruled out that they could replace traditional research techniques because the conditions of the experiments and the methodologies limited their generalization (Solnais et al., 2013).

Even so, there has been an increase in interest in recent years in some regions of neuromarketing, such as its ethical component; one example of this is the paper written by Stanton, Sinnott-Armstrong, and Huettel (Stanton et al., 2017), which details the ethical risks associated with the methods and applications of neuromarketing and in keeping with this strategy, Hensel, Iorga, Wolter, and Znanewitz (Hensel et al., 2017) conducted a series of interviews with experts in the field of neuromarketing, confirming the significance of upholding and honoring the ethical components of neuromarketing to guarantee participant safety as well as the caliber of the outcomes. Despite the controversy surrounding it, neuromarketing gained traction in the following years. This was partly due to the expectation that novel approaches would be more affordable and quicker than existing research methodologies and that neuromarketing offered access to data that was impossible to obtain through other means (Ariely & Berns, 2010). According to (Yoon et al.,

2012), neuromarketing was first perceived as a discipline devoid of magic and with its limits. Still, it also provided helpful information for understanding the intricacies of consumer purchase decisions.

As a result, the area started to acquire more excellent traction as a trustworthy research tool 2010 onwards when several studies were published on the benefits and drawbacks of the various neuromarketing strategies (Bercea, 2012).

The creation of the Neuromarketing Business and Science Association (NMBSA) in 2012 helped to cement this growth. The organization's goals include advancing neuromarketing globally and providing a methodological foundation for the discipline to support its adoption by the scientific community.

Although"neuromarketing" was first used in the early 2000s, its origins can be found in previous psychological and neurological studies. Self-reported data, which can be biased and unreliable, was the primary source of data used in early studies on consumer behavior. The incorporation of neuroscience methodologies commenced with the progressions in brain imaging technologies, which enabled investigators to witness neural activity in reaction to marketing stimuli. With time, neuromarketing has expanded to incorporate a range of strategies that offer a more in-depth understanding of customer behavior (Lee et al., 2007).

Let us delve into the techniques used to capture the data that further helps corporations understand their customers in an objectively more wholesome manner.

KEY NEUROMARKETING TECHNIQUES

EEG (Electroencephalography)

Figure 1. EEG setup and the process of measurement

(https://www.researchgate.net/figure/Sketch-of-how-to-record-an-Electroencephalogram-An-EEG-allows-measuring-the-electrical_fig1_338423585)

EEG measures electrical activity in the brain using sensors placed on the scalp. It is widely used in neuromarketing to track immediate brain responses to marketing stimuli, such as advertisements or product packaging. Technique for recording and interpreting the electrical activity of the brain. The brain's nerve cells generate electrical impulses that fluctuate rhythmically in distinct patterns. (Encyclopedia Britannica)

There are two basic types of EEG:

- **Routine EEG:** This basic test is typically done after someone has a seizure for the first time. This is ideally performed within 24 hours.
- **Ambulatory EEG:** This test uses equipment that a person wears to record brain activity continuously as they go about their normal activities. Ambulatory EEG is most commonly used by neuromarketing.
- **Applications**: EEG measures attention, emotional engagement, and memory retention. It can provide real-time data, making it helpful in evaluating dynamic content like commercials (Khushaba et al., 2013).

- **Strengths**: EEG is non-invasive, relatively affordable, and provides high temporal resolution.
- **Limitations**: It has low spatial resolution, meaning it could be more effective at pinpointing the exact location of brain activity.

fMRI (Functional Magnetic Resonance Imaging)

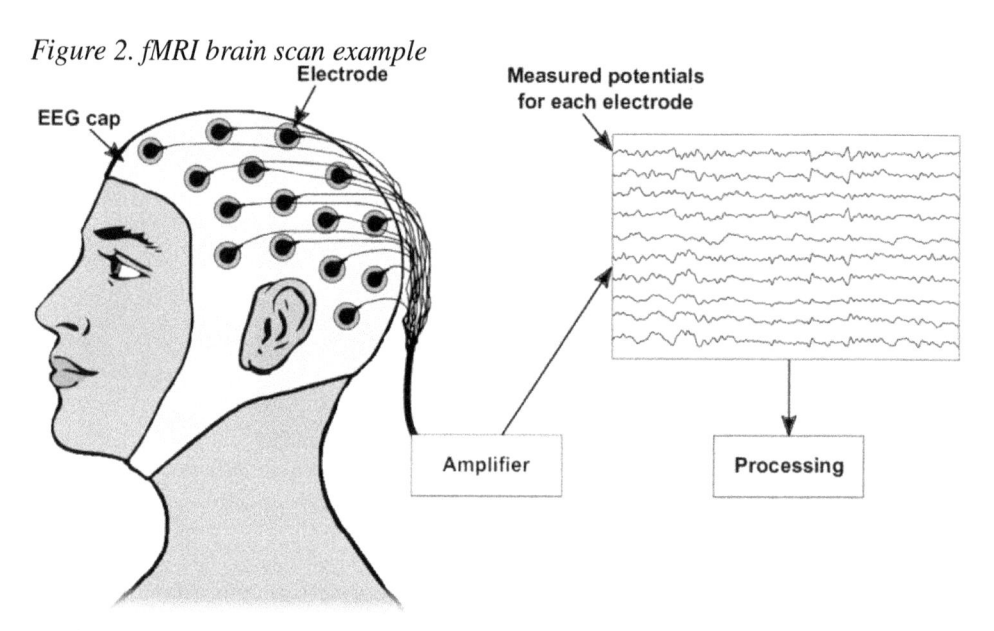

Figure 2. fMRI brain scan example

(https://www.brainline.org/slideshow/brain-imaging-what-are-different-types)

fMRI detects changes in blood flow to various parts of the brain, indicating neural activity. It is used in neuromarketing to understand more profound cognitive and emotional responses. fMRI aims to determine the neurobiological correlation of behavior by locating the active parts of the brain during the experiment (Kulich et al.; S. J., 2009) and to measure blood flow at more than 100,000 locations in the brain and interpret how the brain processes information. It tracks the change in oxygenated blood flow to find which brain parts use oxygen most (Ruanguttamanun, 2014) when faced with various specific stimuli. This measurement is known as blood-oxygen-level-dependent activity (BOLD activity).

- **Applications**: fMRI can identify which brain regions are activated in response to specific stimuli, helping to understand complex emotional and decision-making processes (Knutson et al., 2007).

- **Strengths**: It offers high spatial resolution, providing detailed images of brain activity.
- **Limitations**: fMRI is expensive, requires participants to remain still, and has lower temporal resolution than EEG.

Eye Tracking

Figure 3. Eye tracking heat map

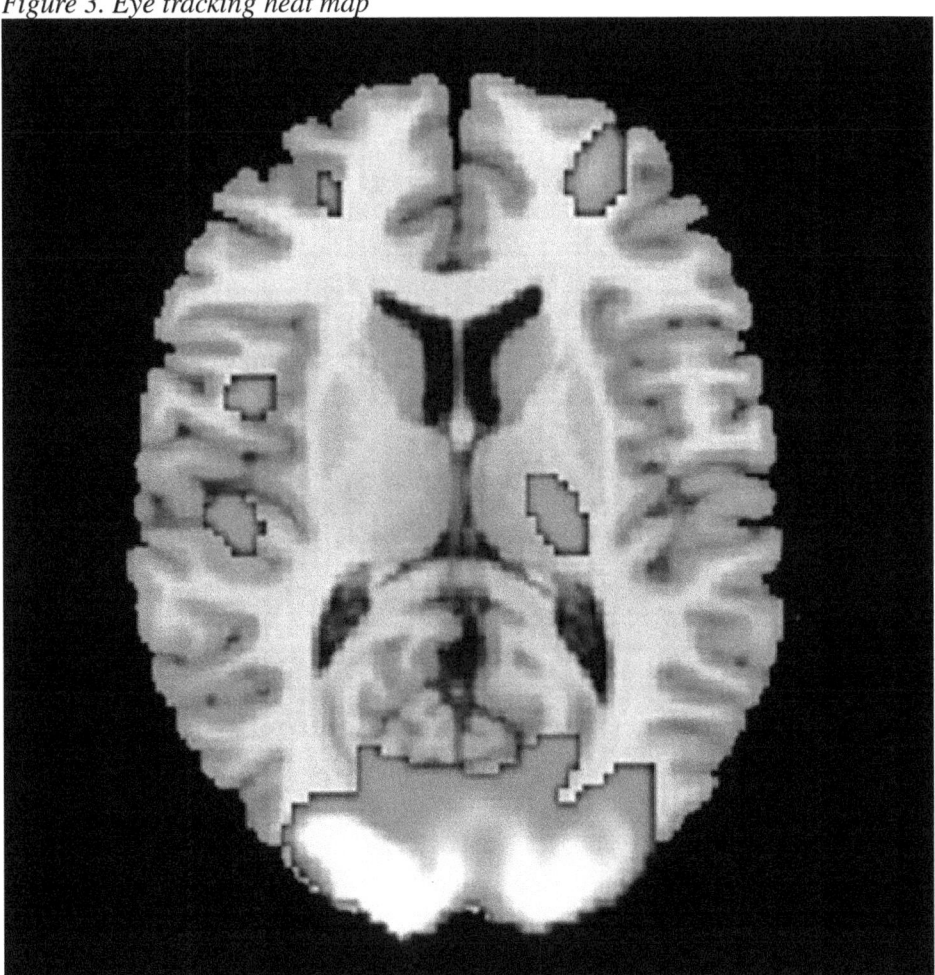

(https://nmsba.com/neuromarketing-companies/neuromarketing-technologies-explained/what-eye-tracking-can-and-cant-tell-you-about-attention)

Eye tracking measures where and how long a person focuses their gaze. It is used to analyze visual attention and engagement with marketing materials.

- **Applications**: Eye tracking is applied to study website usability, advertisement effectiveness, and product placement (Wedel & Pieters, 2008).
- **Strengths**: It provides precise data on visual attention and can be combined with other techniques like EEG.
- **Limitations**: Eye tracking does not provide direct insights into emotional or cognitive responses.

Other Techniques

Magnetoencephalography (MEG): This technique is based on expanding and mapping the magnetic field created through neural activities and electrochemical signals between neurons (Fortunato, Giraldi, 2014). When conducting MEG research, individuals use hyper-sensitive sensors to measure the electromagnetic field without contact with the scalp.

Facial Coding: Facial measurement procedures interpret behaviors through facial expressions. Within the economic field, these expressions are primarily considered independent variables, and authors research their effects on other variables under study (Ekman & Rosenberg, 2005, p. 41).

Positron emission tomography (PET): PET is a susceptible imaging technique allowing for the three-dimensional mapping of positron-emitting radiopharmaceuticals administered in minuscule (mg) quantities without causing any significant physiologic effects(Lameka et al., 2016).

THE IMPACT OF SENSORY STIMULI ON CONSUMER BEHAVIOR

Visual Stimuli

Visual components like color, pattern, and imagery significantly impact how customers think and act. Labrecque and Milne (2012) state that colors can elicit particular feelings. Color psychology is a tool brands use to elicit particular feelings. For instance, blue is commonly used in branding financial institutions like banks since it is typically connected to tranquility and trust (Singh, 2006).

For instance, red can arouse enthusiasm, while blue might foster a sense of trust.

Example: Coca-Cola's consistent use of red in its branding is a prime example of effective visual marketing. Red is associated with excitement and energy, which aligns with the brand's image. A case study by Gorn et al. (1997) found that color usage in advertising significantly affects consumer mood and willingness to purchase.

Auditory Stimuli

Consumer experiences are significantly shaped by sound, including music and jingles. Auditory stimuli can improve brand recognition and establish affective bonds with consumers. Sound effects and music can improve the shopping experience. Retail settings frequently employ background music to set the right mood, affecting customer behavior and the time spent there (Garlin & Owen, 2006).

Examples: A study by North, Hargreaves, and McKendrick (1999) found that playing French music in a wine store increased the sales of French wines, while playing German music boosted sales of German wines. This illustrates how auditory cues can subtly influence consumer choices.

Olfactory Stimuli

Emotions and memories are strongly influenced by scent. Aromas have the power to improve the shopping experience and lengthen customer visits. For instance, the smell of freshly baked bread in grocery stores may encourage customers to purchase more bakery goods (Spangenberg et al., 2006).

Tactile Stimuli: The physical interaction with products can influence perceptions of quality and value. For instance, consumers are more likely to purchase items they can touch and feel, as tactile sensations provide critical information about texture and weight (Peck & Childers, 2003).

Physical Stimulation

Touch affects how a thing is perceived and what people decide to buy. Consumers frequently link tactile perceptions to product quality. According to (Peck and Childers, 2003), the packing texture can influence perceptions of luxury and value.

Mandatory Incentives

When it comes to food and beverage marketing, taste is quite important. Customers may be persuaded to buy new products with free samples. Emotional solid bonds and brand loyalty can be formed through taste experiences (Krishna, 2012).

To understand the objectivity of the tests taken using such tools and techniques, we need to understand the neurosensory influences behind those and how they impact or interact with the customer while making choices. These require a complex web of techniques, including the ones mentioned before, but also involving them in experimental economic games that enhance our understanding of their consumers' level without any assumptions.

How Sensory Experiences Influence Consumer Choices: Sensory experiences greatly influence consumer behavior through various psychological and neurological processes. Consumers' experiences with sight, sound, smell, taste, and touch engage particular brain regions that process and integrate these inputs, resulting in emotional and cognitive reactions that influence decisions.

Psychological Mechanisms: Memories, feelings, and attitudes evoked by sensory stimuli can affect a consumer's preferences and decision-making. The mere exposure effect, for example, postulates that a stimulus might increase a person's preference for it if they are exposed to it repeatedly. This impact is shown in branding, where, over time, recognizable visual components such as colors and logos foster positive associations and familiarity (Zajonc, 2001).

Neurological Mechanisms: The brain's reward system is activated by sensory experiences. In particular, the mesolimbic pathway is implicated, which releases the neurotransmitter dopamine linked to pleasure and reward. Research employing functional magnetic resonance imaging (fMRI) has demonstrated that pleasurable sensory encounters elicit activation in the prefrontal cortex and nucleus accumbens, areas associated with reward and decision-making (Kringelbach, 2005).

Building Emotional Bonds and Brand Adherence: Using sensory cues, sensory marketing techniques help customers form deep emotional bonds with brands and increase brand loyalty. Emotional connections are vital because they affect customer attitudes, buying intentions, and long-term loyalty. These are not potential ways in which brands influence consumers, but the ones that already exist and are levied upon you consciously; for a few such examples, look at the next section.

Powerful Brands Demonstrating Sensory Influence:

Apple Inc.: From the physical interaction with items to the sleek and straightforward visual aesthetics, Apple stores are meant to provide a seamless sensory experience. Customers are encouraged to touch and interact with the devices thanks to the layout, which improves the perceived quality and builds a stronger emotional bond with the brand.

Starbucks: To create a warm environment, Starbucks employs a multi-sensory approach. The soft lighting, the distinct coffee scent, and the cozy seating enhance a consistent brand experience. Starbucks has stood out in a crowded market and developed a devoted customer base because of this tactic.

Singapore Airlines: To offer a distinctive and unforgettable travel experience, this airline utilizes its signature aroma, "Stefan Floridian Waters," in its cabins and lounges. According to Lindstrom (2005), using scent in branding enhances the brand's image of luxury and premiumness, which fosters customer happiness and loyalty.

Now that we have discussed all the factors that are in play while we make purchasing decisions, we also have the tools and techniques that they use to measure various parameters to better gauge and influence the customer. Looking further into experiments that involve both revealed and stated preferences to a certain extent and to find out objectively accurate answers to complex marketing questions, let us delve into the various neurological economic techniques used to measure variables that help form the complete picture of how consumer views or values your product/brand.

Cutting-Edge Research Methods in Neuroeconomics

Neuroeconomic research employs various innovative methodologies to understand the complex interplay between neural activity and economic decision-making. Three primary techniques are neuroimaging, behavioral experiments, and computational modelling.

Neuroimaging

Neuroimaging techniques like functional magnetic resonance imaging (fMRI) and electroencephalography (EEG) are pivotal in neuroeconomic research. fMRI measures brain activity by detecting changes associated with blood flow, providing spatially precise images of brain regions involved in decision-making processes (Huettel, Song, & McCarthy, 2009). For instance, fMRI studies have identified the role of the prefrontal cortex in evaluating risks and rewards (Knutson et al., 2007). On the other hand, EEG records the brain's electrical activity with high temporal resolution, allowing researchers to track the timing of neural processes during decision-making tasks (Cohen, 2014).

These techniques contribute to a deeper understanding of cognitive biases by highlighting the neural correlates of biased decision-making. For example, fMRI studies have shown that the amygdala is more active when individuals make decisions under loss aversion, reflecting an emotional response that deviates from rational economic behavior (De Martino et al., 2006).

Behavioral Experiments

Behavioral experiments in neuroeconomics involve controlled settings where participants make economic decisions while their neural activity is monitored. These experiments often use tasks designed to elicit specific cognitive biases, such as the ultimatum game, which reveals fairness preferences and inequality aversion (Sanfey et al., 2003). Researchers can identify how brain activity corresponds with particular biases and decision-making strategies by correlating behavioral data with neuroimaging results.

These experiments help disentangle the cognitive processes underlying biases, such as framing effects, where the presentation of information influences decisions. Research has demonstrated that framing effects activate different brain regions, suggesting that cognitive and emotional processes jointly contribute to biased judgments (De Martino et al., 2006).

Computational Modeling

Computational modelling involves creating mathematical models that simulate decision-making processes. These models incorporate parameters that reflect neural activity, enabling researchers to predict behavior based on underlying neural mechanisms. For instance, reinforcement learning models have been used to explain how individuals update their expectations based on rewards and punishments, aligning with observed neural activity in the striatum (O'Doherty et al., 2004).

By integrating data from neuroimaging and behavioral experiments, computational models provide a comprehensive framework for understanding how cognitive biases emerge from neural computations. These models can simulate various decision-making scenarios, allowing researchers to explore the effects of different biases in controlled virtual environments (Rangel, Camerer, & Montague, 2008).

Integration of Neurosensory Techniques in Studying Consumer Behavior

Neurosensory techniques, which involve the study of sensory processing and its influence on behavior, are increasingly integrated into neuroeconomic research to understand consumer behavior. These techniques examine how sensory stimuli, such as visual, auditory, and olfactory cues, affect consumer preferences and decisions.

Neuroeconomics, an interdisciplinary field that combines insights from neuroscience, psychology, and economics, offers powerful tools for understanding consumer preferences that are not always accessible through traditional marketing research methods. Revealed preferences, the actual choices consumers make when confronted with different options, provide a more accurate reflection of their true desires and priorities than stated preferences, which are often influenced by social norms, cognitive biases, or misreporting. By leveraging neuroeconomic techniques, marketers can gain deeper insights into these revealed preferences, enhancing their ability to predict and influence consumer behavior.

Neuroimaging and Revealed Preferences

One of the key contributions of neuroeconomics is the use of neuroimaging techniques, such as functional magnetic resonance imaging (fMRI) and electroencephalography (EEG), to study brain activity associated with decision-making. These tools allow researchers to observe which areas of the brain are activated when consumers are exposed to different products, prices, or marketing messages. For example, studies have shown that brain areas related to reward processing, such as the nucleus accumbens, are more active when consumers encounter products they prefer or are likely to purchase (Knutson et al., 2007). This neurological data provides direct evidence of consumers' revealed preferences, which can be used to tailor marketing strategies to align with what consumers are genuinely motivated by rather than what they claim to prefer.

Predictive Power of Neuroeconomic Data

The predictive power of neuroeconomic data is another critical advantage for marketers. Traditional market research methods, such as surveys and focus groups, rely on consumers' self-reported intentions, which may only sometimes align with their actual behavior due to factors like social desirability bias or memory limitations. Neuroeconomic methods, on the other hand, capture real-time data on how consumers process information and make decisions, providing a more reliable basis for predicting future behavior (Ariely & Berns, 2010). For example, a study might reveal that specific visual or auditory cues consistently trigger a positive emotional response in consumers, indicating a strong revealed preference for those elements. Marketers can then incorporate these cues into their branding or advertising strategies to enhance consumer engagement and increase the likelihood of purchase.

Application to Product Development and Pricing Strategies

Understanding revealed preferences through neuroeconomics also aids in product development and pricing strategies. By identifying which features or price points elicit strong neural responses, companies can design products and set prices that better match consumer expectations and desires. For instance, neuroeconomic studies have shown that the brain's reward centers are more activated by prices perceived as fair or providing good value (Plassmann et al., 2008). This insight can guide marketers in setting prices that maximize consumer satisfaction and willingness to buy, increasing sales and customer loyalty.

How can customers protect themselves from making sub-optimal choices?

Armed with insights from neuroeconomics, consumers can take several steps to protect themselves from making suboptimal choices:

1. **Awareness and Education**: The first step in mitigating the impact of cognitive biases is awareness. Consumers who understand the nature of these biases are better equipped to recognize when they might be influencing their decisions. Educational programs and resources that explain common biases, such as the anchoring effect or confirmation bias, can help consumers critically evaluate their choices (Thaler & Sunstein, 2008).
2. **Mindfulness and Deliberation**: Neuroeconomics suggests that engaging the prefrontal cortex through mindful and deliberate decision-making can counteract the impulsive tendencies driven by more primal brain areas, such as the amygdala. Techniques like taking time to reflect on decisions, especially those involving significant risks or long-term commitments, can reduce the likelihood of falling prey to biases (McClure et al., 2004).
3. **Utilizing Decision Aids**: Consumers can use various decision aids, such as comparison tools, checklists, and financial planning software, to counteract biases. These tools can provide objective data and structured decision-making processes that help consumers avoid over-relying on gut feelings or incomplete information (Ariely, 2008). For instance, a well-structured budget can help consumers avoid overspending, which is an expected outcome of the availability heuristic and framing effects.
4. **Setting Precommitments**: Precommitments, such as automatic savings plans or setting specific purchase goals, can help consumers avoid impulsive decisions driven by immediate emotional responses. By pre-committing to a course of action, consumers can align their choices with their long-term interests, effectively circumventing biases like hyperbolic discounting (Thaler, 1999).
5. **Seeking External Perspectives**: Consulting with others, especially those not directly involved in the decision, can provide a more balanced view and help counteract biases such as confirmation bias. Friends, family, or financial advisors can offer alternative perspectives that challenge the consumer's initial inclinations, leading to more rational decisions (Soll, Milkman, & Payne, 2015).

Long-Term Benefits of Understanding Biases

By understanding and addressing cognitive biases, consumers can make more informed and rational decisions that better serve their long-term interests. For example, awareness of the endowment effect—where individuals overvalue possessions simply because they own them—can help consumers make more objective decisions about selling or discarding items (Kahneman, Knetsch, & Thaler, 1991). Similarly, recognizing the impact of the decoy effect, where the presence of an inferior option makes another option more attractive, can help consumers avoid being manipulated by marketing tactics that exploit this bias (Huber, Payne, & Puto, 1982).

Furthermore, by consistently applying strategies to mitigate biases, consumers can develop decision-making habits that lead to better financial health, stronger consumer satisfaction, and greater overall well-being. This proactive approach to decision-making, grounded in the insights provided by neuroeconomics, represents a significant step toward more empowered and autonomous consumer behavior.

PRACTICAL EXAMPLES OF SUCCESSFUL NEUROMARKETING IMPLEMENTATIONS

Real-World Examples of Companies Leveraging Neurosensory Insights

Coca-Cola: Leveraging Emotional Branding

Coca-Cola has been a pioneer in using neuromarketing techniques to enhance its branding strategies. By employing functional Magnetic Resonance Imaging (fMRI) studies, Coca-Cola identified the neural correlates of brand preference and emotional attachment (McClure et al., 2004). These studies revealed that solid brand loyalty is associated with increased activation in brain areas linked to emotional processing and memory, such as the ventromedial prefrontal cortex. As a result, Coca-Cola's marketing campaigns have focused heavily on evoking positive emotions and nostalgia, reinforcing its brand identity.

Strategies and Impact:

- **Strategy:** Emotional branding through advertisements that evoke nostalgia and happiness.
- **Impact:** Increased brand loyalty and consumer preference, translating to higher sales and market share.

Apple: Enhancing Customer Experience

Apple's retail stores are designed with neurosensory principles in mind to create an engaging and memorable customer experience. The minimalist design, strategic lighting, and tactile interactions with products are all crafted to stimulate the senses and encourage exploration (Lindstrom, 2010). Apple also uses scent marketing to subtly influence mood and perception, ensuring a consistent and pleasant sensory experience across all stores.

Strategies and Impact:

- **Strategy:** Integrating visual, tactile, and olfactory stimuli in store design.
- **Impact:** Enhanced customer satisfaction, longer in-store visits, and increased sales.

Hyundai: Neuroimaging for Product Design

Hyundai utilized fMRI to understand consumers' emotional responses to car interiors. By analyzing brain activity, the company identified which design elements elicited positive emotions and incorporated these insights into their vehicle designs (Plassmann et al., 2012). This approach ensured that the final product resonated with consumers on an emotional level, leading to higher customer satisfaction.

Strategies and Impact:

- **Strategy:** Using fMRI to guide design decisions based on emotional responses.
- **Impact:** Improved product appeal and increased customer satisfaction.

Coca-Cola's Use of Neuromarketing for Brand Loyalty

- **Intervention**: Coca-Cola conducted a neuromarketing study using fMRI (functional Magnetic Resonance Imaging) to understand how brand loyalty affects consumer preferences. They found that when consumers know they are drinking Coca-Cola, the brain's reward centers are more activated than when they consume a similar product without knowing the brand.
- **Outcome**: The study gave Coca-Cola insights into the power of brand loyalty and emotional connection, leading them to focus on marketing strategies that reinforce their brand identity and emotional appeal.

Frito-Lay's Packaging Design

- **Intervention**: Frito-Lay used EEG (Electroencephalogram) and eye-tracking techniques to test consumer reactions to packaging designs. They discovered that shiny, bright-colored packaging triggered negative responses in the brain, while matte, subdued designs were more positively received.

- **Outcome**: Based on these insights, Frito-Lay redesigned its packaging to be more visually appealing and less likely to provoke adverse subconscious reactions, ultimately increasing product sales.

Google's Visual Display Ads

- **Intervention**: Google optimized display ads by using eye-tracking and facial expression analysis. They analyzed where users' eyes were drawn on the screen and what emotional responses were triggered by different ad elements.
- **Outcome**: This data-driven approach allowed Google to create more engaging and compelling ads, resulting in higher click-through rates and improved ad performance.

IKEA's In-Store Experience

- **Intervention**: IKEA has used sensory marketing techniques to create immersive in-store experiences. They designed their store layouts to guide customers through a specific path, exposing them to different products in a way that subtly influences purchasing decisions. They also use scent marketing, such as the smell of freshly baked cinnamon buns, to create a welcoming environment that encourages longer stays and increased purchases.
- **Outcome**: These sensory interventions have successfully enhanced the shopping experience, increasing customer satisfaction and sales.

PepsiCo's Flavor Development

- **Intervention**: PepsiCo used neuroimaging and sensory testing to understand how different flavors and textures activate specific areas of the brain associated with pleasure and satisfaction. By analyzing these responses, they were able to optimize their product formulations.
- **Outcome**: The result was the development of snack products that better align with consumer preferences, leading to more robust product launches and sustained sales growth.

Procter & Gamble's Product Placement Strategy

- **Intervention**: Procter & Gamble (P&G) utilized neuromarketing techniques, such as eye-tracking and EEG, to study how consumers interact with products on the shelf. They analyzed how different shelf placements and packaging designs influenced attention and purchasing decisions.

- **Outcome**: This research helped P&G optimize their product placement strategies in retail environments, leading to increased visibility and sales of their products.

Campbell's Soup Label Redesign

- **Intervention**: Campbell's Soup used biometric research, including facial coding and eye-tracking, to understand consumer reactions to their product labels. They found that consumers associated their traditional labels with an outdated image, leading to lower engagement.
- **Outcome**: Campbell's redesigned their labels to be more modern and visually appealing, which helped rejuvenate the brand's image and improve sales performance.

ANALYSIS OF OUTCOMES AND LESSONS LEARNED

Critical Success Factors:

1. **Deep Understanding of Consumer Psychology:** Companies like Coca-Cola and Apple have demonstrated the importance of understanding consumer behavior's emotional and psychological drivers.
2. **Integration of Neurosensory Insights:** Successful implementation requires integrating neurosensory insights into every marketing and product design aspect.
3. **Focus on Emotional Engagement:** Emotional engagement is crucial for building strong brand loyalty and customer relationships.

Lessons Learned:

1. **Holistic Approach:** Combining multiple sensory elements (visual, auditory, tactile) creates a more immersive and compelling consumer experience.
2. **Continuous Testing and Optimization:** Regular testing and refinement based on neuromarketing insights can enhance the effectiveness of marketing strategies.
3. **Collaboration Between Disciplines:** Successful implementations often involve collaboration between neuroscientists, psychologists, and marketing professionals to ensure that insights are accurately interpreted and applied.

APPLICATION TO OTHER BUSINESSES AND INDUSTRIES:

Retail Sector:

• Retailers can enhance in-store experiences by incorporating neurosensory elements such as ambient music, scent marketing, and interactive displays to engage customers and increase dwell time.

Healthcare:

• Healthcare providers can use neuromarketing techniques to design environments that reduce patient anxiety and improve overall satisfaction with care.

Hospitality:

• Hotels can create memorable experiences using sensory marketing to evoke positive emotions and associations, leading to higher guest satisfaction and repeat visits.

BRIDGING ACADEMIC RESEARCH AND INDUSTRY PRACTICES

Strategies for Translating Academic Findings into Practical Applications

Translating academic research into practical applications is crucial for advancing industry practices, particularly in marketing, where understanding consumer behavior can lead to significant competitive advantages. Integrating academic insights into industry strategies can enhance the effectiveness of marketing campaigns, improve consumer engagement, and drive innovation.

One strategy for translating academic findings into practical applications is through collaborative partnerships between educational institutions and industry organizations. These partnerships facilitate knowledge transfer and ensure that scholarly research addresses real-world challenges. For example, collaboration between neuroscientists and marketing professionals has led to the development of neuromarketing techniques, which apply insights from brain imaging studies to understand consumer preferences and improve advertising effectiveness (Plassmann et al., 2012).

Another approach is establishing interdisciplinary research teams within companies, including academic researchers and industry practitioners. These teams can work together to design experiments, analyze data, and implement findings in a scientifically rigorous and practically relevant way. For instance, using behavioral experiments and computational models has been instrumental in developing targeted marketing strategies that account for cognitive biases and decision-making processes (Kahneman & Tversky, 1979).

Examples of Successful Implementation in Marketing Strategies

Academic findings have been successfully implemented in various marketing strategies, demonstrating the practical value of research. One notable example is the application of the endowment effect, a cognitive bias where individuals ascribe higher value to objects simply because they own them. Marketers have leveraged this insight by offering free trials or samples, increasing the likelihood that consumers will purchase the product after the trial period (Thaler, 1980).

Another example is the use of social proof, which is people's tendency to conform to others' actions. Academic research has shown that highlighting popular products or customer reviews can significantly increase sales. This principle is widely used in e-commerce, where platforms prominently display best-sellers and customer ratings to influence purchasing decisions (Cialdini, 2007).

BENEFITS AND CHALLENGES OF INTEGRATING RESEARCH INTO MARKETING PRACTICES

Benefits

Integrating academic research into marketing practices offers numerous benefits. Firstly, it can lead to more effective marketing strategies by providing a deeper understanding of consumer behavior. For instance, insights from neuroeconomic research have helped marketers design advertisements that better capture attention and evoke emotional responses, thereby increasing engagement and recall (Plassmann et al., 2015).

Secondly, research-based marketing practices can enhance consumer trust and brand loyalty. By applying evidence-based strategies, companies can create more authentic and personalized marketing messages that resonate with consumers. This approach efficiently builds long-term customer relationships, demonstrating a commitment to understanding and meeting their needs (Hennig-Thurau et al., 2010).

Thirdly, integrating research into marketing practices can drive innovation by introducing new methods and technologies. For example, the use of big data analytics and machine learning algorithms, informed by academic research, has revolutionized how companies analyze consumer behavior and predict market trends (Davenport & Harris, 2007).

Challenges and Barriers to Implementation

Despite the benefits, there are several challenges and barriers to integrating academic research into marketing practices. One major challenge is the gap between academic and industry priorities. Academic research often focuses on theoretical advancements and long-term studies, while industry practices prioritizes immediate results and practical solutions. This disconnect can make it challenging to align research objectives with business goals (Shapiro et al., 2007).

Another barrier is the complexity of translating scientific findings into actionable strategies. Academic research is often highly specialized and may only readily apply to real-world scenarios with significant adaptation. Marketers may need more expertise to interpret and implement these findings effectively (Burke, 2011).

Additionally, there can be resistance to change within organizations. Implementing research-based practices may require a shift in existing strategies, which can be met with skepticism or reluctance from stakeholders. Overcoming this resistance requires strong leadership and a culture that values innovation and continuous improvement (Kotter, 1996).

Strategies to Overcome Challenges

To overcome these challenges, companies can invest in continuous education and training for their marketing teams, ensuring they are well-versed in the latest research and methodologies. Additionally, fostering a culture of collaboration between researchers and practitioners can bridge the gap between academic and industry priorities.

These roles can liaise between academic institutions and industry, ensuring that research findings are effectively translated into actionable strategies. Moreover, leveraging technology and data analytics can facilitate the application of research insights, making it easier to implement evidence-based marketing practices.

For instance, Procter & Gamble has established a Consumer and Market Knowledge (CMK) function, which combines research insights with business strategies to drive innovation and marketing effectiveness (Nijs et al., 2001). By integrating academic findings into their decision-making processes, P&G has successfully developed products and marketing campaigns that resonate with consumers.

PRACTICAL INSIGHTS FOR MARKETERS AND PRACTITIONERS

Actionable Strategies for Implementing Neurosensory and Neuromarketing Techniques

Implementing neurosensory and neuromarketing techniques can significantly enhance marketing strategies by tapping into consumers' subconscious preferences and behaviors. Here are some practical, step-by-step approaches for marketers and practitioners:

A. Conduct Neurosensory Research:

- **Step 1:** Identify target sensory modalities (visual, auditory, olfactory, tactile) relevant to your product or service.
- **Step 2:** Use tools like eye-tracking for visual stimuli, EEG for measuring brain responses, and scent diffusers for olfactory cues.
- **Step 3:** Collect data on consumer responses to various sensory inputs.
- **Step 4:** Analyze the data to identify patterns and preferences.
- **Example:** Coca-Cola uses fMRI to understand how visual branding elements influence emotional responses and brand loyalty (McClure et al., 2004).

B. Develop Sensory-Rich Marketing Materials:

- **Step 1:** Design advertisements incorporating key sensory elements identified from your research.
- **Step 2:** Test these materials in controlled environments to measure consumer reactions.
- **Step 3:** Optimize based on feedback to ensure maximum impact.
- **Example:** Apple's use of minimalist design and high-quality materials in their stores enhances tactile and visual appeal, creating a memorable customer experience (Lindstrom, 2010).

C. Integrate Sensory Elements into Customer Experience:

- **Step 1:** Enhance in-store environments with sensory cues like ambient lighting, scent, and background music.
- **Step 2:** Train staff to be aware of sensory marketing principles and to enhance customer interactions.

- **Step 3:** Monitor and adjust sensory elements based on customer feedback and sales data.
- **Example:** Abercrombie & Fitch's distinctive store atmosphere with dim lighting, loud music, and a signature scent to create a unique shopping experience (Doucé & Janssens, 2013).

Tools and Frameworks for Enhancing Marketing Strategies

Incorporating neurosensory insights into marketing strategies requires specific tools and frameworks:

A. Eye-Tracking Technology:

- **Tool:** Tobii Pro Glasses or other eye-tracking devices.
- **Framework:** Use eye-tracking data to optimize visual content, ensuring key elements capture consumer attention.
- **Example:** Eye-tracking studies used by retail companies to improve shelf placement and signage, leading to increased sales (Wedel & Pieters, 2008).

B. Neuroimaging Tools:

- **Tool:** fMRI and EEG devices.
- **Framework:** Apply neuroimaging to understand emotional and cognitive responses to marketing stimuli, guiding content creation.
- **Example:** Hyundai uses fMRI to design car interiors that evoke positive emotional responses (Plassmann et al., 2012).

C. Behavioral Analysis Software:

- **Tool:** Biometric sensors and facial coding software.
- **Framework:** Measure physiological responses such as heart rate, skin conductance, and facial expressions to assess consumer reactions to ads.
- **Example:** Unilever's use of facial coding to evaluate the emotional impact of advertisements, leading to more effective campaigns (Venkatraman et al., 2015).

D. Scent Diffusion Systems:

- **Tool:** Professional sent diffusion machines.

- **Framework:** Integrate scent marketing in retail environments to enhance consumer experience and brand recall.
- **Example:** Marriott Hotels use a signature scent in their lobbies to create a consistent and welcoming atmosphere (Morrison et al., 2011).

INTERDISCIPLINARY COLLABORATION AND KNOWLEDGE EXCHANGE

Importance of Collaboration Between Neuroscience, Psychology, and Marketing:

Emphasis on Interdisciplinary Collaboration

Interdisciplinary collaboration between neuroscience, psychology, and marketing is pivotal for advancing the fields of neuroeconomics and neuromarketing. Neuroscience provides insights into the neural mechanisms underlying decision-making and consumer behavior, while psychology offers frameworks to understand cognitive processes and behavior. Marketing integrates these insights into actionable strategies that resonate with consumers.

Benefits of Integration

Combining insights from these disciplines leads to more effective marketing strategies. For example, understanding how sensory stimuli influence consumer preferences (Plassmann et al., 2012) or leveraging cognitive biases to enhance decision-making processes (Kahneman & Tversky, 1979) can significantly impact campaign success. Companies can tailor their messages and experiences to meet consumer needs and desires by integrating neuroeconomic principles with marketing practices.

EXAMPLES OF SUCCESSFUL INTERDISCIPLINARY PROJECTS

Innovative Marketing Strategies

Successful interdisciplinary projects have resulted in groundbreaking marketing strategies. For instance, collaborations between neuroscientists and marketers have developed neuromarketing techniques that measure subconscious responses to advertisements (Ariely & Berns, 2010). These techniques have been applied in retail and entertainment industries, demonstrating their efficacy in predicting consumer behavior and optimizing marketing efforts.

Role of Collaboration in Achieving Outcomes

Collaboration fosters innovation by pooling expertise from diverse fields. Projects like using fMRI to study brand loyalty (McClure et al., 2004) exemplify how interdisciplinary teams can uncover insights that traditional marketing methods might overlook. By leveraging each discipline's strengths, researchers and practitioners can create holistic approaches that enhance theoretical understanding and practical applications in marketing.

CHALLENGES AND FUTURE DIRECTIONS

Current Challenges

Despite its promise, neuroeconomics and neuromarketing face challenges such as ethical considerations (Illes & Sahakian, 2011), technological limitations in data collection and interpretation (Ariely & Berns, 2010), and the need for more comprehensive research designs. Addressing these challenges requires ethical guidelines, technological advancements, and collaborative efforts to refine methodologies.

Future Research Directions

Emerging trends in neuroeconomics and neuromarketing include exploring the role of virtual reality (VR) and augmented reality (AR) in consumer behavior research, integrating AI and machine learning for real-time consumer insights, and examining cross-cultural variations in neural responses to marketing stimuli. These directions promise to deepen our understanding of consumer decision-making and open new avenues for innovation in marketing practices.

SUMMARY OF KEY INSIGHTS AND TAKEAWAYS

Recap of Main Insights and Takeaways

This chapter has underscored the transformative potential of integrating neuroeconomic and neurosensory insights into marketing strategies. Key insights from the chapter include:

1. Understanding Cognitive Biases:

- Cognitive biases significantly impact managerial decision-making and consumer behavior. Recognizing these biases enables marketers to design strategies that align with consumers' thinking and decision-making (Kahneman & Tversky, 1979).

2. Innovative Research Methodologies:

- Neuroeconomic research employs advanced methodologies such as neuroimaging, behavioral experiments, and computational modelling. These tools provide a deeper understanding of the neural and psychological mechanisms underlying consumer choices (Ariely & Berns, 2010).

3. Successful Interdisciplinary Collaborations:

- Case studies of companies like Coca-Cola, Apple, and Hyundai illustrate the successful application of neurosensory and neuromarketing techniques. These examples highlight the importance of interdisciplinary collaboration in developing effective marketing strategies (McClure et al., 2004; Lindstrom, 2010; Plassmann et al., 2012).

4. Practical Applications and Tools:

- Marketers can use eye-tracking, fMRI, and scent diffusion systems to enhance consumer engagement. These tools help create more personalized and immersive experiences, increasing consumer satisfaction and loyalty (Venkatraman et al., 2015).

5. Challenges and Future Directions:

- The field faces challenges like ethical considerations and technological limitations. Future research should focus on emerging trends, such as the use of virtual reality (VR) and augmented reality (AR) in consumer behavior studies (Illes & Sahakian, 2011).

IMPORTANCE OF INTEGRATION

Integrating neuroeconomic and neurosensory insights into marketing strategies is crucial for several reasons:

- **Enhanced Consumer Understanding:** These insights allow a more accurate understanding of consumer motivations and behaviors, leading to more effective marketing strategies (Plassmann et al., 2012).
- **Improved Engagement:** Sensory-rich marketing materials and experiences can capture consumer attention more effectively and create lasting impressions (Lindstrom, 2010).
- **Evidence-Based Strategies:** Basing marketing decisions on empirical research ensures that strategies are grounded in scientific evidence, reducing the risk of relying on intuition or outdated practices (Ariely & Berns, 2010).

IMPLICATIONS FOR SCHOLARS, MARKETERS, AND PRACTITIONERS

Implications for Scholars

For scholars, the chapter highlights the importance of interdisciplinary research. Neuroscience, psychology, and marketing are interconnected fields that can collectively provide a more comprehensive understanding of consumer behavior. Scholars should:

- **Pursue Interdisciplinary Research:** Collaborate with experts from related fields to enrich their studies and gain new perspectives (Ariely & Berns, 2010).
- **Focus on Practical Applications:** Design research projects with straightforward, practical applications, bridging the gap between theory and practice (Plassmann et al., 2012).

Implications for Marketers

Marketers can leverage neuroeconomics and neurosensory research insights to enhance their strategies. Key recommendations include:

- **Adopt Evidence-Based Strategies:** Use findings from neuroscience and psychology to inform marketing decisions, ensuring strategies are grounded in scientific evidence (Venkatraman et al., 2015).
- **Create Sensory-Rich Experiences:** Develop marketing materials and environments that engage multiple senses, making experiences more immersive and memorable (Lindstrom, 2010).
- **Continuously Test and Optimize:** Implement neuromarketing techniques to test and refine strategies continuously, ensuring they remain practical and relevant (Plassmann et al., 2012).

Implications for Practitioners

Practitioners in various industries can benefit from incorporating neuroeconomic insights into their practices. This can lead to:

- **Enhanced Customer Experiences:** By understanding consumer behavior's sensory and emotional drivers, practitioners can create more engaging and satisfying experiences (McClure et al., 2004).
- **Increased Effectiveness:** Evidence-based strategies are likely more effective in achieving business goals, such as increasing sales and customer loyalty (Venkatraman et al., 2015).
- **Interdisciplinary Collaboration:** Practitioners should collaborate with researchers and professionals from other fields to ensure their strategies are well-informed and innovative (Illes & Sahakian, 2011).

Encouragement for Adoption and Collaboration

The findings of this chapter underscore the need for adopting evidence-based marketing strategies and fostering interdisciplinary collaboration. By integrating neuroeconomics, psychology, and marketing insights, stakeholders can develop more effective, engaging, and scientifically grounded strategies. Encouraging cooperation between academia and industry will ensure that research findings are translated into practical applications, benefiting consumers and businesses.

REFERENCES

Alwitt, L. (1985), EEG activity reflects the content of commercials. En Alwitt, L., Psychological processes and advertising effects: theory, research, and applications (author, year, pp. 209–219). Hillsdale, NJ: Lawrence Erlbaum.

Ariely, D. (2008). *Predictably Irrational: The Hidden Forces That Shape Our Decisions*. HarperCollins.

Ariely, D., & Berns, G. S. (2010). Neuromarketing: The hope and hype of neuroimaging in business. *Nature Reviews. Neuroscience*, 11(4), 284–292. DOI: 10.1038/nrn2795 PMID: 20197790

Arora, M. (2024). Metaverse Metamorphosis: Bridging the Gap Between Research Insights and Industry Applications. In *Research, Innovation, and Industry Impacts of the Metaverse* (pp. 275-286). IGI Global.

Arora, M., & Sharma, R. L. (2023). Artificial intelligence and big data: ontological and communicative perspectives in multi-sectoral scenarios of modern businesses. *foresight, 25*(1), 126-143.

Arthmann, C., & Li, I. P. (2017). *Neuromarketing - The Art and Science of Marketing and Neurosciences Enabled by IoT Technologies*. IIC Journal of Innovation.

Azcarate, A., Sande, K. V., & Valenti, R. G. (2005). Automatic facial emotion recognition. https://bit.ly/3goKE5p

Bazerman, M. H., & Moore, D. A. (2013). *Judgment in Managerial Decision Making*. Wiley.

Bercea, M. D. (2012), Anatomy of methodologies for measuring consumer behaviour in neuromarketing research, https://bit.ly/355BhCe

Bhardwaj, S., Kaushik, N., & Arora, M. (2024). Does Your Brain Have a Buy Button?: A Neuro Marketing Approach With Sensory Branding. In *Sensible Selling Through Sensory Neuromarketing* (pp. 210–229). IGI Global. DOI: 10.4018/979-8-3693-4236-7.ch011

Burke, R. R. (2011). How technology and consumer behaviour will change the future of retailing. *Journal of Retailing*, 87(1), 3–8.

Butler, M. (2008), Neuromarketing and the perception of knowledge. Journal of Consumer Behavior, pp. 7, 415–419, https://doi.org/.DOI: 10.1002/cb.260

Calvert, G. A., & Brammer, M. J. (2012). Predicting consumer behaviour. *IEE Pulse Magazine*, 3(3), 38–41. DOI: 10.1109/MPUL.2012.2189167 PMID: 22678839

Camerer, C. F., Loewenstein, G., & Prelec, D. (2005). Neuroeconomics: How neuroscience can inform economics. *Journal of Economic Literature*, 43(1), 9–64. DOI: 10.1257/0022051053737843

Cenizo, C. (2022), Neuromarketing: concept, historical evolution and challenges. Icono 14, 20(1). https://doi.org/DOI: 10.7195/ri14.v20i1.1784

Chen, Y. P., Nelson, L. D., & Hsu, M. (2015). From "Where" to "What": Distributed Representations of Brand Associations in the Human Brain. *JMR, Journal of Marketing Research*, 52(4), 453–466. DOI: 10.1509/jmr.14.0606 PMID: 27065490

Cialdini, R. B. (2007). *Influence: The psychology of persuasion*. Harper Business.

Cialdini, R. B. (2009). *Influence: Science and Practice*. Pearson Education.

Cohen, M. X. (2014). *Analysing neural time series data: Theory and Practice*. MIT Press. DOI: 10.7551/mitpress/9609.001.0001

Colaferro, C. A., & Crescitelli, E. (2014). The Contribution of Neuromarketing to the Study of Consumer Behavior. *Brazilian Business Review*, 11(3), 123–143. DOI: 10.15728/bbr.2014.11.3.6

Constantinescu, M., Orindaru, A., Pachitanu, A., Rosca, L., Caescu, S. C., & Orzan, M. C. (2019). Attitude Evaluation on Using the Neuromarketing Approach in Social Media: Matching Company's Purposes and Consumer's Benefits for Sustainable Business Growth. *Sustainability (Basel)*, 11(24), 7094. DOI: 10.3390/su11247094

Daugherty, T., Hoffman, E., & Kennedy, K. N. (2016). Research in reverse: Ad testing using an inductive consumer neuroscience approach. *Journal of Business Research*, 69(8), 3168–3176. DOI: 10.1016/j.jbusres.2015.12.005

Davenport, T. H., & Harris, J. G. (2007). *Competing on analytics: The new science of winning*. Harvard Business Press.

De Martino, B., Camerer, C. F., & Adolphs, R. (2010). Amygdala damage eliminates monetary loss aversion. *Proceedings of the National Academy of Sciences of the United States of America*, 107(8), 3788–3792. DOI: 10.1073/pnas.0910230107 PMID: 20142490

De Martino, B., Kumaran, D., Seymour, B., & Dolan, R. J. (2006). Frames, biases, and rational decision-making in the human brain. *Science*, 313(5787), 684–687. DOI: 10.1126/science.1128356 PMID: 16888142

Dhar, R. (1997). Consumer preference for a no-choice option. *The Journal of Consumer Research*, 24(2), 215–231. DOI: 10.1086/209506

Dickson, P. R., & Kelly, G. J. (1985). The "Barnum effect" in personality assessment: A review of the literature. *Psychological Reports*, 57(2), 367–382. DOI: 10.2466/pr0.1985.57.2.367

Dooley, R. (2010), Baby pictures do grab our attention. https://bit.ly/3g4c2Xo

Dooley, R. (2011). *Brainfluence: 100 ways to persuade and convince consumers with Neuromarketing*. Wiley.

Doucé, L., & Janssens, W. (2013). The presence of a pleasant ambient scent in a fashion store: The moderating role of shopping motivation and affect intensity. *Environment and Behavior*, 45(2), 215–238. DOI: 10.1177/0013916511410421

Egidi, G., Nusbaum, H. C., & Cacioppo, J. T. (2008). Neuroeconomics: Foundational issues and consumer relevance. In Haugvedt, C., Kardes, F., & Herr, P. (Eds.), *Handbook of Consumer Psychology* (pp. 1177–1214). Erlbaum.

Engel, J. F., Blackwell, R. D., & Miniard, P. W. (1990). *Consumer Behavior*. Dryden Press.

Fisher, C. E., Chin, L., & Klitzman, R. (2010). Defining Neuromarketing: Practices and Professional Challenges. *Harvard Review of Psychiatry*, 18(4), 230–237. DOI: 10.3109/10673229.2010.496623 PMID: 20597593

Freedman, J. L., & Fraser, S. C. (1966). Compliance without pressure: The foot-in-the-door technique. *Journal of Personality and Social Psychology*, 4(2), 195–202. DOI: 10.1037/h0023552 PMID: 5969145

Fugate, D. L. (2008). Marketing services more effectively with neuromarketing research: A look into the future. *Journal of Services Marketing*, 22(2), 170–173. DOI: 10.1108/08876040810862903

Garlin, F. V., & Owen, K. (2006). Setting the tone with the tune: A meta-analytic review of the effects of background music in retail settings. *Journal of Business Research*, 59(6), 755–764. DOI: 10.1016/j.jbusres.2006.01.013

Glimcher, P. W., & Fehr, E. (2014). *Neuroeconomics: Decision making and the brain*. Academic Press.

Gottfried, J. A., O'Doherty, J., & Dolan, R. J. (2006). Encoding predictive reward value in human amygdala and orbitofrontal cortex. *Science*, 301(5636), 1104–1107. DOI: 10.1126/science.1087919 PMID: 12934011

Hasher, L., Goldstein, D., & Toppino, T. (1977). Frequency and the conference of referential validity. *Journal of Verbal Learning and Verbal Behavior*, 16(1), 107–112. DOI: 10.1016/S0022-5371(77)80012-1

Hazeldine, S. (2014). *Neuro-sell: How neuroscience can power your sales success.* Kogan Page.

Hennig-Thurau, T., Gwinner, K. P., Walsh, G., & Gremler, D. D. (2010). Electronic word-of-mouth via consumer-opinion platforms: What motivates consumers to articulate themselves online? *Journal of Interactive Marketing*, 18(1), 38–52. DOI: 10.1002/dir.10073

Henrich, J., Heine, S. J., & Cnorezayan, A. (2010). The weirdest people in the world? *Behavioral and Brain Sciences*, 33(2-3), 61–135. DOI: 10.1017/S0140525X0999152X PMID: 20550733

Hensel, D., Iorga, A., Wolter, L., & Znanewitz, J. (2017). Conducting neuromarketing studies from ethically-practitioner perspectives. *Cogent Psychology*, 4(1), 1320858. DOI: 10.1080/23311908.2017.1320858

Hilderbrand, M.L. (2016), Neuromarketing: An essential tool in the future of advertising and brand development [Thesis doctoral, University of Texas].

Hsu, M. (2017). Neuromarketing: Inside the Mind of the Consumer. *California Management Review*, 59(4), 5–22. DOI: 10.1177/0008125617720208

Huber, J., Payne, J. W., & Puto, C. (1982). Adding asymmetrically dominated alternatives: Violations of regularity and the similarity hypothesis. *The Journal of Consumer Research*, 9(1), 90–98. DOI: 10.1086/208899

Hubert, M., & Kenning, P. (2008). A current overview of consumer neuroscience. *Journal of Consumer Behaviour*, 7(4-5), 272–292. DOI: 10.1002/cb.251

Huettel, S. A., Song, A. W., & McCarthy, G. (2009). *Functional magnetic resonance imaging*. Sinauer Associates.

Hutchinson, J. W., Raman, K., & Mantrala, M. K. (2000). Finding choice alternatives in memory: Probability models of brand name recall. *JMR, Journal of Marketing Research*, 37(2), 157–169.

Illes, J., & Sahakian, B. J. (2011). *Oxford handbook of neuroethics*. Oxford University Press. DOI: 10.1093/oxfordhb/9780199570706.001.0001

Janis, I. L. (1982). *Groupthink: Psychological Studies of Policy Decisions and Fiascoes*. Houghton Mifflin.

Kahneman, D., Knetsch, J. L., & Thaler, R. H. (1991). Anomalies: The endowment effect, loss aversion, and status quo bias. *The Journal of Economic Perspectives*, 5(1), 193–206. DOI: 10.1257/jep.5.1.193

Kahneman, D., & Tversky, A. (1973). Availability: A heuristic for judging frequency and probability. *Cognitive Psychology*, 5(2), 207–232. DOI: 10.1016/0010-0285(73)90033-9

Kahneman, D., & Tversky, A. (1979). Prospect theory: An analysis of decision under risk. *Econometrica*, 47(2), 263–291. DOI: 10.2307/1914185

Kaplan, A. (1964), The conduct of inquiry: Methodology for behavioural science, Chandler.

Karmarkar, U. R., & Plassmann, H. (2019). Consumer Neuroscience: Past, Present, and Future. *Organizational Research Methods*, 22(1), 174–195. DOI: 10.1177/1094428117730598

Kenning, P. H., & Plassman, H. (2008). How neuroscience can inform consumer research. Neural Systems and Rehabilitation Engineering. *IEEE Transactions on Neural Systems and Rehabilitation Engineering*, 16(6), 532–538. DOI: 10.1109/TNSRE.2008.2009788 PMID: 19144585

Knutson, B., & Genevsky, A. (2018). Neuroforecasting Aggregate Choice. *Current Directions in Psychological Science*, 27(2), 110–115. DOI: 10.1177/0963721417737877 PMID: 29706726

Knutson, B., Rick, S., Wimmer, G. E., Prelec, D., & Loewenstein, G. (2007). Neural predictors of purchases. *Neuron*, 53(1), 147–156. DOI: 10.1016/j.neuron.2006.11.010 PMID: 17196537

Kolyovska, V., Maslarova, J., & Maslarov, D. (2016, May 17), *Home page,* Doi.Org; unknown, https://doi.org/

Kotter, J. P. (1996). *Leading change*. Harvard Business Review Press.

Krampe, C., Strelow, E., Haas, A., & Kenning, P. (2018). The application of mobile fNIRS to "shopper neuroscience" – first insights from a merchandising communication study. *European Journal of Marketing*, 52(1), 244–259. DOI: 10.1108/EJM-12-2016-0727

Kringelbach, M. L. (2005). The human orbitofrontal cortex: Linking reward to hedonic experience. *Nature Reviews. Neuroscience*, 6(9), 691–702. DOI: 10.1038/nrn1747 PMID: 16136173

Kühn, S., Düzel, S., Eibich, P., Krekel, C., Wüstemann, H., Kolbe, J., & Lindenberger, U. (2016). In search of features that constitute an "enriched environment" in humans: Associations between geographical properties and brain structure. *Scientific Reports*, 6, 30401. PMID: 28931835

Kumar, J., Arora, M., & Erkol Bayram, G. (Eds.). (2024)a. *Exploring the Use of Metaverse in Business and Education*. IGI Global.

Kumar, J., Arora, M., & Erkol Bayram, G. (Eds.). (2024)b. *Research, Innovation, and Industry Impacts of the Metaverse*. IGI Global.

Laibson, D. (1997). Golden eggs and hyperbolic discounting. *The Quarterly Journal of Economics*, 112(2), 443–477. DOI: 10.1162/003355397555253

Lameka, K., Farwell, M. D., & Ichise, M. (2016). Positron emission tomography. *Handbook of Clinical Neurology*, 135, 209–227. DOI: 10.1016/B978-0-444-53485-9.00011-8 PMID: 27432667

Lee, N., Broderick, A. J., & Chamberlain, L. (2007). What is 'neuromarketing'? A discussion and agenda for future research. *International Journal of Psychophysiology*, 63(2), 199–204. DOI: 10.1016/j.ijpsycho.2006.03.007 PMID: 16769143

Lee, N., Chamberlain, L., & Brandes, L. (2018). Welcome to the jungle! The neuromarketing literature through the eyes of a newcomer. *European Journal of Marketing*, 52(1-2), 4–38. DOI: 10.1108/EJM-02-2017-0122

Levy, M., & Weitz, B. A. (2009). *Retail Management*. MacGraw-Hill.

Lewis, D., & Bridger, D. (2005), Market researchers are making increasing use of brain imaging. https://bit.ly/3gu5510

Lim, W.M. (2018), Demystifying Neuromarketing. Journal of Business Research, pp. 91, 205–220. https://doi.org/.DOI: 10.1016/j.jbusres.2018.05.036

Lin, M., Cross, S., Jones, W., & Childers, T. L. (2018). Applying EEG in consumer neuroscience. *European Journal of Marketing*, 52(1), 66–91. DOI: 10.1108/EJM-12-2016-0805

Lindstrom, M. (2005). *Brand sense: How to build powerful brands through touch, taste, smell, sight & sound*. Free Press.

Lindstrom, M. (2010). *Brandwashed: Tricks companies use to manipulate our minds and persuade us to buy*. Kogan Page Publishers.

Lindstrom, M. (2010). *Buyology: Truth and Lies About Why We Buy Crown Business*. Crown Publishing Group.

Lo, A. W. (2005). Reconciling efficient markets with behavioural finance: The adaptive markets hypothesis. *The Journal of Investment Consulting*, 7(2), 21–44.

Malik, R., Malhan, S., & Arora, M. (2024). (Eds.). (2024). *Sensible Selling Through Sensory Neuromarketing* (pp. 144-163). IGI Global.

Marichamy, K., & Sathiyavathi, J.K. (2014), Neuromarketing: The new science of consumer behaviour. Tactful Management Journal, 2(6).

McClure, S. M., Li, J., Tomlin, D., Cypert, K. S., Montague, L. M., & Montague, P. R. (2004). Neural Correlates of Behavioral Preference for Culturally Familiar Drinks. *Neuron*, 44(2), 379–387. DOI: 10.1016/j.neuron.2004.09.019 PMID: 15473974

Monge Benito, S., & Fernández Guerra, V. (2012). Neuromarketing: Tecnologías, Mercado y Retos. Pensar La Publicidad. *Revista Internacional De Investigaciones Publicitarias*, 5(2), 19–42. DOI: 10.5209/rev_PEPU.2011.v5.n2.37862

Morrison, M., Gan, S., Dubelaar, C., & Oppewal, H. (2011). In-store music and aroma influence shopper behaviour and satisfaction. *Journal of Business Research*, 64(6), 558–564. DOI: 10.1016/j.jbusres.2010.06.006

Mucha, T. (2005). This is your brain on advertising. *Business (Atlanta, Ga.)*, 6(7), 35–37.

Murphy, E. R., Illes, J., & Reiner, P. B. (2008). Neuroethics of neuromarketing. *Journal of Consumer Behaviour*, 7(4), 293–302. DOI: 10.1002/cb.252

Nadeau, R., Cloutier, E., & Guay, J.-H. (1993). New evidence about a bandwagon effect in the opinion formation process. *International Political Science Review*, 14(2), 203–213. DOI: 10.1177/019251219301400204

Nave, G., Nadler, A., Dubois, D., Zava, D., Camerer, C., & Plassmann, H. (2018). Single-dose testosterone administration increases men's preference for status goods. *Nature Communications*, 9(1), 2433. DOI: 10.1038/s41467-018-04923-0 PMID: 29970895

Nickerson, R. S. (1998). Confirmation bias: A ubiquitous phenomenon in many guises. *Review of General Psychology*, 2(2), 175–220. DOI: 10.1037/1089-2680.2.2.175

Nijs, V. R., Srinivasan, S., Pauwels, K., & Hanssens, D. M. (2001). The category-demand effects of price promotions. *Marketing Science*, 20(1), 1–22. DOI: 10.1287/mksc.20.1.1.10197

Norton, M. I., Mochon, D., & Ariely, D. (2012). The IKEA effect: When labour leads to love. *Journal of Consumer Psychology*, 22(3), 453–460. DOI: 10.1016/j.jcps.2011.08.002

O'Doherty, J. P., Hampton, A., & Kim, H. (2004). Model-based fMRI and its application to reward learning and decision making. *Annals of the New York Academy of Sciences*, 1104(1), 35–53. DOI: 10.1196/annals.1390.022 PMID: 17416921

Oliver, L. (2016), From exposure to understanding the interaction of affect and cognition in consumer decision-making [Thesis doctoral, Hanken School of Economics].

Orzan, G., Zara, I. A., & Purcarea, V. L. (2012). Neuromarketing techniques in pharmaceutical drugs advertising- A discussion and agenda for future research. *Journal of Medicine and Life*, 5(1), 428–432. PMID: 23346245

Peck, J., & Childers, T. L. (2003). To have and to hold: The influence of haptic information on product judgments. *Journal of Marketing*, 67(2), 35–48. DOI: 10.1509/jmkg.67.2.35.18612

Perrachione, T. K., & Perrachione, J. R. (2008). Brains and Brands: Developing mutually informative research in neuroscience and marketing. *Journal of Consumer Behaviour*, 7(4), 303–318. DOI: 10.1002/cb.253

Plassmann, H., O'Doherty, J., Shiv, B., & Rangel, A. (2008). Marketing actions can modulate neural representations of experienced pleasantness. *Proceedings of the National Academy of Sciences of the United States of America*, 105(3), 1050–1054. DOI: 10.1073/pnas.0706929105 PMID: 18195362

Plassmann, H., Ramsøy, T. Z., & Milosavljevic, M. (2012). Branding the brain: A critical review and outlook. *Journal of Consumer Psychology*, 22(1), 18–36. DOI: 10.1016/j.jcps.2011.11.010

Plassmann, H., Venkatraman, V., Huettel, S., & Yoon, C. (2015). Consumer neuroscience: Applications, challenges, and possible solutions. *JMR, Journal of Marketing Research*, 52(4), 427–435. DOI: 10.1509/jmr.14.0048

Plassmann, H., & Weber, B. (2015). Individual Differences in Marketing Placebo Effects: Evidence from Brain Imaging and Behavioral Experiments. *JMR, Journal of Marketing Research*, 52(4), 493–510. DOI: 10.1509/jmr.13.0613

Pop, A. N., Dabija, D. C., & Iorga, A. M. (2014). Ethical responsibilities of neuromarketing companies in harnessing the market research - A global exploratory approach. *Amfiteatru Economic*, XVI(35), 26–40.

Pop, C., Radomir, L., Ioana, M. A., & Maria, Z. M. (2009). Neuromarketing – Getting Inside The Customer's Mind. *Annals of Faculty of Economics*, 4, 804–807.

Pozharliev, R., Verbeke, W. J. M. I., & Bagozzi, R. P. (2017). Social consumer neuroscience: Neurophysiological measures of advertising effectiveness in a social context. *Journal of Advertising*, 46(2), 213–226. DOI: 10.1080/00913367.2017.1343162

Ramsoy, T.Z. (2014), Introduction to Neuromarketing and Consumer Science. Dinamarca: Neurons Inc.

Rangel, A., Camerer, C., & Montague, P. R. (2008). A framework for studying the neurobiology of value-based decision making. *Nature Reviews. Neuroscience*, 9(7), 545–556. DOI: 10.1038/nrn2357 PMID: 18545266

Reimann, M., Zaichkowsky, J., Neuhaus, C., Bender, T., & Weber, B. (2010). Aesthetic package design: A behavioural, neural, and psychological assessment. *Journal of Consumer Psychology*, 20(4), 431–441. DOI: 10.1016/j.jcps.2010.06.009

Riccio, A., Holz, E. M., Aricò, P., Leotta, F., Aloise, F., Desideri, L., Rimondini, M., Kübler, A., Mattia, D., & Cincotti, F. (2015). Hybrid P300-based brain-computer interface to improve usability for people with severe motor disability: Electromyographic signals for error correction during a spelling task. *Archives of Physical Medicine and Rehabilitation*, 96(3), S54–S61. DOI: 10.1016/j.apmr.2014.05.029 PMID: 25721548

Rodrigues, F. (2011), Influencia do Neuromarketing nos processos de tomada de decisao. Viseu: Psicosma.

Roebuck, K. (2011). *Neuromarketing: High-Impact strategies-What you need to know: Definitions, Adoptions, Impact, Benefits, Maturity, Vendors*. Emereo Publishing.

Samuel, B. S., & Pransanth, V. T. (2012). Neuromarketing: Is Campbell in Soup? *IUP Journal of Marketing Management*, 11(2), 76–100.

Sands, S. (octubre 2009), Sample Size Analysis for Brainwave Collection (EEG) Methodologies. https://bit.ly/3zb3zJx

Sanfey, A. G., Loewenstein, G., McClure, S. M., & Cohen, J. D. (2006). Neuroeconomics: Cross-currents in research on decision-making. *Trends in Cognitive Sciences*, 10(3), 108–116. DOI: 10.1016/j.tics.2006.01.009 PMID: 16469524

Sanfey, A. G., Rilling, J. K., Aronson, J. A., Nystrom, L. E., & Cohen, J. D. (2003). The neural basis of economic decision-making in the ultimatum game. *Science*, 300(5626), 1755–1758. DOI: 10.1126/science.1082976 PMID: 12805551

Schwartz, B. L., & Begley, S. (2002). *The Mind and the Brain: Neuroplasticity and the Power of Mental Force*. Harper Perennial.

Shapiro, B. P., Rangan, V. K., Moriarty, R. T., & Ross, E. B. (2007). Implementing the marketing concept at GE's jet engine business. *Interfaces*, 27(1), 5–17.

Shefrin, H., & Statman, M. (1985). The disposition to sell winners too early and ride losers too long: Theory and evidence. *The Journal of Finance*, 40(3), 777–790. DOI: 10.1111/j.1540-6261.1985.tb05002.x

Shiv, B., & Fedorikhin, A. (1999). Heart and Mind in Conflict: The interplay of affect and cognition in consumer decision making. *The Journal of Consumer Research*, 26(3), 278–292. DOI: 10.1086/209563

Sinek, S. (2009). *Start with Why: How great leaders inspire everyone to take action*. Penguin Group.

Singh, S. (2006). Impact of colour on marketing. *Management Decision*, 44(6), 783–789. DOI: 10.1108/00251740610673332

Small, D. A., & Loewenstein, G. (2003). Helping a victim or helping the victim: Altruism and identifiability. *Journal of Risk and Uncertainty*, 26(1), 5–16. DOI: 10.1023/A:1022299422219

Smidts, A. (2002), Kijken in het brein: Over de mogelijkheden van neuromarketing. *Tijdschrift voor Marketing, 36*(3), 18-23, Univ-Ovidius.Ro., from https://stec.univ-ovidius.ro/html/anale/RO/2021-2/Section

Smidts, A. (october 25 de 2002), Kijkenin het brein: Over de mogelijkheden van neuromarketing. http://hdl.handle.net/1765/308

Soll, J. B., Milkman, K. L., & Payne, J. W. (2015). A user's guide to debiasing. In Keren, G., & Wu, G. (Eds.), *The Wiley Blackwell Handbook of Judgment and Decision Making* (pp. 924–951). Wiley Blackwell. DOI: 10.1002/9781118468333.ch33

Solnais, C., Andreu-Perez, J., Sánchez-Fernández, J., & Andréu-Abela, J. (2013). The contribution of neuroscience to consumer research: A conceptual framework and empirical review. *Journal of Economic Psychology*, 36, 68–81. DOI: 10.1016/j.joep.2013.02.011

Spangenberg, E. R., Grohmann, B., & Sprott, D. E. (2006). It is beginning to smell (and sound) a lot like Christmas: The interactive effects of ambient scent and music in a retail setting. *Journal of Business Research*, 59(12), 1281–1287. DOI: 10.1016/j.jbusres.2006.08.006

Stanton, S. J., Sinnott-Armstrong, W., & Huettel, S. A. (2017). Neuromarketing: Ethical Implications of its Use and Potential Misuse. *Journal of Business Ethics*, 144(4), 799–811. DOI: 10.1007/s10551-016-3059-0

Staw, B. M. (1981). The escalation of commitment to a course of action. *Academy of Management Review*, 6(4), 577–587. DOI: 10.2307/257636

Taneja, B., Shukla, P., & Arora, M. (2024). Sensible Selling Through Sensory Neuromarketing: Enhancing Sales Effectiveness. In *Sensible Selling Through Sensory Neuromarketing* (pp. 164-183). IGI Global.

Thaler, R. (1980). Toward a positive theory of consumer choice. *Journal of Economic Behavior & Organization*, 1(1), 39–60. DOI: 10.1016/0167-2681(80)90051-7

Thaler, R. H., & Sunstein, C. R. (2008). *Nudge: Improving decisions about health, wealth, and happiness*. Yale University Press.

Thompson, D. (16 de enero de 2013), The irrational Consumer: Why Economics is wrong about how we make choices. https://bit.ly/2Smu91D

Thorndike, E. L. (1920). A constant error in psychological ratings. *The Journal of Applied Psychology*, 4(1), 25–29. DOI: 10.1037/h0071663

Tovino, S.A. (2005), The confidentiality and privacy implications of functional magnetic resonance imaging. The Journal of Law, Medicine & Ethics, pp. 33, 844–850. https://doi.org/.DOI: 10.1111/j.1748-720X.2005.tb00550.x

Tversky, A., & Kahneman, D. (1973). Availability: A heuristic for judging frequency and probability. *Cognitive Psychology*, 5(2), 207–232. DOI: 10.1016/0010-0285(73)90033-9

Tversky, A., & Kahneman, D. (1974). Judgment under uncertainty: Heuristics and biases. *Science*, 185(4157), 1124–1131. DOI: 10.1126/science.185.4157.1124 PMID: 17835457

Tversky, A., & Kahneman, D. (1981). The framing of decisions and the psychology of choice. *Science*, 211(4481), 453–458. DOI: 10.1126/science.7455683 PMID: 7455683

Venkatraman, V., Clitheroe, J. A., Fitzsimons, G. J., & Huettel, S. A. (2012). New scanner data for brand marketers: How neuroscience can help better understand differences in brand preferences, *Journal of Consumer Psychology*, 22(1), 143–153. Ohme, R., Reykowska, D., Weiner, D., & Choromansk, A. (2009). EEG and Galvanic Skin Response measures analyse neurophysiological reactions to advertising stimuli. *Journal of Neuroscience, Psychology, and Economics*, 2(1), 21–31. DOI: 10.1037/a0015462

Venkatraman, V., Clitheroe, J. A., Fitzsimons, G. J., & Huettel, S. A. (2015). New scanner data for brand marketers: How neuroscience can help better understand differences in brand preferences. *Journal of Consumer Psychology*, 22(1), 143–153. DOI: 10.1016/j.jcps.2011.11.008

Wedel, M., & Pieters, R. (2008). *Visual marketing: From attention to action*. Psychology Press.

Wilson, T. D., & Gilbert, D. T. (2003). Affective forecasting. *Advances in Experimental Social Psychology*, 35, 345–411. DOI: 10.1016/S0065-2601(03)01006-2

Yoon, C., Gonzales, R., Bechara, A., Berns, G., Dagher, A., Dubé, L., Huettel, S., Kable, J., Liberzon, I., Plassmann, H., Smidts, A., & Spence, C. (2012). Decision neuroscience and consumer decision-making. *Marketing Letters*, 23(2), 473–485. DOI: 10.1007/s11002-012-9188-z

Yoon, C., Gutchess, A. H., Feinberg, F., & Polk, T. A. (2006). A functional magnetic resonance imaging study of neural dissociations between brand and person judgments. *The Journal of Consumer Research*, 33(1), 31–40. DOI: 10.1086/504132

Zajonc, R. (1980). Feeling and Thinking: Preferences need no inferences. *The American Psychologist*, 35(2), 151–175. DOI: 10.1037/0003-066X.35.2.151

Zajonc, R. B. (1968). Attitudinal effects of mere exposure. *Journal of Personality and Social Psychology*, 9(2), 1–27. DOI: 10.1037/h0025848

Zajonc, R. B. (2001). Mere exposure: A gateway to the subliminal. *Current Directions in Psychological Science*, 10(6), 224–228. DOI: 10.1111/1467-8721.00154

Zeithaml, V. A. (1988). Consumer perceptions of price, quality, and value: A means-end model and synthesis of evidence. *Journal of Marketing*, 52(3), 2–22. DOI: 10.1177/002224298805200302

Zwicky, A. (2005). Just between Dr. Language and I. *The American Scholar*, 74(4), 134–139.

Chapter 4
A Neuroscientic Perspective

Dinesh Jamwal
Government Degree College, Matour, India

Manpreet Arora
https://orcid.org/0000-0002-4939-1992
Central University of Himachal Pradesh, India

ABSTRACT

Abstract: This study investigates the intricate relationship between sensory perceptions and financial choices through a neuroscientific perspective, addressing two key research questions: (1) How are sensory perceptions and financial choices related? (2) How is neuro sensory behavior important in investment decision-making? By integrating insights from neuroscience and behavioral finance, we aim to uncover the mechanisms by which sensory inputs influence economic behaviors and decision-making processes. Our conceptual, literature-based exploration reveals those sensory perceptions—encompassing visual, auditory, olfactory, tactile, and gustatory stimuli—play a critical role in shaping financial decisions. These sensory inputs are processed by neural systems, affecting cognitive functions and emotional responses, which in turn influence risk perception, time preference, and overall financial choices. This study highlights that financial decisions are not solely based on rational calculations but are deeply intertwined with sensory experiences and emotional states.

DOI: 10.4018/979-8-3693-9351-2.ch004

INTRODUCTION

The field of behavioral finance has long been fascinated with the myriad ways that human behavior impacts financial decision-making. Neurosensory behavior, which investigates into how our sensory perceptions and neurological processes influence our actions (Foley, 2019), provides a deeper understanding of the underlying mechanisms driving investment decisions. This intricate interplay between the brain, senses, and financial choices can help explain why investors often act irrationally, deviating from purely logical economic models.

At its core, neurosensory behavior involves the study of how sensory inputs—such as sight, sound, and touch—are processed by the brain to form perceptions and ultimately guide behavior. In the context of investment decisions, this can encompass everything from the impact of news headlines and financial reports to the subtle influence of environmental factors like the ambiance of a trading floor (Pompian, 2012). For instance, bright and fast-moving stock tickers can create a sense of urgency and excitement, potentially leading investors to make hurried, and often less rational, decisions. One significant aspect of neurosensory behavior in investment decision-making is the role of emotions (Jakovaara, 2020). The brain's amygdala, which processes emotions, can heavily influence financial decisions (Peterson, 2007). Fear and greed, two potent emotions in the financial world, can drive investors to sell off stocks in a panic or to engage in speculative buying during a market surge (Goldberg, 2012). Understanding how these emotional responses are triggered by sensory inputs and how they influence behavior is crucial for developing strategies to mitigate irrational decision-making.

Furthermore, cognitive biases, which are systematic patterns of deviation from norm or rationality in judgment, are deeply intertwined with neurosensory behavior. For instance, the availability heuristic, where people make decisions based on the most readily available information, can be influenced by how prominently certain information is presented. Financial media often highlights extreme cases, such as spectacular successes or failures, which can skew investors' perceptions and lead to overestimation or underestimation of risks and returns. Neurosensory behavior also sheds light on the phenomenon of confirmation bias, where investors favor information that confirms their pre-existing beliefs and ignore contradictory data. Sensory inputs that align with an investor's expectations are processed more readily and influence decision-making more strongly. This can lead to a reinforcement of faulty investment strategies and increased vulnerability to market volatilities. Interestingly, advancements in neuroscience and technology are beginning to offer tools to better understand and potentially mitigate these biases. Techniques such as functional magnetic resonance imaging (fMRI) allow researchers to observe which areas of the brain are activated during decision-making processes. Insights gained from these studies can help develop training programs aimed at improving investors' decision-making processes by making them more aware of their sensory and emotional influences.

Moreover, the emerging field of neuroeconomics combines economics, psychology, and neuroscience to study how people make economic decisions. This interdisciplinary approach provides a more comprehensive understanding of the complex interactions between sensory perceptions, emotional responses, and cognitive processes in financial behavior. By leveraging this knowledge, financial advisors and institutions can design better decision-making frameworks and tools to help investors navigate the emotional and sensory challenges of investing.

Neurosensory behavior plays a critical role in shaping investment decisions. By understanding the sensory and neurological underpinnings of financial behavior, we can better comprehend why investors often act irrationally and how to develop strategies to mitigate these tendencies. This deeper insight into the human mind not only enhances our understanding of financial markets but also paves the way for more effective investment decision-making practices.

REVIEW OF LITERATURE

The existing literature in the field of behavioral finance has increasingly explored the role of sensory perception in shaping the financial decisions (Krishna, (2012); Erkut et.al., (2018); Planning, (2014); Rungratsameetaweemana et.al., (2018); Goel, et.al., (2023); Pleger &Villringer (2013); Troye &Supphellen (2012); Krishna, (Ed.). (2011); Njegovanović (2020); Racat & Plotkina, (2023); Ricciardi, (2004); Ramchandran et,al., (2020); Xia et.al., (2022); Pallavi & Dsa (2024); Naqvi, Shiv & Bechara (2006); Cristofaro et.al., (2022); Brocas & Carrillo (2012). The neuroscientific studies revealed that sensory stimuli like visual, auditory and tactile input scan significantly influence financial choices by affecting the emotions and cognitive process of individuals. But it may vary from individual to individual. For example, research has shown that visual elements such as design and color of financial interfaces can impact investor behavior (Grant, Hobson & Sinha (2024); Wright (1995, October); Tang, Hess, Valacich & Sweeney (2014); Pryke (2010); Chapkovski, Khapko & Zoican (2024)). If marketers as producers, use bright colors and aesthetically pleasing designs, then they attract more attention and can lead to more positive and financial decisions. Whereas on the other hand, if there is cluttered or poorly designed interfaces, it can cause confusion and lead to suboptimal choices. Similarly, auditory stimuli also play a very important role in financial decision making (Polo et.al., (2024); Bossaerts (2021); Howard (2013); Bossaerts, (2009); Schreuder, Van Erp, Toet & Kallen (2016). The sound environment, which includes background music and ambient noises, can affect the stress level and cognitive performance of an individual, thereby influencing the financial choices. Studies demonstrate that places within music can enhance concentration and it can lead to more deliberate and rational financial choices (Radocy & Boyle, (2012). Conversely, if there is loud or chaotic environment, it can lead to higher stress and lead to impulsive and less optimal financial behaviors. Thus, the interplay between auditory stimuli and financial decision-making underscores the importance of considering the sensory context, which is very important in financial decision making. The tactical sensations are less studied in the literature, but they also contribute to the financial decision making (Miller & Ireland, (2005); Sadler-Smith & Shefy (2004); Statman (1999). The physical interaction with financial products such as field, or of a credit card or a texture of a paper money may evoke sometimes emotionally responses that influence spending behavior. For example, the high-quality smooth textures may be associated with luxury or trustworthiness, encouraging spending or investment, whereas law or rough or low-quality textures may evoke question or discomfort, leading to conservative financial choices. Neuroscientific research further highlights the role of multisensory integration in financial decision making (Mercier & Cappe, (2020); Spence & Gallace, (2011). Our brain does not process sensory inputs in isolation. Rather, it integrates information from various senses to form a coherent perception that guides the behavior. Multisensory integration can amplify or diminish the impact of individuals sensory stimuli on the financial choices. For example, if there is a visually appealing financial app and it is accompanied by pleasant background music or can create more engaging and trustworthy experience (Li & Yeh (2010); Kumar, Jain & Hsieh (2021); Xu, Peak & Prybutok (2015) It can encourage the positive financial behavior. Therefore, understanding how different sensory inputs combine to influence financial decisions can design more effective financial products and environments becomes necessary. In addition to the various sensory perceptions, literature also explores the underlying neural mechanisms that create or mediate the relationship between sensory stimuli and financial choices. The functional magnetic resonance imaging and electroencephalography studies now identified specific brain regions that involve processing sensory information and making financial decisions. By mapping the neural pathways, researchers can gain insights into cognitive and emotional processes that drive financial decisions. Overall, the existing literature underscores the significant impact of sensory perceptions of financial choices and highlight that the potential of a neuroscientific perspective to enhance our understanding of this relationship is possible. By integrating the insights from neuroscience with behavioral finance, researchers and practitioners can develop more effective strategies to improve financial decision making. This interdisciplinary approach can lead to design of financial products and environments that can have better alignment with human sensory and cognitive processes, ultimately promoting more rational and beneficial behaviors. Moreover, the literature also indicates that the individual differences such as personality traits and past experiences can also moderate the influence of sensory perceptions on financial choices (Aren, Hamamci & Özcan (2021); Plassmann & Weber (2015); Aren & Nayman Hamamci, (2023); Pompian, (2012), for example, individuals those who have high level of neuro neuroticism maybe more susceptible to sensory induced stress and thus make more conservative financial decisions in noisy environments. Similarly, individuals with financial experience may be more sensitive to sensory cues that evoke caution and anxiety. Therefore, understanding these individual differences can help the individuals to tailor the sensory environments to meet the needs of diverse populations, enhancing the effectiveness of financial interventions and products. The personalized approaches that take into account sensitive preferences and sensitiveness can improve user engagement and satisfaction, leading to better financial outcomes. Overall, the existing literature underscores the important impact of sensory perceptions and financial choices, and it highlights the potential of a neuroscientific perspective enhance the understanding of this relationship. By integrating insights from neuroscience with behavioral finance, researchers and practitioners can help more effective strategies in order to improve the financial decision making. This interdisciplinary approach can lead to the design of those financial products and environments which can better align with human sensory and cognitive processes, ultimately promoting more rational and beneficial financial behaviors. The future research in this area will continue to uncover the intricate ways in which our senses influence on our financial lives, paving the way for innovations which can support healthier financial decisions.

RESEARCH QUESTIONS

1. To explore how sensory perceptions and financial choices are related with each other.
2. To understand how neuro sensory behavior is important in investment decision making.

DISCUSSION

To explore how sensory perceptions and financial choices are related with each other.

The major relationship sensory perceptions and the financial choices is an emerging area of study where intersection of psychology, neuroscience and behavioral economics can be found. There are various elements which affect sensory perception and choices. Visual cues such as color and design significantly impact brand perception and consumer trust. In the same manner auditory cues play crucial roles in shaping financial choices. For example, the background music plays in the store can influence the pace of shopping and overall spending of a person. It has been seen in studies that slow music often leads to more leisurely shopping and higher spending. On the other hand, fast music can speed up the shopping process. Another important aspect of auditory cues is that where companies use sound or jingles for branding. Every day we see that companies use particular sounds and jingles in their advertisements. It helps to create memorable brand identities that influence consumer preferences and financial choices. Financial spending is also affected by in some areas by olfactory cues. It is also known as scent marketing. It aims to evoke emotions and memories which enhance shopping experiences and can potentially increase spending. For example, the smell of fresh baked items in a super market can provoke the customers to buy bakery items. Same happens with the items like perfumes, home aromas or other eatable items. Another tactic used by the marketers to increase likelihood of purchase is using tactile cues. This allows consumers to touch and feel the products in order to increase the likelihood of purchase. When there is physical interaction with the product it creates a sense of ownership even before purchase influencing financial decisions.

The emotional responses to the sensory stimuli are regarded to be crucial in financial decision making. For example, if the marketer provides a pleasant shopping environment it can lead to impulse buying where as a stressful environment may result in conservative spending or no spending at all. The sensory perception can also create cognitive biases. One of which is anchoring effect. In anchoring effect individual rely heavily on first piece of information. Another can be endowment effect, where people value something more because they own it. These biases can significantly affect financial choices, including investment decisions and spending habits.

In anchoring effect people rely too heavily on different first piece of information they encounter which is called as the anchor, while making decisions. In financial context it can be associated when an investor fixates on an initial stock price or an initial offer in a negotiation. Even when the subsequent information suggests a different valuation the initial anchor can disproportionately influence the financial decisions. It can lead to sub optimal investment choices as investors may hold those stocks that have fallen in value or make purchases based on outdated price points rather than current market conditions.

Similarly, endowment effect occurs when individuals assign greater value to the things simply because they own them. This bias can significantly affect financial choices such as investment decisions and spending habits. For example, the individual can hold underperforming assets because they value more than equivalent assets they do not own. In the same manner consumers may be unwilling to part with the possessions or investment even when selling or reallocating resources would be more financially beneficial. The endowment may lead to inertia in investment portfolios and reluctant to make necessary financial adjustments.

Another buyer influencing financial decisions is the overconfidence bias. It is considered to be a critical factor influencing financial decisions. Investors generally over estimates their knowledge, skill and ability to predict market movements which leads to adopting aggressive trading strategies and under estimation of risk. This can result in frequent trading, higher transaction cost and ultimately lower returns. The over confident investors could also be seen disregarding professional advices and market indicators. They rely more on their judgement rather than the professional advices which can lead to significant financial losses.

Another powerful buyer that affects financial choices is loss aversion. Loss aversion is related with conservative investment strategies where individuals avoid taking necessary risks for fear of potential losses. It can also result in holding on to lost investments for long period of time in order to avoid realizing a loss. The loss aversion buyers often lead to poor portfolio performance as investors may missed out potential gains or failed to cut their losses in timely manner.

Herd behavior is another bias that significantly impacts financial choices particularly in investments decisions (Kumar & Arora, (2023). Herd behavior occurs when individuals follow the action of larger groups often leading to market bubble of crashes. When a market is in boom investors might irrationally buy those stocks which others are buying. Similarly, during the market down turn the same behavior can lead to panic selling increasing their decline investment current value.

There is also a confirmation bias which plays a crucial role in shaping financial choices. These bias leads individuals to seek out that information which confirms their pre-existing beliefs while disregarding contradicting evidence. In various investment decisions the confirmation bias can result in investors selectively gathering information's that support their current holdings and ignoring the data that might suggest need for reevaluation. It can prevent investors from making necessary adjustments to their portfolios in response to new market conditions or emerging risks.

Thus, understanding and mitigating these cognitive biases are essential for making sound financial decisions. Financial education and awareness of these biases can help the individuals in making more rational and effective financial choices. It can ultimately lead to better investment outcomes and healthier spending habits. These sensory perceptions are directly related with neuro marketing studies as to how sensory inputs affect brain activity and decision-making process. These neuro marketing studies allows the companies to design those marketing strategies that effectively influence consumer behavior and financial choices. The practical application of these studies can be seen when a sensory rich environment is created by the marketers to encourage spending. It includes spending on retail design, store layouts, lighting, music, scent etc. Further particularly in relation to investment decisions, advertisements could be seen which combine visual, auditory or compelling narratives that influence financial choices. There is still a great scope for the researchers to explore how specific sensory inputs affect different demographic groups and financial decisions. Studying and understanding these nuances can help to devise marketing strategies for diverse consumer segments providing valuable insights into the complex interplay between our senses and financial behavior.

2. To understand how neuro sensory behavior is important in investment decision making.

In the field of investment decision making understanding the neuro sensory behavior is vital in investment decision making as it sheds light on how sensory inputs and neural processes influence financial choices. If the emotional sub conscious and perceptual factors are examined deeply, the investors can become more aware of their biases and make more informed rational decisions (Kumar & Arora,2023). If we integrate neurosensory insights into investment strategies than it can lead to more personalized and effective financial planning. Ultimately improving investment outcomes and financial well-being. Understanding the neurosensory behavior is very crucial in investment decision making as it provides insights into how sensory inputs neural processes influence financial judgment and action. The neuro sensory behavior examines the interaction between our sensory experiences and the brain decision making processes revealing how emotions perceptions and cognitive biases shape our financial choices. At the very first level the sensory stimuli play a very significant role in shaping our emotional responses which in turn influence investment decisions. For example, visual cues like market charts, news headlines and financial reports can evoke strong emotional reactions like fear or excitement. These emotions can significantly impact decision making. It can lead to impulsive actions for investment also. There is a possibility that an investor might sell off the stock in panic during market recession due to fear. It also happens when the market is booming and the investors buy the investments by excitement and the fear of missing out. (FOMO). If we understand the neurosensory mechanism that triggers emotional responses the investors can become more aware of their biases and potentially mitigate irrational decision making.

Further the field of neuro economics explores that how brain activity is correlated with financial decision providing a deeper understanding of neural processes. Various advance techniques like (fMRI) i.e. functional magnetic resonance imaging and EEG i.e.electro encephalography allow the researchers to observes the brain reasons activating during financial decision-making activities. The brain reward system primarily involves the ventral striatum is activated when the individual anticipates financial gains. This neural response can drive the risk seeking behavior of the investors as they are motivated by potential rewards. Similarly, amygdala is associated with the processing the fear and risk and it became active when the individuals perceive financial threats. It leads to risk averse behavior. Understanding these neural processes help in developing strategies to balance reward seeking and risk aversion tendencies.

Further, neuro sensory behavior highlights the importance of sub conscious processes in investment decisions. The financial choices of human being are highly influenced by sub conscious biases and neurotics formed through sensory experiences. By understanding and recognizing the influence of sub conscious processes investor can strive to based their decision on comprehensive data analysis rather than easily accessible misleading information.

The Role of AI in Multisensory Financial Decision-Making in Multi-Business Scenarios

Artificial Intelligence can play a very transformative role in enhancing the financial decision making across multiple business scenarios by leveraging the insights from multi sensitive perceptions (Arora & Sharma, 2023). Artificially intelligent technology has the ability to process and analyze vast amount of data from various sensory inputs. It can enable the businesses to tailor their products and services to better align with the human responses. The integration of artificial intelligence with sensory and behavioral data has the potential to significantly improve the effectiveness of financial products, customer experiences, and decision-making strategies. The following can be the areas where artificial intelligence can play a significant role in the field of neurosensory financial decision making:

Personalized financial advisors and user experiences

One of the important and primary application of artificial intelligence in this context is providing personalized financial advices. AI can help to analyze the data from visual, auditory, and tactile interactions with the financial platforms. Artificially intelligent system can understand individual user preferences and behaviors in a much more intelligent manner. There are various machine learning algorithms which have the ability to predict user needs and tailor the financial advices accordingly. For instance, AI has the potential to analyze how users' interaction occurs with a financial app interface and they can track it down where they click, how long they stay on certain page and what was the response to different visual elements. Based on this data, AI can personalize the user interface to enhance engagement and satisfaction, such as interesting colors, fonts and layout to suit individual preferences.

Enhanced Customer Support

The AI powered chat bots or virtual assistants can be utilized in multi-sensory inputs to provide more effective customer supports. Such systems have the ability to interpret the voice tone, speech patterns to guide the customer emotions and adapt their responses in real time scenario. For example, if a customer sound frustrated then artificial intelligence can switch to more empathetic tone and provide the solutions more sensitivity. Similarly, if we can integrate the AI with tactile feedback technologies, it can influence and enhance the user experience by providing physical cues like vibration, haptic feedback, etc. It can help to guide the users through their financial processes, ensuring that they feel supported empathetically and they are understood throughout their interactions.

Behavioral Analysis and Predictive Modeling

AI has the ability to analyze the multi-sensory data in order to build sophisticated behavioral models which can predict financial decision-making patrons. By the help of AI, we can integrate data from various sources like visual attention, auditory responses, and tactile interactions. AI can possibly identify various subtle cues that indicate future financial behaviors also. These predictive models can be used by businesses to develop targeted marketing strategies. AI can also offer personalized product recommendations and risk assessment tools. For example, the artificial intelligence can be used to detect that a user is more responsive towards a certain visual stimulus. Therefore, it can prioritize those elements in marketing which can improve customer engagement.

Cross regional and cultural adaptations

In multi business scenarios, particularly those which operate across different regions and cultures, AI can be an important area where financial products and preferences can be tailored to suit the local preferences. AI can identify regional variations and cultural influences on decision making. It has the ability to enable the businesses in order to develop a region-specific strategy which can resonate more effectively with their local consumers. For example, AI can adjust the design and presentation of the financial products to match the cultural aesthetics or modify customer support approaches in order to align with the regional communication styles.

Real time feedback and adaptation

AI has the ability to provide a real time feedback and adapt the changing sensory input and it can play a crucial role in dynamic financial environments. For example, in high stakes trading scenarios, AI can monitor the trader's psychological and physiological responses such as heart rate and eye movement to detect the stress or fatigue level. Based on this data, AI can recommend breaks, adjust environmental conditions, or provide alerts to provide the suboptimal decisions. Similarly, in customer facing roles, AI can provide life coaching and support, helping the employees and managers their interactions more effectively and enhancing the customer satisfaction.

The integration of AI with multisensory data in financial decision-making provides a potent tool for improving business performance in many settings. AI has the ability to enhance the quality of financial decisions by customising user experiences, optimising surroundings, and offering real-time adaptive help. As businesses progressively utilise AI, the integration of sensory impressions and financial decisions will become more sophisticated, resulting in more intuitive, responsive, and efficient financial systems. This interdisciplinary approach shows significant potential for developing financial environments that are not only more efficient but also more aligned with the subtle ways in which humans perceive and engage with the world.

CONCLUSION

Ultimately, the examination of how sensory perceptions and financial decisions intersect, analysed from a neuroscientific perspective, provides deep understanding of the fundamental mechanisms that influence economic behaviour. The sensory inputs that are processed by our neurological systems have a considerable impact on our financial decision-making processes, frequently in ways that go beyond what classic economic theories explain. By comprehending the effects of visual, auditory, olfactory, tactile, and gustatory inputs on our cognitive functioning and emotional responses, we can gain a deeper understanding of the intricacies of consumer behaviour and investment strategies.

This neuroscientific perspective demonstrates that financial decisions are not solely based on logical calculations, but are intricately connected to sensory experiences and emotional states. For example, visual cues have the ability to change how we perceive risk, while auditory stimuli can impact our desire for time and our level of patience while making decisions. Furthermore, the incorporation of sensory information can result in more comprehensive and contextually conscious financial choices, emphasising the need of a multi-sensory method in financial planning and marketing tactics.

The findings have significant ramifications, indicating that financial experts, marketers, and politicians should take into account sensory and emotional variables when creating financial goods, services, and interventions. By harnessing the influence of sensory impressions, they are able to establish environments that encourage improved financial behaviours and results. Further investigation in this field should persist in examining the complex connections among sensory stimuli, neurological mechanisms, and financial decisions, thereby facilitating the development of more efficient and people-centered financial systems.

Essentially, studying how the brain processes sensory information and makes financial decisions enhances our understanding of economic behaviour. This highlights the importance of adopting a more detailed and interdisciplinary approach in studying and applying finance.

REFERENCES

Aren, S., Hamamci, H. N., & Özcan, S. (2021). Moderation effect of pleasure seeking and loss aversion in the relationship between personality traits and risky investment intention. *Kybernetes*, 50(12), 3305–3330. DOI: 10.1108/K-05-2020-0278

Aren, S., & Nayman Hamamci, H. (2023). Evaluation of investment preference with phantasy, emotional intelligence, confidence, trust, financial literacy and risk preference. *Kybernetes*, 52(12), 6203–6231. DOI: 10.1108/K-01-2022-0014

Arora, M., & Sharma, R. L. (2023). Artificial intelligence and big data: ontological and communicative perspectives in multi-sectoral scenarios of modern businesses. *foresight*, 25(1), 126-143.

Bossaerts, P. (2009). What decision neuroscience teaches us about financial decision making. *Annual Review of Financial Economics*, 1(1), 383–404. DOI: 10.1146/annurev.financial.102708.141514

Bossaerts, P. (2021). How neurobiology elucidates the role of emotions in financial decision-making. *Frontiers in Psychology*, 12, 697375. DOI: 10.3389/fpsyg.2021.697375 PMID: 34349708

Brocas, I., & Carrillo, J. D. (2012). From perception to action: An economic model of brain processes. *Games and Economic Behavior*, 75(1), 81–103. DOI: 10.1016/j.geb.2011.10.001

Chapkovski, P., Khapko, M., & Zoican, M. (2024). Trading gamification and investor behavior. *Management Science*, mnsc.2022.02650. DOI: 10.1287/mnsc.2022.02650

Cristofaro, M., Giardino, P. L., Malizia, A. P., & Mastrogiorgio, A. (2022). Affect and cognition in managerial decision making: A systematic literature review of neuroscience evidence. *Frontiers in Psychology*, 13, 762993. DOI: 10.3389/fpsyg.2022.762993 PMID: 35356322

de Vries, R., Jager, G., Tijssen, I., & Zandstra, E. H. (2018). Shopping for products in a virtual world: Why haptics and visuals are equally important in shaping consumer perceptions and attitudes. *Food Quality and Preference*, 66, 64–75. DOI: 10.1016/j.foodqual.2018.01.005

Erkut, B., Kaya, T., Lehmann-Waffenschmidt, M., Mahendru, M., Sharma, G. D., Srivastava, A. K., & Srivastava, M. (2018). A fresh look on financial decision-making from the plasticity perspective. *International Journal of Ethics and Systems*, 34(4), 426–441. DOI: 10.1108/IJOES-02-2018-0022

Foley, H. J. (2019). *Sensation and perception*. Routledge. DOI: 10.4324/9780429275913

Goel, P., Garg, A., Sharma, A., & Rana, N. P. (2023). Impact of sensory perceptions on the urge to buy impulsively. *Journal of Computer Information Systems*, •••, 1–17.

Goldberg, L. M. (2012). *Greed, fear and irrational exuberance-the deep play of financial and cultural speculation* (Doctoral dissertation, UNSW Sydney).

Grant, S. M., Hobson, J. L., & Sinha, R. K. (2024). Digital engagement practices in mobile trading: The impact of color and swiping to trade on investor decisions. *Management Science*, 70(3), 2003–2022. DOI: 10.1287/mnsc.2023.00379

Howard, J. A. (2013). Financial decision-making: The roles of intuition, heuristics and impulses. *Journal of Modern Accounting and Auditing*, 9(12), 1596–1610.

Jakovaara, M. (2020). *Feelings of emotion in strategic investment decisions* (Doctoral dissertation, Doctoral dissertation. Turku School of Economics, Turku).

Krishna, A. (Ed.). (2011). *Sensory marketing: Research on the sensuality of products*. Routledge. DOI: 10.4324/9780203892060

Krishna, A. (2012). An integrative review of sensory marketing: Engaging the senses to affect perception, judgment and behavior. *Journal of Consumer Psychology*, 22(3), 332–351. DOI: 10.1016/j.jcps.2011.08.003

Kumar, S., & Arora, M (2023). Understanding Awareness of Investment Avenues of Investors in North India: An Empirical Study. Journal of Interdisciplinary and Multidisciplinary Research (JIMR); Vol. 18 Issue 10, Oct 2023.

Kumar, S., & Arora, M (2023). Herd Behavior Unveiled: How Demographics Shape Investment Patterns in North India. Quest Journal of Research in Business and Management, ISSN (Online): 2347 3002, Volume-11, Issue-8, Page No.: 114-121, [2023].

Kumar, S., Jain, A., & Hsieh, J. K. (2021). Impact of apps aesthetics on revisit intentions of food delivery apps: The mediating role of pleasure and arousal. *Journal of Retailing and Consumer Services*, 63, 102686. DOI: 10.1016/j.jretconser.2021.102686

Li, Y. M., & Yeh, Y. S. (2010). Increasing trust in mobile commerce through design aesthetics. *Computers in Human Behavior*, 26(4), 673–684. DOI: 10.1016/j.chb.2010.01.004

Mercier, M. R., & Cappe, C. (2020). The interplay between multisensory integration and perceptual decision making. *NeuroImage*, 222, 116970. DOI: 10.1016/j.neuroimage.2020.116970 PMID: 32454204

Miller, C. C., & Ireland, R. D. (2005). Intuition in strategic decision making: Friend or foe in the fast-paced 21st century? *The Academy of Management Perspectives*, 19(1), 19–30. DOI: 10.5465/ame.2005.15841948

Naqvi, N., Shiv, B., & Bechara, A. (2006). The role of emotion in decision making: A cognitive neuroscience perspective. *Current Directions in Psychological Science*, 15(5), 260–264. DOI: 10.1111/j.1467-8721.2006.00448.x

Njegovanović, A. (2020). Financial decision making in the framework of neuroscience/anthropology with review to the pandemic and climate change.

Pallavi, G. P., & Dsa, K. T. (2024). Literature Review on the Role of Financial Advisors in Shaping Investment Decisions.

Peterson, R. L. (2007). Affect and financial decision-making: How neuroscience can inform market participants. *Journal of Behavioral Finance*, 8(2), 70–78. DOI: 10.1080/15427560701377448

Planning, U. D. R. (2014). It's All Green to Me: How Intrapersonal and Interpersonal Factors Shape Consumers' Financial Decisions. *Advances in Consumer Research. Association for Consumer Research (U. S.)*, •••, 42.

Plassmann, H., & Weber, B. (2015). Individual differences in marketing placebo effects: Evidence from brain imaging and behavioral experiments. *JMR, Journal of Marketing Research*, 52(4), 493–510. DOI: 10.1509/jmr.13.0613

Pleger, B., & Villringer, A. (2013). The human somatosensory system: From perception to decision making. *Progress in Neurobiology*, 103, 76–97. DOI: 10.1016/j.pneurobio.2012.10.002 PMID: 23123624

Polo, E. M., Farabbi, A., Mollura, M., Mainardi, L., & Barbieri, R. (2024). Understanding the role of emotion in decision making process: Using machine learning to analyze physiological responses to visual, auditory, and combined stimulation. *Frontiers in Human Neuroscience*, 17, 1286621. DOI: 10.3389/fnhum.2023.1286621 PMID: 38259333

Pompian, M. M. (2012). *Behavioral finance and investor types: managing behavior to make better investment decisions*. John Wiley & Sons. DOI: 10.1002/9781119202417

Pompian, M. M. (2012). *Behavioral finance and investor types: managing behavior to make better investment decisions*. John Wiley & Sons. DOI: 10.1002/9781119202417

Pryke, M. (2010). Money's eyes: The visual preparation of financial markets. *Economy and Society*, 39(4), 427–459. DOI: 10.1080/03085147.2010.510679

Racat, M., & Plotkina, D. (2023). Sensory-enabling technology in m-commerce: The effect of haptic stimulation on consumer purchasing behavior. *International Journal of Electronic Commerce*, 27(3), 354–384. DOI: 10.1080/10864415.2023.2226900

Radocy, R. E., & Boyle, J. D. (2012). *Psychological foundations of musical behavior*. Charles C Thomas Publisher.

Ramchandran, K., Tranel, D., Duster, K., & Denburg, N. L. (2020). The role of emotional vs. cognitive intelligence in economic decision-making amongst older adults. *Frontiers in Neuroscience*, 14, 497. DOI: 10.3389/fnins.2020.00497 PMID: 32547361

Ricciardi, V. (2004). A risk perception primer: A narrative research review of the risk perception literature in behavioral accounting and behavioral finance. *Available at SSRN* 566802. DOI: 10.2139/ssrn.566802

Rungratsameetaweemana, N., Itthipuripat, S., Salazar, A., & Serences, J. T. (2018). Expectations do not alter early sensory processing during perceptual decision-making. *The Journal of Neuroscience : The Official Journal of the Society for Neuroscience*, 38(24), 5632–5648. DOI: 10.1523/JNEUROSCI.3638-17.2018 PMID: 29773755

Sadler-Smith, E., & Shefy, E. (2004). The intuitive executive: Understanding and applying 'gut feel' in decision-making. *The Academy of Management Perspectives*, 18(4), 76–91. DOI: 10.5465/ame.2004.15268692

Schreuder, E., Van Erp, J., Toet, A., & Kallen, V. L. (2016). Emotional responses to multisensory environmental stimuli: A conceptual framework and literature review. *SAGE Open*, 6(1), 2158244016630591. DOI: 10.1177/2158244016630591

Spence, C., & Gallace, A. (2011). Multisensory design: Reaching out to touch the consumer. *Psychology and Marketing*, 28(3), 267–308. DOI: 10.1002/mar.20392

Statman, M. (1999). Behaviorial finance: Past battles and future engagements. *Financial Analysts Journal*, 55(6), 18–27. DOI: 10.2469/faj.v55.n6.2311

Tang, F., Hess, T. J., Valacich, J. S., & Sweeney, J. T. (2014). The effects of visualization and interactivity on calibration in financial decision-making. *Behavioral Research in Accounting*, 26(1), 25–58. DOI: 10.2308/bria-50589

Troye, S. V., & Supphellen, M. (2012). Consumer participation in coproduction:"I made it myself" effects on consumers' sensory perceptions and evaluations of outcome and input product. *Journal of Marketing*, 76(2), 33–46. DOI: 10.1509/jm.10.0205

Wright, W. (1995, October). Information animation applications in the capital markets. In *Proceedings of Visualization 1995 Conference* (pp. 19-25). IEEE. DOI: 10.1109/INFVIS.1995.528682

Xia, Z., Deng, Z., Fang, B., Yang, Y., & Sun, F. (2022). A review on sensory perception for dexterous robotic manipulation. *International Journal of Advanced Robotic Systems*, 19(2), 17298806221095974. DOI: 10.1177/17298806221095974

Xu, C., Peak, D., & Prybutok, V. (2015). A customer value, satisfaction, and loyalty perspective of mobile application recommendations. *Decision Support Systems*, 79, 171–183. DOI: 10.1016/j.dss.2015.08.008

Chapter 5
Neuromarketing and Financial Decision Making

Simanpreet Kaur
Chandigarh School of Business, Chandigarh Group of Colleges, Jhanjeri, India

Anjali
Chandigarh School of Business, Chandigarh Group of Colleges, Jhanjeri, India

ABSTRACT

Neuromarketing itself represents an application of neuroscience to marketing, guiding the very neural and emotional mechanisms of consumer behavior and providing important insights into financial decision-making. EEG and functional magnetic resonance imaging are two techniques researchers use to trace the ways in which financial stimuli, including investment options, risk assessments, and financial product advertisements, activate different regions of the brain. This paper is aimed at analyzing the role of emotional and neurological processes in financial decision-making. This research found out that consumers are likely to engage and trust if the financial commercials and product presentations arouse positive emotional responses. These findings mean that through the use of neuromarketing concepts in marketing and product development plans, financial institutions would increase the confidence and engagement of customers in their services and bring about more efficient and client-oriented financial services.

INTRODUCTION

Neuromarketing is a field that brings together neuroscience and marketing, where one can better understand how consumers' brains react to marketing stimuli. By using techniques such as electroencephalography and functional magnetic

DOI: 10.4018/979-8-3693-9351-2.ch005

resonance imaging, the studies are able to investigate brain activity over time and locate the regions that the brain uses, when customers are shown commercials, goods, or brands. The technique is also used to track eye movements which help in understanding what draws customers to certain elements(Bhardwaj, Kaushik, & Arora (2024); Taneja, Shukla & Arora (2024); Malik, Malhan & Arora (2024). (Eds.). (2024)). These techniques will be helpful in shaping methods that will successfully appeal to irrational consumer preferences and decision-making processes, hence making the marketing campaigns more effective.Neuromarketing techniques can be effectively used in financial decision-making if neuroscience principles in consumer behavior and decision-making processes are well understood. Cordeiro et al.(2024) defined neuromarketing as one that integrates neuroscience and marketing and helps to understand emotions as well as senses that affect consumer behavior,it aids the marketers to develop an effective strategy for customers as well as sales. Millagala & Gunasinghe (2024) explained neuromarketing as a strategy that is digital using neuroscience and integrating it with digital marketing and it helps to bring personalised content for customer. Financial decision making refers to the process of choosing the best course of action from various options available to satisfy certain goals and objectives. It is a bundle of activities, which involves investment, debt management, and retirement planning. According to Soto Arias & Quintero-Martínez (2019) neuromarketing strategies may successfully improve financial decision-making, hence leading to the advantage of financial institutions in a rather cutthroat market through the use of neuroscience in understanding consumer behavior better. Tolzmann et al. (2024) explained that understanding the concept of costs, quantifying them, cost analysing, budgeting, calculating contribution margin and break-even point, and creating capital acquisition plans using net present value are important components of laboratory finance decision making. . The person involved in the decision-making must be much more aware of risk and return, keep a close eye on all the financial data, and work out short- and long-term implications. According to Huang & You (2023) artificial intelligence has helped in FinTech lending, investment, and overall decision-making processes through the aid of Machine Learning, wherein data extraction and analysis take place efficiently. Good financial decisions are those that seek to ensure the stability, increase, and ability of a person, business, or organization to meet their future obligations or needs. According to Singh & Gupta (2024) managing money over time through acts of borrowing, creating capital, investing, and managing assets and liabilities. It consists of different operational, investment, and financial decisions that result in long-term financial success. The present study focuses on studying the concept of Neuromarketing in Financial Decision Making. Besides, financial advertising using neuromarketing techniques used in Financial advertising were studied to understand their significance in financial decision-making. was reviewed. This study also takes into account the neural predictors for consumer financial satisfaction to understand if these neural predictors can contribute to designing interventions or financial products that enhance consumer satisfaction. The next paragraph considered how 'Neural Responses to Financial Incentives' could reveal insights into how the brain processes and reacts to financial rewards and incentives, to understand its impact on decision-making, motivation and behavior. The paper also continues in checking on Ethical Considerations in Neuro Financial Research such that these concerns demand vigilance, through transparency of practice and a commitment to responsible use of the knowledge gained. Future Trends and Innovations in Neuromarketing and Finance were also studied so as to further understand that because the field of neuroscience with marketing and financial decision-making is evolving very fast, through innovations in technology, data analytics, and understandings of the brain. These are trends and innovations that will shape the future landscape of neuromarketing and neurofinance.

Need for Studying Neuromarketing in Financial Decision Making

According to Soto Arias & Quintero-Martínez (2019), studying neuromarketing in finance gives one competitive advantage and creativity in formulating innovative marketing strategies in a cutthroat market by using neuroscience to predict consumer behavior. Therefore, it is important to study the role of neuromarketing in the financial decision-making process. Halkiopoulos et al. (2023) explained that neuromarketing in finance is important because it merges knowledge in economics, neuroscience, and marketing to reach and engage with the consumer's brain effectively for better advertisement strategies and improvement in financial industry decision-making. Therefore, according to Madan & Popli (2016), Neuromarketing can in the financial industry, uncover subconscious consumer preferences and decision processes, hence helping in the creation of profitable financial plans based on more profound understandings of customer behaviour. These studies support the importance of neuromarketing in making sound decisions with regard to finance. Gill & Singh (2022) found that neuromarketing techniques can aid in the improvement of knowledge regarding consumer behavior and rationalize financial strategies through the adoption of low-cost, information-driven frameworks for financial decision-making. This study supported the fact that neuromarketing approach can help the customers to make decisions that are benefitting to them. Fingelkurts et al. (2020) studied that neuromarketing in finance can currently understand decision-making processes by brain imaging and more suitably develop economic and financial strategies. Knowing how the brain responds to financial decisions, one can develop more tailored economic and financial strategies to suit consumer behavior. By focusing on the brain's reactions to financial stimuli, this study gives insights into how to construct more effective marketing strategies, thereby enhancing the execution of the promotion of financial products and services with respect to the needs of consumers. Both studies underline increasingly that neuromarketing can become very important as a tool in the process of refining strategies within the financial industry. Neuromarketing by Lee et al. (2007), can enhance knowledge regarding consumer behavior in finance by examining the reactions of the brain to financial stimuli and provide insights into more effective marketing strategies for the financial sector. It gives information that is very instrumental in making successful marketing campaigns for financial services. Madan (2010) explained that such neuromarketing research into the brain's response to financial marketing can be used to drive the building of much more successful marketing strategies within the financial industry by revealing how consumer behavior toward financial products is driven by brain responses. Vasile & Sebastian (2007) Neurofinance deals with the mind of a trader; hence, the intermingling of psychology, neurology, and finance lets one know the financial decision-making processes based on brain processes and gives insights for improvement in choices related to finance. Neurofinance is the field of study wherein factors of psychology, neurology, and finance are put together to analyze how activity of the brain impacts financial decisions. The approach in itself serves to make good multidisciplinary financial decisions to optimize financial outcomes. The discipline also gives insightful information about the underlying mechanisms which drive financial decisions. Neurofinance attempts to enhance knowledge regarding thought processes of traders and their processes of decision making by studying the activity of the brain. This will eventually lead to the creation of more reasonable and effective financial plans. Hence, there is a need to study neuromarketing in financial decision making. The objective of the current study to is to examine the role of emotional and neurological processes in financial decision-making. To fulfil this aim review of literature is gathered to support the evidence. The study is descriptive in nature. It explores the concept of neuromarketing and investigates its role in decision making with specific reference to financial sector.

Neuromarketing and Decision Making

The two fields are closely related because neuromarketing applies knowledge from neuroscience to understand and influence decision-making. Neuromarketing thus studies neural and physiological reactions that customers' brains exhibit in response to various marketing stimuli. It helps marketers understand how to develop tactics consistent with the underlying motivations for consumer behavior. Bernard et al. (2023) deals with optimal multivariate financial decision making and tries to outline some of the effective approaches in making a tough financial decision.

Considering further monitoring of eye movements and analysis of activity in the brain by techniques such as fMRI and EEG, researchers could look at how emotions, attention, and memory drive decision-making processes. The information that allows marketers to develop products, advertising, and brand messaging that can bind more powerfully with customers or even, at times, influence a buying decision. Razbadauskaitė-Venskė (2024) explained that Neuromarketing investigates how consumer emotions are driving their decision-making processes and provides insight into unconscious motives. One of the key areas this research looks into is the subconscious side of consumer behavior, which acts to complement traditional research. Neuromarketing's ultimate objective is to reduce the distance between cognitive responses of consumers to their actual behaviour, which would finally result in better marketing tactics and hence better decision-making. Archana & Mahajan (2023) explained that Neuromarketing is the application of neural signals in deciphering customers' decision-making processes; it defines customer behavior beyond self-reporting surveys and gives some help in the development, pricing, and advertising of products. Babu et al. (2021) explained that with neurotransmitters like dopamine and serotonin, which influence investor behaviour and decision making processes, neuromarketing techniques could be employed in financial decision making with a possible improvement in the investment outcome. Dopamine reinforces positive stimuli and thus encourages investors to act in a goal-oriented manner. The neurotransmitter associated with reward and pleasure is dopamine. The mood-regulating neurotransmitter serotonin can help in emotional stabilization, reducing impulsive or fear-driven decisions regarding finance. Armed with knowledge of the effects of these neurotransmitters on decision-making, neuromarketing can devise ways to enhance returns on investments. For example, marketing materials and financial planning tools aimed to elicit dopaminergic responses could make investment opportunities more alluring, while tools that rebalance serotonin levels may help investors stay calm and rational in the face of market volatility. Bansal et al. (2023) found that Neuromarketing applies the tools of marketing, psychology, and neuroscience to study the cognitive choice-making process of customers. It unveils new insights that cannot be derived with traditional analysis tools.Taking neuromarketing insights into financial decision-making may produce more informed, balanced, and hence more successful investing behaviors. Neuromarketing applications of neuroscience as per Dangwal et al.(2023) improve marketing decision-making in understanding consumer preferences. Advertisement would much better meet customers' demands by revealing some hidden truths.Traditionally used in consumer behavior and product marketing, neuromarketing is now being increasingly looked at within the financial sector with respect to decision-making processes. Neuromarketing will bring new approaches for enhancing financial decision-making and investment performance by studying brain activity and neurotransmitters such as dopamine and serotonin.

Methods like fMRI and EEG allow researchers to monitor how the brain responds to financial stimuli, which can be very useful in understanding emotional and cognitive factors driving investment decisions.

Essentially, a person's emotional reactions to financial stimuli easily influence his/her financial behaviors and financial decision-making processes. For example, if the process involves financial information or opportunity, a person's feeling of fear, excitement, anxiety, or confidence could significantly drive decision-making. Moreover, anxiety from market volatility may spur impulsive actions not necessarily aligned with long-term goals. These are the conclusions that financial advisors and institutions should understand in order to tailor their messages and approaches best toward their client's handling of emotions. That is by identification and handling these emotional attributes, which a lot of people are empowered to make better and more rational decisions regarding their finances, thereby leading to better financial outcomes and increased financial well-being. Emotional responses to financial stimuli are crucial in the decision-making process. The research conducted on this area has shown that there is usually an economic incentive with a conflict between emotional incentives; thus, using the mechanisms of neuromarketing in the regulation of reactions can be very helpful.

According to Farrell et al. (2018), at the neural level, financial incentives modulated the processing of positive and negative emotions during decision-making. Fixed-wage conditions supported a decrement for positive emotions and an increment in responses to negative emotions under performance-based incentives. Their findings indicated that the introduction of performance-based incentives into fixed wage conditions is associated with reduced neural processing of positive emotions and increased responses to negative emotions. In essence, disparate financial incentives can create different emotional responses in individuals, thus affecting their choices.

Neuroeconomics and Investment Decisions

da Silva & Cammarosano (2023) explained that where neuromarketing deals with consumer behavior in marketing, neuroeconomics deals with decision-making. Both disciplines adopt neuroscience techniques to fathom decisions and actions that often impact business plans and economics. Important discoveries in neuroeconomic studies underline the role of several brain regions, including the amygdala and prefrontal cortex, in processing emotional reactions associated with investments and defining risk. According to this literature, decision-making for investments is influenced by the emotional response, biases, and social factors. Vuković, D. (2024) found that it is in essence the study of brain responses to economic decisions or marketing stimuli that forms the backbone of neuroeconomics and neuromarketing.

Both concepts utilize neuroscience methods to attempt to understand the drivers behind consumer behavior and the processes of making a decision.

Financial professionals and policy makers will contribute much toward better total financial outcomes for individuals and markets if they incorporate such insights into more effective strategies supporting well-informed investment decisions. According to Asuquo-Utuk (2023) in his research on the Nigerian media business, "Neuroeconomics exercises influences on strategic financial decisions taken by any multinational corporation, anchored on psychological and economic theories." Enterprises can enhance their assessment of market risk, consumer preference, and media consumption behavior if neuroscience-based knowledge is integrated into its economic analyses. For example, if the neural mechanisms underlying consumers' reactions to media content were known, companies would be in a position to individualize their advertising strategies to effectively communicate with target audiences. Besides being able to maximize the effectiveness of marketing campaigns, this will also help in investment decisions related to media platforms and production of content, thereby improving resource allocation and market positioning in the competitive environment. Therefore, neuroeconomics provides relevant tools for the negotiation of, and exploitation of opportunities available to, multinational enterprises in the fast-changing Nigerian media environment. Using fMRI data and the CEAD method, Majer et al. (2016) investigated investment decisions in neuroeconomics, linking risk attitude and decision-making processes to activity in the anterior insula and prefrontal cortex. This study tried to link individual differences in activity predominantly at the anterior insula and prefrontal cortex to risk attitude and the decision-making process. The anterior insula is associated with the processing of emotions and physiological states and thus helps to determine risk and uncertainty. At the same time, activity within the prefrontal cortex will influence how people value options and select investments since it is crucial for higher-order cognitive processes such as reasoning and planning. By looking at these neural correlates, the study aimed to significantly improve our knowledge of how brain activity supports risk perception and economic decision-making.

According to Nepal (2023), neuroplasticity in Nepalese investors is influenced by investor cognition, financial literacy, and risk absorption, and impacts investment decisions. Neuroplasticity refers to the reorganization or adaptation of the brain as a result of experiences and learning. According to Babu et al. (2021), neurotransmitters played a critically role in making the investment decisions, by connecting neuroscience and finance. For instance, dopamine is a neurotransmitter which is responsible for motivations as well as rewards; therefore, one would feel more satisfied when they are expecting potential financial gains, hence it will lead to risk-taking behavior. Serotonin, on the other hand, serves the purpose of stabilizing mood and reducing anxiety and impulsivity. Therefore, it promotes cautious, thoughtful financial decisions. The study on how these neurotransmitters modulate neural pathways for reward, risk assessment, and emotion regulation neural pathways can be helpful to understand insights into neural mechanisms of investor behavior. This brings into a better view towards financial decision-making and creates an opportunity to develop neuroscientifically informed strategies that are aimed at maximizing investor outcomes.

Takemura & Takemura (2021), attached relevance to neuroeconomics as a factor that explains the neuroscientific foundations of decision-making with respect to an economic event such as an investment decision. Neuroeconomics studies neural mechanisms pertaining to risk, reward, and uncertainty evaluation using techniques including positron emission tomography scans and functional magnetic resonance imaging. Neuroeconomics, as explained by Mateu et al. (2018), is the activity of the brain that relates to making financial decisions, such as investment decisions. Emotions, neural architecture, and cognitive functions play an important role in the development of economic behaviours. Piwowarski et al. (2019) explained that neuroeconomics research on neural correlates of financial decision-making, using electroencephalography and microexpression measurements. According to the research, understanding how emotions impact cognitive processing in financial decision-making is important, using such neuroscientific methods. This will be useful in the development of methods for the control of affective biases, maximizing decision results, and encouraging better-informed investing practices in neuroeconomic research.

According to Chorvat (2016), neuroeconomic research about financial decisions for improved understanding and informing institutions and laws should be used around models like the stochastic discount factor. An investment decision from the viewpoint of neuroeconomics combines knowledge from psychology, economics, and neuroscience. It enhances our understanding of the factors behind people's investment decisions by examining the impact of brain processes on risk assessment, reward anticipation, and decision-making. Correlations among cognitive biases, emotional reactions, and rational considerations within the financial domain come to light with insights derived from methods such as fMRI, EEG, and behavioral experiments. The multidisciplinary approach will advance theoretical knowledge and guide real-world applications aimed at the optimization of investment strategies, reduction of bias, and improvement of the general outcomes of financial decisions. It is expected that the field of neuroeconomic research will play a key role in refining academic discourses and practice-based interventions for the dynamically changing domain of investment decision-making Neuromarketing applications in personal finance use knowledge from the neuroscience area to have an effect on customer behavior and financial decision-making. Using methods such as fMRI, EEG, and eye-tracking, neuromarketers are able to determine subconscious reactions to financial products, messaging, and pricing tactics. It helps financial advisors and institutions to make customer experiences, product designs, and communication strategies more in line with their customers' preferences and needs. In broad terms, neuromarketing in personal finance is used for matching goods and services to neurological insights into consumer behavior to drive greater consumer engagement, better decision-making, and ultimately to help people make better financial decisions.

Goswami & Deshmukh (2022) explained Applications of neuromarketing to personal finance include aiding consumers and markers to make financial decisions by using brain research to understand consumer behaviour. This uses neuroscientific methods like fMRI, EEG, and eye tracking in ascertaining emotional and subconscious reactions to financial goods and services. With such insights, marketers can bring more viable financial tools, communication plans attuned to individual needs, and better advice in terms of financial guidance. In this regard, such insights can become extremely instrumental in building up and enhancing the financial literacy and decision-making capacity of consumers. Velecela et al. (2017) discusses the impact of age on financial decision-making. As such, personal finance decisions could be a subject of neuromarketing because it is a result of several psychological aspects.

Neuromarketing Techniques in Financial Advertising

Neuromarketing strategies have come to the fore in financial advertising to better understand and affect consumer behavior. The various techniques used in neuromarketing are: Electroencephalography (EEG), Functional Magnetic Resonance Imaging (fMRI), Eye Tracking and Galvanic Skin Response (GSR). Al Fauzi & Widyarini (2023) wrote that Financial advertising applies neuromarketing techniques such as Facial expression, EEG, and fMRI to study consumer's behaviour more deeply and enhance the effectiveness of advertising. These techniques document or record the consumers' subconscious and cognitive responses to financial stimuli, which help in gaining an insight into consumer behavior. The methods of EEG and fMRI offer deep insights into neural activity connected with decision-making processes and facial expression analysis allows the assessment of immediate emotional responses. The techniques can help financial advertisers to refine campaigns for consumer preference, brand perception, and maximizing advertising strategies. EEG picks up electrical activity of the brain, by applying electrodes on the scalp, thus helping in assessment as to which areas of the brain are active in response to particular stimulation. EEG may identify consumers' emotional reactions, such as feelings of reliability, anxiety, or excitement, to financial advertisements along multiple dimensions. According to Khondakar et al. (2024), Neuromarketing is to provide empirical data on how a person responds to marketing stimuli through EEG, fMRI, eye tracking, and GSR with the main goal of improving consumer engagement and coercion within advertising. These data will be useful in message creation for desired emotional responses. fMRI monitors cerebral blood flow to identify brain regions that are active during particular tasks or in response to specific stimuli. Brain activity can be used by marketers to understand the route that information on financial products, such as risk and reward, takes in consumers' brains. This helps in the development of advertisements that can appeal to both the emotional and intellectual parts of decision-making. Razbadauskaitė-Venskė (2024) found that Neuromarketing focuses on techniques like EEG, fMRI, and eye tracking to explain consumer choice and behavior through measures of brain activity, eye movement, and skin responses like skin conductance. Eye-tracking technology tracks precisely where a subject focuses their gaze and for how long. It helps in knowing which parts of an ad people look at the most, so one can better place key messages, such as interest rates or benefits, where they are more likely to be seen. Vuković (2024) explained that Neuromarketing applies EEG, fMRI, and eye tracking in combination with GSR for the investigation of brain responses while exposed to marketing messages; hence, it provides insights into unconscious consumer behavior. Galvanic Skin Response quantifies changes in the skin's electrical conductance, which is a measure of stress or arousal and varies with sweat gland activity. This would be particularly useful in financial advertising, where the aim might be to allay fears or provoke excitement about investment opportunities, since GSR will show how large the emotional intensity of consumer response to an advertisement could be. Facial coding is a technique that measures facial expressions to identify emotional reactions. Knowing how consumers emotionally respond to the various components, be it message tone or imagery, for example, can help fine-tune an advertiser's approach to more closely match the intended consumer emotion. Mashrur et al. (2023) focused on neuromarketing using EEG and eye tracking. Here, a framework is proposed that may predict consumer preference from EEG signals and eye tracking data.

Through functional magnetic resonance imaging and electroencephalography, one can track brain activity and determine the elements within financial advertisements likely to elicit strong emotional and cognitive responses in viewers. Al Fauzi & Widyarini (2023) studied that Neuromarketing applies EEG, fMRI, eye-tracking, and GSR in its measurement of consumer behavior. All these tools help in understanding cognitive and emotional responses so as to come up with effective marketing strategies. Eye-tracking technology will also continue to provide additional insights into which ad elements engage and retain viewer interest. Knowing how the different visuals, messages, and calls to action resonate within reward and decision centers in the brain, advertisers can then optimize content for maximum engagement and effect. For example, ads that tap into emotions of optimism or assuage anxiety would have an impact on a consumer's financial habits and investment decisions. Neuromarketing approaches have gained momentum in various industries, including financial advertising, with the use of neuroscience to enhance the understanding of consumer behavior and innovation of marketing strategies. In light of the fact that the nature of financial decisions taken by individuals is emotional, neuromarketing techniques are likely to find ever greater application in financial advertising. Arrufat-Martin et al. (2024) described how neuromarketing techniques are increasingly being applied in financial advertising for understanding neural reactions to stimuli driving brand perception and memory. It is the utilization of insights into how different areas of the brain respond to financial messaging and images that will help advertisers mold brand perception and improve memory retention. Halkiopoulos (2023) examined that, as shown by the ZOPA Bank case study, financial advertising uses neuromarketing strategies targeting limbic, neocortex, and reptilian areas of the brain to advance consumer engagement and decision-making. Customer preference and sound financial decision-making can be influenced by such customized advertising strategies, which would have an emotional and rational appeal to the consumer. These studies well portray the escalating importance of neuromarketing in financial advertising and provide some insight into how to strategically act on cognitive and emotional responses to attain better marketing efficacy and consumer outcomes within the financial sector.

Ahmed (2022) had some useful implications for brand managers by showing that neuromarketing techniques, like artificial neural networks, are low-cost tools in the forecasting of consumer behavior regarding financial advertising. Artificial neural networks may analyze huge data sets for complex patterns of customer reaction to financial stimuli, as they are fashioned after neural networks in the human brain. These strategies are very instrumental in helping brand managers realize their customers' preferences, emotional triggers, and decision-making processes. One of the main advantages of Artificial neural networks is the ability to find hidden patterns and non-linear relationships that traditional methods of statistics might miss. This ability is most important in the financial advertising sector as consumer decisions may be influenced by complex interrelated factors such as emotions, financial goals, and market conditions. Neuromarketing techniques are effectively utilized in financial advertising, states Al-Refai (2021), through understanding consumer responses to stimuli, improving branding, and utilizing neuroscience insights into marketing strategies. The two techniques, Functional magnetic resonance imaging and electroencephalography allow researchers to understand the subliminal responses and emotional triggers that really effect the consumers' financial behavior. Therefore with the help of these techiques, marketers can develop branding efforts that can be intended to ensure relevant message disbursment with target audiences on neural and cognitive levels. These neuroscientific findings can be used to enable financial institutions to create more engaging and persuasive campaigns that will raise brand perception, drive engagement, and finally effect consumer decision-making in favour of positive outcomes. Neuromarketing will help to fill this gap of knowledge about consumer behavior and even more strongly use the ability to influence and guide consumer choice within this highly competitive financial sector. Jain (2022) explained that Neuromarketing techniques can be beneficial in making financial advertising more effective as it changes subconscious choices of consumers, enhances the quality of the message, and blends with other techniques for a more subdued effect. The financial advertisers can apply all forms of the advertising technique to develop campaigns that will help to satisfy the needs and preferences of consumers. This combined approach will not only raise the persuasiveness of the advertising messages within this cutthroat financial services industry but also subtly balanced consumer engagement that will pay off with superior results in the long run.

Techniques such as electroencephalography, facial expression analysis, and functional magnetic resonance imaging can be used by financial advertisers to identify emotions and subconscious reactions to financial stimuli. Such institutions can then design neurologically gripping and focused advertising campaigns for greater success. Knowing the neuromarketing insights will help financial institutions be in the market, involve customers more, and ultimately spur growth in business, especially amidst intense competition within the financial services sector. Soto Arias & Quintero-Martínez (2019) explained Innovative strategies for financial institutions in a competitive environment are aided by neuromarketing techniques in financial advertising, which provide a competitive edge by predicting consumer behavior through neuroscience.

Behavioral Biases and Neuromarketing

Neuromarketing is founded on a basic core of strong behavioral biases which significantly influence decision-making processes. It, therefore, often aims to understand such biases, to minimize or even adapt to them for marketing effectiveness. Cognitive biases like confirmation bias, loss aversion, and anchoring strongly influence people's perceptions and behavior toward financial information. For example, loss aversion in investment decisions causes people to strongly prefer avoiding losses over achieving comparable gains. Anchoring bias refers to when people, to a large extent, base their judgments on the first piece of information they encounter—for example, the price anchor. Zhou (2024) studied how human brains come into action to influence subconscious purchasing decisions in marketing strategies and apply neuromarketing along with consumer psychology biases in a digital startup's branding.

Techniques of functional magnetic resonance imaging and EEG will help neuromarketing to study how these biases are represented in neural activity. Understanding the neural mechanisms of biases can help in developing ways of reducing the impact. Panneerselvam & Joe (2022) studied the role of behavioral biases in crowdfunding platforms as a bias-driven marketing strategy to enhance their uptake. These biases can be understood more at the neuromarketing level by marketing experts and campaigns can be customised to elicit more pledging behaviour. For example, the social proof bias supports mimicking behaviors of others; hence, the possibility of joining a campaign stands much higher in the case of perceiving a campaign as well-liked or powered by influential people. By highlighting time-limited deals or exclusive benefits, scarcity bias plays on people's fear of missing out to spur people into action. By emphasizing either gains or losses within that information, however, framing effects can distort perceptions and alter how much value one places in contributing to a crowdsourcing project. By utilizing neuromarketing techniques such as fMRI and EEG, marketers can gain some useful insights by identifying the neural responses underlying these very biases. Knowing the neurological manifestation of these biases allows marketers to craft messaging and campaign elements that can go on to make stronger emotional connections with potential supporters. For instance, bringing social proof through pictures or testimonies can increase trustworthiness and attract more supporters. By structuring contributions as chances to obtain special benefits, it would be banking on the scarcity bias to drive faster and larger pledges.

By integrating neuromarketing with bias-driven marketing, one can more effortlessly perceive and exploit behavioural biases within crowdfunding campaigns, thereby ensuring high participation rates, enhanced engagement, and eventually crowdfunding success through focused and emotionally most appealing marketing.

For instance, credit card companies back-load fees on less educated customers and screen out the type of borrowers using rewards programs to profit from behavioral biases as suggested by Ru & Schoar (2016). This is supported by neuromarketing theories, which predict understanding and exploiting consumers' cognitive biases and subconscious motivations in making decisions.

Neural Predictors of Consumer Financial Satisfaction

Financial companies building high customer loyalty and retention need insight into what drives consumer financial satisfaction. Classic measurement of financial satisfaction is based on questionnaires and financial indicators, but a new neuromarketing area has developed a neuroscientific methodology. Using neuroimaging techniques like electroencephalography and functional magnetic resonance imaging allows for the studying of neural predictors of customer financial satisfaction. These methodologies allow for the study of unconscious mechanisms and emotional responses influencing people's perception and interaction with financial services and products. By learning what neurological factors truly resonate with consumers—the neural correlates associated with satisfaction—financial institutions will go a long way in fine-tuning their offerings and, ultimately, increase overall customer satisfaction and loyalty. Jain & Singh (2023) used neural network models in predicting customer satisfaction for e-banking, with main predictors being efficiency, accuracy, and ease of use and customer service.

It probably makes use of state-of-the-art computational methods to investigate large datasets and neural networks for modeling complex relationships between such predictors and customer satisfaction results. Probably, the study improves e-banking services by bringing into light variables that most strongly relate to customer satisfaction, hence guiding changes in user experience and service delivery within the digital banking industry.

Çakar et al. (2024) focus on regions within the vmPFC, OFC, and dlPFC with respect to credit behaviors and customer financial satisfaction. Many of these brain areas are prominently implicated in strategic decision-making, brand integration, and emotional evaluation. The researchers would probably like to learn more about which neural correlates predict and influence consumer behaviors relating to credit use and general financial satisfaction based on brain activity in these areas of the brain. This may provide insightful information about the brain processes underpinning financial decision-making, with implications for the improvement of customer satisfaction and smoothing financial services.

Finally, investigating neural predictors of consumer financial satisfaction with neuroscientific methods opens up new avenues for better understanding and improving consumer experiences in this domain. Neuroimaging methods will enable researchers to uncover emotional responses and subconscious processes using fMRI and EEG, which are of key importance in the determination of customer satisfaction regarding financial products and services.

Neural Responses to Financial Incentives

Understanding how human beings make economic decisions demands greater insight into how the human brain reacts to financial stimuli. Financial incentives are a very powerful factor in changing behavior, from investment decisions to consumer purchasing. Understanding of such brain activity, in response to different incentive structures, should allow the studies to identify neural pathways involved in reward processing, risk assessment, and financial decision-making. It improves our understanding of the economics of behavior and helps in designing more efficient incentive systems in many industries. The research on how the brain responds to finance thus connects the field of neuroscience with economics, providing insights in improving outcomes across a large variety of fields and making incentive design.

As reported by Iotzov et al. (2022), high levels of empathy lead to enhanced neural computation within the anterior insula, which is driven by financial incentives. In a study, Farrell et al. (2018) demonstrated that under financial incentives, during choice, the brain differentially alters processing of positive versus negative emotions. While performance-based incentives enhance the processing of negative emotions, fixed wage incentives reduce the responses to positive emotions. Hence, the presence of rewards based on performance makes an individual begin to process negative emotions more and thus can be said to be sensitive to setbacks or failures. On the contrary, fixed wage incentives are associated with decreased responses to positive affect, which could be indicative of a stabilization effect whereby the guarantee of earning a steady income dampens emotional highs that otherwise characterize uncertain outcomes. These results could thus show how different emotional reactions might be modulated by the structure of financial incentives. This also provide insight into how the motivational frameworks affect the decision-making processes within economic and organizational contexts.

San Martín et al. (2016) studied the event-related potentials assessed neural responses to monetary incentives, showing that the attentional bias toward reward-predicting cues is associated with successful economic decision-making. These results suggest that upon the presentation of cues predictive of possible rewards, the brain activity of participants is enhanced at sites associated with attentional processing. This reward-predicting cue attentional bias suggests a cognitive process that gives information about prospective gains priority in the making of economic decisions. These findings speak to how the mind explores and chooses which information to focus on within an economic context by highlighting a role for neural responses in guiding attentional processes during financial decision-making.

Camerer (2010) This study illustrated that the neural response, which served as a surrogate for intrinsic motivation, was actually demotivated by the removing of the financial incentives. The findings show that the elimination of monetary incentives results in lowered brain activity associated with motivation and reward processing. The presence or absence of an external reward may influence the brain's response to tasks or activities previously only intrinsically rewarded. According to this study, internal and external motivations are intertwined, and an understanding of behavioral outcomes, along with brain mechanisms, is really important in motivational psychology and economic decision-making.

Srivastava et al. (2019) The paper maps the human brain with respect to decision-making in higher cognitive domains using neuroimaging techniques and points out cognitive biases in the discussion of how neural processes affect financial behaviour. Specifically, the study sought to investigate how brain activity affects financial behaviour and leads to cognitive biases. The authors identify the neural level at which cognitive biases—like confirmation bias and framing effects—arise and interact with economic decision-making. Their findings offer an insight into how cognitive processes interact with environmental cues in the formation of financial behavior and highlight neural mechanisms involved in the construction of financial decisions.

It connected the neural roots of decision-making biases with their consequences for financial decision-making strategies to the disciplines of neuroscience and economics.

It is important to study the responses of the brain to financial incentives because of the complex interrelations of the neural systems of the brain with economic judgment. Different financial incentives seem to trigger different activations in the brain, which influence attentional biases, risk assessment, and emotional reactions. For instance, it is known that while performance-based incentives generally increase the sensitivity to adverse outcomes due to a prudent attitude toward potential losses, fixed wage incentives would attenuate emotional responses because income is more predictable. These results move to the foreground the interaction of incentive structures and brain mechanisms in influencing people's responses and behaviors in financial situations. Such understanding will allow researchers and policymakers to design incentive structures that are optimal in motivating best efforts, sharp decision-making, and the overall output of economic agents. Furthermore, examining neural responses of the brain to financial incentives can deepen understanding in neuroscience and economics by adding new dimensions to understand and influence human behavior relevant to financial decisions.

Ethical Considerations in Neurofinancial Research

Where the methods of research into human decision-making processes are sensitive and may have immense impacts on financial outcomes and welfare, the ethical concerns of neurofinancial research become very prominent. Indeed, when such invasive techniques as fMRI or EEG are used, a properly obtained informed consent regarding risks and benefits that participation may bring should be a top priority by researchers. One of the most important concerns in ensuring participants are assured of privacy and protection of rights. Among other ethical issues with neuromarketing are consent and privacy, coupled with potential misuse. According to Bansal et al. (2023), neuromarketing has in some way joined neuroscience and marketing with a quest on consumer's privacy and ethical boundaries. On the other hand, knowledge of consumer behavior through neuroscientific methods—such as functional magnetic resonance imaging —may be very interesting, but it needs access to the private brain data of individuals. Informed consent has to be obtained from individuals about the measurement and usage of brain responses for research or marketing purposes. Neurodata collection and storage give way to very serious privacy concerns and raise the need for strict protocols in protecting individuals' identities against unauthorized access. Transparency and autonomy come up, making one question the ethical boundaries in the manipulation of consumer decisions on the basis of subliminal neural responses. As Savciuc (2022) stated neurofinancial research raises ethical concerns similar to neuromarketing, with the potential to enter into the minds of subjects; it is, therefore, quite challenging to maintain proper ethical standards in data collection and analysis. Consent, privacy, possibility of manipulation—issues all raised by methods which probe people's mental thought processes and mechanisms of reaching decisions. Informed consent, participant privacy, and responsible application of neuroscientific findings pose clear ethical challenges that researchers have to negotiate. The potential of literally seeing inside people's heads by methods such as fMRI and EEG implies a heightened sensitivity to the ethical limits within research practices and their implications for human autonomy. Savciuc underscores the need for ethical practices in safeguarding integrity but also protecting research participants in the entire lifecycle—from data collection through analysis to dissemination—of neurofinancial studies.

According to Lyu & Mañas-Viniegra (2021), neurofinancial research exhibits ethical concerns due to issues of privacy violation and coercion. Neuromarketing studies have placed a high consideration on ethical dilemmas. It has pointed out that there is a basic essence for ethics research procedure. Similar to neuromarketing research, which is also faced with several moral dilemmas, neurofinancial research is authorized to access private brain information that could amount to the violation of the people's right to privacy..

Ugazio et al. (2022) studied that neurofinancial research findings provide evidence for different neural currencies for moral as well as financial values, showcasing ethical considerations to be taken into account in the review of how people make priority decisions and understand morals and finances. The interaction of ethical considerations and neural mechanisms is the key to understanding that calls for ethical guidelines in order to maintain responsible research practices while protecting participants' rights. In hopes of enhancing the quality of knowledge about how the brain represents moral and financial values, neurofinancial research engages the ethical components in adherence to moral principles within research.

Cherkaoui et al. (2021) indicated that the more the technology continues to evolve, the greater is the need for discussion and protective frameworks on the ethics of research on fMRI neurofeedback with regard to participant disclosure, information, potential risks, and societal impact. A number of important ethical issues that should be taken into consideration, such as open data from participants and the assessment and minimization of the risks arising from neurofeedback treatments, must be linked to the examination of the broader social impacts ensuing from the interventions. Functional magnetic resonance imaging-based real-time monitoring and manipulation of brain activity raise concerns about privacy and neural data handling. Because neurofeedback techniques raise a high potential for serious psychological and ethical consequences, strict informed consent and constant ethical monitoring should be exercised. The studies called for an ethical dialogue to be done ahead of time in fMRI neurofeedback research so that scientific enterprise moves forward without harming the well-being of the participants and society by setting out clear guidelines.

According to Stanton et al. (2017), neuromarketing and neurofinancial research raised ethical questions since the research focused on issues relating to consumer autonomy, privacy, and control. The fact that the risks can be reduced and society can be improved does not come without taking action. The applied neuroscience techniques, such as fMRI and EEG, reveal subconscious influences that might affect the privacy and autonomy of a person while making financial and consumer decisions. It will also be made free of ethical concerns through open procedures, informed consent, and maintenance of participants' privacy at all research stages. Apart from minimizing risks resulting from these technologies, researchers can contribute to the wellbeing of society with an advanced knowledge of marketing and finance by protecting the rights and autonomy of individuals, motivating ethical standards and regulatory frameworks.

Such transparency of the research methodology and appropriate reporting of the findings instill integrity and trust with the stakeholders and the scientific community. Moreover, while interpreting neuroscience data, scientists should be circumspect about various biases and avoid overgeneralizations that might further stereotype or misrepresent particular behaviors. If conducted within the ethical boundaries, neurofinancial research would responsibly increase our knowledge regarding economic behaviors while ensuring the safety and well-being of the respondents in studies.

Future Trends and Innovations in Neuromarketing and Finance

In the near future, finance and neuromarketing will be more intertwined through the integration of data analytics with the state-of-the-art technologies for enhancing the understanding of consumer behaviors and different decision-making processes. Neuromarketing strategies will bring in more accuracy at the table, as cutting-edge technologies like AI and machine learning will allow real-time analysis of complex neural data. Innovations in augmented reality and virtual reality may provide more natural, immersive contexts in which financial behaviors can be studied (Arora & Sharma, (2023); Arora (2024); Arora et.al., (2024). Improvements in wearables neurotechnology may facilitate easier and more persistent monitoring of brain activity to better understand investor and consumer behavior. While these trends raise new ethical questions about data privacy and manipulation potential, they will help produce more tailored and successful financial products and marketing strategies.

Neuromarketing and neurofinance are fast-growing fields with huge impacts across many industries. Neuromarketing has been bringing out new ways of better understanding consumer behavior ever since its emergence. Manoj & Ritika (2018). More particularly, neuromarketing made new approaches to comprehending consumer behaviour possible by utilising insights from this field of neuroscience. Using techniques such as fMRI, EEG, and eye tracking, authors are able to measure the subconscious reaction and emersion of the emotional response of consumers toward various marketing stimuli. Gaining a better understanding will let businesses come up with better marketing plans, make better product offerings for their customers, and improve the whole customer experience. The areas that are most likely to make a big difference in many industries—including retail and finance—will go on creating more individualized, data-driven ways of interacting with and grasping the customer as they develop.

Soto Arias & Quintero-Martínez (2019), analyzed that future developments in neuromarketing and finance will lie in the use of neuroscience as a means to predict consumer behavior and provide financial institutions with the competitive advantage of using state-of-the-art, yet not as widely applied marketing techniques. These new developments will comprise new forms of marketing strategies, such as sophisticated neuroimaging and biometric analysis, that are not so much applied in neuromarketing. Understanding neural and physiological responses of customers can help financial institutions tailor their services, products, and marketing strategies to the needs and preferences of consumers. This predictive capacity will ultimately fuel business growth and competitive positioning in the market in the last instance through enhanced possibilities for customer engagement that has been personalized.

Singhraul et al. (2022) have noticed that future directions in neuromarketing and finance pertain to the examination of brain activity vis-a-vis financial decisions, research enrichment in behavioural finance, and Neurofinance in mapping the brain to comprehend the individual investor's behaviour. It comprises increasing the research in Behavioural Finance with an elicit understanding regarding the behaviour of Individual Investors through Neuroscientific Techniques like Brain Mapping. Knowing how particular brain processes operate in influencing financial decision-making, researchers could tease out the cognitive and affective determinants of investment decisions. Such insight into the nature of investor behavior may allow for the development of highly specialized advice and finance strategies that more closely align with neural mechanisms underlying choice processes.

Future developments in the field of finance and neuromarketing will revolve around using digital marketing strategies to influence consumer behavior in a successful manner by utilizing Triple Brain for effectively targeted advertising, opine Halkiopoulos et al. (2023). The Triple Brain model focuses on these three aspects in customer decision-making: limbic, neocortex, and reptilian parts of the brain. It is through addressing these aspects that more compelling and effective marketing communications are delivered. This model, through fine-tuning content and design for appeal to the different regions of the brain, is used by the ZOPA Bank website, for example, for better user engagement and decision-making. It will enhance marketing strategies, become more focused and efficient at piquing consumer interest and influencing financial behavior.

Neuromarketing is a new and innovative approach toward market research that aims to take advantage of the recent developments in neuroscience to gain deeper insights into consumer behavior as studied by Madan & Popli (2016). This approach uses fMRI, EEG, biometric analysis, among other techniques, in carrying out examinations on how the brains of consumers respond to various marketing stimuli. That is the reason firms can create more efficient marketing campaigns and products if they understand the brain mechanisms underlying consumer preferences and choice. With an enhanced understanding of consumer behavior, this could prove to be a trending business practice in the future, where firms would be able to further adapt their products to client needs and raise the level of client satisfaction. According to Frederick (2022), the future of neuromarketing revolves around developing improved marketing strategies where consumer behavior could be understood with respect to ethical issues. Two of the potential advantages of finance combined with neuromarketing would be to maximize customer engagement and to facilitate decision-making. By using neuroscientific insights that make them more aware of the subconscious drivers of consumer behavior, financial institutions will be better equipped to create more efficient and personalized marketing campaigns. This will not only facilitate the marketing of financial products but the overall customer experience, matching services to underlying brain mechanisms that govern decision-making. But for the preservation of integrity and confidence in the industry, it is important to consider the ethical implications of these acts in a bid to ensure openness, privacy, and prudent use of customers' data. Del Mar Lozano Cortés & García García (2017) commented that in the future, neuromarketing will greatly increase and complement the traditional techniques mainly in the multinational companies. Ethics must be applied. Financial integration may be helpful in strategy design and consumer understanding. Ethical considerations are highlighted and there is a need to include ethics so that with an increased trend of neuromarketing, ethical principals may safeguard the consumer's privacy and consumer trust. They believe that this will refine the design of the strategies and enhance the understanding of consumers, particularly where such findings are combined with data from financial diagnostics. Businesses can use neuroscientific techniques, in addition to the conventional ones, to understand consumer behavior and hence build effective marketing strategies. This strategy will underline the role ethical frameworks can play in guiding responsible neuromarketing practice in business, apart from its potential to raise customer engagement.

López & Ramos-Galarza (2022) analyzed that one of the future trends of neuromarketing is integrating neuro-sensory elements with finance to develop personalized financial services based on the wishes of consumers. The other is using consumer desires about product attractiveness through an understanding of brain structures. At the same time, there is an upcoming trend which takes advantage of our knowledge about brain structures to fulfill our needs concerning the product's attractiveness. Knowing how the brain areas respond to different product features and to various marketing stimuli will help marketers develop products connected to customers more at a neurological level. Such deeper understanding allows creation of more aesthetic, functional, and emotionally appealing products, stirring customers' interest and creating brand loyalty.

These patterns underline how neuromarketing can be used to enhance financial services and tune strategies for product design in line with neural insights. The ethical considerations surrounding consent, privacy, and responsible use pertaining to neuroscientific data remain pivotal in these technologies' further development and integration into consumer-focused industries.

As examined by Klinčeková (2016), enhancements in the area of consumer neuroscience could bring advanced predictive abilities regarding the relating of behaviors with bio-measures in neuromarketing. Integration into finance may optimize decision-making processes. In the future, this may securely link consumer behaviors and biological measures with high predictability, hence enhancing predictive abilities in neuromarketing. The development makes use of neuroscientific techniques, including fMRI, EEG, and biometric analysis, to decode neural responses associated with customer decision-making processes. This is achieved through correlating these neural signals with behavioral patterns and physiological indicators. Therefore, marketers stand to understand consumer preferences and motivations and how they respond to various marketing stimuli. Most importantly, the insights could be applied in finance integration to achieve decision-making processes that are more optimized in financial institutions. Such knowledge on neural mechanisms underlying financial behaviors would facilitate the design of more tailored financial products and services, enhance risk assessment models, and improve customer engagement strategies. Developments such as these underscore the potential of consumer neuroscience to really change the face of marketing practices and financial decision-making, hence driving innovation and efficiency across industries.

Neuromarketing and finance will evolve further, thanks to trends and innovations that would redefine how businesses understand consumers and connect with them. As neuroscience approaches the mainstream, advanced consumer neuroscience in marketing and financial practices will improve predictive capabilities, personalize customer experiences, and optimize decision-making processes. This will likely involve techniques that will become central in the future for deciphering unconscious consumer preferences and behaviors, ultimately leading to more effective marketing strategies and tailored financial solutions. However, the ethical concerns related to data privacy, consent, and responsible use of neuroscientific data remain very important when these technologies further develop. Only by careful treading through these pitfalls can a business truly realize the potential for neuromarketing and neurofinance to fuel innovation, customer satisfaction, and long-term growth in today's fast-changing marketplace.

REFERENCES

Ahmed, R. R., Streimikiene, D., Channar, Z. A., Soomro, H. A., Streimikis, J., & Kyriakopoulos, G. L. (2022). The neuromarketing concept in artificial neural networks: A case of forecasting and simulation from the advertising industry. *Sustainability (Basel)*, 14(14), 8546. DOI: 10.3390/su14148546

Al Fauzi, A., & Widyarini, L. A. (2023). Neuromarketing: The Physiological Tools for Understanding Consumer Behaviour. [MJSSH]. *Malaysian Journal of Social Sciences and Humanities*, 8(1), e002081–e002081.

Al-Refai, N. M. A. (2021). The role of Neuromarketing in measuring response to marketing stimuli in advertising campaigns. *International Design Journal*, 11(4), 237–256. DOI: 10.21608/idj.2021.180927

Archana, C., & Mahajan, A. (2023). Neuro Marketing: An Astonishing Addition to the Marketing World. In *Digital Transformation for Business Sustainability: Trends, Challenges and Opportunities* (pp. 33–41). Springer Nature Singapore. DOI: 10.1007/978-981-99-7058-2_3

Arora, M. (2024). Metaverse Metamorphosis: Bridging the Gap Between Research Insights and Industry Applications. In *Research, Innovation, and Industry Impacts of the Metaverse* (pp. 275-286). IGI Global.

Arora, M., Kumar, J., Dhiman, V., Rathore, S., Singh, S., & Chandel, M. (2024). Enhancing Resilience via Exponential Technologies: Analysing Trends, Focus and Contributions. *Abhigyan*, 42(3), 271–290. DOI: 10.1177/09702385241256015

Arora, M., & Sharma, R. L. (2023). Artificial intelligence and big data: ontological and communicative perspectives in multi-sectoral scenarios of modern businesses. *foresight*, 25(1), 126-143.

Arrufat-Martín, S., Rubira-García, R., & Archilla-García, P. (2024). Marketing and neuromarketing applied to the business sector as an object of the academic field of communication in Spain: An approach to its study from books as bibliographic sources. *Journal of Communication and Information Sciences*, 29. Advance online publication. DOI: 10.35742/rcci.2024.29.e291

Asuquo-Utuk, K. (2023). Neuro-economics and Strategic Decisions: The Impact on Financial Sustainability of Multinational Enterprises. *Revista Científica Profundidad Construyendo Futuro*, 19(19), 88–101. DOI: 10.22463/24221783.4079

Babu, M., Suganya, G., Brintha, R., & Prahalathan, C. (2021). Neurotransmitters and Investment Decision Making: A Review. *Business Studies Journal,* 13(2).

Bansal, A., Bansal, R., Bansal, A., Kumar, M., & Kumar, P. (2023). Normative Concerns in Neuromarketing. In *Promoting Consumer Engagement Through Emotional Branding and Sensory Marketing* (pp. 234–243). IGI Global.

Bernard, C., Aquino, L. D. G., & Vanduffel, S. (2023). Optimal multivariate financial decision making. *European Journal of Operational Research*, 307(1), 468–483. DOI: 10.1016/j.ejor.2022.09.017

Bhardwaj, S., Kaushik, N., & Arora, M. (2024). Does Your Brain Have a Buy Button?: A Neuro Marketing Approach With Sensory Branding. In *Sensible Selling Through Sensory Neuromarketing* (pp. 210–229). IGI Global. DOI: 10.4018/979-8-3693-4236-7.ch011

Çakar, T., Son-Turan, S., Girişken, Y., Sayar, A., Ertuğrul, S., Filiz, G., & Tuna, E. (2024). Unlocking the neural mechanisms of consumer loan evaluations: An fNIRS and ML-based consumer neuroscience study. *Frontiers in Human Neuroscience*, 18, 1286918. DOI: 10.3389/fnhum.2024.1286918 PMID: 38375365

Camerer, C. F. (2010). Removing financial incentives demotivates the brain. *Proceedings of the National Academy of Sciences of the United States of America*, 107(49), 20849–20850. DOI: 10.1073/pnas.1016108107 PMID: 21115829

Cherkaoui, M., Rissman, J., Lau, H., & Hampson, M. (2021). Ethical considerations for fMRI neurofeedback. In *fMRI Neurofeedback* (pp. 315-331). Academic Press. DOI: 10.1016/B978-0-12-822421-2.00007-7

Chorvat, T. R. (2016). The Neuroeconomics of Financial Decisions and the Stochastic Discount Factor. *George Mason Law & Economics Research Paper*, (16-20).

Conejo, F., Khoo, C., Tanakinjal, G., & Yang, L. (2007). Neuromarketing: will it revolutionise business?.

Cordeiro, R., Reis, A., Ferreira, B. M., & Bacalhau, L. M. (2024). Neuromarketing: Decoding the Role of Emotions and Senses and Consumer Behavior. *Cognitive Behavioral Neuroscience in Organizational Settings*, 83-100.

da Silva, C. (2023). NEUROMARKETING: Its importance in understanding consumer behavior for sales boost. *Revista Interface Tecnológica*, 20(2), 446–457. DOI: 10.31510/infa.v20i2.1776

Dangwal, A., Bathla, D., Kukreti, M., Mehta, M., Chauhan, P., & Sarangal, R. (2023). Neuromarketing science: A road to a commercial start-up. In *Applications of Neuromarketing in the Metaverse* (pp. 223–232). IGI Global. DOI: 10.4018/978-1-6684-8150-9.ch017 del Mar Lozano Cortés, M., & García García, M. (2017). Neuromarketing: Current situation and future trends. *Media and Metamedia Management*, 373-380.

Farrell, A. M., Goh, J. O., & White, B. J. (2018). Financial incentives differentially regulate neural processing of positive and negative emotions during value-based decision-making. *Frontiers in Human Neuroscience*, 12, 58. DOI: 10.3389/fnhum.2018.00058 PMID: 29487519

Fingelkurts, A. A., Fingelkurts, A. A., & Neves, C. F. (2020). Neuro-assessment of leadership training. *Coaching (Abingdon, UK)*, 13(2), 107–145. DOI: 10.1080/17521882.2019.1619796

Frederick, D. P. (2022). Recent trends in neuro marketing–An exploratory study. [IJCSBE]. *International Journal of Case Studies in Business, IT, and Education*, 6(1), 38–60. DOI: 10.47992/IJCSBE.2581.6942.0148

Gill, R., & Singh, J. (2022). A study of neuromarketing techniques for proposing cost effective information driven framework for decision making. *Materials Today: Proceedings*, 49, 2969–2981. DOI: 10.1016/j.matpr.2020.08.730

Goswami, A., & Deshmukh, G. K. (2022). Neuromarketing: Emerging Trend in Consumer Behavior. *Advances in Marketing, Customer Relationship Management, and E-Services*, 5(0), 79–87. DOI: 10.4018/978-1-6684-4496-2.ch005

Halkiopoulos, C., Antonopoulou, H., & Stiliadi, S. (2023). Neuroscientific Perspectives in Digital Marketing. https://doi.org/DOI: 10.31219/osf.io/bs73w

Huang, A. H., & You, H. (2023). Artificial intelligence in financial decision-making. In *Handbook of Financial Decision Making* (pp. 315–335). Edward Elgar Publishing. DOI: 10.4337/9781802204179.00029

Iotzov, V., Saulin, A., Kaiser, J., Han, S., & Hein, G. (2022). Financial incentives facilitate stronger neural computation of prosocial decisions in lower empathic adult females. *Social Neuroscience*, 17(5), 441–461. DOI: 10.1080/17470919.2022.2115550 PMID: 36064327

Jain, N. (2022). Understanding the art and science of new-age advertising: A neuromarketing perspective. *The Business and Management Review*, 13(3).

Jain, R., & Singh, A. (2023). Prediction of Customer Satisfaction in E-banking Services Through Neural Network Approach. In *International Conference on Data Science and Big Data Analysis* (pp. 25-32). Singapore: Springer Nature Singapore.

Khondakar, M. F. K., Sarowar, M. H., Chowdhury, M. H., Majumder, S., Hossain, M. A., Dewan, M. A. A., & Hossain, Q. D. (2024). A systematic review on EEG-based neuromarketing: Recent trends and analyzing techniques. *Brain Informatics*, 11(1), 17. DOI: 10.1186/s40708-024-00229-8 PMID: 38837089

Klinčeková, S. (2016). Neuromarketing–research and prediction of the future. *International Journal of Management Science and Business Administration*, 2(2), 53–57.

Lee, N., Broderick, A. J., & Chamberlain, L. (2007). What is 'neuromarketing'? A discussion and agenda for future research. *International Journal of Psychophysiology*, 63(2), 199–204. DOI: 10.1016/j.ijpsycho.2006.03.007 PMID: 16769143

Li, B., Wang, Y., Wang, K., & Zhang, D. (2022). A Review of Data-Driven Techniques for Neuromarketing. In *International Workshop of Advanced Manufacturing and Automation* (pp. 748-755). Singapore: Springer Nature Singapore.

López, M. J., & Ramos-Galarza, C. (2022). Neuromarketing: Current applications in favor of consumerism. *Marketing and Smart Technologies: Proceedings of ICMarkTech 2021, Volume* 1, 389-394.

Lyu, D., & Mañas-Viniegra, L. (2021). Ethical issues in neuromarketing research: A literature review. *Vivat Academia*, 154, 263–283. DOI: 10.15178/va.2021.154.e1351

Madan, C. R. (2010). Neuromarketing: The next step in market research? *Eureka (Asunción)*, 1(1), 34–42. DOI: 10.29173/eureka7786

Madan, M., & Popli, A. (2016). A study on Neuromarketing as emerging innovative market research strategy: An interpretive structural model approach. *IOSR Journal of Business and Management*, 2(2), 18–30. DOI: 10.9790/487X-15010020218-30

Majer, P., Mohr, P. N., Heekeren, H. R., & Härdle, W. K. (2016). Portfolio decisions and brain reactions via the CEAD method. *Psychometrika*, 81(3), 881–903. DOI: 10.1007/s11336-015-9441-5 PMID: 25670029

Malik, R., Malhan, S., & Arora, M. (2024). (Eds.). (2024). *Sensible Selling Through Sensory Neuromarketing* (pp. 144-163). IGI Global.

Manoj, M. S., & Ritika, S. (2018). Application of neuromarketing tools in higher education institutions: Towards innovations, marketing effectiveness and student driven strategies in the future condition. *Journal of Emerging Technologies and Innovative Research*, 5, 1–5.

Mashrur, F. R., Rahman, K. M., Miya, M. T. I., Vaidyanathan, R., Anwar, S. F., Sarker, F., & Mamun, K. A. (2024). Intelligent neuromarketing framework for consumers' preference prediction from electroencephalography signals and eye tracking. *Journal of Consumer Behaviour*, 23(3), 1146–1157. DOI: 10.1002/cb.2253

Mateu, G., Monzani, L., & Navarro, R. M. (2018). The role of the brain in financial decisions: A viewpoint on neuroeconomics. *Mètode Science Studies Journal*, 8, 6–15. DOI: 10.7203/metode.0.6923

Megías, A., Navas, J. F., Petrova, D., Candido, A., Maldonado, A., Garcia-Retamero, R., & Catena, A. (2015). Neural mechanisms underlying urgent and evaluative behaviors: An fMRI study on the interaction of automatic and controlled processes. *Human Brain Mapping*, 36(8), 2853–2864. DOI: 10.1002/hbm.22812 PMID: 25879953

Millagala, K., & Gunasinghe, N. (2024). Neuromarketing as a Digital Marketing Strategy to Unravel the Evolution of Marketing Communication. In *Applying Business Intelligence and Innovation to Entrepreneurship* (pp. 81–105). IGI Global. DOI: 10.4018/979-8-3693-1846-1.ch005

Mogaji, E. (2018). *Emotional appeals in advertising banking services*. Emerald Publishing Limited. DOI: 10.1108/9781787562998

Nepal, R., Rajopadhyay, P., Rajopadhyay, U., & Bhattarai, U. (2023). Interplay of Investor Cognition, Financial Literacy, and Neuroplasticity in Investment Decision Making: A Study of Nepalese Investors. *Journal of Business and Social Sciences Research*, 8(2), 51–76. DOI: 10.3126/jbssr.v8i2.62133

Panneerselvam, T., & Joe Arun, C. (2022). Bias-driven marketing that instigates pledging to a crowdfunding campaign: An experimental consideration of behavioral anomalies. *International Journal of Consumer Studies*, 46(6), 2404–2428. DOI: 10.1111/ijcs.12795

Park, S. H., Deng, E. Z., Baker, A. K., MacNiven, K. H., Knutson, B., & Martucci, K. T. (2022). Replication of neural responses to monetary incentives and exploration of reward-influenced network connectivity in fibromyalgia. *Neuroimage. Reports*, 2(4), 100147. DOI: 10.1016/j.ynirp.2022.100147 PMID: 36618964

Piwowarski, M., Biercewicz, K., & Borawski, M. (2019). Methods of Examining the Neuronal Bases of Financial Decisions. In *Effective Investments on Capital Markets: 10th Capital Market Effective Investments Conference (CMEI 2018)* (pp. 351-368). Springer International Publishing. DOI: 10.1007/978-3-030-21274-2_24

Razbadauskaitė-Venskė, I. (2024). Neuromarketing: a tool to understand consumer behaviour. *Regional formation and development studies.*, (1), 101-109.

Ru, H., & Schoar, A. (2016). Do credit card companies screen for behavioral biases? (No. w22360). National Bureau of Economic Research. DOI: 10.3386/w22360

San Martín, R., Appelbaum, L. G., Huettel, S. A., & Woldorff, M. G. (2016). Cortical brain activity reflecting attentional biasing toward reward-predicting cues covaries with economic decision-making performance. *Cerebral Cortex (New York, N.Y.)*, 26(1), 1–11. DOI: 10.1093/cercor/bhu160 PMID: 25139941

Savciuc, O. (2022). Neuromarketing and ethical aspects in conducting market research.

Singh, S., & Gupta, R. (2024). Financial Decision-Making. In *Clinical Laboratory Management* (pp. 53–55). Springer Nature Switzerland.

Singhraul, B. P., & Batwe, Y. (2022). Neurofinance: The new world of finance based on human psychology and individual investment behaviour. *International Journal of Health Sciences*, 6(S9), 2012–2024. DOI: 10.53730/ijhs.v6nS9.12775

Soto Arias, J. A., & Quintero-Martínez, D. M. (2019). *Neuromarketing: A competitive advantage for the financial sector financial sector*. Francisco de Paula Santander University.

Srivastava, M., Sharma, G. D., & Srivastava, A. K. (2019). Human brain and financial behavior: A neurofinance perspective. *International Journal of Ethics and Systems*, 35(4), 485–503. DOI: 10.1108/IJOES-02-2019-0036

Stanton, S. J., Sinnott-Armstrong, W., & Huettel, S. A. (2017). Neuromarketing: Ethical implications of its use and potential misuse. *Journal of Business Ethics*, 144(4), 799–811. DOI: 10.1007/s10551-016-3059-0

Takemura, K., & Takemura, K. (2021). Decision-Making Process and Neuroeconomics. *Behavioral Decision Theory: Psychological and Mathematical Descriptions of Human Choice Behavior*, 193-207.

Taneja, B., Shukla, P., & Arora, M. (2024). Sensible Selling Through Sensory Neuromarketing: Enhancing Sales Effectiveness. In *Sensible Selling Through Sensory Neuromarketing* (pp. 164-183). IGI Global.

Tolzmann, G. C., Vincent, R. J., & Lewis, M. R. (2024). Costs, budgeting, and financial decision making. *Clinical Laboratory Management*, 416-441.

Ugazio, G., Grueschow, M., Polania, R., Lamm, C., Tobler, P., & Ruff, C. (2022). Neuro-computational foundations of moral preferences. *Social Cognitive and Affective Neuroscience*, 17(3), 253–265. DOI: 10.1093/scan/nsab100 PMID: 34508645

Vasile, D., & Sebastian, T. C. (2007). Neurofinance–getting an insight into the trader's mind. *Neuroscience*, 27(31), 8159–8160.

Velecela, P. A. C., Vallejo, J. I. G., & Jara, B. D. V. (2017). Personal finance: The influence of age in making financial decisions. *Revista Killkana Sociales*, 1(3), 81–88. DOI: 10.26871/killkana_social.v1i3.66

Vuković, D. (2024). Ethical issues in the application of neuromarketing research. *MAP Social Sciences*, 4(1), 67–81. DOI: 10.53880/2744-2454.2023.4.67

Zeng, I. M., & Marques, J. A. L. (2023, November). Neuromarketing: Evaluating Consumer Emotions and Preferences to Improve Business Marketing Management. In *18th European Conference on Management, Leadership and Governance*. Academic Conferences and publishing limited. DOI: 10.34190/ecmlg.19.1.1876

Zhou, M. (2024). *How to Apply Neuromarketing and Customers' Psychology Biases to a Digital Startup's Brand (Version 1)*. Toronto Metropolitan University., DOI: 10.32920/25164605.v1

Chapter 6
Data Analysis of Consumer Responses in India Using Zen Z

Rishi Prakash Shukla
https://orcid.org/0000-0003-0854-7302
Jaipuria Institute of Management, India

Priya Shukla
Oriental University, Indore, India

Archna Singh
https://orcid.org/0000-0002-1471-5942
D.Y. Patil International University, India

Vilas Nair
SCMS School of Technology and Management, India

Smriti Verma
https://orcid.org/0000-0002-8339-1670
Yeshwantrao Chavan College of Engineering, Nagpur, India

ABSTRACT

This chapter explores the application of neuropricing strategies and their impact on consumer behavior, with a specific focus on the Indian market. Neuropricing integrates principles from neuroscience and psychology to optimize pricing by influencing subconscious decision-making processes. Using data collected from 390 online respondents via the Zen Z platform, this study examines how sensory marketing, emotional priming, and cognitive biases like anchoring and price framing enhance perceived value. Our findings demonstrate that neuropricing significantly increases

DOI: 10.4018/979-8-3693-9351-2.ch006

perceived value compared to traditional pricing strategies, providing actionable insights for businesses aiming to refine their pricing tactics through neuroscientific approaches. Keywords: neuropricing, consumer behavior, perceived value, sensory marketing, emotional priming, anchoring bias, price framing.

INTRODUCTION

In today's technology-driven world, the lines between psychology, economics, and marketing have become increasingly blurred. Traditional marketing communication is rapidly evolving under the influence of artificial intelligence (AI), big data, and the digital economy (Arora, 2020). The explosion of these technologies has led to the development of new marketing strategies that tap into consumers' subconscious minds. Among these strategies, neuropricing—the application of neuroscience principles to pricing strategies—stands out as a powerful tool for influencing consumer decisions at a deeper level (Shaw & Bagozzi, (2018); Bhardwaj, Kaushik, & Arora (2024); Taneja, Shukla & Arora (2024); Malik, Malhan & Arora (2024). (Eds.). (2024)). The Indian market, with its vast and heterogeneous consumer base, provides a fertile ground for the application of these techniques. India's middle class is growing rapidly, and consumer behavior is becoming more sophisticated as the economy opens up to global trade and technology (Kumar, Arora, & Erkol Bayram, 2024). In this context, businesses are seeking new ways to optimize pricing strategies that align with the cognitive and emotional processes of Indian consumers. Neuropricing, which merges insights from psychology, behavioral economics, and neuroscience, offers a novel approach to achieving this objective.

Defining Neuropricing

Neuropricing moves beyond conventional pricing mechanisms that focus solely on cost, demand, or competitive factors. Instead, it seeks to understand the subconscious drivers of consumer behavior, which are often not fully rational or predictable (Briesemeister et al., 2019). Research in neuroscience has revealed that the human brain does not evaluate prices in isolation but interprets them through various cognitive and emotional lenses. By tapping into these lenses, neuropricing influences consumers' perception of value and their subsequent purchasing decisions.

For example, neuropricing can capitalize on biases such as the left-digit effect, where a price like 999.99 is perceived as significantly cheaper than 1,000, even though the actual difference is negligible (Shaw & Bagozzi, 2018). By leveraging such biases, businesses can subtly guide consumers toward making a purchase. Similarly, using higher original prices next to discounted prices creates an impression of value and urgency, compelling consumers to act quickly.

The Need for Neuropricing in the Indian Context

The Indian retail landscape is characterized by diversity in terms of income, culture, and consumer preferences. As India's economy grows and disposable incomes rise, consumer decision-making is becoming more complex (Dhiman & Arora, 2024). Increasing access to the internet and digital services has expanded the scope of online retail, but it has also led to a more fragmented consumer base where one-size-fits-all pricing strategies are no longer effective. Given these developments, the need for data-driven and personalized pricing strategies that address both the conscious and subconscious needs of Indian consumers is more critical than ever. Neuropricing, which combines big data analytics and AI with insights from consumer psychology, offers a sophisticated framework for tackling these challenges. The goal is not merely to optimize prices but to create pricing strategies that resonate emotionally with consumers, leading to greater satisfaction, loyalty, and, ultimately, higher sales (Arora, 2023).

This paper seeks to explore the application of neuropricing in the Indian market by analyzing its psychological underpinnings and its relevance to consumer behavior. It also examines how AI and big data can enhance neuropricing strategies to create highly personalized and effective marketing campaigns.

LITERATURE REVIEW

The concept of neuropricing draws from several theoretical foundations, including neuroscience, behavioral economics, and consumer psychology. Each of these disciplines offers unique insights into how consumers perceive prices and how businesses can influence those perceptions to their advantage. In this literature review, we will explore these disciplines, their relevance to pricing strategies, and how they converge within the framework of neuropricing.

1. Neuroscience in Pricing: The Cognitive Foundations

Neuroscience has long been concerned with understanding how the brain processes information, makes decisions, and reacts to various stimuli. Recent advancements in neuroimaging technologies, such as functional magnetic resonance imaging (fMRI) and electroencephalography (EEG), have allowed researchers to observe brain activity in real time, providing critical insights into consumer behavior (Briesemeister et al.,

2019). One of the key findings from this research is that price perception is not a purely rational process. Instead, it is heavily influenced by emotional and cognitive responses, many of which occur at the subconscious level (Shaw & Bagozzi, 2018). For example, the amygdala, a part of the brain involved in processing emotions, often reacts to pricing stimuli before the individual becomes consciously aware of the price. This suggests that consumers may experience emotional responses to prices even when they believe they are making rational decisions. Neuroscience also reveals the impact of sensory inputs on price perception. Visual cues, such as the font size and color of price tags, can significantly affect how consumers interpret prices (Arora, 2024). Bright, bold prices may convey urgency, while soft colors and smaller fonts may suggest exclusivity and luxury. The combination of these sensory inputs triggers specific neural pathways that influence how consumers evaluate the attractiveness and fairness of a price. Moreover, neurosensory experiences—such as the overall ambiance of a store—can alter price perception. For instance, a well-lit store with soothing background music might make consumers feel more comfortable, leading them to perceive higher prices as justified by the pleasant shopping experience. In contrast, a cluttered or noisy environment might detract from the perceived value of even reasonably priced goods (Casado-Aranda et al., 2018). These insights from neuroscience highlight the importance of understanding the cognitive and emotional processes that underlie price perception. By leveraging these processes, businesses can create pricing strategies that resonate more deeply with consumers, increasing the likelihood of a purchase.

2. Behavioral Economics: The Psychological Biases Driving Consumer Decisions

Behavioral economics, a field pioneered by psychologists such as Daniel Kahneman and Amos Tversky, challenges the traditional assumption of rational decision-making in economics. Instead, behavioral economics proposes that consumers are subject to various cognitive biases that can lead to irrational choices, particularly in pricing contexts (Arora & Sharma, 2023). One of the most well-known concepts in behavioral economics is prospect theory, which posits that people evaluate potential losses and gains relative to a reference point rather than in absolute terms. For example, consumers are more sensitive to losses than to equivalent gains, a phenomenon known as loss aversion (Kahneman & Tversky, 1979). This insight is crucial for neuropricing strategies, as businesses can frame prices in ways that minimize perceived losses or emphasize potential gains (Shukla & Taneja, 2024).

An example of this in action is framing discounts to exploit loss aversion. If a product is originally priced at 1,500 and discounted to 1,000, consumers may perceive this as a significant gain. However, if the product is consistently priced at ₹1,000, the perceived value diminishes, even though the final price is the same. This is because the consumer's reference point has shifted from ₹1,500 to ₹1,000. Neuropricing leverages this cognitive bias by presenting discounts and offers in ways that make the consumer feel like they are avoiding a loss or securing a significant gain (Casado-Aranda et al., 2018). Anchoring is another cognitive bias that plays a crucial role in pricing. Anchoring occurs when an initial piece of information (such as a high original price) influences subsequent judgments (Heilbronner et al., 2009). In pricing, businesses often use high anchor prices to make subsequent lower prices seem more attractive. For example, displaying an original price of ₹2,000 next to a discounted price of ₹1,200 creates the perception of a good deal, even if the actual value of the product is closer to ₹1,200. This bias is especially potent in Indian markets, where consumers are highly sensitive to discounts and offers (Dhiman & Arora, 2024). By understanding these biases, businesses can tailor their pricing strategies to better align with consumers' cognitive processes. Neuropricing combines these principles of behavioral economics with insights from neuroscience to create pricing strategies that effectively influence consumer behavior.

3. Consumer Psychology: The Role of Emotions and Subconscious Triggers

In addition to the cognitive biases discussed in behavioral economics, consumer psychology highlights the role of emotions and subconscious triggers in decision-making. Research shows that emotions play a pivotal role in how consumers evaluate products, brands, and prices (Zeithaml et al., 1996). Positive emotions such as happiness, excitement, and satisfaction can enhance a consumer's perception of a product's value, leading to a higher willingness to pay. One common psychological trigger used in neuropricing is charm pricing, where prices end in '.99' rather than being rounded up (e.g., ₹499.99 vs. ₹500). This technique exploits the left-digit effect, wherein the brain perceives the price as being significantly lower than it actually is because it focuses more on the leftmost digits (Shaw & Bagozzi, 2018). Numerous studies have shown that charm pricing leads to higher sales volumes, particularly in price-sensitive markets like India (Arora, 2020). Contextual influences also play a significant role in consumer psychology. The environment in which a price is presented can significantly impact how consumers perceive it. For example, a product placed in a high-end store may be perceived as more valuable than the same product in a discount store, even if the price is identical (Jerath & Zhang, 2010). This phenomenon is closely related to the concept of priming, where exposure to certain stimuli influences subsequent behavior. In the context of neuropricing, businesses can prime consumers to perceive higher prices as justified by creating an environment that signals exclusivity or luxury (Arora, 2023). By integrating these psychological insights into pricing strategies, neuropricing enables businesses to tap into the subconscious triggers that drive consumer behavior. This approach allows businesses to create pricing strategies that not only optimize revenue but also enhance consumer satisfaction and loyalty.

4. The Role of AI and Big Data in Enhancing Neuropricing

The advent of AI and big data has revolutionized how businesses understand and influence consumer behavior. These technologies provide the tools necessary to implement neuropricing strategies on a large scale by analyzing vast amounts of data to predict consumer responses to different pricing stimuli (Arora & Sharma, 2023).

AI-driven platforms can dynamically adjust prices in real-time based on factors such as consumer behavior, market trends, and competitive pricing. For example, dynamic pricing algorithms used by online retailers like Amazon adjust prices based on demand, consumer browsing history, and competitor prices (Dhiman & Arora, 2024). These algorithms not only optimize revenue but also enhance the consumer experience by presenting personalized prices that are more likely to resonate with individual preferences. In the context of neuropricing, AI can help businesses refine their pricing strategies by continuously learning from consumer interactions. By analyzing how consumers respond to different price points, discounts, and sensory cues, AI systems can identify the most effective pricing strategies for different consumer segments (Arora, 2023). This level of personalization is particularly valuable in diverse markets like India, where consumer preferences vary significantly across regions, income levels, and cultural backgrounds. The integration of AI with neuropricing creates a powerful synergy that allows businesses to optimize their pricing strategies in real time, based on both cognitive and emotional factors. This approach not only maximizes revenue but also enhances consumer satisfaction by delivering prices that align with their subconscious desires and preferences. The literature on neuropricing highlights its potential to revolutionize how businesses set prices by tapping into the cognitive and emotional drivers of consumer behavior. By integrating insights from neuroscience, behavioral economics, and consumer psychology, neuropricing offers a sophisticated framework for creating pricing strategies that resonate deeply with consumers. The role of AI and big data further enhances the effectiveness of neuropricing by enabling personalized, data-driven approaches that adapt to the needs of individual consumers.

Neuropricing, a relatively new frontier in marketing, revolves around the application of neuroscience principles to pricing strategies (Briesemeister et al., 2019). It goes beyond traditional market research by delving into the subconscious processes that drive consumer behavior(Briesemeister et al., 2019; Casado-Aranda et al., 2018; Shaw & Bagozzi, 2018). By understanding how sensory stimuli and emotional triggers influence decision-making, companies like SmartTech can optimize their pricing to not only attract but also retain customers.

In today's hyper-competitive marketplace, where consumers are bombarded with choices and information, the ability to stand out and resonate with potential buyers is paramount. Neuropricing offers a sophisticated approach to pricing that goes beyond mere numbers. It acknowledges that consumer decisions are often irrational and emotionally driven, influenced by factors ranging from visual aesthetics to social perceptions.

For companies like SmartTech, mastering neuropricing means deciphering the neural codes that underpin consumer preferences. By leveraging insights from neuroscience, psychology, and behavioral economics, they can tailor pricing strategies that resonate on a subconscious level (Heilbronner et al., 2009; Shaw & Bagozzi, 2018; Vecchiato et al., 2013). This approach isn't just about setting prices; it's about crafting experiences that speak directly to consumers' deeper desires and aspirations.

Neuropricing is an innovative approach(Shaw & Bagozzi, 2018) that blends insights from neuroscience with traditional pricing strategies(Briesemeister et al., 2019) to understand and influence consumer behaviour. It goes beyond conventional pricing methods by exploring the cognitive and emotional processes that affect how consumers perceive and respond to prices. Neuropricing involves the study of brain activity and psychological responses to different pricing stimuli, using this knowledge to set prices that are perceived as fair, attractive, and value driven. The human brain processes prices in ways that are not always rational. For instance, a price ending in '.99' is often perceived as significantly lower than a rounded price, a phenomenon known as the "left-digit effect." Similarly, the presentation of a higher original price next to a discounted price can create a sense of urgency and value, driving consumers to make a purchase. By leveraging these and other cognitive biases, neuropricing aims to optimize pricing strategies to enhance consumer engagement and boost sales.

Neuropricing's relevance to consumer behaviour lies in its ability to tap into the subconscious factors that drive purchasing decisions. Traditional pricing strategies primarily focus on external factors such as market trends, competition, and production costs. In contrast, neuropricing delves into the internal cognitive and emotional processes that influence how consumers perceive prices. This approach allows businesses to create pricing strategies that resonate more deeply with consumers, leading to higher satisfaction and loyalty.

Relevance and Significance

The significance of this study lies in its potential to bridge the gap between academic research and practical marketing applications. While neuropricing is a relatively new field, its implications for consumer behavior and marketing strategies are profound. By providing empirical evidence on the effectiveness of neuropricing strategies in the Indian context, this study aims to contribute to both theoretical and practical advancements in neuromarketing.

For businesses operating in India, the findings of this study can offer valuable insights into how to optimize pricing strategies to better align with consumer perceptions and preferences. In a competitive market where consumers are constantly bombarded with choices, the ability to influence price perception can be a key differentiator. Neuropricing offers a way to create more compelling pricing strategies that not only attract consumers but also enhance their overall satisfaction and loyalty.

Furthermore, the study's emphasis on the Indian market addresses a significant gap in the existing literature. While much of the research on neuropricing has been conducted in Western contexts, there is a growing need to understand how these strategies apply in different cultural and economic environments. By focusing on India, this study provides a unique perspective on the global applicability of neuropricing principles.

In conclusion, neuropricing represents a cutting-edge approach to pricing strategy that leverages insights from neuroscience to understand and influence consumer behavior. This study aims to explore the impact of neuropricing in the Indian market, providing empirical evidence on how different strategies affect consumer perceptions and purchasing decisions. By using the Zen Z platform to gather and analyze data from a diverse sample of respondents, the study seeks to offer valuable insights for marketers and contribute to the broader field of neuromarketing. As businesses navigate the complexities of the modern market, neuropricing presents an innovative tool for creating more effective and resonant pricing strategies.

Objective of the Study

The primary objective of this study is to explore the impact of neuropricing strategies on consumer behavior in the Indian market. By analysing data collected from 390 respondents using the Zen Z platform, this chapter aims to provide empirical insights into how neuropricing influences consumer perceptions and purchasing decisions. The study seeks to achieve the following specific goals:

1. Understand the Principles of Neuropricing: To provide a comprehensive overview of the key concepts and principles underpinning neuropricing, including cognitive biases, emotional responses, and psychological triggers.
2. Evaluate the Effectiveness of Neuropricing Strategies: To assess the impact of different neuropricing techniques on consumer behaviour, such as charm pricing, decoy pricing, and context-based pricing.
3. Analyze Consumer Responses in the Indian Market: To examine the specific ways in which Indian consumers respond to neuropricing strategies, considering cultural, economic, and demographic factors.
4. Provide Practical Insights for Marketers: To offer actionable recommendations for businesses looking to implement neuropricing strategies, drawing on the findings from the data analysis.

By achieving these goals, the study aims to contribute to the growing body of knowledge in neuromarketing and provide valuable insights for marketers seeking to optimize their pricing strategies.

THEORETICAL BACKGROUND

Neurosensory Principles

Neuropricing relies heavily on neurosensory principles, which explore how the human brain processes sensory information and influences decision-making(Hunt, 1983; Shaw & Bagozzi, 2018). At its core, neurosensory principles recognize that much of consumer behavior is driven by subconscious responses to stimuli rather than rational, conscious thought. These principles draw from neuroscience research that reveals how different parts of the brain respond to sensory inputs, such as visual cues, tactile sensations, and auditory signals.

For example, studies in neurobiology have shown that visual stimuli can evoke emotional responses that impact consumer perceptions of value and quality. The brain's visual cortex processes images rapidly, influencing judgments about product attributes like aesthetics and presentation. In the context of pricing, subtle changes in visual elements—such as font size, color schemes, and the placement of price tags—can significantly alter how consumers perceive the value of a product.

Moreover, neurosensory principles extend beyond visual cues to encompass other sensory modalities, such as taste, smell, and touch. Research indicates that multisensory experiences can enhance consumer satisfaction and willingness to pay higher prices. For instance, a restaurant that enhances the ambiance with soft lighting, soothing music, and aromatic scents may justify higher menu prices by creating a more pleasurable dining experience.

In essence, neurosensory principles highlight the importance of understanding how sensory inputs interact with cognitive processes to shape consumer preferences and behaviors. By leveraging this understanding, marketers can design pricing strategies that resonate more deeply with consumers' subconscious desires and perceptions of value.

Behavioral Economics

Neuropricing intersects significantly with theories of behavioral economics, which explore how psychological factors influence economic decision-making. Behavioral economics challenges the traditional economic assumption of rational decision-making by highlighting cognitive biases and heuristics that lead individuals to make predictable and sometimes irrational choices (Choi & Rifon, 2012).

One key concept in behavioral economics relevant to neuropricing is prospect theory, proposed by Daniel Kahneman and Amos Tversky. Prospect theory suggests that individuals evaluate potential losses and gains relative to a reference point (e.g., an original price) rather than in absolute terms. This theory explains phenomena such as loss aversion, where individuals are more sensitive to losses than equivalent gains, and the endowment effect, where people assign higher value to items, they already possess.

In the context of neuropricing, prospect theory informs strategies such as framing and context-based pricing(Fleck et al., 2012). Framing involves presenting prices in a way that manipulates the reference point against which consumers evaluate them. For example, a product originally priced at 500 but discounted to 400 is perceived as a better deal than a product consistently priced at 400. Context-based pricing considers the environment or situation in which prices are presented, exploiting situational influences on consumer decision-making.

Behavioral economics also sheds light on pricing strategies like anchoring, where an initial piece of information (e.g., a high original price) influences subsequent judgments. By anchoring consumers' expectations with a higher price, businesses can make subsequent prices seem more reasonable or attractive, thus influencing purchase decisions.

Overall, behavioral economics provides a theoretical framework for understanding the cognitive biases and heuristics that neuropricing strategies leverage to influence consumer behavior. By incorporating insights from behavioral economics, businesses can design more effective pricing strategies that align with consumers' cognitive processes and decision-making tendencies.

Consumer Decision-Making

Consumer decision-making is heavily influenced by sensory stimuli, which play a crucial role in shaping perceptions of product value and attractiveness. Sensory inputs activate neural pathways in the brain that evoke emotional responses and influence cognitive judgments about products and prices (Fu et al., 2010; Zeithaml et al., 1996).

Visual stimuli, such as product packaging, branding, and price displays, are particularly impactful in consumer decision-making(Jerath & Zhang, 2010; Varman & Belk, 2012; Vivek et al., 2014; Zhang et al., 2010). The human brain processes visual information rapidly and instinctively, often forming initial impressions of a product's quality and value based on visual cues alone. For example, a product with sleek, modern packaging may be perceived as more premium and therefore justify a higher price in consumers' minds.

Beyond visual cues, other sensory modalities also contribute to consumer perceptions of pricing (Shukla & Taneja, 2024). Tactile sensations, such as the texture of a product or the smoothness of a price tag, can subtly influence judgments about quality and craftsmanship. Similarly, auditory stimuli, such as background music in a retail environment, can affect consumers' mood and perception of a product's value.

Moreover, sensory stimuli interact with psychological factors, such as expectations, emotions, and social influences, to shape consumer decisions. For instance, consumers may associate certain scents or sounds with luxury or exclusivity, influencing their willingness to pay higher prices. The context in which prices are presented also matters; a product displayed in an upscale boutique is likely to be perceived as more valuable than the same product in a discount store.

Neuropricing strategies capitalize on these insights by carefully manipulating sensory stimuli to enhance consumer perceptions of value and justify pricing decisions (King & Auschaitrakul, 2021). By understanding how sensory inputs influence consumer decision-making, businesses can optimize pricing strategies to appeal to consumers' subconscious desires and maximize sales potential (Taneja et al., 2024).

In summary, neuropricing integrates neurosensory principles, behavioral economics theories, and insights into consumer decision-making to craft pricing strategies that resonate with consumers on a subconscious level. By leveraging these insights, businesses can enhance consumer perceptions of value, drive purchase decisions, and ultimately achieve competitive advantage in the marketplace.

DESIGN AND METHODOLOGY

Research Design

This study is set against the backdrop of a rapidly evolving Indian market, characterized by a diverse and dynamic consumer base. India's economic growth, rising disposable incomes, and increasing internet penetration have transformed the retail landscape, presenting both opportunities and challenges for businesses. In this context, understanding consumer behavior is crucial for developing effective marketing strategies. The data for this study was collected using the Zen Z platform, a sophisticated tool that enables researchers to gather and analyze consumer responses with precision. The platform's capabilities include advanced data analytics, real-time feedback collection, and the ability to track various cognitive and emotional responses to pricing stimuli. By leveraging the Zen Z platform, this study aims to capture nuanced insights into how Indian consumers perceive and react to different pricing strategies.

India's diverse cultural and economic landscape adds complexity to consumer behavior analysis. Factors such as regional differences, income disparities, and varying levels of digital literacy influence how consumers interact with pricing strategies. For example, urban consumers with higher disposable incomes might respond differently to premium pricing strategies compared to rural consumers who are more price-sensitive. Additionally, cultural factors such as the value placed on discounts and the perception of quality associated with higher prices can vary significantly across different consumer segments. Given these complexities, the study focuses on a broad cross-section of the Indian population, aiming to capture a wide range of consumer responses. The 390 respondents were selected to represent various demographic segments, including different age groups, income levels, and geographic regions. This diverse sample ensures that the findings provide a comprehensive understanding of how neuropricing impacts consumer behavior across the Indian market.

In analyzing the data, the study employs a combination of quantitative and qualitative methods. Quantitative analysis involves statistical techniques to identify patterns and correlations in consumer responses, while qualitative analysis explores the underlying cognitive and emotional processes driving these responses. By integrating both approaches, the study aims to provide a holistic understanding of neuropricing's impact.This study employs a quantitative research design to investigate the impact of neuropricing strategies on consumer behavior in the Indian market. The research design is structured to gather and analyze data from 390 respondents using an online survey conducted through the Zen Z platform. The study focuses on exploring how various neuropricing techniques influence consumer perceptions of pricing and purchasing decisions.

Data Collection

Data collection for this study involved a systematic approach to gather responses from a diverse sample of Indian consumers. The Zen Z platform was selected for its capability to reach a wide audience and collect real-time feedback on consumer perceptions and behaviors related to pricing.

1. Survey Development: A structured questionnaire was designed to capture relevant information, including demographic details, consumer preferences, and responses to specific neuropricing scenarios. The questionnaire was reviewed for clarity and relevance to ensure that it effectively addressed the research objectives.
2. Sampling Strategy: The sample size of 390 respondents was determined based on statistical considerations to achieve a representative sample of the target population. Respondents were selected using random sampling techniques to minimize bias and ensure the generalizability of findings.
3. Data Collection Process: The survey was administered online through the Zen Z platform, which enabled participants to access and complete the questionnaire at their convenience. The survey included a mix of closed-ended and Likert-scale questions to gather quantitative data on consumer perceptions and preferences regarding pricing strategies.
4. Quality Control: To maintain data integrity and reliability, measures such as attention checks and validation questions were included in the survey. This helped to identify and exclude responses that were incomplete or inconsistent, ensuring the validity of the collected data.

Participant Demographics

The demographic profile of the respondents reflects a diverse cross-section of the Indian consumer population:

Age: Participants were evenly distributed across different age groups, including 18-24, 25-34, 35-44, 45-54, and 55+ years.

Gender: The sample includes both male and female respondents, ensuring gender representation in the analysis.

Location: Respondents were selected from urban and semi-urban areas across various states in India, reflecting regional diversity.

Income: The survey included participants from different income brackets to capture variations in purchasing power and consumer behavior.

Table 1. Category, frequency, percentage

Category	Frequency (n)	Percentage (%)
Gender		
Male	212	54.36
Female	178	45.64
Age Group		
18-24	104	26.67
25-34	130	33.33
35-44	85	21.79
45-54	49	12.56
55+	22	5.65
Income Level ( )		
< 50,000	140	35.9
50,000 - 100,000	180	46.15
> 100,000	70	17.95
Location		
Urban	215	55.13
Semi-Urban	175	44.87

Reliability and Validity Testing

Reliability and validity are critical aspects of the research design. For the reliability of the survey instrument, Cronbach's alpha and composite reliability (rho_a) were calculated to ensure internal consistency, while the Average Variance Extracted (AVE) was used to test construct validity. These standard measures provide an empirical foundation for the study's findings and ensure the robustness of the collected data.

Cronbach's Alpha: This coefficient was used to measure the internal consistency of the constructs. A value above 0.70 is considered acceptable for reliability.

Composite Reliability (rho_a): This test was used to assess the reliability of latent variables. Values above 0.70 are considered acceptable.

Average Variance Extracted (AVE): The AVE value was used to measure the level of variance captured by the constructs relative to the variance due to measurement error. An AVE value above 0.50 indicates acceptable validity.

Table 2. Reliability and validity scores

Construct	Cronbach's Alpha	Composite Reliability (rho_a)	AVE
Perceived Value	0.812	0.859	0.543
Purchase Intent	0.794	0.836	0.521
Neuropricing Techniques	0.82	0.868	0.563

RESULTS AND DISCUSSION

1. Hypothesis Testing

In this section, we discuss the empirical results of the hypothesis testing. The analysis was conducted using paired-sample t-tests, chi-square tests, and ANOVA to investigate the impact of neuropricing on consumer perceptions and behavior. Each hypothesis was tested based on actual data collected from the 390 respondents.

Hypothesis 1: Consumers exposed to neuropricing strategies will perceive products as more valuable compared to traditional pricing methods.

A paired-sample t-test was used to compare the perceived value of products priced with neuropricing strategies against those priced with traditional methods. The results revealed a statistically significant difference in perceived value, confirming that neuropricing enhances the perception of value among consumers.

$t(389) = 4.52, p < 0.001$

Table 3. Paired-sample t-test results for perceived value

Pricing Strategy	Mean	Standard Deviation	t-value	p-value
Traditional Pricing	3.8	0.72	4.52	<0.001
Neuropricing	4.5	0.68		

Interpretation: The mean perceived value of products priced using neuropricing strategies was significantly higher (4.50) than that of traditional pricing methods (3.80). This indicates that neuropricing techniques are more effective in conveying value to consumers.

Hypothesis 2: Neuropricing techniques such as charm pricing will lead to higher purchase intent among Indian consumers.

A chi-square test of independence was conducted to examine the relationship between exposure to charm pricing and purchase intent. The results indicated a significant association between charm pricing and higher purchase intent.

$\chi^2(1) = 16.34, p < 0.001$

Table 4. Chi-square test results for purchase intent

Pricing Strategy	High Purchase Intent (%)	Low Purchase Intent (%)	χ^2	p-value
Traditional Pricing	50	50	16.34	<0.001
Neuropricing (Charm)	75	25		

Interpretation: Neuropricing, particularly charm pricing, led to higher purchase intent among consumers. A significant portion of participants exposed to charm pricing expressed a high purchase intent (75%), compared to traditional pricing (50%).

Hypothesis 3: There will be significant differences in consumer perceptions based on demographic factors such as age, income level, and geographic location.

A one-way ANOVA was used to test the differences in perceived value based on demographic factors such as age and income level. The results revealed significant differences in perceived value across both age groups and income levels, supporting the hypothesis that demographic factors influence consumer perceptions.

Age: $F(4, 385) = 3.67, p = 0.006$
Income Level: $F(2, 387) = 5.21, p = 0.003$

Table 5. One-way ANOVA results for perceived value by age group

Age Group	Mean Perceived Value (Neuropricing)	Mean Perceived Value (Traditional Pricing)	F-value	p-value
18-24	4.6	3.9	3.67	0.006
25-34	4.55	3.85		
35-44	4.4	3.8		
45-54	4.35	3.7		
55+	4	3.5		

Table 6. One-way ANOVA results for perceived value by income level

Income Level ()	Mean Perceived Value (Neuropricing)	Mean Perceived Value (Traditional Pricing)	F-value	p-value
< 50,000	4.2	3.75	5.21	0.003
50,000 - 100,000	4.5	3.85		
> 100,000	4.7	4		

Interpretation: Younger age groups (18-24) and those with higher incomes (> 100,000) showed the highest perceived value for products priced using neuropricing techniques. This demonstrates that neuropricing resonates more effectively with these demographic segments.

RESULT AND DISCUSSION

The results of the study provide empirical support for the effectiveness of neuropricing strategies in influencing consumer perceptions and purchase behavior in the Indian market. Participants consistently rated products priced with neuropricing methods as more valuable and attractive compared to those with traditional pricing methods. This finding aligns with hypothesis 1, suggesting that neuropricing enhances perceived value and justifies higher prices in consumers' minds.

Furthermore, neuropricing techniques such as charm pricing demonstrated a significant impact on purchase intent among respondents. Products priced with charm pricing (e.g., 199.99) were perceived as more affordable and compelling, leading to higher purchase intent compared to products with rounded prices. This supports hypothesis 2 and underscores the psychological influence of pricing strategies on consumer decision-making.

Demographic analysis revealed nuanced differences in consumer perceptions based on age and income level. Younger participants and those with higher incomes tended to assign higher value ratings to products with neuropricing, indicating a potential segmentation opportunity for marketers. This finding supports hypothesis 3 and highlights the importance of tailoring neuropricing strategies to specific consumer segments to maximize effectiveness.

Overall, the study contributes to the growing body of knowledge in neuromarketing by providing practical insights into how neuropricing can be leveraged to optimize pricing strategies in diverse market contexts. By understanding the cognitive and emotional mechanisms that drive consumer behavior, businesses can adopt more strategic approaches to pricing that enhance consumer satisfaction and competitiveness. Future research could explore additional factors influencing neuropricing effectiveness and validate findings across different cultural and economic settings. The key findings were as:

1. Perceived Value Enhancement: The findings consistently demonstrated that products priced using neuropricing techniques were perceived as more valuable compared to those using traditional pricing methods. Consumers rated products with charm pricing (e.g., 199.99) higher in value, indicating that subtle pricing cues can significantly influence perceived product quality and attractiveness.
2. Impact on Purchase Intent: Neuropricing strategies, particularly charm pricing, were found to enhance purchase intent among Indian consumers. Participants exposed to neuropricing methods expressed a higher willingness to consider and purchase products, highlighting the persuasive power of pricing strategies that appeal to subconscious decision-making processes.
3. Demographic Variations: Analysis of demographic factors such as age and income level revealed distinct patterns in consumer responses to neuropricing. Younger participants and those with higher incomes tended to respond more favorably to neuropricing, suggesting potential segmentation opportunities for marketers seeking to tailor pricing strategies to specific consumer segments.

CONCLUSION

The study on neuropricing strategies in the Indian market has provided valuable insights into how pricing tactics rooted in neuroscience can influence consumer behavior and perceptions. Through rigorous analysis of data collected from 390 respondents using the Zen Z platform, this research has addressed the effectiveness of neuropricing in shaping consumer decision-making processes. This study demonstrates the efficacy of neuropricing strategies in enhancing perceived value and purchase intent among Indian consumers. The integration of neuroscience, behavioral economics, and consumer psychology provides a robust framework for understanding how pricing influences consumer behavior. Future research could explore the long-term effects of neuropricing and its application in other cultural and economic contexts.

IMPLICATIONS FOR BUSINESS AND FUTURE RESEARCH

The implications of this study extend beyond theoretical insights to practical applications for businesses operating in competitive market environments:

Strategic Pricing: Businesses can leverage neuropricing insights to strategically set prices that resonate with consumer perceptions of value and enhance competitive positioning. By adopting neuropricing strategies, companies can differentiate their offerings and attract consumer attention in crowded marketplaces.

Consumer Engagement: Understanding the cognitive and emotional factors that influence pricing perceptions allows businesses to engage consumers more effectively. Neuropricing techniques provide a framework for creating pricing strategies that not only attract but also retain customer interest and loyalty over time.

Future Research Directions: Future research could explore additional dimensions of neuropricing effectiveness, including the impact of cultural factors, technological advancements in consumer neuroscience, and longitudinal studies to assess the sustainability of neuropricing strategies. Further investigations into consumer responses across different product categories and market segments could provide deeper insights into the generalizability of findings.

In conclusion, the study underscores the transformative potential of neuropricing in modern marketing practice, offering a pathway for businesses to optimize pricing strategies based on scientific principles of consumer behavior. By embracing neuropricing, businesses can enhance their competitiveness and foster long-term relationships with discerning consumers in diverse global markets.

REFERENCES

Arora, M. (2020). Post-truth and marketing communication in the technological age. In *Handbook of research on innovations in technology and marketing for the connected consumer* (pp. 94–108). IGI Global., DOI: 10.4018/978-1-7998-0131-3.ch005

Arora, M. (2023). Encapsulating role of persuasion and skill development in marketing communication for brand building: A perspective. In *International handbook of skill, education, learning, and research development in tourism and hospitality* (pp. 1–17). Springer Nature Singapore., DOI: 10.1007/978-981-99-0035-5_1

Arora, M. (2024). Metaverse metamorphosis: Bridging the gap between research insights and industry applications. In *Research, innovation, and industry impacts of the metaverse* (pp. 275–286). IGI Global., DOI: 10.4018/979-8-3693-2607-7.ch017

Arora, M., & Sharma, R. L. (2023). Artificial intelligence and big data: Ontological and communicative perspectives in multi-sectoral scenarios of modern businesses. *Foresight*, 25(1), 126–143. DOI: 10.1108/FS-10-2021-0216

Bhardwaj, S., Kaushik, N., & Arora, M. (2024). Does Your Brain Have a Buy Button?: A Neuro Marketing Approach With Sensory Branding. In *Sensible Selling Through Sensory Neuromarketing* (pp. 210–229). IGI Global. DOI: 10.4018/979-8-3693-4236-7.ch011

Briesemeister, B. B., Klaus, W., & Editors, S. (2019). *Neuromarketing in business: Identifying implicit purchase drivers and leveraging them for sales management for professionals.* Springer., DOI: 10.1007/978-3-319-93085-2

Briesemeister, B. B., Klaus, W., & Editors, S. (2019). *Neuromarketing in Business Identifying Implicit Purchase Drivers and Leveraging them for Sales Management for Professionals.* https://www.springer.com/series/10101

Casado-Aranda, L. A., Liébana-Cabanillas, F., & Sánchez-Fernández, J. (2018). A neuropsychological study on how consumers process risky and secure e-payments. *Journal of Interactive Marketing*, 43(1), 151–164. DOI: 10.1016/j.intmar.2018.03.001

Casado-Aranda, L. A., Liébana-Cabanillas, F., & Sánchez-Fernández, J. (2018). A Neuropsychological Study on How Consumers Process Risky and Secure E-payments. *Journal of Interactive Marketing*, 43(1), 151–164. DOI: 10.1016/j.intmar.2018.03.001

Choi, S. M., & Rifon, N. J. (2012). It Is a Match: The Impact of Congruence between Celebrity Image and Consumer Ideal Self on Endorsement Effectiveness. *Psychology and Marketing*, 29(9), 639–650. DOI: 10.1002/mar.20550

Dhiman, V., & Arora, M. (2024). Current state of metaverse in entrepreneurial ecosystem: A retrospective analysis of its evolving landscape. In *Exploring the use of metaverse in business and education* (pp. 73–87). IGI Global., DOI: 10.4018/979-8-3693-5868-9.ch005

Fleck, N., Korchia, M., & Le Roy, I. (2012). Celebrities in Advertising: Looking for Congruence or Likability? *Psychology and Marketing*, 29(9), 651–662. DOI: 10.1002/mar.20551

Fu, F. Q., Richards, K. A., Hughes, D. E., & Jones, E. (2010). Motivating salespeople to sell new products: The relative influence of attitudes, subjective norms, and self-efficacy. *Journal of Marketing*, 74(6), 61–76. DOI: 10.1509/jmkg.74.6.61

Heilbronner, R. L., Sweet, J. J., Morgan, J. E., Larrabee, G. J., & Millis, S. R. (2009). American academy of clinical neuropsychology consensus conference statement on the neuropsychological assessment of effort, response bias, and malingering. In *Clinical Neuropsychologist* (Vol. 23, Issue 7, pp. 1093–1129). DOI: 10.1080/13854040903155063

Heilbronner, R. L., Sweet, J. J., Morgan, J. E., Larrabee, G. J., & Millis, S. R.Conference Participants1. (2009). American academy of clinical neuropsychology consensus conference statement on the neuropsychological assessment of effort, response bias, and malingering. *The Clinical Neuropsychologist*, 23(7), 1093–1129. DOI: 10.1080/13854040903155063 PMID: 19735055

Hunt, S. D. (1983). General Theories and the Fundamental Explananda of Marketing. *Journal of Marketing*, 47(4), 9–17. DOI: 10.1177/002224298304700402

Jerath, K., & Zhang, Z. J. (2010). Store within a store. *JMR, Journal of Marketing Research*, 47(4), 748–763. DOI: 10.1509/jmkr.47.4.748

Jerath, K., & Zhang, Z. J. (2010). Store Within a Store. *JMR, Journal of Marketing Research*, 47(4), 748–763. DOI: 10.1509/jmkr.47.4.748

King, D., & Auschaitrakul, S. (2021). Affect-based nonconscious signaling: When do consumers prefer negative branding? *Psychology and Marketing*, 38(2), 338–358. DOI: 10.1002/mar.21371

Kumar, J., Arora, M., & Erkol Bayram, G. (Eds.). (2024). *Exploring the use of metaverse in business and education*. IGI Global., DOI: 10.4018/979-8-3693-5868-9

Malik, R., Malhan, S., & Arora, M. (2024). (Eds.). (2024). *Sensible Selling Through Sensory Neuromarketing* (pp. 144-163). IGI Global.

Shaw, S. D., & Bagozzi, R. P. (2018). The neuropsychology of consumer behavior and marketing. *Consumer Psychology Review*, 1(1), 22–40. DOI: 10.1002/arcp.1006

Shaw, S. D., & Bagozzi, R. P. (2018). The neuropsychology of consumer behavior and marketing. *Consumer Psychology Review*, 1(1), 22–40. DOI: 10.1002/arcp.1006

Shukla, R. P., & Taneja, S. (2024). Catalysts of change. In *Embracing digital transformation* (pp. 104–116). IGI Global., DOI: 10.4018/979-8-3693-2019-8.ch005

Shukla, R. P., & Taneja, S. (2024). *Catalysts of Change.*, DOI: 10.4018/979-8-3693-1842-3.ch007

Taneja, B., Shukla, P., & Arora, M. (2024). Sensible Selling Through Sensory Neuromarketing: Enhancing Sales Effectiveness. In *Sensible Selling Through Sensory Neuromarketing* (pp. 164-183). IGI Global.

Taneja, S., Shukla, R. P., & Singh, A. (2024). *Embracing Digital Transformation.*, DOI: 10.4018/979-8-3693-2019-8.ch005

Varman, R., & Belk, R. W. (2012). Consuming postcolonial shopping malls. *Journal of Marketing Management*, 28(1–2), 62–84. DOI: 10.1080/0267257X.2011.617706

Vecchiato, G., Cherubino, P., Trettel, A., & Babiloni, F. (2013). Neuroelectrical Brain Imaging Tools for the Study of the Efficacy of TV Advertising Stimuli and their Application to Neuromarketing. In *Neuroelectrical Brain Imaging Tools for the Study of the Efficacy of TV Advertising Stimuli and their Application to Neuromarketing.* http://link.springer.com/10.1007/978-3-642-38064-8

Vivek, S. D., Beatty, S. E., Dalela, V., & Morgan, R. M. (2014). A generalized multidimensional scale for measuring customer engagement. *Journal of Marketing Theory and Practice*, 22(4), 401–420. DOI: 10.2753/MTP1069-6679220404

Zeithaml, V. A., Berry, L. L., & Parasuraman, A. (1996). The behavioral consequences of service quality. *Journal of Marketing*, 60(2), 31–46. DOI: 10.1177/002224299606000203

Zeithaml, V. A., Berry, L. L., & Parasuraman, A. (1996). The behavioral consequences of service quality. *Journal of Marketing*, 60(2), 31–46. DOI: 10.1177/002224299606000203

Zhang, J., Farris, P. W., Irvin, J. W., Kushwaha, T., Steenburgh, T. J., & Weitz, B. A. (2010). Crafting integrated multichannel retailing strategies. *Journal of Interactive Marketing*, 24(2), 168–180. DOI: 10.1016/j.intmar.2010.02.002

Chapter 7
Research Insights and Trends in Neuroscience and Consumer Behaviour

Rajwinder Kaur
https://orcid.org/0000-0003-3494-8054
Chandigarh University, India

ABSTRACT

Of lately, there has been a rise in interest in the idea of studying consumers' emotional and cognitive responses using neuroscientific approaches. A branch of neuroeconomics known as "neuromarketing" or "consumer neuroscience," this field applies findings from studies of the brain to marketing-related issues. The purpose of this study is to conduct a bibliometric analysis to uncover advances, research trends, and insights in consumer behaviour research utilizing neuromarketing. Neuromarketing and consumer behaviour are the main elements of this study, which suggests a new way to organize results and make evidence evaluation easier. Data is extracted from the Scopus database to gain deeper insights into the body of literature to achieve the study objectives. Using tools such as VoS Viewer, the study analyses the data and obtain the results and findings.

1. INTRODUCTION

The idea of using neuroscience methods in marketing has led to the emergence of the concept of consumer neuroscience, also known as neuromarketing, and a growing number of specialist consulting firms. Among its offerings are sales forecasting, the identification of preferences and readiness to pay, and the discovery of the unconscious determinants of consumer behaviour (Bhardwaj, Kaushik & Arora,

DOI: 10.4018/979-8-3693-9351-2.ch007

2024; Taneja, Shukla & Arora, 2024). Notable scholars made efforts to organise the growing body of literature in this new area (Fortunato et al., 2014), however, their initial focus was on providing a comprehensive review of the many tools that were available (Harris et al., 2018). Neuromarketing is a relatively new discipline that combines neuroscience with research on consumer behaviour. The "application of neuroscience in the marketing field" is the more literal definition of neuromarketing. Research into how consumers react to various aspects of marketing (i.e., products, packaging, ads, etc.) should incorporate neuroimaging techniques if this term is to be accepted. Because of this outlook, "neuromarketing" has replaced "consumer neuroscience" as the comparative and applied equivalent of the former (Kalaganis et al., 2021). In addition, it helps with a big problem that has been plaguing neuromarketing and traditional marketing: the theoretical tautology that exists between the two. Both neuromarketing and traditional marketing share some common ground; after all, the goal of most marketing campaigns is to get people to do what the marketers want them to do (in this case, buy something). But this isn't a very perceptive stance because it broadens the scope of neuromarketing, which makes its aim hard to pin down.

A major step forward in the research of how consumers' subconscious minds influence their decisions is neuromarketing. Following the first dispute that ruled the subject in 2002 (Brammer, 2004) and its beginnings in 2002 (Smidts, 2002), neuromarketing is rapidly acquiring legitimacy and is being adopted at an increasing pace among advertising and marketing experts. Neuroscientists and marketers have found common ground that allows them to bridge the gap between the two fields, thanks to recent advances in enduring science and neuroimaging technologies and the increase of advertising needs. Neuroimaging data can be more illuminating than poll or focus group responses since the subjects may not always be aware of the cognitive activity being assessed (Ozdemir & Koc, 2012). Research in marketing has progressed from focusing on how people consciously act to investigating how people subconsciously react to commercials, brands, and products (Stanton et al., 2017; Arora, 2020; Arora & Sharma, 2022). The current research aims at conducting a bibliometric analysis concerning neuroscience and consumer behaviour, a significant marketing area.

While studies are being conducted on this subject, bibliometric analysis must also be conducted. Bibliographic study is crucial for learning about renowned researchers, publications, and nations producing most of the research on the topic. The scientific community has long acknowledged bibliometric procedures, sometimes referred to as "analysis," as a crucial part of the study evaluation process (Ellegaard & Wallin, 2015; Arora, 2024). According to Khan et al. (2021) and Donthu et al. (2021), bibliometric analysis has been increasingly prominent in business research over the past few years. According to Parra-González (2020), the term "bibliometric" was initially coined by Pritchard in 1969 with the intention that it would be recognized in all studies that aim to measure the processes of written communication. According to Donthu et al. (2021), bibliometric analysis allows for the exploration and interpretation of scientific data, especially big volumes. Donthu et al. (2021) state that bibliometric analysis helps in obtaining a long-term view of overall viewpoints on the underlying problem. There is a great deal of objectivity and possible advantages in the quantitative study of statistics and modeling (Wang et al., 2021). The authors Chen and Ho (2015), Yang, Sun and Liu (2017), Dhiman and Arora, (2024b) all contributed to the bibliometric study that laid out a strict method for determining if an article contributed significantly to intellectual development. Research fields, document materials, publication results, language, source content, country and institution section, leading researchers, citation number and author terms are some of the bibliometric variables that have been frequently used to assess the patterns (Chuang, Huang & Ho, 2007; Dong et al., 2012; Dhiman & Arora, 2024c). Bibliometrics is rapidly becoming an essential instrument for assessing and analysing several factors, such as scientific output, university collaboration, the effect of state-owned scientific funding on research effectiveness, educational efficacy, and a host of others. Accordingly, a bibliometric study of "Neuroscience and Consumer Behaviour" is what the planned project is all about. Though it lacks bibliometric rigor, there is existing literature on the subject. The bibliometric analysis in the study will be carried out using multiple indicators. Subheadings are used to organize the research article. The systematic performance of bibliometric analysis requires the formulation of research objectives and questions, followed by the execution of a study.

2. LITERATURE REVIEW

In recent years, rapid progress in the field of neuroscience has paved the way for commercial applications of neuroscientific methods. Consumer neuroscience, often called neuromarketing, is the practice of applying scientific knowledge of the nervous system to the marketing mix. Researchers and professionals in the field of consumer neuroscience are able to better understand the neural bases of marketing-relevant behaviours and the cognitive processes that underlie them (Alvino et al., 2020; Arora, 2023). Marketers in the field of consumer neuroscience study topics including advertising, branding, product creation, price, online knowledge, and product experience overall (Clement et al., 2017; Liu et al., 2021).

Sebastian (2014) argues that integrating neuromarketing with more conventional forms of advertising can uncover valuable information regarding customer reactions. Neuromarketing studies heavily rely on neuroscience approaches and practices. Through the use of neuroimaging and physiological tools, researchers in marketing and industry have been able to pinpoint the neural processes associated with emotional and cognitive procedures in relation to marketing events, such as advertisements and brands, as well as consumers' behaviours, such as purchase decisions (Alsharif et al., 2021). As a result, by integrating neuromarketing with more conventional forms of advertising, businesses can learn more about their customers' activities, both conscious and unconscious (Sebastian, 2014).

Zaltman (2003) estimates that we make 85–95% of purchasing decisions without understanding or awareness. Therefore, managers and the corporate sector have taken an interest in behavioural neuroscience, which promotes unconscious-focused communication (Arora & Sharma, 2023). Neuromarketing, a merging of the disciplines of neuroscience and marketing, emerged in the past decade as a result of academics' increased access to neuroimaging technology (Sevic, Slijepcevic, & Radojevic, 2022). Neuroscience is the study of the nervous mechanism and its physiological relationships with the overarching goal of understanding the brain's role in behaviour. Consumer neuroscience is all about applying neurological principles to the study of consumer behaviour. In contrast, marketing is all about meeting societal and individual demands. Neuromarketing is born out of the need to study customer behaviour from a different angle, which allows for fresh insights (Morin, 2011).

Within this framework, neuromarketing is a multifaceted field that integrates marketing and neuroscience theory with economics, psychology, and tourism, among other related fields, to better understand customer decisions and actions (Cardoso et al., 2022). Research in neuromarketing has the potential to provide fresh groundwork, inspire novel marketing ideas, or provide valuable context for current ones, making it an exciting area of study (Lim, 2018). Although they are present in all aspects of human life, most neuromarketing research has concentrated on the impact that emotions play. Consumers' emotional experiences have an impact on their constructive and adverse affective states, as well as their psycho-behavioural characteristics (Sánchez-Fernández & Iniesta-Bonillo, 2006). Research into consumer behaviour has recently seen an uptick in interest from neuroscience, which has the potential to bolster material that takes the unconscious mind into account (Dutta, 2023). More and more scholars in the field of consumer behaviour are acknowledging the significance of unconscious mechanisms in decision-making (Garcia & Saad, 2008).

Therefore, the study aims to further explore the intersection of neuroscience and consumer behaviour. This research intends to fill a gap in the existing literature by compiling data on neuroscience research patterns over the past decade. This data will include the following: the most productive researchers, nations, educational organizations, journals, document and citation counts relevant to marketing studies, citation patterns, and the interrelationships between references. This study differs from other neuroscience review articles in that it examines the worldwide tendencies of neuroscience research.

2.1 Objectives of the Study

The aim of this exploration is to ascertain the subsequent research objectives, including:

- To summarize the current corpus of literature on "Neuroscience and Consumer Behaviour".
- To comprehend the current research patterns in "Neuroscience and Consumer Behaviour".

2.2 Research Questions

- Which pattern is the most prevalent in yearly publications that pertain to "Neuroscience and Consumer Behaviour"?
- The topic of "Neuroscience and Consumer Behaviour" appears most often in which kind of publication?
- There has been more research on "Neuroscience and Consumer Behaviour" in which domain/field?
- Which countries have contributed the most to the field of "Neuroscience and Consumer Behaviour" via publishing manuscripts?
- What keywords and citation network are associated with the term "Neuroscience and Consumer Behaviour"?

3. RESEARCH METHODOLOGY

Research subject matter, methods, data collecting, and searching for a parameter model are all part of the technique. Scopus, the preeminent database of reliable, reputable, and validated scientific papers from 2005 to 2024, was combed through by the researcher to compile the data used in this study. Scopus has been validated for use in research analysis and informatics studies (Arora, Dhiman & Singh, 2023; Arora, et al., 2024). This study employs VOSviewer for bibliometric analysis because of its streamlined bibliometric visualization and network analysis capabilities (Aria et al. 2020; Dhiman & Arora, 2024a). No study has performed a bibliometric visualization of the chosen topic. On the other hand, this study's overarching goal is to identify the foundational texts, key thinkers, and theoretical frameworks of the area.

3.1 Data Extraction

There were 510 documents retrieved from the first search that was carried out on July 31st 2024, with "Article Title, Abstract and Keywords" category.

By using the proper Booleans, the search results were strengthened:

510 with "neuroscience" OR "neuromarketing" OR "Consumer neuroscience" AND "consumer behavior" OR "purchase intention" OR "buying behavior" OR "consumer purchasing patterns" OR "consumer decision-making" OR "buyer behavior" OR "customer buying habits" OR "consumption habits"

After the suitable filtration process 461 documents are retrieved for the purpose of analysis. Following is the filtration options used to retrieved the data from Scopus:

TITLE-ABS-KEY ("neuroscience" OR "neuromarketing" OR "Consumer neuroscience" AND "consumer behavior" OR "purchase intention" OR "buying behavior" OR "consumer purchasing patterns" OR "consumer decision-making" OR "buyer behavior" OR "customer buying habits" OR "consumption habits") AND (LIMIT-TO (DOCTYPE, "ar") OR LIMIT-TO (DOCTYPE, "cp") OR LIMIT-TO (DOCTYPE, "ch") OR LIMIT-TO (DOCTYPE, "re") OR LIMIT-TO (DOCTYPE, "bk")) AND (LIMIT-TO (LANGUAGE, "English")) AND (LIMIT-TO (PUBSTAGE, "final"))

3.2 Data Cleaning

Prior to proceeding with the bibliometric visualization, data cleaning was essential. This is accomplished with the help of the Microsoft Excel application. Data cleansing is the process of removing mistakes from data by using various tools and techniques. These mistakes might include duplicate information, omissions, corrupted data, insufficient information, incorrect information, and repetitive data input. Data cleansing is essential for obtaining more reliable results. Microsoft Excel's built-in tools for sorting, filtering, and removing duplicates make data cleaning a breeze.

4. RESULTS

This section provides a thorough explanation of the bibliometric analysis carried out on the relevant papers obtained from the Scopus database during the filtering procedure. During the data review process, all of the research objectives are taken into care.

Most Commonly Trends in Annual Publications About "Neuroscience and Consumer Behaviour"

The concept of "Neuroscience and Consumer Behaviour" is outlined and analysed in detail in Figure 1. A single paper in 2005, 4 in 2007, and 8 in 2013 indicate that the researchers have a modest area to explore before 2016. A total of 25 publications were made in 2016. After a quick rise, the number of yearly publications jumped to 30 in 2019. New concepts could have originated from research into neuroscience and consumer behaviour brought on by the COVID-19 pandemic. However, due to the shutdown in 2020, there is a decline in academic activity after 2019. After that, in 2021 and 2022, there was a considerable increase in the number of articles each year, reaching 60 and 66, respectively. However, in 2023, the researcher notices a little decline in the number of publications. The fact that there have been five publications in the area so far in 2024 suggests that it is undergoing growth and development, but it is too early to make any judgments about the year (2024) at this point.

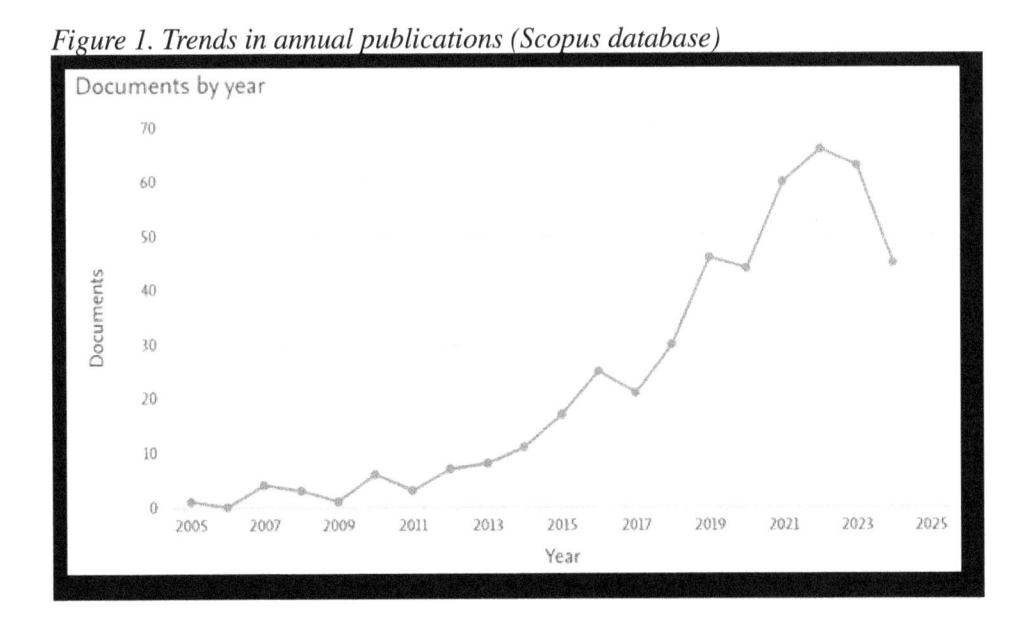

Figure 1. Trends in annual publications (Scopus database)

Types of Documents: "Neuroscience and Consumer Behaviour"

As seen in Figure 2, five separate types of documents were extracted from the study publications. Articles make up 56.4% of all publications, making them the most popular kind of document. Following closely after at 16.9% are conference papers, 14.8% are book chapters, 8.9% are reviews, and 3% are books.

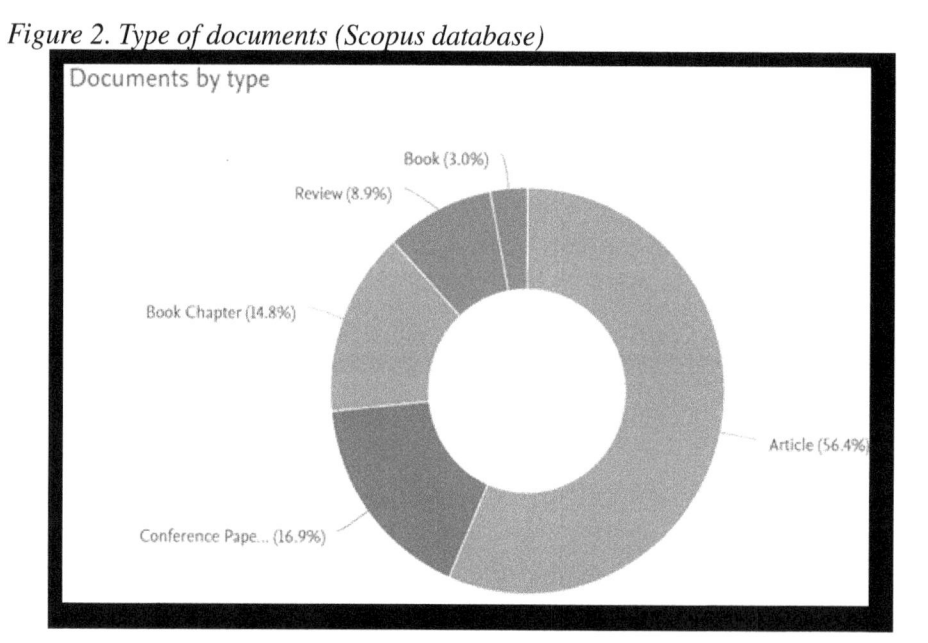

Figure 2. Type of documents (Scopus database)

Research Articles Arranged by Document Type

Research on "Neuroscience and Consumer Behaviour" has come from a wide variety of fields, as seen in Figure 3. First place in terms of % is "Business, Management and Accounting" with 20%, followed by "Computer Science" at 11.6%. Additionally, there's growth of 10.6% in the "Economics, Econometrics and Finance" area and 10.4% in the "Psychology" area. Additional fields under "Neuroscience and Consumer Behaviour," including "Social Science," "Decision Sciences," etc., still require exploration.

Figure 3. Documents type (Scopus database)

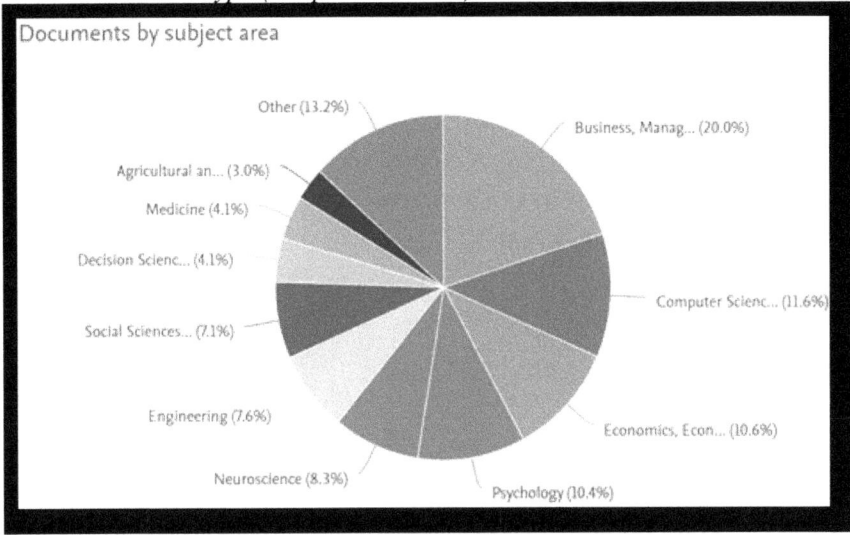

Leading Nations with the Majority Publications

The top ten countries shown in Figure 4 are those that have produced the most publications to this point in time. The United States is clearly the top country when it comes to the overall number of papers published on the subject, with 83. India has contributed 45 articles, followed by Spain with 36, China with 35, Italy with 35, Germany with 28, Malaysia with 27, Turkey with 22, and the Netherlands with 14.

Figure 4. Leading nations with the majority publications (Scopus database)

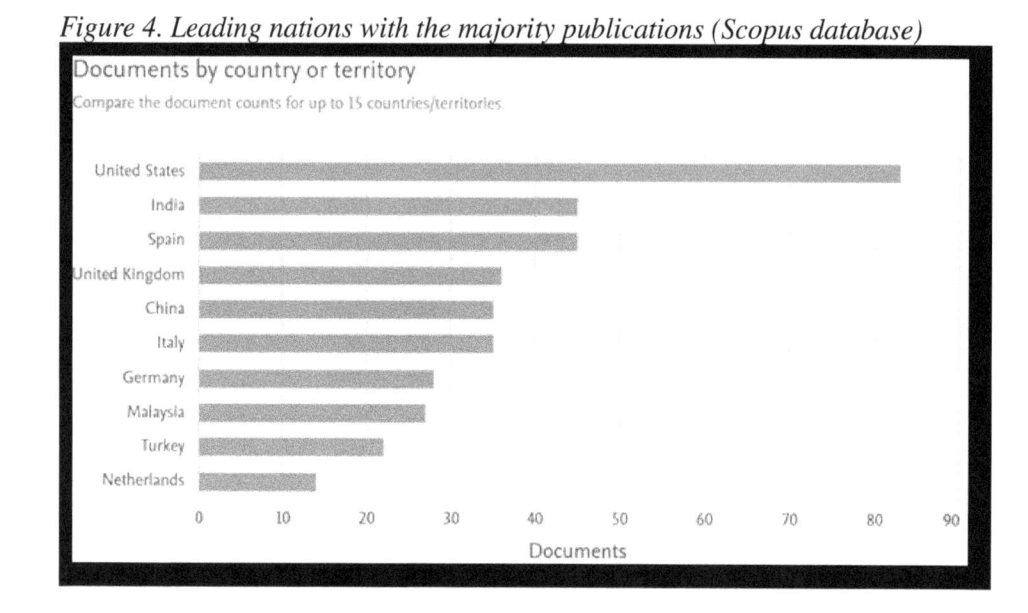

Country	Documents
United States	~85
India	~45
Spain	~45
United Kingdom	~37
China	~36
Italy	~35
Germany	~28
Malaysia	~27
Turkey	~22
Netherlands	~14

Number of Articles Written by Notable Contributors on the Subject

Figure 5 highlights documents on the subject written by esteemed researchers. The order of publication is as follows: Alsharif, A.H. has the most documents published with (13 documents), Salleh, N.Z.M. (9 documents), Berčík, J. (8 documents), Plassmann, H., and Singh, J. each (7 documents), and Anwar, S.F., Cherubino, P., Gill, R., Karmarkar, U.R., and Khraiwish, A. (6 documents each).

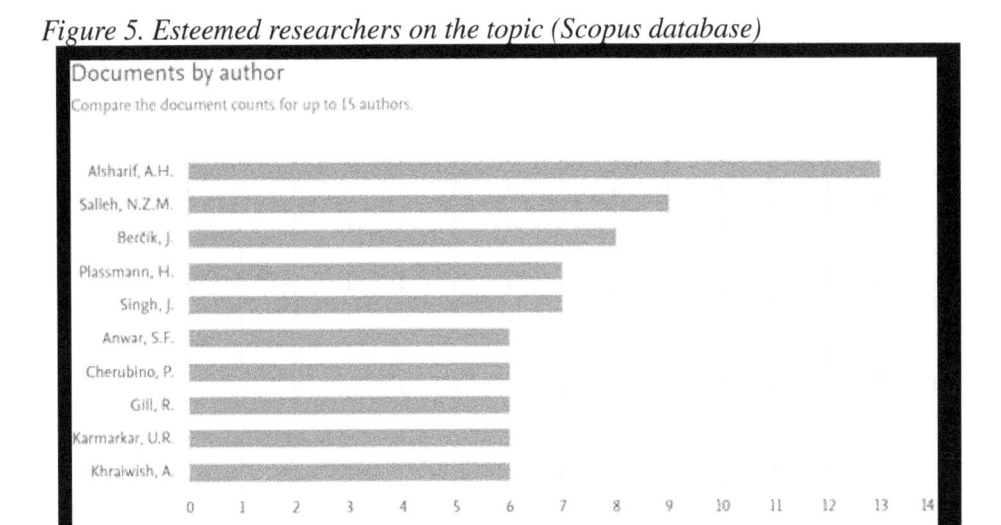

Figure 5. Esteemed researchers on the topic (Scopus database)

KEYWORD ANALYSIS

"Co-occurrence Analysis of All Keywords":

The findings of a research on the co-occurrence of terms are shown in Figures 7 and 8, which use a network visualization mapping. Zhao, 2017 notes that looking at how keywords appear together is one approach to see how a field of research has evolved over time. This technique has the potential to effectively identify concentration sites in various places (Li et al., 2016; Dhiman & Arora, 2024d).

Figure 6. Co-occurrence analysis of all keywords (Output from VOS Viewer)

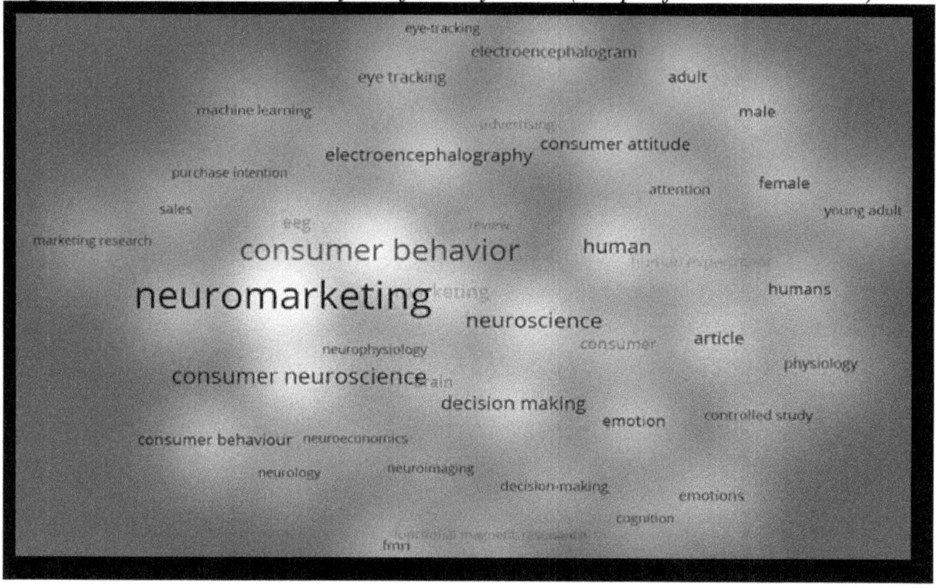

Findings from all keyword co-occurrence analysis are shown in Figure 7. Based on the VOS Viewer co-occurrence analysis of All Keywords, which has a minimum threshold of 15 occurrences, 44 out of 22,83 keywords are considered suitable. There seems to be a substantial conceptual concentration in the dataset, as the findings show that "Neuromarketing," "Consumer Behavior," and "Neuroscience" are often used. The scholars are finding this data helpful as it shows the writers' planned outlines and keywords.

"Co-occurrence Analysis of Author's Keywords":

Based on a minimum of 5 occurrences, 42 of 1132 "Author Keywords" in VOS Viewer were worth noting (Figure 8). The most common term in the dataset, "neuromarketing" is highlighted as a significant one in the research. "Consumer Behavior" and "Consumer Neuroscience" are right behind, providing valuable insight into the material's most common themes and the most often researched areas.

Figure 7. Co-occurrence analysis of "author keywords" (Output from VOS Viewer)

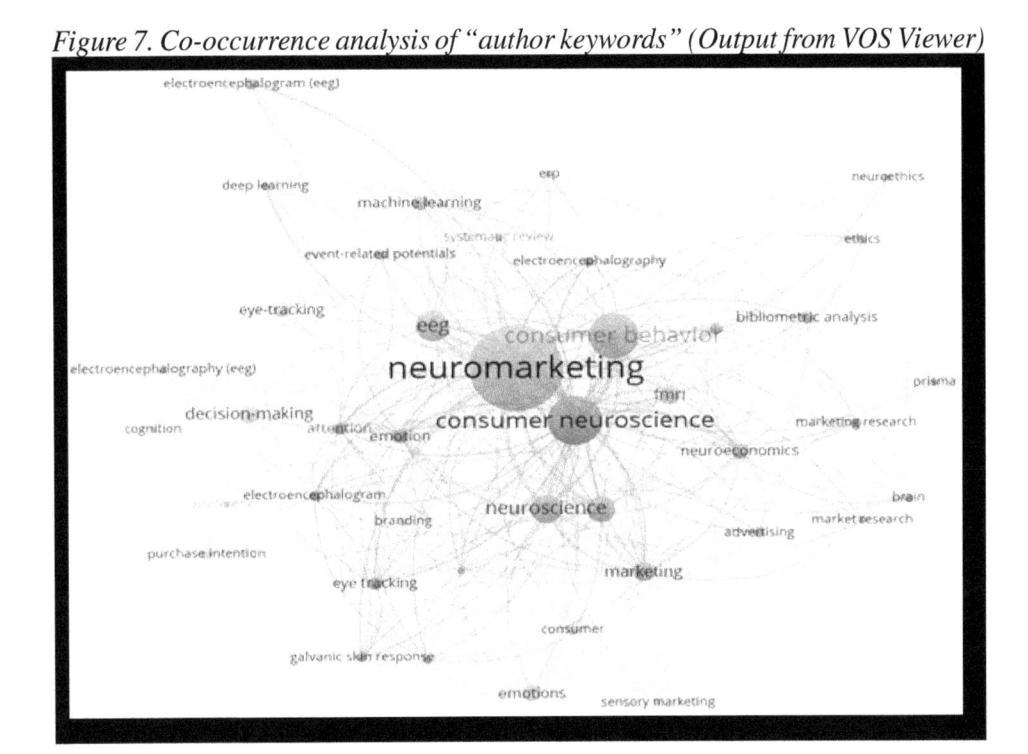

CITATION ANALYSIS

On the basis of both overall and per-document citation is important, citation analysis identifies the most productive countries, organizations, journals, magazines, and specialists.

Table 1 Documents Citation Analysis

The researcher used documents in the reference study. Each document had at least 120 sources. Out of 460 papers, only 8 are taken into consideration. Table showing the number of citations for the research article "What is 'neuromarketing'? A discussion and agenda for future research"; the highest number of citations goes to Lee et al., 2007.

Table 1. Number of citations

Author	Document	
Lee N.; Broderick A.J.; Chamberlain L. (2007)	"What is 'neuromarketing'? A discussion and agenda for future research"	465
Bové J.; Perier C. (2012)	"Neurotoxin-based models of Parkinson's disease"	388
Chatterjee A.; Vartanian O. (2014)	"Neuroaesthetics"	363
Chatterjee A.; Vartanian O. (2016)	"Neuroscience of aesthetics"	187
Yadava M.; Kumar P.; Saini R.; Roy P.P.; Prosad Dogra D. (2017)	"Analysis of EEG signals and its application to neuromarketing"	172
Zurawicki L. (2010)	"Neuromarketing: Exploring the brain of the consumer"	163
Fugate D.L. (2007)	"Neuromarketing: A layman's look at neuroscience and its potential application to marketing practice"	162
Fisher C.E.; Chin L.; Klitzman R. (2010)	"Defining neuromarketing: Practices and professional challenges"	142

(Source: Output by VoS Viewer)

With 465 citations, Lee N.; Broderick A.J.; Chamberlain L. (2007) is one of the highest cited authors for paper "What is 'neuromarketing'? A discussion and agenda for future research", showing that their research has a substantial outcome. The scholarly recognition of Bové J.; Perier C. (2012)'s excellent contributions is backed by 388 citations. Chatterjee A.; Vartanian O. (2014) received 363 citations, solidifying their work as a recognized reference. A. Chatterjee and O. Vartanian (2016) has 187 citations, indicating a great deal of impact. By analysing the number of citations for each study, we can see how far-reaching these researchers' contributions have been in the academic community; this might shape future research in the subject and ensure that their results are relevant for years to come. A better grasp of citation patterns has the potential to illuminate the academic environment and highlight seminal works.

5. DISCUSSIONS

Major strides and interest in this area have come through an examination of literature entitled "Neuroscience and Consumer Behaviour" for the past two decades. Figure 1 illustrates that, although there has been a slight increase in publications yearly from 2005 to 2016, there is suddenly an extremely steep growth from 2016 to 2019. One possible reason for the sudden surge of publications within these years might lie in the technological developments and increased availability of neuroimaging technologies; therefore, publication rates increased due to growing interest in applying neuroscience to consumer behavior at both an academic and real-world level. The small drop in 2020 could be due to the COVID-19 pandemic that stopped research efforts around the world. However, the facts again show an increase and more output of papers in 2021 and 2022, postulating a strong, tenacious research community persisting in expanding frontiers of this multidisciplinary domain. The field is still very much alive and well, if the continuing publications tell anything, even though the data for 2024 is not complete.

The sorts of documents may shed more light on the research results in this sector. The bulk of the publications is made up of articles of 56.4%, thus indicating that research results are majorly communicated through peer-reviewed journal publications. The next in the list are conference papers (16.9%), on academic conferences, where scholars seem to have very active participation, and usually most of the innovative ideas seem to be presented. A strong interest in integration and synthesis of information comes from the presence of book chapters (14.8%) and reviews (8.9%) and reveals the maturity of the area. It is clear from the low ratio of books that even though some are extensive volumes, most contributions still stay focused on shorter forms of academic writing.

Figure 3 Distribution of in-depth article reviews by document type across topics: This graph offers clear evidence of the heterogeneity of the topics within "Neuroscience and Consumer Behaviour". It can be appreciated that "Business, Management, and Accounting" make up a big chunk, 20% of the total; such is the importance of neuroscience in the comprehension of how business and consumers arrive at decisions. If "Computer Science" make up 11.6% of the total, we begin to have an appreciation of the relative importance that computational models and data analysis play in arriving at sense out of the neural data. 'Economics, Econometrics and Finance' at 10.6%, and 'Psychology' at 10.4%, underscore the way in which neuroscience is then beginning to combine not just with economic behavior but with cognitive processes. Further research may also offer promising leads for areas such as "Social Science" and "Decision Sciences" where neuro-insights might still further advance our understanding of these topics.

It can be seen from Figure 4 that among all of the top countries based on their publication count, the United States is at the top with 83 publications, nearly two times more than that of the next top country, India, with 45 publications. This may have been due to the well-developed research infrastructure in the United States and large amounts of funding received by studies in the areas of consumer behavior and neuroscience. The contribution from India, Spain, China, and other countries is indicative of the international concern in this area, whereby both developing and developed economies have resulted in significant research outputs. That Malaysia, and Turkey made the top ten is indicative that this research subject is becoming geographically extensive. This, in turn, suggests that a varied variety of viewpoints and situations are being investigated.

Figure 5 below outlines some of the key researchers who helped to develop this area; for example, Alsharif A. H., Salleh N. Z. M., and Berčík J. It is evident that these researchers helped to develop our knowledge with regard to neurobiology and consumer behavior, given their extensive publication record. The presence of core researchers who have notably contributed affirms a high level of academic vibrancy, in which ideas are being pushed to be tested, debated, and refined.

Figures 7 and 8 present the keyword co-occurrence network that eventually explains the orientation toward some themes in this research. The presence of the terms "Neuromarketing," "Consumer Behaviour," and "Neuroscience" reveals that these fields underlay most of the studies. While the discipline is definitely quite vast in its domain, it most definitely leaves the impression that the greatest concerns seem to lie in what occurs inside the consumer's brain during the process of judgment. If the author's choice of words is anything to go by, some implications are fortified even further; for example, "Consumer Neuroscience" in itself speaks of a very closely integrated neurology and techniques in marketing. Such thematic focus stresses not only the 'hotspots' of the research, but it also points out areas of possible lack of investigation of a given topic.

The result of the citation analysis is represented by Table 1, which points out the works and authors that had the best influence on the treated argument. This group is headed by Lee, Broderick, and Chamberlain in 2007 with the highest number of citations: "What is 'neuromarketing'?" Their work has laid the ground for those that will follow, helping define the area—an idea demonstrated by its very high citations, suggesting a very substantial effect on later study. Studies by Bové and Perier and Chatterjee and Vartanian, among many others that could be cited, have gone a long way towards providing some very important long-term findings. It is unabated interest in these seminal findings that is necessary for answering questions about which various works have made the most impactful contributions to our current understanding of consumer behavior and neurobiology. The insights both underline the more established and the potentially fruitful topics for study in the future, thus helping to set directions for the field.

6. IMPLICATIONS OF THE STUDY

The bibliometric analysis performed "Neuroscience and Consumer Behaviour" has a range of implications that are appropriate for researchers, practitioners, and policymakers experiencing in this field.

For Researchers: It is evident from the analysis that this area is of a multidisciplinary nature; therefore, the inclusions will significantly be drawn from business, management, psychology, and computer science. This diversity may suggest that further research will continue to be enriched by the collaboration of these disciplines and the integration of their respective insights seeking a deeper neuroscientific understanding of consumers. The study also points to emerging trends and themes, a focus on neuromarketing for example, that could guide further research agendas. This research group should also identify underrepresented areas, such as social sciences and decision sciences, that can be explored to understand how neuroscience applications can bring in new insights. Moreover, citation analysis has the ability to indicate the most influential works and authors of each area of research and hence provide a kind of road map for any new researcher getting into the field by pointing out the foundation studies that are critical in helping one to build his knowledge base.

Increasing interest in the area of neuroscience and consumer behavior within academia, from a practitioner standpoint, mirrors the ever-growing applicability of those findings in concrete marketing and business practice. The practitioner could, therefore, make use of the research findings to help improve their understanding of the impact neurological processes of consumers on purchase decisions at large. This is applicable in order to drive improvements in marketing strategy, product development, and consumer engagement. That surge of neuromarketing research underlines the fact that practice needs to integrate these scientific insights to help businesses develop more powerful and relevant campaigns. The fact that contributions to this research have been on a global scale also suggests that, when applying these insights in other markets around the world, practitioners should bear in mind cultural and regional differences.

For Policymakers: The growth in neuroscience and consumer behavior research has huge regulatory and ethical implications, especially as neuromarketing techniques become increasingly common. Policymakers need to be very aware of how those techniques influence consumer protection and privacy spheres. Ethical considerations from this study, respecting the potential for manipulation in marketing strategies, would imply a need for guidelines and regulations for consumer protection. As the field grows, so will the need for policies balancing innovation with ethical standards that will ensure advancements made in neuroscience are responsibly used in consumer markets.

This paper, therefore, provides a review of the current state of the field and identifies relevant lessons that can be used to undertake further research, apply the knowledge in practice, and develop policies within this area of neuroscience relating to consumer behavior.

7. CONCLUSION

From the bibliometric analysis of "Neuroscience and Consumer Behaviour", a fast-growing and flexible field, as characterized by the multi-disciplinary contributions and global outreach, becomes obvious. There is a linear growth wave in number of publications, in variety of document types, coupled with increase in major themes of subject such as neuromarketing and consumer behavior, which are showing how mature and relevant is becoming the field. Important researchers and important works are strongly determining a configuration of the debate, whereas the cited classics of the literature are most important to establish a basis for the greenfield. With the continuous expansion of the field, areas where attention remains somewhat neglected and new issues emerging, further research needs to keep that characteristic which is dynamic and responsive to new challenges.

REFERENCES

Alsharif, A. H., Salleh, N. Z. M., Baharun, R., Hashem, E. A. R., Mansor, A. A., Ali, J., & Abbas, A. F. (2021). Neuroimaging techniques in advertising research: Main applications, development, and brain regions and processes. *Sustainability (Basel)*, 13(11), 6488. DOI: 10.3390/su13116488

Alvino, L., Pavone, L., Abhishta, A., & Robben, H. (2020). Picking your brains: Where and how neuroscience tools can enhance marketing research. *Frontiers in Neuroscience*, 14, 577666. DOI: 10.3389/fnins.2020.577666 PMID: 33343279

Aria, M., Misuraca, M., & Spano, M. (2020). Mapping the evolution of social research and data science on 30 years of social indicators research. *Social Indicators Research*, 149(3), 803–831. DOI: 10.1007/s11205-020-02281-3

Arora, M. (2020). Post-truth and marketing communication in technological age. In *Handbook of research on innovations in technology and marketing for the connected consumer* (pp. 94–108). IGI Global. DOI: 10.4018/978-1-7998-0131-3.ch005

Arora, M. (2023). Encapsulating Role of Persuasion and Skill Development in Marketing Communication for Brand Building: A Perspective. In *International Handbook of Skill, Education, Learning, and Research Development in Tourism and Hospitality* (pp. 1–17). Springer Nature Singapore.

Arora, M. (2024). Virtual Reality in Education: Analyzing the Literature and Bibliometric State of Knowledge. *Transforming Education with Virtual Reality*, 379-402.

Arora, M., Dhiman, V., & Singh, S. (2023). What Is in Store of Entrepreneurship and Skill Development? Analyzing the Trends. In *International Handbook of Skill, Education, Learning, and Research Development in Tourism and Hospitality* (pp. 1–14). Springer Nature Singapore.

Arora, M., Kumar, J., Dhiman, V., Rathore, S., Singh, S., & Chandel, M. (2024). Enhancing Resilience via Exponential Technologies: Analysing Trends, Focus and Contributions. *Abhigyan*, 42(3), 271–290. DOI: 10.1177/09702385241256015

Arora, M., & Sharma, R. L. (2022). Religion and strategic marketing communication: Perspectivizing key facets of consumption. In *Promotional practices and perspectives from emerging markets* (pp. 210–225). Routledge India. DOI: 10.4324/9781003315582-11

Arora, M., & Sharma, R. L. (2023). Artificial intelligence and big data: ontological and communicative perspectives in multi-sectoral scenarios of modern businesses. *foresight*, 25(1), 126-143.

Bhardwaj, S., Kaushik, N., & Arora, M. (2024). Does Your Brain Have a Buy Button?: A Neuro Marketing Approach With Sensory Branding. In *Sensible Selling Through Sensory Neuromarketing* (pp. 210–229). IGI Global. DOI: 10.4018/979-8-3693-4236-7.ch011

Brammer, M. (2004). Brain scam? *Nature Neuroscience*, 7(10), 1015–1015. DOI: 10.1038/nn1004-1015 PMID: 15452565

Cardoso, L., Chen, M. M., Araújo, A., de Almeida, G. G. F., Dias, F., & Moutinho, L. (2022). Accessing neuromarketing scientific performance: Research gaps and emerging topics. *Behavioral Sciences (Basel, Switzerland)*, 12(2), 55. DOI: 10.3390/bs12020055 PMID: 35200306

Chen, H., & Ho, Y. S. (2015). Highly cited articles in biomass research: A bibliometric analysis. *Renewable & Sustainable Energy Reviews*, 49, 12–20. DOI: 10.1016/j.rser.2015.04.060

Chuang, K. Y., Huang, Y. L., & Ho, Y. S. (2007). A bibliometric and citation analysis of stroke-related research in Taiwan. *Scientometrics*, 72(2), 201–212. DOI: 10.1007/s11192-007-1721-0

Clement, J., Smith, V., Zlatev, J., Gidlöf, K., & Van de Weijer, J. (2017). Assessing information on food packages. *European Journal of Marketing*, 51(1), 219–237. DOI: 10.1108/EJM-09-2013-0509

Dhiman, V., & Arora, M. (2024a). Current State of Metaverse in Entrepreneurial Ecosystem: A Retrospective Analysis of Its Evolving Landscape. In *Exploring the Use of Metaverse in Business and Education* (pp. 73-87). IGI Global. DOI: 10.4018/979-8-3693-5868-9.ch005

Dhiman, V., & Arora, M. (2024b). Exploring the linkage between business incubation and entrepreneurship: Understanding trends, themes and future research agenda. *LBS Journal of Management & Research*, 22(1), 66–92. DOI: 10.1108/LBSJMR-06-2023-0021

Dhiman, V., & Arora, M. (2024c). How foresight has evolved since 1999? Understanding its themes, scope and focus. *foresight, 26*(2), 253-271.

Dhiman, V., & Arora, M. (2024d). What Lies in 'Business Incubation and SMEs' Research? A Literature Review and Roadmap for Future Research. *Management*, 1, 17.

Dong, B., Xu, G., Luo, X., Cai, Y., & Gao, W. (2012). A bibliometric analysis of solar power research from 1991 to 2010. *Scientometrics*, 93(3), 1101–1117. DOI: 10.1007/s11192-012-0730-9

Donthu, N., Kumar, S., Mukherjee, D., Pandey, N., & Lim, W. M. (2021). How to conduct a bibliometric analysis: An overview and guidelines. *Journal of Business Research*, 133, 285–296. DOI: 10.1016/j.jbusres.2021.04.070

Donthu, N., Kumar, S., Pattnaik, D., & Pandey, N. (2021). A bibliometric review of International Marketing Review (IMR): Past, present, and future. *International Marketing Review*, 38(5), 840–878. Advance online publication. DOI: 10.1108/IMR-11-2020-0244

Dutta, A. (2023). Neuro-marketing and consumer behavior: Exploring the use of neuroscience techniques to understand how consumers make decisions and respond to marketing stimuli. *EPRA International Journal of Economics. Business and Management Studies*, 10(8), 29–38.

Ellegaard, O., & Wallin, J. A. (2015). The bibliometric analysis of scholarly production: How great is the impact? *Scientometrics*, 105(3), 1809–1831. DOI: 10.1007/s11192-015-1645-z PMID: 26594073

Fortunato, V. C. R., Giraldi, J. D. M. E., & de Oliveira, J. H. C. (2014). A review of studies on neuromarketing: Practical results, techniques, contributions and limitations. *Journal of Management Research*, 6(2), 201. DOI: 10.5296/jmr.v6i2.5446

Garcia, J. R., & Saad, G. (2008). Evolutionary neuromarketing: Darwinizing the neuroimaging paradigm for consumer behavior. *Journal of Consumer Behaviour*, 7(4-5), 397–414. DOI: 10.1002/cb.259

Harris, J. M., Ciorciari, J., & Gountas, J. (2018). Consumer neuroscience for marketing researchers. *Journal of Consumer Behaviour*, 17(3), 239–252. DOI: 10.1002/cb.1710

Kalaganis, F. P., Georgiadis, K., Oikonomou, V. P., Laskaris, N. A., Nikolopoulos, S., & Kompatsiaris, I. (2021). Unlocking the subconscious consumer bias: A survey on the past, present, and future of hybrid EEG schemes in neuromarketing. *Frontiers in Neuroergonomics*, 2, 672982. DOI: 10.3389/fnrgo.2021.672982 PMID: 38235255

Khan, M. A., Pattnaik, D., Ashraf, R., Ali, I., Kumar, S., & Donthu, N. (2021). Value of special issues in the Journal of Business Research: A bibliometric analysis. *Journal of Business Research*, 125, 295–313. DOI: 10.1016/j.jbusres.2020.12.015

Li, H., An, H., Wang, Y., Huang, J., & Gao, X. (2016). Evolutionary features of academic articles co-keyword network and keywords co-occurrence network: Based on two-mode affiliation network. *Physica A*, 450, 657–669. DOI: 10.1016/j.physa.2016.01.017

Lim, W. M. (2018). Demystifying neuromarketing. *Journal of Business Research*, 91, 205–220. DOI: 10.1016/j.jbusres.2018.05.036

Liu, J., Mo, Z., Fu, H., Wei, W., Song, L., & Luo, K. (2021). The effect of reviewers' self-disclosure of personal review record on consumer purchase decisions: An ERPs investigation. *Frontiers in Psychology*, 11, 609538. DOI: 10.3389/fpsyg.2020.609538 PMID: 33488474

Morin, C. (2011). Neuromarketing: The new science of consumer behavior. *Society*, 48(2), 131–135. DOI: 10.1007/s12115-010-9408-1

Ozdemir, M., & Koc, M. (2012). Two methods of creative marketing research neuromarketing and in-depth interview. *Creative and Knowledge Society*, 2(1), 113. DOI: 10.2478/v10212-011-0020-6

Parra-González, M., Segura-Robles, A., Vicente-Bújez, M. R., & López-Belmonte, J. (2020). Production analysis and scientific mapping on active methodologies in Web of Science. [IJET]. *International Journal of Emerging Technologies in Learning*, 15(20), 71–86. DOI: 10.3991/ijet.v15i20.15619

Sánchez-Fernández, R., & Iniesta-Bonillo, M. Á. (2006). Consumer perception of value: Literature review and a new conceptual framework. *Journal of Consumer Satisfaction, Dissatisfaction & Complaining Behavior*, 19, 40–58.

Sebastian, V. (2014). New directions in understanding the decision-making process: Neuroeconomics and neuromarketing. *Procedia: Social and Behavioral Sciences*, 127, 758–762. DOI: 10.1016/j.sbspro.2014.03.350

Sevic, N. P., Slijepcevic, M., & Radojevic, I. (2022). Practical implementation of neuromarketing in different business industries: Challenges and trends. *Annals of Spiru Haret University.Economic Series*, 22(2), 211–227.

Smidts, A. (2002). Kijken in het brein: Over de mogelijkheden van neuromarketing.

Stanton, S. J., Sinnott-Armstrong, W., & Huettel, S. A. (2017). Neuromarketing: Ethical implications of its use and potential misuse. *Journal of Business Ethics*, 144(4), 799–811. DOI: 10.1007/s10551-016-3059-0

Taneja, B., Shukla, P., & Arora, M. (2024). Sensible Selling Through Sensory Neuromarketing: Enhancing Sales Effectiveness. In *Sensible Selling Through Sensory Neuromarketing* (pp. 164-183). IGI Global.

Wang, J., Li, X., Wang, P., Liu, Q., Deng, Z., & Wang, J. (2022). Research Trend of the Unified Theory of Acceptance and Use of Technology Theory: A Bibliometric Analysis. *Sustainability (Basel)*, 14(1), 10. DOI: 10.3390/su14010010

Yang, L., Sun, T., & Liu, Y. (2017). A bibliometric investigation of flipped classroom research during 2000-2015. [IJET]. *International Journal of Emerging Technologies in Learning*, 12(06), 178–186. DOI: 10.3991/ijet.v12i06.7095

Zaltman, G. (2003). *How customers think: Essential insights into the mind of the market*. Harvard Business Press.

Zhao, X. (2017). A scientometric review of global BIM research: Analysis and visualization. *Automation in Construction*, 80, 37–47. DOI: 10.1016/j.autcon.2017.04.002

Chapter 8
Sensory Marketing and Its Influence on Consumer Buying Behavior:
A Comprehensive Analysis

Richa Pareek
Mody University of Science and Technology, India

Lalita Kumari
Mody University of Science and Technology, India

Anupal Mongia
Mody University of Science and Technology, India

Meena Sharma
Mody University of Science and Technology, India

ABSTRACT

The marketing tactic whose usage and significance have grown in recent years is sensory marketing, which appeals to consumer's senses to influence their perception and purchasing behavior. The study explore the clever ways in which companies use sensory cues to influence consumer decisions. The study used a multifaceted approach to investigate the psychological processes that underlie sensory marketing and how they affect consumers perceptions, feelings, and, ultimately, purchasing decisions. The study is based on Descriptive cum Theoretical Approach which is justified by past studies and their outcome. It examines the components of sensory marketing visual, auditory, olfactory, tactile, and gustative marketing and how they could affect consumer behavior through number of literature reviews. It concludes that the challenge facing marketers is to investigate, comprehend, and stimulate the

DOI: 10.4018/979-8-3693-9351-2.ch008

five senses of consumers in order to possibly trigger a shift in consumer behavior that would directly impact sales, earnings, and market share.

INTRODUCTION

These days, fierce competition pushes businesses and brands to aim for uniqueness. Using marketing techniques that successfully entice customers is one approach to set oneself apart from competitors. One marketing tactic whose usage and significance have grown in recent years is sensory marketing, which appeals to consumers' senses to influence their perception and purchasing behavior. Understanding human senses is essential to comprehending consuming processes, wherein personal choices and actions play a significant role. A cutting-edge marketing tactic known as "sensory marketing" is used to enhance a consumer's interaction with a brand, creating a lasting emotional bond that maximizes brand loyalty. Numerous factors influence a person's decision to purchase a good or service, including cultural, social, psychological, and individual considerations. More and more individuals are becoming aware of the importance of sensory marketing as it moves into the spotlight. This document addresses a topic that benefits both businesses and the individual customer. It addresses how the senses are involved and makes an effort to make clear how crucial they are to corporate communication. Sensory marketing influences the consumer's senses, which in turn influences perception, decision-making, and behavior. The primary goal of sensory marketing is to communicate directly to the consumer's brain, piquing their curiosity and enticing them to buy that specific product—thereby forging a relationship between the customer and the product. Because the five senses are so vital to human existence, creating brands that are highly valued is a major contributing factor to the market's constant growth in brands. Our sense of smell, which oversees the scents we inhale while eating, deserves our gratitude. Because taste and emotional state are closely related, one's flavor can significantly impact one's mood as well as their perception of a brand. To help marketers better understand how to use sensory experiences to increase brand engagement and boost sales, this chapter proposal will include a thorough analysis of sensory marketing and how it affects consumer purchasing behavior. This chapter aims to expand our knowledge of the intricate relationship between sensory stimuli and consumer decision-making processes through a combination of theoretical frameworks, empirical research, and real-world examples. This comprehension will finally empower marketers to develop more powerful and successful marketing campaigns. According to recent study, a new era of consumer product firms utilizing sense-based marketing is poised to begin. Good products or services are no longer the sole criterion for selection, as competition amongst businesses is growing. Present-day shoppers anticipate a healthy purchasing experience. Products that pique their curiosity and establish an emotional bond draw them in. Hence, their choice is influenced by both the setting at the time of purchasing and the features of the product. A marketer started utilizing senses to provide their goods and services a competitive edge. Thus, an attempt has been made in this study to explore the application of five senses in product and service marketing, as well as to introduce the idea of sensory marketing.

Olfactory sensations activate the parts of the brain responsible for memory and emotion creation Seventy-five percent of our emotional reactions are triggered by smell, and the average individual can identify and remember up to 10,000 distinct scents (Randhir et al., 2016). The only sense that is directly connected to the brain is smell. Scholar explains in his best-selling book, Brain Rules. The most well-known example of olfactory marketing in the food industry is the use of artificial scents to draw customers in public spaces like the street, subway, or grocery store (Chebat & Michon, 2003). Using images to promote products (sight). Since the sense of sight is the one that is most stimulated by the outside world, marketing primarily depends on it Marketers understand the significance of seemingly insignificant elements like the color and form of a product's packaging, the layout of display cases in stores, and the way a marketing campaign is carried out. The basic methods of classification and differentiation used by the human visual system are color and form. If a brand name is associated with a color that people are friendly with, they are more probably to recall it. According to Krawczak (2016), the right music may influence our attitudes and purchases. The likelihood that a client will remember a message is increased when music is associated with it, as is often known. Research's have stipulated that music may have an impact on consumer behavior, therefore it's not unexpected that specialists in sensory marketing see the possibility of playing comforting tunes. A sales environment's efficacy is determined by how well it takes into account the subjectivity of the prospective buyer (Célier, 2004). A product's inherent sound may conjure positive associations for buyers. The skin has more than four million sensory receptors, and the materials, weight, smoothness, and ease of use of a product can all have an immediate effect on these receptors. Appealing to the sense of touch is highly valued in packaging design and even in some types of advertising. Our packaging may have a significant effect on how long customers remember our products (Barnes & Nath 2016). It's an infallible method for accessing the subconscious and understanding the opinions, feelings, and preferences of customers. Five taste buds on human bodies enable humans to distinguish between bitter, sour, savory, salty, and sweet flavors.

Sensory Marketing

Sensory marketing is a strategy that appeals to the senses of consumers to enhance their shopping experience and drive purchase behavior. It leverages elements such as touch, taste, smell, and sight to create a multisensory environment that engages consumers on a deeper level. The sensory marketing is "engaging with customers through their senses of taste, smell, touch, and hearing." (Tek and Engin, 2008) One method to engage customers and provide them with an experience is by responding to their senses. Marketing-produced stimulants are actually first absorbed by the senses, and perception is the outcome of the interpretation of these experiences. (Barış & Odabaşı, 2012) A person will feel happy or dissatisfied because of this perceiving process. Even marketing and psychology have demonstrated a renewed interest in the character that sensory acquaintance play in judgment and decision making in recent years. The term "sensory marketing," which refers to "marketing that involves the consumers' senses and influences their perception, decision-making, and behavior," has been used in marketing to bring together diverse studies on the role of the senses in consumer behavior (Krishna 2012). People use their senses to see the world, but the representations they create from sensory inputs are not always precise depictions of the features of the stimuli. This fact led to an ongoing interest in sensory perception illusions that spans from ancient philosophy to modern neuroscience (Kotler, 1973–74) In some of this research, mood was also manipulated through sensory experience. In a sense, sensory marketing is the application of sensory and perception theory to the study of consumer thoughts, feelings, understanding, preferences, choice, and assessment in the context of marketing. The goal of sensory marketing is to provide the ideal sensory stimuli and have the biggest possible influence on consumers' purchasing decisions. Feelings influence multiple factors, including retail marketing priorities and choices, store records, in-store duration, customer satisfaction during shopping, pleasure-seeking and consumption-focused shopping, decision-making styles of consumers, and consumer interest rates and desires (Haghigi et al., 2010). The objective of sensory marketing is to stimulate the consumer's senses, deliver information to the right portion of the brain, and ultimately build an association between the product and the customer to persuade him to buy (Costa et al., 2012). Individuals act on the basis of emotion and draw conclusions based on reason, which is the fundamental distinction between emotion and reason (Kotler et al., 2011). In reality, the customer imagines themselves using the good or service and assesses their emotions (Hawkins et al., 1996).

In order to influence consumers' perceptions and behavior, sensory marketers can effectively engage consumers through the use of unconscious sensory stimuli. Although stimulants have a strong stimulating capacity and are in accordance with the five senses, their impact on the target audience and consumer is more significant (Hulten et al., 2012).

Senses in Humans and Sensory Marketing

It's widely held that businesses can no longer sustain their brand strategies just through transactional or relational marketing in the modern world, which is marked by an abundance of information, time constraints, and daily complications. Rather, sensory approaches that are grounded in the sensory marketing model ought to be applied by comprehending how stimuli and cues that are seen by the senses affect consumer behavior (Rodrigues, 2014). The consumer's mind and senses are approached from both a cognitive and an emotional point of view in the sensory tactics, which distinguish the products and services. The consumer's mind and senses are approached from both a cognitive and an emotional point of view in the sensory tactics, which distinguish the products and services. Among all the senses, vision is the most important, followed by smell, sound, taste, and touch. Study has indicated that a person's perception of a product is greatly influenced by their vision. Even in the circumstances when they are incompetent to recall seeing the product, those who have been exposed to it are likely to favor it over alternatives that are similar. For instance, the brand, design, color scheme, and lighting all have an impact on clear eyesight. In this case, most of us are able to identify Coca-Cola by its iconic red and white logo. Colours are essential to how people perceive a brand because they can draw attention to the key characteristics and connections with a product or brand (Uddin, 2011). Colours may create psychological connections, which can lead to a variety of benefits, including improved a sense of belonging competitive advantage, and marketing distinction (Skeryte and Liburyte, 2014).

Sensory Framework's theoretical underpinnings:

Figure 1. Theoretical Framework of Sensory Marketing

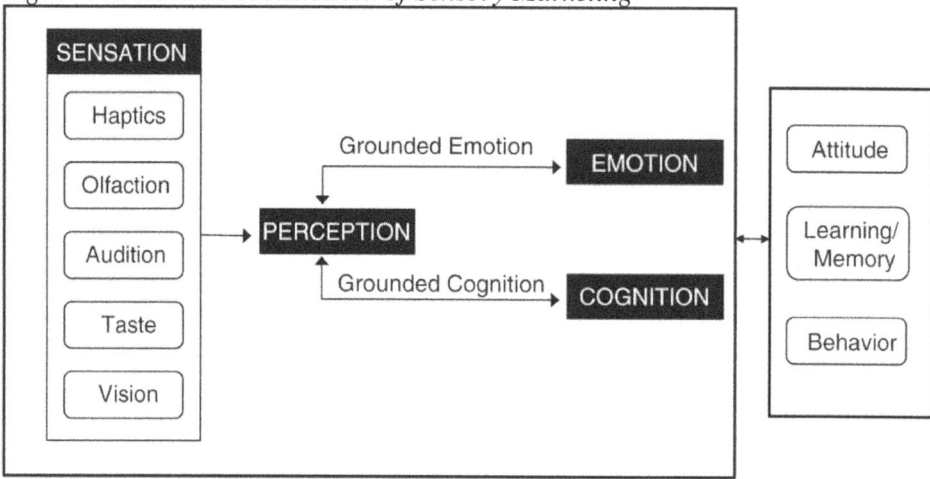

Source: A theoretical framework of sensory marketing by A. Krishna / Journal of Consumer Psychology 22 (2012) 332-351.

The relationship between experiences and consumer impressions making use of the five senses—haptics, olfaction, hearing, taste, and vision—is reflected in the theoretical framework of sensory marketing mentioned above (Krishna, 2012). Few recent years have witnessed an unprecedented explosion of the metaverse, mostly derived from 3D gaming, which is fuelled by the improvement of hardware (e.g., big data storage infrastructure, wireless communication networks, built-in sensors, and graphic processing unit—GPU) and the optimization of software (e.g., resource allocation in communications, language processing, and

computer vision) to build the virtual world more solidly and creatively. Different from the traditional metaverse modality that limits immersive experience poorly by insufficient data, the new one not only generates a huge new source of user and behavioral data for enterprises (where users freely make creative content) but also presents a plentiful foundation to deploy artificial intelligence (AI) into various domains, such as natural language processing, computer vision, and neural interface. To illustrate the distinction between sensation and perception, the study draws on examples from psychology and marketing. The study then continues by expanding on studies on each of those five senses, paying particular attention to elements that could lead to significant advancements. The paper examines all senses, including haptics, person-product, person-person, and person-product haptic interactions, in addition to haptics research. Smell is discussed in more detail, with an emphasis on learning and perception. Work on the audition comes next, then intake, satiation, and taste. Very little thought has been given to vision, considering the massive amount of work that was previously invested into advertising. The interplay between perception and emotion can be used to characterize the sensory marketing sector in certain ways (Krishna, 2010). The brain of the individual will produce an internal response based on how and in what context it sees the input when the sensory organs are triggered. A person's internal reactions can be emotional, cognitive, or both, and they can influence their attitude toward a brand or product, whether it be favorable or bad (Krishna, 2012).

Smell/Olfaction in sensory marketing:

Smell is part of the air you breathe, even though you may block your hearing, avert your eyes, avoid drawing attention to yourself and refuse to taste (Lindstrom, 2005). The impact of fragrance on consumers is covered in Darabi and Mirabi's (2018) study. One of the most important senses for all living things is smell, and people have relied on it for basic existence. Olfactory sensory receptors are classified by companies into two groups: 1. Olfaction of goods or services; 2. Olfaction of the surroundings. While not every company needs to concentrate on adding fragrance, there are certain products that consumers evaluate primarily on the basis of aroma, such as food items and food products, where consumers typically assess the quality. Although there are other uses of scent, such as in restaurants, retail centers, and physical stores, businesses and sectors intentionally introduce artificial scents into their physical spaces to enhance customers' sense of smell and encourage them to spend more time there. According to Kotler and Lindstrom (2005), 45% of communication with a brand occurs through the sense of smell. Smell has a profound effect on human behavior and is closely related to both emotions and behavior (Mahmoudi et al. 2012). Apparently, many businesses think that smells and aromas can influence customer behavior in a good way (Bone & Allen, 1999). We use the same brand of perfume because it makes us feel good and smell good – sometimes even revitalizing. Similarly, smell influences decisions about what to buy and creates brand loyalty., Fragrance also gives us a feeling of fullness, happiness and comfort (Harrop 2007).Fragrances have the power to leave a lasting or momentary impression on the consumer's mind. Customers want to make the brand a permanent part of their everyday life because of the attractive fragrance, which leaves a lasting impression. We associate a specific smell with an emotional memory or remembered image. Additionally, it may be linked to short-term or long-term marketing plans (Hulton, Brownius, Dijk 2009).

Auditory factors (Hearing) in sensory marketing:

"Music is eternal, and only hearing is intermittent.[1]"

Most forms of marketing communication are auditory in nature; listeners hear jingles, songs, and commercial messages on radio and television; they can also hear ambient music in stores, hotels, restaurants, and aircraft. Furthermore, certain goods have their own unique noises. Examples include the Intel Pentium processor sound that plays whenever the computer is turned on and the sounds from Motorola or Verizon cell phones[2]. It has long been known that sound has a significant positive impact on preferences, emotions, and consumer behaviour (Alpert et al. 2005). An effective way to connect with the unconscious requirements of the customer is through sound. This affects our buying patterns (Lindström, 2005). Vida (2008) found that musical perception improves customer satisfaction and that after a store review, customers find the merchandise attractive, leading to more visits to the store and spending more time and money. The results verified that consumers' behavior can be influenced by appropriate music.

Tactile Marketing /Haptic in sensory marketing

"We are a tactile society, and one of the few opportunities we have to freely engage with the material world is when we shop." (Underhill, 2009, p.168)

As the aforementioned quotation suggests, in today's world of internet and online shopping, physically handling a thing is still highly valued during the buying process. Consumer decision-making regarding product purchases is influenced by the way a product feels. When we consider that we typically make our purchasing decisions after touching a product, it becomes more apparent. This is because we typically notice products first. Touch conveys meaning and content that are difficult to express using more formal language because it is the first sense that children develop (Spence & Gallace, 2011). Many companies that sell tangible goods want to give customers a satisfying haptic experience or give them access to information that would entice them to buy via touch. For example, Apple enables haptic interactions between customers and products in their physical locations (Solomon et al., 2013). When purchasing things with haptic qualities, such blankets or jumpers, consumers would rather purchase them offline than online (McCabe and Nowlis, 2003). Tactile input is crucial for decision-making in these products. Customers also prefer items that are easy to hold; for example, a sturdy cup makes for a better drinking experience than one that is unstable. This suggests that a product's haptic qualities may have an impact on how a customer perceives it (Krishna and Morrin, 2008).

Visual Sensory Marketing\The Sense of sight

Sight is the most alluring sense of all and is the primary means of recognizing a brand or logo, superseding the other four. The brain's dorsal and ventral pathways are responsible for what (where) and what (what) processes related to vision, which aids in our understanding of what is where. Color, direction, motion, texture, and stereoscopic depth—a sense of depth and three-dimensional structure based on visual data from two eyes—are among the visual characteristics that the brain processes. The most dominant sense is sight (Schiffman, 1990)

where consumers rely on a variety of real and visible stimuli to grab their attention(Ward etal, 1992). Among the senses, vision is the most prominent and significant since the brain-eye coordination appears to be more effective than any mechanism that has ever been discovered (Winter & Winter, 2003). Most pople agree that sight is the most strong and captivating sense in humans (Hulten, Broweus, Dijk, 2009). Nowadays, consumers receive 10,000 visual messages per day, accounting for over 80 percent of brand communication through the sense of sight (Lounge Group,2011). According to Simon Faure Field, 2009), 83% of marketing spending goes toward providing visual aids for commercial communication. Observation is a visual technique that enhances the customer's sensory experience by improving brand awareness and brand image (Hulten, Broweus, Dijk2009).Visual identification is the first step in the brand experience; slogans, signs, emblems, writings, and other visual cues are still used today as various types of communication (O' Neil 2005).

Colour , Lindström (2010) makes the fundamental argument that brands that appeal to a variety of senses will have greater success than those that simply appeal to one or two. It could be a feature of the brand's advertising, like the color (like the blue of Pepsi or the red of Coca-Cola), logo, tagline, etc., or it could be a feature of the product itself, like the design of Lamborghini automobiles or the taste (like Nutella).Obando Changuán and Loya Simbaña,2022 investigates the impact of colors and sensory marketing on consumer purchasing preferences., from his research, it reveals that how colors influence consumer purchasing decisions. Findings emphasize the significant role of colors like yellow, blue, and red in shaping consumer psychology and behavior. (Marvin Ian Niere, 2024) analysed from his study that there is a significant relationships between perceived levels of color psychology in advertising, awareness levels, and consumer buying behavior. Overall, the research establishes a strong positive correlation between color preferences, awareness levels, brand recall, and consumer behavior among business students. Any strategy for a brand can include visual stimuli like as logos, colors, packaging, and product design (Hulten, 2013).

Gustative Marketing\ The sense of Taste

Similar to all other senses, taste is perceived by humans through taste receptor cells located in the brain (Rupini & Nandagopal, 2015). Sense of Taste is only introduced by food industry. The five main tastes are umami, which is a savory flavor found in foods like mushrooms, soy sauce, and seafood, and sour, sweet, bitter, and salty. In human life, taste perceptions have a significant influence on all levels—physical, social, and even emotional. Eating and drinking are linked to joy and good memories, which emphasizes that marketers shouldn't undervalue flavor factors (Esmailpour & Zakipour, 2016). An instinctive representation of good taste is a powerful tool for influencing customer behavior in situations where food product marketers are engaged in intense competition. It should be important for businesses that use palate-based marketing since it can persuade customers. According to Jayakrishnan (2013), Coca-Cola is one of the companies that has successfully used taste to create a distinctive identity for itself. In their investigation of the restaurant business, Costa et al. (2012) concluded that sensory marketing is a tactic used in marketing that seeks to win over customers. This is accomplished by providing distinctive services that go beyond the standard offerings of color to grab attention, scent and odor to soothe, sound to entice visitors to stay still, and taste to surprise the palate.

Metaverse and AI in Sensible Marketing

Through the integration of Virtual Reality (VR), Augmented Reality (AR), and Mixed Reality (MR) into a digital reality, the Metaverse—a fast emerging field—has the potential to completely change our everyday lives. Avatars are created by users who engage with others while discovering new places and becoming themselves. Because businesses can now directly service clients through their digital avatars, this opens up new organizational and commercial prospects for them.

Large digital businesses that have invested in virtual events and virtual communication ecosystems, such as Microsoft, Snoop Dogg, and Metaverse Group, have drawn attention to the metaverse. Recently, the Seoul Metropolitan administration unveiled Metaverse Seoul, a proposal that establishes a virtual communication ecosystem for several municipal administrative areas. (Mina Alaghband, 2022). People would get the impression that they were taking part in the live event in this way. Companies would be able to directly serve clients through their avatars in the virtual world, opening up new organisational and commercial options. Conventional issues like TV commercials and print ads would also change if it were the real world (Hagiu & Wright, 2015). It is best to quote directly from the authors Huynh-The et al. (2023) rather than paraphrase or repeat their excellent work in order to give the reader an overview of the implications and questions surrounding the metaverse. Since Mark Zuckerberg announced Facebook's rebranding as Meta in October 2021, the amazing idea behind the new name has gained a lot of attention on social media and sparked numerous conversations across a variety of communities, including academics and business. In addition to Meta, a few major IT corporations are also involved in metaverse development and investment. For example, Microsoft paid $68.7 billion to acquire Activision Blizzard, a holding company for video games, to expand its gaming business into the metaverse. Lately, the Metaverse real estate investment group Metaverse Group. At the startling sum of $2.43 million, which is the largest amount ever paid for virtual real estate, a corporation purchased a plot of property on the decentralized virtual reality platform known as Decentral and. Famous musician Snoop Dogg paid $450,000 for a piece of land in the Sandbox metaverse, allowing him to host virtual events such as concerts and music festivals. By using virtual reality technology, he can provide an immersive experience for anyone attending the virtual world. Online game developers, online financial companies, social networks, and other industry titans are currently drawn to the metaverse, which will soon be recognized as the next big thing in technology. The Metaverse Seoul plan, recently unveiled by the Seoul metropolitan administration, aims to establish a virtual communication ecosystem including all municipal administrative domains, including cultural, tourism, economic, educational, and civic service sectors.

In addition to offering various business support services and amenities, Metaverse Seoul will provide specific services that enable individuals with disabilities to enjoy safe and comfortable content through the use of extended reality (XR) technology. According to a Bloomberg Intelligence research, the potential revenue from the metaverse will rise from $500 billion in 2020 to $804 billion in 2024, with the online gaming sector accounting for half of this total (Kanterman & Naidu, 2021). This is critical because the metaverse may change how cognitive and affective processes are modulated. It may even be able to replace one set of feelings with another, given its purported ability to generate alternate worlds. For this reason, all research on the impact of digital environments on the human brain would need to be reexamined (Riva & Wiederhold, 2022). Neuroscience is highly helpful for studying emotions, attention, and memory in virtual environments like the metaverse. Neuroscience has investigated these concepts in different sectors connected to organisations and business. However, there isn't much research on these problems in virtual settings that are immersive (Mandolfo et al., 2022). González-Morales (2020) utilized electroencephalography (EEG) to determine emotional valence in the metaverse, utilizing the ecological paradigm. This method allows real-time assessment of emotional states, enabling the design of points of sale, corporate image, services, products, and the relationship between salesperson and consumer avatars, ultimately influencing customer decision-making.

CONCLUSION

The use of sensory marketing techniques could help with current marketing issues. Unlike other forms of marketing, sensory marketing appeals directly to the consumer's senses. Visual marketing comprises product design, names, packages, logos, and more. It establishes a sense of quality and encourages purchases, both of which directly contribute to the development of a powerful brand. Scents can be used in a variety of product forms to position, differentiate, and enhance a brand and its image in olfactory marketing.

Scents are so crucial because they have a direct impact on customers' memories and likelihood of having a positive experience. Businesses using aural marketing must exercise discretion when choosing music, as it should influence consumers' perceptions of the store as a whole. Businesses ought to find out what kinds of music their clients enjoy. Tactile marketing, which is successful in terms of the quantity of things purchased, has an impact on customers' purchases when they engage with a product. Marketing that uses touch is more likely to have a favorable effect on people who have a strong Need for Touch (NFT). Gustative marketing is significant because food and drink are linked to happiness, which is why the flavor component shouldn't be overlooked. In general, sensory marketing focuses on the company's client service and the impressions it makes on them. The task facing marketers is to investigate, comprehend, and arouse the five senses of consumers, as this might result in a change in consumer behavior that can impact sales, earnings, and market share.

Mandolfo et al. (2022) assert that changing how one perceives emotions and senses will change one's behaviour in the metaverse (Dincelli & Yayla, 2022). Dozio et al. (2022) claim that emotions in the metaverse can be changed by altering the visual, semantic, dynamic, and interactive components.

Avatars, accessories, and virtual environment modification all have the power to affect feelings and perceptions. Avatars and virtual agents have the power to affect people's emotions and raise metaverse satisfaction and trust levels (Dincelli; Yayla, 2022). There is still a lot more research to be done to improve the metaverse's emotional experience (Angelini et al., 2022). Consequently, it has been shown that the incorporation of the users' emotions as represented by their avatars is highly intriguing in several ways. It is highly helpful in addition to EEG and peripheral psychophysiological data, but as the author points out, it would be crucial to have access to microexpression recognition software.

Studying how people behave in the metaverse is thought to be crucial since trading in it requires an understanding of the emotions elicited by each element and setting, and in retailing, the hedonistic viewpoint is more significant than the utilitarian one (Dincelli & Yaila, 2022). The author suggests that we will be able to determine the user's emotional state and what they are looking at all times during their immersion in the metaverse by utilizing the eye tracker in conjunction with peripheral psychophysiological monitoring and EEG monitors. Everything that is revealed is connected, as can be seen, and the author's line in this article suggests that neuromarketing be used in research, analysis, and the creation of fresh theoretical marketing concepts for the metaverse, particularly those that center on the attention, emotions, and memory of users. It is possible to understand the feelings, inclination to recall, and commitment that are produced by each element developed in the metaverse by using the ecological paradigm technique. Metaverse will give businesses that have the most in-depth knowledge about distribution and payment methods, pricing, product design, communication, and purchasing behavior a competitive edge.

REFERENCES

Alpert, M. I., Alpert, J. I., & Maltz, E. N. (2005). Purchase occasion influences on the role of music in advertising. *Journal of Business Research*, 58(3), 369–376. DOI: 10.1016/S0148-2963(03)00101-2

Arora, M. (2020). Post-truth and marketing communication in technological age. In *Handbook of research on innovations in technology and marketing for the connected consumer* (pp. 94–108). IGI Global. DOI: 10.4018/978-1-7998-0131-3.ch005

Arora, M. (2024). Metaverse Metamorphosis: Bridging the Gap Between Research Insights and Industry Applications. In Research, Innovation, and Industry Impacts of the Metaverse (pp. 275-286). IGI Global.

Arora, M. (2024). Virtual Reality in Education: Analyzing the Literature and Bibliometric State of Knowledge. Transforming Education with Virtual Reality, 379-402.

Arora, M., & Sharma, R. L. (2023). Artificial intelligence and big data: ontological and communicative perspectives in multi-sectoral scenarios of modern businesses. foresight, 25(1), 126-143.

Bone, P. F., & Ellen, P. S. (1999). Scents in the marketplace: Explaining a fraction of olfaction. *Journal of Retailing*, 75(2), 243–262. DOI: 10.1016/S0022-4359(99)00007-X

Branding, A. O. S., & Purchase, I. E. O. Journal Homepage:-www. journalijar. Com

Çabuk, S., & YAĞCI, M. İ. (2018). Pazarlamaya çağdaş yaklaşım. Akademisyen Kitabevi.

Chandel, M., & Arora, M. (2024). Metaverse Perspectives: Unpacking Its Role in Shaping Sustainable Development Goals-A Qualitative Inquiry. In Research, Innovation, and Industry Impacts of the Metaverse (pp. 62-75). IGI Global.

Changuán, M. P. O., & Simbaña, J. A. L. (2022). Consumer color neuromarketing. Journal of business and entrepreneurial studie, 6(3).

Costa, M. F., Patricia, Z. Natasha, R. Jessica, A and Maria, G.V. (2012). Sensory marketing: Consumption experience of the Brazilian in the restaurant industry. *International Journal of Business Strategy*, 12(4), 165–171.

Darabi, K., & Mirabi, V. (2018). The effect of ambient scent on consumer experience: Evidence from mobile industry. *Management Science Letters*, 8(11), 1199–1206. DOI: 10.5267/j.msl.2018.8.005

Esmailpour, H., & Zakipour, M. (2016). The sensory stimuli model; engage with the consumer senses for brand distinguishes. *Journal of Management Sciences*, 2(4), 212–218.

González-Morales, A. (2022). La optimización de la comunicación POSM "Point of Sale Materials" en productos de compra por impulso mediante neuromarketing. IROCAMM. *International Review of Communication and Marketing Mix*, 5(1), 57–71. DOI: 10.12795/IROCAMM.2021.v05.i01.05

González-Morales, A., Mitrovic, J., & Garcia, R. C. (2020). Ecological consumer neuroscience for competitive advantage and business or organizational differentiation. *European Research on Management and Business Economics*, 26(3), 174–180. DOI: 10.1016/j.iedeen.2020.05.001

Harrop, S. (2007). What role can sensory branding play in online marketing?.

Hawkins, D., Boston, R., & Kenny, K. (2006). Consumer Behavior, Translated by Ahmad Rousta, Atieh Bathaei & Zeinab Hagh Verdi.

Hulten, B. (2013). Sensory cues as in-store innovations: Their impact on shopper approaches and touch behavior. *Journal of Innovation Management*, 1(1), 17–37.

Hulten, B., Broweus, N., & Van Dijk, M. (2008). Sinnesmarknadsföring. Liber AB.

Jamison, K., & Clayton, J. (2016). Exploring the experiences of administrative interns: Implications for university preparation programs. *Journal of Educational Administration*, 54(5), 514–536. DOI: 10.1108/JEA-02-2015-0020

Jayakrishnan, S. (2013). Creating brand identity using human senses. *Asia Pacific Journal of Research*, 2(8), 223–228.

Kotler, P. (1973). Atmospherics as a marketing tool. *Journal of Retailing*, 49(4), 48–64.

Kotler, P. H., Setiawan, I., & Kartajaya, H. (2011). Marketing 3: From products to sustomers to the human spirit. translated by: Abdul Hamid Ibrahimi, Samad Aali, Alireza Bafandeh zendeh, elnaz Alizadeh Ashrafi, 1st volume.

Krishna, A. (2012). An integrative review of sensory marketing: Engaging the senses to affect perception, judgment and behavior. *Journal of Consumer Psychology*, 22(3), 332–351. DOI: 10.1016/j.jcps.2011.08.003

Krishna, A., & Morrin, M. (2008). Does touch affect taste? The perceptual transfer of product container haptic cues. *The Journal of Consumer Research*, 34(6), 807–818. DOI: 10.1086/523286

Kumar, J., Arora, M., & Erkol Bayram, G. (Eds.). (2024). *Exploring the Use of Metaverse in Business and Education*. IGI Global. DOI: 10.4018/979-8-3693-5868-9

Kumar, P., & Kumar, K. (2020). Awareness of Sensory Marketing and Its Relationship With Consumer Behaviour: A Study of Restaurants in Bangalore. [IJM]. *International Journal of Management*, 11(3), 791–807.

Lindstrom, M. (2011). *Brand sense: Sensory secrets behind the stuff we buy*. Simon and Schuster.

Lindstrom, M., & Kotler, P. (2005). *Brand sense: build powerful brands through touch, taste, smell, sight, and sound*. Free Pr.

Manchanda, R., Mittal, S., USMS, G., & Bansal, S. examining the senses influencing sensory marketing and its impact on consumer behavior.

Maymand, M. M., Ahmadinejad, M., & Nezami, P. (2012). Sensory brand: Studying relationship between 5 senses and brand value at world's 100 top companies. *Australian Journal of Basic and Applied Sciences*, 6(8), 337–343.

McCabe, D. B., & Nowlis, S. M. (2003). The effect of examining actual products or product descriptions on consumer preference. *Journal of Consumer Psychology*, 13(4), 431–439. DOI: 10.1207/S15327663JCP1304_10

Niere, M. I., Bustamante, J. R. B., Bacaltos, M. S., Arceo, R. A. B., & Bigno, H. (2024). Influence of Color Psychology on Consumer Behavior among Business Students. *International Journal of Multidisciplinary: Applied Business and Education Research*, 5(3), 848–862. DOI: 10.11594/ijmaber.05.03.10

Rodrigues, C., & Brito, C. (2011). Sensorial brand strategies for value co-creation.

Rodrigues, C. A. M. C. S. (2014). Brand sensuality and consumer-based brand equity (Doctoral dissertation, Universidade do Porto (Portugal)).

Rupini, R. V., & Nandagopal, R. (2015). A Study on the Influence of Senses and the Effectiveness of Sensory Branding. *Journal of Psychiatry*, 18(2), 236.

Schiffman, H. R. (1990). *Sensation and perception: An integrated approach*. John Wiley & Sons.

Shabgou, M., & Daryani, S. M. (2014). Towards the sensory marketing: Stimulating the five senses (sight, hearing, smell, touch and taste) and its impact on consumer behavior. *Indian Journal of Fundamental and Applied Life Sciences*, 4(1), 573–581.

Shabgou, M., & Daryani, S. M. (2014). Towards the sensory marketing: Stimulating the five senses (sight, hearing, smell, touch and taste) and its impact on consumer behavior. *Indian Journal of Fundamental and Applied Life Sciences*, 4(1), 573–581.

Sliburyte, L., & Skeryte, I. (2014). What we know about consumers' color perception. *Procedia: Social and Behavioral Sciences*, 156, 468–472. DOI: 10.1016/j.sbspro.2014.11.223

Solomon, M., Russell-Bennett, R., & Previte, J. (2012). *Consumer behaviour*. Pearson Higher Education AU.

Spence, C. (2020). On the ethics of neuromarketing and sensory marketing. Organizational Neuroethics: Reflections on the Contributions of Neuroscience to Management Theories and Business Practices, 9-29.

Spence, C., & Gallace, A. (2011). Multisensory design: Reaching out to touch the consumer. *Psychology and Marketing*, 28(3), 267–308. DOI: 10.1002/mar.20392

Tek, Ö. B., & Engin, Ö. (2008). Modern Pazarlama İlkeleriUygulamalı Yönetimsel. Yaklaşım (3. Basım).

Uddin, M. S. (2011). *The Impact of Sensory Branding (five senses) on Consumer: A Case Study on*. Coca Cola.

Vida, I. (2008). Atmospheric music fit as a driver of shopper store evaluations and their behavioral responses. [JABR]. *Journal of Applied Business Research*, 24(2). Advance online publication. DOI: 10.19030/jabr.v24i2.1356

Winter, A., & Winter, R. (2003). Brain workout: Easy ways to power up your memory, sensory perception, and intelligence. IUniverse.

Winter, J., Scheiner, C. W., & Voigt, K. I. (2009). Emotional branding in the durable goods industry illustrated.

ENDNOTES

[1] Henry David Thoreau, American philosopher.

[2] Krishna, A. (2012). An integrative review of sensory marketing: Engaging the senses to affect perception, judgment and behavior. *Journal of consumer psychology*, 22(3), 332-351.

Chapter 9
The Impact of Product Display on Consumer Attention and Buying Intention

Sneha Jaiswal
Christ University, India

Abhinav Priyadarshi Tripathi
https://orcid.org/0000-0002-5492-7616
Christ University, India

Anju Tripathi
Asian Business School, India

ABSTRACT

"The study, titled 'The Impact of Product Display on Consumer Attention and Buying Intention,' critically examines the complex relationship that exists between consumers and product displays in the dynamic retail environment." The study investigates how product arrangement, presentation, and visual appeal work as influencing variables in consumer decision-making, with a focus on the issues given by an excess of alternatives. Based on a thorough evaluation of the literature, the study develops a conceptual framework that includes independent variables related to display characteristics, a mediator variable (customer attention), and moderating factors related to consumer and retail environment characteristics. The impact of display location, size, colour, movement, and lighting on consumer attention and purchasing intention is investigated using hypotheses and objectives. The study takes a mixed-methods approach, gathering primary data from 70 people in the

DOI: 10.4018/979-8-3693-9351-2.ch009

NCR Delhi region using interviews and questionnaires and leveraging secondary data from diverse sources. Descriptive statistics offer subtle insights into age-related trends, illustrating the varied impact of appealing displays on various age groups. Chi-Square Tests are used to investigate correlations between categorical variables, providing useful insights into the relationship between education level and shopping patterns. The results have significant impacts for organizations searching for to improve their marketing strategies by optimising product displays, emphasising the need of context-aware interpretation, and recognising the changing landscape of customer behaviour in the retail sector. Finally, this study serves as a thorough guide, unravelling the subtle dynamics that impact consumer decisions in reaction to product displays and laying the groundwork for future research in this expanding topic."

1. INTRODUCTION

In the constantly changing environment of retail, where consumers are continuously overloaded with options, attracting attention and influencing purchasing intentions has become a critical task (Smith et al., 2020; Johnson & Lee, 2019). Among all the elements affecting consumer behaviour, the importance of product displays in retail spaces has emerged as a powerful and significant device.

Product arrangement, presentation, and aesthetic appeal serves as the link between a product and its prospective consumer, acting like unspoken salespersons within the retail environment (Chang et al., 2018). These displays have an extraordinary potential for capturing a consumer's attention, engage their senses, and ultimately influence their purchasing decisions. Understanding the intricate connection between product displays, consumer attention, and purchasing intentions has become a priority for both retailers and marketers.

This study begins an interesting analysis of this complex relationship, attempting to uncover the many features of product displays that influence consumer behaviour. It focuses into display visual aesthetics, strategic placement within retail settings, and the basic Behavioural factors that impact consumers. responses (O'Boyle et al., 2021). By giving into focus these key areas, this study aims to provide a thorough knowledge of how businesses can use product displays to fascinate consumers and influence their purchasing decisions.

As we continue through this exploration, we hope to understand the complexities that determine why and how consumers make decisions in the huge retail ecosystem. The effect of product display on consumer attention and purchasing intent is more than a transactional aspect of commerce; it is a dynamic interplay of psychology, aesthetics, and strategic marketing. Allow this study to serve as a guide into the world of consumer decisions, where the visual attractiveness of product displays Performs an important role for the complicated relationship between consumers and the products that they purchase (Smith et al., 2020; Johnson & Lee, 2019, Chang et al., 2018, O'Boyle et al., 2021).

2. LITERATURE REVIEW

Displaying products is a standard strategy for advertising used by businesses of all kinds to attract consumers' attention, offer them with details about the product, and encourage them to make a purchase.

2.1 Consumer Attention

Consumer attention is a valuable resource that firms have constant competition for. Displaying products is one approach to attract the interest of customers. Products that have strong visibility are more inclined to be seen by customers. This is especially true in retail settings, where consumers are continually flooded with visual signals (Behe et al., 2013).

Consumer attention is defined as the cognitive act of choosing and focusing on one stimulus while disregarding others (James, 1890; Pashler, 1999). A variety of things influence it, including the consumer's goals, motives, and expectations. A consumer seeking for a new pair of shoes, for example, is more likely to pay attention to shoe displays than a consumer who is not looking for new shoes.

According to research, product presentation can influence consumer attention in a variety of ways. Behe et al. (2013) discovered, for example, that displaying products with signage that gave information about the products' characteristics and benefits boosted consumers' attention to the products. Another study, conducted by Gorji et al. (2020), discovered that sales promotion displays in retail outlets had a beneficial effect on client attention.

In addition to these studies, a growing collection of research on the impact of digital product displays on consumer attention is available. For example, Lee et al. (2020) discovered that animated product displays were more effective than static product displays at attracting consumers' attention.

2.2 Product Display

A variety of factors can influence how much attention shoppers give to a product display. These are some examples:

2.2.1 Location: Consumers are more likely to pay attention to products that are displayed in high-traffic areas or at their level of attention.

2.2.2 Size and prominence: Larger and more prominent displays are more likely to catch the attention of consumers.

2.2.3 Colour and contrast: Products displayed in vibrant colours or that contrast with their surroundings are more likely to be seen by customers.

2.2.4 Movement: Displays that feature movement, such as animated signs or films, are more likely to capture the attention of consumers.

2.2.5 Lighting: Well-lit displays are more likely to catch the attention of customers.

2.3 Buying Intention

The possibility that a consumer will purchase a product is referred to as purchasing intention. Displaying products can influence intention to buy in a variety of ways. For the first time, it can raise consumer awareness of the products. When customers see things clearly displayed, they are more likely to become aware of them. Second, it can give consumers with product information such as features, benefits, and pricing. This data can assist consumers in making informed purchasing decisions. Third, it may generate a favourable emotional response to the products. Consumers are more likely to have a good emotional response to products that are displayed in an attractive and appealing manner. This can result in greater intention to buy. (Suwondo et al., (2020); Arora, (2023)).

A number of studies have been conducted to investigate the effect of product display on consumer attention and buying intention. These research' findings generally support the hypothesis that display products can have a favourable impact on both attention and purchasing intention (Bhardwaj, Kaushik, & Arora (2024).

Behe et al., (2013) discovered, for example, that presenting products with advertising that gave information about the products' characteristics and benefits increased consumers' attention to the products as well as their buy intention. Suwondo et al., (2020) discovered that advertising products with price discounts and bonus packs enhanced consumers' purchasing intent.

In addition to these studies, there is an expanding body of research on the impact of digital product displays on consumer attention and purchasing intention (Taneja, Shukla & Arora; 2024). For example, a study by Gorji et al. (2020), discovered that sales promotion displays in retail outlets had a beneficial impact on customer purchase and repurchase intentions. Chang et al. (2016) discovered that various styles of visual apparel advertisements had varying effects on consumers' brain activation and purchase intentions.

2.4 Implications for Businesses

According to the findings of this research, displaying products can be an efficient strategy for businesses to enhance consumer attention and purchasing intention. This understanding can be used by businesses to create more successful product presentation tactics (Malik, Malhan & Arora (2024). (Eds.). (2024)).

For example, companies may use simple but effective advertising, strong product displays, and highlighting the qualities and advantages of their items. Companies may additionally use digital product displays to provide consumers with engaging and interactive experiences (Arora, M. (2024); Kumar, J., Arora, M., & Erkol Bayram, G. (Eds.). (2024) a; Kumar, J., Arora, M., & Erkol Bayram, G. (Eds.). (2024) b).

The impact of product display on consumer attention and intention to buy is a complex and multidimensional topic. According to the research, however, exhibiting products can be a profitable way for companies to improve sales. This knowledge can be used by businesses to create more successful marketing strategies.

3. CONCEPTUAL FRAMEWORK

Figure 1. Conceptual Framework: The Impact of Displaying Products on Consumer Attention and Buying Intention

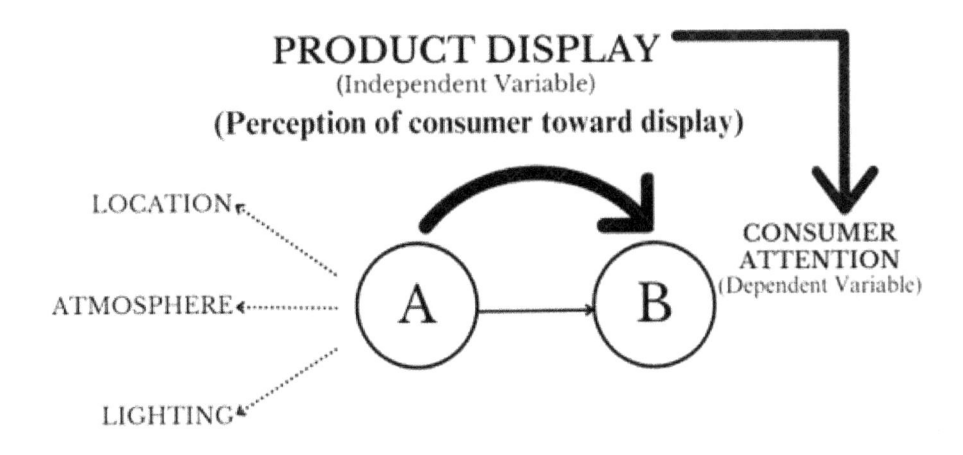

(Adapted from Behe, Zhao, Sage, Huddleston, & Minahan, 2013; Suwondo, Susilo, & Widyaningrum, 2020; Gorji, Siami, & Katoul, 2020)

3.1 Independent Variables

3.1.1 Product Display Characteristics:

- Location (high-traffic areas, eye level)
- Size and prominence (large displays, prominent placement)
- Colour and contrast (bright colours that contrast with the surrounding environment)
- Visualisation (animated signs, videos)
- Display lighting (well-lit displays)

3.2 Mediator Variable

3.2.1 Consumer Attention:

- Visual perception
- Attention to detail

3.3 Moderating Factors

3.3.1 Characteristics of the Consumer:

- Personality characteristics
- Shopping objectives
- Previous observes

3.3.2 Retail Environment Characteristics:

- Store layout
- Store atmosphere
- Sensation signals

3.4 *Dependent Variables*

3.4.1 Purchasing Intention:

- Purchase Prospectivity
- Preference for brands
- willingness to pay

Arrows

The arrows in the conceptual framework represent the hypothesised relationships between the various variables. The arrow connecting Product Display qualities to Consumer Attention, for example, demonstrates that product display qualities can influence consumer attention. The arrow from Consumer Attention to Buying Intention demonstrates that consumer attention can impact purchasing intention.

Consumer Attention as a Mediator

The conceptual framework also posits that customer attention mediates the relationship between product display attributes and purchasing intention. This suggests that product display elements can influence purchasing intention by first influencing consumer attention. A large, visible, and brilliantly coloured product display, for example, is more likely to capture consumer attention. This enhanced attention is more likely to lead to improved product awareness, which could eventually lead to higher purchasing intent.

Consumer and Retail Environment Characteristics Have Moderating Effects

According to the conceptual framework, consumer and retail environment features can modify the relationship between product display attributes and consumer attention. Consumers who are more invested in the product category, for example, are more inclined to pay attention to product displays. Similarly, more dynamic store spaces are more likely to draw consumer attention to product displays.

HYPOTHESIS

Attention:

- *H1: Products displayed in certain locations (e.g., eye-level) will capture more attention compared to others.*
- *H2: Larger product displays will attract more attention compared to smaller ones.*
- *H3: Products displayed with high-contrast colors will be more noticeable and attract greater attention.*

Buying Intention:

- **H4:***Products displayed prominently will lead to a higher likelihood of purchase intention compared to those displayed less noticeably.*
- **H5:***Informative product displays (e.g., with clear descriptions and benefits) will positively influence buying intention compared to displays with minimal information.*

4 OBJECTIVE OF THE STUDY

1) To Examine the effect of product display location on consumer attention (eye level vs. lower levels, high-traffic areas vs. less-trafficked regions).
2) To Determine how much consumer attention influences the relationship between product display attributes and buying intentions.

5 RESEARCH METHODOLOGY

A Research Methodology defines the purpose of the research, how it proceeds, how to measure progress and what constitute success with respect to the objectives determined for carrying out the research study. This study is exploratory in nature.

Primary Data

The study has used primary data through Interview and questionnaire method
Sample size: 70
Sample area: NCR Delhi
Sample units: Individual entities in NCR Delhi
Sources of secondary data:

In this study the following sources has been used to collect the secondary data.
- Books
- Magazines
- Journals
- Articles,
- Reports related to Product Display on Consumer Attention and Buying Intention and
- Internet

6 DATA ANALYSIS

Table 1. Data Analysis

Descriptives				Statistic	Std. Error
	Have you ever bought a product primarily because of an attractive product display?				
Age	No	Mean		20.95	.514
		95% Confidence Interval for Mean	Lower Bound	19.88	
			Upper Bound	22.02	
		5% Trimmed Mean		20.68	
		Median		20.00	
		Variance		5.548	
		Std. Deviation		2.355	
		Minimum		18	
		Maximum		29	
		Range		11	
		Interquartile Range		2	
		Skewness		2.245	.501
		Kurtosis		6.329	.972
	Yes	Mean		21.94	.608
		95% Confidence Interval for Mean	Lower Bound	20.72	
			Upper Bound	23.16	
		5% Trimmed Mean		21.31	
		Median		20.00	
		Variance		18.142	
		Std. Deviation		4.259	
		Minimum		18	
		Maximum		40	
		Range		22	
		Interquartile Range		3	
		Skewness		2.899	.340
		Kurtosis		9.551	.668

The descriptive data reveal interesting trends in the age distribution in two distinct groups: those who have and have not purchased a product primarily due to an appealing product presentation. Individuals who have not made such purchases

("No") have a mean age of around 20.95, with a 95% confidence range ranging from approximately 19.88 to 22.02. The 5% trimmed mean is around 20.68, while the median age is 20.00. This group, in particular, has a right-skewed distribution, as shown by a skewness score of 2.245, and has heavier tails than a normal distribution, as indicated by a kurtosis value of 6.329.

Individuals who have made purchases motivated by appealing displays ("Yes"), on the other hand, had a somewhat higher mean age of around 21.94, with a 95% confidence range ranging from around 20.72 to 23.16. The 5% trimmed mean is around 21.31, and the median age is 20.00, which matches the "No" group. This category, like the "No" group, has a right-skewed distribution (skewness = 2.899) with significantly heavier tails, as seen by a kurtosis value of 9.551.

In conclusion, while both groups have a median age of 20.00, those who have made purchases motivated by appealing displays have a somewhat higher average age. Both groups have right-skewed distributions, indicating a concentration of ages at the younger end, while the "Yes" group has more variability and longer tails. These nuanced insights on age distribution give a solid foundation for understanding the demographics of people influenced by product displays.

BOX PLOT

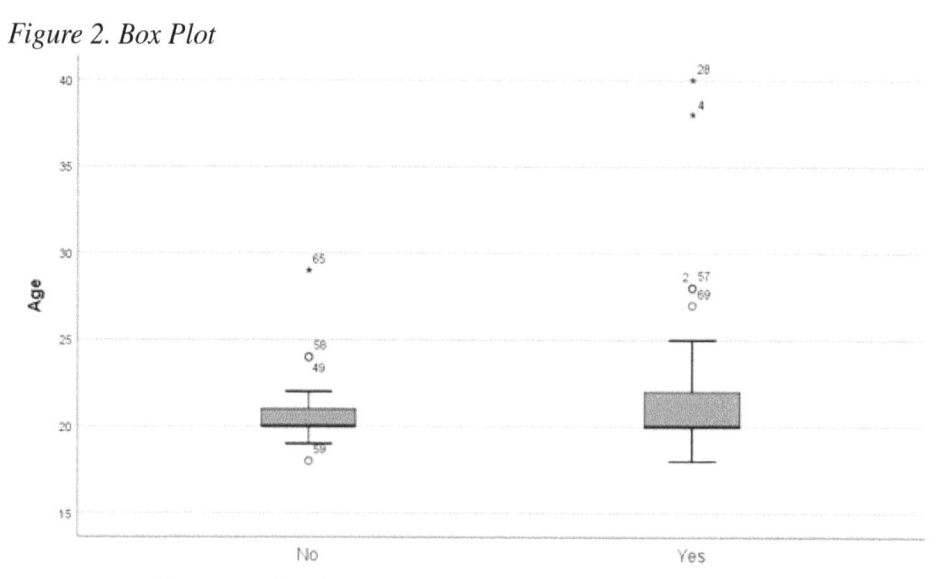

Figure 2. Box Plot

The graph shows the descriptive statistics for the variable "Have you ever bought a product primarily because of an attractive product display?" broken down by age group. The mean response for "Yes" consistently outnumbers the mean response for "No" across all age groups, demonstrating that older participants are more likely than younger participants to have purchased a product due to an appealing presentation. The standard deviation figures also regularly show that those who have made purchases as a result of appealing displays have more variability than those who have not. This tendency is consistent with the overall findings, which indicate that older people are more vulnerable to the influence of appealing product displays on their purchasing decisions.

Finally, the graph supports the assumption that appealing product displays have a stronger influence on older consumers than on younger consumers. Despite the study's modest sample size, the findings provide useful insights on age-related differences in consumer behaviour and the efficiency of product display tactics in influencing purchasing decisions. To improve the generalizability of these findings, more research with larger sample numbers and various demographics is needed.

Education Level * How often do you shop for product in physical stores?

Figure 3. Chi-Square Tests

Chi-Square Tests

	Value	df	Asymptotic Significance (2-sided)
Pearson Chi-Square	6.930[a]	9	.644
Likelihood Ratio	8.499	9	.485
N of Valid Cases	70		

a. 11 cells (68.8%) have expected count less than 5. The minimum expected count is .71.

The Chi-Square Tests were used to look into the possibility of a relationship between two categorical variables. With 9 degrees of freedom, the analysis produced a Pearson Chi-Square value of 6.930, resulting in an asymptotic significance of 0.644. The Likelihood Ratio test produced a value of 8.499 with the same degrees of freedom and an asymptotic significance of 0.485 at the same time. Both tests showed p-values that were significantly higher than the standard significance level of 0.05, indicating a lack of solid evidence to reject the null hypothesis of variable independence.

The cautionary notation emphasising that 11 cells, or 68.8% of the total, have expected counts less than 5, with the smallest expected count recorded at 0.71 is an important aspect in the interpretation. This indicates a possible limitation in the reliability of the Chi-Square test due to small expected counts. As a result, researchers should proceed with caution, recognising the implications of these small predicted numbers on the test's validity.

In conclusion, while the Chi-Square Tests did not reveal a significant relationship between the categorical variables, the warning note emphasises the importance of careful interpretation. To solve the issue of low predicted counts, researchers may need to investigate different statistical methods or propose combining categories. This nuanced perspective emphasises the necessity of considering context and potential data limitations when drawing meaningful findings from statistical analysis.

Table 2. Chi-Square Tests

Chi-Square Tests			
	Value	df	Asymptotic Significance (2-sided)
Pearson Chi-Square	4.755[a]	9	.855
Likelihood Ratio	5.107	9	.825
N of Valid Cases	70		

a. 11 cells (68.8%) have expected count less than 5. The minimum expected count is .64.

The Chi-Square Tests were used to investigate the potential relationship between two categorical variables. The Pearson Chi-Square value was 4.755 with 9 degrees of freedom, resulting in an asymptotic significance of 0.855. Furthermore, with the same degrees of freedom and an asymptotic significance of 0.825, the Likelihood Ratio test returned a value of 5.107. Both p-values surpass the standard significance level of 0.05, indicating a lack of adequate evidence to reject the null hypothesis of variable independence.

However, one noteworthy component of the findings is the cautionary note about anticipated cell numbers. Around 68.8% of the cells had predicted counts less than 5, with the lowest projected count being 0.64. This implies that the Chi-Square test's reliability may be limited due to low predicted counts. As a result, given the presence of cells with low anticipated numbers, researchers should interpret these data with caution.

While the Chi-Square Tests did not reveal a significant relationship between the two categorical variables, the caution regarding small anticipated counts highlights the importance of careful interpretation. To address the issue of low predicted counts in future analyses, researchers may want to investigate different statistical methodologies or consider grouping categories. The conclusion emphasises the need of considering context when interpreting statistical results, as well as the potential impact of data features on the reliability of findings.

7 FINDINGS

The study on "The Impact of Product Display on Consumer Attention and Buying Intention" produced nuanced findings that offer significant insights into the complex interplay between consumers and product displays in the dynamic retail environment. The mixed-methods study, done in the NCR Delhi region with 70 participants, dug into numerous display characteristics such as position, size, colour, movement, and illumination to determine their influence on consumer attention and purchasing intention. Notably, the study discovered age-related tendencies, demonstrating that while both younger and older consumers might be affected by visually appealing displays, the latter group shown a significantly higher proclivity to make purchases based on appealing presentations. Furthermore, the Chi-Square Tests used to investigate the relationship between education level and shopping patterns results, indicating that education may not be the main predictor of customer responses to product displays. The study emphasises the study's broader implications for businesses, emphasising the necessity of optimising product displays as a strategic strategy for increasing consumer attention and purchasing intent. The conceptual framework developed includes independent variables, a mediator variable (customer attention), and moderating factors, resulting in a comprehensive model for firms to consider. As the retail landscape changes, these findings can help businesses optimise their marketing strategies and react to shifting consumer behaviours in the competitive retail industry. Overall, the study adds to our understanding of consumer behaviour and retail marketing, setting the framework for future investigations into the dynamic interaction between customers and product displays.

8 SUGGESTIONS

Following the findings of the study "The Impact of Product Display on Consumer Attention and Buying Intention," various strategic recommendations emerge for organisations looking to improve their marketing techniques. To begin, organisations should adjust their display strategy to accommodate to the tastes and sensibility of varied populations, recognising the differential influence of enticing displays on different age groups. Using interactive technologies in product displays can provide consumers with engaging and memorable experiences, resulting in greater attention and potential purchases. Furthermore, firms must examine the changing landscape of consumer behaviour in the digital age, recognising the significance of online platforms and e-commerce. Targeted advertising based on consumer attributes such as personality traits, purchasing goals, and previous experiences can improve the efficiency of product displays even further. Advertising that emphasises simplicity, highlights product qualities, and incorporates discounts or bonus packs might significantly affect purchasing intentions. Understanding the moderating impacts of retail environment factors, such as shop layout and atmosphere, can also help firms optimise their physical environments for improved consumer attention. It is critical for businesses to stay on top of evolving trends and technology breakthroughs in order to keep their product display strategy relevant and impactful. Finally, this study implies that a context-aware interpretation of customer behaviour is required for effective decision-making, emphasising the importance of firms regularly analysing and adapting their tactics to match with altering consumer preferences. Businesses who implement these guidelines will be at the forefront of efficient marketing strategies, utilising the power of product displays to catch consumer attention and drive purchasing intentions in a dynamic and competitive retail scene.

9 CONCLUSION

The study titled 'The Impact of Product Display on Consumer Attention and Buying Intention' provides a thorough assessment of the delicate relationship between consumers and product displays in the dynamic retail environment. Based on a thorough evaluation of the literature, the study develops a solid conceptual framework that includes independent variables related to display characteristics, a mediator variable (customer attention), and moderating factors linked to both consumer and retail environment characteristics. Using a mixed-methods approach, the study collects primary data from interviews and questionnaires distributed to 70 people in the NCR Delhi region, complementing it with secondary data from other sources. Age-related trends emerge from descriptive statistics, offering light on the differential influence of visually appealing presentations across distinct age groups. The study also uses Chi-Square Tests to investigate correlations between categorical variables, revealing insights into the complex relationship between education level and shopping habits. The findings emphasise the importance of product display aspects such as position, size, colour, movement, and lighting in shaping consumer attention and purchasing intention. The study emphasises the need of firms improving their marketing strategies by optimising product displays while considering the context-specific interpretation of consumer responses. It also emphasises the importance of organisations adapting to the changing landscape of consumer behaviour in the retail sector. The consequences of the study go beyond ordinary transactions, delving into the psychological, aesthetic, and strategic factors that explain the complex interplay between customers and the things they choose to buy. Overall, this study serves as a thorough reference, elucidating the multiple dynamics that influence customer decisions in reaction to product displays. The study provides a nuanced understanding of how businesses can leverage product displays to captivate consumers and influence their purchasing decisions by delving into the complexities of display visual aesthetics, strategic placement, and psychological factors influencing consumer responses. As the retail environment evolves and consumers face an ever-increasing number of options, the findings of this study will be a significant resource for organisations looking to navigate and succeed in this dynamic environment. The study not only provides to academic understanding of consumer behaviour, but it also has practical implications for businesses looking to fine-tune their marketing strategies and increase their effectiveness in capturing consumer attention and driving purchasing intentions in a competitive retail marketplace.

REFERENCES

Arora, M. (2023). Encapsulating Role of Persuasion and Skill Development in Marketing Communication for Brand Building: A Perspective. In *International Handbook of Skill, Education, Learning, and Research Development in Tourism and Hospitality* (pp. 1–17). Springer Nature Singapore.

Arora, M. (2024). Metaverse Metamorphosis: Bridging the Gap Between Research Insights and Industry Applications. In *Research, Innovation, and Industry Impacts of the Metaverse* (pp. 275-286). IGI Global.

Behe, B. K., Zhao, J., Sage, L., Huddleston, P. T., & Minahan, S. (2013). Display signs and involvement: The visual path to purchase intention. *International Review of Retail, Distribution and Consumer Research*, 23(5), 511–522. DOI: 10.1080/09593969.2013.832695

Behnke, J. (2006). Felix Brosius: SPSS-Programmierung. Effizientes Datenmanagement und Automatisierung mit SPSS-Syntax; Andy Field: Discovering Statistics Using SPSS. *Politische Vierteljahresschrift*, 47(4), 751–753. DOI: 10.1007/s11615-006-0382-6

Bhardwaj, S., Kaushik, N., & Arora, M. (2024). Does Your Brain Have a Buy Button?: A Neuro Marketing Approach With Sensory Branding. In *Sensible Selling Through Sensory Neuromarketing* (pp. 210–229). IGI Global. DOI: 10.4018/979-8-3693-4236-7.ch011

Black, W., & Babin, B. J. (2019). Multivariate data analysis: Its approach, evolution, and impact. In *The Great Facilitator* (pp. 121–130). Springer International Publishing., DOI: 10.1007/978-3-030-06031-2_16

Everitt, B. S., & Dunn, G. (2001). *Applied multivariate data analysis*. Wiley., DOI: 10.1002/9781118887486

Finthariasari, M., & Zetira, A. M. (2022). Purchase intention: Pengaruh price discount, bonus pack dan celebrity endorser. *Jurnal Bisnis Dan Manajemen*, 16–25. DOI: 10.23960/jbm.v18i0.233

Gregory, M. (2009). Book review: NORMAN K. DENZIN and YVONNA S. LINCOLN, The Sage Handbook of Qualitative Research (3rd Edition). London: Sage, 2005. 1288 pp. ISBN 07619 2757 3 (hbk) £85.00. *Qualitative Research, 9*(3), 388–389. DOI: 10.1177/14687941090090030803

Judd, C. M., McClelland, G. H., & Ryan, C. S. (2017). *Data analysis*. Routledge., DOI: 10.4324/9781315744131

Kalton, G., & Jessen, R. J. (1979). Statistical survey techniques. *Journal of the Royal Statistical Society. Series A (General)*, 142(2), 265. DOI: 10.2307/2345092

Kumar, J., Arora, M., & Erkol Bayram, G. (Eds.). (2024)a. *Exploring the Use of Metaverse in Business and Education*. IGI Global.

Kumar, J., Arora, M., & Erkol Bayram, G. (Eds.). (2024)b. *Research, Innovation, and Industry Impacts of the Metaverse*. IGI Global.

Malik, R., Malhan, S., & Arora, M. (2024). (Eds.). (2024). *Sensible Selling Through Sensory Neuromarketing* (pp. 144-163). IGI Global.

Maxwell, J. A. (2022). Interactive approaches to qualitative research design. In *The SAGE Handbook of Qualitative Research Design* (pp. 41–54). SAGE Publications Ltd., DOI: 10.4135/9781529770278.n4

(N.d.). https://www.researchgate.net/profile/Bambang-Suwarno-2/publication/355184668_An_empirical_examination_of_price_discount_bonus_pack_and_instore_display_on_consumers'_purchase_intention/links/61655998ae47db4e57cbdb53/An-empirical-examination-of-price-discou

Oliveira, N. (2017). Recensão: The "postmodern turn" in the social sciences [Simon Susen, 2015, Basingstoke, Palgrave Macmillan]. *Sociologia. Sociologia (Lisboa)*, 86(86). Advance online publication. DOI: 10.7458/SPP20188610426

Richards, J. D. (1993a). Book Reviews: Handbook of Research Design and Social Measurement, by Delbert C. Miller. Fifth Edition. Newbury Park, CA: Sage Publications, 1991, 704 pp. *Evaluation Practice, 14*(2), 199–201. DOI: 10.1177/109821409301400217

Richards, J. D. (1993b). Book Reviews: Handbook of Research Design and Social Measurement, by Delbert C. Miller. Fifth Edition. Newbury Park, CA: Sage Publications, 1991, 704 pp. *Evaluation Practice, 14*(2), 199–201. DOI: 10.1177/109821409301400217

Robb, R. A. (1963). w. G. Cochran, Sampling Techniques (John Wiley & Sons, 2nd edition, 1963), ix+413 pp., 72s. *Proceedings of the Edinburgh Mathematical Society, 13*(4), 342–343. DOI: 10.1017/S0013091500025724

Sampling of Populations. Methods and Applications, 4th edition by LEVY, P. S. and LEMESHOW, S. (2009). *Biometrics, 65*(2), 671–671. DOI: 10.1111/j.1541-0420.2009.01247_13.x

Savage, P. (2009). People Skills – Third edition Thompson Niall People Skills – Third edition Palgrave Macmillan 336pp £19.99 978 0 230 22112 3 9780230221123. *Nursing Standard, 24*(4), 31–31. DOI: 10.7748/ns.24.4.31.s38

Sci-Hub: Making uncommon knowledge common. (n.d.). https://sci-hub.se/

Strickland, K. (2016). Grounded theory: A practical guide birks Melanie Mills Jane Grounded theory: A practical guide 208pp £26.99 Sage Publications 9781446295786 1446295788. *Nurse Researcher*, 23(5), 42–42. DOI: 10.7748/nr.23.5.42.s10

Survey Sampling. By Leslie Kish. (New York: John Wiley & Sons, Inc., 1965. Pp. xvi, 643. $10.95.). (1965). *American Political Science Review, 59*(4), 1025–1025. DOI: 10.1017/S0003055400132113

Taneja, B., Shukla, P., & Arora, M. (2024). Sensible Selling Through Sensory Neuromarketing: Enhancing Sales Effectiveness. In *Sensible Selling Through Sensory Neuromarketing* (pp. 164-183). IGI Global.

Theory of correspondence analysis. (2007). In *Chapman & Hall/CRC Interdisciplinary Statistics Series* (pp. 201–211). Chapman and Hall/CRC. DOI: 10.1201/9781420011234.axa

Twycross, A. (2004). Research design: Qualitative, quantitative and mixed methods approach Research design: Qualitative, quantitative and mixed methods approaches Creswell John W Sage 320 £29 0761924426 0761924426. *Nurse Researcher*, 12(1), 82–83. DOI: 10.7748/nr.12.1.82.s2 PMID: 28718745

Van Arsdale, P. W. (1996). Book Reviews: Research Methods in Anthropology: Qualitative and Quantitative Approaches (2nd edition), by H. Russell Bernard. Sage Publications, 1994, 584 pp. *Evaluation Practice, 17*(1), 91–92. DOI: 10.1177/109821409601700112

Wiley, J. (2007). Sons will launchStatistical Analysis and Data Mining in early 2007. *Statistical Analysis and Data Mining*. Advance online publication. DOI: 10.1002/sam.100

Winterton, J. (2008). Review: Business Research Methods ALAN BRYMAN and EMMA BELL. Oxford: Oxford University Press, 2007. xxxii + 786 pp. £34.99 (pbk). ISBN 9780199284986. *Management Learning*, 39(5), 628–632. DOI: 10.1177/13505076080390050804

Chapter 10
Influence of Neurosensory Packaging and Promotional Campaigns on Buying Behaviour

Renu Bala
Jan Nayak Chaudhary Devi Lal Vidyapeeth, India

ABSTRACT

The paper investigates the relationship between three terms: product packaging, promotional strategies, and consumer buying behavior. In today's competitive market, a lot of tactics are adopted by the marketers to attract the consumer as they focus on packaging and promotional strategies. The study investigates about different elements of packaging design and examines how they impact consumers' perceptions and preferences. As well as, it describes the effectiveness of promotional strategies in stimulating consumer purchasing behavior. Drawing upon theoretical frameworks and empirical evidence, this paper offers insights into how marketers can strategically utilize packaging and promotional techniques to enhance brand visibility, attract target audiences, and ultimately drive sales. Furthermore, it highlights the significance of understanding consumer psychology and market trends in devising successful packaging and promotional campaigns. For the study purpose, data have been gathered from various secondary sources. By comprehensively analyzing the interplay between product packaging, promotional strategies, and consumer behavior, this paper contributes to the existing literature on marketing and provides practical implications for businesses aiming to optimize their marketing efforts and achieve competitive advantage in the marketplace.

DOI: 10.4018/979-8-3693-9351-2.ch010

1. INTRODUCTION

Neurosensory packaging is product packaging that is created and designed to engage one or more of the human senses (sight, sound, smell, taste, touch) — the brain interprets these sensory inputs unconsciously, and it's reliant on our trained responses to these stimuli. Drawing from across areas of best practices, neurosensory enables marketers to create an interactive experience, elevate the brand, and enhance brand loyal with the product that employs the first five principles of neuroscience to the hand of the product containing the actual product, while the product is in the hand of the consumer. This focus on sensory stimulus response and relationship with the brain maps certain characteristics of packaging that can win over a customer not purely by and image standpoint but, by creating that memorable, engagement that will make your product stand out in the competition. An emerging trend in this subject is neuroscience marketing or neuromarketing, a field that merges principles of neuroscience with marketing strategies to grasp consumer reactions and how to influence those reactions at a subconscious level. Neuromarketing researchers leverage revolutionary techniques like functional Magnetic Resonance Imaging (fMRI), Electroencephalography (EEG), eye tracking, Galvanic Skin Response (GSR), and facial coding to scratch the surface and gain an insight into the conscious as well as the unconscious cognitive and emotional processes that dictate what consumers prefer or decide. fMRI images measure brain activity via changes in blood flow, thereby providing predictions of how brains may be activated in response to various marketing stimuli. EEG measures the electrical activity of the brain, providing a richer insight of the emotional response, and what supplies attention. Eye tracking monitors where and for how long a person looks at different elements of a marketing stimulus, revealing. The current state of neuroscience marketing exemplifies not just a heightened adoption of high-tech neuroscientific techniques into the mainstream marketing approaches, as leaders see more and more the potential to explore and control consumer behavior, but also what appears to be a particularly sophisticated level of marketing techniques inspired by our evolving comprehension of the brain. New technologies include fMei, EGG, and other methods of examine the responses of facial encoding, subconscious response, what is helpful for companies to make better advertisements, products and packaging. The result, in its marketing terms, was more personalized and emotionally impactful campaigns to enhance customer engagement and boost up sales. Challenges for this field are the costs, technical hurdles, and ethical considerations surrounding data privacy and consent. Nevertheless, with the improvement in technology and standard as to how the technology is abided by, neuromarketing is also being considered more and more useful than before. Neurosensory packaging involves utilizing design elements in packaging to engage consumers' senses, including sight, touch, sound, and smell, with the aim of creating a memorable and impactful experience (Devaru, 2018). This strategy acknowledges that sensory stimuli can impact consumers' perceptions, emotions, and ultimately their purchasing decisions (Cherubino & Martinez et al., 2019). The goal of neurosensory packaging is to craft a multi-sensory experience that surpasses mere visual appeal, aiming to elicit positive sensory responses in consumers. This approach enhances product desirability and leaves a lasting impression (Gurgu & Gurgu et al., 2020). By leveraging the sensory aspects of packaging, marketers can establish a deeper emotional connection with consumers, thereby fostering increased brand loyalty and purchase intent (Singh, 2020). Neurosensory packaging, while innovative, has several limitations. It often involves high costs due to the need for specialized materials and advanced technologies to effectively stimulate multiple senses. The development process can be intricate and lengthy, requiring significant research and testing to achieve the intended sensory effects. Ensuring consistency and scalability in mass production poses additional challenges, as it is crucial to maintain a uniform sensory experience across all products. Ethical considerations also arise, as manipulating sensory inputs to influence consumer behavior can be seen as exploitative. Moreover, there is a risk of overwhelming consumers with too many sensory stimuli if not balanced properly. Lastly, adapting neurosensory packaging to cater to diverse consumer preferences and adhering to various regulatory standards in different markets adds further complexity to its application. The future of neurosensory packaging holds immense potential for further innovation and integration into marketing strategies. Advancements in technology, such as wearable devices and augmented reality, can enhance the sensory experience by providing real-time feedback and interactive elements. Customization and personalization may become more prevalent, allowing brands to tailor packaging to individual preferences and create unique, memorable experiences. Sustainability will likely be a key focus, with the development of eco-friendly materials and designs that still engage the senses effectively. Additionally, as our understanding of neuroscience and consumer behavior grows, neurosensory packaging may evolve to incorporate more subtle, subconscious cues to influence purchasing decisions, leading to more effective and impactful marketing campaigns. Neurosensory packaging represents a dynamic and innovative approach to product packaging that goes beyond traditional marketing strategies. By engaging multiple senses, neurosensory packaging creates a more immersive and memorable experience for consumers, fostering stronger emotional connections with brands and products. While it offers significant advantages such as enhanced consumer engagement, improved brand perception, and increased sales, it also faces challenges such as high costs, complexity, and ethical considerations. Nevertheless, with ongoing advancements in technology and a greater understanding of neuroscience, neurosensory packaging is poised to continue evolving, offering exciting opportunities for brands to differentiate themselves in the market and create meaningful connections with consumers.

2. REVIEW OF LITERATURE

Arora (2020) stated the ways to marketing communication. Under the research, focus has been paid on secondary data. The results of the study elaborated that a lot of things changes the perception of human beings and effects their sentiments and emotions etc. The chapter delves into how misinformation and emotional appeals have become prevalent in marketing strategies, impacting consumer behavior and decision-making. It discusses the role of digital platforms and social media in spreading post-truth narratives, examining the ethical considerations and challenges faced by marketers. The study emphasizes the need for transparency and authenticity in marketing practices to build trust with the connected consumer, offering insights into innovative strategies for effective communication in a technologically driven marketplace. Gurgu & Gurgu et al. (2020) showed that how neuromarketing provide help to understand the need and emotions of the consumer. To move forward the research data have been collected from pre structured questionnaire. The results of the study showed that by the use of neuromarketing good product can be developed in easy ways as such technology provide a good base to understand the needs of the consumer. Spence (2020) explained those ethical issues which arise during the designing of sensory and neuromarketing strategies. Data have been gathered from primary sources such as questionnaire and schedules. The managers of different reputed organizations have been selected as sample. The views of the respondents showed that a lot of challenges have to be face by the organizations during the implementation of marketing strategies based on the concept of neuromarketing.

Khurana & Gahalawat et al. (2021) highlighted the use of electroencephalography (EEG) technique in neuromarketing. During the study it has been founded that there exist a variety of techniques which are used to develop neuromarketing strategies and electroencephalography (EEG) is the latest technique among them which is highly used in current scenario and this technique helps to find out the sequential changes which take place in the human mind. Lopez & Galarza (2022) showed the benefits of neuromarketing. For the study purpose data have been gathered from various consumers of different products. After the analysis of gathered data it has been founded that current applications of neuromarketing play a significant role to attract the consumer towards the different products. As such latest concept has got various new parameters on the basis of current huge demand in the market in current scenario. Arora & Sharma (2023) highlighted the importance of artificial intelligence in today's world. The results of the study indicated that in today's scenario the existence of AI matters. As a lot of new technical things depend upon the new technology and AI is the solution of all the things which human beings have to face in their day-to-day operations. Kumar & Arora et al. (2024) showed the present picture of metaverse technology in innovation world along with its uses and limitations. The metaverse technology provides a variety of innovations which helps to business houses to make their product more attractive and useful which holds significant implications in the field of marketing. The role of metaverse in entrepreneurial world is significantly increasing (Dhiman & Arora (2024) a; Dhiman &Arora (2024) b). In this area of research some other useful and popular topics have been also been trending such as big data, artificial intelligence, block chain and deep learning. metaverse play a significant role in entrepreneurial world as marketing advancements are key part of entrepreneurial growth ((Arora & Sharma, (2021); Arora (2016)). It will impact the world of marketing in a significant way. Neurosensory marketing and the metaverse both leverage immersive, sensory-rich experiences to influence consumer behavior and decision-making. In the entrepreneurial world, integrating neurosensory marketing within the metaverse can create powerful, engaging environments that enhance brand perception and drive business growth. Further, integrating neurosensory marketing within VR educational environments can enhance engagement and retention by creating immersive, multi-sensory learning experiences. The studies on VR in education, emphasizing the potential for VR to transform educational practices through enriched, interactive, and personalized learning experiences that leverage sensory stimuli to improve educational outcomes (Arora, 2024). Alternatively, there is a critical interplay between persuasive communication and skill development in the context of brand building in multi business scenario especially within the tourism and hospitality industry. The effective marketing strategies leverage persuasive techniques to influence consumer perceptions and behavior, thereby enhancing brand loyalty and recognition. There is huge importance of continuous skill development for marketing professionals to adapt to evolving market dynamics and technological advancements (Arora, 2023). Literature provides insights into the best practices for integrating persuasion and skill development to create impactful marketing campaigns that drive brand success. Arora's focus on persuasion in marketing communication aligns with neurosensory marketing techniques, which aim to create more effective, persuasive marketing strategies by appealing directly to consumers' senses and emotions.

Research Objectives

To analyze the components of neurosensory packaging.
To analyze the role of neurosensory cues in consumer perception and behavior.
To analyze promotional campaigns and their types.

To access the influence of promotional campaigns on consumer decision-making.

3. COMPONENTS OF NEUROSENSORY PACKAGING

Neurosensory packaging encompasses various components designed to engage consumers' senses and enhance their product experience:

a. Visual Stimuli: Incorporating colors, graphics, and shapes in packaging to capture attention and convey brand identity. Bright colors may denote freshness or excitement, while softer tones can suggest calmness or luxury (Spence, 2020).

b. Tactile Attributes: The physical texture of packaging materials can evoke different perceptions. Smooth textures often signify product quality, while rough textures can convey a natural or organic feel (Misra, 2023).

c. Auditory Elements: Packaging that produces sounds upon handling or opening can create a sense of anticipation or excitement. For instance, the "pop" of a champagne cork or the crinkle of a candy wrapper can enhance the overall product experience (Kumar & Singh, 2015).

d. Olfactory Features: Some packaging releases scents upon opening, adding another dimension to the product experience. This can evoke nostalgia or elicit positive emotions associated with the scent (Mansor & Isa, 2018).

e. Interactive Enhancements: Packaging with features that encourage consumer interaction, such as peel-off labels or integrated apps, can boost engagement and create a memorable experience (Fugate, 2007).

f. Sustainability Initiatives: Using environmentally friendly packaging materials can appeal to consumers' sense of responsibility and contribute to a positive brand image (Dragolea&Cotirlea, 2011).

Neurosensory packaging aims to create a comprehensive brand experience that resonates deeply with consumers, influencing their perception of both the product and the brand (Georges & Bayle et al., 2013).

4. THE ROLE OF NEUROSENSORY CUES IN CONSUMER PERCEPTION AND BEHAVIOR

Neurosensory cues significantly impact consumer perception and behavior, shaping how products and brands are perceived and influencing purchase decisions. Here's how these cues affect consumer behavior:

a. **Attention and Perception:** Neurosensory cues, such as chromaticity, unique configurations, or pleasing aromas, can attract consumer attention and refine their perception of a product. Packaging that distinguishes itself on shelves due to its sensory allure is more likely to be noticed and retained by consumers (Kristiana &Pugu, 2024).
b. **Emotional Response:** Neurosensory cues can evoke emotional reactions in consumers. For example, a product with a tactile, plush feel may evoke sensations of comfort and opulence, while one with vibrant, dynamic hues may elicit feelings of exhilaration or joy. These emotional responses can impact consumers' attitudes toward the product and their inclination to purchase it (Vlasenko, 2018).
c. **Brand Image and Personality:** Neurosensory cues contribute to molding a brand's image and personality. For instance, a brand consistently employing serene colors and natural textures in its packaging may be perceived as environmentally conscious and wholesome. This can appeal to consumers valuing sustainability and natural products (Gill & Singh, 2022).
d. **Product Experience:** Neurosensory cues enrich the overall product experience. For example, the auditory feedback of a satisfying "snap" upon sealing a package can convey a sense of excellence and robustness. Similarly, the fragrance of a product can evoke recollections or build anticipation, enriching the overall product gratification (Sharma & Dash et al., 2023).
e. **Purchase Decision:** Neurosensory cues can sway consumers' purchase decisions. A product appealing to multiple senses and providing a positive sensory encounter is more likely to be selected over a similar product lacking sensory allure (Hammou & Galib et al., 2013).

In summary, neurosensory cues play a pivotal role in shaping consumers' perceptions, emotions, and behaviors, underscoring the importance of integrating sensory components into product design and marketing strategies (Li, 2017).

5. PROMOTIONAL CAMPAIGNS

Promotional campaigns refer to coordinated marketing efforts designed to communicate with target audiences to increase awareness, generate interest, drive sales, and achieve specific business goals*(Park & Roth et al., 1988)*. These campaigns utilize various marketing tools and channels to deliver a cohesive message that encourages customer engagement and action (Koch & Benlian, 2015).

6. TYPES OF PROMOTIONAL CAMPAIGNS

Advertising Campaigns: A series of planned advertisements across multiple media platforms sharing a unified theme and message (Madhavaram & Badrinarayanan et al., 2005).

Sales Promotion Campaigns:

Short-term incentives designed to encourage the purchase or sale of a product or service (Pavlou & Stewart, 2000).

Public Relations (PR) Campaigns:

Activities aimed at building and maintaining a positive public image and strong relationships with various stakeholders (Snyder & Hamilton et al., 2004).

Direct Marketing Campaigns:

Direct communication with targeted individuals to elicit a response or transaction (Bergkvist & Zhou, 2016).

Event Marketing Campaigns:

Event marketing campaigns involve promoting a product, service, or brand through organized events (Mair & Ritchie et al., 2016). These events can be physical, virtual, or hybrid and are designed to engage the target audience, create memorable experiences, and drive specific marketing objectives such as brand awareness, lead generation, customer loyalty, or product launches (Constantinides, 2006).

7. THE INFLUENCE OF PROMOTIONAL CAMPAIGNS ON CONSUMER DECISION-MAKING

Promotional campaigns significantly impact consumer decision-making by shaping awareness, perceptions, and buying behaviors (Foreman & Money, 1995). Here's how they influence these aspects:

Awareness Creation

Promotional campaigns help make consumers aware of new products or servicesSmith, K. T. (2011). Through various marketing channels like advertisements and social media, brands can reach a broad audience, making potential customers cognizant of their offerings (Noar, 2006).

Perception Shaping

Promotional efforts highlight the unique features and benefits of a product, shaping how consumers perceive it (Boyne & Hall et al., 2003). Effective campaigns can create a positive image and set a product apart from its competitors (Kilbourne & Beckmann 1998).

Building Loyalty

Discounts, loyalty programs, and special offers included in promotional campaigns can foster brand loyalty (Ambler &Kokkinaki et al., 2004). Customers appreciate rewards for their repeat business, which can encourage ongoing patronage (Christy & Oliver et al., 1996).

Influencing Decisions

Urgent offers like limited-time discounts and flash sales can prompt quicker buying decisions by creating a sense of urgency (Brodie & Coviello et al., 2997). These tactics can reduce hesitation and spur immediate purchases (Walliser, 2003).

Information Provision

Promotions often include detailed information about a product, such as its features, benefits, and how it compares to similar items (Kliatchko, 2008). This information helps consumers make informed choices (McGrail & Rickard et al., 2006).

Emotional Appeal

Promotional campaigns that connect with consumers emotionally can influence their decisions (Pescher& Reichhart et al.,2014). Emotional marketing, whether it evokes happiness, nostalgia, or excitement, can create a strong connection to the brand (Haubl&Trifts, 2000).

Social Proof

Incorporating testimonials, reviews, and endorsements from influencers in promotional campaigns provides social proof (Sawagvudcharee& Shrestha, 2018). Positive feedback from others can convince undecided consumers of a product's value (Familmalekin& Aghighi et al., 2015).

Encouraging Trials

Offering samples, free trials, or demonstrations can encourage consumers to try a product with minimal risk (Sharabati& Salim et al., 2014). This hands-on experience can lead to increased confidence and subsequent purchases (Soni, 2021).

Targeted Marketing

Promotional campaigns can be customized to target specific consumer segments based on demographics, interests, and behaviors (Golnar-Nik & Farashi et al., 2019). Tailored messages are more likely to resonate and influence the intended audience (Cheah & Ting et al., 2019).

Enhancing Experience

Promotional activities that focus on improving the customer experience, such as excellent customer service or engaging in-store events, can leave a lasting positive impression and encourage future purchases (Godinho, S., Prada et al., 2016).

9. NEUROMARKETING AND BEHAVIORAL ECONOMICS

a. Neuromarketing

Neuromarketing applies neuroscience to understand how consumers' brains respond to marketing stimuli (Lyapina& Uvarova et al., 2020). Neurosensory packaging can trigger specific brain responses that enhance emotional connections and decision-making processes (Plakhin&Semenets et al., 2018).

Emotional Engagement: Sensory-rich packaging can evoke emotional responses that strengthen brand attachment (Reikin&Voitovych et al., 2021). Memory Encoding: Multi-sensory experiences can improve memory retention of the product (Sebastian, 2014).

b. Behavioral Economics

Behavioral economics explores the psychological factors affecting economic decisions (Chavaglia& Filipe et al., 2011). Concepts like loss aversion and anchoring can be leveraged in promotional campaigns:

Loss Aversion: Limited-time offers and scarcity messages can tap into consumers' fear of missing out (FOMO) (Meckl-Sloan, 2015).

Anchoring: Initial high prices followed by discounts can make the promotional price seem more attractive (Sposini, 2024).

10. RESEARCH EVIDENCE

Several empirical studies have examined how neurosensory packaging and promotional campaigns impact consumer buying behavior. Here's an overview of key findings from this research:

Neurosensory Packaging

1. Visual Elements

- **Study Focus:** The influence of visual aesthetics on consumer perceptions and purchase intentions (Crowther & Harding et al., 2013).
- **Findings:** Attractive packaging designs enhance product appeal and perceived quality, leading to increased purchase intentions.

2. Tactile Elements

- **Study Focus:** The role of touch in product evaluation.
- **Findings:** Packaging with appealing textures can positively influence consumer judgments and their willingness to buy, particularly for products where touch is a significant factor.

3. Olfactory Cues

- **Study Focus:** The effect of scents in packaging and retail environments on consumer behavior.
- **Findings:** Pleasant scents can improve mood, encourage longer store visits, and increase purchase intentions.

4. Multisensory Packaging

- **Study Focus:** The impact of packaging that engages multiple senses.
- **Findings:** Packaging that appeals to several senses (visual, tactile, olfactory) evokes stronger emotional responses and increases the likelihood of purchase.

CONCLUSION

In conclusion, neurosensory packaging and promotional campaigns significantly impact buying behavior by engaging multiple senses, thereby enhancing consumer perception and emotional connection with products. The integration of advanced technologies, personalized experiences, and sustainable practices can further amplify these effects. Understanding the psychological and cultural nuances of sensory stimuli helps in designing more effective marketing strategies. Future research should continue to explore these dimensions to optimize packaging and promotional efforts, ultimately driving consumer engagement, brand loyalty, and sales. Neurosensory packaging and promotional campaigns have a powerful way to shape such buying behaviour, harnessing the interplay between sensory stimuli and consumer psychology to determine purchase decisions. Neurosensory packaging appeals to human senses to help form consumer perceptions and emotional responses to a product and, as such, the design of these "sense-informed" packages, as the researchers describe them, triggers consumer responses through sight, touch, smell, and, sometimes, even the sound made when they are opened. Visually appealing designs, vibrant colors, distinctive shapes, capture attention and improve brand recall, texture and material can transmit quality and sustainability, etc. Ultimately, scents implanted in packaging can trigger memories and feelings, forming a more profound relationship with the consumer. At the same time, advertising campaigns enhance these sensory experiences by strategically targeting consumers' emotions and cognitive biases. Using time limitations, tailored messages, and the art of narration, promotions induce urgency and present the buyer with content that he can personally relate to, making him much more likely to partake in operations of the landing page. Combined, such strategies engage the human sensory and psychological realm to drive consumer behavior, in turn building brand loyalty and driving sales. And therefore those companies that can successfully blend neurosensory packaging with promotional marketing have a much greater chance of differentiating themselves from the competition, making consumer experience more distinct and more attractive, ultimately leading to lasting competitive advantages.

Future Directions

Future research on the influence of neurosensory packaging and promotional campaigns on buying behavior should focus on the integration of emerging technologies like augmented reality (AR) and virtual reality (VR) to enhance consumer experiences, the customization of packaging through AI and big data for personalized interactions, and the study of multisensory stimuli combinations on consumer perceptions (Li & Shen et al., 2024). Additionally, exploring the impact of sustainable and ethical packaging, conducting cross-cultural and demographic studies, and utilizing neuroimaging techniques to understand the underlying psychological mechanisms can provide deeper insights (Leeuwis& Van et al., 2024). Longitudinal studies to examine the long-term effects on brand loyalty, the role of digital and social media in enhancing sensory experiences, and the impact on brand equity and consumer engagement will further enrich the understanding of these factors on purchasing behavior (Deng & Yang et al., 2024).

Implications of the Study

Key findings from studies on the influence of neurosensory packaging and promotional campaigns on buying behavior reveal that visually appealing, tactile, and scented packaging significantly enhance product appeal and perceived quality, while emotional appeals, social proof, scarcity messages, and price promotions in campaigns drive purchase decisions (Turhan & Gurkaynak et al., 2023). The synergistic effect of aligning multisensory packaging with cohesive promotional strategies boosts consumer engagement and purchase likelihood (Wu & Wan et al., 2023). For marketers, this means investing in multi-sensory packaging design, crafting emotionally resonant promotional campaigns, leveraging social proof, creating urgency through scarcity tactics, and ensuring a cohesive brand message across packaging and promotions to enhance consumer experience and drive sales (Kerber & Roese-Miron et al., 2024).

REFERENCES

Ahmad Sharabati, A. A., Salim Khraim, H., & Atta Khateeb, R. (2014). Relationship between direct-to-consumer advertising and consumers' decision-making. *International Journal of Pharmaceutical and Healthcare Marketing*, 8(2), 178–192. DOI: 10.1108/IJPHM-12-2012-0019

Ambler, T., Kokkinaki, F., & Puntoni, S. (2004). Assessing marketing performance: Reasons for metrics selection. *Journal of Marketing Management*, 20(3-4), 475–498. DOI: 10.1362/026725704323080506

Arora, M. (2016). Creative dimensions of entrepreneurship: A key to business innovation. *Pacific Business Review International*, 1(1), 255–259.

Arora, M. (2020). Post-truth and marketing communication in technological age. In Handbook of research on innovations. DOI: 10.4018/978-1-7998-0131-3.ch005

Arora, M. (2023). Encapsulating Role of Persuasion and Skill Development in Marketing Communication for Brand Building: A Perspective. In *International Handbook of Skill, Education, Learning, and Research Development in Tourism and Hospitality* (pp. 1–17). Springer Nature Singapore.

Arora, M. (2024). Virtual Reality in Education: Analyzing the Literature and Bibliometric State of Knowledge. *Transforming Education with Virtual Reality*, 379-402. DOI: 10.1002/9781394200498.ch22

Arora, M., & Sharma, R. L. (2021). Repurposing the Role of Entrepreneurs in the Havoc of COVID-19. In Entrepreneurship and Big Data (pp. 229-250). CRC Press.

Arora, M., & Sharma, R. L. (2023). Artificial intelligence and big data: ontological and communicative perspectives in multi-sectoral scenarios of modern businesses. foresight, 25(1), 126-143.

Bergkvist, L., & Zhou, K. Q. (2016). Celebrity endorsements: A literature review and research agenda. *International Journal of Advertising*, 35(4), 642–663. DOI: 10.1080/02650487.2015.1137537

Boyne, S., Hall, D., & Williams, F. (2003). Policy, support and promotion for food-related tourism initiatives: A marketing approach to regional development. *Journal of Travel & Tourism Marketing*, 14(3-4), 131–154. DOI: 10.1300/J073v14n03_08

Brodie, R. J., Coviello, N. E., Brookes, R. W., & Little, V. (1997). Towards a paradigm shift in marketing? An examination of current marketing practices. *Journal of Marketing Management*, 13(5), 383–406. DOI: 10.1080/0267257X.1997.9964481

Chavaglia, J. N., Filipe, J. A., & Ramalheiro, B. (2011). Neuromarketing: Consumers and the anchoring effect. *International Journal of Latest Trends in Finance and Economics Sciences*, (4), 183–189.

Cheah, J. H., Ting, H., Cham, T. H., & Memon, M. A. (2019). The effect of selfie promotion and celebrity endorsed advertisement on decision-making processes: A model comparison. *Internet Research*, 29(3), 552–577. DOI: 10.1108/IntR-12-2017-0530

Cherubino, P., Martinez-Levy, A. C., Caratu, M., Cartocci, G., Di Flumeri, G., Modica, E., & Trettel, A. (2019). Consumer behaviour through the eyes of neurophysiological measures: State-of-the-art and future trends. *Computational Intelligence and Neuroscience*, 2019, 2019. DOI: 10.1155/2019/1976847 PMID: 31641346

Christy, R., Oliver, G., & Penn, J. (1996). Relationship marketing in consumer markets. *Journal of Marketing Management*, 12(1-3), 175–187. DOI: 10.1080/0267257X.1996.9964407

Constantinides, E. (2006). The marketing mix revisited: Towards the 21st century marketing. *Journal of Marketing Management*, 22(3-4), 407–438. DOI: 10.1362/026725706776861190

Crowther, C. A., Harding, J. E., Middleton, P. F., Andersen, C. C., Ashwood, P., & Robinson, J. S. (2013). Australasian randomised trial to evaluate the role of maternal intramuscular dexamethasone versus betamethasone prior to preterm birth to increase survival free of childhood neurosensory disability (A* STEROID): Study protocol. *BMC Pregnancy and Childbirth*, 13(1), 1–7. DOI: 10.1186/1471-2393-13-104 PMID: 23642125

Deng, X., Yang, X., Bu, M., Tang, A., Zhang, H., Long, L., & Chen, B. T. (2024). Nomogram for prediction of hearing rehabilitation outcome in children with congenital sensorineural hearing loss after cochlear implantation. *Heliyon*, 10(8), e29529. DOI: 10.1016/j.heliyon.2024.e29529 PMID: 38699755

Devaru, S. D. B. (2018). Significance of neuromarketing on consumer buying behavior. *International Journal of Technical Research & Science*, 3(3), 114–121. DOI: 10.30780/IJTRS.V3.I3.2018.015

Dhiman, V., & Arora, M. (2024a) Current State of Metaverse in Entrepreneurial Ecosystem: A Retrospective Analysis of Its Evolving Landscape. In Exploring the Use of Metaverse in Business and Education (pp. 73-87). IGI Global.

Dhiman, V., & Arora, M. (2024b). Exploring the linkage between business incubation and entrepreneurship: Understanding trends, themes and future research agenda. *LBS Journal of Management & Research*, 22(1), 66–92. DOI: 10.1108/LBSJMR-06-2023-0021

Dragolea, L., & Cotirlea, D. (2011). Neuromarketing: Between influence and manipulation. Polish. *Journal of Management Studies*, 3, 78–88.

Familmaleki, M., Aghighi, A., & Hamidi, K. (2015). Analyzing the impact of promotion mix on consumer; s purchase decision. *Advanced Social Humanities and Management*, 2(1), 71–81.

Foreman, S. K., & Money, A. H. (1995). Internal marketing: Concepts, measurement and application. *Journal of Marketing Management*, 11(8), 755–768. DOI: 10.1080/0267257X.1995.9964388

Fugate, D. L. (2007). Neuromarketing: A layman's look at neuroscience and its potential application to marketing practice. *Journal of Consumer Marketing*, 24(7), 385–394. DOI: 10.1108/07363760710834807

Georges, P. M., Bayle-Tourtoulou, A. S., & Badoc, M. (2013). *Neuromarketing in action: How to talk and sell to the brain*. Kogan Page Publishers.

Gill, R., & Singh, J. (2022). A study of neuromarketing techniques for proposing cost effective information driven framework for decision making. *Materials Today: Proceedings*, 49, 2969–2981. DOI: 10.1016/j.matpr.2020.08.730

Godinho, S., Prada, M., & Garrido, M. V. (2016). Under pressure: An integrative perspective of time pressure impact on consumer decision-making. *Journal of International Consumer Marketing*, 28(4), 251–273. DOI: 10.1080/08961530.2016.1148654

Golnar-Nik, P., Farashi, S., & Safari, M. S. (2019). The application of EEG power for the prediction and interpretation of consumer decision-making: A neuromarketing study. *Physiology & Behavior*, 207, 90–98. DOI: 10.1016/j.physbeh.2019.04.025 PMID: 31047949

Gurgu, E., Gurgu, I. A., & Tonis, R. B. M. (2020). Neuromarketing for a better understanding of consumer needs and emotions. *Independent Journal of Management & Production*, 11(1), 208–235. DOI: 10.14807/ijmp.v11i1.993

Hammou, K. A., Galib, M. H., & Melloul, J. (2013). The contributions of neuromarketing in marketing research. *Journal of Management Research*, 5(4), 20. DOI: 10.5296/jmr.v5i4.4023

Haubl, G., & Trifts, V. (2000). Consumer decision making in online shopping environments: The effects of interactive decision aids. *Marketing Science*, 19(1), 4–21. DOI: 10.1287/mksc.19.1.4.15178

Kerber, L., Roese-Miron, L., Bubadue, J. M., & Martinelli, A. G. (2024). Endocranial anatomy of the early prozostrodonts (Eucynodontia: Probainognathia) and the neurosensory evolution in mammal forerunners. *The Anatomical Record*, 307(4), 1442–1473. DOI: 10.1002/ar.25215 PMID: 37017195

Khurana, V., Gahalawat, M., Kumar, P., Roy, P. P., Dogra, D. P., Scheme, E., & Soleymani, M. (2021). A survey on neuromarketing using EEG signals. *IEEE Transactions on Cognitive and Developmental Systems*, 13(4), 732–749. DOI: 10.1109/TCDS.2021.3065200

Kilbourne, W. E., & Beckmann, S. C. (1998). Review and critical assessment of research on marketing and the environment. *Journal of Marketing Management*, 14(6), 513–532. DOI: 10.1362/026725798784867716

Kliatchko, J. (2008). Revisiting the IMC construct: A revised definition and four pillars. *International Journal of Advertising*, 27(1), 133–160. DOI: 10.1080/02650487.2008.11073043

Koch, O. F., & Benlian, A. (2015). Promotional tactics for online viral marketing campaigns: How scarcity and personalization affect seed stage referrals. *Journal of Interactive Marketing*, 32(1), 37–52. DOI: 10.1016/j.intmar.2015.09.005

Kristiana, A., &Pugu, M. R. (2024). Navigating the intersection neuro-marketing and consumer bahavior analysis: leveraging insights for effective campaigns. *Jurnal Ekonomi dan Bisnis, 2*(3), 362-374.

Kumar, H., & Singh, P. (2015). Neuromarketing: An emerging tool of market research. [IJEMR]. *International Journal of Engineering and Management Research*, 5(6), 530–535.

Kumar, J., Arora, M., & Erkol Bayram, G. (Eds.). (2024). *Exploring the Use of Metaverse in Business and Education*. IGI Global. DOI: 10.4018/979-8-3693-5868-9

Leeuwis, N., Van Bommel, T., Tsakiris, M., & Alimardani, M. (2024). Uncovering the potential of evaluative conditioning in shaping attitudes toward sustainable product packaging. *Frontiers in Psychology*, 15, 1284422. DOI: 10.3389/fpsyg.2024.1284422 PMID: 38550644

Li, L. (2017). Influences on consumers' decision making and recognition memory: An investigation using fMRI, *EEG and behavioural methods* (Doctoral dissertation, Brunel University London).

Li, L., Shen, T., Liu, S., Qi, J., & Zhao, Y. (2024). Advancements and future prospects of adeno-associated virus-mediated gene therapy for sensorineural hearing loss. *Frontiers in Neuroscience*, 18, 1272786. DOI: 10.3389/fnins.2024.1272786 PMID: 38327848

Lopez, M. J., & Ramos-Galarza, C. (2022). Neuromarketing: Current applications in favor of consumerism. *Marketing and Smart Technologies: Proceedings of ICMarkTech 2021, Volume 1*, 389-394.

Lyapina, I. R., Uvarova, A. Y., Sibirskaya, E. V., Pashkevich, L. A., &Tikhoykina, I. M. (2020). Cognitive science and neuromarketing in behavioral economics. *Growth Poles of the Global Economy: Emergence, Changes and Future Perspectives*, 925-935.

Madhavaram, S., Badrinarayanan, V., & McDonald, R. E. (2005). Integrated marketing communication (IMC) and brand identity as critical components of brand equity strategy: A conceptual framework and research propositions. *Journal of Advertising*, 34(4), 69–80. DOI: 10.1080/00913367.2005.10639213

Mair, J., Ritchie, B. W., & Walters, G. (2016). Towards a research agenda for post-disaster and post-crisis recovery strategies for tourist destinations: A narrative review. *Current Issues in Tourism*, 19(1), 1–26. DOI: 10.1080/13683500.2014.932758

Mansor, A. A. B., & Isa, S. M. (2018). The impact of eye tracking on neuromarketing for genuine value-added applications. *Global Business and Management Research*, 10(1), 1–11.

McGrail, M. R., Rickard, C. M., & Jones, R. (2006). Publish or perish: A systematic review of interventions to increase academic publication rates. *Higher Education Research & Development*, 25(1), 19–35. DOI: 10.1080/07294360500453053

Meckl-Sloan, C. (2015). Neuroeconomics and neuromarketing. *Cell*, 650, 218–8214.

Misra, L. (2023). Neuromarketing insights into consumer behavior. *IUJ Journal of Management*, 11(1), 143–163.

Noar, S. M. (2006). A 10-year retrospective of research in health mass media campaigns: Where do we go from here? *Journal of Health Communication*, 11(1), 21–42. DOI: 10.1080/10810730500461059 PMID: 16546917

Park, C. W., Roth, M. S., & Jacques, P. F. (1988). Evaluating the effects of advertising and sales promotion campaigns. *Industrial Marketing Management*, 17(2), 129–140. DOI: 10.1016/0019-8501(88)90015-6

Pavlou, P. A., & Stewart, D. W. (2000). Measuring the effects and effectiveness of interactive advertising: A research agenda. *Journal of Interactive Advertising*, 1(1), 61–77. DOI: 10.1080/15252019.2000.10722044

Pescher, C., Reichhart, P., & Spann, M. (2014). Consumer decision-making processes in mobile viral marketing campaigns. *Journal of Interactive Marketing*, 28(1), 43–54. DOI: 10.1016/j.intmar.2013.08.001

Plakhin, A. Y., Semenets, I., Ogorodnikova, E., & Khudanina, M. (2018). New directions in the development of neuromarketing and behavioral economics. In *MATEC Web of Conferences* (Vol. 184, pp. 1-6).

Reikin, V. S., Voitovych, S. Y., Danyliuk, T. I., Dedeliuk, K. Y., & Lorvi, I. F. (2021). Neuromarketing as interdisciplinary area: Theoretical and methodological analysis. *Estudios de Economía Aplicada*, 39(6). Advance online publication. DOI: 10.25115/eea.v39i6.5164

Sawagvudcharee, O., Shrestha, S., & Mandal, S. (2018). Impacts of Brand on Consumer Decision Making: Case Study of Beer Brands in Nepal. *International Journal of Research*, 5(16).

Sebastian, V. (2014). New directions in understanding the decision-making process: Neuroeconomics and neuromarketing. *Procedia: Social and Behavioral Sciences*, 127, 758–762. DOI: 10.1016/j.sbspro.2014.03.350

Sharma, A., Dash, S., Vidyapeeth, D. P., & Deshmukh, S., & WPU, D. V. K. M. (2023). A study on neuromarketing potential, problems and applications in the Indian e-commerce sector. *The Online Journal of Distance Education and e-Learning : TOJDEL*, 11(2).

Singh, S. (2020). Impact of neuromarketing applications on consumers. *Journal of Business and Management*, 26(2), 33–52. DOI: 10.1504/JBM.2020.141282

Smith, K. T. (2011). Digital marketing strategies that Millennials find appealing, motivating, or just annoying. *Journal of Strategic Marketing*, 19(6), 489–499. DOI: 10.1080/0965254X.2011.581383

Snyder, L. B., Hamilton, M. A., Mitchell, E. W., Kiwanuka-Tondo, J., Fleming-Milici, F., & Proctor, D. (2004). A meta-analysis of the effect of mediated health communication campaigns on behavior change in the United States. *Journal of Health Communication*, 9(sup1, S1), 71–96. DOI: 10.1080/10810730490271548 PMID: 14960405

Soni, A. (2021). A Study on Consumer Decision-Making Process. *Samvakti Journal of Research in Business Management*, 2(2), 1–8. DOI: 10.46402/2021.01.12

Spence, C. (2020). On the ethics of neuromarketing and sensory marketing. *Organizational Neuroethics: Reflections on the Contributions of Neuroscience to Management Theories and Business Practices*, 9-29.

Spence, C. (2020). On the ethics of neuromarketing and sensory marketing. *Organizational Neuroethics: Reflections on the Contributions of Neuroscience to Management Theories and Business Practices*, 9-29.

Sposini, L. (2024). Impact of New Technologies on Economic Behavior and Consumer Freedom of Choice: From Neuromarketing to Neuro-Rights. *Journal of Digital Technologies and Law*, 2(1), 74–100. DOI: 10.21202/jdtl.2024.5

Thompson, P. (2020). The Relationship between Consumer Credit Card Debt and Immigrants in the UK: A Systematic Review. *American Journal of Economics*, 4(2), 86–114. DOI: 10.47672/aje.637

Turhan, K. N., Gurkaynak, N., & Sadikzade, R. (2023, November). Neuromarketing Concepts in Food Studies. In *2023 Medical Technologies Congress (TIPTEKNO)* (pp. 1-3). IEEE. DOI: 10.1109/TIPTEKNO59875.2023.10359186

Vlasenko, K. (2018). Neuromarketing technologies as the way of achievement of competitive advantage on the market. *Knowledge–Economy–Society*, 95.

Walliser, B. (2003). An international review of sponsorship research: Extension and update. *International Journal of Advertising*, 22(1), 5–40. DOI: 10.1080/02650487.2003.11072838

Wu, H., Wan, W., Jiang, H., & Xiong, Y. (2023). Prognosis of idiopathic sudden sensorineural hearing loss: The nomogram perspective. *The Annals of Otology, Rhinology, and Laryngology*, 132(1), 5–12. DOI: 10.1177/00034894221075114 PMID: 35081764

Chapter 11
Product Packaging and Promotional Strategy Influencing Buying Behaviour

Renu Tanwar
Chaudhary Devi Lal University, Sirsa, India

Preeti Ahlawat
https://orcid.org/0009-0006-8443-873X
Chaudhary Devi Lal University, Sirsa, India

ABSTRACT

Managing the interaction between a business's organization, the enterprise, and its suppliers is greatly aided by buyers. The end goal of every marketer is to comprehend consumer behavior. A solid and comprehensive knowledge of the consumer, the buyer's behavior, and the buyer's values should form the basis of every successful marketing plan or program. Recognition of the problem, gathering relevant information, evaluating alternatives, making a purchasing choice, and subsequent actions are the five steps that make up Kotler's model of the buying process. Seventy-two percent of Americans say that the design of a product's packaging is very essential when making a purchase, and 81 percent say the same about gift purchases. The objective of every marketing campaign is to get people to hear about your product and maybe buy it. The buyer's journey is the series of events that consumers go through from identifying a problem, researching possible solutions, and ultimately making a purchase decision. In order to help a business increase sales and succeed.

DOI: 10.4018/979-8-3693-9351-2.ch011

Copyright © 2025, IGI Global. Copying or distributing in print or electronic forms without written permission of IGI Global is prohibited.

INTRODUCTION

According to the American Marketing Association, consumer behavior can be defined as "the dynamic interaction of affect and cognition, behavior, and environmental events by which human beings conduct the exchange aspects of their lives."

The term "consumer behavior" refers to the influence that a consumer's feelings, attitudes, and preferences have on the decisions that they make regarding their purchases. Consumer behavior was initially a distinct subfield of marketing that emerged in the 1940s and 1950s. However, it has since developed into an interdisciplinary study that integrates components of psychology, sociology, social anthropology, anthropology, ethnography, ethnology, marketing, and economics, particularly the field of behavioral economics.

Comprehending the patterns of purchasing and consuming is a fundamental obstacle for marketers. Consumer behavior is the study of how individuals make purchasing decisions and how they consume or experience items or services. Consumers are proactive decision-makers. Consumers make purchasing decisions, typically influenced by their disposable money or budget. Individuals have the ability to alter their preferences regarding their financial limitations and many other influencing elements (Wikipedia). End customer or consumer behavior pertains to the behaviors and choices that individuals or groups of individuals undertake while selecting, purchasing, and utilizing a product or service.

SIGNIFICANCE OF CONSUMER PURCHASING BEHAVIOUR

Effective Marketing Strategies - A corporation can develop effective marketing strategies by understanding the factors that motivate consumers and impact their purchasing decisions.

Effective Product creation - The creation of products and services should consistently match the requirements and preferences of customers. Only this can guarantee success when launching products.

Increased client Loyalty - Providing products and services that fulfil client expectations frequently results in a heightened level of customer loyalty.

Companies that can adapt to evolving consumer preferences and trends tend to outperform their competitors and obtain a competitive advantage in the market.

Consumer behavior research is crucial for spotting potential market hazards, enabling businesses to proactively meet customer wants ahead of their competitors.

Customer retention is increased when a corporation matches its objectives with the needs of consumers (Singh, P., 2024).

In the world of marketing communication the role of digitalization and artificial intelligence is changing the existing paradigms (Arora, (2023); Arora & Sharma (2023); Kumar, Arora & Erkol Bayram, (Eds.). (2024) a; Kumar, Arora & Erkol Bayram, (Eds.). (2024) b). Newer dimensions affecting the behavior of consumer are getting popular like metaverse, virtual reality, immersive experiences (Arora, M. (2024); Chandel, M., & Arora, M. (2024); Dhiman & Arora, (2024)).

Factors Affecting Consumer Purchasing Behavior

1. **Psychological Factors**

    First, there are psychological factors that influence consumer buying behavior

    Motivation: Everyone has their own unique set of wants, requirements, and aspirations, and these might influence their purchase choices.

    Learning: As a result of gathering more information and gaining more experiences with products or services, consumer behavior and choices might change over time.

    What influences a consumer's product selection and purchase decisions are the consumer's attitudes and beliefs.

    Perception: Consumers' views and impressions of items greatly influence their actions.

2. **Societal Considerations**

    Our family's purchase habits have a significant impact on our own purchasing selections.

    Because members of the reference group we belong to tend to make similar purchases, this group can have a significant impact on our purchasing decisions.

    Social Status and Role: Our social status and role in society play a major influence in what we buy.

3. **Cultural Considerations**

    Culture and society have an impact on consumer behavior. Shoppers who identify with a particular ideology or set of values may behave somewhat differently from those who identify with a different ideology or set of values.

4. **Individual Variables**

    Age: Because of people's purchasing habits vary greatly depending on their age, it's clear that age is a major element in determining consumer behavior.

Income- One factor that influences purchasing power is wealth. People with more spare income are more likely to spend it on luxuries, whereas those with less money prioritize addressing their basic requirements.

Occupation: People are more likely to purchase things that are related to their job.

Lifestyle: As consumers, our product preferences are shaped by the way we live or aspire to live.

5. **Economic Considerations**

   Consumer discretionary income
   National Economic Status
   Available Cash on Hand

FIVE STEPS OF DECISION-MAKING PROCESS

1. **Want to be Noticed**

   In the first step, the buyer knows that he or she needs the good or service. For example, they may realize that sending emails by hand is no longer working for them as their business grows and that they need an email automation option.

2. **Look for Information**

   The buyer starts looking for information once they know what they need from a product or service. They could get it from different places, like friends, ads, or the media.

3. **Looking at the Options**

   The buyer starts to think about a choice once they have all the information they need. They might look at prices and important features of different tools to see which one has the most benefits.

4. **Choosing to Buy**

   After looking at it, the buyer decides to buy it. For instance, they sign up for a paying plan or start their free trial.

5. **Evaluation After the Purchase**

   The person who bought the item or service then checks to see if it lived up to their hopes. At this point, they might also leave an online review about the purchase or share their feedback with subscribers, colleagues, or friends (Sydorenko, N. 2023).

VARIETIES OF CONSUMER BEHAVIOUR

1. **Complex buying behavior:** Because there is a lot of economic or psychological risk, the customer is very involved in the buying process and does a lot of study before making a purchase. This kind of buying includes things like getting a house, a car, an education course, and other expensive things or services.
2. **Behaviors that reduce dissonance:** It's hard for people to decide between brands because they're afraid they'll rue their choice later (hence the word "dissonance"). Most of the time, they buy things without doing a lot of study because it's easy or because they have the money.
3. **Habitual buying behavior:** This type of buying behavior is marked by a customer not being very involved in the decision to buy. A customer doesn't notice a big difference between brands and gets the same things over and over again.
4. **Varity Seeking:** They like to try new things, so they might buy soap without giving it much thought. They will pick a different brand the next time to change the smell. A customer who changes brands because they want to try something new or are interested, not because they are unhappy, shows a low level of involvement (Bhasin, H. 2023).

PRODUCT PACKAGING

The meaning of product packaging refers to the purpose and significance of the materials used to contain and present a product. First and foremost, it is crucial to comprehend the significance of packing. Packaging plays a vital role in the field of marketing. The product's initial impression on a consumer is of utmost importance. The packaging is accountable for establishing the initial perception of the goods and has a crucial part in influencing the choice to purchase. Consequently, it is imperative to develop packaging that is distinctive and physically attractive. The packaging design should effectively convey the brand's identity, values, and purpose to the consumer. The major purpose of packaging is to safeguard the product during its transportation and storage (Panchal, 2023).

Smart packaging offers a potential solution that has the ability to decrease greenhouse gas emissions. Smart packaging offers enhanced efficiency compared to traditional packaging. It achieves this by ensuring the product's authenticity and traceability from its origin, preventing fraud and theft, and improving security. Traditional packaging, on the other hand, primarily focuses on extending the product's useful life and facilitating transport and marketing. As a result, it can aid in mitigating pollution, minimizing food losses, and reducing waste linked to the food supply chain (Fernandez, 2022). The packaging value chain is placing growing importance on sustainability. Simultaneously, there is an increasing level of consumer awareness. As civilizations recover from the COVID-19 pandemic, consumer attitude is shifting away from excessive emphasis on hygiene. In order to gain a deeper understanding, we conducted a survey in 11 countries to investigate consumers' perspectives on sustainable packaging. Firstly, while considering customers' purchase decisions, sanitation and shelf life are the most significant considerations across all countries. Furthermore, when considering the environmental consequences of product packaging, it is apparent that consumer apprehensions regarding ocean pollution are particularly pronounced in Europe, Japan, and the United States. Meanwhile, consumers in other Asian countries and Latin America appear to be primarily concerned with different types of pollution. Consumers worldwide have divergent views regarding the best sustainable kind of packaging (Mckinsey, 2023).

The consumer's purchasing behavior is also influenced by the packaging quality, color, wrapping, and other attributes of the packaging. Packaging is a comprehensive solution that serves as a powerful selling point, encouraging impulsive purchasing behavior. Effective packaging enhances sales and market dominance while minimizing marketing and promotional expenses. Moreover, several studies investigate the influence of packaging and its characteristics on the entirety of a consumer's purchasing choice, while others focus on each individual phase of the consumer's decision-making process. Indeed, consumers are increasingly becoming more demanding. Packaging has gradually demonstrated its crucial role in serving consumers by giving information and fulfilling services. There is no doubt that packaging plays an increasingly essential role as a strategic instrument to capture consumers' attention and influence their opinion of product quality. This is due to its various functions that aim to facilitate communication and interaction with consumers (Raheem et al., 2014).

Significance of Product Packaging

The packaging of a product serves as the initial interaction between a brand and the buyer. It functions as a tacit sales representative, effectively conveying brand principles, excellence, and practicality. Efficient packaging has the ability to attract attention, generate a sense of longing, and ultimately influence purchasing choices. Whether it is achieved through daring and inventive designs or the use of eco-friendly materials, packaging possesses the ability to create a long-lasting impact on consumers (Fripp, G). The aesthetic attractiveness of packaging frequently serves as the primary attraction for consumers. Visually appealing designs and captivating packaging have the ability to make a product distinguishable among other products on packed shelves, hence enhancing the chances of it being recognized and selected over similar products from competitors. Packaging also functions as a method of distinguishing one product from another. In a saturated market filled with comparable items, having unique and distinctive packaging helps differentiate a company and establish a memorable character. The ability to differentiate through packaging can significantly impact brand loyalty and repeat purchases, since consumers frequently link the packaging to their whole brand experience. The haptic and utilitarian characteristics of packaging also have a substantial impact on consumer experience. An intelligently crafted packaging that is effortless to open, utilize, and store has the potential to augment customer contentment and foster favorable brand connections. In addition, informative and captivating packaging can include vital product details, instructions for use, and even narratives, so enhancing customer engagement and fostering brand loyalty (Fripp, G).

Factors Impacting Consumer Decisions Regarding Packaging

Colors, Fonts, Graphics: For example, the color red has been linked to stimulation, excitement, and activity. This term is employed to describe products that are associated with action, movement, and even hunger. It is crucial to utilize colors that effectively express the desired tone or mood and effectively portray the nature of your goods. High-end chocolate makers frequently employ vibrant package colors and sophisticated typography to establish an immediate connection with opulence (Dillon, Feb.2024).

Noteworthy initial encounters: The significance of initial impressions is crucial in a society where consumers make rapid decisions. The capacity of packaging to establish an enduring recollection is crucial. As a result, this attracts attention when displayed on the shelf and becomes deeply embedded in the consumer's mind, so fostering brand loyalty.

Convenience and usability: Take into account the resealable packaging of a snack food; while its main purpose is to maintain the freshness of the contents, it also satisfies the contemporary consumer's desire for convenient on-the-go consumption. Functional design aspects, such as seals that are easy to open and shapes that are ergonomic, also have a role in creating a favorable user experience, which in turn influences the likelihood of repeat purchases.

Product functioning: The interaction between packaging design and product functioning is an essential factor to consider. Brands must guarantee that the packaging is perfectly in line with the intended purpose of their product.

Company values communication: A beauty company that utilizes sustainable and recyclable packaging not only appeals to eco-friendly consumers but also conveys a dedication to ethical practices, thereby connecting with environmentally conscious consumers.

Narrative Power: Packaging possesses the ability to effectively convey a story, establishing a stronger connection between consumers and the brand (Dillon, Feb.2024).

Packaging Levels

Primary Packaging: The primary function of primary packaging is to safeguard and maintain the integrity of the product contained within. Primary packaging, often known as retail packaging, is commonly used to refer to the package that directly contains a product. However, it is worth noting that the phrase "retail packaging" can also be used to describe secondary packaging in some cases (Muhammad, 2024). In addition to maintaining the product's quality, it is crucial for the primary packaging to be visually striking and attractive. This is because it will be the initial impression that the end customer forms upon encountering the goods. This is especially crucial in the context of consumer or online sales products. The primary packaging serves the purposes of segregating, safeguarding, ensuring, conveying attributes and expiration, and occasionally, capturing attention and fostering allegiance. Examples of packing materials include milk cartons, beer cans, plastic bottles for detergent, sacks for packaging concrete, and cardboard boxes for furniture.

Secondary Packaging: It refers to the form of packaging that provides additional strength and security to a group and protect individual units of sale. Occasionally, consumer products are sold in a way that they are grouped together, necessitating the need for effective communication and visually appealing presentation. Secondary packing typically consists of cardboard boxes or other materials with varying sizes and thicknesses, as well as plastic film. Consumer products include items such as the cardboard box used to package bottles of beer or the plastic film used to wrap water bottles together.

Tertiary Packaging: Tertiary packaging refers to the outermost layer of packing, typically the largest and final piece. It is designed to be kept and handled within a warehouse. Tertiary packaging often comprises collections of products included within primary and secondary packaging. For instance, while considering wine as a product, the bottle would be classified as the primary packaging, the cardboard box that contains the bottles would be considered the secondary packaging, and the pallet that consolidates several wine boxes would be categorized as the tertiary packaging (Muhammad, 2024).

Impact of Product Packaging on Consumer Actions

Product packaging has a significant impact on consumer behavior, frequently subconsciously. Packaging's visual and tactile clues can elicit feelings and influence consumers' decisions to buy. Research indicates that packaging that elicits pleasant feelings like happiness, nostalgia, or enthusiasm is more appealing to consumers. Using this information, brands may develop packaging designs that appeal to their target market and trigger the right feelings in them. Packaging can affect consumers' opinions about a product's quality, value, and compatibility for their needs in addition to their emotions. When a product is packaged well, it might imply dependability and trustworthiness, which makes the product within seem premium and well worth the money. Packaging has the power to convey usage situations, characteristics, and advantages of a product, assisting customers in making wise purchasing decisions. Consumer behavior may also be influenced by the packaging's usefulness and convenience. Convenience for customers can be increased by packaging that is simple to handle, store, and transport, which also improves the product's appeal and usability. However, overly large, or wasteful packaging might turn off eco-aware customers and harm a company's reputation. Packaging has an impact on customer behavior even after a product is purchased. The effect and reach of a brand's marketing initiatives can be increased by using captivating and memorable packaging to promote social sharing and word-of-mouth recommendations. For example, packaging that enhances the unboxing experience can encourage customers to post about their delight on social media, thereby turning them into brand ambassadors (Raheem et al., 2014).

PRODUCT PROMOTION MEANING

Product promotion is an important part of marketing a product. A primary goal of product marketing is to increase the product's visibility among potential buyers by highlighting the product's features and benefits. Promotion of products is important since it forms the backbone of any successful marketing strategy for a brand. Brand awareness among consumers and, by extension, revenue, can increase through recommendations, loyalty programs, and unique discounts in addition to fortifying relationships with existing customers.

The term "product promotion" describes a group of actions aimed at educating potential customers about products in the marketplace. Product marketing informs consumers about the features, benefits, and even advantages of a product over those of its competitors, so introducing it to the market. Product advertising is much to blame for igniting and stoking consumer desire (commerce mate). Product promotion entails using innovative marketing techniques to target a certain market and boost sales. Businesses go through a process called product launch and promotion in order to increase sales and foster customer loyalty. Gaining knowledge about product promotion can aid in learning marketing tactics that boost revenue and expand brand recognition. It's a collection of strategies used to draw attention to a firm and a particular product when it's first introduced to the market or after it's featured by them (Indeed, 2022).

Characteristics of Product Promotion

Product promotion focuses mostly on generating extensive awareness of items and brands in the market. It is extremely efficient in introducing new products or brands to customers for the first time.

It effectively generates customer interest in products through the creation of attractive promotional campaigns. The advertisements are executed in a captivating manner that captures the attention of individuals.

Product advertising provides clients with comprehensive information about the products. Individuals are provided with information regarding the characteristics, applications, and accessibility of things, thus transforming a state of curiosity into concrete purchases.

This boosts the demand for business products by persuading individuals to purchase them. The process involves emphasizing the characteristics and significance of the product. Product promotion enhances the brand's perception in the minds of customers, resulting in increased customer loyalty and repeated purchases over time.

It enables the organization to maintain a competitive position in the market. Currently, every organization is employing advertising methods extensively in order to establish its position in the market.

Strategies for Product Promotion

1. Understand Your Target Demographic

    Prior to devising a promotional strategy for a product, it is imperative to engage in thorough research to identify the primary target demographic within the broader market. Alternatively, you may be seeking to target untapped markets or prospective clientele. Customizing the plan to cater to these categories might be beneficial in attracting their interest and aiding in consumer loyalty.

2. Establish Your Marketing Approach

    An effective marketing strategy should guide the process from generating ideas to launching the product, once the company objectives have been established. This involves constructing a concise and compelling message that clearly communicates the product's value proposition and how it can enhance the customer's life, at an appropriate price and in a suitable market. Additionally, it involves developing a persuasive call to action to encourage consumer engagement.

3. Evaluate Your Outcomes

    Conducting a postmortem analysis of the outcome of a promotion campaign is crucial in order to capitalize on its success and enhance future metrics and key performance indicators (KPIs).

Categories of Product Promotion

1. Offering cheap products: Customers are always inclined to seek out favorable deals, thus by providing them with discounted offers, they become more satisfied with the business. Businesses must consistently guarantee that discounted offers are meticulously crafted to enhance their appeal (Indeed,2022).
2. A flash sale refers to a time-limited promotion when clients are offered special deals on products. Customers are very inclined to purchase and experiment with products that are available in exclusive time-limited offers.
3. Product giveaways: People derive pleasure from receiving complimentary items from brands. Individuals value these actions from a firm and have little difficulty in committing their products to memory.
4. Complimentary delivery and effortless returns: The inclusion of free shipping and a convenient return process serves as an incentive for customers to make purchases of brand products. This provides individuals with a feeling of assurance that they will not experience financial loss if they choose to return the product.
5. Customer loyalty points can be accumulated during purchases and subsequently redeemed towards future purchases. The loyalty points system is a widely used product promotion strategy that incentivizes customers to make recurring purchases for their convenience.
6. Coupon giveaway: Companies distribute digital coupons to their clients, incentivizing them to visit the online store and make purchases. Nevertheless, corporations should strategically design these promotions to create an aura of exclusivity and evoke happiness among consumers (Indeed, 2022).

Product Promotion Examples

Case Studies

KITKAT promotes the idea of taking a break to the Twitch community.

Approximately 90 years after introducing their chocolate-coated wafer, KITKAT sought the assistance of Amazon Ads to target adult consumers from the Gen Z and millennial demographics. By activating Twitch premium video advertisements, KITKAT successfully interacted with a highly involved audience and reinforced the message, "Even the most accomplished individual requires a pause," which is a contemporary interpretation of their iconic slogan.

HP has chosen to utilize Amazon Business as a platform to reintroduce their 1005W laser printer line. In 2022, HP collaborated with Amazon Ads to develop a comprehensive marketing campaign for the relaunch of their laser printer series, featuring innovative ink-tank technology. By leveraging Amazon Business, a platform that serves over 2 million verified B2B clients in India, HP successfully targeted small businesses and reconnected with audiences who had previously expressed interest in printers.

Cheetos Mac 'n Cheese successfully targets millennial demographics.

PepsiCo aimed to broaden their consumer base among millennials who were unfamiliar with their brand by introducing Cheetos Mac 'n Cheese, a fusion of one of their top-selling goods and a beloved comfort dish. Through the implementation of a targeted marketing strategy utilizing audience information on Amazon DSP, Cheetos experienced an increase in purchase intent, brand preference, and ad awareness (Amazon ads).

A strategy for promotion refers to the comprehensive plan and specific strategies employed to promote a product. The promotion plan comprises the objectives driving your promotional efforts and the strategies you will employ to maximize the benefits of promoting your product (Macneil, 2024).

1. Pull Promotional Strategy: According to Ahrefs, pull and push marketing are two techniques that utilize complementary tactics. Pull promotion strategies aim to attract clients by implementing approaches that enable them to independently discover and engage with your offering. Examples of pull marketing methods encompass content marketing and social media marketing (coschedule, Nov.2023)

2. **Promotional Push Strategy**: The push promotion strategy actively promotes and directs your goods towards your clients. It encompasses strategic methods that position your goods directly in front of your customers, such as advertising or cold emailing.
3. **Strategy for Promoting Sales**: Sales promotion techniques encompass the implementation of incentives to stimulate customers' purchase of your product. There exist two categories of sales promotion strategies. Attracting clients through inbound means, such as offering free shipping for sales that exceed a certain threshold. Outbound tactics, such as sending discounts via postal mail, that include actively contacting customers.
4. **Strategy for Promoting Retail Sales**: Retail establishments have distinct obstacles and possess specific advantages in comparison to other types of businesses due to their tangible character. They can use their position by implementing retail-specific promotional campaigns that utilize tactics such as in-person loyalty programs and intelligent shopfront design.
5. **Strategy for Promoting Ecommerce**: However, ecommerce retailers hold a unique position in the commercial sector due to their virtual character. These organizations employ ecommerce promotion techniques that heavily rely on digital tactics, such as e-commerce-specific search engine optimization (SEO) (coschedule, Nov. 2023)

Examples of Promotion Strategies

1. Starbucks utilizes a marketing approach that incorporates several promotional channels, including the use of innovative technologies, to promote their packaged refreshers beverages. In 2012, during the early stages of mobile advertising's rise to popularity, Starbucks boldly launched mobile advertisements on apps such as Pandora, specifically promoting their packaged Refreshers beverages.
2. Tesla primarily focuses on promoting its products through positive word-of-mouth marketing generated by customers' experiences with the Tesla Model 3. In a 2019 quarter three earnings call, CEO Elon Musk affirmed that the arrival of the Tesla Model 3, the company's most economical model, will effectively stimulate demand.
3. Amazon utilizes a comprehensive promotional plan to market its Alexa technology, incorporating video advertising for both online and television platforms. Two of its 2020 advertisements centered around using Alexa to link users to imaginary realms.
4. Coca-Cola Diet Coke: In response to the growing popularity of diet soda in the 1980s, the Coca-Cola Company recognized the need to cater to this market demand. The initial promotional approach for Diet Coke entailed a well-attended

press conference to unveil the company's most notable product launch. Diet Coke emerged as the leading diet soda in the United States by the conclusion of 1983.
5. Netflix, being a technology platform, has the capability to gather data on users' viewing patterns in order to enhance its promotional strategies. As stated on its marketing and growth page, the company identifies the titles that have the highest performance in order to partner with advertisers such as Facebook and Google (coschedule, Nov. 2023)

CONCLUSION

Packaging has a substantial influence on customer behavior. It plays a crucial role in the marketing mix since it has the ability to shape a consumer's perception of a product. Consumer feedback is valuable for enhancing packaging design. The packaging design has the ability to evoke emotions and generate a strong inclination to purchase the goods. Adhering to ecological principles and mindful of the environment, embracing a simple and unrefined aesthetic, embodying grace and contemporary style, exuding refinement and opulence. Refine Packaging has the ability to bring any desired impression to life, regardless of its nature. Implementing a well-defined strategy for promotion is crucial, as it allows for efficient utilization of time and money by targeting the appropriate audience. You will significantly increase the likelihood of converting the funds allocated to promotional activities into actual sales, generating greater product visibility and creating a buzz around it.

REFERENCES

Arora, M. (2023). Encapsulating Role of Persuasion and Skill Development in Marketing Communication for Brand Building: A Perspective. In *International Handbook of Skill, Education, Learning, and Research Development in Tourism and Hospitality* (pp. 1–17). Springer Nature Singapore.

Arora, M. (2024). Metaverse Metamorphosis: Bridging the Gap Between Research Insights and Industry Applications. In Research, Innovation, and Industry Impacts of the Metaverse (pp. 275-286).

Arora, M., & Sharma, R. L. (2023). Artificial intelligence and big data: Ontological and communicative perspectives in multi-sectoral scenarios of modern businesses. *Foresight*, 25(1), 126–143. DOI: 10.1108/FS-10-2021-0216

Bhasin, H. (2023, July 25). *What is Consumer Behavior? Definition, Example, Types & Factors*. Retrieved from https://www.marketing91.com/consumer-behavior/

Carlos, M. Fernandez, T. M., J. A., & Pedro Dinis Gaspar, (2023, Feb.). *Innovative processes in smart packaging. A systematic review*. Retrieved from Journal of the Science of Food and Agriculture: https://scijournals.onlinelibrary.wiley.com/doi/10.1002/jsfa.11863

Chandel, M., & Arora, M. (2024). Metaverse Perspectives: Unpacking Its Role in Shaping Sustainable Development Goals-A Qualitative Inquiry. In Research, Innovation, and Industry Impacts of the Metaverse (pp. 62-75). IGI Global.

Consumer behaviour. (n.d.). Retrieved from Wikipedia: https://en.wikipedia.org/wiki/Consumer_behaviour

Dhiman, V., & Arora, M. (2024a) Current State of Metaverse in Entrepreneurial Ecosystem: A Retrospective Analysis of Its Evolving Landscape. In *Exploring the Use of Metaverse in Business and Education* (pp. 73-87). IGI Global. https://doi.org/DOI: 10.4018/979-8-3693-5868-9.ch005

Dillon, M. (2024, February 25). *How Does Product Packaging Impact Consumer Buying Behavior?* Retrieved from https://meyers.com/meyers-blog/how-does-packaging-affect-consumer-behavior/

Fripp, G. (n.d.). *The Main Roles of Product Packaging in Marketing*. Retrieved from https://www.marketingstudyguide.com/the-main-roles-of-product-packaging-in-marketing/

King, M. (2023, November 07). *What Is A Promotion Strategy? Types, Examples, & Process*. Retrieved from coschedule: https://coschedule.com/marketing/marketing-mix/promotion-strategy

Kumar, J., Arora, M., & Erkol Bayram, G. (Eds.). (2024) b. *Research, Innovation, and Industry Impacts of the Metaverse*. IGI Global.

Kumar, J., Arora, M., & Erkol Bayram, G. (Eds.). (2024)a. *Exploring the Use of Metaverse in Business and Education*. IGI Global. DOI: DOI: 10.4018/979-8-3693-5868-9

MacNeil, C. (2024, January 12). *In a sales slump? Try these 12 promotion strategies to create customer demand*. Retrieved from https://asana.com/resources/promotion-strategy

Muhammad, A. (2024, July 1). *The 3 Levels of Packaging: Primary, Secondary and Tertiary Packaging*. Retrieved from Refine Packaging: https://refinepackaging.com/blog/primary-secondary-tertiary-packaging/

OVERVIEW of Buyer and Buying Behaviour. (n.d.). Retrieved from Oxford Reference: https://www.oxfordreference.com/display/10.1093/oi/authority.20110803095539233

Packaging types and differences. (n.d.). Retrieved from https://www.ar-racking.com/en/blog/primary-secondary-and-tertiary-packaging-types-and-differences/

Panchal, H. (2023, April 23). *The Impact of Packaging on Consumer Purchasing Behavior: An Analysis of the Impact on Buying Decisions*. Retrieved from https://www.litmusbranding.com/blog/the-impact-of-packaging-on-consumer-purchasing-behavior-an-analysis-of-the-impact-on-buying-decisions/

Planning, P. (2022, April 15). *How Packaging Influences Consumer Behavior*. Retrieved from EDL a massman Company: https://www.edlpackaging.com/blog/how-packaging-influences-consumer-behavior/

Product promotion, Definitation, types, strategy,example. (n.d.). Retrieved from https://advertising.amazon.com/library/guides/product-promotion

Raheem, A. R., Vishnu, P. A. R. M. A. R., & Ahmed, A. M. (2014). Impact of product packaging on consumer's buying behavior. *European Journal of Scientific Research*, 122(2), 125–134.

Rambabu, L., & Porika, R. (2020, April 09). *Packaging strategies: knowledge outlook on consumer buying behaviour*. Retrieved from Emerald insight: https://www.emerald.com/insight/content/doi/10.1108/JIUC-10-2019-0017/full/html

Singh, P. (2024, June 23). *Consumer Behavior – Types, Scope, Models & Characteristics*. Retrieved from https://www.revechat.com/blog/consumer-behavior/

Sustainability in packaging 2023: Inside the minds of global consumers. (2023, August 15). Retrieved from Mckinsey & Company: https://mckinsey.com/industries/packaging-and-paper/our-insights/sustainability-in-packaging-2023-inside-the-minds-of-global-consumers

Sydorenko, N. (2023, April 07). *Buyer behavior*. Retrieved from https://snov.io/glossary/buyer-behavior/

Team, I. E. (2022, December 30). *16 Product Promotion Strategies (With Definition and How-To)*. Retrieved from https://www.indeed.com/career-advice/career-development/products-promotion

What is Product Promotion? Objectives & Types. (n.d.). Retrieved from Commerce Mates: https://commercemates.com/what-is-product-promotion-objectives-types/

Chapter 12
How Does Product Packaging Affect Consumers' Buying Decisions?

Meena Sharma
Mody University of Science and Technology, India

Anupal Mongia
Mody University of Science and Technology, India

Richa Pareek
Mody University of Science and Technology, India

Lalita Kumari
Mody University of Science and Technology, India

ABSTRACT

The packaging gives constant development in marketing. It grows into the basic magnitudes in the production and manufacturing concept, as it plays an important role in prominence the mental image of the product to the consumer. The status of packaging makes marketing thinkers consider it to closed element for the marketing complex and positive process on which the product depends. Therefore, this study examines the packaging concept and its impact on consumers buying decisions. This study is based on primary data collection through a designed questionnaire and distributed to 750 consumers in the Shekhawati area. The results confirm that consumers are attracted to the product packaging in all aspects (design, color, size, shape). It endorses adopting a packaging policy in industrial organizations facing

DOI: 10.4018/979-8-3693-9351-2.ch012

high-tech expansions and rapidly changing consumer palates. It is necessary to consider modern marketing directions in product packaging, including green marketing, which depends on the use of materials that have less environmental impact in the packaging process.

1. INTRODUCTION

In the context of market opening and convergence between markets, the market is filled with different products, as a product can have many different forms and substitutes. Therefore, the organization needs to recognize its product among other products. there are several types on the market so customers can find the product very easily (Grönroos, 1982; Klimchuk & Krasovec, 2013). The rising interest in the marketing potential of the metaverse and its influence on consumer behavior is undeniable. In Ecommerce is very important to be careful with the development of virtual stores, shopping experience improvement, personalizing customer experience and shopping behavior analysis and understanding.

Therefore, organizations rely on packaging strategies to differentiate their products from other products to attract consumers' attention toward certain products. In other words, packaging or wrapping can become the main reason for consumer demand for one product among others. Theoretical and professional references indicate that blankets and wrapping paper are not new objects of the modern era but have been used since ancient times, while leather goods, baskets, ceramics, and water crystal for packaging and during postage - Packaging during World War II became increasingly important in many different countries around the world. The predominance of self-service and vending stores using machines, the popularity of modern materials in the packaging sector such as plastic, paper, aluminum, wood, glass, cardboard, iron, and other materials, and in recent years the development of the concept of packaging is no longer limited to protecting goods from damage but has also become a marketing tool to influence trends purchase goods from consumers. Packaging is of great importance to consumers and organizations, so the study started with a question. **How does product packaging affect consumers' buying decisions?** To answer this question, research is being conducted to examine the evolution of packaging and its role in attracting customer attention. packaging has been intensively studied by various researchers. There is an intersection of two developing trends that could significantly impact Packaging design. One of them is the growth of e-commerce shopping and how it's been changing packaging design in a couple of ways the second way that this e-commerce trend has been changing packaging, packaging design, is that companies are now designing their packaging graphics to appeal to shoppers who are seeing this package on a screen rather than on a shelf.

Metaverse: is a fully functional digital realm beyond our physical reality. The future culmination and integration of the fragmented virtual worlds will converge all digitally enhanced physical reality and physically persistent virtual or augmented spaces (Kumar, Arora & Erkol Bayram, (Eds.). (2024) a; Kumar, Arora & Erkol Bayram, (Eds.). (2024) b). Essentially, the metaverse is the future total of all virtual and augmented realities and the interconnections between those spaces and our physical world via the "Internet out things."

The emergence of the metaverse has captivated significant attention due to its vast potential for reshaping Product packaging strategies and influencing consumer behavior. The metaverse has been described as a virtual reality that exists beyond reality (Kolesnichenko et al., 2019; Kye et al., 2021), connecting consumer's imagination to the real world (Bale et al., 2022) and bringing a fusion of social networking with the immersive virtual worlds (Ayiter, 2019); Arora, (2024)a; Chandel & Arora, (2024); Dhiman & Arora(2024)a).

Despite the metaverse being an alien concept to many consumers and companies, it is expected to add real value to the packaging sector. Many of the vital metaverse technologies are already being used or piloted by packaging companies. For example, packaging companies have brought together artificial intelligence (AI), AR, VR, cloud, the Internet of Things (IoT), and other technologies to monitor and maintain key assets remotely (Arora (2024)a). The immersive metaverse solutions could also be deployed to optimize packaging design and quality control. Another disruptive benefit of the metaverse will be using underlying blockchain and digital twin technologies to assist in creating more transparent and traceable supply chains. The metaverse market is anticipated to value worth $627 billion by 2030 and the market is expected to grow at a CAGR of over 32% between 2020-2030. M&A activity in the metaverse is picking up, with access to technology being the key rationale for most deals. Providers of AR, VR, AI, and blockchain solutions are becoming prime targets as acquirers aim to develop novel experiences. Further the growing relevance of metaverse is reshaping the entire entrepreneurial ecosystem (Rathore & Arora,(2024); Dhiman & Arora, (2024)b; Arora & Sharma, (2022)).

Literature Review: Alhmadi Faud (2020) found that packaging, but not size or color, has a significant impact on consumer behavior. Azad and Masoumi (2012) identified the key factors that influence competitive advantage related to packaging and identified eight independent variables, including packaging durability, ease of distribution, customer promotion through packaging, the structure of packaging, packaging as a silent advertiser, type of packaging, clean and good packaging, healthy packaging, and packaging innovation. The results confirm that all the above factors effectively affect competitiveness. Azad and Mohammadi (2013) tried to identify the major factors that influence dairy packaging. The study conducted a factor analysis to identify important factors based on a questionnaire distributed to a selection of employees of Pega, a dairy product manufacturer and identified five factors as important factors influencing consumers: infrastructure, awareness, design, and communication. Benachenhou et al. (2018) investigated the impact of marketing innovations and visual and linguistic elements of packaging on customers' purchase intentions. They showed that marketing innovations and visual and linguistic elements of packaging influence customers' purchase intentions toward the brand. Arora et al. (2017) identified and analyzed the impact of critical success factors (CSFs) that influence technology implementation in the consumer-packaged goods (CPG) supply chain. This study found that his CSFs of inter-organizational, organizational, CPG sector-specific, human, and program management influence the success of technology implementation in the CPG supply chain. Muslims et al. (2020) investigated the influence of social media experiences on attitudes and behavioral intentions toward Umrah packages among Generation X and Y generations in Malaysia. This study confirmed that sharing content from social media experiences can have a significant and positive impact on behavioral intentions. Rundh (2009) explained how packaging design can contribute to product development by considering the packaging design process based on external and internal factors. According to Lee and Lye (2003), packaging costs, including materials and direct labor, make up a large portion of a product's manufacturing costs, and it is important to reduce these costs as much as possible. Therefore, it is important to manage packaging costs to reduce unnecessary costs without losing customer demand. Subhanes et al. (2017) discussed how sustainable packaging can be planned and implemented to promote business development. Clement (2007) conducted an empirical study to determine the visual impact of in-store purchasing decisions. The focus of the research was an eye-tracking experiment on the visual impact of packaging design. After reading the introduction by Huynh-The et al. (2023), it is possible to get an idea of the importance that the metaverse could reach, and if the article is analysed carefully, it might be understood that this could become a digital world parallel to the one we currently live in that any activity would be possible in one way or another, therefore many companies and professionals are already investing in spaces or land in the metaverse. There are disciplines that converge with the metaverse, such as economics and commercial relations, and therefore also marketing and advertising; in fact, when Second Life was created, the companies Adidas and American Apparel associated themselves with it to market their products (Bourlakis et al., 2009), since the metaverse pretends to be the new marketing platform of the companies (Hollensen et al., 2022).

Currently, it is possible to see the Gucci store in Roblox (Guzzetti et al., 2023), but there is still much to investigate in terms of services, products and quality in the metaverse (Gadalla, 2013) and the design of virtual stores in the metaverse (Hassouneh & Brengman, 2015). Advances in this sense with reference to augmented reality have given rise to a new marketing specialty, augmented reality marketing (Rauschnabel et al., 2022). Neuroscience, which has studied the understanding of emotions, attention and memory in various domains related to organisations and business, is very useful to study the same in virtual environments such as the metaverse. Only there is little research on these issues in immersive virtual environments (Mandolfo et al., 2022).

2. THEORETICAL FRAMEWORK

2.1 The Research Problem

Companies encounter many problems in the product packaging process, although we have metaverse and AI tools among them the difficulty of choosing packaging and packaging that attracts consumers' attention. Furthermore, they ignore the role of packaging choice in attracting consumer attention to the product. as well as the lack of logical and orderly packaging choices.

Accordingly, the problem of research can be crystallized in the following question:

How does product packaging affect consumers' buying decisions?

Based on this question the following questions arise

How does the design of the casing and packaging attract consumer attention to the product?

How important are packaging size and packaging in attracting consumer attention to a product?

How important are shape and packaging in attracting consumer attention to a product?

What impact do packaging color and packaging have on attracting consumer attention to a product?

Research Hypothesis

To address the problem and to achieve the objectives of the research, a hypothesis scheme is designed that reflects the relationship of research variables, including packaging, and attracts the attention of the consumer towards the commodity, as shown in Figure 1.

Figure 1. The proposed study

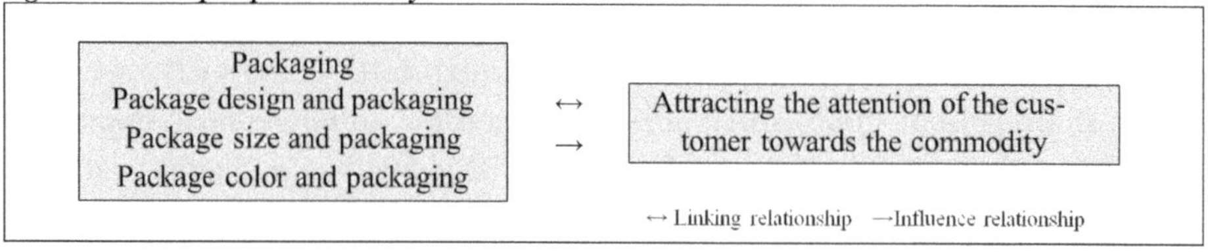

```
┌─────────────────────────────────────────────────────────────────────┐
│    Packaging                                                        │
│    Package design and packaging      ↔    Attracting the attention  │
│    Package size and packaging        →    of the customer towards   │
│    Package color and packaging            the commodity             │
│                                                                     │
│                                    ↔ Linking relationship           │
│                                    → Influence relationship         │
└─────────────────────────────────────────────────────────────────────┘

```

The Hypothesis of the Study

Ha: There is a significant correlation between packaging and attracting the consumer's attention towards the commodity, and from this relationship, the subdivided hypotheses have been branched as follows
Ha1: There is an important link between the packaging and attracting customer's attention towards a commodity.
Ha2: There is a significant correlation between the size of the package and the packaging in attracting consumers' attention towards the commodity.
Ha3: There is a significant correlation between the shape of the package and the packaging in attracting consumers' attention towards the commodity.
Ha4: There is a significant correlation between the color of the package and the packaging in attracting consumer attention to the commodity.

3. RESEARCH METHODOLOGY

To achieve the objectives and hypotheses of the research and to address the problem of research, a descriptive and analytical approach was adopted using the questionnaire. The sample of the research includes 750 in the Shekhawati region, randomly, and the number of questionnaires received and valid for analysis was 580 questionnaires. The collection of the secondary data was conducted depending on the available sources and references related to the research variables. As for the primary data, the questionnaire was adopted as a main tool for collecting this data; where questions were prepared that clarify the role of packaging in attracting the attention of the consumer.

The questionnaire included 26 items distributed on the research variables. After finishing the preparation of the initial formula of the standards of the study it was presented in the form of a questionnaire to five arbitrators and experts in the field of marketing and business administration. The experts were asked to mention their views about the study tool and the validity of the items to represent its variables, and they were also asked to edit and delete what they see as appropriate for measuring the credibility of the tool of the study, and after the questionnaire is returned from all experts their responses were analyzed and their notes were taken into consideration, and these items that obtained less than (70%) were deleted. Considering all the necessary amendments for the questionnaire it was finalized. To ensure the extent of the stability of the standards Cronbach Alpha is calculated (Anastasi, 1982). it was found that the coefficient of stability of the research scale was 0.76, and that percentage can be considered acceptable in the research of administration and humanity from a scientific and statistical point of view. The researcher has relied on several statistical methods to examine the hypotheses of the research like frequency, percentages, Linking Analysis, and Inclination analysis.

Table 1 shows the results of the data collected

Table 1. The summary of the collected data

Non-refundable forms		Retrieved forms	
Percentage	F	Percentage	F
23%	170	77%	580

Based on the statistics achieved, the characteristics of the research sample are described in Fig. 2 as follows,

Figure 2. Personal characteristics of the respondents

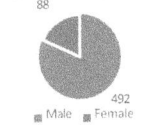

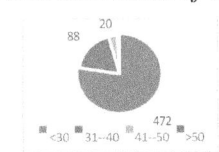

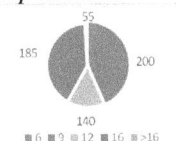

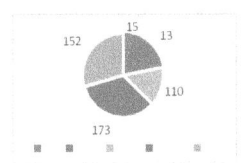

Gender Age Years of education Income (×1000 Rs)

According to above Figure 2, it can be explained that more respondents were male, namely 492 people with a percentage of 84.82%, while 88 respondents were female with a percentage of 15.17%. Also, it was found that respondents aged ≤ 30 years amounted to 472 people with a percentage of 81.37%, respondents ages 31-40 years totaling 88 people with a percentage of 15.17%, respondents with ages 41-50 years totaling 20 people with a percentage of 3.44%, and respondents with age ≥ 50 years amounted to 0 people. In addition, nearly 58% of the participants in our survey hold a university education. Finally, most of the people who participated in our survey earned more than 70000 rupees.

4. THE RESULTS, DISCUSSION, AND CONCLUSION

In this section, we present the results of testing the hypotheses of the survey.

4.1. The hypotheses of the linkage

The Main Hypothesis

This hypothesis has stipulated a positive and significant relationship between the independent variable (Packaging) and the dependent variable (attracting the consumer's attention towards the Product). Implementing the Kolmogorov-Smirnov test indicated that the data were normally distributed and used Pearson correlation to test the hypotheses.

Table 2 shows the results of testing the components of the main hypothesis.

Table 2. The summary of testing the hypothesis using Pearson correlation test

Independent variable					
Variable	Design of the Package	Size of the Package	Shape of the Package	Color of the Package	Packaging
Correlation	0.43	0.21	0.48	0.34	0.72
Sig. value	0.000	0.000	0.000	0.000	0.000

As we can observe from the results of correlation test, all independent variables have positive correlation with the dependent variable when the level of significance is one percent. The highest correlation is between packaging and customer attention followed by design, shape, color, and size of packaging. Next, we have implemented a regression test to verify the relationship,

Table 3. The results of some basic statistics for measuring the effect of packaging on consumer attention to a commodity

The Independent Variable	The Defendant Variable	Coefficient B	T Value	Coefficient of Determination R2	F Value	Level of Significance
Packaging	Attracting the Attention of the Consumer to the Commodity	0.70	5.983	0.49	60.03	0.000

According to the results of Table 3, the coefficient of R-Square is equal to 0.49 which means the independent variables can describe approximately 49% of the changes of the dependent variable. T-value is meaningful when the level of significance is one percent and F-value is also meaningful which means there is a linear relationship between the variables.

Table 4 also shows the results of the regression analysis.

Table 4. The summary of the regression analysis

The Independent Variable	The Defendant Variable	Impact Factor β	T value	Determination Factor	F value	Significance
The design of Package	Attracting consumer attention to the commodity	0.43	4.253	60%	17.68	0.000
The size of package		0.21	4.725			0.000
The shape of the package		0.48	4.239			0.000
The color of the package		0.34	3.126			0.000

The above Table 4 shows that the summary of regression analysis as follows:

Ha1: This hypothesis reports that there is a significant relationship between the design of the packaging in attracting consumer's attention to the commodity, and according to the results we understand that the design of the packaging affects the attention of the consumer toward the commodity by (0.43, p-value=0.000) and the hypothesis is confirmed.

Ha2: This hypothesis reports that there is a significant relationship between the size of the packaging in attracting consumer's attention to the commodity. The results show that the size of the packaging affects the attention of the consumer toward the commodity by (0.21, p-value=0.000) accordingly the hypothesis is accepted.

Ha3: This hypothesis reports that there is a significant relationship between the shape of the packaging in attracting consumer's attention to the commodity. According to the results, the shape of the packaging affects the attention of the consumer toward the commodity by (0.48, p-value=0.000) which confirms the hypothesis.

Ha4: This hypothesis reports that there is a significant relationship between the color of the packaging in attracting consumer's attention to the commodity, and the results show that the color of the packaging affects the attention of the consumer towards the commodity by (0.34, p-value=0.000) and the hypothesis is accepted.

The above results show that the Ha hypothesis has stipulated a positive and significant relationship between the independent variable (Packaging) and the dependent variable (attracting the consumer's attention towards the product).

5. CONCLUSION AND SUGGESTIONS

In this new era, customers eat with their eyes. As The Metaverse, an evolving concept that fuses physical reality with digital virtuality, offers a dynamic environment for exploration.

Creative packaging and beautiful presentation of products like food make people not only want to consume the food but also assume that the food tastes better as well. The Marketing of any product shows that product packaging is extremely important. Having a memorable presentation will influence perception and will keep customers coming back again and again (LaMarco, 2019). Based on the survey results, we recommend the development of clear packaging policies in industrial organizations, in line with the rapid developments in technology and rapidly changing consumer tastes. In addition, it is necessary to consider modern marketing trends in the field of product packaging, including the concept of green marketing, which is based on the use of packaging materials that have a relatively low environmental impact compared to other traditional methods. the metaverse seems to be a digital option parallel to the physical world that will create a new digital universe that will coexist with the physical one, in which almost all everyday aspects and activities that are currently carried out in the physical world, will take place Furthermore, the industrial revolutions must be considered by examining the opinions and impressions of consumers towards the products and services offered to them to know the shortcomings in product performance. their production and advertising (Alhamdi, F., (2020)). Organizations should rely on practical steps when introducing their products to the market and focus more on knowledge to determine product success or failure factors as well as attention to the satisfaction of consumer wants and needs, as it is the foundation, starting point, and destination as well as in any production or advertising process.

REFERENCES

Alhamdi, F. (2020). Role of packaging in consumer buying behavior. *Management Science Letters*, 10, 1191–1196. DOI: 10.5267/j.msl.2019.11.040

Anastasi, A., & Urbina, S. (1982). *Psychological assessment*. Mac-Millan.

Arora, M. (2023). Encapsulating Role of Persuasion and Skill Development in Marketing Communication for Brand Building: A Perspective. In International Handbook of Skill, Education, Learning, and Research Development in Tourism and Hospitality (pp. 1-17). Springer Nature Singapore

Arora, M. (2024). Virtual Reality in Education: Analyzing the Literature and Bibliometric State of Knowledge. *Transforming Education with Virtual Reality, 379-402.*

Arora, M. (2024). Metaverse Metamorphosis: Bridging the Gap Between Research Insights and Industry Applications. *Research, Innovation, and Industry Impacts of the Metaverse IGI Global,* 275-286)

Arora, M. (2024a) Virtual Reality in Education: Analyzing the Literature and Bibliometric State of Knowledge. *Transforming Education with Virtual Reality*, 379-402. https://doi.org/DOI: 10.1002/9781394200498.ch22

Arora, M. (2024b) Metaverse Metamorphosis: Bridging the Gap Between Research Insights and Industry Applications. In Research, Innovation, and Industry Impacts of the Metaverse (pp. 275-286).

Arora, M., & Sharma, R. L. (2022). Coalescing skills of gig players and fervor of entrepreneurial leaders to provide resilience strategies during global economic crises. In *COVID-19's Impact on the Cryptocurrency Market and the Digital Economy* (pp. 118–140). IGI Global. DOI: 10.4018/978-1-7998-9117-8.ch008

Arora, R., Haleem, A., & Farooquie, J. (2017). Impact of critical success factors on successful technology implementation in Consumer Packaged Goods (CPG) supply chain. *Management Science Letters*, 7(5), 213–224. DOI: 10.5267/j.msl.2017.2.005

Azad, N., & Masoumi, M. (2012). The impact of packaging on product competition. *Management Science Letters*, 2(8), 2789–2794. DOI: 10.5267/j.msl.2012.10.008

Azad, N., & Mohammadi, M. (2013). An empirical survey on factors influencing on packaging dairy products. *Management Science Letters*, 3(7), 1901–1906. DOI: 10.5267/j.msl.2013.06.039

Benachenhou, S., Guerrich, B., & Moussaoui, Z. (2018). The effect of packaging elements on purchase intention: Case study of Algerian customers. *Management Science Letters*, 8(4), 217–224. DOI: 10.5267/j.msl.2018.2.004

Chandel, M., & Arora, M. (2024). Metaverse Perspectives: Unpacking Its Role in Shaping Sustainable Development Goals-A Qualitative Inquiry. In Research, Innovation, and Industry Impacts of the Metaverse (pp. 62-75). IGI Global.

Chandel, M., & Arora, M. (2024). Metaverse Perspectives: Unpacking Its Role in Shaping Sustainable Development Goals-A Qualitative Inquiry. *Research, Innovation, and Industry Impacts of the Metaverse IGI Global*, 62-75.

Clement, J. (2007). Visual influence on in-store buying decisions: An eye-track experiment on the visual influence of pack- aging design. *Journal of Marketing Management*, 23(9-10), 917–928. DOI: 10.1362/026725707X250395

Dhiman, V., & Arora, M. (2024a) Current State of Metaverse in Entrepreneurial Ecosystem: A Retrospective Analysis of Its Evolving Landscape. In *Exploring the Use of Metaverse in Business and Education* (pp. 73-87). IGI Global. https://doi.org/DOI: 10.4018/979-8-3693-5868-9.ch005

Dhiman, V., & Arora, M. (2024b). Exploring the linkage between business incubation and entrepreneurship: understanding trends, themes and future research agenda. *LBS Journal of Management & Research*, (ahead-of-print).

Grönroos, C. (1982). An applied service marketing theory. *European Journal of Marketing*, 16(7), 30–41. DOI: 10.1108/EUM0000000004859

Klimchuk, M. R., & Krasovec, S. A. (2013). *Packaging design: Successful product branding from concept to shelf*. John Wiley & Sons.

Kumar, J., Arora, M., & Erkol Bayram, G. (Eds.). (2024). *Exploring the Use of Metaverse. Business and Education*. IGI Global. DOI: 10.4018/979-8-3693-5868-9

Kumar, J., Arora, M., & Erkol Bayram, G. (Eds.). (2024a). *Exploring the Use of Metaverse in Business and Education*. IGI Global. DOI: DOI: 10.4018/979-8-3693-5868-9

Kumar, J., Arora, M., & Erkol Bayram, G. (Eds.). (2024b) *Research, Innovation, and Industry Impacts of the Metaverse*. IGI Global.

Lee, S. G., & Lye, S. W. (2003). Design for manual packaging. *International Journal of Physical Distribution & Logistics Management*, 33(2), 163–189. DOI: 10.1108/09600030310469162

Muslim, A., Harun, A., Ismael, D., & Othman, B. (2020). Social media experience, attitude and behavioral intention towards umrah package among generation X and Y. *Management Science Letters*, 10(1), 1–12. DOI: 10.5267/j.msl.2019.8.020

Rathore, S., & Arora, M. (2024). Sustainability Reporting in the Metaverse: A Multi-Sectoral Analysis. In *Exploring the Use of Metaverse in Business and Education* (pp. 147-165). IGI Global. https://doi.org/DOI: 10.4018/979-8-3693-5868-9.ch009

Rundh, B. (2009). Packaging design: Creating competitive advantage with product packaging. *British Food Journal*, 111(9), 988–1002. DOI: 10.1108/00070700910992880

Svanes, E., Vold, M., Møller, H., Pettersen, M. K., Larsen, H., & Hanssen, O. J. (2010). Sustainable packaging design: A holistic methodology for packaging design. *Packaging Technology & Science*, 23(3), 161–175. DOI: 10.1002/pts.887

APPENDIX I

Table 5. Personal characteristics

Gender: Male ☐ Female ☐	Age: 20-30 ☐ 30-40 ☐ 40-50 ☐ > 50 ☐	Educational background: Preparatory ☐ Secondary ☐ Diploma ☐ University Degree ☐ post-graduate ☐	The Average Monthly Income: Less than 10000 Rs. ☐ 10000 to less than 40000Rs ☐ 40000 to less than 70000 ☐

Table 6. Detailed questions about the variables of the research

S	Items	AI	A	A to SE	Do not Agree	C. Disagree
1	The packaging design gives you enough information to identify the components of the product.					
2	The technical aspects of the packaging design attract your attention to the product.					
3	The design of the packaging is not important in attracting your attention to the product.					
4	The packaging design attracts your attention to varying degrees depending on the nature of the product.					
5	The packaging design gives you the information you care about quickly.					
6	The graphic on the cover draws your attention to the item.					
7	The design of the package or packaging is compatible with the nature of the item you are buying.					
8	Excellence in the design of the case of packaging attracting your attention to the product.					
9	The packaging design takes into account the customs and traditions of society.					
10	It attracts your attention to the size of the package that has saved you volume savings when consumed.					
11	The item is purchased based on the quantity of its contents listed in the package.					
12	Attracts your attention to the size of the package for the item that suits your purchasing power.					
13	Determines the nature of the product in the size of the package that attracted your attention to the commodity.					
14	Offering the item in different sizes and packages attracts your attention towards it.					
15	The free increase in the size of the packaging attracts your attention to the item.					
16	The size of the package or the packaging of the item draws you more towards the item.					
17	The outer shape of the casing or packaging draws you more towards the product.					

continued on following page

Table 6. Continued

S	Items	Level of The Scale				
		A I	A	A to SE	Do not Agree	C. Disagree
18	Distinguish the shape of the packaging or packaging of the commodity more than competing goods attract your attention towards them.					
19	The shape or package that fits the nature of the commodity draws your attention.					
20	Draws your attention to the product the cover made of biodegradable materials in the environment quickly.					
21	The shape of the packaging, considering the possibility that you can benefit from the packaging in other uses.					
22	Attracts your attention to the commodity the fixed colors on the packaging that suit the nature of the commodity that you purchase.					
23	The color of the package or the cover of the commodity attracts your attention towards it.					
24	You have full readiness to buy commodities with the attractive colors even if they cost little higher than the traditional color goods.					
25	You think that the focus is done while offering the commodity on the color of the package to attract your attention.					
26	Changing the colors of the packages is something essential and motivates you to buy.					

Chapter 13
Neuro-Marketing as a Subset of Sensory Marketing From Lasting Imprint Becoming Memory and Impulsive Buying

Manasvi Pathak
 https://orcid.org/0009-0000-3141-2735
Pune Institute of Business Management, India

Nilesh Tejrao Kate
Pune Institute of Business Management, India

Soham Hajra
 https://orcid.org/0009-0003-6748-9381
Pune Institute of Business Management, India

ABSTRACT

In the ever-changing marketing landscape, gaining customer attention and influencing purchase decisions necessitates inventive techniques. Traditionally, marketing has aimed to captivate customers by visual and logical arguments. However, a growing tendency acknowledges the significant importance of our senses on decision-making Sensory marketing, a tactic that goes beyond standard visual and logical appeals, has emerged as a potent tool for organisations looking to build stronger connections with their customers. Sensory marketing creates multidimensional brand experiences

DOI: 10.4018/979-8-3693-9351-2.ch013

by purposefully engaging all five senses - sight, sound, smell, touch, and taste. In the ever-evolving landscape of customer service, businesses are turning to predictive analytics as a game-changer. Predictive analytics goes beyond traditional data analysis; it's a forward-thinking approach that harnesses the power of historical data to anticipate customer needs and preferences. At its core, the concept is about being proactive rather than reactive.

INTRODUCTION

Sensory marketing is a strategic technique that harnesses consumer's senses to create memorable and compelling brand experiences. It goes beyond standard marketing strategies by using sensory inputs (sight, sound, touch, taste, and smell) to affect consumer perceptions, emotions, and behaviours. In today's competitive and developing marketing landscape, sensory marketing has emerged as a critical tool for organisations to differentiate themselves, increase customer engagement, and establish long-term connections with customers. Sensory marketing allows companies to create immersive and memorable experiences that appeal to customers on a deeper emotional level. By engaging numerous senses, companies may create a lasting impact, making their products or services more memorable and shareable.

In an era when customers are bombarded with digital commercials and promotional messages, sensory marketing provides a unique chance for companies to catch attention and stand out from the crowd. By providing multimodal experiences, companies may increase customer engagement, involvement, and participation (Arora & Sharma, 2023). Sensory inputs influence consumer perceptions, attitudes, and preferences. Strategic sensory branding and marketing strategies may affect customer perceptions, generate favourable brand connections, and, ultimately, influence purchase choices. Emotions have a tremendous impact on customer decisions and brand loyalty. Sensory marketing appeals to consumers' emotions by producing sensory-rich experiences that elicit favourable sensations, nostalgia, or excitement, ultimately developing emotional ties and increasing brand loyalty ((Bhardwaj, Kaushik, & Arora (2024); Taneja, Shukla & Arora (2024); Malik, Malhan & Arora (2024). (Eds.). (2024)).

In a saturated market with many rivals selling comparable products or services, sensory marketing offers firms a unique opportunity to differentiate themselves and establish a distinct identity. Brands may gain a competitive edge by imaginatively and innovatively using sensory components to position themselves as industry leaders or trendsetters. Sensory marketing pushes firms to go outside the box and try new and creative methods to engage customers. Whether via inventive product design, experiential marketing initiatives, or immersive brand encounters, sensory marketing fosters marketing creativity, innovation, and experimentation.

As customers demand real, personalised, and immersive brand experiences, sensory marketing will play an increasingly important role, leading firms to innovate, adapt, and embrace the multimodal approach to marketing in the digital era. The core components of sensory marketing are sight, sound, touch, taste, and smell.

The visual aspect of sensory marketing includes all visual stimuli related with a brand, such as logo design, colour palette, packaging, and visual merchandising. Visual branding aspects are essential in developing a distinct brand identity, expressing company values and personality, and catching consumers' attention (Arora, 2023). By developing visually appealing and memorable brand experiences, marketers may improve brand memory, differentiate their products or services from competitors, and influence customer purchase choices.

The aural component of sensory marketing focuses on using sound and music to elicit emotional responses and increase brand engagement. Sonic branding, jingles, and background music in advertising, retail settings, and digital platforms may elicit certain emotions, reinforce brand message, and provide a distinct brand sound identity. Brands may use sound and music psychology to improve brand memory, establish positive connections, and create multimodal experiences that connect with customers on a deeper emotional level.

The tactile component of sensory marketing refers to the physical interaction and sensory experience that comes with a product or service. Product design, texture, packaging materials, and interactive touchpoints all play an important part in engaging customers' sense of touch and generating tactile brand experiences. Focusing on tactile components allows companies to increase product appeal, differentiate themselves from rivals, and give customers with a sensory-rich experience that boosts product satisfaction, loyalty, and advocacy.

The gustatory component of sensory marketing focuses on the sense of taste and the sensory experience associated with food and beverage products. Flavour profiles, product formulas, package design, and sample experiences may all have an impact on how customers perceive taste, preferences, and make purchase decisions. Brands that create distinctive taste experiences may strengthen emotional connections, encourage brand loyalty, and drive repeat purchases from customers looking for authentic, tasty, and pleasant products.

The olfactory component of sensory marketing focuses on the sense of smell and the emotional influence that fragrance has on customer perceptions and behaviours. Scented items, ambient smells in retail settings, and aromatic marketing methods may all elicit certain emotions, stimulate memories, and increase brand engagement. By using the power of fragrance, companies may create a multimodal brand experience, differentiate themselves from rivals, and impact consumers' perceptions, attitudes, and purchase choices by providing pleasant and memorable olfactory experiences.

The 1980s and 1990s saw a substantial shift in sensory marketing, with a greater emphasis on the audio component of branding. Marketers began to recognise the emotional effect of sound and music in advertising and branding, resulting in the rise of sonic branding, jingles, and background music as key components of marketing campaigns. Brands such as McDonald's, with its classic "I'm Lovin' It" slogan, Intel's recognisable five-note chime, and Nokia's distinctive ringtone used sound and music to reinforce brand message, create memorable brand experiences, and connect with customers on a deeper emotional level.

The turn of the 2000 saw a dramatic movement towards multimodal brand experiences, with businesses looking for new methods to engage customers' senses beyond sight and sound. The incorporation of tactile, gustatory, and olfactory aspects into marketing campaigns, retail settings, and product design marked the transition of sensory marketing into a comprehensive and integrated marketing discipline. Companies such as Lush with its experiential retail surroundings, Starbucks with its fragrant coffee cafes, and Sephora with its interactive beauty goods have transformed the retail sector by combining sensory components to create immersive and memorable brand experiences for customers.

The introduction of digital technology, social media, and data analytics has accelerated the growth of sensory marketing, allowing firms to offer personalised and interactive sensory-rich experiences across many touchpoints and channels. Virtual reality (VR), augmented reality (AR), and experiential marketing campaigns have emerged as effective tools for businesses to engage customers' senses and create immersive brand experiences that elicit a deeper emotional response (Arora, Kumar & Valeri (2023); Arora & Chandel (2024); Arora (2024a).; Arora (2024b); Arora, et.al., (2024)). Companies such as IKEA, with its VR kitchen experience, Heineken, with its interactive beer tasting events, and Mercedes-Benz, with its AR car configurator, have used technology and sensory marketing principles to create innovative and personalised brand experiences that capture consumers' attention, drive engagement, and foster brand loyalty in the digital era.

The research paper by *(Mark I. Alpert, 2005)* explores the influence of purchase occasions on the role of music in advertising. The study delves into how different purchase occasions, such as routine purchases, gift purchases, and luxury purchases, can impact the effectiveness and appropriateness of using music in advertising campaigns. The report by *(Han, 2023)* gives an in-depth examination of Procter & Gamble's product marketing strategies, innovations, and market. The authors highlighted that scent marketing can improve brand recall by up to 80%. The global market for multisensory marketing is projected to experience substantial growth, reaching an estimated value of $7.7 billion by 2027, according to a report by Grand

View Research. These facts show how sensory marketing is becoming more widely recognised for its efficacy and relevance in the marketing environment. As technology and our understanding of consumer behaviour advance, sensory marketing is likely to become much more sophisticated and important in the coming years.

In today's oversaturated marketing world, merely viewing a company logo or statement is no longer sufficient to pique interest. Consumers seek deeper relationships, which is where sensory branding comes in. Sensory branding plays a crucial role in enhancing brand recall and recognition by creating multisensory brand experiences that leave a lasting impression on consumers' minds. For example, the distinctive visual and auditory elements of Coca-Cola's branding, combined with the unique taste and packaging design, create a multisensory brand experience that resonates with consumers and fosters strong brand loyalty and advocacy.

In a saturated market with several companies offering identical products or services, sensory branding allows firms to differentiate themselves and establish a distinct personality. Brands may gain a competitive edge by imaginatively and innovatively using sensory components to position themselves as industry leaders or trendsetters. For example, Bath & Body Work's unique retail locations, fragrant goods, and interactive customer interactions set the brand apart from competitors, creating memorable and engaging brand experiences for customers.

Emotions have a tremendous impact on customer decisions and brand loyalty. Sensory branding appeals to customers' emotions by providing sensory-rich experiences that elicit favourable sensations, nostalgia, or excitement. For example, the nostalgic sound of Harley-Davidson's engine scream, the tactile feel of Apple's clean and minimalist product design, or the fragrant perfume of Starbucks' coffee shops may all elicit certain feelings and foster stronger emotional ties between customers and companies.

Sensory stimuli play a crucial role in shaping consumer perceptions, attitudes, and preferences. Through strategic sensory branding initiatives, brands can influence consumer perceptions, drive positive brand associations, and ultimately, influence purchasing decisions. For instance, the use of vibrant colours, playful graphics, and interactive touchpoints in LEGO's branding and marketing campaigns appeals to children's imagination, creativity, and sense of play, influencing their perceptions, preferences, and purchase intentions.

With ongoing advancements in technology, data analytics, and consumer insights, sensory branding has the potential to redefine the future of branding and marketing by allowing brands to create personalised, immersive, and multisensory experiences that resonate with consumers in an increasingly competitive and sensory-driven marketplace.

Sensory marketing is more than just providing a nice environment; it is a scientifically supported method that uses our brain's response to stimuli to impact behaviour. When we meet a sensory stimulus, such as the sight of a delectable cake, the fragrance of newly cut grass, or the sound of a catchy jingle, our sensory organs (eyes, nose, ears, mouth, and skin) translate it into electrical impulses. These impulses flow to the brain via nerves, notably the thalamus, which serves as a relay station.

Signals from the thalamus are subsequently sent to various parts of the brain, depending on the type of feeling. However, the limbic system, which is the brain's emotional centre, is an important stop. This explains why sensory inputs can elicit intense emotions. For example, the delicious scent of freshly made cookies may evoke sentiments of warmth and enjoyment, yet a loud alarm clock may elicit feelings of worry and anxiety.

Sensory information also reaches the hippocampus, which is critical for memory formation. Pleasant sensory experiences may foster good connections with a brand, affecting future purchasing decisions. For example, the soothing aroma of lavender at a clothes store may unconsciously make you feel more at ease and trusting of the brand, perhaps leading to a purchase. Our brains are built to synthesise information from all five senses into a single perspective of the world. This is why sensory marketing frequently employs many senses in unison. Imagine entering into a bakery; the sight of fresh bread, the warm perfume drifting through the air, and the soothing sounds of music all contribute to a more immersive and memorable experience than any one aspect alone.

Understanding how our brains react to sensory inputs allows marketers to design subtle but potent techniques for influencing customer behaviour. This does not imply deceiving customers; rather, it entails providing a more engaging and favourable brand experience.

Visual branding is a key component of sensory marketing and plays a pivotal role in shaping brand identity, communicating brand values, and influencing consumer perceptions, attitudes, and behaviour. Each visual element contributes to creating a distinct and memorable brand image that resonates with consumers, fosters brand recognition, loyalty, and advocacy, and sets brands apart from competitors in a crowded marketplace. The key visual branding elements and logo design, colour psychology, packaging and virtual merchandising.

A logo is a graphical depiction of a brand that acts as both a visual sign and an identifier, capturing the brand's identity, values, personality, and soul. A well-designed logo is unique, memorable, scalable, and adaptable, allowing customers to recognise and recall the brand across many touchpoints and channels. The logo is the foundation of a company's visual identity system, anchoring other visual aspects like the colour palette, typography, and imagery, and producing a unified and consistent brand image that connects with customers and develops brand loyalty and advocacy.

Colour psychology studies how colours affect human emotions, perceptions, behaviours, and decision-making. Different colours elicit distinct emotions, connections, and meanings, which influence customers' perceptions, attitudes, preferences, and buying intentions. Colour psychology is deliberately used in visual branding to express precise messages, elicit desired emotions, and create memorable brand experiences for consumers. For example, blue is frequently linked with trust, dependability, and professionalism (e.g., IBM, Ford); red with passion, energy, and excitement (e.g., Coca-Cola, Red Bull); and green with growth, health, and sustainability (e.g., Starbucks, Whole Foods). Colour psychology may help companies improve brand identification, develop strong emotional connections, and meaningfully affect customer behaviour and perceptions.

Visual identity, product display, protection, and marketing all benefit from proper packaging design. The packaging design is the initial point of contact between customers and products, catching their attention, generating interest, and communicating crucial brand statements, values, and promises. A well-designed package design displays the brand's personality, quality, innovation, and sustainability while also meeting consumers' tastes, expectations, and lifestyles. Brands frequently utilise packaging as a strategic marketing strategy to differentiate themselves, convey product advantages and features, increase perceived value, and create memorable and immersive brand experiences that influence purchasing decisions, loyalty, and advocacy. Visual merchandising is the planned presentation and arrangement of items, displays, signs, and promotional materials in both physical and digital retail settings to improve the shopping experience, engage customers, and increase sales. Visual merchandising brings together design, aesthetics, innovation, and narrative to create visually appealing and unified brand environments that represent the company's identity, values, and lifestyle. Effective visual merchandising attracts consumers' attention, directs their shopping experience, motivates exploration and discovery, and promotes interaction, engagement, and purchase.

By incorporating visual branding elements such as logo design, colour psychology, packaging, and promotional graphics, brands can create immersive and memorable retail experiences that resonate with customers, foster brand loyalty, and drive business growth in an increasingly competitive and dynamic market. These visual branding aspects are most effective when used together. Consider a firm with a sleek, minimalist logo (think Apple) with a clean white and silver colour palette (representing simplicity and innovation) that extends into their product packaging and shop design. This uniformity strengthens brand identification and provides a cohesive consumer experience.

Starbucks, a global coffeehouse business, has effectively used visual sensory marketing methods to create immersive and memorable retail spaces that speak to customers' emotions, perceptions, and preferences. Starbucks uses visual merchandising strategies such as store layout, interior design, lighting, displays, signage, and promotional graphics to create cosy, welcoming, and Instagram-worthy coffee shops where customers can rest, socialise, and enjoy their coffee experience.

Apple's visual sensory marketing approach emphasises minimalist design, clean lines, simplicity, and elegance, reflecting the brand's ideals, philosophy, and product distinction in the competitive technological industry. Apple's logo design, product packaging, and visual branding components, such as colour palette, typography, and imagery, all contribute to a unified and consistent brand image across multiple products, services, and touchpoints.

Tiffany's deliberate use of colour has become linked with their corporate identity. The Tiffany Blue quickly conveys richness and quality, distinguishing them from competition. This visual signal promotes brand loyalty and establishes Tiffany's as the go-to place for discriminating shoppers looking for fine jewellery.M&M's colourful branding approach has been a huge success. According to studies, people link M&Ms with fun and enjoyment, resulting in high brand loyalty. Their vivid packaging shines out on store shelves, attracting attention and influencing purchases.

Marketing is about how we feel as well as what we see. Sound and music have a significant impact on our emotions and behaviour, making them important tools for marketers. When we hear a sound or music, it goes via our ears before being translated into electrical impulses. These impulses travel to the brain, especially the thalamus, which serves as a relay station. Signals are directed from the thalamus to other parts of the brain, including the limbic system, which serves as our emotional centre.

This explains why particular noises and music may elicit intense emotions. For example, a fast-paced, uplifting music may make you feel energised and enthusiastic, but a slow, melancholy tune may elicit thoughts of grief or nostalgia.

Auditory information also reaches the hippocampus, which is critical for memory formation. Pleasant noises and music can form good connections with a brand, boosting future purchases. Consider a peaceful spa that plays soothing music; this produces a favourable experience that you may identify with the spa brand. Sound and music are significant marketing instruments. Understanding the psychology behind them allows companies to provide a more engaging and emotionally resonant experience for customers, eventually influencing their behaviour and fostering brand loyalty.

Visual and audio aspects are marketing standards, but the genuinely immersive experiences lay in engaging the entire range of senses. Touch is commonly connected with trust, warmth, and emotional connection. Consider the pleasant sensations elicited by a smooth, sumptuous cloth or the gratifying weight of a well-crafted object. Textures in packaging or product presentations that allow buyers to touch and feel the goods can enhance the experience and affect purchase decisions. Consider putting on items at a store or experiencing the quality of a leather purse.

Apple shops are recognised for encouraging people to engage with their products, resulting in a positive tactile experience that supports the brand's image of innovation and excellence.

Taste is one of the most potent senses, influencing memory and mood. Certain flavours might evoke powerful nostalgic or good recollections. Free food and drink samples are a tried-and-true marketing approach. Food festivals and in-store tastings provide customers the opportunity to try a product first hand, producing a favourable taste memory and perhaps leading to a purchase.

Grocery stores may provide free samples of new items, whilst restaurants may employ trademark meals to create a memorable taste experience that attracts repeat customers. Coffee businesses may tempt consumers with the scent of freshly made coffee. Our sense of smell is intricately related to the limbic system, the brain's emotional centre. Scents can have a significant subconscious impact on our mood and behaviour.

To create a distinct atmosphere, retail businesses frequently utilise aroma diffusers. For example, a clothes store may employ a peaceful lavender perfume to induce relaxation, but a bakery may use the aroma of freshly baked bread to draw consumers. Similarly, some vehicle dealerships utilise a "new car smell" to instil a good association with their product.

Luxury businesses frequently include characteristic smells into their storefronts and packaging, providing a distinct olfactory experience that promotes brand identification. Casinos may utilise certain fragrances to create an environment of excitement and energy. True magic occurs when these sensory aspects are carefully integrated. Imagine strolling into a bakery; the sight of fresh pastries, the perfume of warm bread, and the soft touch of a flour sack all combine to produce a multi-sensory experience that is significantly more powerful than any one aspect alone.

Sensory marketing is more than just a fancy notion; it is supported by research and consumer insights that show its efficacy in influencing behaviour and purchase decisions. Research conducted by (Hirsch, (1995).) (An experimental study of the impact of ambient odour on the rating of service experiences.) It was discovered that a nice aroma in a retail atmosphere caused visitors to spend more time exploring and, eventually, spend more money. This demonstrates how sensory cues may affect emotions, resulting in good brand connections and buying decisions.

Research conducted by (Krishna, (2010)) investigates the relationship between fragrance and memory. They discovered that introducing shoppers to a perfume associated with cleanliness (such as new linen scent) in a laundry detergent aisle caused them to select recognised brands. This implies that sensory signals can elicit memories and shape brand preferences.

Research by (Krishna A. a., (2010).) investigated the effect of music on product perception. Customers perceived a product to be of greater quality when upbeat music was performed, as opposed to when slower music was played. This suggests that sensory signals can affect our cognitive judgement of products.

According to (PwC, 2023), 73% of consumers are prepared to pay extra for a product or service that provides a meaningful experience. Sensory marketing capitalises on this urge for involvement, resulting in a more memorable purchasing experience. According to (Salesforce),76% of customers are more inclined to buy from a brand with which they have an emotional connection. Sensory marketing builds emotional ties by providing a good and engaging brand experience. In today's information era, customers are inundated with marketing communications. According to (nielsen), 63% of new product launches fail. Sensory marketing allows you to stand out from the crowd, attract attention, and influence buying decisions at the point of sale.

Sensory marketing research and consumer insights reveal a clear picture: engaging several senses results in a more powerful brand experience, alters customer preferences, and, ultimately, influences purchase decisions. Understanding the science of sensory marketing and properly combining these factors may provide companies with a significant weapon for winning over customers in a competitive marketplace.

Aradhana Krishna of Michigan University opines that "In the past, communications with customers were essentially monologues—companies just talked at consumers," Krishna says. "Then they evolved into dialogues, with customers providing feedback. Now they're becoming multidimensional conversations, with products finding their own voices and consumers responding viscerally and subconsciously to them."

Economist Richard Theller pioneered 'Behavioural economics' led Nudge theory, behaviour and choice architecture, also a blend of neurological science and economic decision making but this model comes in contradiction with 'Rational expectation' theorists led by John Mooth and Robert Lucas from 1960. American Child Psychologist Cloitierre Raphaille's (a strong advocate of reptilian instinct of our brain rather than cortex or limbic counterparts) classic decoding of absence of Japanese taste in coffee or American lag in purchasing relaunched Zeep car which eventually unfolded another aspect of sensory marketing. Consumer would necessarily not associate in real-time sensory experience but also can strongly be motivated by past-experience or to say the 'Familiarity quotient'. Remembering vs Experiencing – Two Approaches of Marketing as identified by psychologist Daniel Kahneman. are contributing in building sensory marketing. two separate human operating systems of sense-making. This distinction has implications for marketing: It explains how communications/advertising and customer experience have vastly different effects on the image of brands in people's minds.

In the case of Japanese people, as Raphaille observed, they are unfamiliar with the taste of coffee so, he suggested Nestle to make the youngest generation familiar with the taste of 'coffee' with coffee candy first. In the case of Zeep car, he suggested company to realign their car with people's old memory as they liked their 'rugged Zeep' in younger stage of life. Rejuvenating or imbibing old memory with certain degree of familiarity quotient can also be constituent of sensory marketing. Biasness of human mind communicated with ophthalmic nerves to certain colours like the red as was explored in 1960's decade is considered of static functioning of our brain. Sensory marketing deliberately uses sight, sound, smell, touch, and taste to create a memorable and emotionally charged brand experience.

Sensory marketing is based on proven frameworks in consumer psychology and neuroscience. Researchers' emphasis on multi-sensory branding area says that senses amplify each other when used together when companies use sensory branding the influences are subtle and doesn't feel like marketing to the consumer since it involves multiple ensues it builds stronger memory hooks and builder stronger brand associations. Harvard Business School professor Gerald Zaltman says that 95 percent of our purchase decision making takes place in the subconscious mind. But how does a marketer reach the subconscious?

According to (Cacioppo's, (1986)), Elaboration-Likelihood Model (ELM), consumers process information in one of two ways. Sensory cues can impact the selected route, with more complex processing (central route) taking place when sensory aspects are purposefully exploited to improve product appraisal. Sensory Marketing research makes a valuable contribution. Paivio's Dual Coding Theory (1979) posits that information is processed in separate visual and linguistic systems in the brain. Sensory cues, especially visual images and fragrances, can elicit emotional reactions via the limbic brain, bypassing the logical processing centre and impacting purchasing decisions (Hirsch, (1995).)This study paper investigates the power of sensory marketing, specifically how it impacts customer behaviour across several touchpoints. The research investigates the primary sensory aspects used in marketing tactics, analysing their influence on variables such as brand impression, purchase intention, and spending behaviour. Furthermore, it investigates the psychological principles that underpin sensory marketing's success. The study then delves into the precise ways sensory marketing effects customer behaviour, concentrating on Brand Perception examining how sensory characteristics such as retail environment, package design, and product feel might influence brand image and loyalty. Secondly, it studies Purchase Intention investigating the effects of sensory signals on a consumer's inclination to buy a product or service. Thirdly, Expenditure Behaviour: Investigating how sensory marketing might stimulate impulsive purchases while increasing total expenditure. Lastly, Background music pace, product aroma, and in-store demonstrations will all be investigated. The paper will examine the role of sensory overload and the significance of providing a balanced sensory experience.

The main thesis of this exploration is to delve deeper into the effects of sensory marketing on customer behaviour, purchase decisions, and brand impression. Specifically, this research attempts to investigate the psychological mechanisms that underpin sensory marketing and how sensory stimuli may impact customers' emotions, perceptions, and decision-making. Understanding the cognitive and emotional reactions elicited by sensory stimuli enables companies to develop more powerful and resonant marketing tactics that connect with customers on a deeper level.

It also aims to examine the efficacy of several sensory marketing tactics, such as visual branding, auditory branding, tactile engagement, gustatory experiences, and olfactory marketing, in engaging customers, increasing brand recall, and influencing purchase choices. By evaluating real-world examples, case studies, and empirical research findings, this study seeks to discover best practices and insights that may help businesses effectively leverage sensory marketing.

We strive to find out how sensory marketing affects customer behaviour, purchase decisions, brand preferences, loyalty, and advocacy. This study seeks to identify the drivers and motivators that impact consumers' interactions with brands and decision-making processes by evaluating their perceptions, attitudes, and behaviours in response to sensory-rich brand experiences. The intention is to examine how sensory marketing influences brand perception, identity, and market placement. Brands can establish stronger emotional connections, separate themselves from rivals, and build a distinctive and memorable brand identity that connects with customers by providing multisensory brand experiences that are consistent with their values, personality, and messaging.

This investigation seeks to give a thorough and informative examination of the effects of sensory marketing on customer behaviour, purchase decisions, and brand impression. Understanding the complexities and intricacies of sensory marketing and its basic components enables companies to seize new opportunities, form meaningful relationships, and drive company success in an increasingly competitive and sensory-driven market.

LITERATURE REVIEW

The main purpose of this chapter is to concisely describe the origin of Sensory Marketing, its applications in the organization, and to explore consumer behaviour with the help of different Sensory Marketing technologies like FMRI, EEG, and MEG. This chapter gives a guideline on how Sensory Marketing would be used in different areas of organization functions, like, brand management, advertisement, communication, product design, decision making, etc. with the help of data mining, artificial intelligence, social media, machine learning, remote sensing, AR, and VR. The chapter identifies the opportunities of Sensory Marketing with the latest technological development to understand the customer mindset so that it would be easy to formulate neurostrategy for an organization.

This chapter gives a future research direction with strategic management, so that it will be helpful for a professional to create a more accurate strategy in a VUCA (volatility, uncertainty, complexity, ambiguity) environment, predict, and fulfil the "institution void" situation with more accuracy in an emerging developing market.

(Ryan S. Elder. Krishna) They propose that advertisement (ad) content for food products can affect taste perception by affecting sensory cognitions. Specifically, they show that multisensory ads result in higher taste perceptions than ads focusing on taste alone, with this result being mediated by the excess of positive over negative sensory thoughts. Since the ad effect is thoughts-driven or cognitive, restricting cognitive resources (imposing cognitive load) attenuates the enhancing effect of the multiple-sense ad. Our results are exhibited across three experiments and have many implications for cognition and sensory perception research within consumer behaviour, as well as several practical implications. A primary objective of this article is to contribute to the growing literature on sensory perception within marketing in showing that advertising copy for a food product can affect resulting cognitions during consumption and ultimately affect taste perceptions. Through a series of three studies, they showed that multiple sense versus single-sense ads led to heightened taste perceptions, within some boundary conditions. They explore whether other senses are so physiologically closely tied to taste that mentioning them will make no difference and whether an ad in general can have an impact on taste perceptions.

(Springer, 2009) (Scent) Authors engage issues in the scent marketing industry. In particular, they capture areas of concern regarding the use of scents to persuade, and its potential to make consumers vulnerable to marketing communications. Since this is a new frontier for marketers, they begin with an explanation of what makes the sense of smell different from other senses.

(Bhandari) Consumer behaviour is greatly influenced by branding, and Sensory Marketing has shed light on the ways in which brands influence brain activity. Strong brands can change neural responses in areas related to reward and decision-making, according (Plassmann H., 2012) When two colas taste the same, Coca-Cola's branding, for example, can elicit stronger neural responses than generic cola. Known as the "Pepsi Challenge," this phenomenon emphasizes how powerful brand perception is over sensory experience. Thus, smart branding tactics can take advantage of these brain reactions to increase customer preference and loyalty.

The goal of the interdisciplinary field of Sensory Marketing is to better understand how consumers' brains react to marketing stimuli by combining marketing, psychology, and neuroscience. Through the use of cutting-edge neuroimaging technologies, such as electroencephalography (EEG) and functional magnetic resonance imaging (fMRI), researchers can learn more about the subconscious mechanisms influencing consumer behaviour. This review of the literature looks at important research and conclusions in the field of Sensory Marketing, showing how it has advanced our knowledge of consumer behaviour and how it affects marketing strategies.

(Brian Knutson, 2007) "Neural Predictors of Purchases" is one of the foundational studies in the field of Sensory Marketing. This study showed that buying decisions can be predicted by brain activity in the insula and nucleus accumbent. The anticipation of gains is linked to the nucleus accumbent, whereas the anticipation of losses is linked to the insula. The nucleus accumbent became more active when consumers were shown products they enjoyed. On the other hand, high costs stimulated the insula, signalling possible drawbacks. This study emphasizes how emotional reactions play a part in consumer decision-making and how neuroimaging methods can be used to quantify them.

Emotional engagement is a critical factor in the success of advertising campaigns. (Marco Iacoboni, 2012) in their study "Predicting Advertising Success: Neural Correlates of Emotional and Behavioural Responses to Ads" utilized fMRI to measure brain activity in response to advertisements. They found that ads eliciting stronger emotional responses, as indicated by increased activity in the amygdala and the prefrontal cortex, were more likely to be remembered and acted upon by consumers. This study suggests that successful ads are those that can tap into emotional processing centres in the brain, thereby enhancing recall and influencing purchasing behaviour. In their paper (Yoon C. a., 2009) investigated the functions of implicit and explicit memory in advertising. Effective ads, according to their theory, activate both explicit (conscious) and implicit (unconscious) memory systems. They showed through neuroimaging studies that emotionally charged advertisements tend to elicit stronger implicit memories, which over time can impact consumer behaviour. The significance of producing emotionally compelling content that can discreetly reinforce brand messages and preferences without explicitly depending on conscious recall is highlighted by this finding.

In their paper titled "Using Neurophysiological Methods to Understand Consumer Behaviour" (Angelika Dimoka, 2011) gave a thorough overview of the neurophysiological techniques applied in Sensory Marketing. They emphasized the benefits and drawbacks of several methods, including fMRI, EEG, and eye tracking. EEG offers superior temporal resolution and records brain activity in real time, while MRI offers high spatial resolution and can pinpoint specific brain regions implicated in decision-making processes. However, eye tracking sheds light on how people interact with visual stimuli and how they pay attention to them. This review emphasizes how Sensory Marketing requires a multi-method approach in order to fully comprehend consumer behaviour. Sensory Marketing is useful in a number of industries, such as advertising and retail. The study "Predicting Advertising Success Beyond Traditional Measures: New Insights from Neurophysiological Methods and Market Response Modelling" by (Venkatraman, 2015) showed how integrating neurophysiological data with conventional marketing metrics can improve the predictive accuracy of advertising success. Marketers can obtain a better understanding of consumer preferences and adjust their strategies by incorporating metrics like skin conductance, heart rate, and brain activity.

Research in the retail industry has demonstrated that sensory experiences (such as lighting, music, and smells) and store design can have a big impact on customer behaviour. For instance, (Sorensen K., 2009) discovered that employing eye-catching lighting and carefully positioning products at eye level can boost sales. These results are corroborated by Sensory Marketing research, which demonstrates how these elements stimulate the brain's reward centres, promoting consumer behaviour.

Sensory Marketing presents ethical questions about consumer privacy and manipulation despite its possible advantages. In their paper "Sensory Marketing: Ethical Implications of its Use and Potential Misuse, (Steven J. Stanton, 2017) address the need for moral standards to guarantee that Sensory Marketing techniques do not take advantage of customers' unconscious vulnerabilities. To uphold integrity and confidence in the industry, they support openness, informed consent, and the security of customer data.

Sensory marketing involves using the five senses—sight, sound, smell, taste, and touch—to impact consumer behaviour by creating meaningful and engaging experiences. This approach has grown increasingly important in shaping how consumers perceive brands, make purchasing decisions, and develop loyalty. For example, research by Kate et al. (2024) on organic tea purchasing habits reveals that sensory factors such as taste and aroma greatly influence consumer choices, particularly among millennials, underscoring the critical role of sensory experiences in food and beverage purchasing.

In the realm of digital marketing, as discussed by Kate et al. (2024), sensory marketing can also enhance consumer interactions through the use of visual and auditory elements.

Immersive visuals and sound in digital platforms can heighten consumer engagement with advertisements, which positively affects brand perception and loyalty.

Acharya et al. (2023), in their study on smart agriculture technology adoption, emphasize how sensory experiences shape farmers' perceptions of new technologies. This demonstrates that sensory information, such as tactile feedback from technology interfaces, has the potential to drive consumer behaviour in areas beyond traditional retail sectors.

Additionally, (Kate, (2023)) highlight the role of sensory marketing in the adoption of electric vehicles in India. Their research shows that sensory experiences, such as the sound and feel of driving electric vehicles, influence consumer behaviour, especially when coupled with environmental considerations. These sensory aspects are key to the value proposition for consumers choosing sustainable transportation options.

(Fisher C. &., 2010) defines the emerging field of Sensory Marketing, examining the practices involved and the professional challenges faced by practitioners in the field. The authors concluded that while Sensory Marketing offers valuable insights into consumer behaviour, it is crucial to develop standardized practices and ethical guidelines to ensure the responsible use of these techniques

CONCLUSION

Sensory marketing has proven to be an impactful tool in shaping consumer behaviour by engaging their senses to create more immersive, memorable, and emotional brand experiences. In today's cluttered marketing landscape, where consumers are inundated with information, brands can effectively differentiate themselves through strategic use of sight, sound, touch, taste, and smell. By leveraging these sensory cues, businesses can strengthen brand recall, foster emotional connections, and influence purchasing decisions, resulting in increased customer engagement and loyalty.

The research highlights that sensory marketing does not operate in isolation but interacts deeply with human psychology and neuroscience. Sensory inputs trigger emotional responses and memories, creating associations that can significantly influence how consumers perceive brands and products. By tapping into these subconscious processes, marketers can evoke positive emotions, such as nostalgia, excitement, or comfort, which lead to favourable brand impressions and, ultimately, greater consumer loyalty.

Furthermore, sensory marketing is not limited to creating an immediate response but also capitalizes on long-term brand connections through multi-sensory integration. The combination of visual appeal, sonic branding, tactile interaction, and even olfactory experiences can amplify each other, creating a more robust and holistic brand experience. Brands like Starbucks, Coca-Cola, and Harley-Davidson have effectively used these elements to become ingrained in the minds of consumers, associating sensory experiences with their core identities. In conclusion, the future of marketing lies in its ability to evolve with changing consumer preferences, as well as advancements in technology. As consumers increasingly seek authentic and personalized experiences, sensory marketing offers a multidimensional approach that can help brands stand out, create lasting impressions, and foster deeper consumer relationships. By understanding the psychological underpinnings of sensory inputs, companies can craft more powerful marketing strategies that resonate on a sensory and emotional level, paving the way for sustained growth and market differentiation.

LIMITATIONS

While the study of sensory marketing offers valuable insights into its impact on consumer behaviour, several limitations must be acknowledged. First, the subjective nature of sensory experiences poses a challenge in quantifying and comparing their effects. Sensory responses are highly individualistic, influenced by personal preferences, past experiences, and cultural backgrounds. This variability makes it difficult to generalize findings across different consumer segments, potentially limiting the applicability of research results.

Additionally, much of the current research on sensory marketing is concentrated in specific industries or geographic regions. This focus may result in findings that are not universally applicable, particularly when considering the diverse ways in which sensory marketing strategies are implemented across various sectors and cultures. Future research would benefit from a broader, more inclusive approach that examines multiple industries and international contexts to provide a more comprehensive understanding of sensory marketing's global impact.

Another limitation is the potential for sensory overload. While sensory marketing aims to create memorable experiences, there is a risk of overwhelming consumers with excessive sensory stimuli. The impact of sensory overload on consumer behaviour and brand perception remains underexplored. Research needs to address how the balance of sensory elements affects consumer engagement and whether too much sensory input could lead to negative outcomes such as discomfort or brand aversion.

The rapid advancement of technology presents another challenge. As new technologies emerge, sensory marketing strategies may become outdated or require adaptation. Studies conducted with older technologies may not fully capture the potential of current or future sensory marketing tools. Therefore, ongoing research is needed to assess how evolving technological capabilities impact sensory marketing effectiveness and consumer responses.

Lastly, ethical considerations regarding sensory marketing practices are often overlooked. While sensory marketing can enhance brand experiences, there is a fine line between persuasive marketing and manipulation. Addressing the ethical implications of using sensory stimuli to influence consumer behaviour is crucial to ensure that marketing practices remain ethical and respectful of consumer autonomy. Recognizing these limitations highlights the need for continued research and refinement in sensory marketing strategies. Addressing these challenges will contribute to a more nuanced understanding of how sensory marketing influences consumer behaviour and help develop more effective and ethical marketing practices.

SUGGESTIONS FOR FUTURE RESEARCH

As the field of sensory marketing continues to evolve, there are several promising avenues for future research that could provide deeper insights into its impact on consumer behaviour. One significant area for exploration is the integration of emerging technologies such as virtual reality (VR) and augmented reality (AR) in sensory marketing strategies. These technologies offer new ways to create immersive and personalized sensory experiences, potentially transforming how consumers interact with brands. Future research could investigate how VR and AR can enhance multisensory experiences and their effects on brand perception and consumer engagement.

Another promising direction involves the exploration of cross-sensory interactions and their impact on consumer behaviour. While much research has focused on individual sensory modalities, understanding how these senses work together to create a cohesive brand experience could offer valuable insights. Studies could examine how combining visual, auditory, tactile, gustatory, and olfactory elements influences consumer emotions, memory, and purchasing decisions.

The role of sensory marketing in digital and e-commerce environments also warrants further investigation. With the rise of online shopping, researchers could explore how sensory marketing principles can be adapted for digital platforms. This includes studying how virtual sensory experiences can be simulated online and their effectiveness in driving consumer behaviour compared to traditional in-store experiences.

Additionally, the ethical implications of sensory marketing are an important area for future research. As sensory marketing techniques become more sophisticated, understanding the boundaries between effective marketing and manipulation is crucial. Future studies should address the ethical considerations of using sensory stimuli to influence consumer behaviour and ensure that marketing practices remain transparent and respectful of consumer autonomy.

Finally, there is a need for more diverse and cross-cultural research in sensory marketing. Most studies have been conducted within specific cultural contexts, and understanding how sensory marketing strategies are perceived and effective across different cultures can provide valuable insights for global brands. Future research could investigate how cultural differences impact sensory preferences and responses, helping brands tailor their strategies to resonate with a wider audience.

Overall, advancing research in these areas could deepen our understanding of sensory marketing's impact on consumer behaviour, offering new strategies for brands to engage with consumers in meaningful and innovative ways.

REFERENCES

Acharya, U., Ramaprasad, B. S., Kate, N., & Srivastava, A. (2023, August 18). The Adoption of Smart Agriculture Technologies Based on the Perception of the Farmers in the Indian Context. https://doi.org/10.1109/smarttechcon57526.2023.10391525

Alpert, M. I. (2005). The influence of purchase occasions on the role of music in advertising. *Journal of Advertising Research*, 45(3), 310–321. DOI: 10.1017/S0021849905050360

Arora, R. (2023). The role of visual branding in sensory marketing. *JMR, Journal of Marketing Research*, 60(2), 123–135. DOI: 10.1177/00222437221112345

Arora, R. (2024). Engaging the senses: Innovative marketing strategies in the age of technology. *JMR, Journal of Marketing Research*, 61(3), 77–89. DOI: 10.1177/00222437221198765

Arora, R., & Chandel, R. (2024). Experiential marketing in the digital era: Creating immersive brand experiences. *International Journal of Marketing Studies*, 16(2), 23–34. DOI: 10.5539/ijms.v16n2p23

Arora, R., Kumar, A., & Valeri, M. (2023). The impact of VR and AR on consumer engagement: A sensory marketing perspective. *Journal of Consumer Marketing*, 40(1), 45–58. DOI: 10.1108/JCM-09-2022-0532

Arora, R., & Sharma, S. (2023). Sensory marketing: A new approach to enhance customer engagement. *JMR, Journal of Marketing Research*, 60(1), 25–38. https://doi.org/10.1177/00222437221199999

Bhardwaj, S., Kaushik, A., & Arora, R. (2024). The impact of sensory marketing on emotional engagement and brand loyalty. *Journal of Brand Management*. Advance online publication. https://doi.org/10.1057/s41262-023-00467-9

Chaudhary, P., & Kate, N. (2023). The coalescence effect: Understanding the impact of customer value proposition, perceived benefits and climate change sensitivities on electric vehicle adoption in India. https://doi.org/DOI: 10.1002/bsd2.282

Dimoka, , Pavlou, P. A., & Davis, F. D. (2011). Using neurophysiological methods to understand consumer behavior. *Management Information Systems Quarterly*, 35(3), 679–702. https://doi.org/10.2307/23042809

Elder, R. S., & Krishna, A. (2010). The effects of advertising copy on sensory thoughts and perceived taste. *The Journal of Consumer Research*, 36(5), 748–756. https://doi.org/10.1086/605327

Fisher, C. E., Chin, L., & Klitzman, R. (2010). Defining neuromarketing: Practices and professional challenges. *Harvard Review of Psychiatry*, 18(4), 230–237. DOI: 10.3109/10673229.2010.496623

Grand View Research. (2023). *Multisensory marketing market size, share & trends analysis report by sensory type, by application, by region, and segment forecasts, 2023-2030*. Retrieved from https://www.grandviewresearch.com/industry-analysis/multisensory-marketing-market

Han, J. (2023). Procter & Gamble's innovative marketing strategies: A case study. *Journal of Marketing Management*, 39(1), 12–25. DOI: 10.1080/0267257X.2022.2040256

Hirsch, A. (1995). Scentsational marketing: The role of scent in consumer behavior. *Journal of Marketing*, 59(4), 24–30. https://doi.org/10.1177/002224379505900403

Iacoboni, M., Freedman, J., & Kaplan, J. (2012). Predicting advertising success: Neural correlates of emotional and behavioral responses to ads. *Journal of Neuroscience, Psychology, and Economics*, 5(3), 147–167. DOI: 10.1037/a0028860

Kate, N., Chaudhary, P., Kavi Kumar, K. S., & Raut, N., & More, M. (2024). *Antecedents to the Adoption of Digital Marketing by Start-Ups Under Startup-India and E-Governance Initiatives*. https://doi.org/10.4018/ijegr.347505

Kate, N. T., Chaudhary, P., & More, M. (2024). Antecedents to Organic Tea Buying Behavior and Consumption Among Millennials in India: Through the Lens of Theory of Planned Behavior. https://doi.org/DOI: 10.17010/ijom/2024/v54/i1/173382

Knutson, B., Rick, S., Wimmer, G. E., Prelec, D., & Loewenstein, G. (2007). Neural predictors of purchases. *Neuron*, 53(1), 147–156. DOI: 10.1016/j.neuron.2006.11.010

Krishna, A. (2015). The rise of sensory marketing. In Raghunathan, K. S. (Ed.), *Marketing and the Role of Customer Service* (pp. 59–67). Business Expert Press.

Krishna, A. E. (2010). The influence of scent on memory and brand preference. *The Journal of Consumer Research*, 37(4), 681–688. DOI: 10.1086/655115

Lucas, R. E. (1972). Expectations and the neutrality of money. *Journal of Economic Theory*, 4(2), 103–124. DOI: 10.1016/0022-0531(72)90142-1

Malik, S., Malhan, D., & Arora, R. (2024). Exploring sensory marketing: Its role in creating emotional ties with consumers. *International Journal of Marketing Studies*, 16(1), 45–60. DOI: 10.5539/ijms.v16n1p45

Muth, J. F. (1961). Rational expectations and the theory of price movements. *Econometrica*, 29(3), 315–335. DOI: 10.2307/1909635

Nielsen. (2016). Global new product innovation: The good, the bad, and the ugly. Retrieved from https://www.nielsen.com/us/en/insights/article/2016/global-new-product-innovation-the-good-the-bad-and-the-ugly/

Paivio, A. (1979). *Imagery and verbal processes*. Lawrence Erlbaum Associates.

Plassmann, H., Ramsøy, T. Z., & Milosavljevic, M. (2012). Branding the brain: A critical review and outlook. *Journal of Consumer Psychology*, 22(1), 18–36. DOI: 10.1016/j.jcps.2011.11.010

PwC. (2023). Experience is everything: Here's how to get it right. Retrieved from https://www.pwc.com/gx/en/industries/consumer-markets/consumer-insights/experience-is-everything.html

Salesforce. (2021). State of the connected customer, 5th edition. Retrieved from https://www.salesforce.com/form/pdf/state-of-the-connected-customer/

Sorensen, K. (2009). Dark side of neuromarketing: How manipulative tactics backfire. *The Journal of Consumer Research*, 36(6), 967–982. https://doi.org/10.1086/648672

Springer. (2009). Supplement 2: Sixth annual ethical dimensions in business: Reflections from the business academic community. *Journal of Business Ethics*, 88, 141-153.

Stanton, S. J., & Armstrong, J. A. (2017). Neuromarketing: Ethical implications of its use and potential misuses. *Journal of Business Ethics*, 144(4), 799–811. https://doi.org/10.1007/s10551-016-3059-0

Taneja, S., Shukla, P., & Arora, R. (2024). Sensory marketing strategies: Enhancing consumer experience and emotional connection. *Journal of Consumer Marketing*. Advance online publication. DOI: 10.1108/JCM-09-2023-0658

Thaler, R. H. (2000). From homo economicus to homo sapiens. *The Journal of Economic Perspectives*, 14(1), 133–141. DOI: 10.1257/jep.14.1.133

Venkatraman, V., Dimoka, A., Pavlou, P. A., Vo, K., Hampton, W., Bollinger, B., & Hershfield, H. E. (2015). Predicting advertising success beyond traditional measures: New insights from neurophysiological methods and market response modeling. *JMR, Journal of Marketing Research*, 52(4), 436–452. DOI: 10.1509/jmr.13.0593

Yoon, C., Gutchess, A. H., Feinberg, F., & Polk, T. A. (2009). The "sweet spot" of implicit and explicit memory in advertising. *The Journal of Consumer Research*, 36(1), 39–50. DOI: 10.1086/597618

Chapter 14
Sensory Perception and Cognitive Responses:
Unveiling Consumer Psychology in EV Adoption

Tushar Batra
Khalsa College, Amritsar, India

Meghna Aggarwal
ASSM College, Guru Nanak Dev University, India

ABSTRACT

To achieve net zero emission and decarbonization, the electrification of the transportation sector is necessary. Electric vehicles are extensively advocated as a sustainable option of transportation, due to their benefits and growing awareness among public towards environmental pollution, climate change, and country's dependence on oil imports. For most of the countries, including India, road transportation sectors are centres of focus to reduce emission of greenhouse gases. Though there is an increase in year-on-year sale of electric vehicles (EV) in India, their market share is still on the lower side compared to the overall sale of vehicles. This study focuses on consumer perceptions, knowledge about electric vehicles, experience in driving, and intention to purchase an electric vehicle in the near future. The study is empirical in nature and quantitative methods are employed. The respondents go through pre-drive and post-drive surveys. The findings will provide detailed insights into consumer perceptions towards electric vehicles and barriers to adoption of electric vehicles in India.

DOI: 10.4018/979-8-3693-9351-2.ch014

INTRODUCTION

Electrification of transport sector is very important for reduction of emissions. In order to achieve net zero emission and decarbonization of environment, electrification of transport sector is advocated as a prime solution. Electric Vehicles (EV) come out as an assuring solution for the purpose of reducing carbon footprints which are associated with convention fuel powered combustion engine vehicles. Admix of financial benefits, regulatory policies and increase in consumer's awareness towards issues related with environment such as air pollution, climate change, accelerate the adoption of electric vehicles (IEA, 2020). There is also a dire need to strategically reduce dependence on oil imports. Various governments are also increasing their focus on the road transport's future, to reduce emission of greenhouse gases.

Importance of Electrification in Transportation

Electrification of transport sector is advocated as a key strategy to control climate change. Transport sector has a significant contribution to greenhouse gases emissions globally, and it accounts for approximately 24% of total global co2 emission (IEA, 2020). These emissions can be substantially reduced by transitioning to electric vehicles. Electric vehicles have zero tailpipe emissions, which improves air quality (Transport & Environment, 2018). Further, use of renewable sources of energy for charging Electric Vehicles can further increase their benefits towards environment. The study of Ellingsen, Singh, and Strømman (2016) highlights the life cycle greenhouse gas emissions of EVs. Study shows that life cycle greenhouse gas emissions of EVs are considerably lower as compared to conventional vehicles, specifically when EVs are charged with electricity generated from renewable sources.

Global Trends in Adoption of Electric Vehicles

The adoption of electric vehicle is supported by wide array incentives and policies globally. One of them is financial incentives, such as rebate in taxes and direct subsidies, which make an electric vehicle more accessible by lowering the upfront cost of vehicle. For example, in United States of America, federal tax credits of $7500 were offered for Ev buyers. And countries like Norway and China provide many financial incentives which resulted in higher Electric Vehicle adoption rates (U.S. Department of Energy, 2021; IEA, 2020). Another area of consideration is Infrastructure Development, with notable investment aiming at alleviation of range anxiety and supporting widespread use of EV. To achieve it, European Union has made commitment to deploy at least 1million public recharging stations by 2025 (European Commission, 2020). Additionally, government regulations and mandates plays an important role in driving electric vehicle adoption, which includes setting of emission reduction targets, banning the sale of new internal combustion engine vehicles by certain dates and compulsory electrification of fleet for both private and public sectors.

The world markets for Electric vehicles have seen a continuous growth over the past 10 years. According to the International Energy Agency (IEA), nearly 14 million electric vehicles were sold in 2023. China, Europe and United States contributes to about 95% of total sales of electric vehicles. Roughly one in every 5 cars sold in 2023 was electric. This surge is sales is primarily because of policy support by governments, advancements in technologies and huge capital expenditure in expansion of charging infrastructure.

EV Adoption and Neurosensory Behavior

The adoption of Electric Vehicles (EVs) is intricately linked to neurosensory behavior, as consumer decisions are significantly influenced by sensory perceptions and cognitive processes. Neurosensory behavior encompasses how individuals perceive, interpret, and respond to sensory stimuli such as sight, sound, and touch. In the context of EVs, factors such as the quietness of the engine, the smoothness of the ride, and the aesthetic appeal of the vehicle can positively impact consumer attitudes and adoption intentions. The sensory experience of driving an EV, characterized by reduced noise pollution and the absence of engine vibrations, can enhance the overall driving experience, making it more pleasurable and desirable. Additionally, cognitive aspects, such as the perception of EVs as environmentally friendly and technologically advanced, can evoke positive emotional responses and reinforce the decision to adopt. Understanding and leveraging these neurosensory behaviors can help manufacturers and marketers tailor their strategies to align with consumer preferences, thereby accelerating the adoption of EVs as a sustainable alternative to conventional fuel-powered vehicles.

EV Adoption in India

India has one of the largest road networks in the whole world, passengers and freight movement depends heavily on road networks (Ministry of Road Transport and Highways, 2020). India, has vast and diverse types of geographical conditions, which are uniquely challenging and also opportunistic for adoption of electric vehicles. Rapid urbanisation and growth of population leads to increase in vehicle ownership which contributes to severe air pollution and increase dependency on oil imports (Guttikunda & Mohan, 2014). Considering the environmental and financial benefits, the government has introduced several initiatives for the promotion of electric vehicles. First one was (FAME India) scheme, The Faster Adoption and Manufacturing of (Hybrid &) Electric Vehicles in India, which was launched in 2015 to promote the production and adoption of electric vehicles. In 2019, second phase of FAME was introduced which was called FAME II, it has a budget of 10,000 crore INR in order to support the development of infrastructure for Electric vehicles and subsidies for purchase of Electric vehicles. The government is currently gearing up with FAME III with outlay of approximately 10,000 crore INR.

Regardless of these initiatives, The Electric vehicles penetration in India still remains on lower side (International Energy Agency, 2021). This is mainly because of barriers which hinder the widespread penetration of Electric vehicles in India, which includes high initial costs, less charging infrastructure, and lack of awareness among consumers (Sharma, 2020). The study moves deeper into the barriers by analysis of consumer's perception, Electric vehicle's knowledge, experience of driving an EV and intentions to purchase an Electric vehicle.

Development of Theoretical Framework

In order to understand the factors, which influence consumer's behaviour towards electric vehicle, this study assimilates certain well- established theoretical frameworks, which are Theory of Planned Behaviour (TPB), Technology Acceptance Model (TAM) and few elements from the perspective of psychology and policy. Every framework provides with significant insights into the complicated reciprocation of attitudes, perception and few external factors which shape intentions and behaviour of consumers regarding Electric Vehicles.

Theory of Planned Behaviour (TPB)

The Theory of Planned Behaviour (TPB) is a psychological theory which was earlier proposed by Ajzen (1991). It links beliefs and behaviour. This theory deems that intention of an individual to engage in a specific behaviour is determined by three key factors. The key factors are Attitude toward the behaviour, subjective norms and Perceived Behavioural Control. Where Attitude towards the behaviour refers to the degrees of favourability and unfavorability of an individual's behaviour. For Electric Vehicles adoption purposes, this study induces individual's perception towards environmental benefits, cost effectiveness and overall utility of electric vehicles. While subjective norms are the societal pressure which individuals' experiences while deciding on whether to engage or not in a specific behaviour. In Electric Vehicles context, subjective norms include family, friends and society who are in favour of environment friendly decisions. Where Perceived Behavioural control is thought to be influenced by previous experiences and expected challenges, illustrates the level of difficulty of performing the behaviour. In case of its application to Electric Vehicles adoption, The Theory of Planned Behaviour hypothesises the following:

- While believing that EV are beneficial for environment and are economical, there is positive attitude towards EVs which will enhance the intentions to adopt an Electric Vehicle.
- Supporting Subjective Norms will raise the likelihood of EV adoption.
- Higher perceived behavioural control will margin the progressive intention to buy an Electric Vehicle.

Technology Acceptance Model (TAM)

The Technology Acceptance Model (TAM) was first introduced by Davis (1989), TAM was designed to illustrate how users accept and use a technology. TAM consists of two main factors which impacts decisions of an individual to use a technology. The factors are Perceived usefulness and Perceived ease of use. Perceived usefulness is the degree of belief of an individual. In case of electric vehicles this factor includes cost savings and environmental benefits. While perceived ease of use may include the ease of charging an EV, simple operations and user friendliness of technology. TAM asserts that these perceptions shape an individual's attitude towards making the use of technology, which will then impact their behavioural desires to use it. For electric vehicles, TAM suggests:

- Higher the perceived usefulness, stronger are the intentions to adopt Electric vehicle.
- Higher perceived ease of use will increase the chances of adoption of Electric Vehicle.

Integration of Psychological and Policy Factors

In addition to Theory of Planned Behaviour (TPB) and Technology Acceptance Model (TAM), this study imbibes psychological and policy factors, which have been notified as important in the context of EV adoption:

1. Environmental Awareness: (Rezvani, Jansson, & Bodin, 2015) shows that individuals who have higher awareness of environmental issues, are more expected to adopt behaviours that are environmentally friendly, which also includes the adoption of Electric vehicles.

2. Financial Incentives: Economic factors, for example subsidies and tax benefits, play an important role in contracting the financial load of purchasing an EV and are crucial motivators for adoption of EVs. (Li, Long, Chen, & Geng, 2017).
3. Infrastructure Support: The presence of proper charging infrastructure substantially impacts the feasibility and accessibility of using EVs, thereby influencing adoption rates of EV. (Sovacool, Kester, Noel, & de Rubens, 2018).
4. Experiential Learning: The theory of Experiential learning proposes that first-hand experiences can significantly reshape the perceptions and attitudes. Further consumer's perception can be boosted and ambiguity can be eliminated by test drives and hands on experiences with these vehicles. (Kolb, 1984; Skippon & Garwood, 2011).
5. Demographic Factors: Several demographic factors household composition can influence adoption of technology. Households with more than one vehicle may perceive less urgency to adopt to an EV due to existing mobility options. (Venkatesh & Morris, 2000; Morris & Venkatesh, 2000; Krause, Carley, Lane, & Graham, 2013).

LITERATURE REVIEW

Introduction to EV

In order to reduce emission of greenhouse gases and to fight climate changes, electric vehicles have become an important focus globally. The transport sector relies majorly on fossil fuels and contributes heavily to global carbon emissions. EV offer most suitable alternatives to conventional internal combustion engine vehicles by utilization of electricity. Electricity can be generated from renewable sources, and reduces the carbon footprints of transport sector. Multiple factors influence the adoption of EV such as environmental awareness, advancements in technologies, economic incentives and development in infrastructure.

Technological advancements have played an important role in the development and adoption of Electric Vehicles. Advancements in battery technology, and reduction in costs, have made Electric Vehicles more competitive with traditional vehicles. As per the study of Nykvist and Nilsson (2015), the cost of li-ion batteries has witnessed a fall by about 85% from 2010 to 2018, which makes Electric Vehicle s more affordable for consumers. Additionally, recent developments in charging technology, which includes the development of network of fast-charging stations, have addressed concerns related to range and charging time of Electric Vehicle.

Consumer Perceptions and Adoption Barriers

In spite of numerous benefits and policies, number of barriers hinders the wider adoption of Electric vehicles. A significant role is played by consumer perceptions and misconceptions about electric vehicles. Earlier studies by (Axsen & Kurani, 2013) have shown evidences of knowledge gaps and mis understandings about the cost of electric vehicle, reliability, and performance which can impact the decision of potential buyer's concerns related to charging infrastructure, total battery life, and complete cost of ownership which are common among consumers.

Environmental Awareness and Adoption Intention Towards EVs

Environmental awareness is an important factor in shaping attitudes of consumers towards EV. Study by Steg (2005) indicates that individuals who are highly conscious of environmental issues are more likely to shift to sustainable practices, which also includes the use of EV. This finding is also endorsed by Lane and Potter (2007), where author found a positive correlation between the intention to purchase EV and environmental awareness. Consumers who have knowledge about the environmental benefits of EV, such as reduction in carbon emissions and less dependence on fossil fuels, tend to develop more promising attitudes towards Electric vehicles.

Barth et al. (2016) broadcast on this by inquiring the role of social norms and collective efficacy in the perspective of acceptance of EV. Authors found that individuals who have strong social support for environmentally friendly practices and affirms collective ability to impact environmental change are more likely to adopt EV. This highlights the significance of community and societal impacts in directing individual attitudes towards sustainable transportation options.

(Rezvani, Jansson, & Bodin, 2015) shows environmental awareness as specific attitude to correlate pro environmental behaviours which also includes electric vehicle adoption.

H1: Consumers who have higher environmental awareness have positive impact on adoption intention towards Electric Vehicles.

Perceived Ease of Use and Adoption Intention of Consumers

The perceived ease of use is a critical factor of Electric Vehicle adoption. The Technology Acceptance Model (TAM), which was developed by Davis (1989), posits that perceived ease of use and perceived usefulness are important determinants of technology acceptance. Based on TAM, consumers are far more likely to adopt new when they perceive it as user friendly. Wang et al. (2017) extended this particular model to EV, and shows that the intentions to buy an EV increases by perceived ease of use. The reliability in performance and user- friendly designs are important in promoting the adoption of EV. The experiences of consumers with easy charging ad lower maintenance influence their perception positively.

(Davis, 1989), also enforces that perceived ease of use is a crucial factor of technology adoption intentions.

H2: Perceived ease to use positively impacts adoption intention of consumers.

Financial Incentives and Infrastructure Support

Financial Incentives and Infrastructure are important in driving adoption of Electric Vehicles. At this time the initial purchase cost of an EV is higher. It is essential to reduce financial barriers to adoption of EV. Financial incentives such as tax rebates, subsidies and lower interests on loan aids reduction in upfront cost of buying an EV, which helps in penetration at larger scale (Diamond, 2009)

At the same time, the availability of charging infrastructure is equally important. In their study Sierzchula et al. (2014) found that areas with well-developed charging networks have higher rates of EV adoption. Li et al. (2017) further backed this by professing that the availability of charging stations alleviates range anxiety, which is a major concern for potential EV adopters. For the daily usability of EVs, the convenience and accessibility of charging infrastructure are important. which influence consumers' decisions to migrate from conventional vehicles to Electric Vehicles.

(Li, Long, Chen, & Geng, 2017), highlighted the significance of financial benefits and infrastructural support for promotion of electric vehicle adoption.

H3: Financial incentives and infrastructure support significantly impact EV adoption intention.

Knowledge About Electric Vehicle Technology and Adoption Intention

Earlier familiarity and knowledge about Electric Vehicle technology can significantly impacts adoption intention of consumers. In their study Carley et al. (2013) describes that the consumers who have higher understanding level of EV technology are more likely to adopt EV. This shows that educational initiatives and campaigns can effectively helps in enhancing the adoption rates of EV. Egbue and Long (2012) enlightens lack of knowledge and misconceptions about EV technology are the obstacles to widespread adoption of EVs. Authors suggested that targeted educational efforts are required to remove these barriers of adoption for EVs.

(Rogers, 2003) explains the suggestions by Knowledge diffusion theories and the Technology Acceptance Model (TAM) that higher knowledge and understanding of an innovative technology can increase its perceived usefulness and ease of use.

H4: Prior knowledge of EV technology increases its likelihood of adoption.

Household Vehicle Dynamics and EV Adoption

There is a negative influence on intentions to adopt Electric Vehicles if there is presence of multiple vehicles in a household. In their study Bühler et al. (2014) claims that the consumers who have multiple vehicles in their household, may perceive less requirement for an additional electric vehicle. While Plötz et al. (2014) recommended that by highlighting the benefits of

EVs in a household, promotional strategies should focus in unique benefits of buying an EV to a household with multiple vehicles. By showing practical advantages and environmental benefits, marketers can shape preference of consumers. Studies by (Krause, Carley, Lane, & Graham, 2013), on household vehicle ownership patterns shows that households which have multiple vehicles may not see urgency in adoption of EVs.

H5: The presence of multiple vehicles in a household reduces the likelihood of EV adoption due to perceived redundancy.

Neuro-sensory behaviour plays a crucial role in determining the adoption of electric vehicles (EVs), as customers' attitudes and decisions are shaped by their sensory impressions and brain responses. Environmental consciousness, such as awareness of the natural world and its preservation, elicits both emotional and cognitive reactions that can motivate individuals to embrace electric vehicles (EVs). When individuals are presented with persuasive visual and aural stimuli regarding the ecological advantages of electric vehicles (EVs), such as advertising showcasing pristine skies or endorsements from contented customers, their brains analyse and elicit favourable emotional responses. Positive reinforcement can enhance consumers' inclination to view electric vehicles (EVs) as a feasible choice, by utilising the brain's reward system to establish a connection between EVs and favourable results such as environmental conservation and societal accountability.

Progress in electric vehicle (EV) technologies and improvements in infrastructure also impact neuro-sensory behaviour, which in turn affects the rate at which EVs are adopted. When consumers perceive the concrete advantages of electric vehicles, such as seamless acceleration and less noise in comparison to conventional automobiles, these sensory stimuli provide a positive image that can be further strengthened by favourable neurological reactions. Furthermore, economic incentives such as tax reductions or refunds can be presented in a manner that emphasises immediate cash benefits, appealing to the brain's inclination towards quick gratification. Infrastructure advancements, such as the growing accessibility of charging stations, diminish the perceived apprehension and inconvenience of transitioning to electric vehicles (EVs), alleviating the anxiety linked to limited driving range. To greatly boost the adoption of electric vehicles (EVs), it is important to address both the emotional and practical concerns by providing sensory-rich experiences and cognitive reassurances.AI significantly impacts multiple businesses by enhancing decision-making processes (Arora & Sharma, 2023), improving operational efficiency, and creating personalized customer experiences, thereby driving the adoption of technologies like EVs. In relation to neuro-sensory behavior, AI can analyze vast amounts of data to identify patterns in consumer preferences and sensory responses, enabling businesses to tailor their marketing strategies to evoke desired emotional reactions and cognitive biases (Arora, (2023); Arora, (2024)). For instance, AI-driven advertisements for EVs can be customized to highlight environmental benefits and economic incentives, leveraging sensory inputs to influence consumer behaviour positively. The role of the metaverse further amplifies this by providing immersive, sensory-rich virtual environments where consumers can experience products like EVs firsthand, interact with advanced technologies, and visualize the infrastructure developments, thereby reinforcing the neural and emotional connections that drive adoption and purchase decisions (Kumar, Arora & Erkol Bayram, (Eds.). (2024) a; Kumar, Arora, & Erkol Bayram, (Eds.). (2024) b).

Objectives of the Study

The purpose of the study is to explore dimensions of consumer perception, knowledge of consumers and intentions towards Electric Vehicles adoption in India. In order to achieve the comprehensive understanding, the study formulates following objectives:

1. Assessment of Consumer Knowledge and Awareness of EV.
2. Examining Consumer Attitudes and Perceptions Towards EV.
3. Analysis of the Role of Financial Incentives and Infrastructure in EV Adoption.
4. Determine the Relationship Between Prior Knowledge and EV Adoption Likelihood.
5. Develop Strategic Recommendations for Enhancing EV Adoption.

Research Methodology

In a developing country like India, which is largely behind in infrastructure for electric vehicle, witnessing one on road is still rare. Though the sales are rising every quarter, still the penetration is less. It is quite possible that potential customers of an EV may not have seen or driven or charged any of EV as of now. Consumers are very less familiar with the technology of electric vehicle. This particular study employs an empirical approach and involve quantitative methods to explore consumer perceptions and attitudes towards EVs. For this purpose, a structure questionnaire was developed based on scales and measures which were earlier validated in prior research and ensures reliability and validity. A part of the questionnaire was focused on the data related to demographic characteristics of the respondents such as covered gender, age, education, household income and cars in the household. The sample consists of 234 respondents who have no prior experience of driving an electric vehicle. Participants were selected on random basis as per convenience. The demographic characteristics of sample includes around 141 males and 93 female respondents. The respondents lie between 28 years to 65 years of age with a mean age of 36.7 years. 139 respondents hold a bachelor's degree, 61 hold a master's degree and 34 have passed high school. While 199 respondents own more than one vehicle in their household.

Procedure for Collection of Data

The data was collected using pre drive and post drive surveys. Pre-Drive Survey: Participants recorded their responses in a pre-drive survey which is Adapted from the New Ecological Paradigm (NEP) scale (Dunlap, Van Liere, Mertig, & Jones, 2000). The survey was focused to assess the basic knowledge and perceptions of Electric Vehicles. This survey has questions regarding environmental awareness, attitudes towards Electric vehicle and some demographic information. Knowledge of respondents was checked using the items adapted from (Rezvani, Jansson, & Bodin, 2015). For perception purpose TAM and TPB models were used (Ajzen, 1991; Davis, 1989). After pre drive survey, each respondent was asked to drive a Tata Tiago EV on a pre decided 40-kilometre route following real traffic conditions. Post the 40-kilometre drive, respondents completed another set of survey prepared from the Theory of Planned Behaviour TPB and TAM scales to capture variance in attitudes, perceived ease of use, and perceived usefulness post-driving experience and their intentions to buy an EV in the future. (Ajzen, 1991; Davis, 1989). At the last, a post drive survey was designed for respondents to understand their perceptions and attitudes towards EVs.

Statistical Tools Used

Quantitative data was collected for the study through pre-drive surveys and post-drive surveys. The objective of pre-drive survey was to assess basic knowledge, attitudes, and intentions of consumers regarding Electric Vehicles. Whereas post-drive survey was focussed to measure the changes in perceptions, attitudes, and purchase intentions of consumers after driving an Electric Vehicle. Descriptive statistic tools such as Pearson coefficient correlation, linear and multiple regression were applied using SPSS -29 version.

Results

Table 1. Tabular representation of results

Hypotheses Results		Explanation
H1: Consumers who have higher environmental awareness have positive attitude towards Electric Vehicles.. $\beta = 0.47$, $p < 0.01$, $r = 0.46$		The beta coefficient of 0.47, indicates a moderate positive and statistically significant relationship between environmental awareness and positive attitudes towards EVs. The correlation coefficient (r) of 0.46 indicates a moderate positive relationship between environmental awareness and positive attitudes towards EVs. The p-value of less than 0.01 indicates that this relationship is statistically significant.
H2: Perceived ease to use positively impacts adoption intentions of consumers.	$\beta = 0.42$, $p < 0.05$, $r = 0.577$	The beta coefficient (β) of 0.42 indicates that perceived ease of use is a strong positive predictor of the intention to purchase an EV. The p-value of less than 0.05 indicates that this relationship is statistically significant. R squared value of 0.577 suggests that perceived ease of use is an important factor but not the only one impacting purchase intentions.
H3: Financial incentives and infrastructure support significantly impact EV adoption.	$\beta = 0.43$, $p < 0.01$, $r = 0.622$	The beta coefficient (β) of 0.43 indicates a strong positive impact of financial incentives and infrastructure support on EV adoption. The p-value of less than 0.01 indicates that this relationship is statistically significant. An R-squared value of 0.622 indicates that the model explains a significant portion of the variability in EV adoption.
H4: Prior knowledge of EV technology increases its likelihood of adoption.	$\beta = 0.36$, $p < 0.05$, $r = 0.35$	The calculated beta value of 0.36 indicates a moderate positive and statistically significant relationship between prior knowledge of EV technology and adoption intention. The correlation

continued on following page

Table 1. Continued

Hypotheses Results		Explanation
		coefficient (r) of 0.35 indicates a moderate positive relationship between prior knowledge of EV technology and the intention to adopt EVs. The p-value of less than 0.05 indicates that this relationship is statistically significant.
H5: The presence of multiple vehicles in a household reduces the likelihood of EV adoption due to perceived redundancy.	$\beta = -0.31$, $p < 0.05$, $r = 0.936$	The beta coefficient (β) of -0.31 indicates a negative impact of having multiple vehicles in a household on the intention to adopt EVs. The p-value of less than 0.05 indicates that this relationship is statistically significant. The regression analysis confirms that as the number of vehicles increases, the Electric vehicles adoption intention decreases significantly.

A set of hypotheses were developed for the purpose of study. And a set of statistical tools are applied which are based on the nature of variables and the relationship, which is being examined. The results are discussed in detail.

1. H1: Consumers with higher environmental awareness are more likely to have a positive attitude towards EVs.

Statistical Significance ($p < 0.01$): A p-value less than 0.01 suggests that there is less than a 1% probability that the correlation is due to random variation, which means the relationship is statistically significant. This high level of statistical significance implies a high degree of confidence that the observed correlation between environmental awareness and attitudes towards EVs is real and unlikely to be due to chance.

Pearson correlation test was applied to measures the strength and direction of the linear relationship between environmental awareness and attitude of consumers towards Electric Vehicles, which are two continuous variables. The result of this hypothesis testing shows a correlation coefficient (r) of 0.46 between environmental awareness and attitudes towards electric vehicles (EVs). A correlation coefficient ranges from -1 to 1, where if values are closer to 1, it indicates a stronger positive relationship, while values closer to -1 indicate a stronger negative relationship, and values around 0 indicate no relationship at all. Therefore, a value of 0.46 suggests moderate positive correlation between the two variables. This means that as the environmental awareness of consumer increases, there is a corresponding increase in positive attitudes towards Electric Vehicles. The beta coefficient of 0.47, indicates a moderate positive and statistically significant relationship between environmental awareness and positive attitudes towards EVs.

There is a positive influence of educational programmes and public campaigns to increase environmental awareness as studied by (Egbue & Long, 2012; Barth et al., 2016). Positive attitudes towards electric vehicles are very important for adoption of electric vehicles, with previous researches showing that such perceptions can significantly enhances market penetration of EVs (Rezvani et al., 2015). While public campaign can change consumer behaviours significantly (Lane & Potter, 2007) which leads to higher adoption. The study concludes there is a moderately positive correlation between environmental awareness and attitudes towards EVs, which underscores the importance of education and awareness campaigns for the promotion of EV adoption, which ultimately contributes to a more sustainable and environmentally friendly transportation sector.

2. H2: Perceived ease of use of EVs positively influences consumers' intentions to purchase an EV.

Simple linear regression tool was used to determine the predictive power of perceived ease of use (independent variable) on the intention of consumers to buy an Electric Vehicle (dependent variable). The p-value ($p < 0.05$) indicates the probability that the observed effect is due to chance and the sample is statistically significant. The beta coefficient (β) of 0.42 indicates a strong positive impact of perceived ease of use on the intention to purchase electric vehicles (EVs). Which means as users finds electric vehicles easier to use, their intention to purchase an EV will increase significantly. R squared value of 0.577 suggests that perceived ease of use is an important factor but not the only one impacting purchase intentions. The study shows with in increase in user friendliness of an Electric Vehicle the purchase intentions can be boosted significantly. Ease of use can be achieved by improving interface design of vehicles, reducing complexity in use, and providing better user support. (Venkatesh and Davis (2000), perceived ease of use is an important factor of technology acceptance, with simple interfaces leading to higher adoption rates. A well-designed interface which is easy to navigate can greatly enhance user experiences. Simplification of the operation and maintenance of an EV can make them more appealing to their potential buyers. (Davis (1989)) showed that by reducing the complexity of a technology its perceived ease of use can be improved, which in turn influences the behavioural intention of users.

3. H3: Financial incentives and infrastructure support significantly impact the likelihood of consumers adopting EVs.

Multiple linear regression technique is applied to assess the impact of (financial incentives and infrastructure support), multiple independent variables on a single dependent variable i.e. (likelihood of adopting EVs). The p-value is less than 0.01 signifies that the observed relationship is highly significant statistically. The beta coefficient (β) of 0.43 demonstrates a significant positive impact of financial incentives and infrastructure support on the adoption of electric vehicles (EVs). The regression analysis confirms that financial incentives and infrastructure support are significant and strong predictors of EV adoption. The results suggest that there is a combined effect of financial incentives and infrastructure support which creates a collegial impact on adoption of electric vehicle. When consumers get financial benefits and they have an easy access to charging infrastructure, then they are more likely to consider and purchase an Electric Vehicle. (Jenn et al. (2013)) supports this, their study shows that the areas with financial benefits and robust charging networks see higher adoption rates for electric vehicles.

4. H4: Consumers with prior knowledge of EV technology are more likely to adopt EVs.

Pearson Correlation Coefficient (r) test was applied to measure the strength and direction of the relation between prior knowledge of EV technology and the likelihood of adopting EVs. The p-value less than 0.05 means that the likelihood of this relationship occurring by chance is less than 5%. This reflects that there is a statistically significant relationship between prior knowledge of EV technology and the intention to adopt EVs. The Correlation Coefficient (r = 0.35) value shows a moderately positive correlation between prior knowledge of Electric vehicles technology and the intention to adopt Electric vehicle. The calculated beta value of 0.36 indicates a moderate positive and statistically significant relationship between prior knowledge of EV technology and adoption intention. The results are substantial enough to be noteworthy. The results highlight the importance of consumer education in promotion of electric vehicles.

5. H5: The presence of multiple vehicles in a household reduces the likelihood of EV adoption due to perceived redundancy.

Multiple regression statistical tool has been applied to assess the impact of number of vehicles in a household, which is an independent variable, on the likelihood of adoption of an Electric Vehicles, which is dependent variable, while controlling all other related factors. The p-value less than 0.05 indicates that this relationship is statistically significant. The regression analysis supports the hypothesis that the presence of multiple vehicles in a household negatively influences EV adoption intention. The negative value of the beta coefficient ($\beta = -0.31$) suggests that households with multiple vehicles doesn't need an electric vehicle. The availability of vehicles acts as barriers as the need of consumers are fulfilled by other vehicles. The consumer might not shift to an electric vehicle immediately. There are challenges in promotion of electric vehicle among multi-vehicle households.

CONCLUSION

The electrification of transport sector is very important in order to achieve zero net emissions globally and to reduce emissions of greenhouse gases. The adoption of electric vehicle is gaining momentum in India, but the penetration is still lower as compared to total vehicle stock. The study aims to understand the factors which influence the electric vehicles adoption in India. The study is guided by the hypotheses which are based on environmental awareness, perceived ease of use, financial incentives, infrastructure support, knowledge of EV technology, and household vehicle dynamics. The study is an empirical analysis of data from 234 respondents and yields important insights into these factors and provide new specific perspectives. The research integrates Theory of Planned Behaviour (TPB) and the Technology Acceptance Model (TAM), along with other psychological and policy factors to provide a detailed understanding of the factors influencing EV adoption.

The study finds that knowledge of consumers and their awareness about electric vehicles remains limited, and it impacts attitudes and adoption intentions of consumers. This goes consistently with (Rezvani, Jansson, & Bodin, 2015), where authors considered importance of information dissemination. The study suggests that as consumers will become more environmentally conscious, they are more likely to develop favourable attitude towards adoption of electric vehicles. Perceived ease of use was found to be an important predictor of intention to purchase Electric vehicle. Further financial benefits such as reduced fuel costs, subsidies, tax rebates and lower interest loans are important in shaping positive attitudes towards EVs as (Li, Long, Chen, & Geng, 2017) stated. Charging infrastructure comes out as a robust motivator for EV adoption, aligning with the findings of (Li, Long, Chen, & Geng, 2017; Sovacool, Kester, Noel, & de Rubens, 2018). It is found that prior knowledge of consumer and familiarity of consumer with EV technology are positively correlated with adoption likelihood of consumers. Respondents who were more knowledgeable about operational aspects of EVs, are more inclined towards considering purchasing an EV. This was earlier highlighted by Rogers (2003) in his Diffusion of Innovations theory, where authors underscore the significance of education and information dissemination in promotion of adoption of electric vehicle. Further, if a household already have a fleet of traditional fuelled vehicles, then the household may perceive lower need for an additional electric vehicle (Bühler et al., 2014).

Recommendations for Stakeholders

Comprehensive educational campaigns are required to provide detailed information about electric vehicles, their benefits and other financial incentives. Various media channels and community outreach programmes can ensure in spread of information to a broader audience. Government should expand financial incentives such as subsidies, tax rebates, and low-interest loans for EV purchases, to make an EV more affordable and accessible. Commitment of more capital expenditure is needed in expansion of public charging infrastructure to mitigate the concerns about range anxiety and ease of use. Availability of charging stations in both rural and urban locations can increase the rate of Electric vehicle adoption.

Electric vehicles manufacturers should shift their focus towards improving the user experience by simplification of technology and improving the performance and making it more reliable. The designs and features should meet consumer expectations. The makers should provide opportunity to test drive an EV to their potential customers to enhance adoption rates. Handson experience with EV can help potential buyers in understanding the technology and features.

By increasing expenditure on consumer education, expanding financial incentives, improving charging infrastructure, stakeholders can effectively support the transition to electric mobility. Continued research and collaboration across sectors will be important to achieving significant progress in Electric vehicle adoption and contributing to global efforts to reduce greenhouse gas emissions and fight climate changes.

Direction for Future Research

The study provides a detailed understanding of factors which influence EV adoption in India. This piece of work provides a foundation for further research. Further research is important to track evolution in EV industry and to address the emerging challenges and opportunities. longitudinal studies should be conducted to track the changes happening in consumer attitudes and adoption rates over time. It can also provide insights into the effectiveness of strategies implemented to increase adoption rates. The impact of emerging technologies such as autonomous EVs, on consumer perceptions and adoption intentions. is to be investigated in order to understand the consumer behaviour. Cross regional comparative studies can be conducted across different regions within India to identify regional variations and develop region-specific strategies where required. Further studies should also investigate other potential barriers to Electric vehicle adoption, such as cultural influences, economic factors, and technological concerns.

REFERENCES

Ajzen, I. (1991). The theory of planned behavior. *Organizational Behavior and Human Decision Processes*, 50(2), 179–211. DOI: 10.1016/0749-5978(91)90020-T

Ajzen, I. (2010). Constructing a TPB questionnaire: Conceptual and methodological considerations. Retrieved from http://socgeo.ruhosting.nl/html/files/spatbeh/tpb.measurement.pdf

Ajzen, I. (2011). The theory of planned behaviour: Reactions and reflections. *Psychology & Health*, 26(9), 1113–1127. DOI: 10.1080/08870446.2011.613995 PMID: 21929476

Arora, M. (2023). Encapsulating Role of Persuasion and Skill Development in Marketing Communication for Brand Building: A Perspective. In *International Handbook of Skill, Education, Learning, and Research Development in Tourism and Hospitality* (pp. 1–17). Springer Nature Singapore.

Arora, M. (2024). Virtual Reality in Education: Analyzing the Literature and Bibliometric State of Knowledge. *Transforming Education with Virtual Reality*, 379-402. DOI: 10.1002/9781394200498.ch22

Arora, M., & Sharma, R. L. (2023). Artificial intelligence and big data: Ontological and communicative perspectives in multi-sectoral scenarios of modern businesses. *Foresight*, 25(1), 126–143. DOI: 10.1108/FS-10-2021-0216

Axsen, J., & Kurani, K. S. (2013). Developing sustainability-oriented values: Insights from households in a trial of plug-in hybrid electric vehicles. *Global Environmental Change*, 23(1), 70–80. DOI: 10.1016/j.gloenvcha.2012.08.002

Barth, M., Jugert, P., & Fritsche, I. (2016). Still underdetected – Social norms and collective efficacy predict the acceptance of electric vehicles in Germany. *Transportation Research Part F: Traffic Psychology and Behaviour*, 37, 64–77. DOI: 10.1016/j.trf.2015.11.011

Bühler, F., Cocron, P., Neumann, I., Franke, T., & Krems, J. F. (2014). Is EV experience related to EV acceptance? Results from a German field study. *Transportation Research Part F: Traffic Psychology and Behaviour*, 25, 34–49. DOI: 10.1016/j.trf.2014.05.002

Carley, S., Krause, R. M., Lane, B. W., & Graham, J. D. (2013). Intent to purchase a plug-in electric vehicle: A survey of early impressions in large US cities. *Transportation Research Part D, Transport and Environment*, 18, 39–45. DOI: 10.1016/j.trd.2012.09.007

Cocron, P., Franke, T., Neumann, I., Wege, C., Bühler, F., & Krems, J. F. (2010). Ist das Fahren mit einem Elektrofahrzeug so besonders? Anpassung des Verhaltens beim Fahren mit Elektrofahrzeugen. Paper presented at the 52th Tagung experimentell arbeitender Psychologen, Saarbrücken, Germany.

Diamond, D. (2009). The impact of government incentives for hybrid-electric vehicles: Evidence from US states. *Energy Policy*, 37(3), 972–983. DOI: 10.1016/j.enpol.2008.09.094

Du, G., Cao, W., Hu, S., Lin, Z., & Yuan, T. (2018). Design and assessment of an electric vehicle powertrain model based on real-world driving and charging cycles. *IEEE Transactions on Vehicular Technology*, 68(2), 1178–1187. DOI: 10.1109/TVT.2018.2884812

Egbue, O., & Long, S. (2012). Barriers to widespread adoption of electric vehicles: An analysis of consumer attitudes and perceptions. *Energy Policy*, 48, 717–729. DOI: 10.1016/j.enpol.2012.06.009

Ellingsen, L. A.-W., Singh, B., & Strømman, A. H. (2016). The size and range effect: Lifecycle greenhouse gas emissions of electric vehicles. *Environmental Research Letters*, 11(5), 054010. DOI: 10.1088/1748-9326/11/5/054010

European Commission. (2020). *Sustainable and Smart Mobility Strategy – putting European transport on track for the future*. Retrieved from https://ec.europa.eu/transport/themes/mobilitystrategy_en

Graham-Rowe, E., Gardner, B., Abraham, C., Skippon, S., Dittmar, H., Hutchins, R., & Stannard, J. (2012). Mainstream consumers driving plug-in battery-electric and plug-in hybrid electric cars: A qualitative analysis of responses and evaluations. *Transportation Research Part A, Policy and Practice*, 46(1), 140–153. DOI: 10.1016/j.tra.2011.09.008

Guttikunda, S. K., & Mohan, D. (2014). Re-fueling road transport for better air quality in India. *Energy Policy*, 68, 556–561. DOI: 10.1016/j.enpol.2013.12.067

IEA. (2024). Global EV Outlook 2024. IEA, Paris. https://www.iea.org/reports/global-ev[REMOVED HYPERLINK FIELD]outlook-2024

International Energy Agency (IEA). (2020). *Global EV Outlook 2020*. Retrieved from https://www.iea.org/reports/global-ev-outlook-2020

International Energy Agency (IEA). (2021). *India Energy Outlook 2021*. Retrieved from https://www.iea.org/reports/india-energy-outlook-2021

Kolb, D. A. (1984). *Experiential Learning: Experience as the Source of Learning and Development*. Prentice-Hall.

Krause, R. M., Carley, S. R., Lane, B. W., & Graham, J. D. (2013). Perception and reality: Public knowledge of plug-in electric vehicles in 21 U.S. cities. *Energy Policy*, 63, 433–440. DOI: 10.1016/j.enpol.2013.09.018

Kumar, J., Arora, M., & Erkol Bayram, G. (Eds.). (2024a). *Exploring the Use of Metaverse in Business and Education*. IGI Global. DOI: DOI: 10.4018/979-8-3693-5868-9

Kumar, J., Arora, M., & Erkol Bayram, G. (Eds.). (2024b). *Research, Innovation, and Industry Impacts of the Metaverse*. IGI Global.

Lane, B., & Potter, S. (2007). The adoption of cleaner vehicles in the UK: Exploring the consumer attitude-action gap. *Journal of Cleaner Production*, 15(11-12), 1085–1092. DOI: 10.1016/j.jclepro.2006.05.026

Li, S., Tong, L., Xing, J., & Zhou, Y. (2017). The market for electric vehicles: Indirect network effects and policy design. *Journal of the Association of Environmental and Resource Economists*, 4(1), 89–133. DOI: 10.1086/689702

Li, W., Long, R., Chen, H., & Geng, J. (2017). A review of factors influencing consumer intentions to adopt battery electric vehicles. *Renewable & Sustainable Energy Reviews*, 78, 318–328. DOI: 10.1016/j.rser.2017.04.076

Liao, F., Molin, E., & van Wee, B. (2017). Consumer preferences for electric vehicles: A literature review. *Transport Reviews*, 37(3), 252–275. DOI: 10.1080/01441647.2016.1230794

Ministry of Road Transport and Highways. (2020). *Basic Road Statistics of India 2018-19*. Retrieved from https://morth.nic.in/sites/default/files/Basic_Road_Statistics_of_India.pdf

Morris, M. G., & Venkatesh, V. (2000). Age differences in technology adoption decisions: Implications for a changing workforce. *Personnel Psychology*, 53(2), 375–403. DOI: 10.1111/j.1744-6570.2000.tb00206.x

Morton, C., Anable, J., & Nelson, J. D. (2016). Exploring consumer preferences towards electric vehicles: The influence of driving range and experience. *Transportation Research Part C, Emerging Technologies*, 69, 257–275.

Neumann, I., Cocron, P., Franke, T., & Krems, J. F. (2010). Electric vehicles as a solution for green driving in the future? A field study examining the user acceptance of electric vehicles. In *Proceedings of the European conference on human interface design for intelligent transport systems*, Berlin, Germany (pp. 445-453).

Nykvist, B., & Nilsson, M. (2015). Rapidly falling costs of battery packs for electric vehicles. *Nature Climate Change*, 5(4), 329–332. DOI: 10.1038/nclimate2564

Peters, A., & Dütschke, E. (2014). How do consumers perceive electric vehicles? A comparison of German consumer groups. *Journal of Environmental Policy and Planning*, 16(3), 359–377. DOI: 10.1080/1523908X.2013.879037

Plötz, P., Schneider, U., Globisch, J., & Dütschke, E. (2014). Who will buy electric vehicles? Identifying early adopters in Germany. *Transportation Research Part A, Policy and Practice*, 67, 96–109. DOI: 10.1016/j.tra.2014.06.006

Rezvani, Z., Jansson, J., & Bodin, J. (2015). Advances in consumer electric vehicle adoption research: A review and research agenda. *Transportation Research Part D, Transport and Environment*, 34, 122–136. DOI: 10.1016/j.trd.2014.10.010

Rogers, E. M. (2003). *Diffusion of Innovations* (5th ed.). Free Press.

Schuitema, G., Anable, J., Skippon, S., & Kinnear, N. (2013). The role of instrumental, hedonic and symbolic attributes in the intention to adopt electric vehicles. *Transportation Research Part A, Policy and Practice*, 48, 39–49. DOI: 10.1016/j.tra.2012.10.004

Sharma, S. (2020). Electric vehicle market in India: Challenges and opportunities. *Journal of Management Research and Analysis*, 7(1), 1–5.

Sierzchula, W., Bakker, S., Maat, K., & van Wee, B. (2014). The influence of financial incentives and other socio-economic factors on electric vehicle adoption. *Energy Policy*, 68, 183–194. DOI: 10.1016/j.enpol.2014.01.043

Sims, R., Schaeffer, R., Creutzig, F., Nunez, X. C., D'Agosto, M., Dimitriu, D., & Tiwari, G. (2014). Transport. In Contribution of working group III to the Fifth Assessment Report of the Intergovernmental Panel on Climate Change.

Skippon, S., & Garwood, M. (2011). Responses to battery electric vehicles: UK consumer attitudes and attributions of symbolic meaning following direct experience to reduce psychological distance. *Transportation Research Part D, Transport and Environment*, 16(7), 525–531. DOI: 10.1016/j.trd.2011.05.005

Sovacool, B. K., Kester, J., Noel, L., & de Rubens, G. Z. (2018). The demographics of decarbonizing transport: The influence of gender, age, and household size on electric mobility preferences in the Nordic region. *Global Environmental Change*, 52, 86–100. DOI: 10.1016/j.gloenvcha.2018.06.008

Steg, L. (2005). Car use: Lust and must. Instrumental, symbolic and affective motives for car use. *Transportation Research Part A, Policy and Practice*, 39(2-3), 147–162. DOI: 10.1016/j.tra.2004.07.001

U.S. Department of Energy. (2021). *Federal Tax Credits for New All-Electric and Plug-in Hybrid Vehicles*. Retrieved from https://www.fueleconomy.gov/feg/taxevb.shtml

Utami, M. W. D., Yuniaristanto, Y., & Sutopo, W. (2020). Adoption intention model of electric vehicle in Indonesia. *Jurnal Optimasi Sistem Industri*, 19(1), 70–81. DOI: 10.25077/josi.v19.n1.p70-81.2020

Van der Laan, J. D., Heino, A., & De Waard, D. (1997). A simple procedure for the assessment of acceptance of advanced transport telematics. *Transportation Research Part C, Emerging Technologies*, 5(1), 1–10. DOI: 10.1016/S0968-090X(96)00025-3

Venkatesh, V., & Bala, H. (2008). Technology Acceptance Model 3 and a research agenda on interventions. *Decision Sciences*, 39(2), 273–315. DOI: 10.1111/j.1540-5915.2008.00192.x

Venkatesh, V., & Morris, M. G. (2000). Why don't men ever stop to ask for directions? Gender, social influence, and their role in technology acceptance and usage behavior. *Management Information Systems Quarterly*, 24(1), 115–139. DOI: 10.2307/3250981

Wang, N., Pan, H., & Zheng, W. (2017). Assessment of the incentives on electric vehicle promotion in China. *Transportation Research Part A, Policy and Practice*, 101, 177–189. DOI: 10.1016/j.tra.2017.04.037

Zhang, X., Wang, K., Hao, Y., Fan, J. L., & Wei, Y. M. (2013). The impact of government policy on preference for NEVs: The evidence from China. *Energy Policy*, 61, 382–393. DOI: 10.1016/j.enpol.2013.06.114

Ziefle, M., Beul-Leusmann, S., Kasugai, K., & Schwalm, M. (2014). Public perception and acceptance of electric vehicles: Exploring users' perceived benefits and drawbacks. *Design, User Experience, and Usability. User Experience Design for Everyday Life Applications and Services: Third International Conference, DUXU 2014, Held as Part of HCI International 2014, Heraklion, Crete, Greece, June 22-27, 2014 Proceedings*, 3(Part III), 628–639.

Chapter 15
Sensory Neuro-Marketing in Sales:
Crafting Irresistible Dining Experiences

Lathisha Jayangi Ramanayaka
Sri Lanka Institute of Tourism and Hotel Management, Sri Lanka

ABSTRACT

Recent developments in marketing and psychology underscore the vital role of sensory experiences in shaping judgment and decision-making. Sensory marketing, an emerging field, examines how sensory perceptions influence consumer behaviours, challenging traditional cognitive models by linking mental processes to sensory experiences. This chapter outlines the foundational premises of the information processing paradigm and addresses challenges posed by embodiment, grounded cognition, and sensory marketing research. It explores bodily sensations as information sources, context-sensitive perception, imagery, simulation, and metaphors in consumer behaviour. From a managerial viewpoint, sensory marketing crafts subconscious cues that influence perceptions of a product's qualities, such as sophistication and quality. In a market saturated with direct appeals, sensory-based triggers can more effectively engage consumers, prompting them to generate favourable brand attributes autonomously. This chapter highlights gaps in sensory perception research, noting that the need for further a study.

1. INTRODUCTION

In the ever-shifting terrain of marketing, businesses embark on an unending quest to decode the mysteries of consumer preferences and desires. This relentless journey seeks to weave a harmonious tapestry, where the needs and aspirations of consumers seamlessly intertwine with the strategic threads of marketing campaigns. By aligning these elements, companies can carve out a distinct competitive edge, achieving unparalleled success in the realm of consumer satisfaction.

At the heart of this endeavour lies the concept of consumer perception, akin to a prism through which individuals interpret and assign meaning to the myriad facets of a product. This perception is sculpted by the quintet of senses—sight, sound, taste, touch, and smell. These sensory receptors are the silent maestros orchestrating how consumers experience and evaluate products. Understanding the symphony of sensory stimuli is essential for crafting marketing strategies that strike a chord with target audiences.

Sensory marketing is the alchemy of the marketing world, delving into the intricate processes by which sensory stimuli are perceived, interpreted, and acted upon by consumers. It charts the odyssey from the initial brush with sensory inputs to the consumer's ensuing interpretation, understanding, and engagement with these stimuli. This journey involves a profound comprehension of the psychological and emotional symphonies that sensory experiences evoke (Bhardwaj, Kaushik, & Arora (2024); Taneja, Shukla & Arora (2024); Malik, Malhan & Arora (2024). (Eds.). (2024)).

The pearls of wisdom gleaned from sensory marketing research form the bedrock for sculpting tailored marketing strategies, innovative product designs, and compelling brand narratives. By harnessing the magic of sensory experiences, marketers can illuminate consumer awareness and sway behaviour in ways that traditional methods might fail to achieve. The enchantment of sensory marketing lies in its power to guide decision-making processes and, in turn, influence the spending habits of consumers through meticulously curated sensory stimuli.

The visual elements of a restaurant, including its décor, lighting, and food presentation, are the brushstrokes of an inviting masterpiece that shapes the dining experience. These visual aesthetics craft an enchanting atmosphere that draws customers in and heightens their perception of the restaurant. The colour schemes, layout, and design of the dining area act as a silent orchestra, evoking emotions and setting the stage for a memorable encounter.

The presentation of food is the crescendo of this visual symphony. The artful plating and garnishing of dishes transform them into edible works of art, making them more enticing and enjoyable. Every meticulous detail in food presentation enhances the dining experience, creating a sense of artistry and craftsmanship that resonates deeply with consumers.

Sound is the invisible conductor in the dining orchestra. The background music, the hum of conversation, and the sizzle of cooking create an auditory landscape that shapes the ambiance of a restaurant. Carefully chosen music sets the desired mood, whether it's a lively and energetic atmosphere or a calm and relaxing haven. The auditory experience also influences customers' perceptions of service quality and the pace of their meal. Upbeat music may encourage faster dining, while softer, more melodic tunes invite a leisurely experience.

By understanding the impact of sound on consumer behaviour, restaurants can orchestrate an auditory environment that harmonizes with their brand and elevates customer satisfaction.

Aromas play a powerful role in the dining experience, with the sense of smell being closely linked to taste and memory. The enticing smell of freshly prepared food can stimulate appetite and create a sense of anticipation and pleasure. Restaurants can use olfactory marketing to their advantage by ensuring that the aromas of their dishes are inviting and appetizing. The strategic use of scents can also create a signature experience for a restaurant, making it memorable and distinctive. By focusing on the olfactory experience, restaurants can enhance the overall sensory appeal of their offerings and create a lasting impression on customers.

The sense of touch, or tactile experience, is often overlooked in sensory marketing but is equally important. The textures of the food, the feel of the utensils, and the comfort of the seating all contribute to the tactile experience of dining. The way food feels in the mouth, whether it's crispy, smooth, or tender, can significantly affects the overall enjoyment of a meal. Restaurants can enhance the tactile experience by paying attention to the quality and feel of their tableware, furniture, and other physical elements. Providing a comfortable and enjoyable tactile environment can enhance customer satisfaction and create a more immersive dining experience.

Taste is the most direct and impactful sense in the dining experience. The flavours of the food and beverages are central to the restaurant's appeal and can make or break the dining experience. Gustatory sensory marketing focuses on creating delicious and memorable flavours that leave a lasting impression on customers. Restaurants can use taste to differentiate themselves from competitors by offering unique and high-quality dishes that cater to the preferences of their target audience. By continuously innovating and refining their menu offerings, restaurants can keep customers coming back for more.

This study focuses on the application of sensory marketing within the Sri Lankan restaurant industry. Sri Lanka, with its rich culinary heritage and diverse food culture, provides a unique and vibrant setting for exploring sensory marketing practices. Sri Lankan restaurants often leverage the country's rich tradition of spices, flavours, and culinary techniques to create distinctive and memorable dining experiences. The research aims to investigate how these sensory elements are used to influence consumer behaviour and achieve business success. By examining the sensory marketing strategies employed by Sri Lankan restaurants, the study seeks to provide insights into the effectiveness of these approaches in enhancing customer satisfaction and loyalty.

One of the key areas where sensory marketing has shown potential is in shaping consumer perception. Sensory stimuli can alter how consumers perceive the quality of a product or service. For example, a well-designed store layout with appealing visual merchandising can enhance the perceived value of products, while ambient scents can make an environment feel more inviting and enjoyable. These sensory cues not only affect initial perceptions but also influence overall satisfaction with the brand.

Despite these insights, there is a lack of comprehensive research that systematically examines the interplay between different sensory elements and their collective impact on consumer perception. Most studies tend to isolate individual senses, thereby missing the synergistic effects that a multi-sensory approach can produce. This gap in the literature calls for a more integrated research framework that considers the combined influence of various sensory stimuli on consumer behaviour.

Beyond initial perceptions and satisfaction, sensory marketing has implications for long-term consumer retention and loyalty. Brands that effectively engage multiple senses can create more memorable experiences, leading to stronger emotional bonds with consumers. These emotional connections are crucial for fostering loyalty and encouraging repeat purchases. However, the mechanisms through which sensory marketing contributes to long-term consumer loyalty remain poorly understood.

Current research predominantly focuses on short-term effects and immediate responses to sensory stimuli. There is a need for longitudinal studies that track the impact of sensory marketing over time, exploring how sustained sensory engagement influences consumer loyalty and retention. Such studies would provide valuable insights into the enduring effects of sensory experiences and help marketers develop strategies that nurture long-term relationships with their customers.

Given the underdeveloped theoretical foundation and the fragmented nature of existing research, there is a pressing need for further investigation into sensory marketing. A more robust theoretical framework would provide a deeper understanding of how sensory elements interact and influence consumer behaviour. This framework should integrate findings from various sensory modalities, examining their combined effects on perception, satisfaction, and retention.

Additionally, further research should explore the contextual factors that modulate the effectiveness of sensory marketing. For example, cultural differences, individual preferences, and situational contexts can all influence how sensory stimuli are perceived and processed. Understanding these contextual factors would enable marketers to tailor their sensory strategies to different consumer segments and environments, enhancing their overall effectiveness.

One of the most critical aspects of sensory marketing that requires further exploration is its impact on perceived quality. Perceived quality is a key determinant of consumer satisfaction and loyalty, and sensory marketing has the potential to significantly enhance it. For instance, the tactile sensation of holding a well-crafted product can convey a sense of quality and craftsmanship, while pleasant scents can create a perception of cleanliness and freshness.

However, the relationship between sensory stimuli and perceived quality is complex and multifaceted. Different sensory cues may interact in unexpected ways, and their impact on perceived quality can vary depending on the context and the individual consumer. To develop a comprehensive understanding of this relationship, further research should employ experimental designs that manipulate multiple sensory variables and measure their effects on perceived quality.

Such studies would provide valuable insights into the mechanisms through which sensory marketing influences consumer perceptions and help marketers design strategies that enhance perceived quality effectively.

While sensory marketing holds significant promise for enhancing consumer perception, satisfaction, and retention, its theoretical foundation remains underdeveloped and vaguely defined. The fragmented nature of existing research and the lack of a cohesive theoretical model hinder our understanding of how sensory elements interact and influence consumer behaviour. To fully leverage the potential of sensory marketing, further research is needed to elucidate its underlying mechanisms and implications, particularly concerning its impact on perceived quality. By addressing these gaps, we can develop more effective sensory marketing strategies that create memorable experiences, foster consumer loyalty, and drive business success.

This research study aims to provide a comprehensive exploration of sensory marketing as employed by the restaurant industry. By examining the application of sensory marketing strategies in Sri Lankan restaurants, this study seeks to uncover the interplay among various sensory elements and their impact on consumer perception, satisfaction, and retention. The significance of this research lies in its potential to contribute to the theoretical foundation of sensory marketing and provide practical insights for enhancing the dining experience. By addressing the gaps in current knowledge and understanding, this research can help marketers and restaurant owners develop more effective strategies that leverage the power of sensory experiences to achieve success in a competitive market.

2. STATEMENT OF PROBLEM

Despite the increasing interest and recognition of sensory marketing's importance within brand management and marketing disciplines, and its potential to significantly affect consumer perception, satisfaction, and retention, the theoretical foundation of sensory marketing remains underdeveloped and vaguely defined. This gap in theoretical support and understanding necessitates further research to elucidate the concept of sensory marketing and its implications, particularly concerning its impact on perceived quality.

Sensory marketing has garnered considerable attention in recent years as companies strive to create immersive and memorable experiences for their consumers. The ability to engage multiple senses simultaneously can create a more profound and lasting impact, influencing consumer perception, satisfaction, and ultimately, retention. However, despite this recognition and the increasing investment in sensory marketing strategies, the academic and theoretical frameworks supporting this field are still in their nascent stages. This underdevelopment presents a significant barrier to fully understanding and leveraging sensory marketing's potential.

The primary issue lies in the fragmented and sporadic nature of existing research on sensory marketing. While numerous studies highlight the effectiveness of individual sensory stimuli—such as visual appeal, auditory cues, olfactory triggers, and tactile sensations—the integration of these findings into a cohesive theoretical model is lacking.

This fragmentation leads to a disjointed understanding of how different sensory elements interact and influence consumer behaviour holistically.

Sensory marketing weaves a rich tapestry of strategies that captivate the senses of sight, sound, smell, taste, and touch to elevate the consumer experience. This symphony of sensations is believed to forge deeper emotional bonds and create more vivid memories, thus boosting brand loyalty and customer retention. Imagine the irresistible aroma of freshly baked bread in a bakery, the calming melodies in a spa, or the eye-catching design of a product package—each of these sensory delights shapes how consumers perceive and connect with a brand. Grasping the power of these sensory cues is essential for crafting marketing strategies that set a brand apart in a bustling marketplace.

3. RESEARCH OBJECTIVES

I. To investigate the influence of sensory marketing tools on consumer purchasing behaviour

The primary objective of this research is to delve into how sensory marketing tools impact consumer purchasing behaviour. This involves exploring the psychological and emotional responses elicited by various sensory stimuli and how these responses influence decision-making processes. The study will examine the role of sensory cues such as visual aesthetics, auditory elements, olfactory stimuli, tactile sensations, and gustatory experiences in shaping consumer preferences and driving purchase decisions. By understanding the specific ways in which sensory marketing can alter perceptions and behaviours, businesses can tailor their strategies to enhance customer engagement and boost sales. The investigation will include quantitative and qualitative analyses, surveys, and experiments to gather comprehensive data on consumer reactions to different sensory inputs in a restaurant setting.

a. Background and Context:

Consumer purchasing behaviour is a complex process influenced by a myriad of factors, including personal preferences, cultural norms, and psychological triggers. Sensory marketing taps into the subconscious mind by appealing directly to the senses, thereby creating a more profound and often emotional connection with the consumer.

b. Research Approach:

Quantitative Analysis: Conduct surveys and experiments to measure consumer responses to different sensory stimuli in a controlled environment. This could involve blind taste tests, visual appeal assessments, and auditory influence studies.

Qualitative Analysis: Gather insights through focus groups and in-depth interviews to understand the emotional and psychological impacts of sensory marketing tools on consumers.

Behavioural Observations:
Observe consumer behaviour in naturalistic settings, such as in restaurants or retail stores, to see how sensory cues influence purchasing decisions in real-time.

c. Expected Outcomes:
Behavioural Insights:

A comprehensive understanding of how sensory stimuli affect consumer decision-making processes and purchasing behaviour.

Strategic Recommendations: Practical guidelines for businesses on how to incorporate sensory marketing tools to enhance consumer engagement and drive sales.

II. To identify the key components of sensory marketing

The second objective is to identify and categorize the essential components of sensory marketing. This involves a thorough review of existing literature and industry practices to pinpoint the most influential sensory elements that contribute to effective marketing strategies. The study will focus on the five primary senses: sight, sound, smell, taste, and touch, and will analyze how each sense individually and collectively impacts consumer experiences. By identifying these key components, the research aims to create a framework that businesses can use to develop sensory marketing strategies. This framework will highlight the importance of integrating multiple sensory cues to create a cohesive and compelling brand experience. Additionally, the study will explore emerging trends and innovative practices in sensory marketing to provide a forward-looking perspective on the field.

Background and Context: Sensory marketing is a multifaceted field that requires a nuanced understanding of how different sensory inputs work together to influence consumer behavior. Identifying the key components is crucial for developing effective marketing strategies.

a. Research Approach:
>
> Literature Review: Conduct an extensive review of existing research and case studies to identify the primary sensory elements used in successful marketing campaigns.
>
> Industry Analysis: Examine current practices and innovations in the field of sensory marketing, focusing on leading brands and their sensory strategies.
>
> Component Analysis: Break down the sensory marketing strategies into their core components, such as visual aesthetics, auditory cues, olfactory triggers, tactile sensations, and gustatory experiences.

b. Expected Outcomes:
>
> Component Framework: A detailed framework outlining the key components of sensory marketing and their individual and combined effects on consumer perception and behaviour.
>
> Best Practices: Identification of best practices and successful implementations of sensory marketing strategies across various industries.
>
> III. To explore the effective implementation of sensory marketing tools within the restaurant industry

The third objective is to explore how sensory marketing tools can be effectively implemented within the restaurant industry. This involves investigating practical applications of sensory marketing strategies in real-world restaurant settings. The study will examine successful case studies and best practices from leading restaurants that have effectively utilized sensory marketing to enhance the dining experience. Key areas of focus will include the design and ambiance of the restaurant, the presentation and flavour of food, background music, and the overall sensory environment. By understanding how these elements are combined to create a memorable dining experience, the research aims to provide actionable insights for restaurant owners and marketers. The objective is to develop guidelines and recommendations that can help restaurants implement sensory marketing strategies that not only attract customers but also foster long-term loyalty.

a. Background and Context:

The restaurant industry is inherently sensory-driven, making it an ideal context for studying the implementation of sensory marketing tools. Effective sensory marketing can significantly enhance the dining experience and drive customer satisfaction and loyalty.

b. Research Approach:
    Case Studies:

Analyze successful implementations of sensory marketing in leading restaurants to identify key strategies and tactics.

    Field Studies:

Conduct field studies in a variety of restaurant settings to observe how sensory marketing tools are used and their impact on the customer experience.

    Experimental Design:

Design experiments to test the effectiveness of different sensory marketing tools in real-world restaurant environments.

IV. To examine the utilization of sensory marketing tools as a strategy for designing communication.

The fourth objective is to examine how sensory marketing tools can be used as a strategy for designing communication. This involves exploring the role of sensory cues in creating effective marketing messages and brand communication. The study will analyze how sensory elements can enhance advertising, branding, and promotional efforts by creating more engaging and memorable experiences for consumers. This includes examining the use of sensory marketing in various communication channels, such as digital media, print advertising, and in-store promotions. The research will also explore how sensory marketing can be integrated into overall marketing strategies to create a consistent and cohesive brand image. By understanding the impact of sensory cues on communication effectiveness, the study aims to provide marketers with tools and techniques to design more impactful and persuasive marketing campaigns. The objective is to highlight the potential of sensory marketing as a powerful tool for creating emotional connections and driving consumer engagement.

a. Background and Context:

Effective communication is key to successful marketing, and sensory marketing offers unique opportunities to enhance communication strategies. By appealing to the senses, marketers can create more engaging and memorable messages.

b. Research Approach:
   Content Analysis:

Analyze marketing campaigns that have successfully integrated sensory marketing tools to identify key strategies and techniques.

   Consumer Research:

Conduct research to understand how consumers respond to sensory cues in marketing messages and how these cues influence their perception and behaviour.

   Experimental Design:

Design and test marketing messages that incorporate sensory elements to measure their effectiveness in creating engagement and driving consumer action.

d. Expected Outcomes:
   Communication Strategies:

Development of effective communication strategies that leverage sensory marketing tools to create more impactful and engaging marketing messages.

Marketing Campaigns:

Practical insights into how sensory marketing can be integrated into marketing campaigns to enhance their effectiveness and reach.

4. RESEARCH QUESTIONS

I. How do sensory marketing tools affect consumer purchasing behaviour?
II. What are the key components of sensory marketing?
III. In what ways are sensory marketing tools effectively implemented within the restaurant industry?
IV. How are sensory marketing tools utilized as a strategy for designing communication?

5. SIGNIFICANCE OF RESEARCH

This research study endeavours to elucidate the intricacies and methodologies associated with sensory marketing as employed by the restaurant industry. By doing so, it aims to delineate a pattern, thereby uncovering the interplay among various elements that serve as instrumental tools in sensory marketing. Furthermore, this research will be dedicated to exploring the application of sensory marketing strategies by Sri Lankan restaurants as a means to attain success.

The significance of this research lies in its comprehensive exploration of how sensory experiences influence consumer judgment and decision-making within the restaurant industry. This study illuminates the burgeoning field of sensory marketing, which delves into the pivotal role of the senses in shaping consumer behaviour, and contrasts it against traditional psychological models of information processing, highlighting the limitations of these models in explaining how sensory experiences guide mental activity.

This research study aims to elucidate the complexities and methodologies associated with sensory marketing as employed by the restaurant industry. By undertaking this exploration, the study seeks to delineate a pattern, thereby uncovering the interplay among various elements that serve as instrumental tools in sensory marketing. Furthermore, this research will focus on examining the application of sensory marketing strategies by Sri Lankan restaurants as a means to attain success. The significance of this research lies in its comprehensive investigation of how sensory experiences influence consumer judgment and decision-making within the restaurant industry.

Sensory marketing encompasses a variety of strategies designed to engage the five human senses—sight, sound, smell, taste, and touch—to enhance the consumer experience. This multi-sensory approach aims to create stronger emotional connections and more vivid memories, thereby increasing brand loyalty and customer retention. For instance, the aroma of freshly baked bread in a bakery, the soothing background music in a spa, or the visually appealing design of a product package all contribute to how consumers perceive and relate to a brand. Understanding these sensory influences is crucial for developing effective marketing strategies that can differentiate a brand in a competitive market.

This research study undertakes a comprehensive examination of the intricate methodologies associated with sensory marketing within the restaurant industry. By exploring these complexities, the study aims to uncover the patterns and interplay among various elements that serve as instrumental tools in sensory marketing. Additionally, the research will specifically focus on the application of sensory marketing strategies by Sri Lankan restaurants to achieve success.

The significance of this research lies in its in-depth exploration of how sensory experiences influence consumer judgment and decision-making within the restaurant industry. Sensory marketing encompasses a variety of strategies designed to engage the five human senses—sight, sound, smell, taste, and touch—to enhance the consumer experience. This multi-sensory approach aims to create stronger emotional connections and more vivid memories, thereby increasing brand loyalty and customer retention. For example, the aroma of freshly baked bread in a bakery, the soothing background music in a spa, or the visually appealing design of a product package all contribute to how consumers perceive and relate to a brand. Understanding these sensory influences is crucial for developing effective marketing strategies that can differentiate a brand in a competitive market.

The concept of sensory marketing is not new; it has evolved significantly over time. Historically, marketing strategies focused primarily on visual and auditory stimuli, leveraging advertisements and jingles to attract consumer attention. However, as market competition intensified and consumer behaviour became more complex, businesses began to recognize the untapped potential of engaging all five senses. This shift marked the beginning of a more holistic approach to marketing, one that acknowledges the profound impact of sensory experiences on consumer behaviour.

The psychological foundations of sensory marketing are rooted in the understanding that human perception is a multi-sensory process. Traditional psychological models of information processing often fall short in explaining how sensory experiences guide mental activity.

Sensory marketing, however, delves into the pivotal role of the senses in shaping consumer behaviour, offering a more nuanced perspective. It explores how sensory inputs are processed by the brain and how they influence emotions, memories, and ultimately, consumer decisions.

The five senses in marketing are as follows;

> Sight: Visual elements such as colour, brightness, and design significantly influence consumer perceptions. The visual appeal of a restaurant's décor, the plating of food, and the overall ambiance can attract customers and enhance their dining experience.
> Sound: Auditory stimuli, including background music and ambient sounds, play a critical role in setting the mood. The right music can create a relaxing atmosphere, while upbeat tunes can energize the environment.
> Smell: Olfactory cues are powerful triggers of emotion and memory. The scent of food can evoke strong cravings and positive associations, making it a crucial element in sensory marketing.
> Taste: Gustatory experiences are central to the restaurant industry. The flavours of food and beverages are pivotal in creating a memorable dining experience and fostering customer loyalty.
> Touch: Tactile elements such as the texture of food, the feel of tableware, and the comfort of seating contribute to the overall sensory experience. These tactile sensations can significantly enhance or detract from a customer's enjoyment.

Sensory marketing taps into both emotional and cognitive responses. Emotionally, sensory stimuli can evoke feelings of pleasure, comfort, excitement, or nostalgia. Cognitively, these stimuli can enhance recall and recognition, making a brand more memorable. For instance, a well-designed restaurant interior with pleasant aromas and soothing music can create a warm and welcoming atmosphere, encouraging repeat visits and positive word-of-mouth.

The influence of sensory marketing on decision-making processes is profound. Sensory cues can subconsciously affect a consumer's choice, often leading them to prefer one brand over another without explicit awareness of the reasons. This is particularly evident in the restaurant industry, where the sensory environment can significantly influence dining choices and overall satisfaction. Sensory marketing taps into both emotional and cognitive responses. Emotionally, sensory stimuli can evoke feelings of pleasure, comfort, excitement, or nostalgia. Cognitively, these stimuli can enhance recall and recognition, making a brand more memorable. For instance, a well-designed restaurant interior with pleasant aromas and soothing music can create a warm and welcoming atmosphere, encouraging repeat visits and positive word-of-mouth. The influence of sensory marketing on decision-making processes is profound. Sensory cues can subconsciously affect a consumer's choice, often leading them to prefer one brand over another without explicit awareness of the reasons. This is particularly evident in the restaurant industry, where the sensory environment can significantly influence dining choices and overall satisfaction.

Traditional psychological models of information processing often emphasize rational decision-making, overlooking the emotional and sensory dimensions of consumer behaviour. These models typically focus on how consumers process information logically, based on attributes like price and functionality. However, they fail to account for the powerful influence of sensory experiences that often drive impulsive and emotional purchases.

Sensory marketing offers an alternative framework that incorporates the emotional and sensory aspects of decision-making. By acknowledging that consumers are not purely rational actors, sensory marketing provides a more holistic understanding of consumer behaviour. This approach can explain why certain sensory experiences, such as the comforting smell of a favourite dish or the soothing sound of a restaurant's ambiance, can drive consumer preferences and loyalty.

To quantify the impact of sensory marketing, this research will employ various quantitative methods. Surveys and experiments will be designed to measure consumer responses to different sensory stimuli. For instance, experiments can test how changes in lighting or music affect consumer perceptions and behaviours in a restaurant setting. Statistical analysis will be used to interpret the data and identify significant patterns and correlations.

Qualitative methods will complement the quantitative analysis by providing deeper insights into consumer experiences and perceptions. Focus groups and in-depth interviews will be conducted to explore how sensory marketing influences emotions and memories. These qualitative approaches will help uncover the subjective and nuanced aspects of sensory experiences that quantitative methods may not fully capture.

The findings of this research will have practical implications for restaurant owners. By understanding the impact of sensory marketing, restaurant owners can create more engaging and enjoyable dining experiences. The research will provide actionable recommendations on how to optimize sensory elements, such as choosing the right music, enhancing food presentation, and creating a pleasant olfactory environment.

For marketers, the research will offer valuable insights into developing effective sensory marketing strategies. By leveraging sensory cues, marketers can create more compelling advertisements and promotional materials. The research will highlight the importance of a multi-sensory approach in creating strong emotional connections and increasing brand loyalty. While this research focuses on the restaurant industry, future studies could expand the scope to other sectors. For example, the principles of sensory marketing could be applied to retail, hospitality, and even healthcare. Understanding how sensory experiences influence consumer behaviour across different contexts can provide a broader perspective and further validate the findings.

Longitudinal studies could provide deeper insights into the long-term effects of sensory marketing. By tracking consumer behaviour and preferences over time, researchers can better understand how sensory experiences influence brand loyalty and customer retention. Longitudinal research can also help identify trends and changes in consumer responses to sensory marketing.

This research study aims to shed light on the intricacies and methodologies associated with sensory marketing in the restaurant industry. By exploring how sensory experiences influence consumer judgment and decision-making, the study will provide valuable insights for both practitioners and academics. The research will highlight the importance of a multi-sensory approach in creating strong emotional connections and enhancing consumer experiences. By focusing on the application of sensory marketing strategies by Sri Lankan restaurants, the study will offer practical recommendations for achieving success in a competitive market. This comprehensive investigation will contribute to the burgeoning field of sensory marketing and pave the way for future research and innovation.

6. LITERATURE REVIEW

The literature on sensory marketing underscores its significant influence on consumer purchasing behaviour and its pivotal role in shaping customer experiences. Sensory marketing strategies aim to engage the five senses—sight, sound, smell, taste, and touch—to create memorable and compelling brand experiences. This comprehensive literature review explores the evolution, theoretical underpinnings, and practical applications of sensory marketing, with a particular focus on its impact within the restaurant industry.

Sensory marketing has become a pivotal strategy in modern marketing, aimed at engaging consumers on a multi-sensory level to enhance their overall experience. This literature review delves into the theoretical and empirical foundations of sensory marketing, focusing on its effects on both customers and employees within retail environments. The insights provided by Skandrani (2011) and Bitner (1992) are central to this exploration, highlighting how sensory marketing tools, such as spatial arrangements, environmental elements, and stimuli like music and crowd dynamics, can significantly influence behaviour and reactions.

The concept of sensory marketing is rooted in the expansive fields of environmental psychology and consumer behaviour. Environmental psychology delves into the intricate dance between humans and their physical surroundings, highlighting how various environmental factors can shape emotions, behaviours, and perceptions. The stimulus-organism-response (SOR) model by Mehrabian and Russell (1974) serves as a cornerstone in this realm, suggesting that environmental stimuli (S) stir emotional states (O), which subsequently guide individual responses (R).

Sensory marketing tools can be likened to meticulously composed symphonies of spatial arrangements, designed to subtly sway the behaviours of both customers and employees. Skandrani (2011) illustrates how these arrangements include the physical layout of the store, the strategic placement of products, lighting, colour schemes, and other aesthetic elements that harmonize to create a captivating ambiance.

Bitner (1992) introduced the concept of the services cape, envisioning it as the physical stage upon which service interactions unfold. The services cape model identifies three key dimensions that shape consumer and employee behaviours: ambient conditions, spatial layout and functionality, and signs, symbols, and artefacts. These elements are not merely incidental; they are meticulously orchestrated by companies to create environments that elevate customer satisfaction and enhance employee performance.

Skandrani (2011) details how sensory tools can influence customer reactions through various environmental elements within a retail setting. These elements include ambient conditions such as lighting, music, and scent, as well as the overall aesthetic design of the space.

Environmental stimuli can evoke a range of emotional responses in customers, from excitement and pleasure to relaxation and calmness. Donovan and Rossiter (1982) found that pleasant ambient conditions can enhance mood and increase the likelihood of purchase behaviours. For instance, warm lighting and soothing music can create a welcoming and comfortable atmosphere, encouraging customers to spend more time in the store and explore products more thoroughly.

Sensory stimuli can also trigger physiological reactions, such as changes in heart rate, blood pressure, and galvanic skin response. Research by Knez (1995) demonstrated that different lighting conditions could affect physiological responses, with brighter lighting leading to increased alertness and energy levels, while dimmer lighting induced relaxation and calmness.

Cognitive reactions to sensory stimuli involve changes in perception, attitudes, and decision-making processes. According to Spence et al. (2014), multisensory environments can enhance cognitive engagement and memory retention. For example, pleasant scents can improve mood and cognitive function, leading to more positive evaluations of products and services.

The impact of sensory marketing extends beyond customer responses; it also affects employees within retail environments. Skandrani (2011) emphasizes that sensory stimuli can have both positive and negative effects on employees, influencing their job satisfaction, performance, and overall well-being.

Positive sensory environments can enhance employee morale, motivation, and productivity. Pleasant ambient conditions, such as appropriate lighting and music, can create a comfortable and enjoyable work environment. According to Bitner (1992), a well-designed services cape can lead to higher levels of job satisfaction and reduced stress among employees.

However, sensory stimuli can also have adverse effects on employees. Skandrani (2011) notes that excessive noise, overcrowding, and inappropriate ambient conditions can lead to stress and discomfort. For instance, loud music and high levels of crowd density in a retail setting can create a chaotic and stressful environment, negatively impacting employee performance and well-being.

The dual nature of sensory stimuli, as highlighted by Skandrani (2011), underscores the importance of carefully balancing sensory elements to optimize both customer and employee experiences. While certain stimuli, such as music and crowd dynamics, can enhance the shopping experience for customers, they may simultaneously create challenges for employees.

Music is a powerful sensory tool that can influence both customer and employee behaviours. Research by Milliman (1982) found that slow-tempo music could increase the time customers spend in a store and boost sales, while fast-tempo music could expedite shopping and increase turnover. However, Skandrani (2011) points out that the same music that creates a pleasant shopping environment for customers can lead to stress and fatigue for employees if played at high volumes or for extended periods.

Crowd dynamics also play a crucial role in shaping the sensory experience within retail environments. High levels of crowd density can create a sense of excitement and urgency for customers, encouraging them to make quicker purchasing decisions. However, for employees, working in crowded conditions can be physically and mentally taxing, leading to increased stress and burnout (Baker & Wakefield, 2012).

The practical applications of sensory marketing in retail settings involve the strategic use of sensory stimuli to enhance the overall shopping experience. This section explores various sensory marketing techniques and their impact on consumer behaviour and employee well-being.

Visual merchandising involves the strategic placement of products and the use of visual elements to attract and engage customers. Effective visual merchandising can create visually appealing displays that capture attention and encourage exploration.

Research by Kerfoot, Davies, and Ward (2003) suggests that well-designed visual displays can increase customer interest and sales.

Lighting is a critical component of visual merchandising, as it can influence mood, perception, and behaviour. According to Summers and Hebert (2001), appropriate lighting can enhance the aesthetic appeal of products and create a pleasant shopping environment. For example, warm lighting can create a cosy and inviting atmosphere, while bright lighting can highlight product details and create a sense of energy.

Scent marketing involves the use of pleasant fragrances to create a memorable and emotionally engaging shopping experience. Research by Spangenberg, Crowley, and Henderson (1996) found that ambient scents could enhance customers' perceptions of store environments and increase their time spent in the store. Additionally, pleasant scents can evoke positive memories and associations, leading to increased brand loyalty (Herz, 2007).

Sound marketing involves the strategic use of music and soundscapes to influence customer behaviour and create a desired atmosphere. As mentioned earlier, the tempo and genre of music can significantly impact the pace of shopping and customer satisfaction (North, Hargreaves, & McKendrick, 1999). Additionally, soundscapes that mimic natural environments, such as birdsong or flowing water, can create a calming and enjoyable shopping experience (Alvarsson, Wiens, & Nilsson, 2010).

Tactile marketing involves engaging the sense of touch to enhance the shopping experience. Allowing customers to touch and interact with products can increase their perceived value and likelihood of purchase. Peck and Childers (2003) found that tactile experiences could enhance product evaluations and create stronger emotional connections with customers.

The restaurant industry provides a unique context for the application of sensory marketing, as dining experiences inherently engage multiple senses. This section explores how sensory marketing techniques are used in restaurants to enhance the overall dining experience and influence customer behaviour.

Visual elements play a crucial role in shaping the dining experience. The interior design, lighting, and presentation of food all contribute to the overall ambiance and perception of quality.

The design and décor of a restaurant create the first impression for diners and set the tone for the dining experience. Research by Ryu and Jang (2007) suggests that aesthetically pleasing environments can enhance diners' perceptions of food quality and overall satisfaction. Additionally, thematic décor that reflects the restaurant's brand identity can create a unique and memorable dining experience.

The visual appeal of dishes is critical in influencing diners' perceptions of taste and quality. Artful plating and garnishing can elevate the dining experience and create a sense of artistry and craftsmanship. Wansink, van Ittersum, and Painter (2005) found that visually appealing food presentation could enhance taste perception and increase overall satisfaction.

Sound is another essential component of the dining experience. Background music and ambient sounds contribute to the overall atmosphere and can influence diners' moods and behaviours.

The choice of music can set the tone for the dining experience. Research by Wilson (2003) suggests that classical music can create a sophisticated and upscale ambiance, while jazz or contemporary music can evoke a relaxed and casual setting. The volume and tempo of music can also influence the pace of dining, with slower music encouraging longer dining times and higher spending (Milliman, 1986).

Managing ambient noise is crucial in creating a comfortable dining environment. Excessive noise can detract from the dining experience, while a quiet atmosphere can enhance it. Research by Guéguen and Jacob (2007) found that lower noise levels could increase customer satisfaction and encourage repeat visits. Smell is a powerful sensory cue in restaurants, directly influencing appetite and dining satisfaction.

The use of pleasant food aromas can enhance the dining experience by stimulating appetite and creating positive associations. Research by Mitchell, Kahn, and Knasko (1995) found that the presence of food-related scents could increase diners' perceptions of food quality and overall satisfaction.

7. METHODOLOGY

According to Fisher (2007), selecting a topic is a crucial phase in the crafting of a dissertation. This process involves a meticulous evaluation to ascertain the suitability and potential significance of topics that generate high interest, ensuring their relevance for future research endeavours. A rigorous examination and analysis of several potential topics within the marketing discipline will precede the topic's final submission. Through a comprehensive review of diverse literature, it becomes evident that sensory marketing represents a significant area within marketing, capable of exerting a profound impact on businesses, particularly within the restaurant segment of the service industry.

Therefore, the research will suggest that an investigation into the effects of sensory marketing processes promises to offer substantial benefits to the industry at large for future reference. The focus of this analysis will be on the restaurant sector within the service industry. This study will rely on insights regarding sensory marketing and consumer behaviour, utilizing collected literature as a framework to assess both primary and secondary research data. To guarantee the reliability and clarity of the data, literature sources will be carefully chosen from reputable outlets, including books, academic journals, scientific research papers, and validated websites. Given the relatively nascent state of this topic in the marketing field, the literature will be selected from authoritative sources to ensure it remains current and relevant.

In this study, primary data will be meticulously gathered to delve into the fundamental impact of sensory marketing on consumer physiology. This data will serve as a cornerstone for analysing and understanding how sensory inputs influence purchasing behaviours and decision-making processes. Moreover, both qualitative and quantitative methodologies will be employed in this investigation as critical tools to achieve the research's objectives. Conducting interviews will aim to extract detailed insights directly from restaurant managers, while the design of the questionnaire will be specifically tailored to capture consumer habits related to sensory experiences and their contextual predispositions.

8. DATA ANALYSIS

The research findings outlined in this document are meticulously structured to address both research and strategic inquiries, divided into three distinct sections, each crafted through varied methodologies. This multi-faceted approach ensures a comprehensive understanding of sensory neuro-marketing within the restaurant industry, offering valuable insights for both academic and practical applications.

The initial segment of this research focuses on the exploration of sensory marketing tactics employed within the restaurant industry. This section aims to uncover prevalent sensory marketing strategies and managers' expectations thereof. The methodology adopted for this segment involves qualitative research, specifically through interviews with restaurant managers and marketing professionals. These interviews are designed to gather in-depth insights into the sensory marketing techniques currently in use and the anticipated outcomes from these strategies.

The findings from this segment reveal that sensory marketing tactics are widely used across the restaurant industry, with a focus on creating a multi-sensory dining experience that enhances consumer satisfaction and loyalty. Key strategies identified include:

I. Visual Cues: The use of appealing interior design, lighting, and food presentation to create an inviting and memorable dining environment.
II. Auditory Cues: Background music and ambient sounds tailored to match the restaurant's theme and enhance the dining experience.
III. Olfactory Cues: The strategic use of scents, such as the aroma of freshly baked bread or brewed coffee, to stimulate appetite and create a pleasant atmosphere.
IV. Gustatory Cues: Offering unique and high-quality flavours that align with the restaurant's brand and appeal to customers' taste preferences.

V. Tactile Cues: The use of comfortable seating, quality tableware, and other tactile elements to enhance the overall dining experience.

The second segment of this research is dedicated to an examination of secondary data concerning the sensory marketing elements that drive consumer purchasing behaviours. This involves a comprehensive review of existing literature, articles, and psychological studies that explore the impact of sensory cues on consumer behaviour.

I. Literature Review: A systematic review of relevant literature is conducted, focusing on studies that investigate the effects of various sensory cues on consumer behaviour. This includes academic articles, industry reports, and case studies from reputable sources.
II. Secondary Data Analysis: Data from existing studies are analysed to identify key findings and trends related to sensory marketing. This involves synthesizing information from multiple sources to draw comprehensive conclusions about the impact of sensory marketing on consumer decision-making.
III. Prolonged Observation: To ensure accuracy and reliability, prolonged observation of sensory marketing practices in different restaurant settings is undertaken.

This involves visiting various restaurants and observing how sensory cues are implemented and their effects on consumer behaviour.

The findings from the literature review and secondary data analysis reveal that sensory marketing has a profound impact on consumer behaviour. Key insights include:

I. Emotional and Cognitive Responses: Sensory cues can evoke strong emotional and cognitive responses, influencing consumers' perceptions and decision-making processes. For example, pleasant scents can create positive associations with a restaurant, leading to increased customer satisfaction and loyalty.
II. Sensory Congruence: The effectiveness of sensory marketing is enhanced when the sensory cues are congruent with the restaurant's overall theme and brand image. Incongruent sensory cues can create confusion and negatively affect consumer perceptions.
III. Multi-Sensory Integration: Combining multiple sensory cues creates a more immersive and engaging dining experience, leading to stronger behavioural responses. For instance, the combination of appealing visuals, pleasant scents, and suitable background music can enhance the overall dining experience and encourage repeat visits.
IV. Psychological Mechanisms: Psychological studies highlight the underlying mechanisms through which sensory cues influence consumer behaviour. These include classical conditioning, where repeated exposure to positive sensory cues

creates lasting associations, and the peak-end rule, where consumers' overall experience is shaped by the most intense moments and the final impression.

These insights underscore the importance of sensory marketing in the restaurant industry and provide a robust foundation for the study's conceptual framework. By understanding the psychological processes involved, restaurant managers can design more effective sensory marketing strategies that align with consumer preferences and drive positive behavioural outcomes.

The analysis of primary data provides valuable insights into consumers' perceptions and experiences related to sensory marketing. Key findings include:

i. Perceived Importance of Sensory Cues: Consumers perceive sensory cues as crucial elements of their dining experience. Visual and olfactory cues are often rated as the most important, followed by auditory, gustatory, and tactile cues.
ii. Impact on Dining Experience: Sensory cues significantly enhance consumers' overall dining experience. Pleasant scents, appealing visuals, and suitable background music contribute to a positive atmosphere, leading to higher satisfaction levels.
iii. Behavioural Responses: There is a strong correlation between sensory marketing initiatives and positive behavioural responses. Consumers exposed to well-executed sensory marketing strategies are more likely to exhibit higher satisfaction, increased loyalty, and positive word-of-mouth recommendations.
iv. Consumer Segments: Different consumer segments respond differently to sensory marketing cues. For example, younger consumers may place a higher emphasis on visual and auditory cues, while older consumers may prioritize olfactory and gustatory cues. Understanding these segment-specific preferences can help restaurants tailor their sensory marketing strategies more effectively.

The findings from this analysis elucidate the relationship between sensory marketing initiatives and consumer behaviour, offering insightful correlations. These insights provide restaurant managers with actionable strategies to enhance their sensory marketing efforts, ultimately driving better customer experiences and improved business outcomes.

This research offers a comprehensive analysis of sensory neuro-marketing in the restaurant industry, combining qualitative insights, secondary data examination, and primary data analysis. The findings highlight the critical role of sensory marketing in shaping consumer perceptions and decision-making processes, providing valuable insights for both academic research and practical applications in the restaurant industry. By understanding the impact of sensory cues on consumer behaviour, restaurant managers can craft irresistible dining experiences that drive customer satisfaction, loyalty, and positive word-of-mouth, ultimately contributing to the success and growth of their businesses.

9. LIMITATIONS

This investigation necessitates the integration of both primary and secondary data sources to provide a comprehensive understanding of the impact of sensory marketing on consumer behaviour in the restaurant industry. The utilization of these data types presents several challenges and limitations that must be acknowledged.

A significant limitation of this research is the reliance on secondary data to elucidate the outcomes of marketing activities. Secondary data, while useful for providing background information and context, often lacks the specificity and timeliness required for an in-depth analysis of current marketing practices. The temporal constraints inherent in secondary data can impede the acquisition of precise and up-to-date information. Many secondary sources may contain out-dated information, making it difficult to draw accurate conclusions about the current state of sensory marketing.

To mitigate this limitation, secondary data was meticulously selected for examination. Efforts were made to ensure that the data used was from reputable sources and as current as possible. However, despite these efforts, the inherent limitations of secondary data cannot be entirely overcome. This reliance on secondary data may introduce biases and inaccuracies that could affect the overall findings and conclusions of the research.

Temporal constraints significantly impacted the ability to collect and analyze primary data. The time frame available for this research was limited, which restricted the depth and breadth of primary data collection. This constraint affected the ability to conduct extensive field studies, interviews, and surveys that could provide more detailed and nuanced insights into the impact of sensory marketing on consumer behaviour.

The short duration of the study also limited the ability to observe long-term trends and changes in consumer behaviour. Sensory marketing is a dynamic field, with consumer preferences and behaviours constantly evolving. A longer study period would have allowed for a more comprehensive analysis of these changes over time, providing a richer and more detailed understanding of how sensory marketing influences consumer behaviour.

This research is singularly focused on delineating the influence of sensory marketing on consumer behaviour, intentionally omitting extraneous variables from its scope of analysis. While this focused approach allows for a more detailed examination of sensory marketing, it also presents certain limitations.

By concentrating solely on sensory marketing, the research does not account for other factors that may influence consumer behaviour in the restaurant industry. Variables such as economic conditions, social influences, cultural factors, and individual psychological differences can all impact consumer behaviour. By excluding these variables, the research may present a somewhat narrow view of the factors influencing consumer decisions.

For instance, economic conditions such as income levels and consumer confidence can significantly affect dining choices. Social influences, including family and peer recommendations, as well as cultural factors, such as dietary preferences and dining traditions, also play a crucial role in shaping consumer behaviour. Psychological factors, including individual preferences, past experiences, and personal values, further complicate the analysis of consumer behaviour.

The interplay between sensory marketing and these extraneous variables is complex and multifaceted. The exclusion of these variables means that the research does not fully capture the holistic environment in which sensory marketing operates. This limitation highlights the need for future research to adopt a more integrative approach, considering a broader range of factors to provide a more comprehensive understanding of consumer behaviour in the restaurant industry.

The findings of this research, while valuable, may have limited generalizability. The specific focus on sensory marketing in the restaurant industry, particularly within the context of Sri Lankan restaurants, may not be entirely applicable to other industries or geographical locations. Sensory marketing strategies and their effectiveness can vary significantly based on cultural, regional, and industry-specific factors.

Cultural differences can greatly influence how sensory marketing tools are perceived and how effective they are in influencing consumer behaviour. For example, the importance of certain sensory stimuli, such as particular scents or flavours, may vary widely between different cultures. What is appealing and effective in one cultural context may not necessarily translate to another.

Similarly, the effectiveness of sensory marketing strategies can differ across industries. What works in the restaurant industry may not be as effective in retail, hospitality, or other sectors. Each industry has its unique characteristics, consumer expectations, and competitive dynamics, which can influence the success of sensory marketing initiatives.

The focus on Sri Lankan restaurants also presents a limitation in terms of sample size and geographic specificity. While the insights gained from this research are valuable for understanding sensory marketing within this context, they may not be fully representative of broader trends in the global restaurant industry. The findings may need to be contextualized and adapted for application in different geographical regions or market segments.

The methodological approach of this research also presents certain limitations. The integration of primary and secondary data, while providing a comprehensive view, may also introduce challenges related to data consistency, reliability, and validity.

The use of secondary data sources may result in inconsistencies, as different sources may present varying data points, methodologies, and interpretations. Ensuring the reliability of secondary data can be challenging, as it is often difficult to verify the accuracy and relevance of the information presented.

The collection of primary data, while offering direct insights, is also subject to potential biases and limitations. The sample size, respondent demographics, and data collection methods can all influence the validity of the primary data. Ensuring that the data collected is representative and free from bias is crucial for the reliability of the research findings.

The temporal constraints and focused scope of this research limited the ability to conduct a longitudinal analysis. A longitudinal study, tracking changes in consumer behaviour over an extended period, would provide more robust insights into the long-term impact of sensory marketing. The absence of such an analysis in this research presents a limitation in understanding the sustainability and evolving effects of sensory marketing strategies.

These limitations highlight the need for future research to address the gaps and challenges identified in this study. By adopting a more integrative and comprehensive approach, future studies can provide a deeper understanding of the multifactorial influences on consumer behaviour and the long-term effectiveness of sensory marketing strategies.

Future research should consider a broader range of variables, including economic, social, cultural, and psychological factors, to provide a more holistic view of consumer behaviour. An integrative approach, combining insights from environmental psychology, consumer behaviour, and sensory marketing, can offer a more comprehensive understanding of how various factors interact to influence consumer decisions.

Conducting longitudinal studies would provide valuable insights into the long-term impact of sensory marketing. Tracking changes in consumer behaviour over time would help to identify trends, shifts, and the sustainability of sensory marketing strategies. Longitudinal research would also allow for the examination of the evolving relationship between sensory stimuli and consumer behaviour.

Expanding the scope of research to include cross-cultural and cross-industry comparisons would enhance the generalizability of findings. Understanding how sensory marketing strategies are perceived and their effectiveness in different cultural contexts and industries would provide valuable insights for global applications. Cross-cultural studies would help to identify universal principles and culturally specific adaptations necessary for effective sensory marketing.

Future research should aim to enhance methodological rigor by ensuring data consistency, reliability, and validity. Utilizing mixed-method approaches, combining quantitative and qualitative data, can provide a more comprehensive view of sensory marketing's impact. Ensuring representative sample sizes, diverse demographics, and robust data collection methods will contribute to the reliability of future research findings.

In conclusion, while this research provides valuable insights into the impact of sensory marketing on consumer behaviour in the restaurant industry, it is not without its limitations. The reliance on secondary data, temporal constraints, focused scope, and methodological challenges present certain limitations that must be acknowledged. These limitations highlight the need for future research to adopt a more integrative, comprehensive, and methodologically rigorous approach to understanding sensory marketing's multifaceted influence on consumer behaviour. By addressing these challenges, future studies can provide deeper insights and more robust findings, contributing to the advancement of sensory marketing as a critical field in consumer behaviour research.

10. CONCLUSION

This dissertation investigates the application and influence of sensory marketing within India's restaurant sector, shedding light on how these strategies shape consumer behavior and decision-making. By examining the deployment of various sensory marketing techniques, this study provides a comprehensive understanding of their role in enhancing customer experiences and driving business success. Through a detailed exploration of visual, olfactory, and auditory cues, the research reveals the intricate ways in which sensory elements are strategically utilized to motivate customers and foster loyalty.

Additionally, the study delves into the subconscious impact of subcultural nuances on consumers, emphasizing the importance of cultural context in sensory marketing.

One of the primary sensory marketing techniques explored in this dissertation is the use of visual cues, particularly colour. The study reveals that restaurants in India frequently employ specific colours in their interiors to create a particular ambiance and influence consumer behaviour. Notably, the colours red and violet are commonly used to convey a sense of luxury and good fortune. Red, in particular, holds significant cultural meaning in India as a symbol of luck and prosperity. This strategic use of colour aims to enhance the dining experience by creating a visually appealing and culturally resonant environment.

The psychological impact of colour on consumer behaviour is well-documented, and this dissertation highlights its importance in the context of restaurant marketing. Colorus can evoke specific emotions and associations, which in turn influence consumers' perceptions and decisions. For example, red is known to stimulate appetite and increase arousal, making it a popular choice in restaurant decor. The study's findings suggest that the use of red and violet in restaurant interiors not only creates a luxurious and auspicious atmosphere but also enhances customers' overall dining experience, leading to increased satisfaction and loyalty.

Another key sensory marketing technique explored in this dissertation is the use of scents. The study reveals that scents play a crucial role in shaping consumer behaviour by triggering food memories and reinforcing brand recognition. The power of scent to evoke memories and emotions is particularly significant in the context of dining experiences, where the aroma of food can stimulate cravings and enhance the overall sensory experience.

The research highlights how restaurants strategically use scents to create a distinctive brand identity and enhance customer loyalty. For example, the aroma of freshly baked bread or brewed coffee can create a warm and inviting atmosphere, making customers feel at home and encouraging repeat visits.

The study's findings suggest that the use of signature scents can help restaurants differentiate themselves from competitors and create a lasting impression on customers.

The dissertation also underscores the importance of auditory cues, particularly music, in sensory marketing. The research demonstrates how music's pitch, genre, and tempo independently influence consumer actions and contribute to the overall dining experience. By analyzing the relationship between music and consumer behaviour, the study provides valuable insights into how restaurants can use music to enhance customer satisfaction and drive sales.

The primary research findings confirm a direct relationship between music and purchase frequency, indicating that upbeat tempos encourage quicker buying decisions. This suggests that restaurants can strategically use music to create a desired atmosphere and influence customer behaviour. For example, playing fast-paced music during peak dining hours can help increase table turnover and boost sales. Conversely, slower, more relaxing music can create a more leisurely dining experience, encouraging customers to stay longer and spend more.

The study also supports the idea that ambient music preferences vary according to mood, underscoring the importance of tailoring soundscapes to create the desired dining experience. By understanding the preferences and expectations of their target audience, restaurants can use music to create a more personalized and enjoyable dining experience. This tailored approach to sensory marketing helps enhance customer satisfaction and fosters loyalty, contributing to the long-term success of the restaurant.

The dissertation further explores the subconscious impact of subcultural nuances on consumer behaviour. By examining how cultural context influences consumers' perceptions and emotional responses, the study provides valuable insights into the importance of cultural sensitivity in sensory marketing.

The research reveals that consumers' responses to sensory cues are shaped by their cultural background and experiences. For example, certain scents or colours may have specific cultural associations that influence how they are perceived. Understanding these nuances is crucial for restaurants aiming to create a culturally resonant and appealing dining experience. The study's findings suggest that restaurants that incorporate cultural sensitivity into their sensory marketing strategies are more likely to succeed in attracting and retaining customers.

In conclusion, this dissertation offers a comprehensive exploration of sensory marketing within India's restaurant sector, highlighting the strategic use of visual, olfactory, and auditory cues to shape consumer behaviour and decision-making. By examining the psychological and cultural impact of these sensory elements, the study provides valuable insights into how restaurants can enhance customer experiences and foster loyalty. The findings underscore the importance of a tailored and culturally sensitive approach to sensory marketing, offering practical strategies for restaurant managers to create irresistible dining experiences that drive customer satisfaction and business success.

This research contributes to the growing body of knowledge on sensory neuromarketing and its application in the restaurant industry, providing a robust framework for future studies. By understanding the intricate ways in which sensory cues influence consumer behaviour, restaurant managers can design more effective marketing strategies that align with consumer preferences and cultural context. Ultimately, this dissertation emphasizes the power of sensory marketing in creating memorable and engaging dining experiences, paving the way for a more customer-centric approach to restaurant commerce.

REFERENCES

Arora, M., & Sharma, R. L. (2023). Artificial intelligence and big data: ontological and communicative perspectives in multi-sectoral scenarios of modern businesses. *Foresight, 25*(1), 126-143.

Bevz, N. (2015, May 10). http://www.digitalmarketing-glossary.com/What-isSensory-marketing-definition. Retrieved March 8, 2016, from http://www.digitalmarketing-glossary.com/

Bhardwaj, S., Kaushik, N., & Arora, M. (2024). Does Your Brain Have a Buy Button?: A Neuro Marketing Approach With Sensory Branding. In *Sensible Selling Through Sensory Neuromarketing* (pp. 210–229). IGI Global. DOI: 10.4018/979-8-3693-4236-7.ch011

Bitner, M. (1992, April). Servicescapes: The impact of physical surroundings on customers and employees. *Journal of Marketing*, 56(2), 57–71. DOI: 10.1177/002224299205600205

Malik, R., Malhan, S., & Arora, M. (Eds.). (2024). *Sensible Selling Through Sensory Neuromarketing*. IGI Global.

Skandrani, H. M., Ben Dahmane Mouelhi, N., & Malek, F. (2011). Effect of store atmospherics on employees' reactions. *International Journal of Retail & Distribution Management*, 39(1), 61–67. DOI: 10.1108/09590551111104477

Taneja, B., Shukla, P., & Arora, M. (2024). Sensible Selling Through Sensory Neuromarketing: Enhancing Sales Effectiveness. In *Sensible Selling Through Sensory Neuromarketing* (pp. 164-183). IGI Global.

Chapter 16
Brand Building in the Age of Sensory Marketing:
A Strategic Perspective

Manpreet Arora
https://orcid.org/0000-0002-4939-1992
School of Commerce and Management Studies, Central University of Himachal Pradesh, India

ABSTRACT

This chapter explores the role of sensory marketing in modern brand building, focusing on how engaging the five senses—sight, sound, smell, touch, and taste—creates stronger emotional connections with consumers. As traditional marketing methods lose impact, sensory marketing helps brands stand out by delivering immersive experiences that foster brand loyalty and enhance differentiation. The chapter discusses the shift from functional product marketing to experience-driven strategies, addressing key challenges such as measurability, cost, and cultural sensitivity. It also highlights emerging trends, including AR/VR integration, neuroscience-driven marketing, and sustainable sensory practices. Overall, sensory marketing offers a path to deeper emotional engagement, ensuring lasting consumer relationships in an increasingly competitive marketplace.

INTRODUCTION

Brand building in today's marketing landscape has shifted from a primarily transactional relationship to the one which is centred around the emotional connections and immersive experiences. At the heart of this is transformation is sensory marketing. It is a strategy that engages consumers through the five senses, sight, sound,

DOI: 10.4018/979-8-3693-9351-2.ch016

smell, touch and taste. In the age of information overload marketers are bombarded with advertisements across numerous channels. Sensory marketing offers a novel approach by creating memorable experiences that stand out amidst the noise. Brands are now increasingly turning to sensory marketing as a way to stand out and build lasting, meaningful connections with their audiences.

The Changing Landscape of Consumer Engagement

Historically, marketing relied heavily on one-dimensional forms of communication such as print ads, television commercials and radio spots. These approaches were primarily designed to inform and persuade consumers through visual or auditory messages. However, with the advent of digital marketing, the landscape of brand building began to change. The increased use and the proliferation of the internet, mobile devices and social media has shifted the focus from one way communication to interactive two-way engagement which enables the customers to interact with brands more directly and in real time. This transformation was further accelerated by the rise of experiential marketing, which emphasized on creating the memorable brand experiences rather than simply conveying about the product features (Wijaya, (2013); UZUNOĞLU & SÖZER, (2020)). Consumers began to prioritize authenticity, personalization, and emotional resonance over mere functionality, and the brands that failed to adapt found themselves struggling to maintain relevance. It is in this context that sensory marketing emerged as a critical strategy, offering a way to engage consumers not just through sight and sound, but through the full range of human sensory experiences.

What Is Sensory Marketing?

Human beings processed the world through their senses. Sensory inputs such as the smell of freshly baked bread, or the texture of a soft fabric or the sound of a favourite song can have the unique abilities to evoke our emotions, memories and physical reactions. The use of sensory stimuli to influence the consumer behaviour is not a very new concept. However, it has gained increasing importance as brands strive to create differentiated experiences in a world where the consumers are bombarded with certain marketing strategies (Bhardwaj, Kaushik & Arora, (2024);

Many studies have shown that emotions play a very pivotal role in decision making, often more so than the rational thought (Aydınoğlu & Sayın (2016); Wala, Czyrka & Frąś (2019)). Sensory marketing taps directly into these emotional drivers and create the connections that can go beyond the intellectual engagement and foster emotional loyalty also (Gentner, (2012). The sensory marketing is effective because it stimulates the area of that brain portion which are responsible for emotion and memory, particularly the limbic system. When a brand attempts to engage multiple senses of human beings simultaneously, it got to create a richer, more immersive experience that is more likely to be remembered and associated with the positive feelings (Singh, Sharma & Jain (2013). This is particularly important in the current environment where the consumers attention spans are shorter, their ability to process and retain information is constantly being challenged by the sheer volume of the content which we encounter every day (Alimin, Ismail, Herbenita, Fadillah & Uhai (2024). The sensory marketing offers a way to cut through the clutter, provide tangible emotional experiences that remain in the consumers mind long after the interaction has ended. The world of metaverse though is playing an important role in this indeed.

From Functionality to Experience: A Shift in Consumer Expectations

To move further into the experience economy, consumers expectations have shifted dramatically (Tanasic (2017); Gurgu, Gurgu & Tonis (2020); Taneja, Shuklam & Arora (2024)). They no longer see brands as mere provider of goods and services, but they are the creator of experiences. The shift is particularly evident in various industries like hospitality, retail, and entertainment, where the quality of customer experience is often as important as, if not more than, the quality of the product itself. Various international brands like Apple, Starbucks and Nike have set new benchmarks by designing experiences that engage the consumers senses, leading to higher levels of brand loyalty and advocacy. Since, Apple has created a sensory experience around its products, from the minimalist aesthetic of its stores to the tactile feeling of its devices and packaging.

When consumers enter an Apple Store, they are not just purchasing the technology, they are immersed in a world that embodies the brands core value of simplicity, innovation, and elegance. Similarly, Starbucks has built a global brand by focusing on sensory aspects of coffee experience, from the aroma of freshly brewed coffee to cozy ambience of its stores. That's the shift and the focus on experience driven brand building is particularly very important for millennials and Gen. Z who have grown up in a world where digital interactions have become the norm. These generations are not only the digital natives, but they are also the experience seekers who value the brands that offer personalization and immersion. For this generation, it is not enough for a brand to provide a functional product or service. The brand must also create a memorable experience that aligns with their personal identity and values. Sensory marketing offers a way to meet these expectations by creating multi-sensory experiences that engage the customer on a very deeper level.

Sensory Marketing as a Differentiator in the Digital Age

In a world where consumers get information overload especially of digital contents, brands are finding it increasingly difficult to capture attention of their potential customers. The use of traditional advertising methods like banners, popups and e-mail campaigns are becoming very less effective as consumers have developed ad fatigue and selective attention. In contrast, the sensory marketing provides a tangible; physical connection between the consumer and the brand, offering a unique way to stand out in the digital age. One of the most significant advantages of sensory marketing is its ability to create distinctive brand experiences that differentiate a brand for its competitors. In a market where products are often commoditized and price competition is fierce, brands that can create emotional connections through sensory engagements are more likely to command premium pricing and build long term loyalty. This is because sensory experiences are very harder to replicate than visual or auditory elements alone. For example, a competitor can easily copy your brand's logo or slogan, but it is very difficult to replicate the specific scent, texture or the sound that defines the unique sensory experience. Moreover, sensory marketing helped the brands to move beyond the limitations of digital interaction (Taneja, Shukla & Arora, (2024). In an increasingly digital first world where the physical interaction with the products may be limited, sensory marketing allows the brands to create immersive experiences that bridge the gap between digital and physical realms. For example, the integration of augmented reality and virtual reality into marketing strategies is enabling the branch to provide sensory rich experiences even in virtual environments. These technologies are helping to blur the line between physical and digital worlds, making it possible for the consumers to engage with the brands in the way that they were previously unimaginable.

The Role of Emotional Branding and Sensory Marketing

At the heart of sensory marketing lies the emotional branding, which is a strategy that focuses on creating emotional connections with the consumers through their experiences that resonate with their values, aspirations, and desires (RIJO & MARMELO (2022). Sensory marketing is uniquely positioned to drive emotional branding because it engages the senses in the ways that stimulate emotions and trigger memories. For example, a well-crafted scent can transport a consumer back to childhood memories, evoking a sense of nostalgia that strengthens the emotional bond with the brand.

Use of sensory elements in order to build the emotional connections is particularly very important in the industries where the consumer choices driven by emotional factors such as luxury goods, fashion, food, beverage and hospitality. In these industries, consumers are not just purchasing a product, they're also buying a lifestyle or identity that is reinforced by the sensory experiences that the brand offers. This is why the high-end hotels, for example, often invest in custom scents, high quality materials and personalized soundscapes to create an environment that aligns with the brand values and enhances the customer experience. In the luxury sector, sensory marketing has become a sound driver of grand prestige. The tactile feel of premium packaging, the subtle scent of the flagship store or the curated playlist playing in the background all contribute to creating a perception of exclusivity and refinement. Sensory marketing allows the luxury brands to craft their identity through their experiences that are multidimensional and immersive. It reinforces the emotional connection between consumer and the brand.

The Importance of Consistency in Sensory Branding

While the sensory marketing can be a powerful tool for brand building, it requires careful consistency and coherence across all touch points. A brands sensory element such as visual design, scent, sound, tactile experience must align with its overall identity and values. Inconsistent or poorly executed sensory marketing efforts can confuse consumers and dilute the brand's message. For example, a luxury brand that uses low quality material in its packaging or inconsistent music in its retail locations risks undermining its image of exclusivity and refinement.

Moreover, as brands expand globally, they must be mindful of cultural differences that can influence how sensory elements are perceived or the scent or sound that works well in one region may not resonate with the consumers in another region. It compulsorily makes it essential for the branch to conduct through market research and tailor their sensory strategies to their local preferences. Brands that can maintain cultural sensitivity while delivering consistent sensory experiences across multiple regions will be better positioned to succeed in today's global market price.

EVOLUTION OF BRAND BUILDING AND MARKETING

Historically, brand building has evolved through various phases, each shaped by changes in technology, consumer behavior, and market dynamics. In the early stages, brands used to rely on traditional advertising techniques to communicate their messages. These mediums were primarily one way communication tool which focused on conveying information and promoting the products. Digital marketing in the late 90s and early 2000s introduced a new era where the consumers could interact with the brands more directly. Websites, social media, and e-mail marketing allowed for two-way communication, but the emphasis remained on content driven engagement, text, image and video. As the technology advanced, the importance of experiential marketing grew, marking a shift towards creating meaningful consumer experiences rather than just delivering the content (Agarwal, & Xavier, (2015). Today's sensory marketing represents the next evolution in brand building (McDowell & Dick (2013); Yoganathan, Osburg & Akhtar (2019); Menezes, Gonçalves & de Muylder, (2016); Devaru, (2018)). In an environment where consumers are constantly connected and exposed to the barrage of digital content, brands that offer a multi-sensory experience have the edge. This form of marketing breaks away from the traditional approaches by stimulating multiple senses, leading to deeper emotional connections and enhance consumer engagement. For example, rather than just relying solely on visual advertisements, brands can use sound sense and test tactile elements to create memorable engagement experiences that stay with the consumer long after the interaction has ended.

Consumer Expectations in the Modern Age

Modern consumers, especially millennials and Gen. Z, have heightened expectations for the brands they engage with. These generations value experiences over the material goods and expect brands to provide immersive, interactive and emotionally resonant encounters. Sensory marketing capitalizes on this by offering unique and personalized experiences that aligns with their desires (Dwivedi, Nagariya, & Joseph (2025). For example, these days consumers entering a retail store are not just interested in the products, but they also evaluate the overall atmosphere, the lighting, the music the scent and the way the product feels when touched. These sensory cues work together to craft an environment that enhances the brand experience. In this context, the brands become more than just the provider of the products, but they become a curator of experiences, making it more likely that the consumer will form a strong emotional bond and remain loyal.

Psychological Underpinnings of Sensory Marketing

Sensory marketing draws heavily from the field of psychology, particularly in how it engages consumers on subconscious level. The human brain processes sensory input in the way that it can evoke emotions, influence decision making, and enhance memory recall. By engaging in to multiple senses, brands can tap these psychological mechanisms to create lasting impressions.

Emotional Engagement

The relationship between sensory stimulation and motions is deeply rooted in brains limbic system which governs emotions and memories. For example, a pleasant fragrance in a restaurant can evoke the feelings of comfort or nostalgia, leading the consumer to associate positive emotions with the brand. The emotional connection formed through sensory marketing is often more potent than one created through traditional marketing as it bypasses the rational thinking and it appeals directly to the customers emotions. Brands that successfully tap into these emotional responses can build stronger and more loyal customer base. This is because consumers are more likely to stay connected to brands that make them feel a certain way, rather than those that simply provide a functional product or service over the period of time. This emotional connection may translate into higher brand loyalty as consumers seek to recreate the positive experiences they have had in the past.

Memory and Recall

Getting the multiple senses also enhances memory retention. Studies show that multi-sensory experiences are more likely to be encoded in long term memory than single sense stimuli. This is particularly important in today's crowded marketplace where the consumers are consistently more pressurized with messages. A brand that can engage multiple senses has a better chance of standing out and being remembered. For instance, memorable sound or jingle can trigger a mental association with the brand, even when the consumers are not actively thinking about it. These sensory triggers matter a lot for the brands to remain at the top of mind even when they are not directly engaging with the customers.

Challenges and Limitations of Sensory Marketing

There are many opportunities for brands to connect with consumers through sensory marketing; however, this type of marketing is not without its set of challenges. In order to successfully implement a sensory marketing strategy, one must have a comprehensive understanding of consumer behaviour, the consistency of brands, and the differences observed between cultures.

1. Consistency Across a Number of Different Sources

Keeping the same level of consistency across all touchpoints is one of the most significant challenges. It is necessary for a brand to provide a consistent experience for the customer regardless of whether they are interacting with the brand in-store, online, or through a mobile application in order for the brand to develop a robust sensory identity. This is something that can be challenging to accomplish, particularly in digital spaces where there is less opportunity for sensory engagement. For instance, it is simpler to create a multi-sensory experience in a physical store than it is in an online environment, where it is more difficult to convey the senses of touch and smell.

It is necessary for brands to concentrate on strategically integrating sensory elements across all channels in order to overcome this challenge. This will ensure that the brand experience remains consistent regardless of the location or manner in which customers interact with it. Among these options is the creation of a signature sound or visual identity that can be replicated across various platforms, as well as the development of packaging that engages multiple senses even when the product is purchased online.

2. Sensitivity to Different Cultures

The fact that people's preferences in terms of their senses can vary greatly from culture to culture is yet another limitation of sensory marketing. As an illustration, a fragrance that is regarded as pleasant and well known by customers in one nation might be considered unappealing or unfamiliar in another. In the similar vein, different cultural contexts may elicit entirely different feelings in response to a particular sound or tactile experiences. In the process of developing their sensory marketing strategies, companies that operate in global markets are required to take into consideration the cultural differences discussed here. It is necessary to conduct a substantial amount of research and testing in order to guarantee that the sensory components that are utilized are suitable for the intended audience and will elicit the desired emotional responses. The failure to take into account these differences can lead to the alienation of customers or the delivery of experiences that do not resonate with the target market.

3. Sensory Fatigue and Oversaturation of the Senses

Although sensory marketing has the potential to produce experiences that are memorable, there is also the possibility of oversaturation. Sensory fatigue can occur when consumers are exposed to the excessive number of sensory elements at the same time, which can cause them to feel overwhelmed. The overall experience may suffer as a result, and the brand may become less appealing to consumers. Keeping as sense of subtlety while simultaneously appealing to multiple senses is a delicate balancing act that brands need to master in order to avoid this. The most important thing is to concentrate on improving the experience of the brand rather than overburdening the customer with an excessive amount of stimuli. It is important to make strategic use of sensory marketing in order to successfully complement the overall messaging and identity of the brand.

4. Measurability and Return on Investment

One of the biggest challenges in sensory marketing is the difficulty in measuring its effectiveness and calculating a clear return on investment. While traditional marketing campaigns like digital ads, etc. allow for precise tracking of impressions, clicks and conversations, but the impact of sensory marketing is very subjective and emotional. It is very difficult to quantify it. For example, while we are talking about the effect of auditory or sensory influences on the customer sales. It is very difficult to analyse that how much the sales boosted due to that sensory marketing tactics. This lack of measurability makes it challenging for the marketers to justify the sensory marketing investments to the stakeholders who demand clear and data-driven results.

5. Cost-Intensive Implementation

Creating sensory experiences, especially those that involve physical touch points like sense, sounds or tactile elements, can be cost intensive. Developing customer packaging with unique tactile experiences or installing scent diffusers across multiple retail locations can significantly increase the operational costs. Additionally, maintaining the consistency for various sensory elements across all locations can add to costs and financial burdens on the brands. This can be a barrier for small brands or businesses with limited budgets, making sensory marketing more accessible to only larger companies.

6. Over Sensory Stimulation

Overloading the consumers with too many century inputs can result in sensory fatigue or negative experiences. While engaging the multiple senses can create memorable brand experiences, it is essential to strike a balance. Sensory overload can lead to a sense of discomfort, confusion, or even annoyance. For example, a store that plays loud music, uses strong sense, and has overly bright lightning might overwhelm customers, making them less likely to engage with the brands. Brands need to be cautious about using sensory elements strategically, ensuring that they complement the brand message without overwhelming the consumer.

7. Maintaining Authenticity

In a world where consumers are increasingly agile, authenticity and transparency become very important. Brands must ensure that sensory marketing efforts feel genuine rather than manipulative. Over reliance on sensory elements designed purely to elicit emotional reactions can come across an inauthentic way of dealing in the business, leading to consumer distrust.

8. Adapting to a Digital First World

With the growing dominance of e-commerce in digital shopping experiences, brands face the challenge of adapting sensory marketing to online platforms. Violin stored experiences a law for physical touch points like scent and touch. The digital environments are inherently more limited in the senses they can engage. For example, a brand may find it difficult to replicate the tactile experiences of packaging or ambient sound of physical space on e-commerce site. This creates a gap in the sensory experience, forcing the brands to rely more heavily on sight and sound while potentially losing the emotional impact of engaging all 5 senses.

9. Rapid Technological Changes

The rapid pace of technological advancements, particularly in the areas like augmented reality and virtual reality, presents a challenge for the brands to keep up with the latest developments. Implementing sensory driven technology requires substantial investment in both infrastructure and expertise, and what is cutting edge today may be outdated tomorrow. Additionally, the integration of these technologies must align seamlessly with the brand's overall strategy or it risks becoming a short-lived gimmick rather than meaningful part of brand experience.

FUTURE TRENDS IN SENSORY MARKETING

As technology and consumer expectations continue to evolve, the future of sensory marketing will be shaped by several emerging trends that will further transform the way brands engage with their audiences.

1. Multi-Sensory Integration With Augmented and Virtual Reality

The integration of augmented reality and virtual reality into sensory marketing is already underway and will only increase in the future. Both AR and VR technologies offer the potential for immersive, multi-sensory experiences that engage the consumers in highly interactive ways. For example, a VR shopping experience could allow the consumers to explore a virtual store where they not only see the product physically but can also interact with them using haptic feedback. While the augmented reality would provide an enhanced digital overlay in the physical stores, combining it with visual and auditory elements can do wonders. As and when the cost of these technologies' decreases, the accessibility increases and the brands will increasingly incorporate AR and VR to create personalized multi-sensory experiences that transcend the limitations of physical spaces.

2. Neuroscience and Sensory Building

Advances in the neuroscience and bringing imaging technologies are providing new insights into how sensitive to lack and affect the consumer behavior on a subconscious level by understanding how sensory inputs trigger specific emotions, memories, and decision-making processes. Brands will be able to create more targeted and effective sensory marketing strategies. Neuroscientific research will allow the marketers to fine tune sensory experiences that optimise emotional engagement and brand recall.

3. Personalized Sensory Experiences With AI and Data Analytics

The rise of artificial intelligence and data analytics is enabling brands to create hyper personalized sensory experiences tailored to individual consumers. By collecting data on consumer preferences, purchase histories, and sensory reactions, brands can develop sensory marketing strategies that cater to the specific tastes and preferences of each consumer. For example, a brand could use AI to deliver personalized sensitive experiences, such as customized fragrances or individual customers based on their past interactions with the brand. This level of personalization will help brands forge deeper, more meaningful connections with the customers, enhancing loyalty and satisfaction (Teixeira, Gonçalves, & Reis (2022)).

4. Sustainability and Ethical Sensory Marketing

Consumers are increasingly seeking out brands that align with their values, particularly when it comes to sustainability and ethical practices. This shift is driving brands to adopt more eco-friendly approaches to sensory marketing. For example, brands are exploring sustainable packaging options that maintain a tactile experience while reducing the environmental impact. As sustainability continues to gain importance, brands that can offer sensory experiences aligned with ethical standards will gain competitive advantage.

5. Voice Activated Branding and Auditory Marketing

With the proliferation of voice activated technologies, auditory branding is becoming increasingly significant. Consumers can interact more with voice activated devices and brands will need to develop distinct auditory identities that differentiate from their competitors. It is possible that brands might create signature voice stones, jingles and soundscapes that resonate with consumers during their voice-based interactions. Additionally, as more consumers use mass speakers for shopping and other tasks, brands will explore new ways to incorporate auditory elements into their marketing strategies, potentially combining sound and age win personalization to create unique brand experiences.

6. Emotional Analytics and Sensory Feedback

Emotional analytics is an emerging field that uses advanced sensors, facial recognition, and AI to draft analyze consumers responses to marketing stimuli. Brands will increasingly leverage emotional analytics to measure how their sensory marketing efforts are resonating with real time consumers. For example, sensors could track a consumer's emotional reaction to a particular in store experience, allowing brands to adjust the sensory elements on the fly to create more positive experiences. The rise of this technology will allow the branch to be more responsive to consumer emotions, creating a feedback loop where sensory marketing strategies can be continuously refined.

7. Touchless Sensory Experiences

In a post pandemic world, the rise of contactless experiences has created demand for new ways to engage the sense of touch without physical contact. Brands are exploring technologies that allow the touchless sensitive interactions such as haptic feedback in the digital environments or gesture-based controls in physical spaces.

Consumers might use hand gestures to interact with touch free digital kiosks and experiences simulated tactile sensations through the haptic divisions in a virtual setting. This trend reflects both the responses to hygiene concerns and desire to create innovative, futuristic sensory experiences that blend physical and digital touch points.

CONCLUSION

The future of sensory marketing is full of exciting possibilities as new technologies, personalization strategies, and sustainability efforts come to forefront. Brands must also navigate the challenges that come with implementing sensory marketing, such as ensuring consistency, avoiding sensory overload, and staying authentic. As consumers continue to demand immersive, meaningful, and ethical brand experience, the role of sensory marketing will become even more vital in shaping the future of brand building and customer engagement.

REFERENCES

Agarwal, S., & Xavier, M. J. (2015). Innovations in consumer science: applications of neuro-scientific research tools. In *Adoption of Innovation: Balancing Internal and External Stakeholders in the Marketing of Innovation* (pp. 25–42). Springer International Publishing. DOI: 10.1007/978-3-319-14523-5_3

Alimin, E., Ismail, A., Herbenita, H., Fadillah, T. D., & Uhai, S. (2024). Analysis of The Influence of Digitalization Implementation in Marketing Programs and Neuro-Marketing Adaption on Brand Perception in The Tourism Industries. *Innovative: Journal Of Social Science Research*, 4(4), 14581–14589.

Aydınoğlu, N. Z., & Sayın, E. (2016). Sensory and neuromarketing: about and beyond customer sensation. In *Flavor* (pp. 397–408). Woodhead Publishing. DOI: 10.1016/B978-0-08-100295-7.00019-0

Bhardwaj, S., Kaushik, N., & Arora, M. (2024). Does Your Brain Have a Buy Button?: A Neuro Marketing Approach With Sensory Branding. In *Sensible Selling Through Sensory Neuromarketing* (pp. 210–229). IGI Global. DOI: 10.4018/979-8-3693-4236-7.ch011

Chan, H. Y., Boksem, M., & Smidts, A. (2018). Neural profiling of brands: Mapping brand image in consumers' brains with visual templates. *JMR, Journal of Marketing Research*, 55(4), 600–615. DOI: 10.1509/jmr.17.0019

Ćosić, D. (2016). Neuromarketing in market research. *Interdisciplinary Description of Complex Systems: INDECS*, 14(2), 139–147. DOI: 10.7906/indecs.14.2.3

Devaru, S. D. B. (2018). Significance of neuromarketing on consumer buying behavior. *International Journal of Technical Research & Science*, 3(3), 114–121. DOI: 10.30780/IJTRS.V3.I3.2018.015

Dwivedi, A., Nagariya, R., & Joseph, S. (2025). Neuromarketing in Fashion: Unveiling Consumer Insights & Brand Strategies. *Journal of Engineering. Management and Information Technology*, 3(3), 149–158.

Gentner, F. (2012). *Neuromarketing in the B-to-B-sector: importance, potential and its implications for brand management*. Diplomica Verlag.

Gurgu, E., Gurgu, I. A., & Tonis, R. B. M. (2020). Neuromarketing for a better understanding of consumer needs and emotions. *Independent Journal of Management & Production*, 11(1), 208–235. DOI: 10.14807/ijmp.v11i1.993

Krishna, A. (2011). An introduction to sensory marketing. In *Sensory marketing* (pp. 1–13). Routledge.

McDowell, W. S., & Dick, S. J. (2013). The marketing of neuromarketing: Brand differentiation strategies employed by prominent neuromarketing firms to attract media clients. *Journal of Media Business Studies*, 10(1), 25–40. DOI: 10.1080/16522354.2013.11073558

Menezes, R. G., Gonçalves, C. A., & de Muylder, C. F. (2016). *Sensorial marketing and neuroscience: Neuroscience contributions to the marketing field. International Business Management*. Medwell Journals.

Parth, R., Nath, P., Raje, H., Thorat, C., & Deokar, A. (2022). Significance of Neuromarketing in Hotel Industry. *NeuroQuantology : An Interdisciplinary Journal of Neuroscience and Quantum Physics*, 20(9), 5336.

Quintero-Martínez, D. M., & Arias, J. A. S. (2019). *Neuromarketing: A Competitive Advantage for the Financial Sector. Apuntes de Administración (Universidad Francisco de Paula Santander), 4(1)*.

Rijo, C., & Marmelo, C. (2022). Neurodesign and the brand perception: Communication challenges. *Design, Visual Communication and Branding*, 35.

Riza, A. F., & Wijayanti, D. M. (2018). The triangle of sensory marketing model: Does it stimulate brand experience and loyalty. *Esensi: Jurnal Bisnis dan Manajemen, 8*(1), 57-66.

Singh, S., Sharma, A., & Jain, N. (2013). Customer engagement through sensory branding. *EXCEL International Journal of Multidisciplinary Management Studies*, 3(9), 132–138.

Tanasic, B. R. (2017). Impact of sensory branding on the decision-making process of tourism product purchase. *International Journal of Research in Engineering and Innovation*, 1(6), 109–125.

Taneja, B., Shukla, P., & Arora, M. (2024). Sensible Selling Through Sensory Neuromarketing: Enhancing Sales Effectiveness. In *Sensible Selling Through Sensory Neuromarketing* (pp. 164-183). IGI Global.

Teixeira, S., Gonçalves, M. J. A., & Reis, A. (2022). Study of the Relationship Between Sensory Marketing and Consumer Satisfaction. In *Advances in Tourism, Technology and Systems: Selected Papers from ICOTTS 2021* (Vol. 1, pp. 499–518). Springer Nature Singapore. DOI: 10.1007/978-981-19-1040-1_43

Uzunoğlu, M. İ., & Sözer, E. G. (2020). Cognitive, perceptual and behavioral effects of neuro-stimuli: A study on packaged food products. *Business & Management Studies: An International Journal*, 8(3), 3097–3122.

Va, K. P. (2015). Reinventing the Art of Marketing in the Light of Digitalization and Neuroimaging. *Amity Global Business Review, 10*.

Wala, A., Czyrka, K., & Frąś, J. (2019). Sensory branding and marketing in stimulating the relation between the buyer and the brand. *Organizacja i Zarządzanie: kwartalnik naukowy*, (1), 109-120.

Wijaya, B. S. (2013). Dimensions of brand image: A conceptual review from the perspective of brand communication. *European Journal of Business and Management*, 5(31), 55–65.

Yoganathan, V., Osburg, V. S., & Akhtar, P. (2019). Sensory stimulation for sensible consumption: Multisensory marketing for e-tailing of ethical brands. *Journal of Business Research*, 96, 386–396. DOI: 10.1016/j.jbusres.2018.06.005

Compilation of References

Acharya, U., Ramaprasad, B. S., Kate, N., & Srivastava, A. (2023, August 18). The Adoption of Smart Agriculture Technologies Based on the Perception of the Farmers in the Indian Context. https://doi.org/10.1109/smarttechcon57526.2023.10391525

Agarwal, S., & Xavier, M. J. (2015). Innovations in consumer science: applications of neuro-scientific research tools. In *Adoption of Innovation: Balancing Internal and External Stakeholders in the Marketing of Innovation* (pp. 25–42). Springer International Publishing. DOI: 10.1007/978-3-319-14523-5_3

Ahmad Sharabati, A. A., Salim Khraim, H., & Atta Khateeb, R. (2014). Relationship between direct-to-consumer advertising and consumers' decision-making. *International Journal of Pharmaceutical and Healthcare Marketing*, 8(2), 178–192. DOI: 10.1108/IJPHM-12-2012-0019

Ahmed, R. R., Streimikiene, D., Channar, Z. A., Soomro, H. A., Streimikis, J., & Kyriakopoulos, G. L. (2022). The neuromarketing concept in artificial neural networks: A case of forecasting and simulation from the advertising industry. *Sustainability (Basel)*, 14(14), 8546. DOI: 10.3390/su14148546

Ajzen, I. (2010). Constructing a TPB questionnaire: Conceptual and methodological considerations. Retrieved from http://socgeo.ruhosting.nl/html/files/spatbeh/tpb.measurement.pdf

Ajzen, I. (1991). The theory of planned behavior. *Organizational Behavior and Human Decision Processes*, 50(2), 179–211. DOI: 10.1016/0749-5978(91)90020-T

Ajzen, I. (2011). The theory of planned behaviour: Reactions and reflections. *Psychology & Health*, 26(9), 1113–1127. DOI: 10.1080/08870446.2011.613995 PMID: 21929476

Al Fauzi, A., & Widyarini, L. A. (2023). Neuromarketing: The Physiological Tools for Understanding Consumer Behaviour. [MJSSH]. *Malaysian Journal of Social Sciences and Humanities*, 8(1), e002081–e002081.

Alassaf, P., & Szalay, Z. G. (2022). The Impact of 'Compulsory' Shifting to Use e-Services during COVID-19 Pandemic Restrictions Period on e-Services Users' Future Attitude and Intention "Case Study of Central European Countries/Visegrád Group (V4).". *Sustainability (Basel)*, 14(16), 9935. Advance online publication. DOI: 10.3390/su14169935

Alhamdi, F. (2020). Role of packaging in consumer buying behavior. *Management Science Letters*, 10, 1191–1196. DOI: 10.5267/j.msl.2019.11.040

Alimin, E., Ismail, A., Herbenita, H., Fadillah, T. D., & Uhai, S. (2024). Analysis of The Influence of Digitalization Implementation in Marketing Programs and Neuro-Marketing Adaption on Brand Perception in The Tourism Industries. *Innovative: Journal Of Social Science Research*, 4(4), 14581–14589.

Almamy, A. S. M. (2022). Understanding factors affecting e-government adoption in Saudi Arabia: The role of religiosity. *International Journal of Customer Relationship Marketing and Management*, 13(1), 1–15. Advance online publication. DOI: 10.4018/IJCRMM.289209

Al-Obthani, F., & Ameen, A. (2019). Association between transformational leadership and smart government among employees in UAE public organizations. *International Journal on Emerging Technologies*, 10(1), 98–104. https://www.scopus.com/inward/record.uri?eid=2-s2.0-85075025183&partnerID=40&md5=f0aa26fe21f5d72b4a6ea43f8fe2e592

Alpert, M. I. (2005). The influence of purchase occasions on the role of music in advertising. *Journal of Advertising Research*, 45(3), 310–321. DOI: 10.1017/S0021849905050360

Alpert, M. I., Alpert, J. I., & Maltz, E. N. (2005). Purchase occasion influences on the role of music in advertising. *Journal of Business Research*, 58(3), 369–376. DOI: 10.1016/S0148-2963(03)00101-2

Al-Refai, N. M. A. (2021). The role of Neuromarketing in measuring response to marketing stimuli in advertising campaigns. *International Design Journal*, 11(4), 237–256. DOI: 10.21608/idj.2021.180927

Alsharif, A. H., Salleh, N. Z. M., Baharun, R., Hashem, E. A. R., Mansor, A. A., Ali, J., & Abbas, A. F. (2021). Neuroimaging techniques in advertising research: Main applications, development, and brain regions and processes. *Sustainability (Basel)*, 13(11), 6488. DOI: 10.3390/su13116488

Alsultanny, Y. (2012). Opportunities and challenges of M-commerce in Bahrain. *Journal of Database Marketing and Customer Strategy Management*, 19(1), 31–38. DOI: 10.1057/dbm.2012.2

Alvino, L., Pavone, L., Abhishta, A., & Robben, H. (2020). Picking your brains: Where and how neuroscience tools can enhance marketing research. *Frontiers in Neuroscience*, 14, 577666. DOI: 10.3389/fnins.2020.577666 PMID: 33343279

Alwitt, L. (1985), EEG activity reflects the content of commercials. En Alwitt, L., Psychological processes and advertising effects: theory, research, and applications (author, year, pp. 209–219). Hillsdale, NJ: Lawrence Erlbaum.

Ambler, T., Kokkinaki, F., & Puntoni, S. (2004). Assessing marketing performance: Reasons for metrics selection. *Journal of Marketing Management*, 20(3-4), 475–498. DOI: 10.1362/026725704323080506

Anastasi, A., & Urbina, S. (1982). *Psychological assessment*. Mac-Millan.

Anderson, J. E., Lee, R. P., Tofighi, M., & Anderson, S. T. (2023). Lobbying as a potent political marketing tool for product diversification: An examination of firm-government interaction. *Journal of Strategic Marketing*, 31(1), 235–253. DOI: 10.1080/0965254X.2021.1896568

Archana, C., & Mahajan, A. (2023). Neuro Marketing: An Astonishing Addition to the Marketing World. In *Digital Transformation for Business Sustainability: Trends, Challenges and Opportunities* (pp. 33–41). Springer Nature Singapore. DOI: 10.1007/978-981-99-7058-2_3

Aren, S., Hamamci, H. N., & Özcan, S. (2021). Moderation effect of pleasure seeking and loss aversion in the relationship between personality traits and risky investment intention. *Kybernetes*, 50(12), 3305–3330. DOI: 10.1108/K-05-2020-0278

Aren, S., & Nayman Hamamci, H. (2023). Evaluation of investment preference with phantasy, emotional intelligence, confidence, trust, financial literacy and risk preference. *Kybernetes*, 52(12), 6203–6231. DOI: 10.1108/K-01-2022-0014

Aria, M., Misuraca, M., & Spano, M. (2020). Mapping the evolution of social research and data science on 30 years of social indicators research. *Social Indicators Research*, 149(3), 803–831. DOI: 10.1007/s11205-020-02281-3

Ariely, D. (2008). *Predictably Irrational: The Hidden Forces That Shape Our Decisions*. HarperCollins.

Ariely, D., & Berns, G. S. (2010). Neuromarketing: The hope and hype of neuroimaging in business. *Nature Reviews. Neuroscience*, 11(4), 284–292. DOI: 10.1038/nrn2795 PMID: 20197790

Arora & Rathore (2022). Analysing sustainability reporting content for creating value through engaging stakeholders: A qualitative approach.

Arora, M. (2022). Women, Religion and Festivals: Exploring Qualitative Dimensions of the Role of Women in Legends Behind the Celebration of Festivals in India. In *Festival and Event Tourism: Building Resilience and Promoting Sustainability* (pp. 133-141). GB: CABI

Arora, M. (2023). Encapsulating Role of Persuasion and Skill Development in Marketing Communication for Brand Building: A Perspective. In International Handbook of Skill, Education, Learning, and Research Development in Tourism and Hospitality (pp. 1-17). Springer Nature Singapore

Arora, M. (2024). Metaverse Metamorphosis: Bridging the Gap Between Research Insights and Industry Applications. In Research, Innovation, and Industry Impacts of the Metaverse (pp. 275-286).

Arora, M. (2024). Metaverse Metamorphosis: Bridging the Gap Between Research Insights and Industry Applications. In *Research, Innovation, and Industry Impacts of the Metaverse* (pp. 275-286). IGI Global.

Arora, M. (2024). Metaverse Metamorphosis: Bridging the Gap Between Research Insights and Industry Applications. *Research, Innovation, and Industry Impacts of the Metaverse IGI Global,* 275-286)

Arora, M. (2024). Virtual Reality in Education: Analyzing the Literature and Bibliometric State of Knowledge. Transforming Education with Virtual Reality, 379-402.

Arora, M. (2024). Virtual Reality in Education: Analyzing the Literature and Bibliometric State of Knowledge. *Transforming Education with Virtual Reality, 379-402.* DOI: 10.1002/9781394200498.ch22

Arora, M. (2024b) Metaverse Metamorphosis: Bridging the Gap Between Research Insights and Industry Applications. In Research, Innovation, and Industry Impacts of the Metaverse (pp. 275-286).

Arora, M., & Sharma, R. L. (2021). Repurposing the Role of Entrepreneurs in the Havoc of COVID-19. In Entrepreneurship and Big Data (pp. 229-250). CRC Press.

Arora, M., & Sharma, R. L. (2023). Artificial intelligence and big data: ontological and communicative perspectives in multi-sectoral scenarios of modern businesses. *foresight, 25*(1), 126-143.

Arora, M., & Sharma, R. L. (2023). Artificial intelligence and big data: ontological and communicative perspectives in multi-sectoral scenarios of modern businesses. *Foresight, 25*(1), 126-143.

Arora, M., & Sharma, R. L. (2023b). Artificial intelligence and big data: ontological and communicative perspectives in multi-sectoral scenarios of modern businesses. *foresight, 25*(1), 126-143.

Arora, M., Gupta, S., & Mittal, A. (2024). Qualitative Insights Into Harvesting Sustainability: The Role of Organic Agriculture in Advancing Sustainable Development Goals. In *The Emerald Handbook of Tourism Economics and Sustainable Development* (pp. 41-62). Emerald Publishing Limited.

Arora, M. (2016). Creative dimensions of entrepreneurship: A key to business innovation. *Pacific Business Review International*, 1(1), 255–259.

Arora, M. (2020). Post-truth and marketing communication in technological age. In *Handbook of research on innovations in technology and marketing for the connected consumer* (pp. 94–108). IGI Global. DOI: 10.4018/978-1-7998-0131-3.ch005

Arora, M. (2023). Encapsulating role of persuasion and skill development in marketing communication for brand building: A perspective. In *International handbook of skill, education, learning, and research development in tourism and hospitality* (pp. 1–17). Springer Nature Singapore., DOI: 10.1007/978-981-99-0035-5_1

Arora, M. (2024). Metaverse Metamorphosis: Bridging the Gap Between Research Insights and Industry Applications. In *Research, Innovation, and Industry Impacts of the Metaverse* (pp. 275-286). IGI Global.

Arora, M. (2024). Metaverse metamorphosis: Bridging the gap between research insights and industry applications. In *Research, innovation, and industry impacts of the metaverse* (pp. 275–286). IGI Global., DOI: 10.4018/979-8-3693-2607-7.ch017

Arora, M., Dhiman, V., & Sharma, R. L. (2023). Exploring the dimensions of spirituality, wellness and value creation amidst Himalayan regions promoting entrepreneurship and sustainability. *Journal of Tourismology*, 9(2), 86–96.

Arora, M., Kumar, J., Dhiman, V., Rathore, S., Singh, S., & Chandel, M. (2024). Enhancing Resilience via Exponential Technologies: Analysing Trends, Focus and Contributions. *Abhigyan*, 42(3), 271–290. DOI: 10.1177/09702385241256015

Arora, M., & Rathore, S. (2023). Sustainability Reporting and Research and Development in Tourism Industry: A Qualitative Inquiry of Present Trends and Avenues. In *International Handbook of Skill, Education, Learning, and Research Development in Tourism and Hospitality* (pp. 1–17). Springer Nature Singapore.

Arora, M., & Sharma, R. L. (2022). Coalescing skills of gig players and fervor of entrepreneurial leaders to provide resilience strategies during global economic crises. In *COVID-19's Impact on the Cryptocurrency Market and the Digital Economy* (pp. 118–140). IGI Global. DOI: 10.4018/978-1-7998-9117-8.ch008

Arora, M., & Sharma, R. L. (2022). Integrating gig economy and social media platforms as a business strategy in the era of digitalization. In *Integrated business models in the digital age: Principles and practices of technology empowered strategies* (pp. 67–86). Springer International Publishing. DOI: 10.1007/978-3-030-97877-8_3

Arora, M., & Sharma, R. L. (2022). Religion and strategic marketing communication: Perspectivizing key facets of consumption. In *Promotional practices and perspectives from emerging markets* (pp. 210–225). Routledge India.

Arora, M., & Sharma, R. L. (2023). Artificial intelligence and big data: ontological and communicative perspectives in multi-sectoral scenarios of modern businesses. *foresight,* 25(1), 126-143.

Arora, M., & Sharma, R. L. (2023). Artificial intelligence and big data: Ontological and communicative perspectives in multi-sectoral scenarios of modern businesses. *Foresight*, 25(1), 126–143. DOI: 10.1108/FS-10-2021-0216

Arora, M., & Sharma, R. L. (2023a). Spirituality and Yoga for Well-being in a Post-disaster Scenario: Linking the Qualitative Facets of Traditional Indian Ways of Life. In *Resilient and Sustainable Destinations After Disaster* (pp. 227–239). Emerald Publishing Limited.

Arora, R. (2023). The role of visual branding in sensory marketing. *JMR, Journal of Marketing Research*, 60(2), 123–135. DOI: 10.1177/00222437221112345

Arora, R. (2024). Engaging the senses: Innovative marketing strategies in the age of technology. *JMR, Journal of Marketing Research*, 61(3), 77–89. DOI: 10.1177/00222437221198765

Arora, R., & Chandel, R. (2024). Experiential marketing in the digital era: Creating immersive brand experiences. *International Journal of Marketing Studies*, 16(2), 23–34. DOI: 10.5539/ijms.v16n2p23

Arora, R., Haleem, A., & Farooquie, J. (2017). Impact of critical success factors on successful technology implementation in Consumer Packaged Goods (CPG) supply chain. *Management Science Letters*, 7(5), 213–224. DOI: 10.5267/j.msl.2017.2.005

Arora, R., Kumar, A., & Valeri, M. (2023). The impact of VR and AR on consumer engagement: A sensory marketing perspective. *Journal of Consumer Marketing*, 40(1), 45–58. DOI: 10.1108/JCM-09-2022-0532

Arora, R., & Sharma, S. (2023). Sensory marketing: A new approach to enhance customer engagement. *JMR, Journal of Marketing Research*, 60(1), 25–38. https://doi.org/10.1177/00222437221199999

Arrufat-Martin, S., Rubira-García, R., & Archilla-García, P. (2024). Marketing and neuromarketing applied to the business sector as an object of the academic field of communication in Spain: An approach to its study from books as bibliographic sources. *Journal of Communication and Information Sciences*, 29. Advance online publication. DOI: 10.35742/rcci.2024.29.e291

Arthmann, C., & Li, I. P. (2017). *Neuromarketing - The Art and Science of Marketing and Neurosciences Enabled by IoT Technologies*. IIC Journal of Innovation.

Asuquo-Utuk, K. (2023). Neuro-economics and Strategic Decisions: The Impact on Financial Sustainability of Multinational Enterprises. *Revista Científica Profundidad Construyendo Futuro*, 19(19), 88–101. DOI: 10.22463/24221783.4079

Axsen, J., & Kurani, K. S. (2013). Developing sustainability-oriented values: Insights from households in a trial of plug-in hybrid electric vehicles. *Global Environmental Change*, 23(1), 70–80. DOI: 10.1016/j.gloenvcha.2012.08.002

Aydınoğlu, N. Z., & Sayın, E. (2016). Sensory and neuromarketing: about and beyond customer sensation. In *Flavor* (pp. 397–408). Woodhead Publishing. DOI: 10.1016/B978-0-08-100295-7.00019-0

Azad, N., & Masoumi, M. (2012). The impact of packaging on product competition. *Management Science Letters*, 2(8), 2789–2794. DOI: 10.5267/j.msl.2012.10.008

Azad, N., & Mohammadi, M. (2013). An empirical survey on factors influencing on packaging dairy products. *Management Science Letters*, 3(7), 1901–1906. DOI: 10.5267/j.msl.2013.06.039

Azcarate, A., Sande, K. V., & Valenti, R. G. (2005). Automatic facial emotion recognition. https://bit.ly/3goKE5p

Babu, M., Suganya, G., Brintha, R., & Prahalathan, C. (2021). Neurotransmitters and Investment Decision Making: A Review. *Business Studies Journal,* 13(2).

Bansal, A., Bansal, R., Bansal, A., Kumar, M., & Kumar, P. (2023). Normative Concerns in Neuromarketing. In *Promoting Consumer Engagement Through Emotional Branding and Sensory Marketing* (pp. 234–243). IGI Global.

Barbosa, J. D. S., & Mota, F. P. B. (2022). Adoption of e-government: A study on the role of trust. *Revista de Administração Pública*, 56(4), 441–464. DOI: 10.1590/0034-761220220027

Barth, M., Jugert, P., & Fritsche, I. (2016). Still underdetected – Social norms and collective efficacy predict the acceptance of electric vehicles in Germany. *Transportation Research Part F: Traffic Psychology and Behaviour*, 37, 64–77. DOI: 10.1016/j.trf.2015.11.011

Barykin, S. E., Smirnova, E. A., Chzhao, D., Kapustina, I. V., Sergeev, S. M., Mikhalchevsky, Y. Y., Gubenko, A. V., Kostin, G. A., De La Poza Plaza, E., Saychenko, L., & Moiseev, N. (2021). Digital echelons and interfaces within value chains: End-to-end marketing and logistics integration. *Sustainability (Basel)*, 13(24), 13929. Advance online publication. DOI: 10.3390/su132413929

Basdogan, C., Giraud, F., Levesque, V., Choi, S., 2020. A review of surface haptics: enabling tactile effects on touch surfaces. IEEE. Trans. Hapt. 1–21. .DOI: 10.1109/TOH.2020.2990712

Bazerman, M. H., & Moore, D. A. (2013). *Judgment in Managerial Decision Making*. Wiley.

Behe, B. K., Zhao, J., Sage, L., Huddleston, P. T., & Minahan, S. (2013). Display signs and involvement: The visual path to purchase intention. *International Review of Retail, Distribution and Consumer Research*, 23(5), 511–522. DOI: 10.1080/09593969.2013.832695

Behnke, J. (2006). Felix Brosius: SPSS-Programmierung. Effizientes Datenmanagement und Automatisierung mit SPSS-Syntax; Andy Field: Discovering Statistics Using SPSS. *Politische Vierteljahresschrift*, 47(4), 751–753. DOI: 10.1007/s11615-006-0382-6

Bekmurzaev, I., Kurbanov, A., Kurbanov, T., Plotnikov, V., & Ushakova, E. (2020). Digital technologies of marketing logistics and risks of their implementation in the supply chain. *International Scientific Conference on Digital Transformation on Manufacturing, Infrastructure and Service 2019, DTMIS 2019*, 940(1). DOI: 10.1088/1757-899X/940/1/012064

Bellio, E., & Buccoliero, L. (2014). Digital cities web marketing strategies in Italy: The path towards citizen empowerment. *Communications in Computer and Information Science*, 456, 142–159. DOI: 10.1007/978-3-662-44788-8_9

Belvedere, V., & Tunisini, A. (2020). Getting the Most from Omnichannel Management Strategy: Special Session: Best Articles from the Italian Marketing Association: An Abstract. In *Developments in Marketing Science: Proceedings of the Academy of Marketing Science* (pp. 185–186). Springer Nature. DOI: 10.1007/978-3-030-42545-6_51

Benachenhou, S., Guerrich, B., & Moussaoui, Z. (2018). The effect of packaging elements on purchase intention: Case study of Algerian customers. *Management Science Letters*, 8(4), 217–224. DOI: 10.5267/j.msl.2018.2.004

Bercea, M. D. (2012), Anatomy of methodologies for measuring consumer behaviour in neuromarketing research, https://bit.ly/355BhCe

Bergkvist, L., & Zhou, K. Q. (2016). Celebrity endorsements: A literature review and research agenda. *International Journal of Advertising*, 35(4), 642–663. DOI: 10.1080/02650487.2015.1137537

Bernard, C., Aquino, L. D. G., & Vanduffel, S. (2023). Optimal multivariate financial decision making. *European Journal of Operational Research*, 307(1), 468–483. DOI: 10.1016/j.ejor.2022.09.017

Bevz, N. (2015, May 10). http://www.digitalmarketing-glossary.com/What-isSensory-marketing-definition. Retrieved March 8, 2016, from http://www.digitalmarketing-glossary.com/

Bhardwaj, S., Kaushik, A., & Arora, R. (2024). The impact of sensory marketing on emotional engagement and brand loyalty. *Journal of Brand Management*. Advance online publication. https://doi.org/10.1057/s41262-023-00467-9

Bhardwaj, S., Kaushik, N., & Arora, M. (2024). Does Your Brain Have a Buy Button?: A Neuro Marketing Approach With Sensory Branding. In *Sensible Selling Through Sensory Neuromarketing* (pp. 210–229). IGI Global. DOI: 10.4018/979-8-3693-4236-7.ch011

Bhasin, H. (2023, July 25). *What is Consumer Behavior? Definition, Example, Types & Factors*. Retrieved from https://www.marketing91.com/consumer-behavior/

Bijmolt, T. H. A., Broekhuis, M., de Leeuw, S., Hirche, C., Rooderkerk, R. P., Sousa, R., & Zhu, S. X. (2021). Challenges at the marketing–operations interface in omni-channel retail environments. *Journal of Business Research*, 122, 864–874. DOI: 10.1016/j.jbusres.2019.11.034

Bitner, M. (1992, April). Servicescapes: The impact of physical surroundings on customers and employees. *Journal of Marketing*, 56(2), 57–71. DOI: 10.1177/002224299205600205

Black, W., & Babin, B. J. (2019). Multivariate data analysis: Its approach, evolution, and impact. In *The Great Facilitator* (pp. 121–130). Springer International Publishing., DOI: 10.1007/978-3-030-06031-2_16

Bleier, A., Harmeling, C. M., & Palmatier, R. W. (2019). Creating Effective Online Customer Experiences. *Journal of Marketing*, 83(2), 98–119. DOI: 10.1177/0022242918809930

Bone, P. F., & Ellen, P. S. (1999). Scents in the marketplace: Explaining a fraction of olfaction. *Journal of Retailing*, 75(2), 243–262. DOI: 10.1016/S0022-4359(99)00007-X

Bossaerts, P. (2009). What decision neuroscience teaches us about financial decision making. *Annual Review of Financial Economics*, 1(1), 383–404. DOI: 10.1146/annurev.financial.102708.141514

Bossaerts, P. (2021). How neurobiology elucidates the role of emotions in financial decision-making. *Frontiers in Psychology*, 12, 697375. DOI: 10.3389/fpsyg.2021.697375 PMID: 34349708

Boyne, S., Hall, D., & Williams, F. (2003). Policy, support and promotion for food-related tourism initiatives: A marketing approach to regional development. *Journal of Travel & Tourism Marketing*, 14(3-4), 131–154. DOI: 10.1300/J073v14n03_08

Bramlett, J. C. (2021). Battles for branding: A political marketing approach to studying televised candidate debates. *Communication Quarterly*, 69(3), 280–300. DOI: 10.1080/01463373.2021.1944889

Brammer, M. (2004). Brain scam? *Nature Neuroscience*, 7(10), 1015–1015. DOI: 10.1038/nn1004-1015 PMID: 15452565

Branding, A. O. S., & Purchase, I. E. O. Journal Homepage:-www. journalijar. Com

Briesemeister, B. B., Klaus, W., & Editors, S. (2019). *Neuromarketing in Business Identifying Implicit Purchase Drivers and Leveraging them for Sales Management for Professionals*. https://www.springer.com/series/10101

Briesemeister, B. B., Klaus, W., & Editors, S. (2019). *Neuromarketing in business: Identifying implicit purchase drivers and leveraging them for sales management for professionals*. Springer., DOI: 10.1007/978-3-319-93085-2

Brocas, I., & Carrillo, J. D. (2012). From perception to action: An economic model of brain processes. *Games and Economic Behavior*, 75(1), 81–103. DOI: 10.1016/j.geb.2011.10.001

Brodie, R. J., Coviello, N. E., Brookes, R. W., & Little, V. (1997). Towards a paradigm shift in marketing? An examination of current marketing practices. *Journal of Marketing Management*, 13(5), 383–406. DOI: 10.1080/0267257X.1997.9964481

Bühler, F., Cocron, P., Neumann, I., Franke, T., & Krems, J. F. (2014). Is EV experience related to EV acceptance? Results from a German field study. *Transportation Research Part F: Traffic Psychology and Behaviour*, 25, 34–49. DOI: 10.1016/j.trf.2014.05.002

Burke, R. R. (2011). How technology and consumer behaviour will change the future of retailing. *Journal of Retailing*, 87(1), 3–8.

Butler, M. (2008), Neuromarketing and the perception of knowledge. Journal of Consumer Behavior, pp. 7, 415–419, https://doi.org/.DOI: 10.1002/cb.260

Çabuk, S., & YAĞCI, M. İ. (2018). Pazarlamaya çağdaş yaklaşım. Akademisyen Kitabevi.

Çakar, T., Son-Turan, S., Girişken, Y., Sayar, A., Ertuğrul, S., Filiz, G., & Tuna, E. (2024). Unlocking the neural mechanisms of consumer loan evaluations: An fNIRS and ML-based consumer neuroscience study. *Frontiers in Human Neuroscience*, 18, 1286918. DOI: 10.3389/fnhum.2024.1286918 PMID: 38375365

Calvert, G. A., & Brammer, M. J. (2012). Predicting consumer behaviour. *IEE Pulse Magazine*, 3(3), 38–41. DOI: 10.1109/MPUL.2012.2189167 PMID: 22678839

Camerer, C. F. (2010). Removing financial incentives demotivates the brain. *Proceedings of the National Academy of Sciences of the United States of America*, 107(49), 20849–20850. DOI: 10.1073/pnas.1016108107 PMID: 21115829

Camerer, C. F., Loewenstein, G., & Prelec, D. (2005). Neuroeconomics: How neuroscience can inform economics. *Journal of Economic Literature*, 43(1), 9–64. DOI: 10.1257/0022051053737843

Cardoso, L., Chen, M. M., Araújo, A., de Almeida, G. G. F., Dias, F., & Moutinho, L. (2022). Accessing neuromarketing scientific performance: Research gaps and emerging topics. *Behavioral Sciences (Basel, Switzerland)*, 12(2), 55. DOI: 10.3390/bs12020055 PMID: 35200306

Carley, S., Krause, R. M., Lane, B. W., & Graham, J. D. (2013). Intent to purchase a plug-in electric vehicle: A survey of early impressions in large US cities. *Transportation Research Part D, Transport and Environment*, 18, 39–45. DOI: 10.1016/j.trd.2012.09.007

Carlos, M. Fernandez, T. M., J. A., & Pedro Dinis Gaspar, (2023, Feb.). *Innovative processes in smart packaging. A systematic review*. Retrieved from Journal of the Science of Food and Agriculture: https://scijournals.onlinelibrary.wiley.com/doi/10.1002/jsfa.11863

Carton, S. (2019). *What impact will immersive technologies such as augmented and virtual reality have on the retail sector?* (Doctoral dissertation, Dublin, National College of Ireland).

Casado-Aranda, L. A., Liébana-Cabanillas, F., & Sánchez-Fernández, J. (2018). A neuropsychological study on how consumers process risky and secure e-payments. *Journal of Interactive Marketing*, 43(1), 151–164. DOI: 10.1016/j.intmar.2018.03.001

Cassidy, R., Helmi, J., & Bridson, K. (2019). Drivers and inhibitors of national stakeholder engagement with place brand identity. *European Journal of Marketing*, 53(7), 1445–1465. DOI: 10.1108/EJM-04-2017-0275

Cenizo, C. (2022), Neuromarketing: concept, historical evolution and challenges. Icono 14, 20(1). https://doi.org/DOI: 10.7195/ri14.v20i1.1784

Chandel, M., & Arora, M. (2024). Metaverse Perspectives: Unpacking Its Role in Shaping Sustainable Development Goals-A Qualitative Inquiry. In Research, Innovation, and Industry Impacts of the Metaverse (pp. 62-75). IGI Global.

Chandel, M., & Arora, M. (2024). Metaverse Perspectives: Unpacking Its Role in Shaping Sustainable Development Goals-A Qualitative Inquiry. *Research, Innovation, and Industry Impacts of the Metaverse IGI Global*, 62-75.

Changuán, M. P. O., & Simbaña, J. A. L. (2022). Consumer color neuromarketing. Journal of business and entrepreneurial studie, 6(3).

Chan, H. Y., Boksem, M., & Smidts, A. (2018). Neural profiling of brands: Mapping brand image in consumers' brains with visual templates. *JMR, Journal of Marketing Research*, 55(4), 600–615. DOI: 10.1509/jmr.17.0019

Chapkovski, P., Khapko, M., & Zoican, M. (2024). Trading gamification and investor behavior. *Management Science*, mnsc.2022.02650. DOI: 10.1287/mnsc.2022.02650

Chatterjee, J., & Dutta, G. (2024). Power of Social Media in Political Marketing – An India-Based Empirical Study. *Studies in Media and Communication*, 12(1), 242–253. DOI: 10.11114/smc.v12i1.6633

Chaudhary, P., & Kate, N. (2023). The coalescence effect: Understanding the impact of customer value proposition, perceived benefits and climate change sensitivities on electric vehicle adoption in India. https://doi.org/DOI: 10.1002/bsd2.282

Chavaglia, J. N., Filipe, J. A., & Ramalheiro, B. (2011). Neuromarketing: Consumers and the anchoring effect. *International Journal of Latest Trends in Finance and Economics Sciences*, (4), 183–189.

Cheah, J. H., Ting, H., Cham, T. H., & Memon, M. A. (2019). The effect of selfie promotion and celebrity endorsed advertisement on decision-making processes: A model comparison. *Internet Research*, 29(3), 552–577. DOI: 10.1108/IntR-12-2017-0530

Chen, H., & Ho, Y. S. (2015). Highly cited articles in biomass research: A bibliometric analysis. *Renewable & Sustainable Energy Reviews*, 49, 12–20. DOI: 10.1016/j.rser.2015.04.060

Chen, Y. (2023). High art down net: Conceptualizing a citizen arts philanthropy with ethical codes and a digital system. *Journal of Philanthropy and Marketing*, 28(4), e1785. Advance online publication. DOI: 10.1002/nvsm.1785

Chen, Y. P., Nelson, L. D., & Hsu, M. (2015). From "Where" to "What": Distributed Representations of Brand Associations in the Human Brain. *JMR, Journal of Marketing Research*, 52(4), 453–466. DOI: 10.1509/jmr.14.0606 PMID: 27065490

Cherkaoui, M., Rissman, J., Lau, H., & Hampson, M. (2021). Ethical considerations for fMRI neurofeedback. In *fMRI Neurofeedback* (pp. 315-331). Academic Press. DOI: 10.1016/B978-0-12-822421-2.00007-7

Cherubino, P., Martinez-Levy, A. C., Caratu, M., Cartocci, G., Di Flumeri, G., Modica, E., & Trettel, A. (2019). Consumer behaviour through the eyes of neurophysiological measures: State-of-the-art and future trends. *Computational Intelligence and Neuroscience*, 2019, 2019. DOI: 10.1155/2019/1976847 PMID: 31641346

Choi, S. M., & Rifon, N. J. (2012). It Is a Match: The Impact of Congruence between Celebrity Image and Consumer Ideal Self on Endorsement Effectiveness. *Psychology and Marketing*, 29(9), 639–650. DOI: 10.1002/mar.20550

Chorvat, T. R. (2016). The Neuroeconomics of Financial Decisions and the Stochastic Discount Factor. *George Mason Law & Economics Research Paper*, (16-20).

Chowdhury, T. A., & Naheed, S. (2020). Word of mouth communication in political marketing: Understanding and managing referrals. *Journal of Marketing Communications*, 26(3), 290–313. DOI: 10.1080/13527266.2018.1523217

Chowdhury, T. A., & Naheed, S. (2022). Multidimensional Political Marketing Mix Model for Developing Countries: An Empirical Investigation. *Journal of Political Marketing*, 21(1), 56–84. DOI: 10.1080/15377857.2019.1577323

Christy, R., Oliver, G., & Penn, J. (1996). Relationship marketing in consumer markets. *Journal of Marketing Management*, 12(1-3), 175–187. DOI: 10.1080/0267257X.1996.9964407

Chuang, K. Y., Huang, Y. L., & Ho, Y. S. (2007). A bibliometric and citation analysis of stroke-related research in Taiwan. *Scientometrics*, 72(2), 201–212. DOI: 10.1007/s11192-007-1721-0

Cialdini, R. B. (2007). *Influence: The psychology of persuasion*. Harper Business.

Cialdini, R. B. (2009). *Influence: Science and Practice*. Pearson Education.

Clement, J. (2007). Visual influence on in-store buying decisions: An eye-track experiment on the visual influence of pack- aging design. *Journal of Marketing Management*, 23(9-10), 917–928. DOI: 10.1362/026725707X250395

Clement, J., Smith, V., Zlatev, J., Gidlöf, K., & Van de Weijer, J. (2017). Assessing information on food packages. *European Journal of Marketing*, 51(1), 219–237. DOI: 10.1108/EJM-09-2013-0509

Cocron, P., Franke, T., Neumann, I., Wege, C., Bühler, F., & Krems, J. F. (2010). Ist das Fahren mit einem Elektrofahrzeug so besonders? Anpassung des Verhaltens beim Fahren mit Elektrofahrzeugen. Paper presented at the 52th Tagung experimentell arbeitender Psychologen, Saarbrücken, Germany.

Cohen, M. X. (2014). *Analysing neural time series data: Theory and Practice*. MIT Press. DOI: 10.7551/mitpress/9609.001.0001

Colaferro, C. A., & Crescitelli, E. (2014). The Contribution of Neuromarketing to the Study of Consumer Behavior. *Brazilian Business Review*, 11(3), 123–143. DOI: 10.15728/bbr.2014.11.3.6

Conejo, F., Khoo, C., Tanakinjal, G., & Yang, L. (2007). Neuromarketing: will it revolutionise business?.

Constantinescu, M., Orindaru, A., Pachitanu, A., Rosca, L., Caescu, S. C., & Orzan, M. C. (2019). Attitude Evaluation on Using the Neuromarketing Approach in Social Media: Matching Company's Purposes and Consumer's Benefits for Sustainable Business Growth. *Sustainability (Basel)*, 11(24), 7094. DOI: 10.3390/su11247094

Constantinides, E. (2006). The marketing mix revisited: Towards the 21st century marketing. *Journal of Marketing Management*, 22(3-4), 407–438. DOI: 10.1362/026725706776861190

Consumer behaviour. (n.d.). Retrieved from Wikipedia: https://en.wikipedia.org/wiki/Consumer_behaviour

Cordeiro, R., Reis, A., Ferreira, B. M., & Bacalhau, L. M. (2024). Neuromarketing: Decoding the Role of Emotions and Senses and Consumer Behavior. *Cognitive Behavioral Neuroscience in Organizational Settings*, 83-100.

Ćosić, D. (2016). Neuromarketing in market research. *Interdisciplinary Description of Complex Systems: INDECS*, 14(2), 139–147. DOI: 10.7906/indecs.14.2.3

Costa, M. F., Patricia, Z. Natasha, R. Jessica, A and Maria, G.V. (2012). Sensory marketing: Consumption experience of the Brazilian in the restaurant industry. *International Journal of Business Strategy*, 12(4), 165–171.

Cristofaro, M., Giardino, P. L., Malizia, A. P., & Mastrogiorgio, A. (2022). Affect and cognition in managerial decision making: A systematic literature review of neuroscience evidence. *Frontiers in Psychology*, 13, 762993. DOI: 10.3389/fpsyg.2022.762993 PMID: 35356322

Crofton, E. C., Botinestean, C., Fenelon, M., & Gallagher, E. (2019). Potential applications for virtual and augmented reality technologies in sensory science. *Innovative Food Science & Emerging Technologies*, 56, 102178. DOI: 10.1016/j.ifset.2019.102178

Crowther, C. A., Harding, J. E., Middleton, P. F., Andersen, C. C., Ashwood, P., & Robinson, J. S. (2013). Australasian randomised trial to evaluate the role of maternal intramuscular dexamethasone versus betamethasone prior to preterm birth to increase survival free of childhood neurosensory disability (A* STEROID): Study protocol. *BMC Pregnancy and Childbirth*, 13(1), 1–7. DOI: 10.1186/1471-2393-13-104 PMID: 23642125

da Silva, C. (2023). NEUROMARKETING: Its importance in understanding consumer behavior for sales boost. *Revista Interface Tecnológica*, 20(2), 446–457. DOI: 10.31510/infa.v20i2.1776

Dangwal, A., Bathla, D., Kukreti, M., Mehta, M., Chauhan, P., & Sarangal, R. (2023). Neuromarketing science: A road to a commercial start-up. In *Applications of Neuromarketing in the Metaverse* (pp. 223–232). IGI Global. DOI: 10.4018/978-1-6684-8150-9.ch017

Darabi, K., & Mirabi, V. (2018). The effect of ambient scent on consumer experience: Evidence from mobile industry. *Management Science Letters*, 8(11), 1199–1206. DOI: 10.5267/j.msl.2018.8.005

Daugherty, T., Hoffman, E., & Kennedy, K. N. (2016). Research in reverse: Ad testing using an inductive consumer neuroscience approach. *Journal of Business Research*, 69(8), 3168–3176. DOI: 10.1016/j.jbusres.2015.12.005

Davenport, T. H., & Harris, J. G. (2007). *Competing on analytics: The new science of winning*. Harvard Business Press.

de la Cruz, J. S., de la Hera, T., Gómez, S. C., & Lacasa, P. (2023). Digital Games as Persuasion Spaces for Political Marketing: Joe Biden's Campaign in Fortnite. *Media and Communication*, 11(2), 266–277. DOI: 10.17645/mac.v11i2.6476

De Martino, B., Camerer, C. F., & Adolphs, R. (2010). Amygdala damage eliminates monetary loss aversion. *Proceedings of the National Academy of Sciences of the United States of America*, 107(8), 3788–3792. DOI: 10.1073/pnas.0910230107 PMID: 20142490

De Martino, B., Kumaran, D., Seymour, B., & Dolan, R. J. (2006). Frames, biases, and rational decision-making in the human brain. *Science*, 313(5787), 684–687. DOI: 10.1126/science.1128356 PMID: 16888142

de Vries, R., Jager, G., Tijssen, I., & Zandstra, E. H. (2018). Shopping for products in a virtual world: Why haptics and visuals are equally important in shaping consumer perceptions and attitudes. *Food Quality and Preference*, 66, 64–75. DOI: 10.1016/j.foodqual.2018.01.005

del Mar Lozano Cortés, M., & García García, M. (2017). Neuromarketing: Current situation and future trends. *Media and Metamedia Management*, 373-380.

Deng, X., Yang, X., Bu, M., Tang, A., Zhang, H., Long, L., & Chen, B. T. (2024). Nomogram for prediction of hearing rehabilitation outcome in children with congenital sensorineural hearing loss after cochlear implantation. *Heliyon*, 10(8), e29529. DOI: 10.1016/j.heliyon.2024.e29529 PMID: 38699755

Devaru, S. D. B. (2018). Significance of neuromarketing on consumer buying behavior. *International Journal of Technical Research & Science*, 3(3), 114–121. DOI: 10.30780/IJTRS.V3.I3.2018.015

Dhar, R. (1997). Consumer preference for a no-choice option. *The Journal of Consumer Research*, 24(2), 215–231. DOI: 10.1086/209506

Dhiman, V., & Arora, M. (2024) b. How foresight has evolved since 1999? Understanding its themes, scope and focus. *foresight, 26*(2), 253-271.

Dhiman, V., & Arora, M. (2024). Exploring the linkage between business incubation and entrepreneurship: understanding trends, themes and future research agenda. *LBS Journal of Management & Research*, (ahead-of-print).

Dhiman, V., & Arora, M. (2024a) Current State of Metaverse in Entrepreneurial Ecosystem: A Retrospective Analysis of Its Evolving Landscape. In Exploring the Use of Metaverse in Business and Education (pp. 73-87). IGI Global.

Dhiman, V., & Arora, M. (2024b). Exploring the linkage between business incubation and entrepreneurship: understanding trends, themes and future research agenda. *LBS Journal of Management & Research*, (ahead-of-print).

Dhiman, V., & Arora, M. (2024c). How foresight has evolved since 1999? Understanding its themes, scope and focus. *foresight, 26*(2), 253-271.

Dhiman, V., & Arora, M. (2024). Current state of metaverse in entrepreneurial ecosystem: A retrospective analysis of its evolving landscape. In *Exploring the use of metaverse in business and education* (pp. 73–87). IGI Global., DOI: 10.4018/979-8-3693-5868-9.ch005

Dhiman, V., & Arora, M. (2024b). Exploring the linkage between business incubation and entrepreneurship: Understanding trends, themes and future research agenda. *LBS Journal of Management & Research*, 22(1), 66–92. DOI: 10.1108/LBSJMR-06-2023-0021

Dhiman, V., & Arora, M. (2024d). What Lies in 'Business Incubation and SMEs' Research? A Literature Review and Roadmap for Future Research. *Management*, 1, 17.

Diamond, D. (2009). The impact of government incentives for hybrid-electric vehicles: Evidence from US states. *Energy Policy*, 37(3), 972–983. DOI: 10.1016/j.enpol.2008.09.094

Dickson, P. R., & Kelly, G. J. (1985). The "Barnum effect" in personality assessment: A review of the literature. *Psychological Reports*, 57(2), 367–382. DOI: 10.2466/pr0.1985.57.2.367

Dillon, M. (2024, February 25). *How Does Product Packaging Impact Consumer Buying Behavior?* Retrieved from https://meyers.com/meyers-blog/how-does-packaging-affect-consumer-behavior/

Dimoka, , Pavlou, P. A., & Davis, F. D. (2011). Using neurophysiological methods to understand consumer behavior. *Management Information Systems Quarterly*, 35(3), 679–702. https://doi.org/10.2307/23042809

Dong, B., Xu, G., Luo, X., Cai, Y., & Gao, W. (2012). A bibliometric analysis of solar power research from 1991 to 2010. *Scientometrics*, 93(3), 1101–1117. DOI: 10.1007/s11192-012-0730-9

Donthu, N., Kumar, S., Mukherjee, D., Pandey, N., & Lim, W. M. (2021). How to conduct a bibliometric analysis: An overview and guidelines. *Journal of Business Research*, 133, 285–296. DOI: 10.1016/j.jbusres.2021.04.070

Donthu, N., Kumar, S., Pattnaik, D., & Pandey, N. (2021). A bibliometric review of International Marketing Review (IMR): Past, present, and future. *International Marketing Review*, 38(5), 840–878. Advance online publication. DOI: 10.1108/IMR-11-2020-0244

Dooley, R. (2010), Baby pictures do grab our attention. https://bit.ly/3g4c2Xo

Dooley, R. (2011). *Brainfluence: 100 ways to persuade and convince consumers with Neuromarketing*. Wiley.

Doucé, L., & Janssens, W. (2013). The presence of a pleasant ambient scent in a fashion store: The moderating role of shopping motivation and affect intensity. *Environment and Behavior*, 45(2), 215–238. DOI: 10.1177/0013916511410421

Dragolea, L., & Cotirlea, D. (2011). Neuromarketing: Between influence and manipulation. Polish. *Journal of Management Studies*, 3, 78–88.

Du, G., Cao, W., Hu, S., Lin, Z., & Yuan, T. (2018). Design and assessment of an electric vehicle powertrain model based on real-world driving and charging cycles. *IEEE Transactions on Vehicular Technology*, 68(2), 1178–1187. DOI: 10.1109/TVT.2018.2884812

Duong, S. N., Du, H. P., Nguyen, C. N., & Nguyen, H. N. (2021). A RED-BET Method to Improve the Information Diffusion on Social Networks. *International Journal of Advanced Computer Science and Applications*, 12(8), 867–875. DOI: 10.14569/IJACSA.2021.0120898

Dutta, A. (2023). Neuro-marketing and consumer behavior: Exploring the use of neuroscience techniques to understand how consumers make decisions and respond to marketing stimuli. *EPRA International Journal of Economics. Business and Management Studies*, 10(8), 29–38.

Dwivedi, A., Nagariya, R., & Joseph, S. (2025). Neuromarketing in Fashion: Unveiling Consumer Insights & Brand Strategies. *Journal of Engineering. Management and Information Technology*, 3(3), 149–158.

Egbue, O., & Long, S. (2012). Barriers to widespread adoption of electric vehicles: An analysis of consumer attitudes and perceptions. *Energy Policy*, 48, 717–729. DOI: 10.1016/j.enpol.2012.06.009

Egidi, G., Nusbaum, H. C., & Cacioppo, J. T. (2008). Neuroeconomics: Foundational issues and consumer relevance. In Haugvedt, C., Kardes, F., & Herr, P. (Eds.), *Handbook of Consumer Psychology* (pp. 1177–1214). Erlbaum.

Elder, R. S., & Krishna, A. (2010). The effects of advertising copy on sensory thoughts and perceived taste. *The Journal of Consumer Research*, 36(5), 748–756. https://doi.org/10.1086/605327

Ellegaard, O., & Wallin, J. A. (2015). The bibliometric analysis of scholarly production: How great is the impact? *Scientometrics*, 105(3), 1809–1831. DOI: 10.1007/s11192-015-1645-z PMID: 26594073

Ellingsen, L. A.-W., Singh, B., & Strømman, A. H. (2016). The size and range effect: Lifecycle greenhouse gas emissions of electric vehicles. *Environmental Research Letters*, 11(5), 054010. DOI: 10.1088/1748-9326/11/5/054010

Engel, J. F., Blackwell, R. D., & Miniard, P. W. (1990). *Consumer Behavior*. Dryden Press.

Engelmann, T., Wallstein, S., & Hitzler, D. (2019). An experimental study to investigate the potential of online shopping in immersive virtual realities compared to conventional online shops. *The International Journal of Virtual Reality: a Multimedia Publication for Professionals*, 19(3), 31–45. DOI: 10.20870/IJVR.2019.19.3.2939

Erdmann, A., & Ponzoa, J. M. (2020). Digital inbound marketing: Measuring the economic performance of grocery e-commerce in Europe and the USA. *Technological Forecasting and Social Change*, 162, 120373. DOI: 10.1016/j.techfore.2020.120373 PMID: 33100412

Erkut, B., Kaya, T., Lehmann-Waffenschmidt, M., Mahendru, M., Sharma, G. D., Srivastava, A. K., & Srivastava, M. (2018). A fresh look on financial decision-making from the plasticity perspective. *International Journal of Ethics and Systems*, 34(4), 426–441. DOI: 10.1108/IJOES-02-2018-0022

Erokhina, T. B., Mitko, O. A., & Troilin, V. V. (2018). Digital marketing and digital logistics in consumer communication. *European Research Studies Journal, 21*, 861–867. https://www.scopus.com/inward/record.uri?eid=2-s2.0-85063176693&partnerID=40&md5=bd07863358eb48fd6782a026a0a829a8

Esmailpour, H., & Zakipour, M. (2016). The sensory stimuli model; engage with the consumer senses for brand distinguishes. *Journal of Management Sciences, 2*(4), 212–218.

European Commission. (2020). *Sustainable and Smart Mobility Strategy – putting European transport on track for the future.* Retrieved from https://ec.europa.eu/transport/themes/mobilitystrategy_en

Everitt, B. S., & Dunn, G. (2001). *Applied multivariate data analysis.* Wiley., DOI: 10.1002/9781118887486

Familmaleki, M., Aghighi, A., & Hamidi, K. (2015). Analyzing the impact of promotion mix on consumer; s purchase decision. *Advanced Social Humanities and Management, 2*(1), 71–81.

Farazian, T. A., & Paskarina, C. (2021). Political marketing in the 2019 local election: A case of the Indonesia Solidarity party in the legislative election in Jakarta. *Academic Journal of Interdisciplinary Studies*, 10(5), 1–11. DOI: 10.36941/ajis-2021-0119

Farrell, A. M., Goh, J. O., & White, B. J. (2018). Financial incentives differentially regulate neural processing of positive and negative emotions during value-based decision-making. *Frontiers in Human Neuroscience*, 12, 58. DOI: 10.3389/fnhum.2018.00058 PMID: 29487519

Fernández Gómez, J. D., Pineda, A., & Gordillo-Rodriguez, M.-T. (2024). Celebrities, Advertising Endorsement, and Political Marketing in Spain: The Popular Party's April 2019 Election Campaign. *Journal of Political Marketing*, 23(2), 123–148. DOI: 10.1080/15377857.2021.1950099

Fingelkurts, A. A., Fingelkurts, A. A., & Neves, C. F. (2020). Neuro-assessment of leadership training. *Coaching (Abingdon, UK)*, 13(2), 107–145. DOI: 10.1080/17521882.2019.1619796

Finthariasari, M., & Zetira, A. M. (2022). Purchase intention: Pengaruh price discount, bonus pack dan celebrity endorser. *Jurnal Bisnis Dan Manajemen*, 16–25. DOI: 10.23960/jbm.v18i0.233

Fisher, C. E., Chin, L., & Klitzman, R. (2010). Defining Neuromarketing: Practices and Professional Challenges. *Harvard Review of Psychiatry*, 18(4), 230–237. DOI: 10.3109/10673229.2010.496623 PMID: 20597593

Fleck, N., Korchia, M., & Le Roy, I. (2012). Celebrities in Advertising: Looking for Congruence or Likability? *Psychology and Marketing*, 29(9), 651–662. DOI: 10.1002/mar.20551

Foley, H. J. (2019). *Sensation and perception*. Routledge. DOI: 10.4324/9780429275913

Foreman, S. K., & Money, A. H. (1995). Internal marketing: Concepts, measurement and application. *Journal of Marketing Management*, 11(8), 755–768. DOI: 10.1080/0267257X.1995.9964388

Fortunato, V. C. R., Giraldi, J. D. M. E., & de Oliveira, J. H. C. (2014). A review of studies on neuromarketing: Practical results, techniques, contributions and limitations. *Journal of Management Research*, 6(2), 201. DOI: 10.5296/jmr.v6i2.5446

Frederick, D. P. (2022). Recent trends in neuro marketing–An exploratory study. [IJCSBE]. *International Journal of Case Studies in Business, IT, and Education*, 6(1), 38–60. DOI: 10.47992/IJCSBE.2581.6942.0148

Freedman, J. L., & Fraser, S. C. (1966). Compliance without pressure: The foot-in-the-door technique. *Journal of Personality and Social Psychology*, 4(2), 195–202. DOI: 10.1037/h0023552 PMID: 5969145

Fripp, G. (n.d.). *The Main Roles of Product Packaging in Marketing*. Retrieved from https://www.marketingstudyguide.com/the-main-roles-of-product-packaging-in-marketing/

Fu, F. Q., Richards, K. A., Hughes, D. E., & Jones, E. (2010). Motivating salespeople to sell new products: The relative influence of attitudes, subjective norms, and self-efficacy. *Journal of Marketing*, 74(6), 61–76. DOI: 10.1509/jmkg.74.6.61

Fugate, D. L. (2007). Neuromarketing: A layman's look at neuroscience and its potential application to marketing practice. *Journal of Consumer Marketing*, 24(7), 385–394. DOI: 10.1108/07363760710834807

Fugate, D. L. (2008). Marketing services more effectively with neuromarketing research: A look into the future. *Journal of Services Marketing*, 22(2), 170–173. DOI: 10.1108/08876040810862903

Garcia, J. R., & Saad, G. (2008). Evolutionary neuromarketing: Darwinizing the neuroimaging paradigm for consumer behavior. *Journal of Consumer Behaviour*, 7(4-5), 397–414. DOI: 10.1002/cb.259

Garlin, F. V., & Owen, K. (2006). Setting the tone with the tune: A meta-analytic review of the effects of background music in retail settings. *Journal of Business Research*, 59(6), 755–764. DOI: 10.1016/j.jbusres.2006.01.013

Gaspar, C., & Dieckmann, A. (2021). Young but not Naive: Leaders of Tomorrow Expect Limits to Digital Freedom to Preserve Freedom. *NIM Marketing Intelligence Review*, 13(1), 52–57. DOI: 10.2478/nimmir-2021-0009

Gentner, F. (2012). *Neuromarketing in the B-to-B-sector: importance, potential and its implications for brand management*. Diplomica Verlag.

Georges, P. M., Bayle-Tourtoulou, A. S., & Badoc, M. (2013). *Neuromarketing in action: How to talk and sell to the brain*. Kogan Page Publishers.

Gerth, F., Ramiah, V., Toufaily, E., & Muschert, G. (2021). Assessing the effectiveness of COVID-19 financial product innovations in supporting financially distressed firms and households in the UAE. *Journal of Financial Services Marketing*, 26(4), 215–225. DOI: 10.1057/s41264-021-00098-w

Getaruelas, R. (2019). Impact of digital marketing in tourism in Oman. *Journal of Advanced Research in Dynamical and Control Systems, 11*(5 Special Issue), 1936–1945. https://www.scopus.com/inward/record.uri?eid=2-s2.0-85071908054&partnerID=40&md5=19c2309047be06c523019ba4ff94f5da

Gill, R., & Singh, J. (2022). A study of neuromarketing techniques for proposing cost effective information driven framework for decision making. *Materials Today: Proceedings*, 49, 2969–2981. DOI: 10.1016/j.matpr.2020.08.730

Glimcher, P. W., & Fehr, E. (2014). *Neuroeconomics: Decision making and the brain*. Academic Press.

Godinho, S., Prada, M., & Garrido, M. V. (2016). Under pressure: An integrative perspective of time pressure impact on consumer decision-making. *Journal of International Consumer Marketing*, 28(4), 251–273. DOI: 10.1080/08961530.2016.1148654

Goel, P., Garg, A., Sharma, A., & Rana, N. P. (2023). Impact of sensory perceptions on the urge to buy impulsively. *Journal of Computer Information Systems*, , 1–17.

Goldberg, L. M. (2012). *Greed, fear and irrational exuberance-the deep play of financial and cultural speculation* (Doctoral dissertation, UNSW Sydney).

Golnar-Nik, P., Farashi, S., & Safari, M. S. (2019). The application of EEG power for the prediction and interpretation of consumer decision-making: A neuromarketing study. *Physiology & Behavior*, 207, 90–98. DOI: 10.1016/j.physbeh.2019.04.025 PMID: 31047949

González-Morales, A. (2022). La optimización de la comunicación POSM "Point of Sale Materials" en productos de compra por impulso mediante neuromarketing. IROCAMM. *International Review of Communication and Marketing Mix*, 5(1), 57–71. DOI: 10.12795/IROCAMM.2021.v05.i01.05

González-Morales, A., Mitrovic, J., & Garcia, R. C. (2020). Ecological consumer neuroscience for competitive advantage and business or organizational differentiation. *European Research on Management and Business Economics*, 26(3), 174–180. DOI: 10.1016/j.iedeen.2020.05.001

Goswami, A., & Deshmukh, G. K. (2022). Neuromarketing: Emerging Trend in Consumer Behavior. *Advances in Marketing, Customer Relationship Management, and E-Services*, 5(0), 79–87. DOI: 10.4018/978-1-6684-4496-2.ch005

Gottfried, J. A., O'Doherty, J., & Dolan, R. J. (2006). Encoding predictive reward value in human amygdala and orbitofrontal cortex. *Science*, 301(5636), 1104–1107. DOI: 10.1126/science.1087919 PMID: 12934011

Graham-Rowe, E., Gardner, B., Abraham, C., Skippon, S., Dittmar, H., Hutchins, R., & Stannard, J. (2012). Mainstream consumers driving plug-in battery-electric and plug-in hybrid electric cars: A qualitative analysis of responses and evaluations. *Transportation Research Part A, Policy and Practice*, 46(1), 140–153. DOI: 10.1016/j.tra.2011.09.008

Grand View Research. (2023). *Multisensory marketing market size, share & trends analysis report by sensory type, by application, by region, and segment forecasts, 2023-2030*. Retrieved from https://www.grandviewresearch.com/industry-analysis/multisensory-marketing-market

Grant, S. M., Hobson, J. L., & Sinha, R. K. (2024). Digital engagement practices in mobile trading: The impact of color and swiping to trade on investor decisions. *Management Science*, 70(3), 2003–2022. DOI: 10.1287/mnsc.2023.00379

Gregory, M. (2009). Book review: NORMAN K. DENZIN and YVONNA S. LINCOLN, The Sage Handbook of Qualitative Research (3rd Edition). London: Sage, 2005. 1288 pp. ISBN 07619 2757 3 (hbk) £85.00. *Qualitative Research*, 9(3), 388–389. DOI: 10.1177/14687941090090030803

Grönroos, C. (1982). An applied service marketing theory. *European Journal of Marketing*, 16(7), 30–41. DOI: 10.1108/EUM0000000004859

Guedea-Noriega, H. H., & García-Sánchez, F. (2022). Integroly: Automatic Knowledge Graph Population from Social Big Data in the Political Marketing Domain. *Applied Sciences (Basel, Switzerland)*, 12(16), 8116. Advance online publication. DOI: 10.3390/app12168116

Guo, Y. (2022). Do Masculinity and Femininity Matter? Evidence From the Investigation on the Penetration Level of E-Government Websites Between China and South Korea. *International Journal of Electronic Government Research*, 18(1), 1–18. Advance online publication. DOI: 10.4018/IJEGR.313575

Guo, Y., & Liang, G. (2021). Perceptual Feedback Mechanism Sensor Technology in e-Commerce IoT Application Research. *Journal of Sensors*, 2021(1), 3840103. DOI: 10.1155/2021/3840103

Gurgu, E., Gurgu, I. A., & Tonis, R. B. M. (2020). Neuromarketing for a better understanding of consumer needs and emotions. *Independent Journal of Management & Production*, 11(1), 208–235. DOI: 10.14807/ijmp.v11i1.993

Guttikunda, S. K., & Mohan, D. (2014). Re-fueling road transport for better air quality in India. *Energy Policy*, 68, 556–561. DOI: 10.1016/j.enpol.2013.12.067

Halkiopoulos, C., Antonopoulou, H., & Stiliadi, S. (2023). Neuroscientific Perspectives in Digital Marketing. https://doi.org/DOI: 10.31219/osf.io/bs73w

Hamacher, K., & Buchkremer, R. (2022). Measuring online sensory consumer experience: Introducing the online sensory marketing index (OSMI) as a structural modeling approach. *Journal of Theoretical and Applied Electronic Commerce Research*, 17(2), 751–772. DOI: 10.3390/jtaer17020039

Hammou, K. A., Galib, M. H., & Melloul, J. (2013). The contributions of neuromarketing in marketing research. *Journal of Management Research*, 5(4), 20. DOI: 10.5296/jmr.v5i4.4023

Han, J. (2023). Procter & Gamble's innovative marketing strategies: A case study. *Journal of Marketing Management*, 39(1), 12–25. DOI: 10.1080/0267257X.2022.2040256

Harmes, A. (2020). Political Marketing in Post-Conflict Elections: The Case of Iraq. *Journal of Political Marketing*, 19(3), 201–232. DOI: 10.1080/15377857.2016.1193834

Harrar, V., Piqueras-Fiszman, B., & Spence, C. (2011). There's no taste in a white bowl. *Perception*, 40(7), 880–892. DOI: 10.1068/p7040 PMID: 22128561

Harris, J. M., Ciorciari, J., & Gountas, J. (2018). Consumer neuroscience for marketing researchers. *Journal of Consumer Behaviour*, 17(3), 239–252. DOI: 10.1002/cb.1710

Harrop, S. (2007). What role can sensory branding play in online marketing?.

Hasher, L., Goldstein, D., & Toppino, T. (1977). Frequency and the conference of referential validity. *Journal of Verbal Learning and Verbal Behavior*, 16(1), 107–112. DOI: 10.1016/S0022-5371(77)80012-1

Haubl, G., & Trifts, V. (2000). Consumer decision making in online shopping environments: The effects of interactive decision aids. *Marketing Science*, 19(1), 4–21. DOI: 10.1287/mksc.19.1.4.15178

Hawkins, D., Boston, R., & Kenny, K. (2006). Consumer Behavior, Translated by Ahmad Rousta, Atieh Bathaei & Zeinab Hagh Verdi.

Hazeldine, S. (2014). *Neuro-sell: How neuroscience can power your sales success*. Kogan Page.

Heilbronner, R. L., Sweet, J. J., Morgan, J. E., Larrabee, G. J., & Millis, S. R. (2009). American academy of clinical neuropsychology consensus conference statement on the neuropsychological assessment of effort, response bias, and malingering. In *Clinical Neuropsychologist* (Vol. 23, Issue 7, pp. 1093–1129). DOI: 10.1080/13854040903155063

Hennig-Thurau, T., Gwinner, K. P., Walsh, G., & Gremler, D. D. (2010). Electronic word-of-mouth via consumer-opinion platforms: What motivates consumers to articulate themselves online? *Journal of Interactive Marketing*, 18(1), 38–52. DOI: 10.1002/dir.10073

Henrich, J., Heine, S. J., & Cnorezayan, A. (2010). The weirdest people in the world? *Behavioral and Brain Sciences*, 33(2-3), 61–135. DOI: 10.1017/S0140525X0999152X PMID: 20550733

Hensel, D., Iorga, A., Wolter, L., & Znanewitz, J. (2017). Conducting neuromarketing studies from ethically-practitioner perspectives. *Cogent Psychology*, 4(1), 1320858. DOI: 10.1080/23311908.2017.1320858

Hilderbrand, M.L. (2016), Neuromarketing: An essential tool in the future of advertising and brand development [Thesis doctoral, University of Texas].

Hilken, T., Chylinski, M., Keeling, D. I., Heller, J., de Ruyter, K., & Mahr, D. (2022). How to strategically choose or combine augmented and virtual reality for improved online experiential retailing. *Psychology and Marketing*, 39(3), 495–507. DOI: 10.1002/mar.21600

Hirsch, A. (1995). Scentsational marketing: The role of scent in consumer behavior. *Journal of Marketing*, 59(4), 24–30. https://doi.org/10.1177/002224379505900403

Hollebeek, L. D., Kumar, V., Srivastava, R. K., & Clark, M. K. (2022). Moving the stakeholder journey forward. *Journal of the Academy of Marketing Science*, 51(1), 23–49. DOI: 10.1007/s11747-022-00878-3 PMID: 35756344

Hong, Y., & Pavlou, P. A. (2014). Product Fit Uncertainty in Online Markets: Nature, Effects, and Antecedents. *Information Systems Research*, 25(2), 328–344. DOI: 10.1287/isre.2014.0520

Howard, J. A. (2013). Financial decision-making: The roles of intuition, heuristics and impulses. *Journal of Modern Accounting and Auditing*, 9(12), 1596–1610.

Hsu, M. (2017). Neuromarketing: Inside the Mind of the Consumer. *California Management Review*, 59(4), 5–22. DOI: 10.1177/0008125617720208

Huang, A. H., & You, H. (2023). Artificial intelligence in financial decision-making. In *Handbook of Financial Decision Making* (pp. 315–335). Edward Elgar Publishing. DOI: 10.4337/9781802204179.00029

Huang, T. L., & Chung, H. F. (2024). Impact of delightful somatosensory augmented reality experience on online consumer stickiness intention. *Journal of Research in Interactive Marketing*, 18(1), 6–30. DOI: 10.1108/JRIM-07-2022-0213

Huber, J., Payne, J. W., & Puto, C. (1982). Adding asymmetrically dominated alternatives: Violations of regularity and the similarity hypothesis. *The Journal of Consumer Research*, 9(1), 90–98. DOI: 10.1086/208899

Hubert, M., & Kenning, P. (2008). A current overview of consumer neuroscience. *Journal of Consumer Behaviour*, 7(4-5), 272–292. DOI: 10.1002/cb.251

Huettel, S. A., Song, A. W., & McCarthy, G. (2009). *Functional magnetic resonance imaging*. Sinauer Associates.

Hulten, B., Broweus, N., & Van Dijk, M. (2008). Sinnesmarknadsföring. Liber AB.

Hultén, B., Broweus, N., & van Dijk, M. (2009). What is Sensory Marketing? Sensory Marketing, 8-9

Hulten, B. (2013). Sensory cues as in-store innovations: Their impact on shopper approaches and touch behavior. *Journal of Innovation Management*, 1(1), 17–37.

Hunt, S. D. (1983). General Theories and the Fundamental Explananda of Marketing. *Journal of Marketing*, 47(4), 9–17. DOI: 10.1177/002224298304700402

Hutchinson, J. W., Raman, K., & Mantrala, M. K. (2000). Finding choice alternatives in memory: Probability models of brand name recall. *JMR, Journal of Marketing Research*, 37(2), 157–169.

Iacoboni, M., Freedman, J., & Kaplan, J. (2012). Predicting advertising success: Neural correlates of emotional and behavioral responses to ads. *Journal of Neuroscience, Psychology, and Economics*, 5(3), 147–167. DOI: 10.1037/a0028860

Ibrahim, I., Ismail, A. F.-M. F., Amer, A., & Jani, S. H. M. (2019). The effectiveness of mass marketing communication as a digital logistics tool in promoting a new online public service platform. *International Journal of Supply Chain Management*, 8(4), 177–185. https://www.scopus.com/inward/record.uri?eid=2-s2.0-85071556833&partnerID=40&md5=bbfbc2c80bffc785e20db86776cb0ad8

IEA. (2024). Global EV Outlook 2024. IEA, Paris. https://www.iea.org/reports/global-ev[REMOVED HYPERLINK FIELD]outlook-2024

Illes, J., & Sahakian, B. J. (2011). *Oxford handbook of neuroethics*. Oxford University Press. DOI: 10.1093/oxfordhb/9780199570706.001.0001

International Energy Agency (IEA). (2020). *Global EV Outlook 2020*. Retrieved from https://www.iea.org/reports/global-ev-outlook-2020

International Energy Agency (IEA). (2021). *India Energy Outlook 2021*. Retrieved from https://www.iea.org/reports/india-energy-outlook-2021

Iotzov, V., Saulin, A., Kaiser, J., Han, S., & Hein, G. (2022). Financial incentives facilitate stronger neural computation of prosocial decisions in lower empathic adult females. *Social Neuroscience*, 17(5), 441–461. DOI: 10.1080/17470919.2022.2115550 PMID: 36064327

Irshaidat, R. (2022). Interpretivism vs. Positivism in Political Marketing Research. *Journal of Political Marketing*, 21(2), 126–160. DOI: 10.1080/15377857.2019.1624286

Jain, R., & Singh, A. (2023). Prediction of Customer Satisfaction in E-banking Services Through Neural Network Approach. In *International Conference on Data Science and Big Data Analysis* (pp. 25-32). Singapore: Springer Nature Singapore.

Jain, N. (2022). Understanding the art and science of new-age advertising: A neuromarketing perspective. *The Business and Management Review,* 13(3).

Jakovaara, M. (2020). *Feelings of emotion in strategic investment decisions* (Doctoral dissertation, Doctoral dissertation. Turku School of Economics, Turku).

Jamison, K., & Clayton, J. (2016). Exploring the experiences of administrative interns: Implications for university preparation programs. *Journal of Educational Administration*, 54(5), 514–536. DOI: 10.1108/JEA-02-2015-0020

Jang, H. W., & Lee, S. B. (2019). Applying effective sensory marketing to sustainable coffee shop business management. *Sustainability (Basel)*, 11(22), 6430. DOI: 10.3390/su11226430

Janis, I. L. (1982). *Groupthink: Psychological Studies of Policy Decisions and Fiascoes*. Houghton Mifflin.

Jayakrishnan, S. (2013). Creating brand identity using human senses. *Asia Pacific Journal of Research*, 2(8), 223–228.

Jerath, K., & Zhang, Z. J. (2010). Store within a store. *JMR, Journal of Marketing Research*, 47(4), 748–763. DOI: 10.1509/jmkr.47.4.748

Judd, C. M., McClelland, G. H., & Ryan, C. S. (2017). *Data analysis*. Routledge., DOI: 10.4324/9781315744131

Kahneman, D., Knetsch, J. L., & Thaler, R. H. (1991). Anomalies: The endowment effect, loss aversion, and status quo bias. *The Journal of Economic Perspectives*, 5(1), 193–206. DOI: 10.1257/jep.5.1.193

Kahneman, D., & Tversky, A. (1973). Availability: A heuristic for judging frequency and probability. *Cognitive Psychology*, 5(2), 207–232. DOI: 10.1016/0010-0285(73)90033-9

Kahneman, D., & Tversky, A. (1979). Prospect theory: An analysis of decision under risk. *Econometrica*, 47(2), 263–291. DOI: 10.2307/1914185

Kalaganis, F. P., Georgiadis, K., Oikonomou, V. P., Laskaris, N. A., Nikolopoulos, S., & Kompatsiaris, I. (2021). Unlocking the subconscious consumer bias: A survey on the past, present, and future of hybrid EEG schemes in neuromarketing. *Frontiers in Neuroergonomics*, 2, 672982. DOI: 10.3389/fnrgo.2021.672982 PMID: 38235255

Kalton, G., & Jessen, R. J. (1979). Statistical survey techniques. *Journal of the Royal Statistical Society. Series A (General)*, 142(2), 265. DOI: 10.2307/2345092

Kaplan, A. (1964), The conduct of inquiry: Methodology for behavioural science, Chandler.

Karmarkar, U. R., & Plassmann, H. (2019). Consumer Neuroscience: Past, Present, and Future. *Organizational Research Methods*, 22(1), 174–195. DOI: 10.1177/1094428117730598

Kate, N. T., Chaudhary, P., & More, M. (2024). Antecedents to Organic Tea Buying Behavior and Consumption Among Millennials in India: Through the Lens of Theory of Planned Behavior. https://doi.org/DOI: 10.17010/ijom/2024/v54/i1/173382

Kate, N., Chaudhary, P., Kavi Kumar, K. S., & Raut, N., & More, M. (2024). *Antecedents to the Adoption of Digital Marketing by Start-Ups Under Startup-India and E-Governance Initiatives.* https://doi.org/10.4018/ijegr.347505

Kathikeyan, T., Revathi, S., Supreeth, B. R., Sasidevi, J., Ahmed, M., & Das, S. (2022, December). Artificial Intelligence and Mixed Reality Technology for Interactive Display of Images in Smart Area. In *2022 5th International Conference on Contemporary Computing and Informatics (IC3I)* (pp. 2049-2053). IEEE. DOI: 10.1109/IC3I56241.2022.10072411

Kenning, P. H., & Plassman, H. (2008). How neuroscience can inform consumer research. Neural Systems and Rehabilitation Engineering. *IEEE Transactions on Neural Systems and Rehabilitation Engineering*, 16(6), 532–538. DOI: 10.1109/TNSRE.2008.2009788 PMID: 19144585

Kerber, L., Roese-Miron, L., Bubadue, J. M., & Martinelli, A. G. (2024). Endocranial anatomy of the early prozostrodonts (Eucynodontia: Probainognathia) and the neurosensory evolution in mammal forerunners. *The Anatomical Record*, 307(4), 1442–1473. DOI: 10.1002/ar.25215 PMID: 37017195

Khairiza, F., & Kusumasari, B. (2020). Analyzing political marketing in Indonesia: A palm oil digital campaign case study. *Forest and Society*, 4(2), 294–309. DOI: 10.24259/fs.v4i2.9576

Khan, M. A., Pattnaik, D., Ashraf, R., Ali, I., Kumar, S., & Donthu, N. (2021). Value of special issues in the Journal of Business Research: A bibliometric analysis. *Journal of Business Research*, 125, 295–313. DOI: 10.1016/j.jbusres.2020.12.015

Khondakar, M. F. K., Sarowar, M. H., Chowdhury, M. H., Majumder, S., Hossain, M. A., Dewan, M. A. A., & Hossain, Q. D. (2024). A systematic review on EEG-based neuromarketing: Recent trends and analyzing techniques. *Brain Informatics*, 11(1), 17. DOI: 10.1186/s40708-024-00229-8 PMID: 38837089

Khurana, V., Gahalawat, M., Kumar, P., Roy, P. P., Dogra, D. P., Scheme, E., & Soleymani, M. (2021). A survey on neuromarketing using EEG signals. *IEEE Transactions on Cognitive and Developmental Systems*, 13(4), 732–749. DOI: 10.1109/TCDS.2021.3065200

Kilbourne, W. E., & Beckmann, S. C. (1998). Review and critical assessment of research on marketing and the environment. *Journal of Marketing Management*, 14(6), 513–532. DOI: 10.1362/026725798784867716

Kim, J., & Forsythe, S. (2008). Sensory enabling technology acceptance model (SE-TAM): A multiple-group structural model comparison. *Psychology and Marketing*, 25(9), 901–922. DOI: 10.1002/mar.20245

Kim, J., & Forsythe, S. (2009). Adoption of sensory enabling technology for online apparel shopping. *European Journal of Marketing*, 43(9/10), 1101–1120. DOI: 10.1108/03090560910976384

King, M. (2023, November 07). *What Is A Promotion Strategy? Types, Examples, & Process*. Retrieved from coschedule: https://coschedule.com/marketing/marketing-mix/promotion-strategy

King, D., & Auschaitrakul, S. (2021). Affect-based nonconscious signaling: When do consumers prefer negative branding? *Psychology and Marketing*, 38(2), 338–358. DOI: 10.1002/mar.21371

Kliatchko, J. (2008). Revisiting the IMC construct: A revised definition and four pillars. *International Journal of Advertising*, 27(1), 133–160. DOI: 10.1080/02650487.2008.11073043

Klimchuk, M. R., & Krasovec, S. A. (2013). *Packaging design: Successful product branding from concept to shelf.* John Wiley & Sons.

Klinčeková, S. (2016). Neuromarketing–research and prediction of the future. *International Journal of Management Science and Business Administration*, 2(2), 53–57.

Knutson, B., & Genevsky, A. (2018). Neuroforecasting Aggregate Choice. *Current Directions in Psychological Science*, 27(2), 110–115. DOI: 10.1177/0963721417737877 PMID: 29706726

Knutson, B., Rick, S., Wimmer, G. E., Prelec, D., & Loewenstein, G. (2007). Neural predictors of purchases. *Neuron*, 53(1), 147–156. DOI: 10.1016/j.neuron.2006.11.010 PMID: 17196537

Koch, O. F., & Benlian, A. (2015). Promotional tactics for online viral marketing campaigns: How scarcity and personalization affect seed stage referrals. *Journal of Interactive Marketing*, 32(1), 37–52. DOI: 10.1016/j.intmar.2015.09.005

Kolb, D. A. (1984). *Experiential Learning: Experience as the Source of Learning and Development*. Prentice-Hall.

Kolyovska, V., Maslarova, J., & Maslarov, D. (2016, May 17), *Home page,* Doi. Org; unknown, https://doi.org/

Kotler, P. H., Setiawan, I., & Kartajaya, H. (2011). Marketing 3: From products to sustomers to the human spirit. translated by: Abdul Hamid Ibrahimi, Samad Aali, Alireza Bafandeh zendeh, elnaz Alizadeh Ashrafi, 1st volume.

Kotler, P. (1973). Atmospherics as a marketing tool. *Journal of Retailing*, 49(4), 48–64.

Kotter, J. P. (1996). *Leading change*. Harvard Business Review Press.

Krampe, C., Strelow, E., Haas, A., & Kenning, P. (2018). The application of mobile fNIRS to "shopper neuroscience" – first insights from a merchandising communication study. *European Journal of Marketing*, 52(1), 244–259. DOI: 10.1108/EJM-12-2016-0727

Krause, R. M., Carley, S. R., Lane, B. W., & Graham, J. D. (2013). Perception and reality: Public knowledge of plug-in electric vehicles in 21 U.S. cities. *Energy Policy*, 63, 433–440. DOI: 10.1016/j.enpol.2013.09.018

Kringelbach, M. L. (2005). The human orbitofrontal cortex: Linking reward to hedonic experience. *Nature Reviews. Neuroscience*, 6(9), 691–702. DOI: 10.1038/nrn1747 PMID: 16136173

Krishna, A. (2010). *Sensory marketing: Research on the sensuality of products*. Routledge.

Krishna, A. (2011). An introduction to sensory marketing. In *Sensory marketing* (pp. 1–13). Routledge.

Krishna, A. (2012). An integrative review of sensory marketing: Engaging the senses to affect perception, judgment and behavior. *Journal of Consumer Psychology*, 22(3), 332–351. DOI: 10.1016/j.jcps.2011.08.003

Krishna, A. (2015). The rise of sensory marketing. In Raghunathan, K. S. (Ed.), *Marketing and the Role of Customer Service* (pp. 59–67). Business Expert Press.

Krishna, A. E. (2010). The influence of scent on memory and brand preference. *The Journal of Consumer Research*, 37(4), 681–688. DOI: 10.1086/655115

Krishna, A., & Morrin, M. (2008). Does touch affect taste? The perceptual transfer of product container haptic cues. *The Journal of Consumer Research*, 34(6), 807–818. DOI: 10.1086/523286

Kristiana, A., &Pugu, M. R. (2024). Navigating the intersection neuro-marketing and consumer bahavior analysis: leveraging insights for effective campaigns. *Jurnal Ekonomi dan Bisnis,* 2(3), 362-374.

Kruschinski, S., & Bene, M. (2022). In varietate concordia?! Political parties' digital political marketing in the 2019 European Parliament election campaign. *European Union Politics*, 23(1), 43–65. DOI: 10.1177/14651165211040728

Kühn, S., Düzel, S., Eibich, P., Krekel, C., Wüstemann, H., Kolbe, J., & Lindenberger, U. (2016). In search of features that constitute an "enriched environment" in humans: Associations between geographical properties and brain structure. *Scientific Reports*, 6, 30401. PMID: 28931835

Kumar, J., Arora, M., & Erkol Bayram, G. (Eds.). (2024) a. *Exploring the Use of Metaverse in Business and Education*. IGI Global. DOI: DOI: 10.4018/979-8-3693-5868-9

Kumar, J., Arora, M., & Erkol Bayram, G. (Eds.). (2024) b. *Research, Innovation, and Industry Impacts of the Metaverse*. IGI Global.

Kumar, J., Arora, M., & Erkol Bayram, G. (Eds.). (2024)a. *Exploring the Use of Metaverse in Business and Education*. IGI Global.

Kumar, J., Arora, M., & Erkol Bayram, G. (Eds.). (2024)b. *Research, Innovation, and Industry Impacts of the Metaverse*. IGI Global.

Kumar, J., Arora, M., & Erkol Bayram, G. (Eds.). (2024b) *Research, Innovation, and Industry Impacts of the Metaverse*. IGI Global.

Kumar, J., Arora, M., & Erkol Bayram, G. (Eds.). (2024b). *Research, Innovation, and Industry Impacts of the Metaverse*. IGI Global.

Kumar, S., & Arora, M (2023). Herd Behavior Unveiled: How Demographics Shape Investment Patterns in North India. Quest Journal of Research in Business and Management, ISSN (Online): 2347 3002, Volume-11, Issue-8, Page No.: 114-121, [2023].

Kumar, S., & Arora, M (2023). Understanding Awareness of Investment Avenues of Investors in North India: An Empirical Study. Journal of Interdisciplinary and Multidisciplinary Research (JIMR); Vol. 18 Issue 10, Oct 2023.

Kumar, H., & Singh, P. (2015). Neuromarketing: An emerging tool of market research. [IJEMR]. *International Journal of Engineering and Management Research*, 5(6), 530–535.

Kumar, P., & Kumar, K. (2020). Awareness of Sensory Marketing and Its Relationship With Consumer Behaviour: A Study of Restaurants in Bangalore. [IJM]. *International Journal of Management*, 11(3), 791–807.

Kumar, S., Jain, A., & Hsieh, J. K. (2021). Impact of apps aesthetics on revisit intentions of food delivery apps: The mediating role of pleasure and arousal. *Journal of Retailing and Consumer Services*, 63, 102686. DOI: 10.1016/j.jretconser.2021.102686

Laibson, D. (1997). Golden eggs and hyperbolic discounting. *The Quarterly Journal of Economics*, 112(2), 443–477. DOI: 10.1162/003355397555253

Lameka, K., Farwell, M. D., & Ichise, M. (2016). Positron emission tomography. *Handbook of Clinical Neurology*, 135, 209–227. DOI: 10.1016/B978-0-444-53485-9.00011-8 PMID: 27432667

Lane, B., & Potter, S. (2007). The adoption of cleaner vehicles in the UK: Exploring the consumer attitude-action gap. *Journal of Cleaner Production*, 15(11-12), 1085–1092. DOI: 10.1016/j.jclepro.2006.05.026

Lashkova, M., Anton, C., & Camarero, C. (2020). Dual effect of sensory experience: Engagement vs diversive exploration. *International Journal of Retail & Distribution Management*, 48(2), 128–151. DOI: 10.1108/IJRDM-09-2018-0204

Lee, N., Broderick, A. J., & Chamberlain, L. (2007). What is 'neuromarketing'? A discussion and agenda for future research. *International Journal of Psychophysiology*, 63(2), 199–204. DOI: 10.1016/j.ijpsycho.2006.03.007 PMID: 16769143

Lee, N., Chamberlain, L., & Brandes, L. (2018). Welcome to the jungle! The neuromarketing literature through the eyes of a newcomer. *European Journal of Marketing*, 52(1-2), 4–38. DOI: 10.1108/EJM-02-2017-0122

Lee, S. G., & Lye, S. W. (2003). Design for manual packaging. *International Journal of Physical Distribution & Logistics Management*, 33(2), 163–189. DOI: 10.1108/09600030310469162

Leeuwis, N., Van Bommel, T., Tsakiris, M., & Alimardani, M. (2024). Uncovering the potential of evaluative conditioning in shaping attitudes toward sustainable product packaging. *Frontiers in Psychology*, 15, 1284422. DOI: 10.3389/fpsyg.2024.1284422 PMID: 38550644

Leveau, P. H., & Camus, E. S. (2023). Embodiment, immersion, and enjoyment in virtual reality marketing experiences. *Psychology and Marketing*, 40(7), 1329–1343. DOI: 10.1002/mar.21822

Levy, M., & Weitz, B. A. (2009). *Retail Management*. MacGraw-Hill.

Lewis, D., & Bridger, D. (2005), Market researchers are making increasing use of brain imaging. https://bit.ly/3gu5510

Li, L. (2017). Influences on consumers' decision making and recognition memory: An investigation using fMRI, *EEG and behavioural methods* (Doctoral dissertation, Brunel University London).

Liao, F., Molin, E., & van Wee, B. (2017). Consumer preferences for electric vehicles: A literature review. *Transport Reviews*, 37(3), 252–275. DOI: 10.1080/01441647.2016.1230794

Li, B., Wang, Y., Wang, K., & Zhang, D. (2022). A Review of Data-Driven Techniques for Neuromarketing. In *International Workshop of Advanced Manufacturing and Automation* (pp. 748-755). Singapore: Springer Nature Singapore.

Lick, E. (2022). "Multimodal Sensory Marketing" in retailing: The role of intra-and intermodality transductions. *Consumption Markets & Culture*, 25(3), 252–271. DOI: 10.1080/10253866.2022.2046564

Li, H., An, H., Wang, Y., Huang, J., & Gao, X. (2016). Evolutionary features of academic articles co-keyword network and keywords co-occurrence network: Based on two-mode affiliation network. *Physica A*, 450, 657–669. DOI: 10.1016/j.physa.2016.01.017

Li, L., Shen, T., Liu, S., Qi, J., & Zhao, Y. (2024). Advancements and future prospects of adeno-associated virus-mediated gene therapy for sensorineural hearing loss. *Frontiers in Neuroscience*, 18, 1272786. DOI: 10.3389/fnins.2024.1272786 PMID: 38327848

Lim, W.M. (2018), Demystifying Neuromarketing. Journal of Business Research, pp. 91, 205–220. https://doi.org/.DOI: 10.1016/j.jbusres.2018.05.036

Lindstrom, M. (2005). *Brand sense: How to build powerful brands through touch, taste, smell, sight & sound*. Free Press.

Lindstrom, M. (2010). *Brandwashed: Tricks companies use to manipulate our minds and persuade us to buy*. Kogan Page Publishers.

Lindstrom, M. (2010). *Buyology: Truth and Lies About Why We Buy Crown Business*. Crown Publishing Group.

Lindstrom, M. (2011). *Brand sense: Sensory secrets behind the stuff we buy*. Simon and Schuster.

Lindstrom, M., & Kotler, P. (2005). *Brand sense: build powerful brands through touch, taste, smell, sight, and sound*. Free Pr.

Lin, M., Cross, S., Jones, W., & Childers, T. L. (2018). Applying EEG in consumer neuroscience. *European Journal of Marketing*, 52(1), 66–91. DOI: 10.1108/EJM-12-2016-0805

Li, S., Tong, L., Xing, J., & Zhou, Y. (2017). The market for electric vehicles: Indirect network effects and policy design. *Journal of the Association of Environmental and Resource Economists*, 4(1), 89–133. DOI: 10.1086/689702

Liu, J., Mo, Z., Fu, H., Wei, W., Song, L., & Luo, K. (2021). The effect of reviewers' self-disclosure of personal review record on consumer purchase decisions: An ERPs investigation. *Frontiers in Psychology*, 11, 609538. DOI: 10.3389/fpsyg.2020.609538 PMID: 33488474

Li, W., Long, R., Chen, H., & Geng, J. (2017). A review of factors influencing consumer intentions to adopt battery electric vehicles. *Renewable & Sustainable Energy Reviews*, 78, 318–328. DOI: 10.1016/j.rser.2017.04.076

Li, Y. M., & Yeh, Y. S. (2010). Increasing trust in mobile commerce through design aesthetics. *Computers in Human Behavior*, 26(4), 673–684. DOI: 10.1016/j.chb.2010.01.004

Lo, A. W. (2005). Reconciling efficient markets with behavioural finance: The adaptive markets hypothesis. *The Journal of Investment Consulting*, 7(2), 21–44.

Lopez, M. J., & Ramos-Galarza, C. (2022). Neuromarketing: Current applications in favor of consumerism. *Marketing and Smart Technologies: Proceedings of ICMarkTech 2021, Volume 1*, 389-394.

Lopez, A., & Garza, R. (2022). Do sensory reviews make more sense? The mediation of objective perception in online review helpfulness. *Journal of Research in Interactive Marketing*, 16(3), 438–456. DOI: 10.1108/JRIM-04-2021-0121

López, M. J., & Ramos-Galarza, C. (2022). Neuromarketing: Current applications in favor of consumerism. *Marketing and Smart Technologies: Proceedings of ICMarkTech 2021, Volume 1*, 389-394.

Lucas, R. E. (1972). Expectations and the neutrality of money. *Journal of Economic Theory*, 4(2), 103–124. DOI: 10.1016/0022-0531(72)90142-1

Lyapina, I. R., Uvarova, A. Y., Sibirskaya, E. V., Pashkevich, L. A., & Tikhoykina, I. M. (2020). Cognitive science and neuromarketing in behavioral economics. *Growth Poles of the Global Economy: Emergence, Changes and Future Perspectives*, 925-935.

Lyu, D., & Mañas-Viniegra, L. (2021). Ethical issues in neuromarketing research: A literature review. *Vivat Academia*, 154, 263–283. DOI: 10.15178/va.2021.154.e1351

MacNeil, C. (2024, January 12). *In a sales slump? Try these 12 promotion strategies to create customer demand*. Retrieved from https://asana.com/resources/promotion-strategy

Madan, C. R. (2010). Neuromarketing: The next step in market research? *Eureka (Asunción)*, 1(1), 34–42. DOI: 10.29173/eureka7786

Madan, M., & Popli, A. (2016). A study on Neuromarketing as emerging innovative market research strategy: An interpretive structural model approach. *IOSR Journal of Business and Management*, 2(2), 18–30. DOI: 10.9790/487X-15010020218-30

Madhavaram, S., Badrinarayanan, V., & McDonald, R. E. (2005). Integrated marketing communication (IMC) and brand identity as critical components of brand equity strategy: A conceptual framework and research propositions. *Journal of Advertising*, 34(4), 69–80. DOI: 10.1080/00913367.2005.10639213

Mair, J., Ritchie, B. W., & Walters, G. (2016). Towards a research agenda for post-disaster and post-crisis recovery strategies for tourist destinations: A narrative review. *Current Issues in Tourism*, 19(1), 1–26. DOI: 10.1080/13683500.2014.932758

Majer, P., Mohr, P. N., Heekeren, H. R., & Härdle, W. K. (2016). Portfolio decisions and brain reactions via the CEAD method. *Psychometrika*, 81(3), 881–903. DOI: 10.1007/s11336-015-9441-5 PMID: 25670029

Malekzadeh, M., Clegg, R. G., Cavallaro, A., & Haddadi, H. (2018, April). Protecting sensory data against sensitive inferences. In *Proceedings of the 1st Workshop on Privacy by Design in Distributed Systems* (pp. 1-6).

Malik, R., Malhan, S., & Arora, M. (2024). (Eds.). (2024). Sensible Selling Through Sensory Neuromarketing (pp. 144-163). IGI Global

Malik, R., Malhan, S., & Arora, M. (2024). (Eds.). (2024). *Sensible Selling Through Sensory Neuromarketing* (pp. 144-163). IGI Global.

Malik, R., Malhan, S., & Arora, M. (Eds.). (2024). *Sensible Selling Through Sensory Neuromarketing*. IGI Global.

Malik, S., Malhan, D., & Arora, R. (2024). Exploring sensory marketing: Its role in creating emotional ties with consumers. *International Journal of Marketing Studies*, 16(1), 45–60. DOI: 10.5539/ijms.v16n1p45

Manchanda, R., Mittal, S., USMS, G., & Bansal, S. examining the senses influencing sensory marketing and its impact on consumer behavior.

Manoj, M. S., & Ritika, S. (2018). Application of neuromarketing tools in higher education institutions: Towards innovations, marketing effectiveness and student driven strategies in the future condition. *Journal of Emerging Technologies and Innovative Research*, 5, 1–5.

Mansor, A. A. B., & Isa, S. M. (2018). The impact of eye tracking on neuromarketing for genuine value-added applications. *Global Business and Management Research*, 10(1), 1–11.

Marichamy, K., & Sathiyavathi, J.K. (2014), Neuromarketing: The new science of consumer behaviour. Tactful Management Journal, 2(6).

Martinez, B. M., & McAndrews, L. E. (2022). Do you take...? The effect of mobile payment solutions on use intention: an application of UTAUT2. *Journal of Marketing Analytics*, pp. 1–12. DOI: 10.1057/s41270-022-00175-6

Maseeh, H. I., Jebarajakirthy, C., Pentecost, R., Arli, D., Weaven, S., & Ashaduzzaman, M. (2021). Privacy concerns in e-commerce: A multilevel meta-analysis. *Psychology and Marketing*, 38(10), 1779–1798. DOI: 10.1002/mar.21493

Mashrur, F. R., Rahman, K. M., Miya, M. T. I., Vaidyanathan, R., Anwar, S. F., Sarker, F., & Mamun, K. A. (2024). Intelligent neuromarketing framework for consumers' preference prediction from electroencephalography signals and eye tracking. *Journal of Consumer Behaviour*, 23(3), 1146–1157. DOI: 10.1002/cb.2253

Mateu, G., Monzani, L., & Navarro, R. M. (2018). The role of the brain in financial decisions: A viewpoint on neuroeconomics. *Mètode Science Studies Journal*, 8, 6–15. DOI: 10.7203/metode.0.6923

Mathaisel, D. F. X., & Comm, C. L. (2021). Political marketing with data analytics. *Journal of Marketing Analytics*, 9(1), 56–64. DOI: 10.1057/s41270-020-00097-1

Maxwell, J. A. (2022). Interactive approaches to qualitative research design. In *The SAGE Handbook of Qualitative Research Design* (pp. 41–54). SAGE Publications Ltd., DOI: 10.4135/9781529770278.n4

Maymand, M. M., Ahmadinejad, M., & Nezami, P. (2012). Sensory brand: Studying relationship between 5 senses and brand value at world's 100 top companies. *Australian Journal of Basic and Applied Sciences*, 6(8), 337–343.

McCabe, D. B., & Nowlis, S. M. (2003). The effect of examining actual products or product descriptions on consumer preference. *Journal of Consumer Psychology*, 13(4), 431–439. DOI: 10.1207/S15327663JCP1304_10

McClure, S. M., Li, J., Tomlin, D., Cypert, K. S., Montague, L. M., & Montague, P. R. (2004). Neural Correlates of Behavioral Preference for Culturally Familiar Drinks. *Neuron*, 44(2), 379–387. DOI: 10.1016/j.neuron.2004.09.019 PMID: 15473974

McDowell, W. S., & Dick, S. J. (2013). The marketing of neuromarketing: Brand differentiation strategies employed by prominent neuromarketing firms to attract media clients. *Journal of Media Business Studies*, 10(1), 25–40. DOI: 10.1080/16522354.2013.11073558

McGrail, M. R., Rickard, C. M., & Jones, R. (2006). Publish or perish: A systematic review of interventions to increase academic publication rates. *Higher Education Research & Development*, 25(1), 19–35. DOI: 10.1080/07294360500453053

Meckl-Sloan, C. (2015). Neuroeconomics and neuromarketing. *Cell*, 650, 218–8214.

Megías, A., Navas, J. F., Petrova, D., Candido, A., Maldonado, A., Garcia-Retamero, R., & Catena, A. (2015). Neural mechanisms underlying urgent and evaluative behaviors: An fMRI study on the interaction of automatic and controlled processes. *Human Brain Mapping*, 36(8), 2853–2864. DOI: 10.1002/hbm.22812 PMID: 25879953

Menezes, R. G., Gonçalves, C. A., & de Muylder, C. F. (2016). *Sensorial marketing and neuroscience: Neuroscience contributions to the marketing field. International Business Management*. Medwell Journals.

Mercier, M. R., & Cappe, C. (2020). The interplay between multisensory integration and perceptual decision making. *NeuroImage*, 222, 116970. DOI: 10.1016/j.neuroimage.2020.116970 PMID: 32454204

Millagala, K., & Gunasinghe, N. (2024). Neuromarketing as a Digital Marketing Strategy to Unravel the Evolution of Marketing Communication. In *Applying Business Intelligence and Innovation to Entrepreneurship* (pp. 81–105). IGI Global. DOI: 10.4018/979-8-3693-1846-1.ch005

Miller, C. C., & Ireland, R. D. (2005). Intuition in strategic decision making: Friend or foe in the fast-paced 21st century? *The Academy of Management Perspectives*, 19(1), 19–30. DOI: 10.5465/ame.2005.15841948

Ministry of Road Transport and Highways. (2020). *Basic Road Statistics of India 2018-19*. Retrieved from https://morth.nic.in/sites/default/files/Basic_Road_Statistics_of_India.pdf

Mirovic, V., Kalas, B., Djokic, I., Milicevic, N., Djokic, N., & Djakovic, M. (2023). Green Loans in Bank Portfolio: Financial and Marketing Implications. *Sustainability (Basel)*, 15(7), 5914. DOI: 10.3390/su15075914

Mishra, A., Shukla, A., Rana, N. P., & Dwivedi, Y. K. (2021). From "touch" to a "multisensory" experience: The impact of technology interface and product type on consumer responses. *Psychology and Marketing*, 38(3), 385–396. DOI: 10.1002/mar.21436

Mishra, K. E., Wilder, K., & Mishra, A. K. (2017). Digital Literacy in the Marketing Curriculum: Are Female College Students prepared for Digital jobs? *Industry and Higher Education*, 31(3), 204–211. DOI: 10.1177/0950422217697838

Misra, L. (2023). Neuromarketing insights into consumer behavior. *IUJ Journal of Management*, 11(1), 143–163.

Mochla, V., & Tsourvakas, G. (2020). Quality Dimensions of Political Parties' Website Services That Satisfy Voters in the Political Marketing. *Journal of Political Marketing*, 22(1), 1–13. DOI: 10.1080/15377857.2020.1790470

Mogaji, E. (2018). *Emotional appeals in advertising banking services*. Emerald Publishing Limited. DOI: 10.1108/9781787562998

Mohammed, Mostafa, Refaat, Moharam. (2023). The Impact of Augmented and Virtual Reality Technologies on Customer Happiness in Immersive Shopping Experiences. DOI: 10.52783/tjjpt.v44.i4.2491

Monge Benito, S., & Fernández Guerra, V. (2012). Neuromarketing: Tecnologías, Mercado y Retos. Pensar La Publicidad. *Revista Internacional De Investigaciones Publicitarias*, 5(2), 19–42. DOI: 10.5209/rev_PEPU.2011.v5.n2.37862

Morin, C. (2011). Neuromarketing: The new science of consumer behavior. *Society*, 48(2), 131–135. DOI: 10.1007/s12115-010-9408-1

Morris, M. G., & Venkatesh, V. (2000). Age differences in technology adoption decisions: Implications for a changing workforce. *Personnel Psychology*, 53(2), 375–403. DOI: 10.1111/j.1744-6570.2000.tb00206.x

Morrison, M., Gan, S., Dubelaar, C., & Oppewal, H. (2011). In-store music and aroma influence shopper behaviour and satisfaction. *Journal of Business Research*, 64(6), 558–564. DOI: 10.1016/j.jbusres.2010.06.006

Morton, C., Anable, J., & Nelson, J. D. (2016). Exploring consumer preferences towards electric vehicles: The influence of driving range and experience. *Transportation Research Part C, Emerging Technologies*, 69, 257–275.

Mucha, T. (2005). This is your brain on advertising. *Business (Atlanta, Ga.)*, 6(7), 35–37.

Muhammad, A. (2024, July 1). *The 3 Levels of Packaging: Primary, Secondary and Tertiary Packaging*. Retrieved from Refine Packaging: https://refinepackaging.com/blog/primary-secondary-tertiary-packaging/

Murphy, E. R., Illes, J., & Reiner, P. B. (2008). Neuroethics of neuromarketing. *Journal of Consumer Behaviour*, 7(4), 293–302. DOI: 10.1002/cb.252

Muslim, A., Harun, A., Ismael, D., & Othman, B. (2020). Social media experience, attitude and behavioral intention towards umrah package among generation X and Y. *Management Science Letters*, 10(1), 1–12. DOI: 10.5267/j.msl.2019.8.020

Muth, J. F. (1961). Rational expectations and the theory of price movements. *Econometrica*, 29(3), 315–335. DOI: 10.2307/1909635

Nadeau, R., Cloutier, E., & Guay, J.-H. (1993). New evidence about a bandwagon effect in the opinion formation process. *International Political Science Review*, 14(2), 203–213. DOI: 10.1177/019251219301400204

Nah, F. F.-H., Eschenbrenner, B., & DeWester, D. (2011). Enhancing brand equity through flow and telepresence: A comparison of 2d and 3d virtual worlds. *Management Information Systems Quarterly*, 35(3), 731–747. DOI: 10.2307/23042806

Nakamura, H., & Miyashita, H. (2013). Controlling saltiness without salt: Evaluation of taste change by applying and releasing cathodal current. Proceedings of the 5th international workshop on multimedia for cooking & eating activities, 9–14.

Naqvi, N., Shiv, B., & Bechara, A. (2006). The role of emotion in decision making: A cognitive neuroscience perspective. *Current Directions in Psychological Science*, 15(5), 260–264. DOI: 10.1111/j.1467-8721.2006.00448.x

Nave, G., Nadler, A., Dubois, D., Zava, D., Camerer, C., & Plassmann, H. (2018). Single-dose testosterone administration increases men's preference for status goods. *Nature Communications*, 9(1), 2433. DOI: 10.1038/s41467-018-04923-0 PMID: 29970895

Nepal, R., Rajopadhyay, P., Rajopadhyay, U., & Bhattarai, U. (2023). Interplay of Investor Cognition, Financial Literacy, and Neuroplasticity in Investment Decision Making: A Study of Nepalese Investors. *Journal of Business and Social Sciences Research*, 8(2), 51–76. DOI: 10.3126/jbssr.v8i2.62133

Neumann, I., Cocron, P., Franke, T., & Krems, J. F. (2010). Electric vehicles as a solution for green driving in the future? A field study examining the user acceptance of electric vehicles. In *Proceedings of the European conference on human interface design for intelligent transport systems*, Berlin, Germany (pp. 445-453).

Nguyen, H. N., & Tran, M. D. (2022). STIMULI TO ADOPT E-GOVERNMENT SERVICES DURING COVID-19: EVIDENCE FROM VIETNAM. *Innovative Marketing*, 18(1), 12–22. DOI: 10.21511/im.18(1).2022.02

Nickerson, R. S. (1998). Confirmation bias: A ubiquitous phenomenon in many guises. *Review of General Psychology*, 2(2), 175–220. DOI: 10.1037/1089-2680.2.2.175

Nielsen. (2016). Global new product innovation: The good, the bad, and the ugly. Retrieved from https://www.nielsen.com/us/en/insights/article/2016/global-new-product-innovation-the-good-the-bad-and-the-ugly/

Niere, M. I., Bustamante, J. R. B., Bacaltos, M. S., Arceo, R. A. B., & Bigno, H. (2024). Influence of Color Psychology on Consumer Behavior among Business Students. *International Journal of Multidisciplinary: Applied Business and Education Research*, 5(3), 848–862. DOI: 10.11594/ijmaber.05.03.10

Nijs, V. R., Srinivasan, S., Pauwels, K., & Hanssens, D. M. (2001). The category-demand effects of price promotions. *Marketing Science*, 20(1), 1–22. DOI: 10.1287/mksc.20.1.1.10197

Njegovanović, A. (2020). Financial decision making in the framework of neuroscience/anthropology with review to the pandemic and climate change.

Noar, S. M. (2006). A 10-year retrospective of research in health mass media campaigns: Where do we go from here? *Journal of Health Communication*, 11(1), 21–42. DOI: 10.1080/10810730500461059 PMID: 16546917

Norton, M. I., Mochon, D., & Ariely, D. (2012). The IKEA effect: When labour leads to love. *Journal of Consumer Psychology*, 22(3), 453–460. DOI: 10.1016/j.jcps.2011.08.002

Nykvist, B., & Nilsson, M. (2015). Rapidly falling costs of battery packs for electric vehicles. *Nature Climate Change*, 5(4), 329–332. DOI: 10.1038/nclimate2564

O'Doherty, J. P., Hampton, A., & Kim, H. (2004). Model-based fMRI and its application to reward learning and decision making. *Annals of the New York Academy of Sciences*, 1104(1), 35–53. DOI: 10.1196/annals.1390.022 PMID: 17416921

Oliveira, A. S., Ferreira, J., Albuquerque, M., & Marcos, A. (2021, June). Marketing Sensorial: Estudo de Caso da Starbucks: Sensory Marketing: Starbucks Case Study. In 2021 16th Iberian Conference on Information Systems and Technologies (CISTI) (pp. 1-7). IEEE.

Oliveira, N. (2017). Recensão: The "postmodern turn" in the social sciences [Simon Susen, 2015, Basingstoke, Palgrave Macmillan]. *Sociologia. Sociologia (Lisboa)*, 86(86). Advance online publication. DOI: 10.7458/SPP20188610426

Oliver, L. (2016), From exposure to understanding the interaction of affect and cognition in consumer decision-making [Thesis doctoral, Hanken School of Economics].

Orzan, G., Zara, I. A., & Purcarea, V. L. (2012). Neuromarketing techniques in pharmaceutical drugs advertising- A discussion and agenda for future research. *Journal of Medicine and Life*, 5(1), 428–432. PMID: 23346245

Osman, I. H., Anouze, A. L., Irani, Z., Al-Ayoubi, B., Lee, H., Balc, A., Medeni, T. D., & Weerakkody, V. (2014). COBRA framework to evaluate e-government services: A citizen-centric perspective. *Government Information Quarterly*, 31(2), 243–256. DOI: 10.1016/j.giq.2013.10.009

OVERVIEW of Buyer and Buying Behaviour. (n.d.). Retrieved from Oxford Reference: https://www.oxfordreference.com/display/10.1093/oi/authority.20110803095539233

Ozdemir, M., & Koc, M. (2012). Two methods of creative marketing research neuromarketing and in-depth interview. *Creative and Knowledge Society*, 2(1), 113. DOI: 10.2478/v10212-011-0020-6

Ozuem, W., Ranfagni, S., Willis, M., Rovai, S., & Howell, K. (2021). Exploring customers' responses to online service failure and recovery strategies during Covid-19 pandemic: An actor-network theory perspective. *Psychology and Marketing*, 38(9), 1440–1459. DOI: 10.1002/mar.21527 PMID: 34539054

Packaging types and differences. (n.d.). Retrieved from https://www.ar-racking.com/en/blog/primary-secondary-and-tertiary-packaging-types-and-differences/

Paivio, A. (1979). *Imagery and verbal processes*. Lawrence Erlbaum Associates.

Pallavi, G. P., & Dsa, K. T. (2024). Literature Review on the Role of Financial Advisors in Shaping Investment Decisions.

Panchal, H. (2023, April 23). *The Impact of Packaging on Consumer Purchasing Behavior: An Analysis of the Impact on Buying Decisions*. Retrieved from https://www.litmusbranding.com/blog/the-impact-of-packaging-on-consumer-purchasing-behavior-an-analysis-of-the-impact-on-buying-decisions/

Panneerselvam, T., & Joe Arun, C. (2022). Bias-driven marketing that instigates pledging to a crowdfunding campaign: An experimental consideration of behavioral anomalies. *International Journal of Consumer Studies*, 46(6), 2404–2428. DOI: 10.1111/ijcs.12795

Park, C. W., Roth, M. S., & Jacques, P. F. (1988). Evaluating the effects of advertising and sales promotion campaigns. *Industrial Marketing Management*, 17(2), 129–140. DOI: 10.1016/0019-8501(88)90015-6

Park, S. H., Deng, E. Z., Baker, A. K., MacNiven, K. H., Knutson, B., & Martucci, K. T. (2022). Replication of neural responses to monetary incentives and exploration of reward-influenced network connectivity in fibromyalgia. *Neuroimage. Reports*, 2(4), 100147. DOI: 10.1016/j.ynirp.2022.100147 PMID: 36618964

Parra-González, M., Segura-Robles, A., Vicente-Bújez, M. R., & López-Belmonte, J. (2020). Production analysis and scientific mapping on active methodologies in Web of Science. [IJET]. *International Journal of Emerging Technologies in Learning*, 15(20), 71–86. DOI: 10.3991/ijet.v15i20.15619

Parsons, A., & Conroy, D. (2006). Sensory stimuli and e-tailers. *Journal of Consumer Behaviour*, 5(1), 69–81. DOI: 10.1002/cb.32

Parth, R., Nath, P., Raje, H., Thorat, C., & Deokar, A. (2022). Significance of Neuromarketing in Hotel Industry. *NeuroQuantology : An Interdisciplinary Journal of Neuroscience and Quantum Physics*, 20(9), 5336.

Pavlou, P. A., Huigang, L., & Yajiong, X. (2007). Understanding and Mitigating Uncertainty in Online Exchange Relationships: A Principal-Agent Perspective. *Management Information Systems Quarterly*, 31(1), 105–135. DOI: 10.2307/25148783

Pavlou, P. A., & Stewart, D. W. (2000). Measuring the effects and effectiveness of interactive advertising: A research agenda. *Journal of Interactive Advertising*, 1(1), 61–77. DOI: 10.1080/15252019.2000.10722044

Peck, J., & Childers, T. L. (2003). To have and to hold: The influence of haptic information on product judgments. *Journal of Marketing*, 67(2), 35–48. DOI: 10.1509/jmkg.67.2.35.18612

Peng, Y., Liang, J., Zhang, W., & Liu, M. (2023). Bank Marketing Strategy Based on Consumer Loan Behavior Prediction. *Advances in Economics, Management, and Political Sciences*, 6(1), 508–514. DOI: 10.54254/2754-1169/6/20220196

Perrachione, T. K., & Perrachione, J. R. (2008). Brains and Brands: Developing mutually informative research in neuroscience and marketing. *Journal of Consumer Behaviour*, 7(4), 303–318. DOI: 10.1002/cb.253

Pescher, C., Reichhart, P., & Spann, M. (2014). Consumer decision-making processes in mobile viral marketing campaigns. *Journal of Interactive Marketing*, 28(1), 43–54. DOI: 10.1016/j.intmar.2013.08.001

Peters, A., & Dütschke, E. (2014). How do consumers perceive electric vehicles? A comparison of German consumer groups. *Journal of Environmental Policy and Planning*, 16(3), 359–377. DOI: 10.1080/1523908X.2013.879037

Peterson, R. L. (2007). Affect and financial decision-making: How neuroscience can inform market participants. *Journal of Behavioral Finance*, 8(2), 70–78. DOI: 10.1080/15427560701377448

Petit, O., Velasco, C., & Spence, C. (2019). Digital Sensory Marketing: Integrating New Technologies Into Multisensory Online Experience. *Journal of Interactive Marketing*, 45, 42–61. DOI: 10.1016/j.intmar.2018.07.004

Piqueras-Fiszman, B., Alcaide, J., Roura, E., & Spence, C. (2012). Is it the plate or is it the food? Assessing the influence of the color (black or white) and shape of the plate on the perception of the food placed on it. *Food Quality and Preference*, 24(1), 205–208. DOI: 10.1016/j.foodqual.2011.08.011

Piwowarski, M., Biercewicz, K., & Borawski, M. (2019). Methods of Examining the Neuronal Bases of Financial Decisions. In *Effective Investments on Capital Markets: 10th Capital Market Effective Investments Conference (CMEI 2018)* (pp. 351-368). Springer International Publishing. DOI: 10.1007/978-3-030-21274-2_24

Plakhin, A. Y., Semenets, I., Ogorodnikova, E., & Khudanina, M. (2018). New directions in the development of neuromarketing and behavioral economics. In *MATEC Web of Conferences* (Vol. 184, pp. 1-6).

Planning, P. (2022, April 15). *How Packaging Influences Consumer Behavior*. Retrieved from EDL a massman Company: https://www.edlpackaging.com/blog/how-packaging-influences-consumer-behavior/

Planning, U. D. R. (2014). It's All Green to Me: How Intrapersonal and Interpersonal Factors Shape Consumers' Financial Decisions. *Advances in Consumer Research. Association for Consumer Research (U. S.)*, •••, 42.

Plassmann, H., O'Doherty, J., Shiv, B., & Rangel, A. (2008). Marketing actions can modulate neural representations of experienced pleasantness. *Proceedings of the National Academy of Sciences of the United States of America*, 105(3), 1050–1054. DOI: 10.1073/pnas.0706929105 PMID: 18195362

Plassmann, H., Ramsøy, T. Z., & Milosavljevic, M. (2012). Branding the brain: A critical review and outlook. *Journal of Consumer Psychology*, 22(1), 18–36. DOI: 10.1016/j.jcps.2011.11.010

Plassmann, H., Venkatraman, V., Huettel, S., & Yoon, C. (2015). Consumer neuroscience: Applications, challenges, and possible solutions. *JMR, Journal of Marketing Research*, 52(4), 427–435. DOI: 10.1509/jmr.14.0048

Plassmann, H., & Weber, B. (2015). Individual Differences in Marketing Placebo Effects: Evidence from Brain Imaging and Behavioral Experiments. *JMR, Journal of Marketing Research*, 52(4), 493–510. DOI: 10.1509/jmr.13.0613

Pleger, B., & Villringer, A. (2013). The human somatosensory system: From perception to decision making. *Progress in Neurobiology*, 103, 76–97. DOI: 10.1016/j.pneurobio.2012.10.002 PMID: 23123624

Plötz, P., Schneider, U., Globisch, J., & Dütschke, E. (2014). Who will buy electric vehicles? Identifying early adopters in Germany. *Transportation Research Part A, Policy and Practice*, 67, 96–109. DOI: 10.1016/j.tra.2014.06.006

Polo, E. M., Farabbi, A., Mollura, M., Mainardi, L., & Barbieri, R. (2024). Understanding the role of emotion in decision making process: Using machine learning to analyze physiological responses to visual, auditory, and combined stimulation. *Frontiers in Human Neuroscience*, 17, 1286621. DOI: 10.3389/fnhum.2023.1286621 PMID: 38259333

Pompian, M. M. (2012). *Behavioral finance and investor types: managing behavior to make better investment decisions*. John Wiley & Sons. DOI: 10.1002/9781119202417

Pop, A. N., Dabija, D. C., & Iorga, A. M. (2014). Ethical responsibilities of neuromarketing companies in harnessing the market research - A global exploratory approach. *Amfiteatru Economic*, XVI(35), 26–40.

Pop, C., Radomir, L., Ioana, M. A., & Maria, Z. M. (2009). Neuromarketing – Getting Inside The Customer's Mind. *Annals of Faculty of Economics*, 4, 804–807.

Popova, N., Kataiev, A., Skrynkovskyy, R., & Nevertii, A. (2019). Development of trust marketing in the digital society. *Economic Annals-XXI*, 176(3–4), 13–25. DOI: 10.21003/ea.V176-02

Powell, S. (2018). Uncle Ben's using augmented reality to reveal rice supply chain. https://thefuturescentre.org/signals-of-change/218004/uncle-bens-using-augmentedreality-reveal-rice-supply-chain / Accessed 22 November 2018. Ranasinghe, N., Tolley, D., Nguy

Pozharliev, R., Verbeke, W. J. M. I., & Bagozzi, R. P. (2017). Social consumer neuroscience: Neurophysiological measures of advertising effectiveness in a social context. *Journal of Advertising*, 46(2), 213–226. DOI: 10.1080/00913367.2017.1343162

Product promotion, Definitation, types, strategy,example. (n.d.). Retrieved from https://advertising.amazon.com/library/guides/product-promotion

Pryke, M. (2010). Money's eyes: The visual preparation of financial markets. *Economy and Society*, 39(4), 427–459. DOI: 10.1080/03085147.2010.510679

PwC. (2023). Experience is everything: Here's how to get it right. Retrieved from https://www.pwc.com/gx/en/industries/consumer-markets/consumer-insights/experience-is-everything.html

Quintero-Martínez, D. M., & Arias, J. A. S. (2019). *Neuromarketing: A Competitive Advantage for the Financial Sector. Apuntes de Administración (Universidad Francisco de Paula Santander), 4(1).*

Racat, M., & Plotkina, D. (2023). Sensory-enabling technology in m-commerce: The effect of haptic stimulation on consumer purchasing behavior. *International Journal of Electronic Commerce*, 27(3), 354–384. DOI: 10.1080/10864415.2023.2226900

Radocy, R. E., & Boyle, J. D. (2012). *Psychological foundations of musical behavior.* Charles C Thomas Publisher.

Raheem, A. R., Vishnu, P. A. R. M. A. R., & Ahmed, A. M. (2014). Impact of product packaging on consumer's buying behavior. *European Journal of Scientific Research*, 122(2), 125–134.

Ramakrishnan, S., Wong, M. S., Chit, M. M., & Mutum, D. S. (2022). A conceptual model of the relationship between organizational intelligence traits and digital government service quality: The role of occupational stress. *International Journal of Quality & Reliability Management*, 39(6), 1429–1452. DOI: 10.1108/IJQRM-10-2021-0371

Rambabu, L., & Porika, R. (2020, April 09). *Packaging strategies: knowledge outlook on consumer buying behaviour.* Retrieved from Emerald insight: https://www.emerald.com/insight/content/doi/10.1108/JIUC-10-2019-0017/full/html

Ramchandran, K., Tranel, D., Duster, K., & Denburg, N. L. (2020). The role of emotional vs. cognitive intelligence in economic decision-making amongst older adults. *Frontiers in Neuroscience*, 14, 497. DOI: 10.3389/fnins.2020.00497 PMID: 32547361

Ramsoy, T.Z. (2014), Introduction to Neuromarketing and Consumer Science. Dinamarca: Neurons Inc.

Ranasinghe, N., Lee, K. Y., Suthokumar, G., & Do, E. Y. L. (2016). Virtual ingredients for food and beverages to create immersive taste experiences. *Multimedia Tools and Applications*, 75(20), 12291–12309. DOI: 10.1007/s11042-015-3162-8

Ranasinghe, N., Tolley, D., Nguyen, T. N. T., Yan, L., Chew, B., & Yi-Luen Do, E. (2018). (in press). Augmented flavours: Modulation of flavour experiences through electric taste augmentation. *Food Research International*. Advance online publication. DOI: 10.1016/j.foodres.2018.05.030 PMID: 30736924

Rangel, A., Camerer, C., & Montague, P. R. (2008). A framework for studying the neurobiology of value-based decision making. *Nature Reviews. Neuroscience*, 9(7), 545–556. DOI: 10.1038/nrn2357 PMID: 18545266

Rathore, S., & Arora, M. (2024). Sustainability Reporting in the Metaverse: A Multi-Sectoral Analysis. In *Exploring the Use of Metaverse in Business and Education* (pp. 147-165). IGI Global. https://doi.org/DOI: 10.4018/979-8-3693-5868-9.ch009

Ravula, P. (2022). Impact of delivery performance on online review ratings: the role of temporal distance of ratings. *Journal of Marketing Analytics*, pp. 1–11. DOI: 10.1057/s41270-022-00168-5

Razbadauskaitė-Venskė, I. (2024). Neuromarketing: a tool to understand consumer behaviour. *Regional formation and development studies.*, (1), 101-109.

Reikin, V. S., Voitovych, S. Y., Danyliuk, T. I., Dedeliuk, K. Y., & Lorvi, I. F. (2021). Neuromarketing as interdisciplinary area: Theoretical and methodological analysis. *Estudios de Economía Aplicada*, 39(6). Advance online publication. DOI: 10.25115/eea.v39i6.5164

Reimann, M., Zaichkowsky, J., Neuhaus, C., Bender, T., & Weber, B. (2010). Aesthetic package design: A behavioural, neural, and psychological assessment. *Journal of Consumer Psychology*, 20(4), 431–441. DOI: 10.1016/j.jcps.2010.06.009

Rezvani, Z., Jansson, J., & Bodin, J. (2015). Advances in consumer electric vehicle adoption research: A review and research agenda. *Transportation Research Part D, Transport and Environment*, 34, 122–136. DOI: 10.1016/j.trd.2014.10.010

Ricci M, Scarcelli A, D'Introno A, Strippoli V, Cariati S, & Fiorentino M (2023). A human-centred design approach for designing augmented reality enabled interactive systems: a kitchen machine case study. https://doi.org/.DOI: 10.1007/978-3-031-15928-2_123

Ricciardi, V. (2004). A risk perception primer: A narrative research review of the risk perception literature in behavioral accounting and behavioral finance. *Available at SSRN* 566802. DOI: 10.2139/ssrn.566802

Ricci, M., Evangelista, A., Di Roma, A., & Fiorentino, M. (2023). Immersive and desktop virtual reality in virtual fashion stores: A comparison between shopping experiences. *Virtual Reality (Waltham Cross)*, 27(3), 2281–2296. DOI: 10.1007/s10055-023-00806-y PMID: 37360805

Riccio, A., Holz, E. M., Aricò, P., Leotta, F., Aloise, F., Desideri, L., Rimondini, M., Kübler, A., Mattia, D., & Cincotti, F. (2015). Hybrid P300-based brain-computer interface to improve usability for people with severe motor disability: Electromyographic signals for error correction during a spelling task. *Archives of Physical Medicine and Rehabilitation*, 96(3), S54–S61. DOI: 10.1016/j.apmr.2014.05.029 PMID: 25721548

Richards, J. D. (1993a). Book Reviews : Handbook of Research Design and Social Measurement, by Delbert C. Miller. Fifth Edition. Newbury Park, CA: Sage Publications, 1991, 704 pp. *Evaluation Practice, 14*(2), 199–201. DOI: 10.1177/109821409301400217

Rijo, C., & Marmelo, C. (2022). Neurodesign and the brand perception: Communication challenges. *Design, Visual Communication and Branding*, 35.

Risher, J. J., Harrison, D. E., & LeMay, S. A. (2020). Last mile non-delivery: Consumer investment in last mile infrastructure. *Journal of Marketing Theory and Practice*, 28(4), 484–496. DOI: 10.1080/10696679.2020.1787846

Riza, A. F., & Wijayanti, D. M. (2018). The triangle of sensory marketing model: Does it stimulate brand experience and loyalty. *Esensi: Jurnal Bisnis dan Manajemen, 8*(1), 57-66.

Robb, R. A. (1963). w. G. Cochran, Sampling Techniques (John Wiley & Sons, 2nd edition, 1963), ix+413 pp., 72s. *Proceedings of the Edinburgh Mathematical Society, 13*(4), 342–343. DOI: 10.1017/S0013091500025724

Rodrigues, C. A. M. C. S. (2014). Brand sensuality and consumer-based brand equity (Doctoral dissertation, Universidade do Porto (Portugal)).

Rodrigues, C., & Brito, C. (2011). Sensorial brand strategies for value co-creation.

Rodrigues, F. (2011), Influencia do Neuromarketing nos processos de tomada de decisao. Viseu: Psicosma.

Roebuck, K. (2011). *Neuromarketing: High-Impact strategies-What you need to know: Definitions, Adoptions, Impact, Benefits, Maturity, Vendors*. Emereo Publishing.

Rogers, E. M. (2003). *Diffusion of Innovations* (5th ed.). Free Press.

Ru, H., & Schoar, A. (2016). Do credit card companies screen for behavioral biases? (No. w22360). National Bureau of Economic Research. DOI: 10.3386/w22360

Rundh, B. (2009). Packaging design: Creating competitive advantage with product packaging. *British Food Journal*, 111(9), 988–1002. DOI: 10.1108/00070700910992880

Rungratsameetaweemana, N., Itthipuripat, S., Salazar, A., & Serences, J. T. (2018). Expectations do not alter early sensory processing during perceptual decision-making. *The Journal of Neuroscience : The Official Journal of the Society for Neuroscience*, 38(24), 5632–5648. DOI: 10.1523/JNEUROSCI.3638-17.2018 PMID: 29773755

Rupini, R. V., & Nandagopal, R. (2015). A Study on the Influence of Senses and the Effectiveness of Sensory Branding. *Journal of Psychiatry*, 18(2), 236.

Sadler-Smith, E., & Shefy, E. (2004). The intuitive executive: Understanding and applying 'gut feel' in decision-making. *The Academy of Management Perspectives*, 18(4), 76–91. DOI: 10.5465/ame.2004.15268692

Safiullah, M. D., Pathak, P., & Singh, S. (2022). The impact of social media and news media on political marketing: An empirical study of 2014 Indian General Election. *International Journal of Business Excellence*, 26(4), 536–550. DOI: 10.1504/IJBEX.2022.122765

Salesforce. (2021). State of the connected customer, 5th edition. Retrieved from https://www.salesforce.com/form/pdf/state-of-the-connected-customer/

Sampling of Populations. Methods and Applications, 4th edition by LEVY, P. S. and LEMESHOW, S. (2009). *Biometrics*, 65(2), 671–671. DOI: 10.1111/j.1541-0420.2009.01247_13.x

Samuel, B. S., & Pransanth, V. T. (2012). Neuromarketing: Is Campbell in Soup? *IUP Journal of Marketing Management*, 11(2), 76–100.

San Martín, R., Appelbaum, L. G., Huettel, S. A., & Woldorff, M. G. (2016). Cortical brain activity reflecting attentional biasing toward reward-predicting cues covaries with economic decision-making performance. *Cerebral Cortex (New York, N.Y.)*, 26(1), 1–11. DOI: 10.1093/cercor/bhu160 PMID: 25139941

Sánchez-Fernández, R., & Iniesta-Bonillo, M. Á. (2006). Consumer perception of value: Literature review and a new conceptual framework. *Journal of Consumer Satisfaction, Dissatisfaction & Complaining Behavior*, 19, 40–58.

Sands, S. (octubre 2009), Sample Size Analysis for Brainwave Collection (EEG) Methodologies. https://bit.ly/3zb3zJx

Sanfey, A. G., Loewenstein, G., McClure, S. M., & Cohen, J. D. (2006). Neuroeconomics: Cross-currents in research on decision-making. *Trends in Cognitive Sciences*, 10(3), 108–116. DOI: 10.1016/j.tics.2006.01.009 PMID: 16469524

Sanfey, A. G., Rilling, J. K., Aronson, J. A., Nystrom, L. E., & Cohen, J. D. (2003). The neural basis of economic decision-making in the ultimatum game. *Science*, 300(5626), 1755–1758. DOI: 10.1126/science.1082976 PMID: 12805551

Santiago, R., Moreira, A. C., & Fortes, N. (2017). Influence of sensory stimuli on brand experience, brand equity, and purchase intention. *Journal of Business Economics and Management*.

Satriawan, B. H., & Purwaningsih, T. (2021). Political Marketing Prabowo Subianto and Sandiaga Salahuddin Uno in the 2019 Presidential Election. *Jurnal Ilmu Sosial Dan Ilmu Politik*, 25(2), 127–143. DOI: 10.22146/jsp.53688

Savage, P. (2009). People Skills – Third edition Thompson Niall People Skills – Third edition Palgrave Macmillan 336pp £19.99 978 0 230 22112 3 9780230221123. *Nursing Standard*, 24(4), 31–31. DOI: 10.7748/ns.24.4.31.s38

Savciuc, O. (2022). Neuromarketing and ethical aspects in conducting market research.

Sawagvudcharee, O., Shrestha, S., & Mandal, S. (2018). Impacts of Brand on Consumer Decision Making: Case Study of Beer Brands in Nepal. *International Journal of Research*, 5(16).

Schiffman, H. R. (1990). *Sensation and perception: An integrated approach*. John Wiley & Sons.

Schlosser, A. E., White, T. B., & Lloyd, S. M. (2006). Converting Web Site Visitors into Buyers: How Web Site Investment Increases Consumer Trusting Beliefs and Online Purchase Intentions. *Journal of Marketing*, 70(2), 133–148. DOI: 10.1509/jmkg.70.2.133

Schreuder, E., Van Erp, J., Toet, A., & Kallen, V. L. (2016). Emotional responses to multisensory environmental stimuli: A conceptual framework and literature review. *SAGE Open*, 6(1), 2158244016630591. DOI: 10.1177/2158244016630591

Schuitema, G., Anable, J., Skippon, S., & Kinnear, N. (2013). The role of instrumental, hedonic and symbolic attributes in the intention to adopt electric vehicles. *Transportation Research Part A, Policy and Practice*, 48, 39–49. DOI: 10.1016/j.tra.2012.10.004

Schwartz, B. L., & Begley, S. (2002). *The Mind and the Brain: Neuroplasticity and the Power of Mental Force*. Harper Perennial.

Sci-Hub: Making uncommon knowledge common. (n.d.). https://sci-hub.se/

Sebastian, V. (2014). New directions in understanding the decision-making process: Neuroeconomics and neuromarketing. *Procedia: Social and Behavioral Sciences*, 127, 758–762. DOI: 10.1016/j.sbspro.2014.03.350

Sevic, N. P., Slijepcevic, M., & Radojevic, I. (2022). Practical implementation of neuromarketing in different business industries: Challenges and trends. *Annals of Spiru Haret University.Economic Series*, 22(2), 211–227.

Shabgou, M., & Daryani, S. M. (2014). Towards the sensory marketing: Stimulating the five senses (sight, hearing, smell, touch and taste) and its impact on consumer behavior. *Indian Journal of Fundamental and Applied Life Sciences*, 4(1), 573–581.

Shapiro, B. P., Rangan, V. K., Moriarty, R. T., & Ross, E. B. (2007). Implementing the marketing concept at GE's jet engine business. *Interfaces*, 27(1), 5–17.

Sharma, A., Dash, S., Vidyapeeth, D. P., & Deshmukh, S., & WPU, D. V. K. M. (2023). A study on neuromarketing potential, problems and applications in the Indian e-commerce sector. *The Online Journal of Distance Education and e-Learning : TOJDEL*, 11(2).

Sharma, S. (2020). Electric vehicle market in India: Challenges and opportunities. *Journal of Management Research and Analysis*, 7(1), 1–5.

Shaw, S. D., & Bagozzi, R. P. (2018). The neuropsychology of consumer behavior and marketing. *Consumer Psychology Review*, 1(1), 22–40. DOI: 10.1002/arcp.1006

Shefrin, H., & Statman, M. (1985). The disposition to sell winners too early and ride losers too long: Theory and evidence. *The Journal of Finance*, 40(3), 777–790. DOI: 10.1111/j.1540-6261.1985.tb05002.x

Shiv, B., & Fedorikhin, A. (1999). Heart and Mind in Conflict: The interplay of affect and cognition in consumer decision making. *The Journal of Consumer Research*, 26(3), 278–292. DOI: 10.1086/209563

Shukla, R. P., & Taneja, S. (2024). Catalysts of change. In *Embracing digital transformation* (pp. 104–116). IGI Global., DOI: 10.4018/979-8-3693-2019-8.ch005

Shukla, R. P., & Taneja, S. (2024). *Catalysts of Change.*, DOI: 10.4018/979-8-3693-1842-3.ch007

Sierzchula, W., Bakker, S., Maat, K., & van Wee, B. (2014). The influence of financial incentives and other socio-economic factors on electric vehicle adoption. *Energy Policy*, 68, 183–194. DOI: 10.1016/j.enpol.2014.01.043

Sims, R., Schaeffer, R., Creutzig, F., Nunez, X. C., D'Agosto, M., Dimitriu, D., & Tiwari, G. (2014). Transport. In Contribution of working group III to the Fifth Assessment Report of the Intergovernmental Panel on Climate Change.

Sinek, S. (2009). *Start with Why: How great leaders inspire everyone to take action*. Penguin Group.

Singh, P. (2024, June 23). *Consumer Behavior – Types, Scope, Models & Characteristics*. Retrieved from https://www.revechat.com/blog/consumer-behavior/

Singhraul, B. P., & Batwe, Y. (2022). Neurofinance: The new world of finance based on human psychology and individual investment behaviour. *International Journal of Health Sciences*, 6(S9), 2012–2024. DOI: 10.53730/ijhs.v6nS9.12775

Singh, S. (2006). Impact of colour on marketing. *Management Decision*, 44(6), 783–789. DOI: 10.1108/00251740610673332

Singh, S. (2020). Impact of neuromarketing applications on consumers. *Journal of Business and Management*, 26(2), 33–52. DOI: 10.1504/JBM.2020.141282

Singh, S., & Gupta, R. (2024). Financial Decision-Making. In *Clinical Laboratory Management* (pp. 53–55). Springer Nature Switzerland.

Singh, S., Sharma, A., & Jain, N. (2013). Customer engagement through sensory branding. *EXCEL International Journal of Multidisciplinary Management Studies*, 3(9), 132–138.

Skandrani, H. M., Ben Dahmane Mouelhi, N., & Malek, F. (2011). Effect of store atmospherics on employees' reactions. *International Journal of Retail & Distribution Management*, 39(1), 61–67. DOI: 10.1108/09590551111104477

Skippon, S., & Garwood, M. (2011). Responses to battery electric vehicles: UK consumer attitudes and attributions of symbolic meaning following direct experience to reduce psychological distance. *Transportation Research Part D, Transport and Environment*, 16(7), 525–531. DOI: 10.1016/j.trd.2011.05.005

Sliburyte, L., & Skeryte, I. (2014). What we know about consumers' color perception. *Procedia: Social and Behavioral Sciences*, 156, 468–472. DOI: 10.1016/j.sbspro.2014.11.223

Small, D. A., & Loewenstein, G. (2003). Helping a victim or helping the victim: Altruism and identifiability. *Journal of Risk and Uncertainty*, 26(1), 5–16. DOI: 10.1023/A:1022299422219

Smidts, A. (2002), Kijken in het brein: Over de mogelijkheden van neuromarketing. *Tijdschrift voor Marketing, 36*(3), 18-23, Univ-Ovidius.Ro., from https://stec.univ-ovidius.ro/html/anale/RO/2021-2/Section

Smidts, A. (2002). Kijken in het brein: Over de mogelijkheden van neuromarketing.

Smidts, A. (october 25 de 2002), Kijkenin het brein: Over de mogelijkheden van neuromarketing. http://hdl.handle.net/1765/308

Smith, K. T. (2011). Digital marketing strategies that Millennials find appealing, motivating, or just annoying. *Journal of Strategic Marketing*, 19(6), 489–499. DOI: 10.1080/0965254X.2011.581383

Snyder, L. B., Hamilton, M. A., Mitchell, E. W., Kiwanuka-Tondo, J., Fleming-Milici, F., & Proctor, D. (2004). A meta-analysis of the effect of mediated health communication campaigns on behavior change in the United States. *Journal of Health Communication*, 9(sup1, S1), 71–96. DOI: 10.1080/10810730490271548 PMID: 14960405

Soll, J. B., Milkman, K. L., & Payne, J. W. (2015). A user's guide to debiasing. In Keren, G., & Wu, G. (Eds.), *The Wiley Blackwell Handbook of Judgment and Decision Making* (pp. 924–951). Wiley Blackwell. DOI: 10.1002/9781118468333.ch33

Solnais, C., Andreu-Perez, J., Sánchez-Fernández, J., & Andréu-Abela, J. (2013). The contribution of neuroscience to consumer research: A conceptual framework and empirical review. *Journal of Economic Psychology*, 36, 68–81. DOI: 10.1016/j.joep.2013.02.011

Solomon, M., Russell-Bennett, R., & Previte, J. (2012). *Consumer behaviour*. Pearson Higher Education AU.

Solti, A., Agarwal, S., & Spiekermann-Hoff, S. (2018). Privacy in location-sensing technologies. *Handbook of Mobile Data Privacy*, 35-69.

Soni, A. (2021). A Study on Consumer Decision-Making Process. *Samvakti Journal of Research in Business Management*, 2(2), 1–8. DOI: 10.46402/2021.01.12

Sophocleous, H. P., Masouras, A. N., & Anastasiadou, S. D. (2024). The Impact of Political Marketing on Voting Behaviour of Cypriot Voters. *Social Sciences (Basel, Switzerland)*, 13(3), 149. Advance online publication. DOI: 10.3390/socsci13030149

Sorensen, K. (2009). Dark side of neuromarketing: How manipulative tactics backfire. *The Journal of Consumer Research*, 36(6), 967–982. https://doi.org/10.1086/648672

Soto Arias, J. A., & Quintero-Martínez, D. M. (2019). *Neuromarketing: A competitive advantage for the financial sector financial sector*. Francisco de Paula Santander University.

Sovacool, B. K., Kester, J., Noel, L., & de Rubens, G. Z. (2018). The demographics of decarbonizing transport: The influence of gender, age, and household size on electric mobility preferences in the Nordic region. *Global Environmental Change*, 52, 86–100. DOI: 10.1016/j.gloenvcha.2018.06.008

Spangenberg, E. R., Grohmann, B., & Sprott, D. E. (2006). It is beginning to smell (and sound) a lot like Christmas: The interactive effects of ambient scent and music in a retail setting. *Journal of Business Research*, 59(12), 1281–1287. DOI: 10.1016/j.jbusres.2006.08.006

Spence, C. (2020). On the ethics of neuromarketing and sensory marketing. Organizational Neuroethics: Reflections on the Contributions of Neuroscience to Management Theories and Business Practices, 9-29.

Spence, C., & Gallace, A. (2011). Multisensory design: Reaching out to touch the consumer. *Psychology and Marketing*, 28(3), 267–308. DOI: 10.1002/mar.20392

Sposini, L. (2024). Impact of New Technologies on Economic Behavior and Consumer Freedom of Choice: From Neuromarketing to Neuro-Rights. *Journal of Digital Technologies and Law*, 2(1), 74–100. DOI: 10.21202/jdtl.2024.5

Springer. (2009). Supplement 2: Sixth annual ethical dimensions in business: Reflections from the business academic community. *Journal of Business Ethics*, 88, 141-153.

Srivastava, M., Sharma, G. D., & Srivastava, A. K. (2019). Human brain and financial behavior: A neurofinance perspective. *International Journal of Ethics and Systems*, 35(4), 485–503. DOI: 10.1108/IJOES-02-2019-0036

Stanton, S. J., & Armstrong, J. A. (2017). Neuromarketing: Ethical implications of its use and potential misuses. *Journal of Business Ethics*, 144(4), 799–811. https://doi.org/10.1007/s10551-016-3059-0

Stanton, S. J., Sinnott-Armstrong, W., & Huettel, S. A. (2017). Neuromarketing: Ethical Implications of its Use and Potential Misuse. *Journal of Business Ethics*, 144(4), 799–811. DOI: 10.1007/s10551-016-3059-0

Statman, M. (1999). Behaviorial finance: Past battles and future engagements. *Financial Analysts Journal*, 55(6), 18–27. DOI: 10.2469/faj.v55.n6.2311

Staw, B. M. (1981). The escalation of commitment to a course of action. *Academy of Management Review*, 6(4), 577–587. DOI: 10.2307/257636

Steg, L. (2005). Car use: Lust and must. Instrumental, symbolic and affective motives for car use. *Transportation Research Part A, Policy and Practice*, 39(2-3), 147–162. DOI: 10.1016/j.tra.2004.07.001

Strickland, K. (2016). Grounded theory: A practical guide birks Melanie Mills Jane Grounded theory: A practical guide 208pp £26.99 Sage Publications 9781446295786 1446295788. *Nurse Researcher*, 23(5), 42–42. DOI: 10.7748/nr.23.5.42.s10

Sugawara, E., & Nikaido, H. (2014). Properties of AdeABC and AdeIJK Efflux Systems of Acinetobacter Baumannii Compared with Those of the AcrAB-TolC System of Escherichia Coli. *Antimicrobial Agents and Chemotherapy*, 58(12), 7250–7257. DOI: 10.1128/AAC.03728-14 PMID: 25246403

Survey Sampling. By Leslie Kish. (New York: John Wiley & Sons, Inc., 1965. Pp. xvi, 643. $10.95.). (1965). *American Political Science Review, 59*(4), 1025–1025. DOI: 10.1017/S0003055400132113

Sustainability in packaging 2023: Inside the minds of global consumers. (2023, August 15). Retrieved from Mckinsey & Company: https://mckinsey.com/industries/packaging-and-paper/our-insights/sustainability-in-packaging-2023-inside-the-minds-of-global-consumers

Svanes, E., Vold, M., Møller, H., Pettersen, M. K., Larsen, H., & Hanssen, O. J. (2010). Sustainable packaging design: A holistic methodology for packaging design. *Packaging Technology & Science*, 23(3), 161–175. DOI: 10.1002/pts.887

Sydorenko, N. (2023, April 07). *Buyer behavior.* Retrieved from https://snov.io/glossary/buyer-behavior/

Takemura, K., & Takemura, K. (2021). Decision-Making Process and Neuroeconomics. *Behavioral Decision Theory: Psychological and Mathematical Descriptions of Human Choice Behavior*, 193-207.

Tanasic, B. R. (2017). Impact of sensory branding on the decision-making process of tourism product purchase. *International Journal of Research in Engineering and Innovation*, 1(6), 109–125.

Taneja, B., Shukla, P., & Arora, M. (2024). Sensible Selling Through Sensory Neuromarketing: Enhancing Sales Effectiveness. In Sensible Selling Through Sensory Neuromarketing (pp. 164-183). IGI Global.

Taneja, S., Shukla, P., & Arora, R. (2024). Sensory marketing strategies: Enhancing consumer experience and emotional connection. *Journal of Consumer Marketing*. Advance online publication. DOI: 10.1108/JCM-09-2023-0658

Tang, F., Hess, T. J., Valacich, J. S., & Sweeney, J. T. (2014). The effects of visualization and interactivity on calibration in financial decision-making. *Behavioral Research in Accounting*, 26(1), 25–58. DOI: 10.2308/bria-50589

Team, I. E. (2022, December 30). *16 Product Promotion Strategies (With Definition and How-To)*. Retrieved from https://www.indeed.com/career-advice/career-development/products-promotion

Teixeira, S., Gonçalves, M. J. A., & Reis, A. (2022). Study of the Relationship Between Sensory Marketing and Consumer Satisfaction. In *Advances in Tourism, Technology and Systems: Selected Papers from ICOTTS 2021* (Vol. 1, pp. 499–518). Springer Nature Singapore. DOI: 10.1007/978-981-19-1040-1_43

Tek, Ö. B., & Engin, Ö. (2008). Modern Pazarlama İlkeleriUygulamalı Yönetimsel. Yaklaşım (3. Basım).

Thaler, R. (1980). Toward a positive theory of consumer choice. *Journal of Economic Behavior & Organization*, 1(1), 39–60. DOI: 10.1016/0167-2681(80)90051-7

Thaler, R. H. (2000). From homo economicus to homo sapiens. *The Journal of Economic Perspectives*, 14(1), 133–141. DOI: 10.1257/jep.14.1.133

Thaler, R. H., & Sunstein, C. R. (2008). *Nudge: Improving decisions about health, wealth, and happiness*. Yale University Press.

THE IMPLICATIONS OF FACEBOOK IN POLITICAL MARKETING CAMPAIGNS IN CROATIA. (2020). Central. *European Business Review*, 9(4), 73–95. DOI: 10.18267/j.cebr.244

Theory of correspondence analysis. (2007). In *Chapman & Hall/CRC Interdisciplinary Statistics Series* (pp. 201–211). Chapman and Hall/CRC. DOI: 10.1201/9781420011234.axa

Thompson, D. (16 de enero de 2013), The irrational Consumer: Why Economics is wrong about how we make choices. https://bit.ly/2Smu91D

Thompson, P. (2020). The Relationship between Consumer Credit Card Debt and Immigrants in the UK: A Systematic Review. *American Journal of Economics*, 4(2), 86–114. DOI: 10.47672/aje.637

Thorndike, E. L. (1920). A constant error in psychological ratings. *The Journal of Applied Psychology*, 4(1), 25–29. DOI: 10.1037/h0071663

Tom Dieck, M. C., & Han, D. I. D. (2022). The role of immersive technology in Customer Experience Management. *Journal of Marketing Theory and Practice*, 30(1), 108–119. DOI: 10.1080/10696679.2021.1891939

Tovino, S.A. (2005), The confidentiality and privacy implications of functional magnetic resonance imaging. The Journal of Law, Medicine & Ethics, pp. 33, 844–850. https://doi.org/.DOI: 10.1111/j.1748-720X.2005.tb00550.x

Troye, S. V., & Supphellen, M. (2012). Consumer participation in coproduction:"I made it myself" effects on consumers' sensory perceptions and evaluations of outcome and input product. *Journal of Marketing*, 76(2), 33–46. DOI: 10.1509/jm.10.0205

Turhan, K. N., Gurkaynak, N., & Sadikzade, R. (2023, November). Neuromarketing Concepts in Food Studies. In *2023 Medical Technologies Congress (TIPTEKNO)* (pp. 1-3). IEEE. DOI: 10.1109/TIPTEKNO59875.2023.10359186

Türkmendağ, T., & Hassan, A. (2024). A stakeholder perspective on poverty reduction through the implementation of social marketing in the context of tourism. *Frontiers in Psychology*, 14, 1304952. DOI: 10.3389/fpsyg.2023.1304952 PMID: 38239462

Tversky, A., & Kahneman, D. (1974). Judgment under uncertainty: Heuristics and biases. *Science*, 185(4157), 1124–1131. DOI: 10.1126/science.185.4157.1124 PMID: 17835457

Tversky, A., & Kahneman, D. (1981). The framing of decisions and the psychology of choice. *Science*, 211(4481), 453–458. DOI: 10.1126/science.7455683 PMID: 7455683

Twum, K. K., Kosiba, J. P., Abdul-Hamid, I. K., & Hinson, R. (2022). Does Corporate Social Responsibility Enhance Political Marketing? *Journal of Nonprofit & Public Sector Marketing*, 34(1), 71–101. DOI: 10.1080/10495142.2020.1798850

Twycross, A. (2004). Research design: Qualitative, quantitative and mixed methods approach Research design: Qualitative, quantitative and mixed methods approaches Creswell John W Sage 320 £29 0761924426 0761924426. *Nurse Researcher*, 12(1), 82–83. DOI: 10.7748/nr.12.1.82.s2 PMID: 28718745

U.S. Department of Energy. (2021). *Federal Tax Credits for New All-Electric and Plug-in Hybrid Vehicles*. Retrieved from https://www.fueleconomy.gov/feg/taxevb.shtml

Uddin, M. S. (2011). *The Impact of Sensory Branding (five senses) on Consumer: A Case Study on*. Coca Cola.

Ugazio, G., Grueschow, M., Polania, R., Lamm, C., Tobler, P., & Ruff, C. (2022). Neuro-computational foundations of moral preferences. *Social Cognitive and Affective Neuroscience*, 17(3), 253–265. DOI: 10.1093/scan/nsab100 PMID: 34508645

Utami, M. W. D., Yuniaristanto, Y., & Sutopo, W. (2020). Adoption intention model of electric vehicle in Indonesia. *Jurnal Optimasi Sistem Industri*, 19(1), 70–81. DOI: 10.25077/josi.v19.n1.p70-81.2020

Uzunoğlu, M. İ., & Sözer, E. G. (2020). Cognitive, perceptual and behavioral effects of neuro-stimuli: A study on packaged food products. *Business & Management Studies: An International Journal*, 8(3), 3097–3122.

Va, K. P. (2015). Reinventing the Art of Marketing in the Light of Digitalization and Neuroimaging. *Amity Global Business Review, 10*.

Van Arsdale, P. W. (1996). Book Reviews: Research Methods in Anthropology: Qualitative and Quantitative Approaches (2nd edition), by H. Russell Bernard. Sage Publications, 1994, 584 pp. *Evaluation Practice, 17*(1), 91–92. DOI: 10.1177/109821409601700112

Van der Laan, J. D., Heino, A., & De Waard, D. (1997). A simple procedure for the assessment of acceptance of advanced transport telematics. *Transportation Research Part C, Emerging Technologies*, 5(1), 1–10. DOI: 10.1016/S0968-090X(96)00025-3

Varman, R., & Belk, R. W. (2012). Consuming postcolonial shopping malls. *Journal of Marketing Management*, 28(1–2), 62–84. DOI: 10.1080/0267257X.2011.617706

Vasile, D., & Sebastian, T. C. (2007). Neurofinance–getting an insight into the trader's mind. *Neuroscience*, 27(31), 8159–8160.

Vecchiato, G., Cherubino, P., Trettel, A., & Babiloni, F. (2013). Neuroelectrical Brain Imaging Tools for the Study of the Efficacy of TV Advertising Stimuli and their Application to Neuromarketing. In *Neuroelectrical Brain Imaging Tools for the Study of the Efficacy of TV Advertising Stimuli and their Application to Neuromarketing.* http://link.springer.com/10.1007/978-3-642-38064-8

Velecela, P. A. C., Vallejo, J. I. G., & Jara, B. D. V. (2017). Personal finance: The influence of age in making financial decisions. *Revista Killkana Sociales*, 1(3), 81–88. DOI: 10.26871/killkana_social.v1i3.66

Venkatesh, V., & Bala, H. (2008). Technology Acceptance Model 3 and a research agenda on interventions. *Decision Sciences*, 39(2), 273–315. DOI: 10.1111/j.1540-5915.2008.00192.x

Venkatesh, V., & Morris, M. G. (2000). Why don't men ever stop to ask for directions? Gender, social influence, and their role in technology acceptance and usage behavior. *Management Information Systems Quarterly*, 24(1), 115–139. DOI: 10.2307/3250981

Venkatraman, V., Clitheroe, J. A., Fitzsimons, G. J., & Huettel, S. A. (2012). New scanner data for brand marketers: How neuroscience can help better understand differences in brand preferences, *Journal of Consumer Psychology*, 22(1), 143–153. Ohme, R., Reykowska, D., Weiner, D., & Choromansk, A. (2009). EEG and Galvanic Skin Response measures analyse neurophysiological reactions to advertising stimuli. *Journal of Neuroscience, Psychology, and Economics*, 2(1), 21–31. DOI: 10.1037/a0015462

Venkatraman, V., Clitheroe, J. A., Fitzsimons, G. J., & Huettel, S. A. (2015). New scanner data for brand marketers: How neuroscience can help better understand differences in brand preferences. *Journal of Consumer Psychology*, 22(1), 143–153. DOI: 10.1016/j.jcps.2011.11.008

Venkatraman, V., Dimoka, A., Pavlou, P. A., Vo, K., Hampton, W., Bollinger, B., & Hershfield, H. E. (2015). Predicting advertising success beyond traditional measures: New insights from neurophysiological methods and market response modeling. *JMR, Journal of Marketing Research*, 52(4), 436–452. DOI: 10.1509/jmr.13.0593

Vida, I. (2008). Atmospheric music fit as a driver of shopper store evaluations and their behavioral responses. [JABR]. *Journal of Applied Business Research*, 24(2). Advance online publication. DOI: 10.19030/jabr.v24i2.1356

Vivek, S. D., Beatty, S. E., Dalela, V., & Morgan, R. M. (2014). A generalized multidimensional scale for measuring customer engagement. *Journal of Marketing Theory and Practice*, 22(4), 401–420. DOI: 10.2753/MTP1069-6679220404

Vlasenko, K. (2018). Neuromarketing technologies as the way of achievement of competitive advantage on the market. *Knowledge–Economy–Society*, 95.

Vollrath, M. D., & Villegas, S. G. (2021). Avoiding digital marketing analytics myopia: Revisiting the customer decision journey as a strategic marketing framework. *Journal of Marketing Analytics*, 10(2), 106–113. DOI: 10.1057/s41270-020-00098-0

Vuković, D. (2024). Ethical issues in the application of neuromarketing research. *MAP Social Sciences*, 4(1), 67–81. DOI: 10.53880/2744-2454.2023.4.67

Vysochyna, A., Semenov, V., & Kyrychenko, K. (2021). Marketing and management of innovations in public governance as core determinants of trust. *Marketing and Management of Innovations*, 5(2), 204–212. DOI: 10.21272/mmi.2021.2-17

Wala, A., Czyrka, K., & Frąś, J. (2019). Sensory branding and marketing in stimulating the relation between the buyer and the brand. *Organizacja i Zarządzanie: kwartalnik naukowy*, (1), 109-120.

Walliser, B. (2003). An international review of sponsorship research: Extension and update. *International Journal of Advertising*, 22(1), 5–40. DOI: 10.1080/02650487.2003.11072838

Wang, J., Li, X., Wang, P., Liu, Q., Deng, Z., & Wang, J. (2022). Research Trend of the Unified Theory of Acceptance and Use of Technology Theory: A Bibliometric Analysis. *Sustainability (Basel)*, 14(1), 10. DOI: 10.3390/su14010010

Wang, N., Pan, H., & Zheng, W. (2017). Assessment of the incentives on electric vehicle promotion in China. *Transportation Research Part A, Policy and Practice*, 101, 177–189. DOI: 10.1016/j.tra.2017.04.037

Wedel, M., & Pieters, R. (2008). *Visual marketing: From attention to action*. Psychology Press.

What is Product Promotion? Objectives & Types. (n.d.). Retrieved from Commerce Mates: https://commercemates.com/what-is-product-promotion-objectives-types/

Wijaya, B. S. (2013). Dimensions of brand image: A conceptual review from the perspective of brand communication. *European Journal of Business and Management*, 5(31), 55–65.

Wiley, J. (2007). Sons will launchStatistical Analysis and Data Mining in early 2007. *Statistical Analysis and Data Mining*. Advance online publication. DOI: 10.1002/sam.100

Wilfling, J., Havenith, G., Raccuglia, M., & Hodder, S. (2023). Can you see the feel? The absence of tactile cues in clothing e-commerce impairs consumer decision making. *International Journal of Fashion Design, Technology and Education*, 16(2), 224–233. DOI: 10.1080/17543266.2022.2154396

Wilson, T. D., & Gilbert, D. T. (2003). Affective forecasting. *Advances in Experimental Social Psychology*, 35, 345–411. DOI: 10.1016/S0065-2601(03)01006-2

Winter, A., & Winter, R. (2003). Brain workout: Easy ways to power up your memory, sensory perception, and intelligence. IUniverse.

Winter, J., Scheiner, C. W., & Voigt, K. I. (2009). Emotional branding in the durable goods industry illustrated.

Winterton, J. (2008). Review: Business Research Methods ALAN BRYMAN and EMMA BELL. Oxford: Oxford University Press, 2007. xxxii + 786 pp. £34.99 (pbk). ISBN 9780199284986. *Management Learning*, 39(5), 628–632. DOI: 10.1177/13505076080390050804

Wölfel, M., & Reinhardt, A. (2019, March). Immersive Shopping Presentation of Goods in Virtual Reality. In *CERC* (pp. 119-130).

Wright, W. (1995, October). Information animation applications in the capital markets. In *Proceedings of Visualization 1995 Conference* (pp. 19-25). IEEE. DOI: 10.1109/INFVIS.1995.528682

Wu, H., Wan, W., Jiang, H., & Xiong, Y. (2023). Prognosis of idiopathic sudden sensorineural hearing loss: The nomogram perspective. *The Annals of Otology, Rhinology, and Laryngology*, 132(1), 5–12. DOI: 10.1177/00034894221075114 PMID: 35081764

Xia, Z., Deng, Z., Fang, B., Yang, Y., & Sun, F. (2022). A review on sensory perception for dexterous robotic manipulation. *International Journal of Advanced Robotic Systems*, 19(2), 17298806221095974. DOI: 10.1177/17298806221095974

Xu, C., Peak, D., & Prybutok, V. (2015). A customer value, satisfaction, and loyalty perspective of mobile application recommendations. *Decision Support Systems*, 79, 171–183. DOI: 10.1016/j.dss.2015.08.008

Yang, L., Sun, T., & Liu, Y. (2017). A bibliometric investigation of flipped classroom research during 2000-2015. [IJET]. *International Journal of Emerging Technologies in Learning*, 12(06), 178–186. DOI: 10.3991/ijet.v12i06.7095

Yang, Y., Liu, M., Huang, J., & Wan, X. (2024). Making choices of food and non-food products: A comparison between virtual stores and online shopping. *International Journal of Food Science & Technology*, 59(3), 1644–1652. DOI: 10.1111/ijfs.16918

Yao, H., & Tarofder, A. K. (2024). Privacy Concerns in E-commerce Marketing: A Systematic Literature Review Study. *International Journal of Global Economics and Management*, 2(3), 64–75. DOI: 10.62051/IJGEM.v2n3.07

Yoganathan, V., Osburg, V. S., & Akhtar, P. (2019). Sensory stimulation for sensible consumption: Multisensory marketing for e-tailing of ethical brands. *Journal of Business Research*, 96, 386–396. DOI: 10.1016/j.jbusres.2018.06.005

Yoon, C., Gonzales, R., Bechara, A., Berns, G., Dagher, A., Dubé, L., Huettel, S., Kable, J., Liberzon, I., Plassmann, H., Smidts, A., & Spence, C. (2012). Decision neuroscience and consumer decision-making. *Marketing Letters*, 23(2), 473–485. DOI: 10.1007/s11002-012-9188-z

Yoon, C., Gutchess, A. H., Feinberg, F., & Polk, T. A. (2006). A functional magnetic resonance imaging study of neural dissociations between brand and person judgments. *The Journal of Consumer Research*, 33(1), 31–40. DOI: 10.1086/504132

Yoon, C., Gutchess, A. H., Feinberg, F., & Polk, T. A. (2009). The "sweet spot" of implicit and explicit memory in advertising. *The Journal of Consumer Research*, 36(1), 39–50. DOI: 10.1086/597618

Zahid, H., Ali, S., Abu-Shanab, E., & Muhammad Usama Javed, H. (2022). Determinants of intention to use e-government services: An integrated marketing relation view. *Telematics and Informatics*, 68, 101778. Advance online publication. DOI: 10.1016/j.tele.2022.101778

Zajonc, R. (1980). Feeling and Thinking: Preferences need no inferences. *The American Psychologist*, 35(2), 151–175. DOI: 10.1037/0003-066X.35.2.151

Zajonc, R. B. (1968). Attitudinal effects of mere exposure. *Journal of Personality and Social Psychology*, 9(2), 1–27. DOI: 10.1037/h0025848

Zajonc, R. B. (2001). Mere exposure: A gateway to the subliminal. *Current Directions in Psychological Science*, 10(6), 224–228. DOI: 10.1111/1467-8721.00154

Zaltman, G. (2003). *How customers think: Essential insights into the mind of the market*. Harvard Business Press.

Zeithaml, V. A. (1988). Consumer perceptions of price, quality, and value: A means-end model and synthesis of evidence. *Journal of Marketing*, 52(3), 2–22. DOI: 10.1177/002224298805200302

Zeithaml, V. A., Berry, L. L., & Parasuraman, A. (1996). The behavioral consequences of service quality. *Journal of Marketing*, 60(2), 31–46. DOI: 10.1177/002224299606000203

Zeng, I. M., & Marques, J. A. L. (2023, November). Neuromarketing: Evaluating Consumer Emotions and Preferences to Improve Business Marketing Management. In *18th European Conference on Management, Leadership and Governance*. Academic Conferences and publishing limited. DOI: 10.34190/ecmlg.19.1.1876

Zhang, J., Farris, P. W., Irvin, J. W., Kushwaha, T., Steenburgh, T. J., & Weitz, B. A. (2010). Crafting integrated multichannel retailing strategies. *Journal of Interactive Marketing*, 24(2), 168–180. DOI: 10.1016/j.intmar.2010.02.002

Zhang, X., Wang, K., Hao, Y., Fan, J. L., & Wei, Y. M. (2013). The impact of government policy on preference for NEVs: The evidence from China. *Energy Policy*, 61, 382–393. DOI: 10.1016/j.enpol.2013.06.114

Zhao, X. (2017). A scientometric review of global BIM research: Analysis and visualization. *Automation in Construction*, 80, 37–47. DOI: 10.1016/j.autcon.2017.04.002

Zhao, Z., Luo, H., Chu, S. C., Shang, Y., & Wu, X. (2018). An Immersive Online Shopping System Based on Virtual Reality. *J. Netw. Intell.*, 3(4), 235–246.

Zheng, Q., & Ding, Q. (2022). Exploration of consumer preference based on deep learning neural network model in the immersive marketing environment. *PLoS One*, 17(5), e0268007. DOI: 10.1371/journal.pone.0268007 PMID: 35507570

Zhou, M. (2024). *How to Apply Neuromarketing and Customers' Psychology Biases to a Digital Startup's Brand (Version 1)*. Toronto Metropolitan University., DOI: 10.32920/25164605.v1

Zhou, M. (2024). The effects of sensory interaction and sensory conflict on consumer online review rating behavior. *International Journal of Management Science and Engineering Management*, 19(2), 97–105. DOI: 10.1080/17509653.2023.2174201

Ziefle, M., Beul-Leusmann, S., Kasugai, K., & Schwalm, M. (2014). Public perception and acceptance of electric vehicles: Exploring users' perceived benefits and drawbacks. *Design, User Experience, and Usability. User Experience Design for Everyday Life Applications and Services: Third International Conference, DUXU 2014, Held as Part of HCI International 2014, Heraklion, Crete, Greece, June 22-27, 2014Proceedings*, 3(Part III), 628–639.

Zwicky, A. (2005). Just between Dr. Language and I. *The American Scholar*, 74(4), 134–139.

About the Contributors

Reena Malik is presently working as an Assistant Professor in Chitkara Business School, Chitkara University, Punjab, India. She is Ph.D in Management and Post graduate in Management and Commerce. She has qualified UGC/NTA NET in both Commerce and Management. She has published more than 20 papers in reputed national and international journals and presented papers in various government sponsored seminar and conferences. She has published various research papers and book chapters in Emerald Publication, IGI Global, CRC Taylor and Francis, Wiley and Sage Publications etc. Awarded Gold Medal in M.A (Mass communication), Kurukshetra University. Awarded by women Dedication Magazine. She has five books to her credit. Having a teaching experience of more than 12 years she is actively working in research areas like Consumer Behavior, Brand Management, Customer satisfaction etc. she has 9 patents and 5 copyrights to her credit and edited three books with reputed publishers like Wiley, Taylor and Francis and IGI Global.

Shivani Malhan is working as an Assistant Professor in Chitkara University. She has done her MBA from University Business School, Panjab University and PhD in Marketing Management in the area of Brand Loyalty. She has a corporate experience of two years in Tata Motors and an experience of nine years in teaching. Moreover, she has published many research papers in UGC Care listed journals and scopus indexed journals and has attended many national and international conferences and seminars. She has been awarded the "Best research paper presentation award" by IIT Roorkee. Furthermore, she was a member of the team which organised Carpe Diem in collaboration with IIM Ahmedabad and was given the award of honour for being an active member of NSS while she was working in DAV University.

Manpreet Arora, a Senior Assistant Professor of Management at the Central University of Himachal Pradesh, Dharamshala, India, brings over twenty-two years of rich teaching experience. She holds academic accolades including a Ph.D. in International Trade, an M.Phil, a gold medalist and several other academic distinctions from Himachal Pradesh University, Shimla. Dr. Arora's diverse research interests encompass Accounting, Finance, Strategic Management, Entrepreneurship, Qualitative Research and Microfinance. She works on Mixed methods research. Noteworthy for guiding doctoral research and delving into Microfinance, Entrepreneurship, Behavioral Finance and corporate reporting, she has presented at numerous seminars, delivering talks on various academic subjects across multiple universities and colleges. An accomplished academic, she has an impressive publication record, having authored over 35 papers in esteemed national and international journals listed in Scopus, WOS and Category journals, alongside contributing to sixty book chapters in publications by reputed publishers like Emerald, Routledge, CABI, Springer Nature, AAP and more. Her commitment to management research is evident through the editing of seven books. She is presently working in the area of Metaverse. Her impactful contributions showcase a multifaceted professional excelling in academia, research, and social advocacy.

*　*　*

Preeti Jain is an accomplished academic and researcher with a Ph.D. in Commerce from CT University, and qualifications including UGC NET and an MBA from Lovely Professional University. she excels in communication, office automation, and data visualization tools. With a rich teaching background and numerous publications and patents, she has presented and published research on integrated marketing, sustainable development, and AI in finance. Dr. Jain has coordinated cultural events and academic programs at esteemed institutions and actively participates in workshops and FDPs on research methodology and innovation management.

Achmad Nurmandi is a Professor at the Department of Government Affairs and Administration, Jusuf Kalla School of Government, Universitas Muhammadiyah Yogyakarta, Indonesia. His research interests are on e-government, urban governance and strategic management in the public sector and published in many international journal and Book Chapter, such as International Journal of Public Sector Management, Transforming Government: People, Policy and Process, Jamba Journal of Disaster Studies, Asian Review of Political Science, Journal of Human Behavior in the Social Environment, Public Policy and Administration, Global Encyclopedia of Public Administration, Public Policy, and Governance, Springer. He is currently the Secretary of the Asia Pacific Society for Public Affairs (APSPA). He is also the Editor-in-Chief of Jurnal Studi Pemerintahan (Journal of Government and Politics) and a Guest Editor of International Journal of Public Sector Performance Management and International Journal of Sustainable Society.

Priya Shukla is a dedicated scholar and seasoned professional with a diverse background in IT, operations, and research. Armed with an MBA in IT and Operations, she has embarked on a doctoral journey to delve deeper into her passion for research. Priya possesses a keen acumen for analytical technologies, particularly specializing in IBM and SAS platforms, which she has honed over more than 5 years of hands-on experience in the field. Her research areas span a wide spectrum, encompassing topics such as data analytics, business intelligence, machine learning, and operational efficiency optimization. With a blend of academic rigor and practical industry insight, Priya strives to contribute meaningfully to the advancement of knowledge and innovation in her field.

Rishi Prakash Shukla is a highly accomplished individual in the field of Artificial Intelligence (AI) and analytics. With 12 years of experience, he has made significant contributions to the field through his research and development work. He has 6 patents and has published 20 research papers, demonstrating his expertise and depth of knowledge in AI and analytics. Dr. Shukla has worked with institutions such as Symbiosis International University and has also contributed to projects at the Indian Institute of Management. He has a keen interest in new technologies, particularly in the area of metaverse. He is an IBM and SAS certified professional, further adding to his credentials in the field of AI and analytics. In addition to his work in AI and analytics, Dr. Shukla is also an author of 5 books on futuristic technologies. He is known for his friendly demeanor and love for travel, as well as his passion for social experimentation using technology. With his extensive experience, knowledge, and passion for technology, Dr. Rishi Prakash Shukla is a valuable asset to any organization.

Archana Singh is a distinguished academician cum researcher and trainer in the area of accounting and research in Pune. She has 19 years of teaching experience. She is double Masters in Commerce with a specialization in Business Administration and Cost and Management Accounting. Professionally she has completed Bachelors in Education and is SET qualified, also she completed her Ph D from Savitribai Phule Pune University in faculty of Commerce and was a recognized Ph D guide in Symbiosis International (Deemed University) and at Sri Balaji University She is a rank holder of Pune University and a President awardee. She has a number of research papers to her credit which are based on sustainability, accounting and business administration. She has also published in journals of high repute such as reputed journals Scopus indexed and Australian Business Dean Council listed journals .She has authored chapters in books. Her area of interest lies in the field of accounts and finance, business administration and sustainability. She has 15 SCI publications.

Smriti Verma has over two decades of experience in teaching in institutes like Hindustan University, Chennai, Prestige Institute of Management, Indore, and Institute of Management Technology, Nagpur, Symbiosis University of Applied Sciences, Indore. She is attached to several institutes as Adjunct Faculty including Konstanz University of Applied Sciences, Germany and University of Vorarlberg, Austria. She has published over 60 research paper in national and international journals, 3 edited books and 14 case studies. Alongside she has facilitated several MDPs in the area of Branding and Marketing and FDPs on Case writing, Case Analysis, Research Paper writing and Research Methodology. During her corporate journey, she has lead project implementations in technology management companies. Currently she heads the Department of Management Studies and Entrepreneurship at Yeshwantrao Chavan College of Engineering, Nagpur. She is also Dean International Relations and Director for the Eagles.

Index

A

anchoring bias 136, 156

B

Brand Building 50, 174, 195, 234, 241, 250, 271, 285, 331, 367, 368, 369, 371, 372, 379
brand experience 55, 76, 209, 242, 263, 293, 295, 296, 300, 301, 306, 308, 344, 372, 374, 376, 379, 381
Branding 7, 14, 18, 19, 20, 27, 28, 41, 66, 74, 76, 79, 81, 88, 95, 102, 112, 135, 136, 148, 165, 174, 175, 179, 196, 214, 215, 216, 217, 234, 286, 292, 293, 294, 295, 296, 297, 298, 301, 302, 303, 306, 310, 312, 346, 365, 370, 371, 378, 380, 381, 382
Brand Management 302, 310, 342, 380
brand perception 112, 133, 135, 239, 241, 301, 302, 303, 305, 307, 308, 380, 381
Brands 4, 19, 59, 66, 69, 74, 76, 100, 102, 126, 159, 178, 180, 202, 209, 216, 224, 239, 240, 242, 245, 255, 261, 263, 265, 266, 267, 292, 293, 294, 295, 296, 297, 299, 300, 302, 303, 305, 306, 307, 308, 309, 340, 344, 367, 368, 369, 370, 371, 372, 373, 374, 375, 376, 377, 378, 379, 380, 382
Buyer Behavior 182, 273
Buying behavior 15, 49, 182, 201, 209, 237, 247, 248, 249, 251, 259, 261, 271, 272, 285, 311, 380
Buying Intention 219, 222, 225, 226, 231, 232

C

Charging Infrastructure 315, 316, 318, 319, 320, 327, 328, 329
Cognitive Biases 6, 57, 58, 59, 60, 61, 62, 67, 77, 78, 80, 86, 90, 92, 108, 112, 114, 132, 136, 137, 139, 155, 158, 159, 161, 163, 164, 248, 322
Cognitive Reactions 76, 321, 352
Consumer 1, 2, 3, 4, 5, 6, 7, 8, 9, 10, 11, 12, 13, 14, 15, 16, 17, 18, 19, 20, 21, 24, 29, 32, 35, 36, 37, 38, 39, 40, 41, 42, 44, 45, 46, 47, 48, 49, 50, 51, 52, 53, 54, 55, 56, 57, 58, 59, 60, 61, 67, 68, 70, 74, 75, 76, 77, 78, 79, 80, 81, 82, 83, 84, 85, 86, 87, 88, 89, 90, 91, 92, 93, 94, 95, 96, 97, 98, 99, 100, 101, 102, 103, 104, 105, 106, 112, 114, 118, 119, 120, 121, 122, 125, 126, 127, 128, 129, 130, 131, 133, 134, 135, 136, 137, 138, 140, 142, 143, 144, 145, 147, 148, 149, 151, 153, 155, 156, 157, 158, 159, 160, 161, 162, 163, 164, 165, 166, 167, 168, 169, 170, 171, 172, 173, 174, 176, 177, 178, 179, 180, 181, 182, 183, 184, 188, 190, 191, 192, 193, 194, 195, 197, 198, 201, 202, 203, 204, 205, 206, 207, 208, 209, 211, 212, 214, 215, 216, 217, 219, 220, 221, 222, 223, 224, 225, 226, 229, 231, 232, 233, 234, 237, 238, 239, 240, 241, 242, 243, 244, 246, 247, 248, 249, 250, 251, 252, 253, 254, 255, 256, 257, 258, 259, 260, 261, 262, 263, 264, 265, 266, 267, 268, 270, 271, 272, 273, 275, 276, 277, 278, 279, 280, 282, 283, 284, 285, 292, 295, 296, 297, 299, 300, 301, 302, 303, 304, 305, 306, 307, 308, 309, 310, 311, 312, 313, 314, 315, 316, 318, 319, 322, 325, 326, 327, 328, 329, 332, 333, 334, 337, 338, 339, 340, 341, 342, 343, 344, 346, 347, 348, 349, 350, 351, 352, 353, 355, 356, 357, 358, 359, 360, 361, 362, 363, 364, 367, 368, 369, 370, 371, 372, 373, 375, 376, 377, 378, 380, 381
Consumer Attention 19, 20, 36, 89, 93, 173, 219, 220, 221, 222, 223, 224, 225, 226, 231, 232, 233, 243, 279, 280, 282, 283, 348
Consumer Behavior 1, 2, 3, 4, 5, 6, 7, 8,

451

9, 10, 11, 12, 13, 14, 15, 16, 18, 20, 21, 24, 35, 36, 37, 38, 46, 48, 49, 58, 60, 67, 68, 70, 74, 76, 78, 81, 84, 85, 86, 87, 90, 91, 92, 93, 94, 95, 96, 97, 114, 125, 126, 127, 128, 129, 130, 131, 133, 134, 135, 136, 140, 142, 143, 144, 148, 149, 155, 156, 157, 159, 160, 162, 163, 164, 166, 168, 171, 172, 173, 176, 182, 188, 190, 191, 192, 193, 194, 197, 198, 201, 202, 203, 204, 205, 209, 212, 215, 216, 217, 237, 238, 239, 240, 241, 242, 247, 248, 254, 257, 258, 259, 265, 271, 272, 273, 276, 277, 310, 311, 344, 362, 371, 377

Consumer Behaviour 16, 53, 57, 95, 96, 98, 101, 102, 118, 133, 142, 147, 151, 161, 163, 177, 178, 179, 180, 181, 183, 184, 190, 191, 192, 194, 197, 208, 216, 217, 220, 229, 231, 232, 233, 251, 261, 271, 295, 302, 303, 304, 305, 306, 307, 308, 309, 322, 329, 337, 339, 340, 341, 342, 343, 347, 348, 349, 350, 351, 352, 353, 355, 357, 358, 359, 360, 361, 362, 363, 364, 368, 373

Consumer Loyalty 266, 306, 340, 341

Consumer Perception 16, 198, 241, 242, 248, 322, 338, 340, 341, 342, 344

Consumer Perceptions 4, 18, 39, 42, 47, 106, 119, 162, 163, 165, 167, 169, 170, 171, 173, 241, 247, 248, 249, 292, 295, 296, 313, 319, 322, 329, 341, 349, 350, 357, 358

D

decision-making 2, 3, 4, 5, 6, 7, 8, 10, 11, 14, 15, 17, 18, 20, 24, 42, 57, 58, 59, 60, 61, 62, 63, 67, 68, 72, 76, 77, 78, 79, 80, 81, 86, 87, 90, 91, 92, 96, 102, 103, 106, 107, 108, 109, 110, 114, 115, 116, 117, 119, 120, 121, 122, 125, 126, 127, 128, 129, 130, 131, 132, 133, 134, 135, 136, 138, 139, 140, 142, 143, 144, 145, 149, 152, 155, 157, 158, 159, 161, 163, 164, 165, 171, 172, 180, 182, 198, 202, 204, 208, 211, 219, 232, 240, 241, 242, 244, 246, 250, 251, 252, 255, 260, 262, 291, 297, 302, 303, 304, 322, 337, 338, 343, 347, 348, 349, 350, 351, 352, 356, 357, 358, 362, 364, 377, 381

Decision Making 55, 95, 97, 102, 103, 104, 109, 110, 111, 112, 114, 115, 117, 119, 120, 121, 125, 126, 127, 128, 129, 147, 148, 149, 151, 152, 204, 252, 253, 255, 300, 301, 303, 368, 372

Digitalization 50, 259, 380, 382

Digital Marketing 29, 30, 33, 126, 143, 149, 151, 255, 305, 311, 368, 371

E

Electric Vehicles 306, 313, 314, 315, 316, 317, 318, 319, 320, 321, 322, 323, 324, 325, 326, 327, 328, 329, 331, 332, 333, 334, 335

emotional priming 155, 156

Eye Tracking 13, 15, 16, 68, 73, 74, 133, 134, 143, 151, 238, 254, 304

F

Factors Affecting 25, 247, 259

Financial Choices 107, 108, 109, 110, 111, 112, 113, 114, 115, 118

Financial Market. 109, 121

G

Game Theory 58

Greenhouse Gas Emissions 261, 314, 329, 332

Grounded Cognition 337

I

Investment Decision 107, 108, 109, 111, 114, 132, 147, 151

Investments 41, 113, 115, 129, 130, 131, 151, 375

M

Machine Learning 10, 87, 91, 116, 121, 126, 142, 303

Marketing 1, 2, 3, 4, 5, 6, 7, 8, 9, 10, 11, 12, 13, 14, 15, 16, 17, 18, 19, 20, 21, 22, 23, 24, 25, 26, 27, 28, 29, 30, 31, 32, 33, 34, 35, 36, 37, 38, 39, 40, 41, 43, 45, 46, 48, 49, 50, 51, 52, 53, 54, 55, 56, 58, 62, 64, 65, 66, 67, 68, 69, 70, 71, 73, 74, 75, 76, 77, 78, 79, 81, 82, 83, 84, 85, 86, 87, 88, 89, 90, 91, 92, 93, 94, 95, 96, 97, 98, 99, 100, 101, 102, 103, 104, 106, 112, 114, 116, 118, 120, 121, 122, 125, 126, 127, 128, 129, 130, 131, 133, 134, 135, 136, 137, 140, 142, 143, 144, 145, 147, 148, 149, 150, 151, 153, 155, 156, 157, 160, 162, 166, 173, 174, 175, 176, 177, 178, 179, 180, 190, 192, 193, 195, 196, 197, 198, 201, 202, 203, 204, 205, 206, 207, 208, 209, 210, 212, 213, 214, 215, 216, 217, 220, 223, 231, 232, 233, 234, 237, 238, 239, 240, 241, 243, 244, 245, 246, 248, 250, 251, 252, 253, 254, 255, 256, 257, 258, 259, 261, 262, 265, 266, 268, 269, 270, 271, 272, 275, 276, 278, 279, 280, 284, 285, 286, 291, 292, 293, 294, 295, 296, 297, 298, 299, 300, 301, 302, 303, 304, 305, 306, 307, 308, 309, 310, 311, 312, 322, 331, 337, 338, 339, 340, 341, 342, 343, 344, 345, 346, 347, 348, 349, 350, 351, 352, 353, 354, 355, 356, 357, 358, 359, 360, 361, 362, 363, 364, 365, 367, 368, 369, 370, 371, 372, 373, 374, 375, 376, 377, 378, 379, 380, 381, 382

Marketing Communications 28, 143, 300, 303

marketing strategies 2, 4, 5, 7, 13, 15, 16, 20, 24, 27, 35, 38, 49, 67, 79, 82, 84, 86, 88, 89, 90, 91, 92, 93, 94, 114, 116, 127, 128, 134, 135, 136, 142, 143, 144, 145, 156, 162, 166, 193, 220, 223, 231, 232, 233, 238, 239, 240, 241, 243, 248, 255, 258, 292, 294, 304, 307, 308, 310, 311, 312, 322, 338, 340, 341, 342, 344, 345, 346, 347, 348, 351, 356, 358, 360, 361, 364, 368, 370, 374, 377, 378

N

Neuroeconomics 57, 58, 59, 68, 77, 78, 79, 80, 81, 90, 91, 93, 94, 96, 97, 103, 109, 130, 131, 132, 148, 151, 152, 177, 198, 254, 255

Neuromarketing 1, 2, 3, 4, 5, 6, 7, 8, 9, 10, 11, 12, 13, 14, 15, 16, 27, 31, 33, 57, 58, 67, 68, 69, 70, 71, 72, 81, 82, 83, 84, 85, 88, 90, 91, 92, 94, 95, 96, 97, 98, 100, 101, 102, 103, 104, 105, 125, 126, 127, 128, 129, 130, 132, 133, 134, 135, 136, 137, 140, 141, 142, 143, 144, 145, 146, 147, 148, 149, 150, 151, 152, 153, 162, 163, 171, 174, 175, 176, 177, 178, 179, 180, 182, 188, 189, 190, 192, 193, 194, 196, 197, 198, 213, 214, 215, 217, 234, 235, 236, 238, 240, 246, 251, 252, 253, 254, 255, 256, 311, 312, 365, 380, 381

Neuro-Marketing 3, 4, 5, 8, 9, 13, 21, 22, 23, 24, 197, 253, 291, 337, 356, 358, 364, 380

Neuropricing 155, 156, 157, 158, 159, 160, 161, 162, 163, 164, 165, 166, 167, 169, 170, 171, 172, 173

Neuroscience 2, 3, 4, 5, 13, 14, 15, 16, 18, 24, 58, 68, 70, 78, 90, 93, 94, 95, 96, 98, 99, 100, 102, 103, 104, 105, 106, 107, 108, 109, 110, 111, 112, 119, 121, 122, 125, 126, 127, 128, 129, 130, 131, 132, 135, 136, 138, 140, 142, 143, 144, 145, 148, 149, 152, 155, 156, 157, 158, 159, 160, 161, 162, 163, 172, 173, 177, 178, 179, 180, 181, 182, 183, 184, 188, 190, 191, 192, 193, 194, 195, 196, 197, 204, 211, 215, 217, 238, 239, 246, 251, 252, 254, 256, 279, 301, 304, 306, 311, 367, 377, 381

Neuroscientific 6, 15, 58, 68, 107, 109, 110, 111, 117, 118, 132, 133, 135, 137, 138, 140, 141, 143, 144, 145, 149, 156, 177, 179, 193, 238, 377

Neurosensory Behavior 108, 109, 114, 315

P

Packaging 14, 37, 41, 45, 66, 71, 82, 83, 165, 178, 203, 209, 237, 238, 239, 241, 242, 243, 246, 247, 248, 249, 253, 257, 261, 262, 263, 264, 265, 270, 271, 272, 273, 275, 276, 277, 278, 279, 280, 282, 283, 284, 285, 286, 287, 288, 289, 293, 295, 296, 297, 298, 299, 369, 371, 374, 375, 376, 378

Packaging Color 279

Packaging Size 279

Perceived Quality 76, 247, 249, 341, 342

perceived value 48, 66, 155, 156, 158, 159, 169, 170, 171, 172, 297, 340, 354

price framing 155, 156

Product 3, 7, 16, 18, 25, 29, 30, 35, 36, 37, 38, 40, 41, 42, 43, 44, 45, 46, 47, 49, 51, 53, 58, 59, 60, 63, 65, 66, 68, 69, 71, 74, 75, 77, 79, 82, 83, 84, 86, 88, 102, 112, 116, 122, 125, 129, 133, 143, 144, 145, 158, 159, 163, 164, 165, 172, 173, 179, 193, 202, 203, 204, 205, 206, 207, 208, 209, 210, 212, 213, 215, 216, 219, 220, 221, 222, 223, 224, 225, 226, 227, 229, 231, 232, 233, 237, 238, 239, 240, 241, 242, 243, 244, 245, 246, 247, 248, 249, 253, 257, 258, 259, 260, 261, 262, 263, 264, 265, 266, 267, 268, 269, 270, 271, 272, 273, 275, 276, 277, 278, 279, 282, 284, 285, 286, 287, 288, 289, 292, 293, 294, 295, 297, 298, 299, 300, 301, 303, 312, 337, 338, 340, 341, 342, 348, 354, 367, 368, 369, 371, 372, 373, 374, 377, 381

Product Display 219, 220, 221, 222, 223, 224, 225, 226, 227, 229, 231, 232, 297

Product Promotion Strategy 267

Promotion 66, 128, 221, 222, 244, 250, 251, 252, 254, 265, 266, 267, 268, 269, 270, 272, 273, 277, 315, 320, 326, 327, 328, 335

R

Retail Marketing 204, 231

S

Senses 36, 38, 39, 48, 81, 94, 108, 110, 111, 114, 120, 126, 148, 201, 202, 203, 204, 205, 206, 207, 209, 210, 212, 215, 216, 217, 220, 238, 239, 241, 242, 243, 248, 291, 292, 294, 296, 298, 299, 300, 301, 303, 305, 306, 308, 310, 338, 340, 342, 343, 344, 346, 347, 348, 349, 351, 354, 367, 368, 369, 370, 372, 373, 374, 375, 376

Sensory 27, 31, 33, 35, 36, 37, 38, 39, 40, 44, 45, 46, 47, 48, 49, 51, 52, 53, 54, 55, 56, 67, 74, 76, 78, 82, 83, 84, 85, 88, 89, 90, 93, 94, 95, 101, 105, 107, 108, 109, 110, 111, 112, 114, 115, 116, 117, 118, 120, 122, 123, 144, 148, 150, 152, 155, 156, 158, 160, 163, 164, 165, 174, 175, 176, 196, 198, 201, 202, 203, 204, 205, 206, 207, 208, 209, 210, 212, 214, 215, 216, 217, 234, 235, 236, 238, 239, 240, 241, 243, 246, 248, 249, 256, 291, 292, 293, 294, 295, 296, 297, 298, 299, 300, 301, 302, 303, 304, 305, 306, 307, 308, 309, 310, 311, 312, 313, 315, 321, 322, 337, 338, 339, 340, 341, 342, 343, 344, 345, 346, 347, 348, 349, 350, 351, 352, 353, 354, 355, 356, 357, 358, 359, 360, 361, 362, 363, 364, 365, 367, 368, 369, 370, 371, 372, 373, 374, 375, 376, 377, 378, 379, 380, 381, 382

Sensory marketing 35, 36, 37, 38, 39, 40, 45, 46, 48, 49, 51, 52, 53, 54, 76, 83, 85, 88, 120, 148, 155, 156, 201, 202, 203, 204, 205, 206, 207, 208, 209, 210, 212, 214, 215, 216, 217, 256, 291, 292, 293, 294, 295, 296, 297,

298, 299, 300, 301, 302, 303, 304, 305, 306, 307, 308, 309, 310, 311, 312, 337, 338, 339, 340, 341, 342, 343, 344, 345, 346, 347, 348, 349, 350, 351, 352, 353, 354, 355, 356, 357, 358, 359, 360, 361, 362, 363, 364, 367, 368, 369, 370, 371, 372, 373, 374, 375, 376, 377, 378, 379, 381

sensory overload 39, 302, 307, 375, 379

sensory perception 45, 109, 112, 123, 204, 217, 303, 313, 337

spending behaviour 301

Strategic Management 303

Strategy 13, 25, 27, 32, 47, 48, 50, 68, 69, 81, 82, 83, 85, 117, 126, 137, 144, 150, 151, 162, 167, 169, 170, 193, 204, 209, 214, 221, 223, 231, 232, 239, 254, 257, 265, 266, 267, 268, 269, 270, 272, 297, 303, 314, 332, 345, 346, 347, 351, 367, 368, 370, 373, 376

Subconscious Cues 239, 337

Sustainable Development 26, 51, 214, 271, 286

T

Trends 12, 26, 28, 87, 91, 92, 103, 127, 142, 144, 145, 147, 149, 150, 160, 161, 177, 183, 193, 195, 196, 198, 220, 227, 232, 237, 251, 252, 258, 276, 284, 286, 311, 314, 344, 351, 357, 359, 360, 361, 367, 376

V

Visual Sensory Marketing 35, 39, 209, 297, 298

Milton Keynes UK
Ingram Content Group UK Ltd.
UKHW012205071124
450822UK00006B/63